Past Convictions

THE MIDDLE AGES SERIES

RUTH MAZO KARRAS, SERIES EDITOR
EDWARD PETERS, FOUNDING EDITOR

A complete list of books in the series is available from the publisher.

Past Convictions

The Penance of Louis the Pious and the Decline of the Carolingians

Courtney M. Booker

PENN

University of Pennsylvania Press
Philadelphia

Publication of this book has been aided by a grant from the Medieval Academy of America

Published by
University of Pennsylvania Press
Philadelphia, Pennsylvania 19104-4112

Printed in the United States of America on acid-free paper

10 9 8 7 6 5 4 3 2 1

Library of Congress Cataloging-in-Publication Data
Booker, Courtney M.
  Past convictions : the penance of Louis the Pious and the decline of the Carolingians / Courtney M. Booker.
    p. cm. — (The Middle Ages series)
  Includes bibliographical references and index.
  ISBN 978-0-8122-4168-6 (alk. paper)
    1. Louis I, Emperor, 778–840. 2. Louis I, Emperor, 778–840—Historiography.
3. France—Kings and rulers—Biography. 4. France—History—To 987. I. Title.
DC74.B66   2009
944'.01092—dc22   2009017735
[B]

For Susan

CONTENTS

It would be absurd that a Guardian should need a guard.
—Plato, *The Republic*

Who will guard the guardians themselves?
—Juvenal, *Sixth Satire*

Introduction

For a great many years there lived in Rue de la Harpe one of those men of stay-at-home habits for whom the only distraction consisted in occasional visits to the flower market and who, on returning home, would rediscover with ever-renewed pleasure his modest lodgings where order and cleanliness reigned everywhere. One day, as he hurried home, his landlord stopped him in the stairway and told him that the house had to be demolished because of some street repairs and that he would have to find another place to live for the next trimester. On hearing the news the poor lodger remained paralyzed with surprise and chagrin. Returning to his apartment, he immediately took to his bed and stayed there several months, the victim of a profound sadness accompanied by a raging fever. In vain his landlord tried to console him, promising him a more comfortable lodging in the new house that was going to be built on the land of the old one: "It will no longer be my lodging," he responded with bitterness, "the one I loved so much, that I embellished with my own hands, where, for thirty years, I had all my habits and where I cherished the hope of finishing my life!"

The eve of the day fixed for the demolition, he was warned that he must absolutely give back his keys the following day by noon at the latest. "I will not return them," he responded coldly. "If I leave here, it will only be feet first." Two days later, the *commissaire* was required to force open the door of the stubborn lodger. He found the poor man dead; he had suffocated from the despair of having to leave the abode he cherished too much.[1]

HERE WAS A "textbook" case, from Jean-Baptiste-Felix Descuret's 1841 volume, *La médecine des passions*, exemplifying symptoms of an ailment over which Descuret and many others of the scientific community in the early to mid-nineteenth century were engaged in heated debate. Coming to the conclusion that they were witnessing the symptoms of a disease, doctors struggled over the correct pathology and proper treatment for what had long been known as the affliction of "nostalgia," an illness "that doctors regarded as potentially fatal, contagious, and somehow deeply connected to French life in the middle of the nineteenth century."[2] Central to the debate over this disease was the question of what constituted a person's "healthy" or "normal" relationship with the past. Clearly, too much nostalgia could prove fatal in an era deeply committed to the idea of progress. The inertia caused by this disease, it was argued, allowed the expanse between the victim's static, "inhabited" past and the ongoing present to widen beyond reach. Responding to changes in the present became impossible to those paralyzed by their "malignant" memories. Beset with nostalgia, the poor lodger diagnosed by Descuret could not tolerate such a shock to his system as the changing of his cherished environment and routine. Rather than cope with the fickle present, he became a passive casualty of circumstance—a kind of living anachronism—rendered immobile by his "pathologically" deep attachment to a gilded past.[3]

If this brief account of doctors operating in the field of the historian seems strange, one might first consider the fact that historians themselves have, from the earliest times, borrowed from the lexicon of the physician.[4] When speaking of a society or a state, historians have often utilized an organic metaphor, providing themselves with a flexible model that encapsulates the complex in the simple. As Paul Dutton has observed, "whenever we find the state compared to a diseased body, a poisoned body, or a body naturally growing old, we are in the presence of this organic metaphor."[5] By extension, historians thus become the (often hypochondriacal) "physicians" of this social organism, rendering "diagnoses" and evaluating its "health" by using additional medical metaphors. For example, the concept of a "crisis" has been widely used in historiography since the seventeenth century, referring to moments of particular stress upon the normative equilibrium—or "homeostasis"—of a society.[6] Yet the word *crisis* itself is an ancient Greek medical term, used most often to describe the point at which a disease will, according to Hippocrates, "increase in intensity or go away or change into another disease or end altogether."[7]

Carolingian Europe, the great empire of Charlemagne and his family, during the ninth century is the subject of this study. I have begun with Descuret's nineteenth-century account of the nostalgic lodger not only because it serves as a vivid reminder of the influence that doctors have traditionally had upon historians in their analyses of change but also because it offers a particularly apt illustration of the specific form of metaphorical thinking that has long influenced and shaped Carolingian historiography. Indeed, the precedent for this kind of metaphorical analysis was set by the Carolingians themselves.[8] Agobard, bishop of Lyon, lamented in 833 that, rather than subjugating the barbarian nations that were threatening from every side, all the kingdoms of the realm were instead focusing their attention upon the empire's center, preparing to tear its "intestinal innards" to pieces with civil war.[9] By 863, however, Ermentarius, a monk of Saint-Philibert, despaired that the civil wars were so frequent and fearful they resembled nothing so much as "tightly-packed intestines."[10] Evidently, the empire had not yet disemboweled itself. Regino, a monk, chronicler of the monastery at Prüm, and contemporary witness in 888, famously described what he perceived as the end of the Carolingian empire using similar terms, but this time to suggest a kind of mitosis: "After Charles [the Fat's] death, the kingdoms which had obeyed his will, as if devoid of a legitimate heir, were loosened from their bodily structure into parts and now awaited no lord of hereditary descent, but each set out to create a king for itself from its own innards."[11]

Over a millennium later, modern Carolingian historiography continues to bear the stamp of this very metaphor. James Westfall Thompson employed organic imagery when speaking about the "decomposition" of the Carolingian "body politic and body social," while Marc Bloch, Louis Halphen, and Jan Dhondt would discuss the later years of the realm beneath a rubric of "dismemberment."[12] Other historians would offer more detailed diagnoses. For Heinrich Fichtenau, who made ironic use of a metaphor that Europeans had long applied to the Ottoman empire, the Carolingian empire "was like a sick man who could not live, but could not die."[13] Gerald Simons was more certain about the nature of this peculiar illness: "Charlemagne's empire was, in fact," he pronounced, "a giant dying of its own great size—and of his very efforts to preserve it."[14] François Louis Ganshof, however, saw these same efforts by Charlemagne not as cause of the empire's illness but as its cure: "Even a rapid reading of the capitularies reveals all the symptoms of a defective administration," explained Ganshof. "Excesses and irregularities became endemic. The seriousness of the situation gave Charlemagne cause for constant concern, and he did what he could to apply a remedy."[15]

As their incredible persistence attests, such metaphors, once adopted, become increasingly difficult to dispense with owing to their attractive conceptual economy.[16] In addition, when used frequently and habitually, metaphors often subtly impose a situational construct upon their user, circumscribing all analysis within their confines, if not directing the course of the analysis itself.[17] For example, when one speaks of a society as "sick," there remains the possibility of a recovery. Yet when the metaphor of decline into old age is used, there can be no such reversal. Moreover, the notion of senescence in this latter case could also predetermine a pattern of analysis, organizing it according to related metaphors of organic decrepitude. Because a society is in its "old age," it should not be able to "see" and "hear" as well as it once had; hence, an examination of the society's communication network is demanded.[18]

These consequences of adopting organic metaphors for historical analysis bring us back to our nineteenth-century doctors and the poor, nostalgic lodger. Just as historians long ago appropriated biological and medical terminology for their use as metaphors, so too have they often observed within the larger social body the doctors' pathology of nostalgia as an enervating disease.[19] The case of the nineteenth-century Swiss historian J.-C.-L. Simonde de Sismondi is instructive of this tendency. In the introduction to his history of early medieval France, Sismondi justified his general approach to the study of the past as follows:

> It is true that the study of history [that I propose] too often arrests the mind upon sorrowful remembrances, and nourishes painful feelings. We shall have to recount atrocious crimes which never drew upon their authors the deserved chastisement, of harrowing sufferings, a state of misery and despair, from which we should be eager to turn our eyes if it were presented to us in a fiction. But a friend of mankind ought to approach the study of history with that species of firmness, that he who wishes to relieve his fellow-man carries to the study of medicine or surgery.[20]

Later in the same work, Sismondi abides by this rigorous methodology, detailing with a doctor's "firmness" a whole host of political, social, economic, religious, and genetic factors deemed responsible for the "degeneration" and "decline" of his patient, the Carolingian empire. Yet, despite all his clinical observations, his final diagnosis of the "ailing giant" recalls nothing so much as Descuret's description of the poor, nostalgic lodger: "The empire appears to be nothing more than a great body," concluded Sismondi, "in which we perceive the last convulsion of failing sensibility, when thought has fled, and the soul ceases to be present."[21] Given this vivid, suggestive assessment of pathogenesis, the fact that Sismondi's own mother, years earlier, had fallen gravely ill from nostalgia is perhaps of more than passing interest.[22] To what extent did the latent memory of his mother's illness inform his diagnosis of a nearly comatose Carolingian Europe?

Certainly Sismondi was not the only scholar to internalize the symptoms and pathology of nostalgia and to invoke them in his historical analysis. Indeed, much like the cases of Descuret's lodger and Sismondi's mother, Carolingian society has been diagnosed repeatedly by historians as having succumbed to a particularly virulent strain of this debilitating disease: unable to deal "realistically" with change, struggling in traditional—and thus ineffectual—ways against its own "dissolution" over the course of the ninth century, Carolingian society vociferously bemoaned its fate in nostalgic tones.[23] It is little wonder that historians have arrived at such a diagnosis, for the Carolingian literary corpus is replete with nostalgic laments. Take, for example, the following mid-ninth-century jeremiad of Paschasius Radbertus, a bitter abbot of the monastery of Corbie:

> And who would have been able to guess that such a glorious realm,
> one so spacious and fortified, so populated and powerful, was destined
> to be humbled and disgraced by the atrocities of such men? . . . And
> so among us the sword of the barbarian rages, unsheathed from the
> scabbard of the Lord! And we, wretched creatures, live as though
> paralyzed, not only among the hideous evils done by savages, but as
> well among the wars fought without pity between our own peoples,
> amid pillaging and plundering, sedition and fraud. Day by day men's
> hearts burn with new ardor to commit greater and more wicked
> crimes![24]

In the 840s, Nithard, a disgruntled nobleman and grandson of Charlemagne, similarly decried the present state:

> In the times of Charles the Great of good memory, who died almost
> thirty years ago, peace and concord ruled everywhere because our
> people were treading the one proper way, the way of the common
> welfare, and thus the way of God. But now since each goes his separate

way, dissension and struggle abound. Once there was abundance and happiness everywhere, now everywhere there is want and sadness.[25]

Evaluating the latter passage, the historian Janet Nelson once wrote that Nithard's "final comparison of the wretched present with the golden past of the 'great Charles' [could never] have been thought fit for the eyes of Nithard's former patron and confidant [King Charles the Bald]."[26] Taking his lament at face value, Nelson understood Nithard to be so despondent over his day and age that he opted to escape into the past by way of nostalgic recollection—a move that implicitly condemned the present and thereby could offend the current king; hence, Nelson's conclusion that Nithard could not have intended such an account for royal eyes.

However, to base any diagnosis of a debilitating Carolingian nostalgia on texts such as Nithard's is to ignore not only the implications of nostalgia itself but also the rich tradition of rhetoric in which the Carolingians were steeped.[27] Nelson would later change her mind about Nithard's intended audience, and thus about the nature of nostalgia: "Could [Nithard] ever have contemplated Charles [the Bald] as a reader? Perhaps yes . . . Nithard may indeed have intended Charles himself to read his 'Histories.'" Nelson attributed this new perspective to her enhanced sensitivity to Carolingian historiography and the function of nostalgia within it. Rather than viewing nostalgia as a passive, escapist response to historical change, she now understood its use by Carolingian authors as an active form of criticism: by "harking back to the golden days of Charlemagne," Nelson assures us, "Nithard did very effectively criticise Charles's hard times."[28] A comparison of the base present with the golden past illustrated the need for current reform and, if shown to the proper person, could even effect such desired, salutary change.[29] As she decorously put it, a golden age was not just a stick with which to beat the present but "perhaps as much a carrot as a stick."[30] One understands, then, why Nelson attempted to show that the king was a possible reader of Nithard's nostalgic critique of his troubled present. All the courtier's hopes for reform depended on his account of current wrongs gaining the attention of the king—the one person who could right them.

This understanding of the nostalgic lament as instrumental, as a type of strategic, suggestive criticism of the present, endows the nostalgist with agency. Far from the notion of a bedridden, wistful body, Carolingian society is now being reevaluated in light of this "dynamic" paradigm.[31] Remarkably resourceful in reacting to the many challenges of the ninth century, the Carolingians are now seen as having employed a whole host of strategies not just for coping with social and political change but also for anticipating and often implementing it. Yet, in light of this apparent resourcefulness, it is important to remember that change in the Carolingian world was generally understood and expressed by the literate and learned in pessimistic, if not outright pejorative, terms of decline.[32] Bringing our discussion full circle, this somber belief even underlay and informed the practice of medicine; Carolingian doctors perceived any change in the equilibrium of an organism as indicative of a decline in health.[33] To believe that someone like Nithard was exploiting nostalgic rhetoric simply because he deemed it the most expedient means to achieve his ends would, thus, be a rather cynical misrepresentation of mentality during the ninth century, a specious view of "liberation" and empowerment as wide of the mark as that of a paralyzing nostalgia.[34] People really did believe that things were getting worse. The signs could be seen everywhere.[35] But this did not mean that they believed themselves helpless in the face of such uncertain times.[36] Again, early medieval medical practice provides a good example. Using a formula that required the letters of a patient's name and the number of the particular lunar day on which the patient had fallen ill, Carolingian doctors would occasionally appeal to "ancient" (i.e., pagan) charts in order to prognosticate the outcome of a sickness (Figure 1). The desire to establish with certainty the time of death and thereby secure the performance of last rites for a proper and peaceful transition from this world to the next evidently outweighed any fears of damnation for practicing vaticination.[37] Yet, for most such worriers, the solutions to current problems lay not in the nebulous future but in the proven past, not in augury, nor even in novelty, but in reform.[38]

These are just a few of the many problems and issues one encounters when undertaking broad analyses of social and political change. Language and terminology—especially of the medical variety—can act as obstacles when applied as metaphors. More specifically, when used without caution, the state-as-organism metaphor can predetermine and circumscribe patterns of analysis and interpretation. As I have outlined briefly above, this has been the overriding problem with Carolingian historiography for centuries.[39] Unfortunately, the recent historiographical reaction against the traditional, metaphor-ridden grand narrative of Carolingian rise and decline, growth and decay—for all its sophisticated argumentation—has often tended to extremes in its attack upon this inveterate narrative, leading to another problematic representation of the Carolingian past. Just as the narrative of Carolingian emaciation and

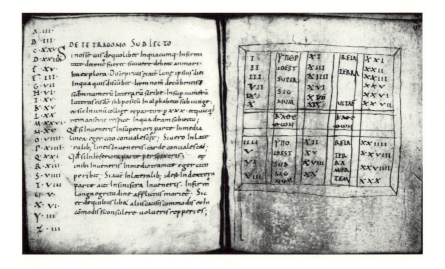

Figure 1. Ninth-century copy of a medical prognostication formula and chart. Laon, Bibliothèque municipale 407, fols. 136v–137r. Courtesy Bibliothèque municipale Laon, IRHT-CNRS.

dissolution had long been received as the ineluctable result of a kind of medieval paralysis in the face of change,[40] the current trend to correct this view by underscoring Carolingian agency has itself produced a skewed narrative of early medieval "strategists," tacticians who proactively maneuvered through their difficult times in accordance with suspiciously modern notions of pragmatism and utility.[41] From this perspective, the Carolingians paid little heed to Christ's injunction on the Mount that so moved men such as Saints Anthony and Francis at the opposite ends of the Middle Ages—to "be not solicitous for tomorrow; for the morrow will be solicitous for itself. Sufficient for the day is the evil thereof" (Matt. 6:34).[42]

In the following pages, I wish to respond to this anachronistic hypercorrection by arguing for a more balanced view—one that sees the actions of the Carolingians as having taken place within a dialectic between "untidy" circumstances and contingencies and a "more tidy" complex of received norms. Thus, my narrative is processual rather than judgmental, emphasizing improvisation and transformation (paradoxically in terms of reform) rather than evaluating achievement and failure, growth and decay, rise and decline.[43] Put another way, I wish to show that the Carolingians were, to use John J. Contreni's felicitous phrase, "innovative despite themselves."[44]

The abandonment of Charlemagne's son, Emperor Louis the Pious, by his troops and his controversial public penance in 833 are ideal incidents with which to demonstrate the advantages provided by a narrative of process. As sole heir to the imperial throne in 814, Louis is often blamed in historical accounts for both causing and allowing the nominally unified empire established by his grandfather Pippin the Short and father Charlemagne to disintegrate into a patchwork of independent territories and autonomous lordships.[45] This process, whose point of no return is usually seen in the events of 833, is often represented as the product of a series of poor choices by Louis, themselves the result of his allegedly mercurial character, being on the one hand a weak and indecisive monarch, on the other hand a religious zealot blind to the consequences of his actions.[46] For instance, arriving at the imperial court in Aachen shortly after his father's death, Louis purged the palace of its "filth," an act that included the destruction of the old Germanic pagan tokens and texts collected by Charlemagne and the exile and enclaustration of the court's morally "dissolute," a number of whom were members of his own kindred. This abrasive "cleansing of the palace" is often taken as the new emperor's first error. In the following years of his reign, Louis is alleged to have made a long series of other mistakes, including the (unintentional) execution of his nephew King Bernard of Italy for treason in 818; his marriage in 819 to the "bad" Judith of Bavaria following the death of his "good" first wife, Ermengard; his performance of a public penance in 822 to atone for, among his other sins and those of his father, the murder of Bernard; fathering a son by Judith in 823, thereby jeopardizing the arrangement of his first three sons' patrimony (established and divinely ordained in 817); the replacement of his closest counselors with Count Bernard of Septimania, an ambitious favorite of the empress, in 829; the granting of the rich territory of Alemannia in the same year to Charles, his youngest son, thereby diminishing Lothar's inheritance and sparking a civil war with his allied elder children; and finally, emerging victorious after a momentary defeat in 830, only to show clemency to many who had rebelled against him.

These deeds are typically taken as Louis' major "errors,"[47] though his liberality in the dispensation of the lands and property of the imperial fisc is often adduced as another factor contributing to the realm's "dissolution" under his command.[48] Yet, in most narratives of Louis' reign, these past mistakes serve merely as prologue to what occurred in 833.[49] For in that year Louis met his first three sons in open rebellion once again, only this time to be deserted by his own forces in a dramatic display of greed, fear, and disfavor toward his years of alleged misrule. To add insult to injury, Louis' sons then purportedly coerced him in secret to undertake another public penance for his many "crimes," after which he was said by the rebels to have willingly forfeited the throne for a life of pentitential self-reflection and prayer. Unfortunately for the new emperor, Lothar, dispute and division among his brothers soon followed in the wake of these unsettling events, which resulted in Louis' restoration and official recovery of the throne early in 835. For the next five years, Louis would maintain possession of the realm, though he was often forced to fight with his sons to keep it. Shortly after his death from illness in June 840, the empire would erupt into full-fledged civil war.

For centuries, these dramatic events sketched above have been judged by historians,[50] and it is their stern, summary judgment that has itself often formed a critical fulcrum upon which pivot both the older decline/decay narratives and the modern narratives of pragmatism, ambition, and interest. What happens if the "pivotal" events of Louis' reign—and the events of 833, in particular—are instead seen within a continuum of process and transformation? My conviction is that they become understandable on their own terms, rather than tendentious in ours.

One major theme of this study is the shift in the interpretation and representation of historical events, moving from the evaluation and judgment of competing narratives of the past, to the isolation and historicization of the narratives' rhetorical elements, to the understanding of the historical beliefs and value systems that justified and informed them. It is a shift from the despair born of a vain search for truth amid a tangle of conflicting narratives, to the hope arising from the discernment of common threads woven throughout the narratives themselves.[51]

Another prominent theme is the complex relationships among experience, memory, and identity. To what extent does the remembrance of an experience contribute to one's identity? To what extent do the demands of identity shape the remembrance of one's experience?[52] The ways in which a worldly king with his changing needs (Charles the Bald) and an ecclesiastical advisor with his hardening convictions (Hincmar of Reims) each remembered and remembered again the events of 833 are only two of the many examples that will attend to these questions.

A third theme that emerges regularly is the idea of foresight and acting proactively. A great variety of means for coping with change (believed to be detrimental) were adopted during the ninth century. Yet the reliance on any one or combination of such means was in most cases prudently ad hoc and conservative in character, rather than impudently premeditated and transformative.[53] While the Carolingians may appear at times to have been a superficially Christian people, rarely did they forget Christ's teaching to forsake anxiety about the future. Whether viewed with optimism or (more often) with pessimism, with hope or with fear, the morrow would look after itself.[54] One did not have to be a saint to take this sentiment seriously. When they did attempt a concerted, creative plan for the future—and ironically, it would take a fortuitous, nearly fatal fall by the emperor to prompt such forward thinking—their inexperience and the considerable force of custom would together prove to be their own undoing.[55]

A final theme is neatly summed up in an aphorism by the Roman satirist Juvenal: "Who will guard the guardians themselves?"[56] A line well known during the Middle Ages, the sentiment it expressed was pervasive and deep. Methods and techniques were constantly sought by which those in positions of power and responsibility might govern their own actions in accordance with truth, justice, and equity and keep from going astray. How could one penetrate the dense fog of self-delusion and know oneself truly?[57] One way was to submit oneself to external scrutiny and seek the advice of trusted counselors and critics. Yet, as Saint Paul had warned, this method always ran the risk of having one's itching ears scratched by the flattery of fawning courtiers (2 Tim. 4:3). Another way was to allow one's inner tribunal of justice and equity, one's conscience, to render corrective judgment in accordance with a strict scale of comparison.[58] Models, both typological and historical, were perpetually desired, exalted, and emulated as guides: Charlemagne was said to have listened to Saint Augustine's *City of God* read aloud each night, while his son Louis the Pious was known to meditate daily on scripture and exegesis.[59] Codes of conduct and self-correction were also frequently adopted, such as Saint Benedict's Rule for abbots, Pope Gregory the Great's *Pastoral Care* and Saint Peter's standard of equity for bishops, and the numerous edifying "mirrors of princes" for secular rulers. Such models and codes served to goad one's conscience through their constant and explicit reminders that to whom more is entrusted by God, more is expected. Anxiety and dread over the final account that must be rendered on the day of reckoning both for oneself and for one's stewardship of others were expected to make the careful consideration of behavior a ceaseless, imperative task.

As privileged guardians of the past and speakers for the dead, historians have an equally grave responsibility.[60] How do we keep from going astray, from misleading not only others but even—but especially—ourselves? It is not enough to offer self-conscious, belated caveats about the subjectivity of our intervention in the ordering and reordering of the historical record.[61] A more proactive approach is necessary. As in the Middle Ages, one way is to rely on models as guides. In the following pages, it should become rather clear who my guides have been. Submitting one's work to the counsel and criticism of others is likewise of vital importance. In this respect, I have been fortunate to receive scrupulous and candid comments from numerous—though by no means mutually exclusive—counselors, critics, and friends. None have been afraid to speak freely, and for that they have my warmest and lasting gratitude. In the end, or, rather, to begin, I can only echo what Augustine once wrote to Jerome: "I find it hard to judge properly what I have written, because I am either excessively diffident or more partial than I should be. I do also sometimes see my own faults but I prefer to be told of them by someone better in case, after having rightly taken myself to task, I should delude myself again and think that I have been pedantic rather than fair in my judgment."[62]

PART I

Remembering

When you tell about life . . .
—Jean-Paul Sartre, *Nausea*

CHAPTER I

Telling the Truth About the Field of Lies

*Do you imagine that you could relate anything that would please
everybody equally and that everybody would believe?*
  —*Adeodatus,* Epitaphium Arsenii

Shadows present, foreshadowing deeper shadows to come.
  —*Herman Melville,* Benito Cereno

ON THE FEAST day of Saint John the Baptist, June 24, in the year 833, Emperor Louis the Pious (b. 778), Charlemagne's sole surviving heir, readied himself for battle against a terrible foe. Amassed in the distance stood an armed coalition led by his three elder sons, Pope Gregory IV, and part of the Frankish clergy. Dismayed over what they alleged was Louis' chronic negligence and increasing misconduct,[1] his sons Lothar (b. 795), Pippin (b. 797), and Louis the German (b. 810) had for years sought to preserve their grandfather Charlemagne's great empire of western Europe through more peaceful means. Yet, because all their entreaties had failed to make Louis aware of his many sins, ill feelings only continued to escalate. Now the two factions found themselves squared for battle upon a ferrous red plain aptly— and in the present context, ominously—called the Rotfeld. It appeared that the familial dispute would be settled by nothing less than civil war.

Unfortunately for Louis, this precarious stalemate was soon resolved neither by battle nor by diplomacy but by treachery. One night, during the week-long course of negotiations on the Alsatian plain, most of the emperor's sworn *fideles* furtively abandoned his camp, some returning to their own lands, others defecting to the entourage of his sons.[2] Louis' most recent bid to reconfigure the future political landscape of the empire—the creation of a kingdom for Charles, his youngest son, at the expense of the three older half brothers' patrimony—had failed. Bereft of support, Louis dispatched his sole term of surrender: that his young wife, Judith (b. ca. 805), and their ten-year-old son, Charles, remain unharmed. His captors readily complied, spiriting Judith away to Tortona, north of Genoa in Italy, while Prince Charles was confined to the monastery of Prüm near Trier—"something that," according to one contemporary annalist, "grieved his father very much indeed."[3] From the Rotfeld (known only a few years later as the *campus mentitus*, the "Field of Lies") Louis himself was taken by way of Metz to Soissons, and left there by Lothar under the strict custody of the abbot of the monastery of Saint-Médard. The pope, Pippin, and Louis the German returned to their own realms of Rome, Aquitaine, and Bavaria, respectively.

Three months later, following a summer of game hunting, Lothar met at Compiègne with a great assembly of lay and ecclesiastical dignitaries, led by the Emperor Louis' foster brother, Archbishop Ebbo of Reims.[4] After much discussion, the assembly moved within the abbey church of Saint-Médard in Soissons, gathering there with a large number of the general populace. According to the record left by the participating bishops, the captive emperor soon came forward.[5] Prostrating himself on a hair cloth before the altar, Louis tearfully confessed to a whole host of crimes, including perjury, sacrilege, and murder, and referred to himself as nothing less than a *divinarum seu humanarum legum violator*, a violator of divine and human laws.[6] He had scandalized the church, forsaken oaths, and compelled his people to do the same, he admitted, and now sought absolution for these and still other misdeeds through the performance of a public penance. Wishing to set an example of a worthy penitent, explains the episcopal narrative, Louis handed to the bishops a document detailing his wrongs for posterity. After they placed this indictment on the altar, the contrite emperor laid his sword-belt (*cingulum militiae*) beside it. He then exchanged his noble raiment for humble garb, a ritual act that (as the bishops' account is careful to note) symbolized his irrevocable transformation from warrior to penitent, and was confirmed in his new station by the laying on of hands by the bishops, together with prayers and chanting. Henceforth, Louis was excluded from those martial activities that defined a Frankish warlord and king. He had forsaken them for a life of penance and prayer, with the hope that he might still win salvation, both for himself and his people. Or so ends the episcopal *Relatio* of the proceedings at Saint-Médard in October of 833.[7] Yet, despite its tidy conclusion, as scripted by the attendant bishops, the story of Louis' abandonment, penance, and abdication was far from over. On the contrary, the contest over establishing the "correct" tale of 833 had only just begun.

At an address to his fellow savants in 1863, Augustin Ingold argued that the events of 833 had, without doubt, deeply captured the imagination of contemporary witnesses.[8] Over the course of a millennium, he explained, it was the intense memory of the betrayal of Louis the Pious on the Rotfeld that, in particular, had been passed down among the local populace of the site from generation to generation, appearing during his own day in the muddled form of legends and vague traditions. Most striking in this regard was the toponym of a field not far from the Alsatian town of Cernay, a place that, as Ingold pointed out, was believed by many to be the "Field of Lies" itself. Called *der Lügner*, the Liar, its very name still evoked the infamy of the event. Moreover, noted Ingold, local legend had it that a terrible crime once occurred on the neighboring heath of Ochsenfeld, one so heinous that even the land itself had cried out for vengeance from heaven. God, in his just anger, said the tale, had responded to this terrestrial appeal by cleaving the bowels of the earth and hurling those who were culpable into its foul depths. For centuries, the guilty—entire battalions of men, clad in iron— slumbered in the vast caverns beneath the plain. But occasionally, at certain hours of the night, these same ancient warriors would awaken, rise to the surface, and tour the stretches of the Ochsenfeld, led at their vanguard by a certain "Prince Charles." Those travelers unlucky enough to have chanced upon this phantom army, Ingold reported, told of being overcome by their plaintive cries of despair—macabre laments that ceased only upon reaching the outskirts of the haunted plain.

Other manifestations of this same legend, continued Ingold, could also be found within various local traditions. When a man died in the region, he was said "to have gone to join the soldiers of Prince Charles." Similarly, the people of the nearby town of Cernay were themselves known by the customary nickname "Ochsenfeld-Ritter," the Knights of the Ochsenfeld. In 1852, a decade before Ingold's lecture, a laborer digging a reservoir for the local mills unearthed the remains of some ancient weapons. A rumor immediately spread through the countryside that the "armor of Prince Charles" had just been discovered.[9]

Interpreting these strange vestiges of the past, Ingold suggested that the hoary legend of Prince Charles and his phantom army was an imaginative way of accounting for Louis the Pious's abandonment by his men in the middle of the night. How else could one explain the fact that, on that fateful June evening in 833, there had been two armies, while the next morning there was only one? Evidently, the local populace believed that God himself had joined the struggle, explained Ingold, and cast into the earth those men who were in the process of breaking their sworn oaths of fidelity by furtively abandoning their lord, Louis. Behold, in the morning there was now but one (much larger) army—that of the sons. All those faithful to Louis had disappeared! Moreover, continued Ingold, because the young Prince Charles (known later as Charles "the Bald") had caused the discord—the need for a kingdom of his own had ultimately led his father to confront his elder half brothers on the Rotfeld—it was this same Charles who was forever damned to lead the army of traitors across the cursed plain.[10]

On June 18, 1809, Napoleon called to his chambers at Saint-Cloud a number of his French and Italian bishops, whom he suspected of collusion and treason with the pope.[11] Upon entering the room, the bishops beheld not just Napoleon but an audience consisting of Empress Marie Louise and her attendants, the viceroy of Italy, and several other high-ranking officials. Finishing his coffee as though on cue, Napoleon strode with choreographed steps to a nearby table, reached for a prop he had readied there, and confronted the startled bishops. Brandishing the day's newspaper, the *Moniteur*, as evidence of their "treason," the emperor suddenly burst into a rage, hurling insults and accusations while wringing the paper in his hands. As Talleyrand, Napoleon's senior advisor, would later recount with distaste, "the excited countenance he assumed, the violence and confusion of his expressions and the attitude of those whom he addressed, made of this singular conference a scene such as he delighted in playing, and in which he displayed his brutal coarseness."

Incensed by the outcome of the bishops' meeting with the pope as reported by the newspaper, Napoleon first attacked Cardinal Fesch, his maternal uncle, launching into a confused tirade about "proper" ecclesiastical principles and customs. Fesch's behavior at the council, he proclaimed, betrayed a plot to elevate himself within the church and cow any opposition through his kinship with Napoleon. Wounded, the cardinal responded firmly that the emperor's melodramatic notion of a plot was the result of a simple misunderstanding—as the archbishop of Lyon, his assumption of the title "primate of Gaul" at the council was a traditional, well-precedented, and hardly exceptional episcopal practice. Yet even after Fesch's explanation, which received the unanimous agreement of the other bishops, Napoleon refused to listen. Instead, the emperor, irked and growing defensive, only generalized his increasing anger. Confusing the word *obéissance* for *obédience* in the oath sworn by the bishops at the previous day's assembly, he now accused them all of conspiring with the pope against him. "For one is a traitor," he added, "when he takes two oaths of fidelity at the same time, and to two sovereigns, enemies." Again the bishops protested, trying desperately to make Napoleon recognize both the difference between the two words and that their oath of *obédience* should be understood not as outright submission but only as the obedience owed by any Roman Catholic to the pope. Again their efforts proved futile. Indeed, they served only to inflame the emperor, who now threw one of those violent tantrums for which he was notorious (Figure 2). According to Talleyrand, the seething, exasperated emperor

> continued to talk for an hour with an incoherence, which would have left no recollection other than astonishment at his ignorance and his loquacity, if the phrase which follows, and which he repeated every three or four minutes, had not revealed the depth of his thought. "Messieurs," he exclaimed to them, "you wish to treat me as if I were Louis le Débonnaire. Do not confound the son with the father. You see in me Charlemagne. . . . I am Charlemagne, I, . . . yes, I am Charlemagne!" This "I am Charlemagne" recurred at each instant.

Only fatigue finally brought an end to his rant around midnight. At that point, concluded Talleyrand, of those witnessing the scene "each one went his way, carrying from Saint-Cloud strange impressions." Just what these impressions were one can only guess, but the events of 833 likely loomed large in the depth of Napoleon's thought—that his own bishops, like those on the Rotfeld, had betrayed their oaths of fidelity and were plotting with the pope against him.[12] Desperately wanting to be seen as Charlemagne,[13] the insecure emperor was wracked by fears that he was instead being seen as Louis the Pious and that his haughty bishops were acting on this appearance. He, however, would not be "treated," i.e., humbled, like the debonair son.[14] "I am Charlemagne," he announced again and again—words that were meant both

Figure 2. *Maniac-Raving's, or Little Boney in a Strong Fit*. Caricature of Napoleon by James Gillray, published May 24, 1803.

as an attestation and a threat. There would be no confusion over their respective roles in the present drama. He would make certain of that.

The Beginning of the End?

Much like their presence in the popular imagination, the events at the Field of Lies along with Louis' contrition at the feet of his clergy at Saint-Médard have together long been stamped into the scholarly imagination, appearing as central to many narratives concerned with the decline or disintegration of the Carolingian realm. Traditionally seen as a moment of crisis for the Carolingian monarchy, they are consistently invoked by historians to mark the beginning of a steady dissipation of its "universal" sovereignty. Despite the fact that Louis would quickly regain the support of most of his sons and magnates the following year and be reinstated as emperor in 835 by having the judgment of penance officially overturned at assemblies in Thionville and

Metz,[15] in the eyes of generations of historians his rule would never again be the same. For example, in 1765 the Abbé de Mably's description of Louis, following the events of 833, was nothing if not ominously foreboding: "confused by his good and bad fortune, he was more timid than ever." Equally dire was J.-C.-L. Simonde de Sismondi's languid portrait of Louis: "[after 833] his character appeared still weaker than in the preceding period, his policy more vacillating, and his projects, almost all abandoned before they were put in execution, were less worthy of remembrance." For James Prichard, Louis' penance at Soissons was simply the emperor's "greatest error of all," while for Thomas Greenwood the "detestable transaction" on the Field of Lies was the "starting-point of one of the boldest experiments upon the credulity of mankind ever devised." The remainder of Louis' reign following that "instructive chapter in the history of human depravity" upon the Rotfeld, he concluded, could "be dismissed in a few sentences."[16]

Twentieth-century historiography saw little change in this inveterate characterization of Louis and the ruinous effects of 833. In 1902, Arthur Kleinclausz could still describe that fateful year as a "grave" moment in the history of the Carolingian empire, a description Ferdinand Lot would support in 1948 by representing Louis in his years after 833 as a monarch both "incorrigible" and "incurable."[17] Nearly a decade later, Theodor Schieffer estimated Louis' abandonment and fall at the hands of the bishops as having been the "heaviest blow" to the empire and monarchy, an event whose "irrevocable" consequences were described by Jacques Boussard and Robert Folz shortly thereafter in terms of "chaos" and "confusion."[18] Even after a major reevaluation in 1990 of Louis and his problematic career, one that sought to "expose the inadequacy of the clichés with which the reign of Charlemagne's heir has customarily been dismissed," many scholars have continued to paint Louis' later years in dismal tones.[19]

In short, for modern Carolingian historiography, "833 tends to appear as definitive," observes Janet Nelson, a fateful year signaling "the fall of monarchy; the end of peace and concord; a trauma from which neither the Carolingians nor the Franks ever recovered."[20] Yet this definitive appearance is deceiving, for, as Nelson has shown, the last seven years of Louis' reign following 833 were hardly those of an ineffectual "shadow king." On the contrary, they were filled with Louis' continuous efforts to keep his eldest son, Lothar, out of Francia and reassert his own control over the imperial succession—arduous activities whose success did much to restore the confidence and commitment of Louis' magnates and faithful men.[21] Indeed, in the face of what contemporary stargazers took to be a dire portent, Louis, like his father Charlemagne, was optimistic about the course of his reign, interpreting the appearance in 837 of what would later be dubbed Halley's comet as a salutary admonition from God, an auspicious sign compelling all to hasten in the improvement of their knowledge and abilities.[22] Why then, in light of such observations, have scholars continually focused on 833 as the definitive moment signaling the commencement of Carolingian decline?[23]

The Beginning of the Story of the End

Certainly the factor that contributes most to the allure of 833 has been the long historiographical shadow cast by the events of that year.[24] Throughout the past millennium of their telling and retelling, the circumstances of Louis' abandonment and penance have repeatedly been the subject of emplotment by historians, beginning with the Carolingians themselves.[25] Whether interpreted as a tragedy or a comedy, the events of 833 have nearly always been organized and expressed as a kind of didactic drama, one which, for the purposes of modern historians, eloquently showcases those pernicious elements that would appear with ever greater frequency during the course of the ninth century, ultimately leading to the downfall of the realm.

In the following pages of Part I, we shall survey the tradition of emplotment connected to the dramatic events of 833 and evaluate the considerable influence it has exerted upon modern attempts to understand the transformations that took place in the ninth century.[26] That is, rather than explore what the events of 833 can tell us about broad patterns of continuity and change within Carolingian culture per se, we shall first trace the enduring memory of Louis the Pious's abandonment and penance over the succeeding centuries and plot a history of remembrance revealing broad patterns all its own. Above all, what must be kept in mind is the great difference between the aims of later historians' representations of the events and the goals of those ninth-century writers who first gave the events their dramatic complexion.

To be sure, writers both past and present believed 833 to have been a momentous year; that they have shared this conviction for radically different reasons, however, is a fact rarely acknowledged by modern historians. As we have seen, the events of 833 have consistently been deemed central to many historical narratives concerned with the achievement and failure of the Carolingians. I shall argue that this seemingly central role in fact arises from an

unwittingly contrived congruence between, on the one hand, the vivid, polemical accounts of 833 supplied by the Carolingian sources and, on the other
hand, the elements begged both by the narrative strategy of achievement and
failure and by a pervasive interest in the dramatic.[27] Historians writing on the
rise and decline of the Carolingians have traditionally looked for culpability
and motive in their efforts to explain the empire's ruin—a pattern of analysis
suggested by the narrative strategy itself.[28] If the once-great empire had risen
on the powerful and magnanimous shoulders of Charlemagne (the "shoulders of a Titan," in the words of one scholar), its fall (it seems to follow) must
likewise be attributable both to weakness and to the self-serving interests
of individuals.[29] And as the following impressionistic portrait—already rendered with assurance over a century ago—makes clear, historians have long
been convinced of who such "guilty" parties were:

> Louis the Pious, who is also called the Debonnair, presents the
> melancholy spectacle of a man essentially good by nature, full of lofty
> intentions, amiable and magnanimous in private life, quick to repent
> when he had done amiss, and quicker to forgive injury, yet wanting
> in vigour and resolution, easily relying on the advice of others, and
> destitute of the worldly wisdom which would have enabled him to
> choose his advisers well. Men of his character are numerous in every
> age; they are doomed to suffer themselves and to bring suffering on
> others; and when they are born, as Louis was born, to hold the reins of
> government, their life is apt to be a tragedy. So it was with the son of
> Charles the Great, who . . . experienced the fate of our own Henry II at
> the hands of his turbulent and ambitious sons.[30]

To historians of Carolingian decline in need of a fateful, dramatic moment,
one punctuated by a melancholy spectacle involving such reckless delinquents
and their tragically feckless father, the year 833 has been particularly alluring,
for Carolingian writers themselves spared little effort in blaming individuals
and providing motives in their many striking depictions of that year's extraordinary events.[31]

However, while the contemporary accounts of 833 have served the purposes of generations of historians by revealing the ominous undercurrents
that would eventually drag down the realm, they have rarely been understood in terms of their authors' own sensibilities and immediate concerns—
concerns hardly congruent with the priorities of later narrators of the realm's

decline.[32] Carolingian authors, in telling their story of what happened in 833, represented the events in accordance with particular mimetic modes (such as biblical stories and/or classical genres), a highly subjective, interpretive process that led them—inasmuch as it allowed them—to collect, organize, and present details and assign roles to individuals in accordance with the modes' decorum of possibilities and constraints.[33] What the following pages will stress is that this emplotment within what modern historians call the historical record, while subjective, was never arbitrary[34]; that each Carolingian author had his own set of experiences, circumstances, and motivations, which collectively contributed to make certain modes seem most apt for both understanding and representing the events of 833.[35] Whether the doers and their deeds were cast and emplotted in accordance with the scriptural trials of Job's faith or in terms of the classical absurdities of the Roman playwright Terence, the reliance upon any one or combination of such modes in every instance says as much about the cultural milieu in which they were used as it does about those who used them.[36] Indeed, the enduring dramatic quality of the events of 833—the very aspect that, as we shall see, brings to the fore issues of culpability and motive seized upon by later historians of rise and decline in need of a turning point—itself amply attests to the rhetorical skills possessed by Carolingian authors, as well as to the complexity of their culture.[37]

Writing a Wrong

Before undertaking any survey of the stories about the events of 833, it is imperative to recall that Louis the Pious soon regained the throne. Rescued from his captors within months, the emperor crushed the rebellion and was ritually reinvested with his regalia by February of 835, less than two years after his abandonment and public penance.[38] Moreover, Louis retained firm control over the empire for another five years; only his death by illness in the year 840 would wrest it from him again.[39] This fact of Louis' swift recovery and triumph over the rebellion is significant, for it has profoundly influenced the particular perspective from which the events of 833 have nearly always been viewed.

Among the many ninth-century texts that make mention of the events of 833, six narrative sources treat them in vivid detail: the "Annals of Saint-Bertin," the *Gesta Hludowici imperatoris* by Thegan, the *Vita Hludowici imperatoris* by the Astronomer, the *Historiae* of Nithard, the *Epitaphium Arsenii*

TABLE 1. TEXTS DETAILING AND DISPUTING THE ABANDONMENT OF LOUIS THE PIOUS AND HIS SUBSEQUENT PENANCE IN 833

Texts	Key events
	June 829, Reform council of Paris
	August 829, Louis the Pious redivides the empire
	April 830, First rebellion of Lothar, Pippin, and Louis the German
	February 831, Louis the Pious redivides the empire
	September 832, Louis the Pious redivides the empire
	June 833, Louis the Pious is abandoned on the Rotfeld
	October 833, Louis the Pious undertakes penance
	March 834, Louis the Pious is restored at Saint-Denis
	February 835, Louis the Pious is re-crowned at Metz
Annales Bertiniani Thegan, *Gesta Hludowici imperatoris*	
	June 840, Louis the Pious dies
Astronomer, *Vita Hludowici imperatoris* Nithard, *Historiae*	June 841, Battle of Fontenoy
	August 843, Treaty of Verdun
Paschasius Radbertus, *Epitaphium Arsenii*	
	Beginning of the tenth century
Odilo of Soissons, *Translatio Sancti Sebastiani*	

by Paschasius Radbertus, and the *Translatio sancti Sebastiani* by Odilo (Table 1).[40] As we shall see in the chapters to follow, later authors have drawn consistently and selectively from these same six accounts to tell their own stories about 833 and its momentous place in the history of the Carolingian realm. For example, of the nine modern authors mentioned at the beginning of this chapter—Mably, Sismondi, Prichard, Greenwood, Kleinclausz, Lot, Schieffer, Boussard, and Folz—nearly all rely on some combination of these six Carolingian accounts as the basis for their own narratives.[41] Yet, if it has long been known what these six accounts say about 833, rarely has it been asked how, and only then perhaps why, each tells the story of that year in its own particular (and, to later authors, particularly appealing) fashion.[42] Robert Stein has put the matter succinctly: "Rather than picking and choosing only those aspects of the [sources'] content that are plausible for us to believe and because they are plausible seem true for us, let us try to look *at* [these sources] rather than *through* [them]. How [do these narratives] go about the business of securing belief in [their] representation of experience?"[43] It is to these questions—of narrative content, form, and the dynamic relationship between them—that we shall now turn.

The Annals of Saint-Bertin

In what are now known as the "Annals of Saint-Bertin," the anonymous ecclesiastic who recorded the yearly events of the Frankish realm during the early 830s told a dismal tale of contumacy and greed, loss and redemption.[44] To be sure, the annalist clearly made an attempt to keep his entries consistent with those written by the annals' previous custodian, for he continued the practice of recording the specific details of the ruler's itinerary, such as where Louis celebrated Easter and Christmas, the time and location of public assemblies, and the like.[45] But during the early 830s, these regularizing activities around which the annalist organized each year's other events were overshadowed by the story of Louis' fall and recovery. Janet Nelson once remarked that the entries between 830 and 834, rather than written as typical annual installments, appear to have been composed in their present form all at once, and only after the restoration of Louis to the throne in March 834. This is an insight with rather significant implications, for the retrospective entries of these years work together as a sad, yet edifying, account of right over wrong: of equity over iniquity, clemency over severity, and patience over reckless haste.[46] Indeed, the degree to which the events were emplotted by this annalist of the Annals of Saint-Bertin becomes all the more evident when one compares his representation of these years with a parallel account provided by a contemporary annalist. In the "Annals of Xanten," for instance, the following entry appears for the year 833:

> Then, in the summer, the sons of the emperor—Lothar, Pippin, and Louis—met in the region of Alsace, bringing Pope Gregory with them.

And there the emperor's men disregarded their oaths, and, leaving him
alone, they turned back to Lothar, [and] pledged an oath of loyalty
to him. The emperor—by their command deprived at the same time
of his wife and his kingdom—distressed and grieving, came into the
control of [his] sons. They sent him into public custody in Soissons,
and a similar thing was done to his wife. And since their plans had
been brought to completion, the realm of the Franks was divided into
three, and the Lord Pope returned to his fatherland. Lothar remained
in Compiègne, but the rest [of the people] returned [home], each to his
own.[47]

Unlike this typical passage by the Xanten annalist, which provides a pithy
record of royal politics during the early 830s, the annalist of the Annals of
Saint-Bertin chose to narrativize the events in considerable detail, shaping
and linking them into a vivid story—one that had heroes and villains, told
of good kingship and bad, and at once illustrated and declared the nature of
proper and improper relationships between fathers and sons.[48] Writing as a
partisan of the emperor, the annalist made decisions about what to include
and exclude in his account that not only fit the moral tale he wished to tell
but made it compellingly dramatic as well.

Above all, the annalist sought to show how his Emperor Louis, even
in times of extreme adversity, acted according to an ecclesiastical model of
perfect kingship.[49] Throughout the account, Louis is portrayed as a king renowned for his mercy (*clementia*) and magnanimity (*pietas*), a sovereign who,
even after being deeply humiliated, repeatedly pardoned those who had risen
against him, commuting their death sentences and returning their confiscated
benefices and lands. He was always one to act in accordance with law, and
was sure to seek the counsel of his advisors and faithful men before decid-
ing upon a course of action. Yet Louis certainly had a strong will of his own;
while he often bore adversity with patience and sought peace with words, he
was also a mighty defender of the faith, guarding his Christian people with
the force of arms. In addition, the annalist took care to underscore the seemly
behavior that Louis practiced in his relationship with his sons, conduct that
befit a loving father and a king. He always received obedient sons honorably
and with paternal affection, but also knew how to treat disobedient children, showing first his deep disquiet and then publicly displaying his disfavor
toward the unruly son. Moreover, as a proper king and father, implied the
annalist approvingly, Louis never let the spite of his children provoke him. If

a son chose to rebel, the patient emperor would pursue him slowly, expecting the child to turn back eventually and pay him the respect that was his right and due.

In contrast to Louis' illustrious virtues, the annalist also evinced the depravity of those responsible for the emperor's many troubles.[50] The pernicious "murmuring" of the populace (a significant, descriptive term, which points to the biblical mode of the events' emplotment)[51] and the wicked scheming of certain magnates—in particular, Matfrid, count of Orléans, and the diabolic *incentor* Ebbo, archbishop of Reims—had turned Louis' sons against him.[52] Once the annalist began to recount the various offenses committed by Louis' sons, however, his focus left such instigators as Matfrid or the populace and fixed strictly upon the wretched examples of kingship demonstrated by the royal brood. If their father was renowned for his mercy and magnanimity, then Lothar, Pippin, and Louis the German, in the annalist's tale, were all the more infamous for their inhuman cruelty and oppression. In the course of their rebellions, they are constantly portrayed as imposing excessive burdens, rendering extreme penalties, and razing the lands of their enemies. And unlike Louis, the contumacious sons neither behaved in accordance with law nor sought the advice of their counselors and faithful men. Rather, they either were led astray by conniving magnates and the murmuring—in the sense of fickle—populace or acted maliciously by following the dictates of their own rash willfulness. Indeed, it was just such poor judgment that had led them to their shameless course of action, one that—contrary to the trust of the emperor—could have done harm to the Christian people. Yet, as the annalist quickly made plain, there had been little to fear, for, given a taste of adversity, the sons' first reaction was craven terror and flight—responses hardly resembling the fortitude shown by their father. Certainly these qualities were reprehensible for kings; but, in the annalist's estimation, perhaps the most offensive trait of Lothar, Pippin, and Louis the German was their behavior as sons. They had dared to scorn the fatherly affection and forgiveness freely offered to them by Louis, wishing instead, remarked the annalist, "to remain fixed in their obstinacy."[53]

If, as Paul Dutton has observed, the Annals of Saint-Bertin's first author sought to portray Louis as an oppressed father in a dreary domestic tragedy,[54] then, to make his "tragic" point most effectively, such a moral tale required the magnification of its principal elements to the point of their figural, if not explicitly typological, signification: the loftiness of Louis' character was duly if inversely matched and accentuated by the abysmal malevolence of his oppressors. Equally important to the efficacy of his narrative, however, were those things the annalist chose to diminish, leave in abeyance, or even efface in its telling.[55] In other words, to a contemporary ecclesiastic, it may have been obvious that "matters that are done or events that occur [are] committed to annals for posterity to learn about"[56]; less obvious was the fact that one still needed to make decisions about what "matters and events" were worthy of mention and thus preservation. Certainly the first annalist of the Annals of Saint-Bertin passed over specific details in his story that, from a modern perspective, would have performed the function of motives. For example, in the entry for the year 831 there is no mention of the new partition of the empire made by Louis in response to the earlier unsuccessful rebellion by his sons in 830—a partition that left only the kingdom of Italy to Lothar, while dividing the greater realm of Francia among Pippin, Louis the German, and the young Charles.[57] Moreover, for the year 832 the entry obscures the fact that Louis had revised his partition of the empire yet again, transferring the kingdom of Aquitaine from Pippin to Prince Charles.[58] To the modern reader, the inclusion of these unsettling events seems necessary, if not crucial, for understanding why the sons continued to rebel against their father and act "willfully." To the Carolingian annalist, however, the edifying story he wished to tell had no need for what we might now understand as a motive: rather, the emperor was most righteous, while his sons sought insolently to finish what they had begun. Their actions were reflections not merely of their "roles" (perhaps as the typological, wicked sons of Jacob[59]) but of their nature—bad sons acted badly.[60] No wonder, then, that when the annalist had Louis wonder aloud "why [Pippin] had fled from his father's presence without permission" in 832, he provided no answer.[61] The reason was clear: Pippin, like his brothers, was just a bad son. His very actions—as carefully remembered and represented by the annalist—betrayed him.

Thegan

In 836/37, Thegan, a nobleman, suffragan bishop of Trier and loyal biographer of Louis, also cast the events of 833 in dramatic fashion, contrasting the pious equanimity of the emperor with the treachery of his servants. In the early parts of the "Deeds of the Emperor Louis," Thegan closely followed—and at times consciously inverted—the pattern of the biography of Louis' father, the *Vita Karoli Magni* by Einhard, dutifully reporting Louis' military expeditions, suppression of rebels, patronage of architecture, and physical characteristics.[62] But as Ernst Tremp has noted, the closer one comes to the events of 833/34—what Tremp calls the focal point of the work—the more original and extensive the biography becomes, a correlation demonstrating Thegan's familiarity with Louis' travails and perhaps the greater significance he accorded them.[63] For instance, it has long been known that Thegan's biography of Louis possesses an "annalistic" form, with the events of the emperor's life organized and described in sequential, yearly sections. As even the biography's first editor, the Carolingian scholar and poet Walafrid Strabo, observed ca. 841, Thegan had composed his work "*in morem annalium*," in the manner of annals.[64] What has not been acknowledged, however, is how Thegan worked within his annalistic format to build anticipation for his tale's focal point of 833/34. For example, in his 821 "entry," Thegan remarks that "at that time [namely, in the year 821] infidelity was already threatening Louis."[65]

A more prominent forecasting of the storm that would break in the 830s comes in the entry for the year 817, significantly, at the point where Thegan abandons the thematic pattern of Einhard's biography and begins to tell his own story. Here Thegan's voice carries an ominous tone, for his account of Louis' life opens with a forbidding sermon, one filled with invective for the insolence of lowborn bishops. Closing emphatically with the word *Amen*, Thegan's entry establishes the worrisome theme of the story that remained to be told: the emperor himself, Thegan lamented, had allowed the execrable, inveterate practice of turning the basest slaves into the highest bishops to continue unabated. And its effects, assured the biographer, were catastrophic.[66] Indeed, Thegan's modern editor has astutely identified the denouement of this allusive "introduction"; while Thegan's sudden, sermonizing diatribe (chap. 20) and his later portrayal of Louis' fall at Soissons in 833 (chap. 44) constitute the only two breaks in the otherwise regular, annalistic format of the biography, it is in the latter that Thegan reveals the terrible outcome anticipated by his earlier remonstrations.[67] For it had been none other than an archbishop "who was originally of servile stock"—that "shameless and most cruel man" Ebbo—who had "savagely crushed Louis," insisted Thegan, and brought "the most pious emperor" to his knees.[68]

Another way Thegan heightened the drama of 833 was to recount the desertion of Louis by his troops on the Rotfeld with a striking, emotive anecdote:

Leaving their tents, [Louis' men] went over to his sons. On the next day those who remained came to the emperor who admonished them, saying "Go to my sons. I do not wish any of you to lose your lives or limbs on account of me." And they, filled with tears, withdrew from him.[69]

Employing direct speech to spotlight Louis' charity and concern, self-sacrifice and fortitude, in the face of desperate circumstances, Thegan further under-scored these royal virtues by noting the emotional reaction of Louis' few remaining men.[70] Certainly, their anguish befit the decorum of the scene. As Thegan remarked so ominously in his prefatory sermon, when the arro-gance of episcopal slaves gains a wide sway, men, "truly, with great sadness, moaning and weeping, count their days."[71] Duly confirming this pronounce-ment, Louis' last adherents, unlike their dignified emperor, were not able to hold back their tears over Louis' deplorable fortune at the hands of the lowborn Ebbo and, thus, over the ensuing fate of the realm. At this point in the story, they (via their author writing in retrospect) knew the very days were numbered.

While Thegan used foreshadowing and rhetorical conventions such as anecdotes and direct speech to focus attention on the events of 833, these techniques simultaneously established that the looming events should be in-terpreted in accordance with scripture.[72] For example, in his allusive sermon of 817, Thegan proved that turning the basest slaves into the highest bishops was "the greatest evil among the Christian people" by explicitly quoting the testimony of the Old Testament (3 Kings 13:33–34).[73] And as Thegan's modern editor has recognized, the tears shed by Louis' best men on the Rotfeld were in fact the biblical tears of Ozias, quoted by Thegan from the book of Judith (7:23).[74]

It is in the representation of the emperor's fall at Soissons, however, that Thegan revealed the specific story he had been telling all along: Louis' inces-sant struggles, proclaimed the biographer, should be seen as "nothing but a test of his goodness, just as the patience of blessed Job."[75] Beginning with his harangue in 817 and culminating in the humiliation of Louis at Soissons in 833, Thegan represented the events of those years in accordance with a particular biblical mode, one that emphasized the righteousness of his most pious emperor. Like another Job, Louis weathered each new affliction during his reign with unwavering faith—a plot given to the emperor's life that led Thegan to include certain details in his story and forego others, to heighten particular qualities of its characters and diminish others. Above all, to un-

derscore the perfect devotion and aplomb of the emperor, this "Jobian" mode
required the amplification of the difficulties of Louis' reign in general and the
events of 833 in particular. Moreover, if 833 was, in Thegan's tale, the year of
Louis' greatest trials, then Archbishop Ebbo was without doubt the emperor's
greatest tormentor. And for Thegan, it was in this fact that the true cause for
concern lay.

Like the experience of Job, Thegan understood Louis' struggles within the
larger context of divine fulfillment.[76] If Louis had been ordained by the Lord
to sit on his father's throne, then his divestiture by Ebbo had equally been the
fulfillment of divine will.[77] Thus, in Thegan's story, while Count Matfrid of
Orléans was named as the kindler of many evils (*incentor malorum*) against
Louis, and the rebel bishops as those who had chosen Ebbo "to savagely crush
Louis with the lies of the others," Ebbo himself harbored no motive behind
his machinations; rather, his insolence and cunning ambition were seen by
Thegan as essential, constitutive qualities of the lowborn. The grasping Ebbo
was simply the divine instrument of Louis' greatest and most difficult trial.[78]
The fact that God—working through the bishops—had chosen one such as
Ebbo for this instrumental function, however, was a deeply disturbing sign,
for, as Thegan grieved, there was a vast difference between the persecutors
of Job and those who had been assigned to beset Louis: "Those who taunted
holy Job are said to have been kings in the Book of Saint Tobias," he explained, "while those who struck at Louis were the legal slaves of him and
his father." Here was the nobleman Thegan's central concern—the present
transgression and overturning of old boundaries, where slaves now played the
part of kings.[79] Certainly the divestiture of the emperor had seemed to him a
terrible event, but it was ultimately a demonstration of divine favor toward a
faithful monarch; as Thegan was quick to report, Louis had not long to wait
before regaining his throne. That the lowborn Ebbo had been Louis' persecu-
tor, however, was nothing short of an abomination, an appallingly clear and
deplorable sign of the realm's current plight. And it was this fact, above all,
that Thegan sought to bring to the fore through his literary skill.

In addition to foreshadowing and rhetorical conventions, Thegan employed biblical testimony and even classical verse specifically within his account of the year 833 to underscore the issue so deserving of lamentation.
The "cruel Ebbo," through his cupidity and mendacity, decried Thegan, had
scorned the apostolic precepts of Peter and Paul on the correct relationship
between masters and servants. Men such as Ebbo—namely, base slaves unnaturally raised to positions of honor ("[Louis] made you free, not noble,

which is impossible"), slaves whose "fathers were goatherds, not counselors of princes"—were not just divine foils but earthly foes. Only if he were the possessor of "an iron tongue and bronze lips," Thegan waxed poetically, could he even begin to enumerate or explain all their wrongs. But if by chance there were anyone who wished to probe all their evils with poetry, he continued, "perhaps he could overcome the bard of Smyrna, old Homer, Mincianus, Virgil, and Ovid."[80]

Thus, the urgent point of Thegan's biography of Louis was to sound a warning. While Ebbo had already been deposed and imprisoned by the time Thegan composed the biography in 836/37—indeed, Thegan closes his work with the fall of that "most vile peasant Ebbo"[81]—the divine message revealed by the events of 833 was nevertheless clear: the ongoing practice of raising the lowborn to positions of power should be anathematized. As Thegan implored, "let the almighty God, along with kings and princes, deign henceforth to stifle and eradicate this very evil practice, so that it may no longer occur among Christian people. Amen."[82] Contrary to the claims of some scholars, Thegan's book concludes not with the reassuring "happy ending" of Ebbo's fate but with this nervous concern: "The greatest discipline [once] taught [an upstart], so that he did not become arrogant. There is the greatest need to follow this example now."[83] Such distress was not just over the specific possibility of Ebbo's regaining his episcopal see but more about the larger problem of transgression that Ebbo's case symbolized.[84] Louis' great devotion to the study of scripture was certainly admirable, but, as Thegan noted, its demands had, unfortunately, caused the emperor to forego the prudence for which he was renowned and "entrust more to his counselors than he should have."[85] Yet, this delegation of authority would not have been a problem, Thegan implied, if only Louis had appointed the right kind of counselors in the first place—not arrogant upstarts, not former slaves who "oppress the nobles and strive to raise themselves along with their most vile relatives," but men of quality and noble birth.[86] Thegan could only hope that the emperor, with the noble counsel of his biography, would now recognize this wrong and right it.

Thegan's work reflected the anxieties of his fellow churchmen and aristocrats and was likely aimed at the constituency of the imperial court.[87] No matter whether the audience there were other "elevated," overbearing counselors or the emperor himself, Thegan's subject matter was absolutely, if notoriously, topical. As he pensively noted in the last lines of his book, these were still discordant times.[88] In 833, God had shown why.

The Astronomer

Another of Louis' biographers, an anonymous author known to modern scholars only as the "Astronomer," also told the story of 833 in dramatic terms. Perhaps he was one of those very men against whom the contemporary abbot of Corbie, Paschasius Radbertus, repeatedly fulminated—an admirer of profane letters, who studied "the carping criticism of tragedies and the vain imagining of poets" in order to charm or soften the reader with "tragic piety."[89] For upon looking back from the winter of 840/41, the Astronomer, employing a rather rare term, specifically described the events of 833 as an "almost unheard-of tragedy" (*pene inaudita traguedia*)—this being the *locus classicus* for the explicitly "tragic" characterization of the entire affair.[90]

Written from the perspective of the imperial palace, the Astronomer's text clearly exhibits the high literary art of a cultivated courtier.[91] As many scholars have observed, this lengthy biography of the recently deceased Emperor Louis (20 June 840) displays not only a dynamic style reminiscent of the church fathers but also its author's readiness to draw from a variety of contemporary sources to tell his story.[92] The long-lost *Vita* of the monk Ademar and the "Royal Frankish Annals" are just the most conspicuous of his many literary influences.[93] Indeed, contrary to most claims, the Astronomer seems to have had access to the Royal Frankish Annals for the years following 829 (modern scholars have dubbed these, as a separate work, the aforementioned Annals of Saint-Bertin), or at least the notes from which they were redacted, as evidenced by the entire sentences he appropriated from them.[94] The biographer also utilized the Annals of Saint-Bertin as an outline around which to construct his larger narrative and develop the dreary domestic tale of Louis and his sons more fully and more explicitly. What the annalist had been content to declare, describe, and suggest, the Astronomer was willing to foreshadow, embellish, and assert—the difficulties of Louis' life, and those of 833 in particular, amounted to nothing less than a tragedy.[95]

Now, to an audience of the twenty-first century steeped in the countless melodramas of Hollywood, the perception of 833 as a tragedy hardly seems surprising.[96] But in the early Middle Ages, with its scraps and vague notions of classical drama, the term *tragoedia* was very rarely invoked.[97] Thus, the Astronomer's specific use of it signals not only the direction and depth of his sympathy but also the presence of a particularly sophisticated interpretive scheme.[98] In the biography Louis is cast in the role of Christ, whose terrestrial life the Astronomer considered a tragedy.[99]

As Walter Berschin has noted, the casting of Louis' life in tragic terms is even adumbrated in the Astronomer's prologue. At once admiring and celebrating the four cardinal virtues that so epitomized the emperor's character—sobriety, prudence, justice, and fortitude—the Astronomer closed his introductory profile by suggesting Louis' single fault (*culpa*): that he had been too mild (*nimis clemens*).[100] In Berschin's estimation, this is the emperor's tragic flaw around which the entire biography turns.[101] The Astronomer himself—in an evocative challenge—may appear to leave it to the reader to ascertain the veracity of this fault: "Whether these things [namely, Louis' virtues and fault] are true or not, whoever reads this [work] carefully should be able to discover."[102] But the clues the biographer left within his text nevertheless strongly suggest the conclusion he wished his reader to reach; "It will become clear, after a few [more words]," confides the Astronomer, that the rebels, to whom Louis showed clemency by sparing their lives, demonstrated their gratitude by bringing nothing but "the greatest slaughter of which they were capable against him."[103] Here, it seems, was the truth of the tragedy: Louis, the most orthodox and Christian emperor, had paid the price for his excessive *clementia* with a reign characterized by revolt—a bitterly tragic irony that was not lost on the Astronomer, who implored the reader, for Louis' sake, to join with the apostle Paul in his sardonic request to "forgive him this wrong!" (Cf. 2 Cor. 12:13).[104] In fact, this mordant appeal with the words of Paul is the key to understanding the Astronomer's narrative; if being too forgiving was Louis' only "fault"—one which, he adds, was ascribed only by "the envious"[105]—then this reflected not an imperfect emperor who had been too mild but rather the utter depravity of the times, an age when Louis' tender clemency had brought him nothing but ridicule and scorn.[106] For those who would read carefully, this was the deeper truth. Louis had been a perfect king in an imperfect era.[107] That was both his ironic and tragic fate (*infortunium*).[108]

Certainly, the Astronomer's biography of Louis was an exculpatory work, but this hardly kept the biographer from imputing blame and explicating motives.[109] Employing a vivid proverb, the Astronomer ascribed culpability for the discord of the realm during the 830s to certain great nobles, men who were "always desirous of change after the manner of greedy dogs and birds which look for another's defeat to add to their satiety."[110] The numerous allegations of these wicked magnates were clearly pretexts and enticements, none of which, remarked the Astronomer, could quite conceal their guilt.[111] Yet, such men were merely intermediaries in a diabolic chain of liability and sin. As the Astronomer discerned, it had been the devil himself who had stirred up and persuaded the nobles to rebel through his cunning instigation.[112] Consequently, figures such as Counts Lambert and Matfrid or Abbots Hilduin and Wala had in their turn joined with the fickle populace, and together—in the opinion of both the emperor and the Astronomer—sought to corrupt the minds of Louis' sons through shouting, urging, and fawning.[113] And sure enough, quipped the Astronomer using another vivid proverb, just as "a gentle drop of water striking very often is wont to bore through the hardest stone, it finally came to pass that [this faction] caused the emperor's sons to form a common league and muster as large an army as they could [against their father]."[114]

In the later years of the Astronomer's tragic tale, however, Louis' wayward sons, unlike their wretched, willful portrayal in the Annals of Saint-Bertin, play a far less insidious role than the ever-iniquitous magnates or the fickle populace. As the biographer was especially careful to note, Lothar, Pippin, and Louis the German—sons hewn from the hardest stone—had given nothing more than their tacit consent to the machinations of their *fideles*; indeed, according to the Astronomer, the overly clement Louis believed that his innocent children were simply being manipulated.[115] For instance, when the sons accused their father of falling prey to perverse delusions, Louis countered with an equivalent charge, reminding them of his paternal affection and begging them "not to confide in the common enemy."[116]

After Louis' abandonment and divestiture, however, such unwitting complicity on the part of his sons was rather hard for the emperor's guilt-ridden, rapidly returning supporters to swallow. Yet, as the Astronomer told it, Lothar, while still holding his father in captivity, was nevertheless willing and able to maintain his innocence in the face of what he deemed hypocritical accusations on the part of the fickle, recreant populace: "No one suffered more in his father's calamity or rejoiced more in his father's prosperity than he did," Lothar "reasonably" (*sane*) told them. But "the ultimate blame (*culpa senioratus*) imputed to him [by the fickle populace] should not be so attributed since they too had deserted and betrayed the emperor."[117]

Like Thegan before him, the Astronomer here shows his hand. For there can be little doubt that the recrimination by Lothar was in fact one that the Astronomer himself felt particularly important to relate. In the biographer's estimation, Lothar's trenchant rebuttal against his accusers had been perfectly "reasonable," a judgment that betrayed the tragedy of Louis' reign as foreshadowed by the Astronomer in the sardonic remarks of his preface—that everyone in the (imperfect) realm was to some degree complicit in the (perfect) emperor's fall, even those who now sought once more to support him.[118] If the pope, leaving the Field of Lies, had returned to Rome "with heavy grief," while, after Louis' penance at Soissons, the factious populace had gone back to their own lands "full of sadness for such deeds," their Judas tears, as carefully depicted by the Astronomer, had come too late.[119] Like Christ, Louis had shown unconditional clemency but was rewarded with nothing but betrayal.[120] Even if sheathed in the words of Lothar's "reasonable" retort, the Astronomer still meant this shamefully tragic truth to cut long and deep.

Before proceeding, we should pause to consider the "dramatic" configuration of the events by the Astronomer, for only recently have a handful of scholars pointed out the marked increase of allusions to drama and theater that occurred in western Europe specifically during the late eighth and ninth centuries.[121] Unfortunately, what such references and their relative frequency might tell us about interpretive modes and the people who used them in the early Middle Ages has largely been overlooked in the rush to determine their value as evidence of actual theatrical performance.[122] Doubtless, the disparaging references to actors and theater by Carolingian ecclesiastics are, for the most part, nothing more than rhetorical commonplaces, themselves dependent on a tradition of moralizing that extends back at least to church fathers such as Jerome and Augustine, if not earlier.[123] Theater and drama had long since disappeared as a living art. Yet, the sum of this textual evidence about drama—despite remaining unreliable as testimony of contemporary performance—nevertheless stands as a powerful and revealing statement about Carolingian culture: drama and actors were frequently, if but figuratively, on the minds of many among the literate and learned.[124] But if this was so, then what did they make of their inherited miscellany of ancient theatrical texts and images, such as the masked and togaed actors of Terence? (Figure 3).[125] When Einhard noted that a woman once yawned so widely that her jaw locked and, to her dismay, "she looked more like a mask (*persona*) than a human being," one wishes he had said more.[126] For like the twelfth-century Andalusian philosopher Averroës, who puzzled over Aristotle's strange words comedy and tragedy in Jorge Luis Borges's famous short story,[127] early medieval authors often devised rather creative definitions for these unfamiliar terms.[128] It is extremely regrettable that we do not know the identity of the Astronomer,[129] for it might shed light on his understanding of tragedy, and consequently on the demands that this concept made on the configuration of his narrative.[130] Certainly, he used the term with a degree of technical pre-

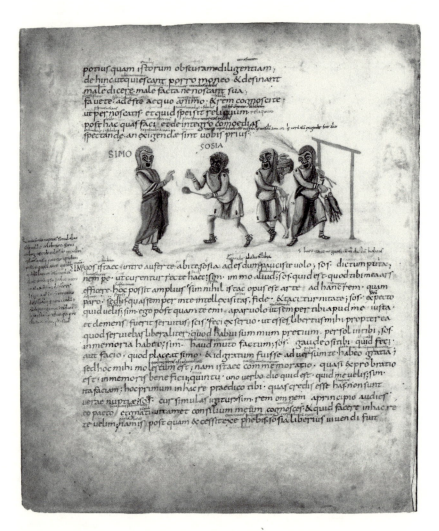

Figure 3. Ninth-century illuminated manuscript of the Comedies of Terence. Rome, Biblioteca Apostolica Vaticana, lat. 3868, fol. 4v. Courtesy Biblioteca Apostolica Vaticana.

cision beyond what Karl Young once enumerated as the three basic criteria understood in the Middle Ages to constitute tragedy: that the story should begin happily but end with misfortune; that it should be written in an elevated style; and that it should treat weighty events in the lives of eminent persons.[131] Moreover, by using the term, the biographer expected his audience to understand him;[132] as we have seen, the Astronomer considered Louis' "unheard-of tragedy" a christological passion. Biblical typology was being fused specifically with an ancient dramatic genre to provide keen insight, a method that has significant implications both for the historiography of the ninth century and for that of the modern era as well.[133] We shall have reason to return to this point in the pages to come.

Nithard

Writing in the autumn of 841 at the behest of the emperor's youngest son, Charles (now eighteen years old), the lay aristocrat and warrior Nithard began a work of history, conceived and executed with the express purposes of both accounting for the recent events of his sovereign's reign and forestalling any competing versions of them.[134] Characterized by one modern author as "a hard-faced historian with a down-to-earth secular intelligence who knew what stirred and drove his own *gens* and the Frankish nobility like the air he breathed," Nithard has only come under major scrutiny in the last century.[135] Doubtless, his "hard-faced" and sparing lay perspective on the events of the 830s–840s has had not a little to do with the utter neglect of his text during the last millennium, as well as its relatively recent popularity among modern scholars confident in their own down-to-earth secular intelligence.[136] For Nithard's explicit aim of his endeavor has a seductively modern ring. In order to expedite faithfully his Lord Charles's command—that is, to reveal, explained Nithard, "why Lothar resolved to pursue you [namely, Charles] and your brother [Louis the German] after your father's death"[137]—Nithard sought "to lay bare the roots" (*explicare initia*) of Charles's present conflicts with his brother. To do so, however, meant beginning his work not with the current events of Charles's reign but with those that occurred during the reign of his father, Louis the Pious. Such insolence—of beginning Charles's own history with an account of someone else's career—was justified, maintained Nithard, if the erstwhile events covered within his opening pages could help to illuminate the truth: "I had initially decided to omit what had occurred in the times of your father," he admitted, "but the truth about your conflicts will appear more clearly to the reader if I summarily point out certain things which came to pass (*contigisse*) during his life."[138]

Foremost among those "certain things" Nithard chose to include in his summary of Louis' life were the events of 833. For if the dire truth about the present, as Nithard insisted repeatedly, was that the once-glorious realm had been ruined through the selfish neglect of the common good—Lothar's current, self-serving belligerence testified to this bitter fact—then the infamous events of 833 had indeed proven to be revelatory. Called by Nithard a "great crime committed against the empire," the abandonment and subsequent divestiture of Louis best illustrated such deplorable, "criminal" negligence.[139] More specifically, the quarrels of the 830s, 833 in particular, exposed to Nithard the underlying reason for the sad neglect of the realm: an opportunistic, "blind cupidity" (*ceca cupiditas*) that was oblivious both to morality and consequentiality.[140] For example, after explaining how Lothar had first seized power from his father in 830, Nithard remarked that "the state of the empire grew worse from day to day, since all were driven by greed and sought only their own advantage." And after describing the circumstances of Louis' restoration in 831, Nithard again observed that the emperor's supporters had acted solely out of self-interest, having been promised a reward of property in exchange for their help. Some, continued Nithard, even expected to be made second in the empire because they had done so much for Louis' restoration.[141]

It was only after Lothar's usurpation of his father in 833, however, that, in Nithard's estimation, the most ruinous effects of such reckless greed finally emerged. Having gained control of the realm under the pretext that it was being run poorly, Lothar's advisors were unable to agree on which of them should become second in the empire; consequently, "they began to argue, and, since each of them looked out for his own," declared Nithard, "they entirely neglected the government."[142] This appears to have been the decisive moment for Nithard, the final blow to a foundering realm. Indeed, the events of 833 made such an impact upon Nithard's mind that one can detect a shift in his political vocabulary: prior to 833, Nithard chose the term *res publica* to signify a united commonwealth; after the events of that year, however, he used *imperium* to describe an empire now ruled (*regere*) by the covetous, rather than governed (*gubernare*) by the magnanimous.[143]

Yet the "great crime" of 833 was for Nithard less definitive than illustrative. It served as a focal point for a work that was, we should remember, "if not quite a tragedy, at least a cautionary tale."[144] By focusing upon the events of 833 to fulfill King Charles's mandate, Nithard not only sought to reveal the truth about the present difficulties but also meant to warn his lord away from the avaricious behavior that caused them. Now, certainly Nithard believed the lasting effects of 833 were dire. The concluding line of his history, composed in March 843, leaves no doubt that Nithard felt he was living in desperate times: "here, there, and everywhere," he observed, "rapines and all kinds of evils have arisen and, thence, the inclemency of the weather has snatched away the hope of all good things."[145] Nithard's death from an ax blow to the head within two years of penning these words—the discovery of his skeleton with its shattered skull a grisly reminder of this violent end[146]—attests to the immediate truth of his work's last words. But as Janet Nelson has recognized, Nithard's gloomy portrait of the present was also an oblique criticism of his king; if 833 marked the ruination of the *res publica*, then not much had changed a decade later under Charles the Bald's reign.[147] And therein lay the contemporary utility of Nithard's prefatory analysis of the events of 833. In revealing the "true" source of that year's criminal events—an all-consuming cupidity—Nithard was illuminating the destructive behavior that was still causing the realm's ills, behavior that, once recognized, could be righted. As Nithard explained, an irrepressible avarice led to the downfall of the realm: "From this history, everyone may gather how mad it is to neglect the common good and to follow only private and selfish desires."[148] More specifically, the lure of becoming second in the empire had incited the greed of Louis' sons (Lothar, Pippin, and Louis the German) as well as Louis' and his sons' advisors (Bernard, Guntbald, Hugh, Lambert, and Matfrid).[149] And the prospect of this chief advisory role itself only appeared, remarked Nithard, because a "distressed" (*anxius*) Louis the Pious had, upon Charles's birth, appealed to his sons for their help and advice in repartitioning the empire.[150] Here was the deepest root uncovered by Nithard. Doubtless, selfishness and avarice lay behind Charles's current troubles, just as they had for his pious father.[151] But such destructive behavior could be checked by a resolute king, one who ruled neither anxiously with the assistance of his children, like Louis,[152] nor rashly with the assistance of untrustworthy counselors, like Charles,[153] but rather with sober determination and an iron will. For such a sure sovereign Nithard had a ready example.

Contrary to his introductory promise, Nithard began his work not with Louis but rather with a brief account of the virtues of Charlemagne. As Nithard said at the end of his prologue, it seemed to him "highly inadvisable to omit altogether the venerable memory of [Charles's] grandfather." Hardly an afterthought, the great emperor of the Franks provided the model of perfect kingship. Through his exemplary embodiment of wisdom and force, asserted Nithard, Charlemagne had instilled love, admiration, and terror in his subjects.[154] And it was this last quality for which he believed the mighty emperor would be best remembered; Charlemagne's tempered severity (*terror moderatus*) had kept both the iron-hearted barbarians and the fiercest Franks in harmony with the public welfare.[155] As a result, "he made his whole reign in every way glorious and salutary, as was apparent to everyone." When Charlemagne died, recalled Nithard in closing, "he left the whole of Europe flourishing."[156] And lest the reader forget the point behind this nostalgic, introductory sketch, Nithard ended his work as he had begun:

> In the times of Charles the Great of good memory, who died almost thirty years ago, peace and concord ruled everywhere because our people were treading the one proper way, the way of the common welfare, and thus the way of God. But now since each goes his separate way, dissension and struggle abound. Once there was abundance and happiness everywhere, now everywhere there is want and sadness.[157]

The lesson was clear. For Nithard, Charlemagne had been the ideal king, the "terrifying" monarch against whom all his successors were measured and found wanting.[158] He was also the ruler who should serve as current inspiration. Like the weather that Nithard described, the present times were horrible but not irremediable.[159] If 833 served to show what a ruler should not do, as well as the consequent depths to which the realm could sink, then Charlemagne demonstrated the extreme opposite—that only a terrifying and righteous king, not the Astronomer's mild one, could restore the realm to the "one proper way, the way of the common welfare, and thus the way of God." Nithard's dismal history was finished but not conclusive. The final chapters were for King Charles to write by his deeds. It had been Nithard's urgent aim to suggest how.[160]

Paschasius Radbertus

Sometime between the mid-830s to mid-850s, Paschasius Radbertus, abbot of Corbie, joined the chorus of lament. Commemorating in a highly allusive text the life of one of Charlemagne's cousins, the great Abbot Wala of Corbie, Paschasius recounted the virtues, deeds, and troubles of his predecessor and friend in lugubrious tones. It was a sad story, to be sure, but by no means a simple one. Written in two parts, at two different periods, the "*epitaphium*," as Paschasius entitled it, grapples with the elusive, transcendental relationships of conscience, truth, and self-knowledge and the reasons for their recent disappearance in his own day.[161] Indeed, the desire for self-knowledge was the catalyst behind the composition of the text itself; as he states at its outset, "no one should mourn who does not know what he is suffering."[162] Aware of the difficulty in achieving self-awareness, Paschasius adopted the rather unusual literary form of a didactic dialogue for his commemoration of Wala. By means of this striking rhetorical device, in which he portrays himself carrying on a conversation with his fellow monks, Paschasius sought to ensure that the true cause of Corbie's collective suffering, and hence of its present mourning, was properly understood.[163] And there was the rub, for the cause of their lasting grief was not just the death of Wala in 836 but more specifically the slander and scorn still attached to that abbot's name after nearly two decades.[164] To mourn properly meant to revisit both the injury and the insult that had been added to it.

In short, Wala had been one of those men standing against Louis the Pious on the Rotfeld, a seemingly defiant posture that soon earned him the bitter reward of exile. Worse yet, his reputation continued to carry the stain of infamy and disgrace, despite his formal, public pardon by Louis in 836.[165] But Paschasius insisted that these unjust consequences of Wala's misunderstood involvement in 833 were less deserving of lamentation than the utter contempt shown by both parties, rebel and loyal, toward Wala's wise counsel during those dark days. That such a perspicacious man, a latter-day Jeremiah, had been both ignored and persecuted and that this treatment had come from the very people he wished to save![166] To Paschasius, the effects of such obdurate, arrogant disdain were clear—"When [Wala] was spurned, when he was not heeded, all these ills [of the 830s] occurred."[167] In this respect, 833 had been especially noteworthy, for, according to Paschasius, Wala had been coerced to join the camp of the rebel sons specifically for the advantage gained by his wise counsel.[168] His advice did not suit the immediate aims of the kings,[169] however, and was ignored to disastrous effect: "Certainly then [833] and thereafter," explained Paschasius, "those ills came openly upon all, ills greater and more savage than those which our flowing pen can or will pursue."[170] Indeed, the ills were so appalling that Paschasius, in the midst of his jeremiad, felt compelled to alter the scope of the work in order to incorporate them within his now broader lamentation:

One thing only we ought to lament [namely, the loss and scorn of
Wala], but harsher events have happened to compel us to include them
in our lamentation. They are so much more bitter and cruel than what
we originally proposed to bewail. It is therefore fitting to subsume them
all under one lament. [Wala] should not be grieved for so much as that
the events themselves should be deplored so that God's wrath may be
averted from us.[171]

Consequently, after a lengthy recounting of the emperor's abandonment and
submission in 833, which includes an otherwise unattested redaction of letters exchanged between Louis and his sons on the Rotfeld,[172] Paschasius not
only recalled the rebels' disdain for Wala's recommendations regarding the
future dispensation of the empire but also underscored the reaction of his
prudent and virtuous hero (a reaction that, in Paschasius's mind, his reader
ought obviously to agree and identify with): Wala "began to be more and
more sorrowful" as he witnessed the consequences of Louis' abandonment
and penance.[173] To be sure, even Paschasius himself could not help but lament, bewail, and grieve profoundly over the shameful matters in the act of
their telling,[174] horrific deeds that required the dauntless words of Job for him
just to relate.[175]

Yet Paschasius believed it was neither the fate of Wala nor the events of
833 in themselves that should be deplored—events about which, he conceded,
his readers had surely "often read" (in the accounts of Thegan, the Astronomer, or Nithard?[176]). Paschasius was a deeper thinker than that. Rather, it
was what these cruel and bitter deeds revealed about his age that deserved
lamentation, a bewildering condition Paschasius described with an arresting
image:

What ought to follow comes first and the head which ought to come
first follows at random. Indecisive and playful authority swells on all
sides. So comes to pass that statement by the comic writer [Terence],
"I will, I won't; I won't, I will." And everyone is possessed by a vastly
unhappy, childish giddiness (*puerilis vertigo*).[177]

Employing imagery of inversion and confusion, Paschasius turned, significantly, to the Roman comic playwright Terence to describe the outcome of
the "sorrowful" events, a lamentable, puerile state of being ultimately characterized with the deliberate, scriptural term *vertigo*.[178] Twice more would

Paschasius use this term in his lament for Wala, in each case invoking it in accordance with Isaiah 19:14 to characterize the "spirit of error" and "faithlessness and discord" demonstrated by the events of the time[179]—the lasting effects of which, noted Paschasius, were still evident in the 850s: "Hence it is [due to this *vertigo*]," he reasoned, "that today no prince has yet been able to straighten the roads of the commonwealth toward justice."[180] Here we see how both a scriptural and a classical, comedic mode could complement one another to provide insight. As several modern scholars have pointed out, Paschasius doubtless quoted Terence frequently throughout the first book of his lamentation both to demonstrate the extent of his learning and to supply a rhetorical intimacy of conversation among his interlocutors.[181] But as a man with keen, if ambivalent, interests in both ancient drama and satire— Paschasius was a rare reader of Senecan satire; remarked that the fate of John the Baptist at the hands of Herod had been a "tragedy" (*tragoedia*) narrated by the evangelists; and railed against those, like the Astronomer, who studied the carping criticism of tragedies and the vain imagining of poets—surely he turned to Terence (whose comedies likely formed part of the Corbie library) for a specific reason.[182]

In fact, the most striking aspect of Paschasius's text is not that its form is a monastic dialogue but that its gossipy monks refer to the characters they are discussing only by way of pseudonyms: Wala is called "Arsenius"; Louis the Pious, "Justinian"; Louis' wife Judith, "Justina"; Lothar, "Honorius"; and Louis the German, "Gratian," to name a few. Since the discovery of the text's lone, ninth-century manuscript by the Benedictine scholar Jean Mabillon in the seventeenth, these pseudonyms have been understood as a precaution taken by Paschasius to avoid potential punishment for the expression of untimely views.[183] As the monks themselves admit within the text, even by the 850s it was still dangerous for one to sympathize openly with Wala and his plight: "It is not yet permitted to disclose all to everyone," explained Paschasius, "particularly to those to whom truth is an object of hatred and to those to whom crimes are pleasing."[184]

The use of pseudonyms also functioned on another level, for with them Paschasius not only cloaked but also typecast the characters in his work. Paschasius may have loathed those who enjoyed reading tragedies and comedies, but clearly he had read and internalized (if not enjoyed) many of these dramas himself. Indeed, in this sense he seems to have known his enemy too well, for Paschasius cast the events from 833 into the age of Ambrose of Milan, giving the *dramatis personae* of his own dark comedy the names of many of the people involved in that famous bishop's conflict with the emperor Theodosius in 390.[185] Here was a strange kind of typology—Honorius and Gratian, like Lothar and Louis the German, were each the son of an emperor; Justina, like Judith, was an emperor's second wife, one who had a holy man educate her son, only to have him persecuted later; and Arsenius, like Wala, was the tutor of an emperor's children who abandoned the pomp of court for an ascetic life as a monk.[186] It is curious that Paschasius chose Justinian rather than Theodosius as a pseudonym for Louis, for there is little doubt that the central event of his larger story, the public penance and self-abasement of an emperor, is what prompted Paschasius's particular "Ambrosian" typology.[187] Ambrose's bold, conscientious demand that Theodosius perform public penance had set an unforgettable precedent.[188] Perhaps Paschasius saw a parallel between Louis and Justinian, in the sense that both men married a "wicked" woman much his junior, and both were the last emperors of united realms.[189] Or perhaps in "Justinian" he conflated the historical emperors Justinian I (483–565) and Justinian II (669–711); the latter, after all, was deposed by divine judgment on account of his dispute with the pope, was restored only to face a second rebellion, and was remembered in the West as a humble quasi-penitent emperor.[190]

None of these typological "roles" should be cast too rigidly, however, for Paschasius appears to have understood them not just in a theatrical sense but in a pictorial sense as well. Invoking a favorite Ciceronian anecdote about the artist Zeuxis, Paschasius claimed that, like that ancient painter, he was selecting attributes from various individuals and combining them to create an ideal form for each of his literary portraits:

> He proposes that in the manner of Zeuxis I depict (*pingere*) as a memorial for the ages a representation of the character (*morum liniamentis imago*) of our Arsenius. He does not think it enough that I, unworthy artist (*pictor*), am afraid to appear even more unworthy by giving through the medium of letters an image (*icon*) of a man so great, so renowned for his virtuous ornaments. . . . A picture of this man's character (*morum imago*), however, will not be fully fashioned from the face of one person, for by his actions he displayed the worth of many illustrious men. It seemed to me, for example, that when he wore the mantle (*conspersionem morum habere*) as Prior Arsenius, he was truly playing the role (*personam gerere*) of Father Benedict. As we have already hinted, he occasionally performed the office (*officium fungi*) of

Jeremiah, pursuing bitterly with inflexible expression although he was gentle in spirit and mildest of men.[191]

Although each person was initially cast in Ambrosian terms, under this historical guise each played a variety of roles (*personae*) that contributed to the fashioning of their "character," that aspect that Paschasius believed to be so essential to the idealized images he was creating.[192] Wala's pseudonym Arsenius was reflective not just of the late antique tutor-turned-holy-man but also—in the ways that this particular Arsenius acted—of both Saint Benedict and the prophet Jeremiah. Characters in a play were themselves playing characters. And what is more, this metadrama unfolded within a fictitious dialogue among monks, whose names strongly hint at being roles as well. For instance, Paschasius's monastic interlocutor Chremes possesses the name of a character found in several plays by Terence, while another interlocutor, Adeodatus, bears the name of Augustine's precocious, inquisitive son, who is present in that saint's own dialogic works.[193] Like his late antique namesake, Adeodatus incessantly prods Paschasius to clarify himself throughout the dialogue, asking insightful questions that often steer its direction. Perhaps even Paschasius himself is a *persona* within the text; as Augustine had once explained in his discussion of Cicero's dialogic works, the character "Cicero" in the text should not necessarily be equated with the work's eponymous narrator.[194]

In sum, the pseudonyms that Paschasius assigned to the leading persons of the early 830s served simultaneously to cloak his representation of the recent conflict, to call forth the memory of a past one, and to project the entire drama onto a plane of timeless values.[195] Remarkable as it may seem, such a multivalent approach is less surprising when one recalls that Paschasius was known first and foremost as an exegete. Renowned—indeed, even sanctified—for his work on the interpretation of scripture, he was extremely adept at articulating the four-fold meaning (literal, allegorical, tropological, anagogical) of God's plan in all its mysterious manifestations.[196] When he cast his gaze upon the events of 833, Paschasius, like Thegan and the Astronomer, saw in them a typological conflation of past and present events in which a deplorable difference between the two ages had been revealed, one that was damning of his own. By dressing the role of Wala in Ambrosian terms, Paschasius was in essence justifying Wala's deeds in terms of conscience and frank speech. In Ambrose's day, he implied, men who had had the ear of the emperor were permitted to speak without fear of reprisal for expressing untimely views.[197] If such men were persecuted, they were considered heroes for having acted with resolve and following their conscience. In Paschasius's day, on the other hand, men such as Wala who had dared to speak freely, who had acted conscientiously, were not merely persecuted but, what was worse, also seen as villains and widely condemned.[198] The very fact that Paschasius had felt compelled to use pseudonyms was demonstrative of how perverse the present age had become. It was still too dangerous to speak freely.

Paschasius was certain that the sad outcome of the struggle between conscience and desire during the events of 833 was the true reason for all the realm's subsequent woes. A blind, mad willfulness had triumphed. This was the reason most people slandered Wala rather than mourned him and the reason frank speech was now impossible. "Whoever pretends that he knows what and how great these matters [of 833] were, or how bad continuing matters are which arose from them," Paschasius pronounced, "is either foolish or mad." Such persons misunderstand the events and Wala's part in them, he explained, because they interpret and judge according to the dictates of their will rather than their conscience.[199] Consequently, when confronted with the uncomfortable truth, such willful people understood it not as historical fact but merely as *fabula*, a fictive account, for their will led them to believe only what they wished to be true. Even with events like the Resurrection, where there were multiple, unimpeachable witnesses, whose accounts align and, as Paschasius says, "point out as if by one finger what has happened," most chose not to believe.[200] As one interlocutor observed, "it seems to me that . . . [to such willful people] everything grounded in truth is a 'story' (*fabula*) and a game (*ludus*). But in your conscience you recognize his account (*historia*) and therefore to you is set forth not a 'story' (*fabula*) but the truth."[201] The difference between the willful and the conscientious—and, thus, the difference between those who saw truth either as *fabula* or as *historia*—was the degree of self-knowledge possessed by each.[202] And as Paschasius ceaselessly stressed, Wala had known himself utterly; he "bore himself with himself, being always present to himself."[203] Most others, especially after the events of 833, were deluded or mad, having been blinded by their desires, led astray by their will and thus, in Paschasius's estimation, "were exiled from themselves, from sense, from counsel."[204] Unlike Wala with his self-knowledge, they had nothing to guide or restrain their will. As one of the monks in the *Epitaphium* lamented,

Alas, how miserable the years of our age in which the will of everyone leads the way. What each one savors and can do is now lawful. He can with degenerate desire bring to completion what is in conflict with this purpose. Formerly it was necessary first (*praesertim*), to discern what one should will; then (*deinde*), to will what one discerned; and finally (*demum*), to accomplish whatever good one could. Now, however, minds give birth to monsters.[205]

This was precisely the context in which Paschasius then invoked the haltingly headlong passage from Terence: "I will, I won't; I won't, I will." At the mercy of their will, people—especially those in the imperial palace, which had itself shamefully become, as Paschasius called it, "a theater" (*theatrum*)[206]—now resembled nothing so much as the ridiculous, deplorable characters from an ancient comedy, made dizzy by their unchecked desire. Yet, as noted earlier, Paschasius, in his capacity as abbot, also understood this vertiginous condition in a scriptural, and more specifically monastic, sense. After all, the point of the Rule of Saint Benedict was to counter vertigo with stability for its monastic adherents, allowing them to pursue perfection, and thus salvation, in the most efficient manner possible. What made Wala so remarkable— and what so many misrepresented, insisted Paschasius—was that he had risked everything not just for the stability of the monastery but for that of the world it sought to deny. He had understood that the two were inextricably intertwined, no matter how much others wished to believe otherwise. As Paschasius grieved again and again, had not Wala striven against such a perverse *vertigo*, working for among other things the *stabilitas et unitas* of the realm?[207] "If he stood nearly alone amidst all the crises," observed Henry Mayr-Harting, "that was not because he was at fault but because others were too faint-hearted to do their duty."[208] Such craven negligence, it seemed, was true even of Louis the Pious, who, in the eyes of both Paschasius and Thegan, devoted excessive time to the study of scripture.[209] This was how backward things had become: an emperor was shirking his duties, retreating from the world, and acting like a monk, forcing a monk to shirk his duties, enter the world, and act as a leader of kings and men. Saint Paul may have declared that "no one fighting for God involves himself in worldly business" (2 Tim. 2:4),[210] but Wala had known that, in the particular business of 833, if he did not involve himself, "one annihilation was surely imminent for all."[211] By the 850s, all Paschasius could do was lament the unjust consequences of this heroic involvement and only then in a kind of code. The conscientious would decipher it and mourn.

Odilo

Fifty years later (ca. 900), Odilo, a monk of Saint-Médard, the very monastery within which Louis had performed his penance, claimed to have made an important discovery. In his account of the translation of the relics of Saints Sebastian and Gregory the Great to his monastery, Odilo inserted an extraordinary confessional narrative, which he claimed was written by none other than Louis the Pious himself.[212] In what the historian Sir Francis Palgrave once called a "curious, but almost forgotten document," Louis describes his summer-long confinement at Saint-Médard and relates his sorrows, hopes, and adventures within the monastery in the first person.[213] With dramatic flair, he carefully notes the smallest details of his surroundings, such as the paneled ceilings or the poles upon which standards were carried during the celebration of Lent, and reports conversations that reveal a remarkable wit for one who, as his biographer Thegan would note, "never showed his white teeth in a smile."[214]

There is much of interest in Odilo's text, and in Louis' narrative in particular, but for those wishing to learn more about Louis the Pious himself, it unfortunately holds little of value. The narrative is almost certainly an invention on the part of Odilo, conceived for the purpose of glorifying Sebastian, the saint whose holy relics were acquired with great fanfare by the monastery of Saint-Médard from Rome in 826.[215] Indeed, Louis' narrative is only one vignette (albeit a rather striking one) among many recorded by Odilo in his lengthy account—over 17,000 words—concerning the wonders worked by his Saints Sebastian and Gregory. The imprisonment of Louis at Saint-Médard in 833 provided an ideal setting for Odilo in this respect, as it supplied a familiar scene within which he could frame the miraculous, thereby lending credibility to the incredible, while simultaneously adding an element of wonder and sanctity to the historical event. As the text's modern editor once noted, the deeds of 833 appear to have been well known at Saint-Médard in Odilo's day.[216]

Indeed, given the major role of Saint Sebastian in the narrative of the events, a role unattested in any other account of them, Odilo's particular hagiographical remembrance of Louis' abandonment, imprisonment, and penance was likely a local, collective one, a social memory shaped over the decades following 833 to suit his monastery's needs and interests.[217] In other words, Odilo's account reflects what he and his brethren believed, wanted to believe, and needed to believe about the pious emperor's special relationship with their house and the saint it venerated and served. The recollection of Louis' imperial favor apparently still brought them more than a little pride and prestige—especially insofar as it could lend support to their present claim to property. For the dependent abbey of Saint-Étienne in Choisy-au-Bac—a prosperous house, Odilo conveniently noted in his account, that Louis had allegedly bestowed upon Saint-Médard—was under threat of alienation when Odilo was writing the *translatio*.[218] The useful memory of Louis' visits to Saint-Médard—specifically as an example of his great love for its saint, of the donations of property (such as Saint-Étienne) that he made in the saint's honor, and of the heavenly rewards granted to him by the saint in return— appears to have outweighed concerns over the remembrance of his captivity as a stain on the reputation of the monastery for its collaboration in treason. As Odilo stated in the chapter's first line, its theme is "the kind and degree of the Emperor Louis' devotion to the saint"—something for which "he ought to be remembered."[219]

Yet, despite his confidence in evoking memories worthy of praise rather than condemnation, Odilo knew there was still a catch. While the audience within the monastery would accept Louis' profession of a singular love for their house and its saint, the outside world might harbor doubts, since Louis was buried not at Saint-Médard but at Metz.[220] How to account for this apparent paradox? Why was Louis not interred near Saint Sebastian if he had so cherished the saint? In fact, Odilo's attempt to address this question explains much about the extraordinary form and content of his narrative. While Louis' story serves within Odilo's much larger work on the saints as yet another example of their power, it has a more specific function within its immediate context, one that, among other things, clarifies the reason for its strange description by Odilo as an account of Louis' "most secret vow" (*secretissimum sacramentum*). Given that Odilo's rather difficult work has never been translated into English, the following summary will prove useful for establishing this intratextual context, which, in turn, will shed light on Louis' mysterious promise.

Hearing that Abbot Hilduin had successfully transferred the relics of Saint Sebastian from Rome to Saint-Médard in Soissons and that many miracles were subsequently occurring there, Louis and Judith visited the monastery during Easter 827. Louis was soon so overcome by what he saw that he divested himself of the regalia of his office and led the monastery in the paschal prayer to the saint. While the emperor was preparing himself for the service, however, Judith learned that several flagellants within the monastery secretly posed a threat to her husband. These men, she was told, had managed to cloak with their cries the hatred that consumed them. If they appeared to be terrified, this was only because they feared that their hidden crimes, for which they had neglected to give confession and undertake penance, might be discovered and they would be consigned to the flames. Distressed and uncertain of what to do, since she knew that she would be unable to keep Louis from proceeding with the ceremony—and thus from falling into the hands of these duplicitous villains—without bringing shame upon herself, Judith decided to devote herself to God. Following the dictates of Psalm 18:13–14 and throwing herself into the arms of her Redeemer, she hoped through confession to be forgiven for her silence regarding the sins of others. Shortly thereafter, Louis and Judith together proceeded through elaborate initiation rituals, with Louis' leading the service for Sebastian, removing his opulent garments, and bestowing to the monastery among other things a lavishly decorated Gospel book and the abbey of Saint-Étienne in Choisy-au-Bac. Mimicking David, explained Odilo, the exultant emperor stopped at the door to the oratory and sang aloud that great king's vow to God, "this is my rest for ever and ever: here will I dwell, for I have chosen it." (Ps. 131:14) Upon hearing these words, all those in the church who were injured or sick suddenly received divine medicine from Sebastian and were miraculously cured.[221]

There was no doubt, remarked Odilo, that Louis had been utterly committed to the saint, for, amid a constant stream of tears, the emperor worshipped Sebastian as though he were present in the flesh. Indeed—and here was the sentence to which all the preceding events had been leading—because of his absolute commitment, Louis believed that whatever he might ask of the saint he would receive. And, in fact, observed Odilo, this belief was proved true. But exactly what Louis asked for, he continued enticingly, can be seen in the narrative of Louis' "most secret vow." It is here that Odilo abruptly inserts Louis' first-person account.

The first part of the narrative provides a record of Louis' trials in 833 and the assistance afforded to him by the saints in return for his devotion. Beginning with the frank admission that he was an emperor "broken from a once vigorous branch," Louis acknowledges that he ruled "too immoderately," allowing people whom he had forgiven to show their gratitude by perversely impugning his piety. These brazen ingrates even coerced his children to rebel against him and plot his murder. As in the Astronomer's account, Louis here is at pains to avoid blaming his sons for their sedition: "The horrid crime entangled my sons in this treason" on the Rotfeld, he explains, "and made them its leaders." Indeed, he rather sees himself, despite averring his own innocence, as somehow still responsible for the wretched events: "Harmed and deluded in many ways by those [whom I] never harmed, I was not unaware of my own foul actions, and bore the events with equanimity, imagining that I was suffering these things deservedly in accordance with the utterly just judgment of God."[222] Louis then observes—and he (i.e., Odilo) is the first to have done so—why his captors brought him specifically to the monastery of Saint-Médard in Soissons.[223] Since his love for the monastery was well known, he reasons, they believed it would be there, if anywhere, that he might lay down his arms willingly (*sponte*) after a period of grieving and take up the monastic habit. To expedite this process, his captors sent messengers to his cell, who informed him that his son, Charles, had been made a monk and his wife had most likely been killed. Overcome by despair, Louis begged the monks, whom he was occasionally allowed to visit, to devote their prayers to the salvation of his wife. Moved by his pious appeal, the brethren assured Louis that, so long as he maintained his faith, all would be well thanks to the power of the saints (whom Louis refers to as "his lords").

Louis' devotion was soon rewarded, for he was heartened by an absurdly auspicious event, which he took to be an omen. The guard assigned to watch a small opening in Louis' cell dozed off, thanks to an excess of wine, and was sleeping so fitfully that he happened to knock away his sword. Seeing his chance, Louis quickly gathered objects in his cell and devised a makeshift fishing rod. Slipping it through the cell's window, he snagged the sword and cast it into a nearby latrine. Pleased with himself, Louis then woke the guard and taunted him about his vigilance. Here, Louis reports the "actual" conversation by using direct speech:

> I called out [the guard's] name and said to him: "O ever vigilant guard, most trustworthy hope of your people, are you awake?"
> To this he said, "I am awake, very awake."
> Again I said, "And what are you doing?"
> "What is that to you?" he shot back.
> I replied, "If by chance you should be confronted by sudden necessity, perhaps your sword will be far from your hand."

[The guard] put his arms to his head and felt here and there
[for the sword he had left on his pillow].

I said, "If you had [always] guarded me in this way, you would
by no means have held me here today."

He replied, "[Despite] whatever was done with my sword, I
have guarded over you [well] enough, as I was ordered, and I shall
take care to guard [you still]."

And I [responded]: "Go then and, in reward for your fidelity
and vigilance in this place, recover from [its] fitting 'armory' the
sword which you foully lost."[224]

Later that day, when Louis was in the abbey church for the daily service,
the monks sympathetic to his plight passed a secret message to him. While
he was praying for the absolution of his wife, whom he believed to be dead,
a monk by the name of Hardinus interrupted him with the cryptic remark,
"It is otherwise in the altar." After everyone had left the church, Louis approached the altar, where he discovered a small roll. Within it, he read that
his wife was still alive and that his son was unharmed. He also learned that
those who had abandoned him on the Rotfeld were ashamed of their actions
and were now seeking his reinstatement as emperor. To Louis, the reason for
this about-face was clear: "That came to happen," he states matter-of-factly,
"by God bestowing his favor and making things better, thanks to the intervention of his saints."[225]

The second part of the narrative, which treats the way Louis reacted to a
premonitory dream of his own demise, begins sometime shortly after he regained the throne. Restored to his former dignity, Louis was soon confronted
with renewed rebellions. Knowing that Saint Sebastian had been his special
advocate in the past, he returned to the monastery of Saint-Médard to pray to
the saint for his assistance. The following night, the emperor received a vision
from Sebastian that was at once saddening and comforting: he foresaw his
own imminent death and the empire's subsequent ruin (fulfilling in fact and
deed, explains Louis, what he had always expected to happen). But he also
learned that he would be found blameless by God for this catastrophic event
and thus avoid eternal damnation.

Leaving the monastery the next day with an ecclesiastic named Teuther,
Louis set out with renewed determination to fight for the welfare of the people entrusted to him by God.[226] When they had travelled some distance from
the monastery, however, Louis looked back and suddenly began to weep,

realizing, thanks to the terminal vision he had received, that he would never see that holy place again. Unable to bear the emperor's sadness, Teuther fell to weeping as well, but still tried as he could to comfort his lord. To show tears, he told Louis, was counterproductive, for an emperor's grief disheartens his faithful men while it emboldens his enemies. Certainly Louis should keep his despair to himself. Perhaps he would find consolation in the suffering his *fideles* were willing to undergo on his behalf; at the very least, granted Teuther, their suffering would allow him to bear his sadness more easily, since it would be a burden now shared by many.

Louis immediately took Teuther's words to heart and chose to conceal from him the true source of his sadness—the premonition of his death and the empire's demise. The reason for his tears, he told Teuther, was their departure from Saint-Médard. He had earlier made a vow to Saint Sebastian, he explained, that, in exchange for the saint's assistance, he would lay down the symbols of his office and join the brethren at Saint-Médard. And he had intended to do just that, except that the recent acts of rebellion urgently demanded his presence in the world. Thus, his sadness stemmed from his neglect of his vow to Sebastian in order to uphold the oath he had sworn to his people as their guardian. To this explanation Teuther responded that Louis' vow was without doubt a good one, but that his desire for renunciation is what truly mattered. Louis may now, due to circumstances, be unable to renounce his secular life as he had intended, but, Teuther continued, there were other ways to attain this goal. That the emperor was ready to fight to the death for God, his saints, and his people would surely be understood by the Almighty as praiseworthy and a fitting form of renunciation. Indeed, concluded Teuther, did not Christ himself show by example that this is the ultimate form of sacrifice—to offer one's soul so that another may live? Comforted only somewhat by Teuther, Louis set out on his way once more, concluding his narrative with a simple, or perhaps—given his foreknowledge—final, "farewell" to the reader.

Following Louis' valediction, Odilo resumed his own narrative by stating that the monks at Saint-Médard learned of Louis' plight (presumably from Teuther) and resolved to praise Sebastian in the hope that their collective prayers would move the saint to come to the emperor's aid. Unfortunately, this was "not what God had predestined." Rather, Louis died on an island in the Rhine while leading his army against his son Louis the German. To be sure, explained Odilo, Louis acquired everlasting life with the saint because of his merits and his sedulous veneration of Sebastian. But—and here was the catch—his mortal remains now rest in the basilica of his ancestor Saint Arnulf in Metz, not in Saint-Médard, "since as we knew through his making it manifest," concluded Odilo, "[Louis] refused to fulfill [his] vow, and so did not deserve to have [his] greatly desired place of burial in the foundation of the martyr."[227]

From this summary of Odilo's account of 833 and its aftermath, the reason for its composition in the form of Louis' confessional narrative becomes clear. By means of this rhetorical device, Odilo was able to provide not only Louis' words but also his thoughts. The first-person perspective allowed him to reveal Louis' inner anxieties about his actions and their consequences and thus to develop—with great moral and psychological drama—the reason Louis was not buried in Saint-Médard. The text is replete with cognitive verbs, such as *believe, cherish, consider, decide, dissemble, enjoy, fear, feel, know, love, perceive, recall,* and *wish*. Louis fought nobly and renounced the world through death but was not assisted by the saint after 833 because he had failed to honor his vow to retire to the monastery. Thanks to the vision from Sebastian, he understood the consequences of his decision to forswear his vow and defend his people, but he chose to proceed anyway; hence his lingering melancholy at his narrative's end. In each instance, the pressure these events placed upon Louis is not just implied but, thanks to the confessional form, fully professed. In Odilo's text we thus have a little-noticed Carolingian (pseudo)autobiography, appearing midway between the medieval landmarks in the genre: Augustine at the close of the fourth century and Guibert of Nogent, Hermann Judaeus, and Peter Abelard in the twelfth.[228]

Odilo also uses the distinction between explicit acts and guarded thoughts, outer appearance and inner truth, to underscore his ambivalent feelings toward Louis and the rebellion. For example, he has Louis confess to the reader that he was innocent in 833 but nonetheless suffered the events because he believed this was in accordance with the judgment of God. Inversely, by means of Judith's "discovery" Odilo reveals that certain people in the monastery were guilty of crimes but that they chose to conceal them. (Perhaps this was Odilo's way of accounting for the reports of Louis' mistreatment during his confinement at Saint-Médard[229]; it was the fault of a few "bad apples.") While it is unclear what Odilo desired the reader to make of Judith's silence about another's sins in order to preserve her honor, the problem of acting on one's conscience is as evident here as it was in Paschasius's account of Wala. It is not the last time we shall encounter this problem in relation to the events of 833. Other examples of Odilo's mixed feelings about the events are found in the way Louis is characterized in the text: as ingenious (devising the fishing rod), humorous (chastising the guard), honorable (not escaping from his cell when the guard was asleep), and pious (praying assiduously to the saint), but also as weak ("broken from a once vigorous branch"), injudicious (ruling immoderately and with disgrace), and sinful (having committed foul deeds).

However, the most effective rhetorical element of Louis' narrative is its first-person perspective, which permits the reader to empathize with Louis' plight and glory in his deliverance. In order to illustrate the intercessory power of Sebastian, Odilo needed to establish that Louis was in a truly dire situation; he was well aware of the direct relationship between the difficulty of a dilemma and the virtue of the saint who helps to resolve it. To this end, Odilo allowed Louis himself to relate his agony over his confinement:

> [While imprisoned I was told by my captors] that my wife either had been made a nun in a monastery of virgins or, and this they had heard as more likely, had died. Moreover, they affirmed that my little son, innocent Charles, a little boy of good character, whom they knew was dearest to me above all else, had been tonsured and admitted to the company of monks. When I heard that, I, who had been robbed of the kingdom and deprived of my wife and child, could not contain myself. For days on end I wailed and had no one to console me. I gradually felt myself being consumed by the fires of the most overwhelming languor because of the enormity of my sadness.[230]

This vivid portrait of the despondent emperor—through its sense of sheer hopelessness—doubtless demonstrated, in inverse proportion, the miraculous powers of emancipation possessed by Saint Sebastian. But in so doing, it also intensified the "tragic" elements of 833. Indeed, here was the private counterpart to Thegan's more public depiction of the strong-willed emperor, whose resolve had seemed so remarkable in comparison with the tears shed by his best men (though, as we have seen, Teuther would also advise this same staunch, imperial comportment). By revealing Louis' "most secret vow" in order to exalt the virtue of his saints, Odilo gave the "unheard-of tragedy" a personal, and thus sympathetic, aspect—the anguish of a king, who was as susceptible as anyone to the effects of despair. So deep was the pathos and impact of this account of Louis' "tragic" imprisonment that, even as late as the nineteenth century, one scholar still found it necessary to refute the age-old conviction that an enigmatic inscription in the crypt of Saint-Médard (the la-

Figure 4. Louis the Pious making an inscription in the prison of the Abbey of Saint-Médard, Soissons. Drawing by Eduard Henri Théophile Pingret. Musée de Soissons, coll. Beauzée, inv. 90.9.25. Courtesy Musée de Soissons.

ment of a self-styled "Prince of Sorrow") had been written by the imprisoned Emperor Louis himself (Figures 4 and 5).[231] To his dismay, the scholar found that the owner of Saint-Médard was capitalizing on (and thereby perpetuating) this erroneous belief, creating a subterranean passageway to "Louis' prison" and leading tours of the place to the likes of the Duchess of Berry in 1821 (Figure 6).[232]

Conclusions

As the preceding pages have demonstrated, the vivid Carolingian accounts of Louis' abandonment and penance are largely loyalist and/or apologetic. While some, such as Nithard and Odilo, saw problems stemming from Louis' diffident character, they were in agreement that the events of 833 had been a "great crime" (*tantum facinus*; *horrendum facinus*). In fact, of the six detailed narratives, only that by Paschasius Radbertus displayed serious ambivalence about the events, at first viewing the rebels' cause with some sympathy before condemning all parties for not having heeded Wala's judicious counsel.

Rhetorical devices, such as direct speech and foreshadowing, and generic forms, such as annals, biography, dialogue, and confession, were adopted for specific purposes within these accounts. Yet, in each case, the work's form affected its content; indeed, in the words of Hayden White, the form itself could be said to *have* content. But unlike White's broad, pessimistic conclusions about the meaningful content of one eighth-century annal's generic form—as reflective of "a culture hovering on the brink of dissolution"[233]—the narrative forms we have surveyed display the mid-ninth-century fruits of the Carolingian revival of learning, a vibrant culture so fluent in rhetorical figures and invention that it could depart with confidence from the first part of Saint Augustine's dictum "that a brief and lucid narrative communicates facts efficiently, and that variety holds the attention without creating boredom."[234] Paschasius's *Epitaphium Arsenii* is neither brief nor lucid, but it is certainly effective at conveying the moral conflicts confronted by Wala—who was later regarded (rather nebulously) as a saint.[235]

This point regarding the use and aims of rhetoric raises two additional, thorny issues: authorial intention and the question of audience. Rather than develop these issues theoretically, we can briefly draw some pregnant conclusions from the texts we have examined thus far. Paschasius doubtless sought to justify Wala's bold engagement with the world, but his text suggests other

Figure 5. The prison of Louis the Pious, including the text of the inscription. Sketch by Souliac, ca. 1844. Ville de Soissons, coll. B Ancien. Courtesy Musée de Soissons.

purposes as well. To defend, to warn, to criticize, to document, and, most explicitly, to mourn—these were all objectives of his work, operating at times singly, at times simultaneously. The same multivalence can be said to characterize most of the other works surveyed above, though which purposes were paramount in each text was as much a function of its potential audience as its author's intentions.[236] To underscore the importance of this realm of negotiation between author and audience in the process of historical interpretation, as well as to stress the stakes involved, Patrick Geary has described it rather as a zone of engagement and struggle, "a battlefield in which a tension exists between proposed meaning and received meanings."[237] The warrior-turned-historian Nithard would no doubt have agreed; thanks to his martial experience, he understood the advantages to be gained by a preemptive attack—whether on the battlefield of warlords or words. "I have agreed to add a third book of the events in which I myself took part," he explained, "lest some misguided man dare to record them inaccurately."[238] The point was to take the initiative, to establish the meaning of the events of his time in the minds of his audience before they had a chance to receive other accounts. All too familiar with the pernicious effects of rumor, Nithard knew that, as in combat, the best defense in reputation and historiography was a strong offense.[239]

Yet, unlike Nithard, some Carolingian authors did not want to be pinned down on "the" meaning of their texts, especially of their critical texts, for they realized then, as we must now, that they were writing works that, once released for copying, were open to circulation and out of their control.[240] Unguarded statements were unwise upon the open "battlefield" of meaning, where candid speech was just a utopian ideal. Given this uncertain, often perilous context, prudence was an especially prized virtue. As Margaret Trenchard-Smith has observed,

> the practice of adopting literary forms toward unspoken ends was especially prevalent in the polemical literature which accompanied the incipient fragmentation of the Carolingian Empire, when direct expression was risky. Hagiography, letters, dream narratives, history, poetry: all were commandeered to give bearings to the foundering ship of state, to settle scores, to put forward suits. It was a form of mannered discourse, in which the writer escaped the consequences of meanings conveyed but not openly claimed, requiring that both writer and audience understand and obey the *règles de jeu*. Contemporary audiences were not incapable of hearing "raging silences" (*furibunda silentia*) in such communications.[241]

With respect to such prudent, mannered works, witness the fact that, of nearly all the texts we have examined, the earliest manuscripts preserving them do not identify their authors. Indeed, centuries of scrupulous analysis have not disclosed the identity of the Astronomer.[242] This anonymity is more than a

Figure 6. Exterior of the prison of Louis the Pious at Saint-Médard, Soissons. Drawing by Danjoy. Musée de Soissons, coll. Beauzée, inv. 90.9.96. Courtesy Musée de Soissons.

mere product of authorial humility or careless work by a copyist.[243] Certainly
these authors were all too familiar with the proverb that books have their own
fates. But they also knew of the often-overlooked clause that qualifies this
proverb: that books have their own fates "depending on the discernment of
their reader."[244] Authors were aware that their audience, possessed of varying
degrees of discernment, held preconceptions about the topic at hand, often
derived from other texts as well as from lingering rumors—textual and oral
sources of information that were rarely mutually exclusive.[245] In this sense,
then, authors knew that their works were competing for authority with other
reports already in circulation and would be interpreted and judged in relation to them. Paschasius reveals as much when he declared to his interlocutors (and thus to his readers) regarding the events of 833, "As you have often
read. . . ." What did he assume they had read in the two decades since the
events? This is a difficult question to answer.[246] While we have seen some authors reveal their awareness of, and at times reliance upon, the works of their
predecessors and contemporaries, rarely are they explicit about the nature of
this intertextual awareness and reliance. One thing, however, is certain: as
we gain distance from the events of 833, so increases the number of texts that
compete for predominance as the authoritative truth about them. As we shall
see, each age, depending on its values and concerns, selects a "winner" in this
competition.

   If we look at the manuscript evidence of the six texts examined above,
we can make some cautious, tentative inferences about the prevailing narrative on 833 in the ninth century and the value system it implies. In terms of
the extant ninth- and tenth-century manuscripts and of attestations within
other texts, the two biographies of Louis by Thegan and the Astronomer were
clearly predominant.[247] The Annals of Saint-Bertin and the texts by Nithard, Paschasius, and Odilo, on the other hand, were transmitted, as far as
we can tell, in only a handful of manuscripts. Given these basic observations on textual reception, we can turn to the diverse modes of interpretation
possessed by the authors of the various narratives and draw some equally
basic conclusions. To be sure, the majority of the authors perceived Louis'
troubles typologically, according to a biblical tale that, through comparison
and contrast, was deemed particularly apt for the timeless truths it revealed
in the present events: the anonymous author of the Annals of Saint-Bertin
understood them in terms of the Old Testament story of Jacob and his sons;
Thegan, in terms of Job and his testing by God; the Astronomer, in terms of
Christ's clemency and bitter reward of betrayal and suffering; and the enco-

Figure 7a. Drawing of the tomb of Louis the Pious. Th. Le Puillon de Boblaye, *Notice historique sur l'ancienne abbaye royale de Saint-Arnould* (Metz, 1857), 26–27. Courtesy Bibliothèque nationale de France.

Figure 7b. The existing fragments of the sarcophagus of Louis the Pious set against a drawing of the lost pieces. La Cour d'Or—Musées de Metz. Courtesy Musées La Cour d'Or—Clichés Jean Munin. All rights reserved.

miast Paschasius Radbertus, largely in terms of Jeremiah's senseless persecution. But it was the comparisons of Louis with Job and Christ that appear to have struck a chord with contemporaries; by way of the biographies of Thegan and the Astronomer, Louis was widely regarded as a figure who had suffered abuse and yet had remained steadfast in his faith. Other ways of interpreting the events were not widely recognized or esteemed. Odilo of Saint-Médard demonstrated the way in which the memory of the events could be configured and expressed through a hagiographic mode of emplotment, while the learned lay aristocrat Nithard showed how the same events appeared when understood in accordance with a martial value system and measured against the yardstick of Charlemagne's "terrifying" kingship. Yet, like the account of Paschasius, these were interpretations made for an immediate, local context, beyond which their meaning lost much of its relevance and force[248]: if Wala was ever really regarded as a saint outside of Corbie, it was only in Corbie's daughter house of Herford; Nithard's terse text, perhaps due to its very terseness, its focus on current events, and its lay perspective on politics, went unread and uncopied throughout most of the Middle Ages; and Odilo's account evidently convinced no one beyond the walls of Saint-Médard that Louis had favored Saint Sebastian as his special heavenly advocate.[249] To the larger literate memory culture of the Middle Ages, the lesson of 833 taken from Thegan and the Astronomer was a simple, timeless, and edifying one: the evils of infidelity are vanquished by the power of true faith.

It has often been observed that interpretation of the past in the early Middle Ages resembles the layered nature of biblical exegesis.[250] In the majority of instances, this is doubtless true. But sometimes, as Paschasius explained using the example of the Greek artist Zeuxis, interpretation was conceived more as a clustering than a layering, as an assemblage of apposite ideals in which the collective whole was greater than the sum of its parts.[251] In the case of the Carolingians, the remarkable part of this hermeneutic strategy lies in what some authors opted to draw upon in the act of their interpretive assemblage. The Astronomer saw Louis' christological passion as an "unheard-of tragedy," while Paschasius Radbertus understood his jeremiad about Wala's suffering as a deplorable, Terentian comedy of the perverse. Biblical typology was being fused specifically with genres of ancient drama to gain insight.[252] Theater may no longer have been performed in the early Middle Ages, but it continued to exert a profound influence upon the clergy who often claimed to abhor it. In alloying with other interpretive modes, drama not only acted to prescribe this thinking along certain paths but paved new roads to the truth as well.

Before concluding, it would be prudent to shine a light on someone who has been lurking in this chapter's thicket of notes. Drogo (801–855), Louis' half brother, bishop of Metz, and archchaplain of the palace from 834 to 840, has been glimpsed through circumstantial evidence as having been involved, either directly or indirectly, in the composition of three of the works examined above. A manuscript of the Annals of Saint-Bertin containing only the entries for the years 830 to 837 is believed to have been copied at Drogo's request. Moreover, some think that Drogo, who was conspicuously at Louis' deathbed, commissioned the Astronomer to write his intimate biography (which contains a vivid depiction of the emperor's final hours and words). And Drogo's actions shortly after Louis' death ultimately led Odilo to compose his unusual text accounting for why Louis was not buried at Saint-Médard; Drogo had taken Louis' body and interred it with Louis' mother, Hildegard, together with two of Louis' sisters and two of Charlemagne's sisters, at the seat of his own bishopric in Metz.[253] A staunch supporter of his half brother in the 830s—he was one of the few who remained with Louis on the Rotfeld and was eventually granted the office of archchaplain in return—Drogo seems to have had a large hand in shaping and preserving Louis' reputation. It is surely no coincidence that Louis' epithet of "the Pious" appears more frequently in those sources having their origins geographically proximate to the city of Metz.[254] Unfortunately, we have virtually nothing written by Drogo himself.[255] This is a pity, for, in many ways, he may be responsible for much of what is to come. The little that we do have is suggestive enough: Drogo is likely behind the selection of the now fragmentary late antique marble sarcophagus in which Louis was buried, one that depicted Moses and the Israelites successfully crossing the divided waters of the Red Sea while their pursuers drown in the deluge of its violent collapse (Figures 7a and 7b).[256] "For Drogo," observes Paul Dutton, "Louis' life had seemed a Mosaic search for salvation. The Pharaonic pursuers, [he] must have thought, were those sins of greed, pride, and impiety that had filled the rebel breast; Louis himself had reached the far shore, there to stand with the saints raised above the churning waters of the world below."[257] Whether as Jacob or Job, Moses or Christ, Louis had defied temptation and shown others the way.

CHAPTER 2

The Shame of the Franks

Fame may or may not represent what men were; but it always
represents what humanity needs them to have been.
    —*Charles Horton Cooley,* Human Nature and the Social Order

Saint Agobard.
    —*Entry in a medieval martyrology from the church of Lyon*

IN THIS CHAPTER, we shall continue the line of inquiry pursued in the previous pages and explore the contexts in which the events of the year 833 were
remembered during the Middle Ages. Unsurprisingly, the recollection of 833
grew increasingly incidental over time, a trend that was already underway in
the early tenth century when Odilo of Saint-Médard inserted "Louis' narrative" within his larger work on the translation and miracles of his monastery's
saints. Yet, although the selective remembrance of 833 by later generations,
like Odilo, exhibits their diminishing interest in the events, it still reveals
much about their concerns and the nature of their historical consciousness.
An epic poem of the twelfth century, the *Couronnement de Louis,* and a set of
"national" chronicles from the thirteenth, the *Grandes Chroniques de France,*
recall 833 to underscore the issue of faith, but do so from different perspectives
and for different ends, imparting the events with new meanings in light of
current events and their concomitant demands. By the early modern era, the
abandonment of Louis and his penance appear as little more than a footnote,
which, when remembered at all, serve simply as a notable precedent from the

past, grouped with any number of like examples to support Protestant arguments against the church or Huguenot attacks upon the monarchy. Ironically, it was precisely in this context of relative indifference that—thanks to a rather fortuitous event—interest in the particulars of 833 would once again become intense. Just as the theologian Paschasius Radbertus of Corbie composed a passionate apology in the ninth century for a leader of the rebellion whom he felt had been undeservedly slandered, so too in the mid-seventeenth century would the theologian Théophile Raynaud of Lyon suddenly feel compelled to defend the repute of another leading figure of 833, one who, like Wala, had sought to correct the iniquity of Louis' court. In this way, this chapter ends much like the last—with the rebels and their deeds gaining renewed attention through the zealous efforts of those who dared to defend them. And in both cases, it was the reputation of a saint that so desperately needed defending.

Regino of Prüm

Near the end of the first decade of the tenth century, Regino (b. ca. 845–d. 915), a former abbot of Prüm residing in Trier, set to work on an elaborate chronicle, in the process sketching a stark, synoptic account of Louis' reign.[1] Dedicating his chronicle to Bishop Adalbero of Augsburg, Regino began with the birth of Christ and worked his way to the year 813 by drawing from an impressive array of sources, including texts by Boethius, Bede, the *Liber Pontificalis*, the *Historia Francorum*, Paul the Deacon, various annals and saints' lives, and the martyrology (but not the chronicle) compiled by Ado of Vienne just a few decades earlier.[2] Like Ado before him, Regino saw the year 814 (that of Charlemagne's death) as the point at which memory, hearsay, and, eventually, personal experience could begin to supplant written records as sources for his chronicle.[3] Unlike Ado, Regino was explicit about the reasons this was so:

> These things, which were described above, I learned in a certain little book written [in] vulgar and rustic speech. I emended some [of its corrupt text] in accordance with the rule of Latin [grammar], and I added certain things that I heard from the tale (*ex narratione*) of old men. What follows [below] was copied with the zeal of my smallness, [either] just as I found [it] noted down in books of chronicles, or [from what] I was able to learn by listening to the report of [my] fathers (*ex*

relatione patrum). And indeed I have put down very little in writing
about the times of Emperor Louis [the Pious], since I did not find
written records (*scripta*), nor did I hear from [my] elders anything that
had been worthy of being committed to memory. But I copied a great
deal about the deeds of Emperor Lothar and his brothers, the kings of
the Franks. Where [my chronicle] approached our times, however, I
brought forward the discourse (*sermo*) of a more detailed story (*latior
narratio*). "For things seen," as [Saint] Jerome said, "are narrated in one
fashion, things heard in another. What we understand better, we also
express better."[4]

Evidently, the "little book" (*libellus*) Regino had been using as a source for
this section of his chronicle (a section he entitled "The Book Concerning the
Deeds of the Frankish Kings") had come to its conclusion, causing him to
turn to other records of the recent past, such as written accounts, the stories
of elders, and even personal experience.[5] Unfortunately, explained Regino,
these new sources gave a rather lopsided shape to the remainder of his chronicle, compelling him to account for the relative paucity of information in
the section on the reign of Louis the Pious, as well as the increasing length
of the chronicle's entries as it approached his own time. The dilation of the
chronicle's later years was entirely warranted, maintained Regino, because
it reflected his personal experience, a source of information which, as Saint
Jerome had once said, demanded a qualitatively different kind of narrative
than those things learned only from hearsay.[6]

A remarkable digression by Regino late in his chronicle suggests that,
apart from the gap in his sources, there was another reason for his abrupt
pause and editorial apology upon reaching the death of Charlemagne in
814—one that would profoundly affect his account of 833. Noting in his entry
for the year 880 that a royal son had been given the name "Arnulf," Regino
was reminded that this was also the name of the seventh-century bishop of
Metz and progenitor of the Carolingian line of kings. That family, he recalled, had gradually swelled over time with the aid of divine providence,
until it crested in Charles the Great, who ruled over an empire of diverse
peoples and kingdoms. After his death, however, the fickleness of fortune
(*varians fortuna*) saw to it that the glory that had given rise to Charles's sublimity began to ebb; not only were the Carolingians slowly abandoned by
their satellite kingdoms, observed Regino, but their royal line was also rapidly
perishing, "partly because of unripe age, partly because of the sterility of their

wives."[7] For Regino the death of Charlemagne clearly marked a terrible turning point, one that was evidenced by the dearth of records immediately following the emperor's demise; he could ascertain relatively little about Louis the Pious, while the data about the remaining years of the empire's decline often had to be provided by Regino himself.[8] Not long after these reflections, Regino even noted that the empire of the Carolingians, in his opinion, had finally come to its end. "After Charles [the Fat's] death," he observed in his entry for the year 888, "the kingdoms which had obeyed his will, as if devoid of a legitimate heir, were loosened from their bodily structure into parts and now awaited no lord of hereditary descent, but each set out to create a king for itself from its own innards." Certainly many wars resulted from this "mitosis" of the Carolingian body politic, but Regino hastened to add that the fateful division had not been due to any want of noble or wise princes among the Franks. To the contrary, the equality of their ancestry, dignity, and power had created the very surfeit that exacerbated the discord, "for no one [among them] so surpassed the others," he continued, "that they considered it fitting to submit themselves to follow his rule. Indeed Francia would have given rise to many princes fit to govern the kingdom had not fortune (*fortuna*) in the pursuit of power armed them for mutual destruction."[9]

Thus, it was as part of the breakup of the empire—beginning with Charlemagne's death in 814 and punctuated by Charles the Fat's death and the empire's division in 888—that Regino understood the events of 833. From such a "post-Carolingian" perspective, Louis' abandonment and penance merited a brief mention and an even more abbreviated explanation. "In the year of the holy incarnation 838," began Regino for the year 833, abiding by the faulty chronology he had adopted previously and would continue to follow for the next several decades,[10]

Louis was deprived of the empire by his own people, and was placed in solitary confinement, while the crown of the kingdom was bestowed upon his son Lothar by the election of the Franks. In turn, he was removed from custody by his son Louis [the German] and by the Franks, and was restored to his imperial seat. This deposition (*deiectio*) was due mainly to the many adulterous liaisons (*propter multimodam fornicationem*) of his wife Judith.

In the year of the holy incarnation 839, Lothar, having forsaken France, sought Italy. Bishop Ebbo of Reims was deposed in a general synod, and many others, who had colluded in the deposition (*deiectio*) of the emperor, were condemned to exile.[11]

These two entries by Regino, which conflate the major political events of the years 833–835, have the rhetorical structure and tone of something obvious and undisputed. Louis' notorious troubles, Regino seems to be saying, were—as everyone knows—clearly due to the improprieties of his wife. No elaboration was necessary. Facing a dearth of source material, Regino appears to have bridged the gap in his chronicle with what he considered common knowledge about the years of Louis' reign. For example, in the five other entries he composed for the years between 814 (Charlemagne's death) and 840 (Louis' death), Regino noted a few additional events: the blinding of Louis' nephew, King Bernard of Italy; the death of Louis' first wife, Ermengard; Louis' defeat on the battlefield by Breton rebels; the subsequent grant of the kingdom of Brittany to a native by the name of Nominoë; and Louis' death by illness.

Despite their long polished appearance, these terse, "common knowledge" anecdotes were also shaped by Regino's immediate ecclesiastical values and literary sensibilities. As Hans-Henning Kortüm has noted, Regino displays a conspicuous interest in those persons and deeds of the past that evinced the qualities of effort (*actio*) and vigorous activity (*strenuitas*), as well as those events in which a Boethian notion of fortune (*fortuna*) appears to have played a hand.[12] Conversely, where he thought these elements lacking, Regino has little to say, and, even then, his laconic remarks still betray his judgment in accordance with a standard of achievement. Thus, there was little worth mentioning about Louis' reign not only (and primarily) due to a dearth of records but also because the emperor had apparently achieved so little.[13] When Regino does speak about Louis, he primarily underscores his passivity and failure: King Bernard was delivered to Louis, blinded, and killed; Louis fought the Bretons only to lose; the king of the Bretons had to die before Louis could act again in Brittany; because of his wife, Louis was deprived of his rule and imprisoned by his sons, only to be rescued and restored to his throne by Louis the German and the populace. And even when Ebbo and the other conspirators were deposed and condemned, Regino conveys this information using the passive voice: punishments were suffered by the conspirators, rather than inflicted upon them by anyone. The wronged Louis is nowhere to be found, except on his deathbed in the very next entry.

Moreover, when Regino offers an explanation that is not dependent upon literary models, he routinely accounts for events paradigmatically, along strict moral-theological criteria.[14] For Regino, Boethian fortune played a role in the empire's eventual dissolution, as did the overabundance of virtue, a classical notion he borrowed from an epitome of Pompeius Trogus. But these interpretations were more the exception than the rule. Less spectacular events, such as the deposition of the indolent emperor, were interpreted by Regino in more typical, Christian fashion as the familiar result of moral depravity.[15] Judith's "many adulterous liaisons" (*multimoda fornicatio*) were cited as the unequivocal reason behind Louis' removal from the throne. And for Regino that was reason enough. In 869, the chronicler Ado of Vienne had carefully bookended with fulsome praise a similar criticism of Judith's wanton behavior during the early 830s, referring to her first as Louis' "dear wife" (*uxor dilecta*) before sententiously denouncing her *malitia,* and then concluding his remarks by referring to her again as Louis' "most gracious wife" (*uxor gratissima*).[16] Like Ado, Regino understood the events in moral terms and readily adopted what appears to have become a standard narrative about the rebellion of 833: Judith's shameless concupiscence was "predominantly" (*ex permaxima parte*) to blame. But unlike Ado, by the beginning of the tenth century, Regino could invoke this explanation frankly, without the need to sugar the pill.[17]

Odbert of Utrecht

After the accounts by Odilo and Regino, the last extended discussion of the events of 833 occurs in the early eleventh century. Sometime near 1024, a monk named Odbert composed a lengthy *passio* text about the virtuous life and brutal assassination of his hero Frideric, bishop of Utrecht, who was allegedly murdered at the command of Louis' wife, Judith, in the wake of the events at Saint-Médard.[18] Odbert is the only source for this rather startling information. While contemporary ninth-century accounts show that Frideric did indeed have an active episcopal career in the 820s–830s, it is uncertain whether he was involved in the events of 833 or their aftermath.[19] Odbert himself provides no clues, for his description of the events at Saint-Médard is both general and vague, being largely dependent on the accounts provided by Thegan, Regino of Prüm, and even the apologies of Ebbo of Reims and the rebel bishops' *Relatio* of 833.[20]

Louis' sons, explains Odbert, convoked an assembly with a number of bishops, nobles, and other dignitaries, and there determined that, on account of the queen's ignominy and Louis' disobedience of a direct order from the pope, the imperial couple deserved to be abandoned and imprisoned. The emperor should then remain in solitary confinement, under heavy guard, they agreed, until he performed penance and placated God with his prayers. After these things were done, continues Odbert, Queen Judith—who had been forced to take the veil by Jesse, bishop of Amiens—was sent to the city of Tortona and threatened with nothing short of death if she should try to escape.[21]

If Odbert's account seems rather straightforward—especially in comparison with the vitriolic narrative of 833 rendered by his main source, Thegan—that is because it does not exhibit the same immediate concerns of the many ninth-century accounts. For Odbert, the events of 833 were of interest only insofar as they helped to illustrate the contemporary priorities addressed by his tale. In fact, the details that Odbert chose to highlight in his narrative—Judith's "ignominy," her enveiling by Bishop Jesse, and Louis' obdurate defiance of the pope—become significantly pronounced when viewed against the backdrop of the entire *passio*.

Throughout the story of Frideric's life and martyrdom, Odbert underscores that same bishop's preoccupation with blood kinship and illegitimate marriage, issues that had far more resonance in the eleventh century than in the ninth.[22] After several chapters detailing Frideric's birth, training, and rise to the episcopate (an office Louis the Pious imposed upon the unwilling, humble Frideric, thereby establishing the hostile tenor of their relationship), Odbert introduces the *passio*'s leitmotif with a spectacular scene. Called to the palace, Frideric was personally commanded by Louis to rid the island of Walcheren (at the Scheldt estuary) of its inhabitants' incestuous marriages.[23] Taking the emperor by surprise, the bishop responded to this order not with obeisance but with two strange questions: "Tell me, I wonder, my Lord Emperor, whether it is more proper to begin to eat a fish at the head or at the tail, or first to build a wall to the top and [only] afterwards to lay [its] foundation?" Louis answered knowingly that it is proper to eat a fish by beginning at its head, and to build a wall by beginning with its foundation, "since without the foundation the work will hardly be sturdy."[24] "You have judged well," agreed Frideric, who then, without warning, proceeded to rebuke the emperor; as the "head" and "foundation" of the church, explained Frideric, it was Louis, and not the people of Walcheren, who required Frideric's immediate attention, for the emperor himself was guilty of an incestuous marriage, endangering the stability of the entire church thereby![25] Queen Judith, proclaimed

Frideric in a voice imbued with the Holy Spirit, was none other than Louis'
cousin (*neptis*) and should be spurned so that the emperor could undergo
a worthy penance for his sin.[26] Ashamed by the bishop's lengthy reproach,
Louis threw himself to the ground, admitted his sin amid a vale of tears, and
begged forgiveness.[27]

Frideric's vigilance for consanguinity drives the rest of Odbert's account,
setting in motion a sequence of events that lead to the death of the conscientious bishop, thereby demonstrating unequivocally the validity of his
concern. After attending to the priorities of Louis' humiliation and Judith's
dismissal from the palace, Frideric returned to Utrecht and soon travelled
to the island of Walcheren. By preaching and ultimately gaining the confidence of the island's elders, the bishop managed to uproot their practice of
incestuous marriage.[28] However, the emperor's own illicit union was still not
fully emended, for Judith continued in her wanton schemes; failing to bribe
Frideric into allowing her unlawful marriage to stand, the queen then tried
to seduce Louis' godson, the court chamberlain Bernard, and—after this also
failed—went spitefully before the emperor to accuse that "innocent youth"
of rape.[29] Even the invasion by the Bretons and Louis' decision to bribe them
with gifts rather than engage them in battle were, in Odbert's opinion, all "on
account of the woman." What was worse, Louis subsequently acted as though
he had achieved a victory—something that hardly fooled the populace, who
knew that God had allowed their realm to be scourged by the Bretons for a
reason: "And so," Odbert explained, "there was great murmuring about the
emperor's illicit marriage."[30]

At this point in the account, Judith's incestuous turpitude begins to
wreak havoc upon the realm as a whole, consequently escalating the kind
and degree of each party's reprisals and compelling the story to its murderous
conclusion. Unwilling to meet with failure, continues Odbert, the queen finally succeeded in seducing Bernard and with him committed the "diabolical
sin" of adultery. However, King Pippin, a son from the emperor's first marriage, soon discovered this "infamy" (*fama*) and, with sadness, alerted several
dignitaries, including Bishop Jesse, Archchaplain Hilduin, Abbot Helisachar,
and Counts Matfrid and Godefrid, who all hastened to the emperor with
their scandalous report. Mortified in the face of their outcries, Louis grimly
nodded his consent, allowing Judith to be seized, enveiled, and sent back into
monastic custody. After only a few months, however, the emperor managed to
free the queen once more, and together they not only deposed many of those
who had condemned Judith but also imprisoned others and cast the remain-

ing conscientious dignitaries into exile. News of these vindictive judgments soon reached Pope Gregory IV, who was so aggrieved that he crossed the Alps to admonish Louis and Judith to come to their senses. After begging his forgiveness, the emperor and his wife were granted indulgence by the pope, who promptly returned to Rome, but not before leaving them with a grave ultimatum: that the penitent couple must follow the admonitions of those bishops whom they had previously deposed and exiled or else be deemed "as heathens" (*veluti ethnicos*) and suffer everlasting excommunication. Soon after the pope's departure, however, Louis and Judith openly displayed their contempt for both the bishops and their papal mandate; Bishop Frideric drew their particular ire, for he more than anyone had striven to expose their iniquity and correct their transgressions.[31]

It is here, within this melancholy chain of events, that Odbert's account of 833—and more specifically, his abrasive treatment of Judith and Louis—should be understood. Louis' sons together agreed that, because of Judith's incestuous ignominy and their father's violation of the pope's command, the imperial couple should once again be deposed and taken into custody—but this time, each would be imprisoned alone and bound under the threat of death. These deeds were quickly accomplished, but to little effect. Louis the German was so wrenched by his feelings for his father that he soon liberated the emperor, who, with as many supporters as he could muster, freed Judith and once more deposed those ecclesiastics who had condemned them—a vengeful deed that, Odbert noted, was done "without cause." Learning of the tumultuous events from afar, Bishop Frideric promptly dispatched a letter to this proud, stray sheep of his flock. Quoting a lengthy passage, Odbert allows the reader an earful of Frideric's invective: the bishop was outraged that the presumptuous emperor, as a self-proclaimed servant of Christ, had himself dared to judge and punish his fellow servants, namely, the ecclesiastics. Had the apostle not said (here quoting Paul's epistle to the Romans, 14:4), "Who art thou that judgest another man's servant? To his own lord he standeth or falleth." Frideric warned Louis to return immediately to his state of penance or face excommunication. Closing his quotation of the letter, Odbert observes that the emperor became extremely angered on account of Frideric's admonitions—so enraged, in fact, that he at last desired what the queen had wanted all along: the death of that man of God.[32] Seizing her opportunity, Judith assembled a number of the emperor's men and, reminding them of the constant suffering Frideric had caused Louis, announced that a large reward awaited those who would avenge their lord emperor and queen by doing away with their common enemy. Two haughty youths leaped at the offer, sealed their murderous pact with an oath, and set out on their errand with knives hidden in their sleeves. Ambushing Frideric in his church shortly after he had conducted the Mass, the youths repeatedly stabbed the bishop—who only invited their blows—and with their cries informed this precursor to Thomas Beckett, "Our Queen is avenged of you!" Yet, even after the fatal blow was delivered, Frideric kindly called his assassins close and informed them of the best route for their escape. Choking on his final breaths—"*Ve, ve, et vach!*" writes Odbert onomatopoeically—the saintly bishop even managed to warn his horrified brethren, who had since discovered their mortally wounded master, of the even greater horrors that awaited them: the Northmen would soon visit their slaughter upon the kingdom, gasped Frideric portentously, "because of the iniquity of the emperor and his wife."[33]

As the preceding summary has illustrated, it was not the divestiture of Louis the Pious and his treatment at the hands of his sons and clergy that were now, two centuries later, deserving of lamentation, but the murderous consequences of the emperor's alleged illegitimate marriage that were rather adduced as the tragedy. By the early eleventh century, the events surrounding 833 were represented in accordance with what was perhaps a hostile regional memory of Louis in Utrecht[34] and in terms that spoke of and to an issue of great moment: the alleged consanguinity (of four degrees) between King Conrad II and his wife, Gisela.[35] Leading ecclesiastics of the day, such as Archbishop Aribo of Mainz, who scrupulously adhered to the sanctions (if not uniform definitions) of canon law, condemned unions within seven degrees of kinship as incestuous.[36] When asked by Conrad to crown Gisela in 1024 (thereby implicitly validating their standing marriage of eight years), the monarch's longtime supporter Archbishop Aribo—having learned of the royal couple's rumored consanguinity—resolutely refused. As Patrick Corbet has argued, it is precisely within this context—of heightened tension between the lay nobility and the clergy over differing notions of kinship and incest—that the composition of Odbert's *passio* text should be understood. Adalbold, the bishop of Utrecht (1010–1026) to whom Odbert dedicated his text, is known to have stood alongside the Lotharingian bishops of Cologne and Liège in their opposition to Conrad's election in September of 1024 as the new German king, one whose coronation would punctuate and supplant the Ottonian dynasty of monarchs with that of a new line, the Salians.[37] Lending support to Aribo and Adalbold's protests, Odbert's tragic tale about Frideric, Louis, and Judith illustrated the dire consequences of unions such as that of

Conrad and Gisela: if left unchecked, consanguineous marriages resulted in suffering, sorrow, and death.[38] Yet, Bishop Frideric's ultimate sacrifice was not meant simply as proof of this axiom but more as a testament to God's approbation of those who acted to abolish such incest. For Odbert, 833 served as an important clause in this divine mandate on the rectitude of ecclesiastical concern and zealous reproach.

The *Couronnement de Louis*

Little more than a century after Odbert's account, a vague recollection of Louis' "failure" as a monarch again appears in the written records, but this time within a particular cycle of epic poems or *chansons de geste* steadily gaining popularity in France. Perhaps recited for untold years but only codified during the middle of the twelfth century, the collection of twenty-four poems concerned with the heroic deeds of the Carolingian warrior William of Orange celebrates his virtue, courage, and might in numerous ways and amid many misfortunes.[39] One theme in particular, however, cuts across several poems in the William cycle: the manifold perils brought about by the empire's transfer from the mighty Charlemagne to the incompetent Louis and the valorous feats by which William dared to brave them.[40] As a royal disappointment, Louis errs in the *chansons* much as he had in the *Historiae* of Nithard: by his diffidence, impotence, and anxiety. Upon assuming the reins of government from his father, Louis quickly shows himself to be an irresolute, cowardly king, an ignoble foil whose troubles time and again serve both to elicit and underscore William's own noble resolve. But if the theme of "Louis' haplessness causing the adversity to be overcome by an able William" runs through several poems to develop plot and character, it also addresses an implicit question about the proper relationship between lords and vassals: what should become of the obligation to serve one's king faithfully, if the king proves himself to be an unfit lord?[41] While this question may reflect contemporary anxieties on the part of the poets and their audience,[42] it may also attest to an enduring, if vague, sentiment of the shameful "problem" with Louis' reign: the specific events of 833 were here sublimated into the categorical wrong of treason.

Several features of one particular poem of the William cycle, the *Couronnement de Louis*, while clearly at odds with the Carolingian historical event they purport to represent, parallel the sudden rise of the young Capetian prince Louis VII in 1131 as heir-apparent to the French throne.[43] Indeed, so great is this resemblance that scholars posited as the poem's date of composition the years between 1131 (the year of Louis VII's coronation and rise as heir-apparent) and 1137 (the year of his father's death and Louis VII's elevation to the throne).[44] Just as Louis the Pious is presented in the *Couronnement* as a boy undergoing royal consecration, Louis VII was a tender youth of only ten years when, upon the untimely death of his elder brother Philip in 1131, he was crowned the incumbent to his father's patrimony. The historical Louis the Pious, however, was already thirty-five years old when he was crowned by his father at Aachen in 813. Another similarity of the poem to the twelfth-century scene is that, like the figure of Charlemagne in the *chanson*, the prince's father, Louis VI, continued to live for several years after his son's coronation. The historical Charlemagne, though, died just four months after the coronation of his son. A third contemporary parallel is the presence of the pope both in the poetic representation of Louis the Pious's coronation and at the coronation ceremony of Louis VII in 1131. The historical Pope Leo III, however, is mentioned nowhere in the ninth-century records describing the Carolingian ceremony of Louis' coronation in 813.[45]

Yet, if we follow scholarly consensus and accept the assignment of the *Couronnement*'s composition to the period of Louis VII's early years,[46] a troubling question still remains: why was Louis the Pious's reign chosen as the setting for the poem if the details of Louis VII's situation—one the poem is thought to address—were so different? Accounting for the poet's reconciliation of the many incongruities between the historical coronation of Louis the Pious and that of Louis VII becomes all the more complicated when one considers the fact that the poet knew (either directly or indirectly) both Einhard's and Thegan's detailed contemporary reports of Louis the Pious's coronation, liberally borrowing from them to flesh out his own fanciful rendering of the event.[47]

More than a century of debate still finds no satisfactory answer to this question.[48] To be sure, the explanation for the poet's seemingly strange choice of mise-en-scène must lie in the nature of his relationship with the past. However one chooses to understand his process of composition—whether as a deliberate exercise or as the inspired expression of a general, unconscious sentiment[49]—the broad features that the poet remembered about Louis the Pious's reign were sufficient to make it, more than any other, seem the reign most apropos of current concerns. Despite the apparently contradictory "historical" information found in the poet's Carolingian sources, a lingering memory of Louis the Pious seems to have accorded with present apprehensions elicited by Louis VII's minority.[50]

Unfortunately, there remains little historical evidence beyond the William cycle that attests to any such coexistent collective memory of Louis the Pious as an unfit monarch. To the contrary, up through the twelfth century Louis appears regularly in the written records of ecclesiastics in an extremely favorable light, and is often cited alongside his father as a paragon of royal conduct in ecclesiastical affairs.[51] Louis' pan-European epithet "the Pious" (French: le Pieux and le Débonnaire; German: der Fromme; Italian: il Pio) had stuck fast and crystallized—for reasons that are still unclear—sometime between the tenth and twelfth centuries.[52] Moreover, the very cognomens "Louis" and "Charles" appear to have been deemed peculiarly significant names by the French nobility of the eleventh and twelfth centuries and were not thought suitable for general use. Indeed, the nearly exclusive adoption of the otherwise "taboo" name Louis by the Capetians was perhaps meant to associate their line through allusion to some lasting prestige of the Carolingians.[53]

Such historical testimony to Louis the Pious's esteemed reputation, however, did not keep the French philologist René Louis from advancing a theory about how the poet of the *Couronnement* had come to know (what René Louis himself believed was) the ugly truth about Charlemagne's son. The "accurate" memory of Louis the Pious as a "feeble, irresolute, wavering slave of his attendants," the philologist explained, was preserved through an unrecorded oral tradition that by the twelfth century had already endured for nearly three hundred years. Wandering minstrels and jongleurs from the south of France kept alive and disseminated with their songs a vague image of both the heroic feats of Louis' faithful chamberlain Bernard of Septimania (who, the philologist believed, would slowly become the "William" of the eponymous *chanson* cycle), and Louis' utter ineptitude as a monarch.[54]

Although the details of his argument have long been considered problematic, René Louis' claim that an unfavorable memory of Louis and his reign persisted beyond the ninth century has not been discredited. For as we have seen, Odbert in his *passio* account of the early eleventh century depicted Louis and his wife as the basest, most contemptible of royalty. Moreover, while its extant manuscript witnesses are few and late, Odbert's tale nevertheless appears to have been read and circulated not long after its composition[55]; the English historian William of Malmesbury knew Odbert's text in the twelfth century (ca. 1125–1140), albeit indirectly, having liberally redacted his own version of the *passio*—which in William's estimation was an "utter tragedy" (*totus tragedia*)—apparently without having had access to a written source.[56]

However, in keeping with the generally favorable memory of Louis held by ecclesiastics, William tempered Odbert's vilification of the emperor (whom he now characterized merely as a petulant monarch), reserving most of his rebuke for Judith.[57] Such an attenuated, ambivalent memory of Louis, coupled with the infamy of his second wife, seems to have gained wide sway: in the eleventh century, for example, the French monk and chronicler Odo Aribert could explain that Charles the Bald had in truth been the foul progeny of an illicit union between Judith and the chamberlain Bernard of Septimania, with Louis implicitly serving as the unwitting cuckold.[58] In the middle of the twelfth century, the historian Otto of Freising (1115–1158), likely following the earlier report of Regino of Prüm, would also recall that Louis the Pious had been "expelled from the kingdom on account of the evil deeds of his wife."[59] When the contemporary biographer of Abbot Suger of Saint-Denis (1081–1151), the royal advisor to both Louis VI and Louis VII,[60] boasted that Suger could recount the deeds of past kings named at random, one wonders what his impromptu response might have been to a query about Louis the Pious—a king, Suger once noted, whose sons had cast the realm into confusion.[61]

Certainly the poet of the *Couronnement de Louis* left little doubt about his own feelings for Charlemagne's heir: Louis had been a feeble, emasculated excuse for a king. While the poet's representation eschews the specific—and as we shall see, specifically Carolingian—notion of Louis as having been another Ahab or Samson, a dupe pandering to the wiles of a wicked wife,[62] the Louis of the *chanson* is still characterized as a victim of circumstance, a king whose indiscretion and diffidence gave rise to revolt. For example, throughout the *Couronnement*, Louis describes himself as but a mere youth, unable to "maintain his honor by deeds" when confronted with adversity.[63] Yet, as the poet's description of the sniveling Louis and his few deeds soon makes manifest, it is more his craven nature than his inexperience that repeatedly places Louis in peril.[64] At the outset of the *chanson*, the poet even has Charlemagne himself lament Louis' "monkish" quality and refuse to recognize him as his son:

the emperor burned in sorrow and ire;
"Alas," he said, "I was deceived by my wife—

a lowly valet lay at her side
and begat on her this cowardly child.
He will have no more from me in his life.
To crown him king would have been a crime.
Rather we shall cut his hair with a knife
and shut him in church to be a prior,
to pull the ropes and follow the rites;
only his food, lest he beg, I shall provide."[65]

By the *chanson*'s end, William's hot-headed nephew Bertrand, having weathered the many vicissitudes brought about by Louis' succession and learning of yet another revolt, calls Louis a "fool" out of exasperation and disgust.[66]

As noted earlier, the correlation between weak kingship and the rise of rebellion appears as a leading motif throughout the cycle of poems about William. Additionally, the depiction of a weak Louis seems to draw on a vague memory and unflattering estimation of that same sovereign. That the majority of Louis' poetic troubles are cast in terms of treason and revolt illustrates a corollary aspect of Louis' royal "ineptitude" and similarly draws on a faint memory. Within the *Couronnement*, Louis is beset by traitors, both lay and ecclesiastic. At first, the young king nearly succumbs to the treachery of "Arneis d'Orleans" upon the cunning nobleman's bid for the crown.[67] Yet, for much of the *chanson*—and like his experience in 833—Louis languishes in the crypt of a monastery, having been toppled from his throne by scheming barons and held captive by their "four score canons and prelates,/bishops and abbots most worthy of fame."[68] To be sure, in the last century there have been numerous efforts to link the rebels in the poem to their historical counterparts, but for our purposes of understanding the *Couronnement* in the twelfth century and the legacy of 833 within it, we can put aside such elusive pursuits.[69] For if the *Couronnement de Louis* was written in the wake of young Louis VII's regency (after 1131), then the mere appearance in it of Louis the Pious as a callow youth was sufficient to evoke a general set of "historical" circumstances (impotent rule, rebellion, and disaster), allude to present, analogous concerns (impotent rule and the prospect of rebellion and disaster), and prompt a line of conduct to address them (steadfast loyalty).[70] "Great ills will come when [Louis] is overthrown," decrees the pope of the *Couronnement* to both William within the poem and the audience outside it, a suggestive pronouncement that referred simultaneously to a vague event from the Carolingian past (833) and a distinct possibility in the Capetian present. After all, rumors abounded that the sudden, untimely death of Louis VII's elder brother Philip in 1131 (the event that had thrust Louis before the throne) was due to the machinations of their father's enemies.[71] The events of 833 provided a harsh reminder of how inaction against, or collusion with, such men would be recollected; between the late ninth and the early twelfth centuries, for instance, numerous annals, which record little else of Louis the Pious's reign, placed just two synoptic, striking words beside the year DCCCXXXIII: *francorum dedecus,* the shame of the Franks.[72]

Certainly, within the world of the *chanson,* the code of conduct demanded by such trying circumstances as the minority of a king was clear. No matter that one's sovereign or lord is, in the words of the hot-headed Bertrand, a "fool," unequivocally unfit for his office—the bonds of loyalty, by remaining unbroken, sustain honor, and allow for triumph, while base treason is to be abhorred and swiftly crushed. Had not Louis VII's father (Louis VI) and grandfather (Philip I) themselves been confronted with the insolence of comital resistance during their own minorities and triumphed, thanks to the unwavering assistance of their faithful men? This is the constant refrain of the poem about the proper relationship between a lord and his vassal, between Louis the Pious and William of Orange, and perhaps between Louis VII and any nobleman reconsidering his fealty now suddenly owed to a child-king: "Who would commit treason against his lord," warns the poem, "it is right he be made to suffer sore."[73] With respect to ecclesiastical traitors, the verses are even more explicit:

> [Count William] summoned his noble knights to speak:
> "I would have you give me your decree.
> If a man is crowned by the church a priest
> and should spend his life with a psalter to read,
> should he then commit treason for a fee?"
> The knights answered: "He should not certainly."
> "If he do so, what should he then receive?"
> "He should be hung like a miserable thief."
> The count answered: "Well have you advised me."[74]

Here, the notion of committing "treason for a fee" serves as an excellent reminder of what Jean Frappier has called the *Couronnement de Louis'* "double reference" to the past and to the present[75]: on the one hand, the imputation to the ecclesiastics of treachery against Louis the Pious sets the *chanson* in the ninth century (recalling Ebbo, Wala, and their like); on the other hand, the sinful motive ascribed to these same ecclesiastics reveals a comprehension of the rebellion in twelfth-century terms—as the result of avarice rather than pride.[76] That the many troubles of Louis' reign were cast in the poem in the categorical terms of treason against an inept king likewise reflects an understanding shaped by a lay historical consciousness of the twelfth century—of concerns over loyalty and the nature of its limits, rather than (as we shall see) ninth-century concerns about a kingdom rife with iniquity.[77]

In 1228, an Italian notary observed that "rumors of the past often cause one to fear what is about to happen."[78] Nearly a century earlier, during the early years of young Louis VII's reign, the *Couronnement de Louis* perhaps served to dispel such phantoms of remembrance or at least to conjure up its own. That it borrowed from the ninth-century account of Thegan to do so—an account that, as we saw in Chapter 1, took the events of 833 as its focal point—gives the face to such twelfth-century ghosts.[79]

Primat and the *Grandes Chroniques de France*

In the late thirteenth century, the French monastic compiler-translator-author Primat made certain to highlight the year 833 in his *Grandes Chroniques de France* with an account not of Louis' ignominy but of his piety.[80] Relating episodes of the French past through a skillful interweaving and redaction of several Latin and vernacular histories, Primat's own vernacular text focused specifically upon the deeds of kings, telling a genealogical, legitimating tale of unbroken royal succession from King Priam and the fall of Troy through the reign of Philip Augustus (1165–1223).[81] Described by one scholar as a "quintessentially royalist text," the *Grandes Chroniques* were likely composed for the court of Louis IX (1214–1270), grandson of Philip Augustus and the French king canonized in 1297 as "Saint Louis."[82] Certainly, the work spoke to the Christian ideals so exalted and valorized by that pious monarch, for Primat's chronicle relates a story about the special place held by France and its rulers in the eyes of God, the outstanding moral of which was the salutary rewards of pure, unyielding faith.[83] In this respect, the events of 833 provided a memorable, "historical" example of the value of unwavering piety for French kings.

In his account of Louis the Pious's reign, Primat seems to have utilized as his sources only the *Vita Hludowici imperatoris* of the Astronomer and the confessional narrative of Louis the Pious first introduced by Odilo of Saint-Médard.[84] Given that the Astronomer's text itself sharply details the events of 833, Primat's supplemental use of Louis' confession was hardly fortuitous.[85] As the modern editor of the *Grandes Chroniques* has noted, Primat's redaction of the Astronomer's biography halts abruptly after the description of Louis' abandonment at the "Field of Lies" and subsequent internment in the monastery of Saint-Médard.[86] At this point, the narrative switches suddenly to an abridged redaction of Louis' confession, an account taken from, explained Primat, the otherwise unknown "croniques Saint Germain des Prez."[87] Prefaced with the remark that Louis speaks of the cruelty of his sons and the treachery and infidelity of his barons and prelates,[88] the confession functioned here for Primat in much the same way as it had for Odilo: both to heighten the drama of the year's events and to stress the "misery and sorrow" of their outcome.[89]

Yet, in Primat's chronicle, the vivid first-person narrative of Louis' tribulations and saintly deliverance served a different purpose than it had for Odilo's text. As we have seen, Odilo inserted Louis' narrative within his larger account, one that was concerned with the translation and miracles of his patron saints Gregory and Sebastian; in this context, the rescue of the emperor was meant as but another instance of the saints' virtuous might. For Primat, however, Louis' narrative provided a perfect example for his moralizing royal history. The predicament and wondrous release of the emperor now emphasized the unrelenting devotion of an otherwise broken king, together with the divine grace such piety had merited. That a century later the French King Charles V (1338–1380) would commission for his personal library a lavish, illuminated copy of the *Grandes Chroniques*—one updated to include the events of his minority and reign between 1350 and 1380—confirms the resonance Primat's genealogical chronicle, and its image of devout kings such as Louis, would continue to obtain with the French monarchy. (Figure 8)[90]

Protestant Reactions

In the sixteenth century, historians looked back to early medieval texts primarily for the light they shed on issues pertaining to the great religious controversies of the time. Combing the records of their past to find nascent signs of Protestant principles, scholars quickly fixed upon (among other things) the accounts concerning the reign of Louis the Pious[91]; for what they found there

on et quil auoleur muerle li mie li para
en la fin · Le · xbiij · chapitie parle Coment
tout le pieuple se tourna deuers son filz et
de la teneptio de lapostoile · Coment ses filz
le priftrent li et sa feme et charlot son pe
tit filz · Et coment il deptirent le royaume
De la complainte quil fait de ses filz · Et
puis coment il gaba le serjant qui le gar
doit a saint maart de soiffons en prison ·

Figure 8. Louis the Pious disarming his guards at Saint-Médard. Illumination
from the copy of the *Grandes Chroniques de France* of King Charles V. Paris,
Bibliothèque nationale de France, fr. 2813, fol. 142r, detail. Courtesy Bibliothèque
nationale de France.

appeared to be outrageous: Louis let slip from his hands the "unique privilege" that had been proffered to his illustrious father by the church—namely, the sole right to "elect" (i.e., to nominate) the pope. Due to the alleged testimony of numerous medieval documents, it was long accepted that, during Charlemagne's siege against the Lombard king at Pavia in 774, a synod was held in Rome, one attended by numerous abbots, bishops (exactly 153, say the sources), and Pope Hadrian I. With the hope of gaining Charlemagne's protection, the council purportedly decided that the election of all the bishops of Christendom, including the papacy itself, should henceforth lie with the Frankish king, an astonishing right that was duly rendered to Charlemagne.[92] Yet, upon his succession, the "overly clement" Louis the Pious had allowed this privilege to lapse, inferred many sixteenth-century historians, by heedlessly granting Popes Stephen IV and Paschal I their former right to canonical elections. In the historians' eyes, this imprudent act born of Louis' slavishness to the church served to reestablish the traditional electoral custom of Rome.[93]

Yet, many Protestant historians also believed that the unsettling events of the 830s demonstrated what was best about Louis the Pious. The troubles during the later years of Louis' reign were understood to have been the result of the jealousy and resentment that the clergy harbored over the pious emperor's assiduously applied program to reform their morals. Not surprisingly, Louis' triumph over and humiliation of the bishops who had forced him to undergo penance in 833 was especially lauded.[94]

Perhaps the most impressive use of the early medieval past by a sixteenth-century scholar was by the Huguenot jurist François Hotman (1524–1590). Written amid the tempest of the French Wars of Religion, Hotman's notoriously inflammatory work *Francogallia* (1573) sought to prove the despotic character of the French monarchy by demonstrating the liberties once enjoyed by the Franks before its establishment.[95] Adducing and reconstructing what he believed was the ancient constitution of the Franks by means of selective historical examples, Hotman methodically built a source-driven case for the people's power over their chosen monarch. And sure enough, numbering among his legion of precedents from the past were references to Louis the Pious's difficulties with his sons. Yet neither side in the inveterate quarrels of the 830s won Hotman's allegiance, for, as his quotations from the sources were meant to reveal, it was rather the decisive authority of the commonwealth that had dictated both the nature of those disputes and the terms of their resolution. As Hotman noted, quoting Regino of Prüm, "Louis was deprived of his authority by his own followers, and the royal title was bestowed on his son Lothar by the election of the Franks."[96] And again, Hotman marshaled evidence to show that, when "the conspirators discovered that they could not depose the king [Louis] without an assembly of the nobles" because they "feared that they might lack public authority" to do it themselves, they enforced the holding of a council at Compiègne, one consisting of bishops and nobility drawn from the entire kingdom.[97] For Hotman, the events of 833 were memorable only insofar as they evidenced the control the Frankish nobility had once exerted over their kings and showed how much the kings themselves had acknowledged this power. That this truth should be realized in the present as much as it had been in the past was the urgent point Hotman sought to make irrefutable.

Diminishing Returns

Doubtless there are many other sustained recollections of the events of 833, but the foregoing medieval and early modern examples are sufficient to illustrate different ways in which the malleable story of Louis' "downfall" could be remembered and recast both in form and content to speak to current concerns.[98] Whether as part of an eleventh-century *passio* justifying the ecclesiastical prohibition of consanguineous marriage among the nobility, a twelfth-century *chanson* celebrating the glory that comes of unconditional devotion to one's lord, or a thirteenth-century *chronique* testifying to the divine rewards bestowed upon French kings for their adamant faith, the events of 833 proved to be particularly adaptable to the historical sensibilities and concerns of generations of authors.

For all their variety and historical specificity, these same accounts also display a line of continuity with the early medieval memories of Louis the Pious. In each instance, Charlemagne's son was recalled as a relatively good king, or at least one who had meant well, despite his misfortunes, ineptitude, and excessive clemency. The same observation can be made with respect to the memory of his second wife, Judith, though in her case this tenacious remembrance fixed not on any such imprudent charity but on her "characteristic" malevolence. In Hotman's final estimation of Louis, for example, the public had exercised its peremptory authority over the king only because it had been persuaded by his sons' accusations of the evils wrought by Judith: "She stirred up a disastrous and fatal war between Louis and her stepsons," he explained, "from which sprang so great a conspiracy against the king that they forced him to abdicate and cede them his office, to the great detriment of nearly all Europe."[99] Just as the medieval conception of a benign Louis persisted into the early modern era, so, too, had the memory, fostered by Regino and Odbert among others, of a pernicious Judith.[100]

Another, far more evident line of continuity is the diminishing attention given by later generations to the events of 833. Although the various deeds of that year continued to be remembered in a multiplicity of forms over the centuries, they were not the preoccupation they once had been for the several contemporary Carolingian authors we have already encountered, such as Thegan, the Astronomer, and Paschasius Radbertus. Indeed, within the late ninth-century account of Odilo of Saint-Médard, Louis' experience in 833 was already being recalled as an *exemplum,* as but one instance among many invoked to reveal his patron saints' power and their intercessions for the faithful. By the beginning of the tenth century, Regino of Prüm remembered the events of 833 as well-known instances of Judith's depravity and Louis' pusillanimity; yet, in doing so, Regino was reflecting not just on a disgraceful year but on the decline of Charlemagne's empire. From this perspective, the events of 833 were evidence of the realm's lassitude under Louis. Odbert's recollection of 833 likewise formed only part of his larger story about Louis, Judith, Bishop Frideric, and the cost of consanguineous marriage, providing another instance of the contumacy bred by the royal couple's incest. Within the *Couronnement de Louis*, Louis and his troubles during the 830s were sublimated into a vague, categorical memory of a reign that had presented a series of trials for his vassals; the rebellion of 833 had now become the murky basis for any number of treasonous plots throughout the *chanson,* set to test a vassal's loyalty to an inept king. In the *Grandes Chroniques*, Primat's carefully tailored memory of Louis' fate in 833 at the hands of his sons, composed of narrative swaths rent from the accounts of the Astronomer and Odilo, was also emblematic, forming one more patch in a broad historical tapestry illustrating the divine rewards bestowed upon the pious kings of France. For all their cries of approbation or reproach, Protestant historians of the sixteenth century viewed Louis' career as just one among the many royal reigns in the annals to be critiqued and judged according to the nature and degree of the monarch's participation with the rapidly "degenerating" church. Perhaps the zenith of this rhetorical practice, of aggregating seemingly analogous incidents to assert an incontestable truth, was reached with Hotman's vast collection of quotations culled from what we would now distinguish as primary and secondary source material; indeed, it would be odd not to find the events of the 830s amid the hundreds of historical examples Hotman indiscriminately enlisted to demonstrate the ancient authority of the Franco-Gallic commonwealth.[101]

Further evidence of the ingrained indifference to the events of 833 is the disregard of several texts produced by members of the rebellion. The summary of the proceedings of Louis' penance at Saint-Médard, jointly composed by the bishops who had presided over the ritual, was transmitted into the early modern period—as far as we know—through only two manuscript copies: one dates to the mid-ninth century, while the other was recognized in the sixteenth century to be a late medieval witness, a *chartaceum exemplar*. Both copies have since been lost. Likewise, the *Epitaphium Arsenii* of Paschasius Radbertus, a sympathetic account of Abbot Wala's role in the rebellion, survived over the centuries in a lone manuscript (itself of the ninth century), which was only "discovered" by Jean Mabillon in 1677.

If the terse remarks left by their medieval and early modern readers are an indication, it is not surprising that these two texts by members of the rebellion, with their alternative, and even counter, narratives to the long-accepted "tragic" story of 833, failed to raise an eyebrow over the centuries.[102] For the texts of the bishops and Paschasius—when they were read at all— appear to have been considered in light of the normative, loyalist narrative of 833, a story that, according to the first annalist of the Annals of Saint-Bertin, was promulgated in February 835 in Thionville and Metz at the time of Louis' restoration ceremony. Louis' half brother Drogo led the proceedings:

> At this council, among other provisions for ecclesiastical discipline, the following events were particularly fully discussed: in the year immediately preceding, the most devout Emperor [Louis] had been deposed undeservedly, through the treachery of evildoers and enemies of God, from the realm, honor, and royal title which he had inherited from his father; then after some time it had been decided and confirmed by everyone in concord and unanimity that since the evildoers' factions had been destroyed by God's help, he, restored now to his ancestral honor and clothed again as he deserved in the royal splendor, should be acknowledged by all in the most loyal and unswerving obedience and subjection as emperor and lord. Each one present at the council drew up with his own hand a full account of these findings and of his own confirmation thereof, and authenticated

it with his own signature. The outcome of the whole affair, how it had been dealt with, discussed, settled, and finally confirmed in suitable fashion by the signatures of everyone: all this was put together, set out in full detail in one collection, bound as a small volume, and agreed by all as an accurate account. They then wasted no time in making it as widely known as possible, bringing it to everyone's attention with most devoted and heartfelt and kind concern, and with an authority most worthy of so many reverend fathers.[103]

Soon thereafter this "accurate account" was disseminated, as we saw in the conclusion to Chapter 1, through the sympathetic narratives of Louis' promoters and defenders, including Thegan, the Astronomer, and the annalist of the Annals of Saint-Bertin himself.[104] Internalized as the truth by successive generations, this entrenched a priori narrative about 833 always already informed the understanding of the rebels' texts (a process Paschasius Radbertus had lamented as early as the 850s), making their justificatory accounts appear as nothing more than further evidence of their "fraudulence," "mendacity," and "vice," rather than as rival or even revelatory witnesses. The same can be said about the survival and reception of a remarkable apology by Archbishop Ebbo of Reims; written in the 840s in defense of his seemingly seditious actions, it was preserved within only three manuscripts, at least one of which included it as additional proof of Ebbo's cunning and guilt. In short, when viewed within the interpretive frame of the loyalist accounts, the rebels' justificatory texts served to further incriminate their authors rather than vindicate them.

An examination of the reception of these texts is instructive of this tendency. But it is also useful insofar as it reveals the recognition of this framing process, both by the framers and by those few who refused to be so framed.

The Bishops' *Relatio*

In the winter of 840/41, the famed poet, scholar, and abbot of Reichenau Walafrid Strabo (808–849) edited both Thegan's biography of Louis the Pious and the rebel bishops' account of Louis' penance in 833.[105] In the former, Walafrid divided the work into chapters with brief titles and appended a prologue that defended its unpolished style.[106] Thegan had been too busy with more important matters, such as preaching and correction, explained

Walafrid, to set down anything but his raw, impassioned feelings about the emperor they both cherished. Moreover, the work's rough style had its own virtues; written "in the manner of annals," without ornament, he continued, it thereby bore a closer accordance with the truth.[107] To the latter text, the bishops' *Relatio*, Walafrid likewise appended a prologue:

> What follows are the things that were done against the most Christian emperor Louis at the palace of Compiègne when he was deprived of the kingdom for a time. These things were done from a partisan zeal for his overthrow, which should not be imitated, by Ebbo, the author of this evil, and by the other bishops who were either working in error or acquiescing out of fear. These things, however, should not be embraced as the decrees of a healthy council, but rejected as the work of a deadly contrivance.[108]

While it is unclear whether Thegan himself appended the bishops' narrative to his text or if Walafrid united the two works when he edited them, a library catalog from Reichenau drawn up between late 840 and 842 suggests that they were by then already paired.[109] Given the contents and arguments of Thegan's work, this particular compilation is unsurprising; passionate in its defense of Louis and excoriation of elevated slaves such as Ebbo, the short biography of the emperor reads as a direct rebuttal to the charges in the bishops' narrative of Louis' iniquity. As Thegan has Louis himself explain, using direct speech, he did not assemble his people on the Rotfeld for the purpose of their mutual destruction—the emperor's greatest sin, imputed the bishops—but rather sent his faithful men away out of concern that they not lose their lives or limbs on his account.[110] More than just evidence of false charges, however, the bishops' *Relatio* also functions in the compilation as "proof" that Thegan's cautionary tale should be taken seriously, for it depicts in vivid hues Archbishop Ebbo's villainy and the consequences of allowing the lowborn to ascend to positions of power. This is certainly how Walafrid understood the relationship between the two texts, as his prologue to the bishops' *Relatio* above makes manifest. Describing the bishops' account as the "work of a deadly contrivance," Walafrid reminds the reader that Ebbo was the "author of this evil." Whether he meant that Ebbo authored the shrewd "contrivance" that sought to depose the emperor through the ruse of a self-imposed penance and abdication or that Ebbo was simply the author of the bishops' collective narrative of the penance—or perhaps both—is ambiguous. What is certain is that Walafrid's prologue didactically established for the reader the loyalist context within which the rebel bishops' account should be understood.[111] Doubtless, it is for this reason that the bishops' damning narrative of Louis and his many wrongs survived, despite the many generations that have viewed the events of 833 as "the shame of the Franks" (one might recall that this specific characterization stemmed from a late ninth-century set of annals also kept at Reichenau[112]). Walafrid's prefatory remarks recast what was originally a justificatory narrative into a cautionary tool, appended not only to underscore the urgency of Thegan's work and expose the lowborn Ebbo's authorship of the "evil" but also, or perhaps especially, to reveal and thus demonstrate the text's duplicitous nature—the seemingly "healthy" language, style, and form that such a "deadly" contrivance could assume.[113] To explain why Walafrid bothered to do this at all must wait for a later chapter. For now, it is sufficient to note that the loyalist narrative, with its depiction of the "evil" events of 833 as an endeavor to deceive, already framed the bishops' narrative by 841.

Turning to the later, meager reception of the *Relatio*, we find that Walafrid's prologue continued to dictate the terms of its interpretation. The two manuscripts that, as far as we know, preserved the bishops' account during the Middle Ages transmitted it only as an appendix to Thegan's work, with both texts carrying Walafrid's didactic prologues.[114] What is more, these manuscripts preserved the texts only as part of a larger compilation, one that offers a history of the world from Creation to the late years of Louis' reign. This compilation was likely assembled by Reginbert, the learned librarian of Reichenau and Walafrid's old friend, sometime during the period of Walafrid's brief exile from Reichenau between 841 and 842.[115] Given the recent shift in the political winds following Louis' death in June 840, it is perhaps no coincidence that Reginbert chose to compile historical texts sympathetic not only to Louis the Pious but also to Louis the German, Reichenau's new overlord.[116] Here was a history book detailing what should be done and what should be avoided and how Louis himself exemplified such prudence in his conduct. Moreover, the form of Walafrid's two-text compilation suited Reginbert's purpose; written in the manner of annals, as Walafrid noted in his preface, Thegan's biography fit neatly with the other annals Reginbert selected to precede it.

Whether Louis the German, like his pious father a ruler with a deep interest in history, ever saw Reginbert's compilation is unknown.[117] What we do know is that, until the sixteenth century, the two manuscripts preserving it appear not to have wandered far beyond the ambit of Reichenau and its nearby towns; Reginbert's codex cataloged at Reichenau in 840/41 was likely seen at Engelberg in the seventeenth century, while a late medieval paper copy was found in the monastery of Petershausen, near Constance, early in the sixteenth.[118] Although the fate of the former manuscript is uncertain, the latter is believed to have come into the hands of the Gallican scholar Pierre Pithou (1539–1596), who used it for his collection of Frankish sources published in 1588, in which the bishops' *Relatio* was given the damning title "The Proceedings of Emperor Louis the Pious's shameful and impious deposition."[119] Like Pithou, the editors of the numerous reprintings of the *Relatio*, which were made in quick succession over the seventeenth century,[120] found it unnoteworthy, as the text confirmed what Walafrid stated in his preface and what they themselves already believed: that "all those things [described in the rebel bishops' account] were done through compulsion and fear, and were colored by the false paint of religion," explained one editor, Severinus Binius, in 1606, just as the familiar testimony of Thegan, he continued, already demonstrated "beyond doubt" (*verissimum*).[121] Others readily seconded this opinion and added that the bishops' text merely verified what they believed Charlemagne's respected biographer Einhard had said about the events of 833: that they amounted to nothing less than a "detestable crime" against a "most gentle ruler," a terrible offense that "ought to be despised for all time."[122] The humanist Isaac Casaubon (1559–1614) succinctly summarized the bishops' *Relatio* in his copy of Pithou's source collection: in the margin beside the text, he scribbled with contempt, "*Orem ridiculam. Plane ingeniosum*" (Absurd, I daresay. Clearly a deceit!).[123]

The Apology of Ebbo of Reims

Within the seventh volume of *Spicilegium* (1666), his massive anthology of medieval texts, Luc d'Achéry (1609–1685), the French Benedictine scholar and librarian of the monastery of Saint-Germain des Prés, published for the first time an apology written by Ebbo of Reims.[124] Discovered a few years earlier in the Vatican library in a ninth-century manuscript, the text was promptly copied and sent to d'Achéry for inclusion in his source collection.[125] In the apology, written in 842, Ebbo vehemently defends his actions during the 830s and argues for his continuing right to the see of Reims, which he had lost in 835 at Louis' restoration ceremony, momentarily regained in 840 after Louis' death, and lost again late in 841.[126] Although the apology survived in at least two additional manuscripts, it attracted little attention during the Middle Ages. A brief examination of the contents of the three manuscripts that contain it suggests why.

In the old Vatican manuscript, the apology is found among several texts that are generally hostile to and refute the many arguments of Hincmar, Ebbo's eventual successor as bishop of Reims and truculent rival.[127]

Another manuscript, this one from the beginning of the eleventh century, is a compilation of texts largely concerned with priestly duties and the penalties for ignoring bans imposed by bishops.[128] It, too, suggests by its particular contents a compiler who was sympathetic to Ebbo's plight—that Louis the Pious not only broke his vow of penance solemnized by Ebbo and the other bishops (a sin deserving of condign punishment, as detailed in the manuscript's list of canons) but also unjustly punished Ebbo, who, as the compilation underscores, had even been given a papal mandate for his missionary duties in the north.[129] The compilation also intimates Louis' misconduct by the inclusion of two contiguous extracts: a short list of twenty-five ethical and military maxims (drawn from the work of the classical author Vegetius) that a ruler (such as Louis) ought to follow and an excerpt from the *Dialogues* of the late antique author Sulpicius Severus on the serious misgivings of a soldier who had entered the monastic life (such as Louis) and the episcopal admonishment he duly received and followed.[130]

The third manuscript containing Ebbo's apology is different from the other two in several respects. First, it is a transcription made in the seventeenth century by the scholar Jacques Sirmond (1559–1651) of a manuscript from the monastery of Hérivaux that has since been lost.[131] Second, it contains a text of the apology that is markedly different from the two witnesses described above; indeed, Albert Werminghoff, who discovered Sirmond's transcription, argued that its text should be understood as a second, revised edition made by Ebbo himself shortly after his initial (and very rough) draft of the apology began to circulate.[132] Finally, the particular assemblage of texts faithfully copied by Sirmond from the lost Hérivaux manuscript suggests a compiler unsympathetic to Ebbo's cause, one who wished to have at hand a book that elucidates and codifies the meaning of Ebbo's abortive restitution and apology. Appearing in Sirmond's transcription immediately after Ebbo's text and likely copied from the same Hérivaux manuscript is a remarkable narrative known as the *Visio Bernoldi*, which reveals Ebbo's posthumous state in purgatory.[133] When taken as a pair with Ebbo's apology, the *Visio Bernoldi* functions as a striking conclusion to that initial text's story, providing the last word on Ebbo's fate and a moral about it as well. Just as we have seen Thegan's biography refute the tale told about Louis in the appended bishops' narrative, the vision text refutes Ebbo's defense of his deeds in this world (and thus his right to the see of Reims) yet does so not by explicit counterargument but by allowing a glimpse of Ebbo's plight in the next world. Framed in this conclusive fashion, the apology appears as nothing but another failed ploy by the sly old bishop. Guile such as Ebbo possessed might be effective against men, the compilation seems to say, but it withered before God, whose judgment ultimately renders each his due.[134] That the *Visio Bernoldi* is believed to have been written by Ebbo's old nemesis Hincmar further underscores the politics behind punctuating the apology in this pointed manner.[135]

Although these meaningful compilations preserved Ebbo's apology and with it an alternative account of 833, they made little impact on the traditional, loyalist narrative about the events of that year. In the case of the last collection, Ebbo's apology itself served to support the traditional narrative. Even the first two manuscripts, despite their texts' solidarity with Ebbo's crusade as a wronged bishop, apparently led few to question their assumptions about Ebbo and the reasons for his quarrels with Hincmar and Louis. Such indifference is not surprising, as the compilations are comprised of texts that have little relevance to concerns beyond those specifically held by Ebbo and his disciples in the ninth century. That they survived at all is likely also due to this indifference; the two books appear to have long remained in the cities of their origin, Reims and Hildesheim respectively—cities directly associated with Ebbo's disputes.[136] While the second volume, compiled in the eleventh century apparently to address broad concerns about a bishop's authority and ministry, had a potentially wider audience, its readers found little of interest in the old episcopal conflict. Indeed, one anonymous reader wrote in the bottom margin of Ebbo's apology the following phrase in Hebrew letters: "Peace be upon Israel and on Judah" (*shalom al yisrael v-al yehudah*).[137] Was this a prayer for heavenly peace between the "divided kingdoms" of Ebbo and his enemies?

In the wake of d'Achéry's first edition of the text in 1666, and for the sake of completeness in the chronological source record, Ebbo's apology was reprinted in at least seven historical and ecclesiastical anthologies in the seventeenth and eighteenth centuries.[138] Yet, if Charles Le Cointe's severe condemnation of the text in 1683 is any indication, its interpretation remained unchanged despite this wide circulation.[139] Looking ahead two centuries, we can perhaps see why. In a rare, spirited defense of the rebels involved in 833, Edouard Dumont and Charles Barthélemy were careful to describe the participants as "men most eminent in intelligence and virtue . . . distinguished by their blood and their sanctity."[140] They then detailed the rebels' names and offices, but Ebbo figures nowhere among them. Even in a work undertaken expressly to remedy the "historical injustices" incurred by the rebels, to vindicate their actions, and to redeem their honor, Ebbo is conspicuously absent. But this omission is not unexpected, given the basis of Dumont and Barthélemy's apology—that the rebels were men most eminent and distinguished. For as Thegan had clamored so insistently in the ninth century, Ebbo was lowborn and "unnaturally" raised to his office of bishop. Such transgressions of status, it seems, were by the mid-nineteenth century still unforgivable. The ignoble Ebbo would find no defenders.

Jean Mabillon and the *Epitaphium Arsenii*

Another sympathetic account of the rebellion was brought to light by d'Achéry's disciple, the Benedictine scholar Jean Mabillon (1632–1707), in 1677.[141] Originating from the monastery of Corbie, the lone, ninth-century manuscript containing Paschasius Radbertus's dramatic defense of Abbot Wala—the *Epitaphium Arsenii* discussed in Chapter 1—was owned at some point in the twelfth or thirteenth century by the monastery of Saint-Arnoul de Crépy, before finding its way into the collection of the priory of Saint-Martin des Champs in Paris, where it was discovered by Mabillon.[142] Although Mabillon called it a "golden work," the fact that the *Epitaphium Arsenii* has survived in only one manuscript, itself dating from the period shortly after the text's completion in the 850s, suggests that few of its medieval owners, whether at Saint-Arnoul de Crépy, Saint-Martin des Champs, or elsewhere, held it in such high regard.[143] Doubtless the alternative story that the *Epitaphium* told about the events of 833 was—like the bishops' *Relatio* and Ebbo's apology—read and understood from the loyalist perspective and thus quickly dismissed. Unlike the bishops' account, which was apparently deemed worthy of additional copies (for admonitory purposes, if Walafrid's prefatory remarks affixed to them are any indication), Paschasius's peculiar apology for Wala was thought to hold little value.

Mabillon praised the *Epitaphium* as a work of moral and historical merit, a text whose incongruities with the traditional, loyalist narrative of 833 deserved consideration rather than contempt. For example, in the preface to his edition of the text, Mabillon explained soberly that one of Paschasius's main objectives was to show that Wala, contrary to the loyalist claim that he was a leading member of the rebellion, in fact had opposed Louis' deposition. It was only when Wala realized the immutability of the rebels' willfulness, continued Mabillon, that he sadly acknowledged the futility of his efforts for a peaceful reconciliation and subsequently withdrew into Italy.[144]

Despite Mabillon's high regard for it, Paschasius's strange and difficult text was rarely reprinted or utilized by subsequent historians to reconfigure the standard narrative about the 830s.[145] Even in those scarce instances when the *Epitaphium* was used as a source, such as by the humanist and philosopher Gottfried Wilhelm Leibniz at the beginning of the eighteenth century, the information it provided was treated with caution. In his monumental history of the imperial house of Brunswick (Braunschweig-Lüneberg), Leibniz often prefaced his employment of the *Epitaphium* with the proviso "if we can believe Paschasius . . ." or simply noted Paschasius's version of an event parenthetically, as an unverifiable alternative to the account given in his master narrative.[146] Paschasius's curious text raised few doubts for Leibniz and others who wrote from the loyalist perspective.[147]

Jean-Papire Masson and the Texts of Agobard of Lyon

While the alternative accounts of 833 given by the rebel bishops, Ebbo, and Paschasius Radbertus continued to be met with antipathy after their respective "discoveries" by Pithou, d'Achéry, and Mabillon in 1588, 1666, and 1677, a fourth alternative account of 833, this one published in 1605, quickly sparked a heated debate. Jean-Papire Masson (1544–1611), like Pithou another French humanist, entered a Lyon bookshop at the beginning of the seventeenth century and found what appeared to be an "ancient" Latin manuscript facing imminent mutilation at the hands of a bookbinder.[148] Immediately procuring the manuscript, Masson discovered that he had serendipitously rescued a ninth-century codex containing numerous unknown texts by the Carolingian archbishop of Lyon, Agobard (769–840).[149] Although Agobard was already known, both through the relatively abundant copies of his polemics with Amalarius (his replacement as bishop of Lyon between 834 and 838) on the correct form of the antiphonary and liturgy[150] and through references to him in the works of his contemporaries,[151] Masson's discovery exclusively supplied the majority of Agobard's extant texts.[152] Publishing an edition of the manuscript in

1605, Masson revealed to the wider public the full scope of Agobard's secular and ecclesiastical activities. It was the former aspect, however, that soon drew the ire of critics, for, as Masson's edition made manifest, the learned Agobard had participated in the rebellion of 833 and even acted as its mouthpiece. Since most scholars were impressed by the "cool common sense" that Agobard seemed to wield against the "barbarism and superstition" of his day, the fact that such a "rational" man could have deliberately taken such a "shameful, erroneous" course in 833 only made him appear all the more despicable.[153] Then again, as some would argue, such appearances could be deceiving.

Unlike the "scandalous" episcopal *Relatio*, Ebbo's "cunning" apology, or Paschasius's "dubious" defense of Wala, the new texts of Agobard soon found a passionate defender of their author's integrity. Among Agobard's works printed by Masson were several that justified the bold steps taken by the rebellion in 833, including a terse affidavit attesting to Agobard's participation in Louis' penance at Saint-Médard.[154] As the episcopal *Relatio* states, each participating bishop had drawn up his own signed document (*cartula*) endorsing the penance, and it was subsequently the sum of these records that was rendered "briefly and concisely" (*breviter strictimque*) as the episcopal narrative.[155] Of the many such affidavits, Agobard's is the only one to survive. As we shall examine this affidavit in detail in Chapter 4, it is sufficient to note here that, of all the texts in Masson's edition, this testament by Agobard was singled out and reprinted repeatedly in source collections by editors of the seventeenth and eighteenth centuries, usually being appended once again to the summary episcopal account it had originally served to validate. Doubtless this reassociation was made not to elucidate the two texts, but rather to condemn their authors all the more with the evidence of the texts' mutually incriminating "fraudulence." Just as the anonymous episcopal *Relatio* was vilified by the compilers of the source collections in which it was printed, so too was Agobard, the author of the sole affidavit that was joined and implicated with the *Relatio*, to suffer editorial scorn.[156]

Agobard's reputation grew worse once his new texts attracted the attention of monarchist scholars of the seventeenth century. Recalled self-righteously as an "abject stain" in the vast record of historical events rapidly being uncovered, edited, and printed in support of nationalistic concerns,[157] the "inexcusably shameful" events of 833 were also characterized by historians as an unpardonable example of lèse-majesté. And as attested by the *editio princeps* of Masson and then a second edition by Étienne Baluze in 1666, Bishop Agobard was one of the chief rebels, behavior seized upon by French monarchist writers such as Scipion Dupleix as illustrative of the "execrable" effrontery the church could display toward the royal majesty if allowed the slightest opportunity.[158] Even ecclesiastical authors, such as Jacques-Bénigne de Bossuet (who served as tutor to the Dauphin, son of Louis XIV), could not deny that the bishops involved in the divestiture of Louis (including Agobard) had perpetrated an exceptional perfidy that—as these same authors were prudent to assert in consideration of their own absolutist milieu—certainly had set no precedent for the future.[159]

By 1662, a Jesuit scholar from Lyon, Théophile Raynaud (1583–1663), had finally heard enough. Publishing a spirited apology on behalf of Agobard, who in the region of Lyon had long been venerated—uncanonically— as a saint, Raynaud sought to uphold the Carolingian bishop's illustrious (if parochial) reputation.[160] The first part of his defense focused on the charges made against Agobard's acerbic treatise denouncing the worship of images. This text only became widely known with the publication of Masson's edition, which quickly caused the volume to be included in the church's Index of Prohibited Books "until corrected."[161] The second part of Raynaud's apology dealt with Agobard's allegiance to the rebel party. Agobard was hardly guilty of conspiracy against the "truly most pious emperor" in 833, Raynaud protested, for by his deeds the bishop had simply tried to remain faithful to the original oaths sworn by Louis and his sons in 817 regarding the future dispensation of the Frankish kingdoms and their governance. In other words, Agobard's seemingly treasonous conduct had been inspired not by any malice on his part but by fear of the divine wrath that Louis' violation of those sacred oaths would soon call down upon everyone if not swiftly corrected. Evidently, Louis himself had come to understand Agobard's motives, observed Raynaud, for the clement emperor had pardoned the bishop and restored him to his see in Lyon in 838. Raynaud continued his defense by pointing out the antiquity of Agobard's veneration in Lyon; surely a saint could not have committed such crimes. Consequently, either Saint Agobard must be innocent, Raynaud reasoned, or else the wrongs must have been washed away with the tears of a penance undertaken sometime before Agobard's death in 840.[162] Agobard's new critics were not convinced, however, and would continue to debate his guilt with other Lyonnais partisans well into the nineteenth century.[163] As Alcuin, Charlemagne's court scholar, had once observed, "There is one thing which people of all ages and of all places have in common. They do not suffer their saints to be dishonored."[164] Raynaud could not have agreed more.

Conclusions

In the preceding medieval and early modern accounts, we have traced several lines of continuity regarding the remembrance of 833, running from Regino of Prüm's anecdotal rehearsal of the events to the drama's revival in the seventeenth century upon the discovery of Agobard's texts. First, medieval and early modern authors chiefly remembered Louis' abandonment and penance in accordance with the sympathetic accounts provided by Louis' defenders. This loyalist counternarrative of the ninth century, which originally sought to refute the rebels' justifications (or pretexts) for their deeds, took many forms, as we saw in Chapter 1, and would eventually assume its firmly embedded place as the master narrative of the events. Yet, this narrative victory by Louis' *fideles* was neither immediate nor absolute. In Odbert's *passio* text, Louis was a reckless monarch who blindly followed the will of his wife into incest, oath breaking, vengeance seeking, and the sanctioning of murder; in the *chansons de geste,* Louis retained the reputation of being Charlemagne's inept son, a king who had meant well but had ultimately been short-sighted and easily influenced by his wicked retinue. While the general contours of the loyalist narratives were largely accepted, it seems that the memory of Louis and the events of 833 was still in a state of flux at the turn of the second millennium.

Another line of continuity we have witnessed relates to the defense of the rebels. Wala and Agobard both garnered apologists—the former in the ninth century, the latter in the seventeenth—because each was regarded (by some) as a scholar and a saint. Ebbo, however, found few defenders beyond certain acolytes he had consecrated as priests in 840. And even they held to his increasingly maligned memory likely because the legitimacy of their office depended upon his repute.[165] In fact, the issue long informing Ebbo's near universal condemnation was less a matter of his "authorship" of the alleged plot against Louis than of class; Thegan saw Ebbo's cruel behavior as a natural consequence of his servile origins, an assumption it seems Dumont and Barthélemy tacitly acknowledged over a millennium later by excluding Ebbo from a defense of the rebels framed largely in terms of their *gentilesse.* Only over the last century, with its gradual change in perspective on the relationship between class and ability, has Ebbo gained apologists—among either those outraged by the elitism of the church or those appreciative of his significant patronage of art.[166]

A third general trend we have noted is the increasingly incidental attention given to the events of 833 over time. Although this neglect would end quite suddenly with the chance discovery of Agobard's texts at the beginning of the seventeenth century, the minor controversy they caused would ultimately have little effect upon either the inveterate reputation of Louis as a benign, pious king or the established narrative about the iniquity of the conspirators.

This third trend of the events' increasingly anecdotal usage is mirrored in the codicological preservation of the rebels' texts. The bishops' *Relatio*, Ebbo's apology, even Agobard's *pièces d'occasion*—all were at various times compiled with other works in a deliberate sequence in order to elicit intertextual dialogues. New meanings unimagined by the texts' authors were generated through juxtapositions designed to suit equally new contexts and concerns.[167] Within a decade of its composition, for instance, the bishops' narrative had been compiled twice. At first, it circulated with Thegan's biography of Louis to refute the rebels' charges, to demonstrate Ebbo's iniquity, to denounce the practice of elevating the lowborn, and to reveal the written guise that evils could assume; in this context, the bishops' *Relatio* testified against itself. By 842, this initial grouping was incorporated into a larger compilation of texts likely meant to disclose the great deeds of the Franks, specifically those of the Carolingian line, and of Louis the Pious and his "beloved son" Louis the German in particular. That Ebbo was briefly reinstated by Lothar in 840 as archbishop of Reims, and that in 841 Louis the German became the new overlord of Reichenau—the site where this second compilation was made—suggest that the timing and contents of these collections were anything but arbitrary. Ebbo's apology was similarly clustered with other texts. One late ninth-century compilation includes it conceivably to adduce yet another example of Hincmar's many injustices. Another compilation, this one from the eleventh century, uses Ebbo's apology as evidence to support the prerogatives of bishops and the insolence of those who defy them, and in so doing seems to incorporate an earlier compilation in which the apology appears. This previous compilation, perhaps assembled by Ebbo himself, is composed of texts that together attest to the propriety of Ebbo's actions against a fickle emperor. In the seventeenth century, Jacques Sirmond had before him a manuscript that contained the apology as part of another cluster of texts about Ebbo; perhaps compiled by Archbishop Hincmar, it paired the apology with Bernold's vision of Ebbo and his fellow bishops in purgatorial torment. Likely the author of the *Visio Bernoldi*, Hincmar sought to leave no doubt about his adversary's deceit and ultimate suffering. Finally, the collection of texts by Agobard of Lyon also suggests editorial intervention. Agobard's works were gathered before the end of the ninth century—the date of the manuscript that preserves them—into a single-author codex that appears to have been created in Lyon, where Masson stumbled upon it in 1604.[168] The high esteem that Agobard long enjoyed in Lyon likely accounts for the existence and survival of this anthology. But who arranged the manuscript's sequence, why it is so arranged, and how the manuscript ended up with a local bookbinder, who, as Masson described with hyperbole, "held in his hand a knife for the purpose of killing it," all remain a mystery.[169]

What is certain is that Masson himself, in his edition of the texts he found in the Agobard manuscript, manipulated their sequence. By clustering (but not reordering) certain texts under the provocative title "On the Comparison of Ecclesiastical and Political Government, and in Which Things the *Dignitas* of the Church Outshines the Majesty of Empires," Masson attempted to show the supra-Roman authority once wielded by Carolingian bishops and thereby demonstrate a ninth-century precedent for the present Gallican movement, of which he was a vocal supporter.[170] The "true Gauls," explained Masson, by gathering together in the 830s "for the purpose of confirming Gallican liberty," opposed the pro-papal rebellion with which Agobard had recklessly allied himself, as his texts made manifest.[171] Masson's edition was seen faulted for its sloppiness and abundance of errors, which, as Étienne Baluze generously noted in his own critical edition of the text published in 1666, were primarily the result of Masson's slavishness to his defective manuscript exemplar.[172] Confident in his own Latinity, Baluze explained that he would emend the manuscript's text in his new edition but that any changes he made would be duly justified in his notes. "For the things [treated by Agobard in his texts]," he concluded, "seem to be of great moment."[173]

The rise of the Enlightenment and its concomitant concerns in the eighteenth century would do little to change the deeply seated memories surveyed above. Rather, it was the specific rhetorical formulation of these traditional beliefs that historians of the Enlightenment would radically transform, resurrecting the vivid Carolingian accounts in accordance with their own predilections for "dramatic" history. In the next chapter, we shall see that the lasting effects of this particular Enlightenment fascination with the theater are what have informed nearly every subsequent interpretation of the events of 833—and thus Carolingian history—to this day. Whether cast in the constitutive terms of a tragedy or a farce, modern narratives of 833 consistently bear as much an Enlightenment as a Carolingian stamp.

CHAPTER 3

Histrionic History, Demanding Drama

*Events are like the foam of history, bubbles large or small that burst
at the surface and whose rupture triggers waves that travel varying
distances. This one has left very enduring traces that are not yet
completely erased today. It is those traces that bestow experience upon
it. Outside of them, the event is nothing. . . .*
        —*Georges Duby,* The Legend of Bouvines

*For a peg, unless it is very strong and attached to something stronger
than itself, quickly falls with everything hanging upon it.*
        —*Hincmar of Reims,* De ordine palatii

IN THE PRECEDING chapters, we have seen two constants associated with
the representation of 833 from the early Middle Ages through the early modern period: Louis' portrayal as a benign king and the intermittent fashioning
of the year's events to support current concerns. The "discovery" between the
late sixteenth and late seventeenth centuries of the justificatory accounts by
the rebellion did little to alter these two trends, for the narratives of Louis'
promoters had long since established their interpretive preeminence, providing a trusted story by which the rebels' texts would be summarily condemned.
Only the discovery of Agobard's texts shed new light on the events of Louis'
abandonment and divestiture, for his writings were soon used to undermine
the emperor's alleged piety. In response to the slandering of Agobard's reputation by monarchist historians—who quickly employed Agobard's texts to

reveal his "shameful" role as the rebellion's apologist—devout writers from Lyon denigrated Louis the Pious's character in kind, initiating a debate over the respective "culpability" of Agobard and Louis that would again make the deeds and developments of 833 central rather than anecdotal. Yet, while the debate drew the controversial events under scrutiny, it failed to move beyond the ad hominem level to have a significant impact upon the traditional historiographical representation of 833 as a year synonymous with treason and disgrace. Rather, it was the reorientation of historiography itself that would truly bring the events of that year to the fore.

A Spectacular Crisis

In the eighteenth century, under the banner of the Enlightenment, a great shift in attitude toward the events of 833 took place. Savants, in their crusade for progress, began to consider the reasons underlying the decline of the Carolingian empire.[1] To such timely concerns about the collective achievement of European—and more specifically, French—society, the year 833 was deemed especially crucial. It was prevalently viewed not only as the key to understanding the historical case of Carolingian decline but also, more important, as an isolated episode, a *crisis* in which to discern the general social factors that were considered detrimental to the progress of Western civilization.[2] No longer incidental, the events of 833 were resurrected and examined once again but now as a revealing part of a troubled whole, a useful synecdoche. Moreover, Enlightenment *philosophes* such as Montesquieu, Voltaire, and Mably, in keeping with the loyalist tradition, began to characterize the participants in the newly critical events of 833 as performers in an opprobrious drama. It was largely from within what they repeatedly called the "spectacle" of Louis' abandonment and penance that certain elements were discovered, abstracted, and generalized onto a broader plane of analysis, there to be used as evidence of the causes responsible for the decline of civilization—be it Carolingian or otherwise.[3]

No longer the result of God's disfavor with a morally bankrupt society, the decline of the Carolingians now began to be conceived in terrestrial—and, thus, in more empirical and predictable—terms of cause and effect.[4] For example, to Montesquieu (1689–1755), who sought to understand the relationship between law and changes in the French monarchy, 833 simultaneously demonstrated the behavior that characterized a poor lawgiver (prodigality, imprudence, precipitate action), the cost of being a poor lawgiver (deposition, "revolution"), and the nature and identity of those parties who would not hesitate to collect on this debt (an ever-avaricious nobility and clergy).[5] Voltaire (1694–1778) saw in the events of 833—an "extraordinary enterprise"— the culmination of a practice that had begun in Louis' time and thenceforth caused all the great disasters that had befallen Europe: the granting of worldly power to those who had renounced the world. He could not help but be "secretly pleased," Voltaire confessed, that Louis' petulant sons ultimately showed their ecclesiastical cronies Abbot Wala and Pope Gregory IV scarcely more gratitude than that they had bestowed upon their own deposed father.[6] For Mably (1709–1785), who wished to expose the causes of the continual "revolutions" in the government of the French, 833 revealed the pernicious factors that Charlemagne had been able to stave off but that had taken their revenge upon his weak son: corruption by wealth, the preference for the private over the public, and the confusion of license with liberty.[7] In short, the "spectacular" events of 833 were now being singled out repeatedly, yet in each case they revealed different causes of decline to each Enlightenment thinker.

A Dramatic Intrigue for a Dramatic Era

What was so special about the events of 833 that isolated them in the minds of these analysts? One suspects that the vivid, dramatic accounts provided by authors of the ninth century resonated with a historical consciousness of the eighteenth century, one that was particularly attuned to theater and drama. Theater of the Enlightenment, such as the Comédie-Française, the Opéra, and the Comédie-Italienne of Paris—known among contemporaries as "the three great spectacles"—is today acknowledged as having deeply influenced, and having been influenced by, French public and intellectual life.[8] As F. W. J. Hemmings has observed, "in the course of the eighteenth century the universality of French as the language of polite society owed as much, perhaps, to the lofty reputation of the Comédie-Française, attended devoutly by every educated visitor from abroad, as to the widely read works of the writers of the Enlightenment who, in a few cases, were also the authors of the tragedies and comedies it produced on its stage."[9] Hemmings' characterization of this widespread interest as a kind of "théatromanie" is no exaggeration, for, even after a relative slump in the first four decades of the eighteenth century, the Comédie-Française alone drew 160,000 spectators a year, a figure that would climb to over 180,000 by 1770.[10]

Given the pervasiveness of the dramatic spectacle within French society, historians of the time, who were a minute but avid fraction of the legion of theatergoers, were not immune to its influence. Indeed, such contemporary theatricality subtly informed the way they apprehended and narrated the past.[11] For example, the three Enlightenment thinkers surveyed above were all involved deeply with the theater, either as critics or playwrights. Not only was Montesquieu well versed in the dramatic genres, but he also tried his hand early in his career at writing plays.[12] For Voltaire, as Marvin Carlson reminds us, "the theatre maintained a central position in his interest and affection from the beginning to the end of his career. . . . He created a total of fifty-six [plays], and there was rarely a period in his long life when he was not actively working on a theatrical script."[13] With Mably, one can detect striking parallels between his description of the events of 833 and the critiques on theater and opera he had made some twenty-four years earlier. In his description of 833, Mably explains that "domestic disputes" (*tracasseries domestiques*) had led to civil war, and, as a result of such banal origins, it was "natural" (*naturel*) that the war should have "conclude[d] by a ridiculous intrigue" (*terminée par une intrigue ridicule*).[14] Within a series of letters on opera written to the Marquise de Pompadour and published in 1741, Mably criticized the conclusion of Philippe Quinault's tragédie-opéra *Proserpine* and attacked the social and political constraints of Greek tragedy. In both instances, he employed language remarkably similar to that which he would utilize later:

> and the play [*Proserpine*], which finally finishes as it started, is concluded (*est terminée*) by a denouement that is not at all natural (*naturel*).

> The necessity that they [the Greeks] felt of giving a role to the multitude, in order to flatter those people enamored of free government, compels them to place in the scene only those things relating to the public interest. A tragic deed [for those Ancients] is not at all, such as for us [Moderns], a small domestic intrigue (*intrigue domestique*) that carries on only among five or six people, who, if they are not kings or princes, then merely enact a comedy.[15]

When Mably later described the events of 833, these thoughts on drama would lend his summary its dramatic shape: Louis' domestic disputes had naturally concluded with a ridiculous intrigue. Yet, despite the involvement of princes and kings in the intrigue, Mably appears to have understood it in the ridiculous terms of a comedy; perhaps Louis and his heirs seemed to Mably such poor excuses for royalty that their deeds hardly qualified as tragedy. Then again, perhaps Mably was undertaking what the contemporary playwright and composer Pierre Beaumarchais had insisted was the noble task of the dramatist: "Vices and abuses are eternal and disguise themselves in a thousand ways," the author of the *Marriage of Figaro* explained. "The noble task of the dramatist is to tear away this mask and expose to public ridicule the evils it disguises."[16]

Given their interests, it is no coincidence that, when combing through medieval annals, chronicles, and narratives, such theatrically minded scholars—many of whom were also prolific playwrights—were repeatedly struck by, to use the Astronomer's words, that "almost unheard-of tragedy" of 833.[17] Montesquieu, for instance, described the events in terms of a "spectacle," and more specifically in a way that clearly evokes the classic—and in the eighteenth century, contemporary—Aristotelian conception of a tragedy: "the situation of affairs at that time," he explained, "is a spectacle really deserving of pity."[18] Voltaire also opted for theatrical language; Wala, he noted, had been the one who "started this memorable scene [of the rebellion and Louis' abandonment and divestiture]."[19] And when Louis the Pious was involved in a public act of state, Mably likewise intimated that such affairs were often a sham: in 822, the bishops were edified by the "spectacle" of Louis' prostration, Mably proclaimed, one that "appeared" (*semblait*) to speak to their great credit, though they in truth deserved none, since it was an act not of Christian humility but of shameful cowardice by their monarch. Later in his reign, Louis was so feeble that he could do nothing but be embarrassed by his slavish role in the spectacle that his public assemblies had become. Consequently, when Mably finally reached the events of 833 in his narrative, he could only see in them the dramaturgical conclusion of such affected, duplicitous behavior—they were the last act of a *comédie d'intrigue* deserving of contempt.[20]

In sum, the "ruse" of the rebels' conscientious actions and Louis' voluntary penance was understood by some Carolingian and many Enlightenment interpreters specifically in *theatrical* terms, such as a tragedy. An illuminating comparative case is found in the early fifth century, in perhaps the most famous dispute between Saints Jerome and Augustine: on whether Galatians

2:11–14 should be understood to suggest a prearranged, pious dissimulation on the parts of Saints Peter and Paul.[21] Jerome believed benevolent pretense to have been the case and likened the apostles' duplicity to the fictitious debates practiced by the orators he had observed as a youth in the Roman Forum. These oratorical disputants, Jerome recalled, would often avoid suspicion of their collusion and fool bystanders by their feigned severity with one another. While Augustine's counterargument (that such collusion and dissimulation by the apostles could never have happened, even if done with pious intentions) won acceptance as the orthodox view, Jerome's argument reveals how a discourse of his day could shape his interpretation of dissimulation—in his case, not in theatrical terms but in terms of Roman oratory and rhetorical disputation. In other words, for Jerome the *theatrum mundi* was not necessarily the preferred or primary metaphor among those available to him to articulate a false or frank performance.[22] There were other options, as Augustine himself would attest. In one of his replies to Jerome, for instance, he self-consciously described their correspondence, and the private dispute its widespread circulation consequently disclosed, as taking place "in the theater of this world," with all Christendom as their audience.[23] But in another letter, this time in reply to a Spanish monk's report about an orthodox Christian who went "undercover" to expose the duplicity of heretics feigning orthodoxy, Augustine both characterized and condemned such "pious" dissimulation by inverting Christ's well-known pastoral metaphor: Jesus, he explained, nowhere instructed his sheep to "come clad in wolves' clothing to the wolves" (cf. Matt. 7:15).[24]

Such modes of pretense culled from scripture or legal oratory held far less appeal in an age obsessed with the spectacle of the theater and stagecraft. To gain a sense of the extent to which the discourse of theater and dramaturgy pervaded Enlightenment thinking about power politics and their manifestation in the events of 833, one need only revisit, for example, the anecdote by Talleyrand about the dramatic confrontation between Napoleon and his bishops in 1809. In an effort to upstage them, Napoleon had summoned the bishops before an audience of his choosing and delivered a pompous harangue, making it clear (both by the harangue and the raving into which it devolved) that he would not be cast as the lead in a restaging of Louis the Pious's humiliating defeat.[25] Yet, while Napoleon's performance had its intended effect on his captive audience, other interpreters, free of censure, were quick to adduce his life's dramatic plot. Within five years, the philosopher Georg W. F. Hegel, recalling nothing so much as the Astronomer's tragic depiction of 833, would specifically describe the melodramatic Napoleon's eventual defeat in 1814 as a *tragikotaton* (τραγικώτατον), a most tragic event (here in the ancient Greek sense).[26] Hegel prided himself on the fact that his grand theory had accurately predicted this tragedy (or so he claimed).[27] Hegel's formidable powers of discernment may have allowed him to recognize in Napoleon a "world-historical" figure, one in the grip of forces beyond his control (the "Cunning of Reason") and ultimately—indeed, tragically—expendable,[28] but both men still gripped tightly (and tellingly) to a theatrical metaphor to describe this process, Napoleon from within it and Hegel from without.

Same Drama, Different Plots

While Louis' abandonment and divestiture were readily understood by both Carolingian and Enlightenment interpreters in terms of a dramatic intrigue, the specific meaning and import of the drama differed radically for each era. These differences must not be overlooked. For Carolingian loyalist authors, the machinations of the rebellion seemed especially appalling and "tragic" because they demonstrated not just an insidious insolence on the part of the rebels but a brazen, "almost unheard-of" Christian sacrilege[29]: the solemn ritual of public penance had been deviously exploited, Louis' supporters insisted, in order to impart upon the emperor the false semblance of a transgressor, wrongfully strip him of his regalia, make the fraudulent deed "irrevocably" binding, and at the same time perversely allow the cruel leaders of the rebellion to play the part of Louis' attentive "spiritual doctors."[30] Their appearance and deeds at Saint-Médard had merely been the histrionics of contrived *personae*—immediate roles masking ulterior motives.[31] Worse still, the very men who had hypocritically participated in the travesty were, in the eyes of Louis' *fideles*, formerly honored alongside the most upright figures of the realm. In short, feelings ran high among contemporaries when discussing the almost unheard-of intrigue against Louis, for the sooner and more completely the sanctimony of the rebels could be revealed, the sooner and more completely could their charges of negligence and iniquity against Louis be exposed as part of the ruse and consequently discredited.[32] While hypocrisy, conspiracy, rebellion, and other works of Satan were considered a perennial part of providential history, Carolingian authors saw the significance of the diabolical intrigue of 833 in terms that were also immediate and personal.[33]

Enlightenment *philosophes*, by contrast, valued the intrigue for its seemingly timeless and universal secular qualities—qualities seen to be the sine qua non of drama itself (which suggests one reason for drama's great popularity with intellectuals of the time). Within its twists and turns, the pernicious forces responsible for the decline of civilization had been momentarily unmasked, which made the "spectacle" of 833 an extremely useful didactic drama. Not only had the reasons for the collapse of Carolingian achievement been evinced in the intrigue, but impediments to the progress of civilization had been glimpsed as well. Of course, ninth-century Carolingian critics also discerned in the drama the larger reasons behind their present and future ills, but for them these were matters of morality and purity, equity and iniquity—considerations that formed the basis of an intimate, contractual relationship with God.[34] In 833, there was no doubt that divine punishment for a breach in this contract had been swift. Nearly a millennium later, however, when Enlightenment thinkers focused on the Carolingian drama, they removed God from the affairs. Indeed, in an ironic twist, the Astronomer's Christian tragedy was resurrected and restaged by fervent anticlericalists, thanks to the superficial congruence of a theatrical discourse. The drama's plot, however, now stripped of its religious mise-en-scène, was decidedly different.[35]

Performing the Past

To a greater or lesser degree, the broad, universalizing Enlightenment interpretation of Louis' abandonment and penance has guided the events' representation and function to the present day. As we have seen, in the eighteenth century the "shameful" events began to be depicted again in dramatic terms, at once signaling the beginning of the end for the Carolingians and making manifest the latent reasons for the empire's eventual perdition. Not coincidentally, also during this period, the events were for the first time literally dramatized for the stage, being cast as an intrigue of such epic proportions as to have transcended history for the loftier, more perennial plane of the human condition and its vain struggle against fate.

In 1726, the composer Georg Caspar Schürmann debuted his opera *Ludovicus Pius oder Ludewig der Fromme*, offering repeat performances in 1727 and 1734.[36] Given the survey of the enduring memory of 833 conducted in the previous pages, the plot of the opera's libretto, by Christian Ernst Simonetti, should come as no surprise. Doubtless it was even less surprising to Schürmann's contemporary Brunswick audience, who were accustomed to

the historical and mythical fare of his operas.[37] Even the stage directions for
the opening scene indicate what Simonetti considered the defining moment
of Louis' reign (recall that the opera was simply entitled, in Latin and German, "Louis the Pious") and suggest what was to come in the following acts:
"The scene is set before a great imperial hall with numerous princes, knights,
and soldiers," explains the note, "who have joined the rebel party of Lothar
and Pippin."[38] Simonetti's libretto is no lugubrious tragedy, however, for the
opera concludes happily with the scheming Lothar and Pippin apprehended,
humiliated, released from their chains, and married to princesses, thanks
both to the renowned clemency of their father and a good deal of timely "fortune" (*Glück*).[39] As one critic explained, the kind of pleasure such an opera
provided was timeless, rendering nothing less than "a cure of the souls, highly
necessary for the preservation of human life."[40]

Over the next two and a half centuries, the dramatic and incriminatory
interpretation of the rebels' actions would become all the more entrenched
through a vicious circle of influence between such "ahistorical" dramatiza-
tions of the events and the truth claims made by dramatic historical narratives. To be sure, the effects of nationalism upon historiography of the
nineteenth and early twentieth centuries—and especially that concerned
with the rise and decline of the Carolingians—were lasting and deep. As
Gene Marx, Paul Dutton, and Robert Morrissey have shown in detail, the
rise and fall of Napoleon's "neo-Carolingian" empire ("I am Charlemagne,
I, . . . yes, I am Charlemagne!"), and the impact it had upon the national historical consciousness of French and German intellectuals, gave birth to a host
of fresh analyses of the Carolingian past, studies that sought to uncover the
relationship between the developments of the ninth century and the medieval
origins of France and Germany.[41] Yet, in all these nationalistic accounts—no
matter their arguments for the decline of the Carolingians—the events of 833
retained their dramatic guise, continuing to betray the rebels' duplicity. If
the events' wider historical or social implications were not explicated to the
degree that they had been by Enlightenment scholars, Louis' abandonment
and divestiture were nevertheless accepted unequivocally as the result of a
shameful plot—a damning view sensationalized in, and itself redoubled by,
the events' concurrent representation in other genres and media.[42]

In 1815, Louis Antoine François de Marchangy, an admirer of Napoleon,
would include the events of 833 among the numerous programmatic, historical essays for painters, sculptors, dramatists, and poets in his eight-volume
series *La Gaule poétique*.[43] In the chapter he titled "Louis the Debonair: Beau-

ties of Historical Contrasts, Subject of a Tragedy," Marchangy began by explaining the advantages afforded by the method of comparison and contrast.
The use of this methodology—one especially favorable to poetry, he noted,
which, by definition, contrasts human destiny with our personal desires—is
profitable because it allows a pattern, or what Marchangy called a "universal
harmony," to be discerned. One such "beautiful contrast" could be found in
the historical succession of the "mighty" Charlemagne by the "weak" Louis.
Counter to most historical characterizations of Louis, protested Marchangy,
the son of Charlemagne was not only an interesting person but a poetic and
theatrical figure as well.[44] Indeed, the poet—who has the right to modify
historical facts as he sees fit, Marchangy insisted, and who is not beholden
to strict chronology—could derive from the historical events of Louis' life
(which Marchangy knew well) the excellent subject for a tragedy.[45] Such a
tragedy based on Louis' life would be comparable, assured the irrepressible
Marchangy, to *Oedipus at Colonus* by Sophocles or *The Death of Adam* by
Klopstock.[46] In all three plays the conflict revolves around a son rebelling
against his father: "Cain, Polynice, and Lothar," Marchangy explained,
"have equally tragic traits."[47] Lothar, in fact, was "an impious and headstrong
prince, a more fitting descendent of Clovis than of Charlemagne," and a "fu-
rious prince, whose life was nothing but a series of revolts and perjuries."[48]
Consequently, in order to cast a foil worthy of such a powerful antagonist,
Marchangy opposed Louis' traditional image as a feckless monarch by demonstrating that the emperor had possessed sufficiently majestic qualities to
qualify as a tragic hero.[49]

The similarities between the plays did not end with their lofty *dramatis
personae*. In all three tragedies, continued Marchangy, an omen of the father's
demise was featured: the death of Adam was intimated by an angel, the death
of Oedipus was foretold by an oracle, and the death of Louis was heralded by
the appearance of Halley's comet.[50] Inspired by the "universal harmonies" he
had discerned, Marchangy even hazarded a rough sketch of a script for the
"tragedy of Louis the Pious."[51] Beginning with the tragic death of Bernard of
Italy at the hands of his uncle, Louis the Pious, the drama reaches its climax
with the "pompous spectacle" of Louis' divestiture at Saint-Médard before his
sons and their sycophantic crony Archbishop Ebbo.[52] Marchangy admitted
that this scene, while humiliating for Louis in historical terms, was nevertheless utterly "theatrical." His sad script concluded with a prophetic deathbed
speech by Louis, warning of the devastation to be visited upon the realm by
the Northmen, and of the sacrilegious wars that would soon be fought among

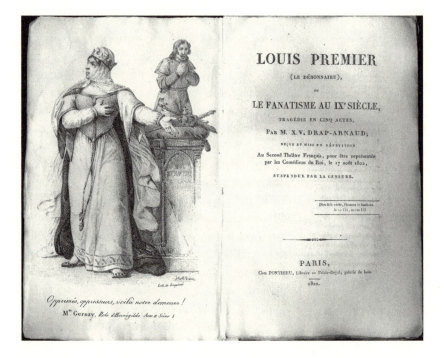

Figure 9. Frontispiece and title page of Marc-Xavier-Victor Drap-Arnaud, *Louis Premier (Le Débonnaire), ou Le fanatisme au IXe siècle, Tragédie en cinq actes* (Paris, 1822).

his children.[53] If, as Andrew Taylor has stated, Marchangy's goal was to revitalize France and restore its political harmony by evoking lost glories, then his vision of Louis the Pious—a vision he compared to that of Sophocles or Klopstock—revealed the stirring heights to which he had set his aim.[54]

In 1822, M. X. V. Drap-Arnaud took up what he called Marchangy's "elegant" lead and dramatized for the Parisian stage Louis' struggles with his sons (Figure 9).[55] To his chagrin, however, the play was quickly banned by state censors. Titled *Louis Premier, (Le Débonnaire), ou Le fanatisme au IXe siècle, Tragédie en cinq actes*, the drama's "appalling" tale about the French monarchy's being forced to bow before "fanaticism cloaked by the mantle of religion" was, in the wake of the French Revolution and its series of precarious, fragile governments, considered too potentially subversive to be performed.[56] Drap-Arnaud's plea that his "national tragedy" was "totally imaginary" fell upon deaf ears: "I write in the nineteenth century a tragedy," he implored "whose subject is drawn from the ninth. I present therefore a picture of local manners of that time, whose resemblance should not be supposed in our own, without [a sense of] the utmost absurdity."[57] Indeed, insisted Drap-Arnaud, he could not even read about the divestiture of Louis by depraved men such as Ebbo—an event that seemed to him the "heartrending convulsion" that signaled the empire's fall—"without horror."[58] Nevertheless, the censors evidently discerned in Drap-Arnaud's tragedy something tantamount to those "universal harmonies" so dear to Marchangy; it seemed Drap-Arnaud's play had been composed too well, laying bare man's propensity for fanaticism and the bold steps such zeal could inspire.[59] The deposition of a king at the hands of fanatics was judged a transhistorical phenomenon, a great crime against (French) humanity that was utterly execrable but that itself did not meet the standards of a tragedy. Objecting to this interpretation (which suggested that the real purpose of his play was to foment insurrection), Drap-Arnaud justified his work on the grounds of his civic vigilance and loyal service,[60] defining his tragedy as a dramatic attempt to expose the "poison" of fanaticism. By banning his play, he concluded, the censors only served the fanatics' interests: "All [fanatics] are equally odious; all are the poison of the people, the scourge of sovereigns," harangued Drap-Arnaud, "and when you condemn to perish without glory the works of writers who keep watch in order to destroy [such fanaticism], CENSORS, remember that they serve humanity!"[61]

French and German historians could not as easily censor the dramatic events of 833 from their own narratives of the national past, for Louis' troubles were too ingrained in the popular consciousness to omit without notice. (One need only recall the popularity as a tourist attraction of the alleged site of Louis' penitential imprisonment at Saint-Médard.[62]) But if historians could not ignore the events, they could still malign the intrigue even as they vividly represented it. The historical spectacle of 833 began to be explicitly defined as a specific kind of drama and its performers critiqued accordingly for their respective roles in the tragedy or comedy. For instance, within his monumental history of France published in 1833, Jules Michelet was, if more discerning than Marchangy and Drap-Arnaud, no less histrionic in his representation of the events of 833. Viewing the abandonment and final, moving speech of "the poor Louis" (in the "theater" of the Rotfeld) as a "disgraceful scene," Michelet characterized the emperor's divestiture at Soissons as having been "absurd," suggesting that the ostensibly solemn ritual had been nothing more than a rude pretense, manifest to all.[63] Yet, unlike Marchangy, Michelet believed these vivid scenes from the national past to evoke not Sophocles or

Klopstock but rather Shakespeare: when speaking of Louis and his struggles with his sons, Michelet was moved to remark, "poor old Lear, who found no Cordelia among his children!"[64]

Michelet's contemporary J.-M.-F. Frantin, in his biography of Louis the Pious, held little doubt that the Rotfeld had been a "horrible scene of ingratitude and deceit," a "lamentable spectacle" that was simply a prelude to the "scandalous scene" that would take place in the "theater" of Saint-Médard.[65] In 1849, after quoting Louis' farewell speech to his men, "sad" and "cruel" were the adjectives Auguste Himly chose to describe the emperor's fate on the Field of Lies; it was rather the "scene" at Saint-Médard—"a sacrilegious ceremony" that was a "degradation without equal in history"—that had been truly "disgraceful."[66] In 1862, X. Boyer, councilor of the imperial court of Colmar, published a highly defensive, nationalistic essay on the historical "stain" left by the "perfidy" that had taken place on the nearby Field of Lies: "Alsace," his essay begins, "served as a theater for one of the most woefully celebrated dramas of history."[67] Employing the theatrical, hierarchical language of scene and act to order the discrete parts of the historical drama both chronologically and by significance, Boyer revealed the kind of play he had been rehearsing: the abandonment of Louis on the Rotfeld was nothing less than "the first station of [a] veritable passion," he explained, the place where Louis' antagonists finally "raise[d] their masks."[68] Such a dolorous passion play deserves to be remembered, Boyer stressed, because, even if the shame perpetrated on the Rotfeld could somehow affix itself there, the glory of the Alsatian French in the past millennium was certainly sufficient to "erase every last trace of it."[69] Here we would do well to recall Augustin Ingold's lecture published only a year later (1863) on the Field of Lies as a haunted, accursed place still shrouded in legend during his own day.[70] Evidently, Boyer's glorious erasure had not yet occurred.

In 1862, the year of Boyer's emotional essay, scholars Leopold Warnkönig and Pierre Gerard described Lothar's "sacrilegious triumph" as an "injury inflicted upon the nation" and admitted that "the history of this sad drama [of 833] is well known,"[71] a familiarity no doubt widespread through both the literary medium of historiography and staged, theatrical performances. In the same year, the playwright Karl Robe debuted (in Berlin?) his drama *Ludwig der Fromme* (Louis the Pious)—the fourth eponymous dramatization of the emperor and his familial struggles since the early eighteenth century.[72] Demonstrating a detailed knowledge of the primary and secondary accounts of Louis' career, Robe crafted a nationalistic play recounting the fateful last years of Louis' reign and the subsequent birth of the German nation. All the usual characters appear, though in sometimes slightly reconfigured roles—Wala rather than Ebbo is the leader of the rebellion; Charles the Bald is a petulant, unforgiving son—and all deliver hyperbole-laden dialogue: Judith describes herself as a "lioness" in her struggle to secure Charles's inheritance; Louis the Pious cries out in frustration, "a duchy for Wala's head!"; and Lothar refers both to himself as "Caesar" and to a river running across the Rotfeld as "my Rubicon."[73] No fewer than one hundred thousand men are made to abandon Louis on the Rotfeld, while later, during a moment of introspection in his cell, Louis acknowledges his own surprising passivity toward what he self-consciously sees as a "sad play indeed" taking place around him.[74] Like Wala's ill-treatment as cast within Paschasius's remarkable jeremiad a millennium earlier, Louis' tribulations had now become a drama within a drama.

For our purposes, however, it is Robe's deliberate attempts at historical foreshadowing that are of most interest, for these seemingly slight intimations (relative to the overriding hyperbole of the play) lend certain events their gravity, suggesting episodes considered by Robe to have historical import. For instance, Wala shows to the emperor the rebellion's document detailing his wrongs and (suddenly gaining the hindsight of a nineteenth-century German playwright) calls it "a poison for kings that should still remain potent after a thousand years." Likewise, after he performs his penance and the bishops endorse their charters, Louis tells them that they have written "the cowardice of [his] heart in the Book of World History."[75]

Unlike these intimations, the significance of one element foreshadowed by Robe is made perfectly manifest throughout the play: the birth of the Western nations and the grand destiny that awaits Germany. Although little is known about Robe himself, this nationalistic aspect of his drama reveals much about his historical consciousness, for Germany is invoked time and again by the characters in the play as the particularly special "child" born from Charlemagne's great empire, an empire that had "died" in the process of giving birth to the triplets Germany, France, and Italy.[76] Consequently, the turmoil of the 830s, observes one of the rebels in hindsight, should be understood as having been the sharp—but entirely natural—"labor pains" (*Geburtswehen*) suffered by the "pregnant" realm. Germany alone, proclaims a triumphant Louis the German in the closing speech of Robe's play, would be the "cradle of valiant men," invigorating Europe's "tired pulse" with young, fresh blood.[77]

Nineteen years later, in 1881, the events of 833 would once again be cast as a play, or in this instance as a *Trauerspiel*. Written by the German pseudoromantic Ernst von Wildenbruch, the drama, simply titled *Die Karolinger* (The Carolingians), was ostensibly his poetic attempt to read between the lines of the historical record and explain what he saw there.[78] Armed with this artistic license, Wildenbruch sought to dramatize the historically unattested events in the early months of 833 that had served as prelude to the confrontation on the Rotfeld. Both the family and the realm of the Carolingians, suggests his play, were caught in a tragic struggle between "Nature" and "Law," the former represented by the scheming chamberlain Bernard of Septimania and his adulterous dupe Queen Judith, the latter by all four of the royal sons.[79] By the drama's end, Louis the Pious is poisoned by Bernard (who describes himself as a ruthless "child of Nature" and thus "beyond" blame[80]), and Bernard, being a creature of passion, is in turn killed by Louis' righteous sons. Law ultimately prevails but at a terrible cost: Charles and Lothar's fraternal relationship is irrevocably transformed into one based solely on law; they (and, thus, their subjects) recognize each other no longer in the "natural" sense of their love for one another or their blood kinship.[81] The world they knew—a united Carolingian Europe—was dead. For Wildenbruch, the events of 833 marked not just the defining moment of Louis the Pious's career, but—as the title of his play suggested—the point of no return for the entire Carolingian era.

Certainly the two plays of Robe and Wildenbruch exhibit similarities, but their perspectives on the Carolingians and the fate of Europe also evince the different concerns inspiring the two playwrights. Like Robe before him, Wildenbruch had his dramatic characters self-consciously imagine themselves as actors within a drama—in this case, the events of 833 were a "tragedy" taking place within the larger "farce of the world" (*Possenspiel der Welt*).[82] And also like Robe, Wildenbruch invoked the notion of the "Book of World History"; during a moment of reverie, the gloating Bernard admits that "in the Book of World History there is only one law, it is called Success (*Erfolg*)."[83] Yet, if this maxim is how Wildenbruch himself conceived of history, then the birth of Europe from Charlemagne's world-historical achievement had, in his view, been an event unworthy of note. For Wildenbruch's play presents the creation of the European nations as the "unnatural" result of a tragic failure on the part of Louis' sons. Unlike Robe's vision of the empire pregnant with the glorious future, Wildenbruch's nostalgic image of the Carolingian past contained only a bitter sense of loss.

Historiography of the late nineteenth and twentieth centuries would only continue to be influenced by such dramatic accounts. Engelbert Mühlbacher, one of the foremost scholars of Carolingian Europe, understood Louis' "confession" by Odilo as the equivalent of a chapter taken from a modern paperback thriller (*Schauderroman*), while the events at Saint-Médard were yet again a "tragedy" with "acts" and "leading actors."[84] Even Leopold von Ranke, no less than Michelet before him, would rehearse that "vile drama" of 833, with its "dark, dreary scene" at Soissons, once again.[85] Indeed, Ranke's dramatic representation of the events in his monumental and definitive "Book of World History" verified the theatrical remarks of Robe's and Wildenbruch's actors about the "world-historical" quality of 833, bearing out the playwrights' convictions.[86] That Ranke owned a copy of Robe's rare play suggests that this particular rehearsal on his part was more than mere coincidence.[87]

In the Shadow of the Enlightenment

By the beginning of the twentieth century, the dramatic representation of Louis' abandonment and divestiture had become deeply if unintentionally established as a historiographical norm. To be sure, other media such as theater and the historical novel continued to reinforce the dramatic formulation of 833.[88] The events of 833 had become an explanatory commonplace, functioning as a discrete unit by which to make sense of the chaos characterizing Louis the Pious's reign and the subsequent decline of the Carolingians. Yet, in addition to its defining traits as a dramatic moment and a historiographical benchmark for Carolingian history, the nineteenth-century representation of 833 also exhibits two other attributes. First, because it served as an event that could illustrate and provide answers about Louis' difficult reign (and simultaneously foreshadow reasons for the empire's fall), the drama of 833 was often dwelled on in historical narratives.[89] Within these extended pages, however, one senses that, during their spirited rehearsal and critique of the drama, historians were using it to enliven what was otherwise becoming a dull and depressing narrative about the Carolingians. Certainly this dreary quality was recognized by contemporaries as characteristic of medieval history in general; in 1865, Lewis Carroll even parodied what was to the English sensibility the tediousness so common to modern accounts of the medieval past. Attempting to dry Alice's drenched clothes in Wonderland, a mouse proceeds to recite, in a supercilious tone, a typical nineteenth-century narrative of medieval history (which Carroll excerpted from a book by a contemporary historian);

when asked to justify its unusual method of desiccation, the mouse explains matter-of-factly, "this is the driest thing I know."[90] Even the grave master of scientific history, Leopold von Ranke, recognized the importance of an adroit and felicitous delivery for describing how things "really were" in the past.[91] Within narratives of Carolingian history, the dramatic events of 833 were frequently found to be conducive to satisfying such rhetorical concerns and were elaborated accordingly.

Another feature long associated with the drama of Louis' abandonment and divestiture was moral rebuke, for historians consistently felt compelled to demonstrate their disapproval of the events while in the act of narrating them. Such condemnation allowed historians to convey their own scrupulousness to the reader, inspiring confidence in their common allegiance to the truth. In this respect, historians of the twentieth century have been only slightly more reserved in their moral judgments than their predecessors.[92] Nonetheless, they have been decidedly unanimous in their representation of 833 as an instructive drama—a power play that sets in bold relief those immanent forces that would tear the realm apart.

Less prudent historians have been unable to repress their moral outrage. In 1947, for example, Louis Halphen made what was probably the most influential statement of the century about 833. Describing Louis' troubles in his survey of Carolingian Europe, Halphen referred to the events as both an "odious comedy" and a "tragic affair." Not long after, Eleanor Shipley Duckett "saw the opening of tragedy" upon the Rotfeld, a drama whose conclusion Robert Folz would describe in similar terms: "the outcome of this tragedy was nothing more nor less than the overthrow of Louis the Pious, Judith and Charles," he explained. "The empress was shut up in an Italian monastery and her son at Prüm, whilst the unfortunate emperor was made to go through the show of a voluntary abdication in the sinister comedy staged at Saint-Médard de Soissons by Archbishop Ebbo of Rheims in October 833." For Gene Marx, however, the "hideous, unjust event" of 833 was clearly the "infamous cheap ruse of the dramatically-staged arrival" by Pope Gregory IV on the Rotfeld. Paul Zumthor thought Louis' divestiture a "sordid scene" out of a "comedy," while for Karlheinz Deschner this same utterly "shameful" deed was a "Christian tragedy"—one "worse than Canossa." While Philippe Depreux could hardly agree that 833 had served as a dress rehearsal for the infamous humiliation of Emperor Henry IV at Canossa in 1077, he was nevertheless certain that in the months between 830 and 833 the "masks" of the rebels at last had "fallen."[93] Such quotations can easily be multiplied.[94]

In a recent historiographical characterization of 833, the malevolence of Louis' antagonists has reached new heights. In 1976, Élisabeth Magnou-Nortier declared that the judgment and excommunication of Louis in 833 was a "genuine tragedy," an opinion she repeated in 1995 with the addition that the clerics who orchestrated the drama were the equivalent of "fanatics" (here one is reminded of Drap-Arnaud's 1822 play).[95] In 1999, Magnou-Nortier again called the events of 833 a "veritable tragedy"; this time, however, she revealed the model that informed her understanding of the entire affair. She declares with distaste that the "trial" within Saint-Médard was the first of the "Stalinesque type in the history of the West."[96] Lothar and his "party members" have now become associated with Josef Stalin's regime and its odious, apparently Carolingian techniques.[97] In a modern world increasingly populated with corrupt states and political prisoners, Machiavellian hypocrisy and travesties of justice, the "portentous" events of 833 are seemingly more relevant than ever. It appears we get the Carolingians we deserve.

Conclusions

Enlightenment historians and their successors have often been unable to resist thinking of Louis' abandonment and penance as a revealing melodrama, a spectacle with despicable antagonists playing essentialized, categorical roles.[98] Certainly the notion of theatrical duplicity has long been useful to historians thinking in terms of rise and decline or growth and decay, for, if the moment of crisis in their arcing narratives is viewed as a dramatic intrigue, then assigning blame for the onset of decline/decay becomes a matter of casting the drama's protagonists (whose motives are pure and candid) and antagonists (whose motives are corrupt and concealed).[99] Accordingly, since the rise of those grand narratives in the eighteenth century concerned with the exclusively temporal, terrestrial factors responsible for Carolingian decline/decay, Louis' eldest son, Lothar, bishops Agobard of Lyon and Ebbo of Reims, and several others have consistently been characterized as scheming villains.[100] Viewed in the hindsight of the empire's ruin, the rebels' justification that their bold measures were taken for the good of the realm appears to be a feeble pretext to mask their greed and lust for power, an apparent ruse made all the more contemptible by its disastrous consequences.[101] Put another way, Louis, Judith, and the leaders of the rebellion in 833 have together traditionally been seen as *dramatis personae* almost too good to be true—characters not just revealing but embodying those very factors held liable for the decline/decay of Carolingian civilization.[102] And depending on how one values Carolingian civilization, perhaps they are responsible for much more.[103]

The problem with such dramatic and ultimately damning interpretations is that they ignore the historicity of cognitive horizons, assuming rather that the referents that frame an event were employed by contemporaries *solely* for their strategic efficacy. Consequently, as Mayke de Jong has observed, scholars have been all too ready to see Louis' desertion and subsequent penance "as a sort of political theatre which barely masked episcopal arrogance and aristocratic craving for power."[104] Confronted by his sons' military might and their moral pretext of defending the realm's virtue, Louis lost most of his men on the Rotfeld not because of any qualms in their conscience about doing what was right but rather due to the baser motives of fickleness, avarice, and fear. According to this traditional narrative (based, as we have seen, on the works of Louis' defenders), the emperor was deposed by sanctimonious bishops who shrewdly masked their profane, immoral tactics with the supernatural explanation that God had rendered his judgment upon Louis' alleged iniquity and increasingly flagrant scandals. To make the deposition legitimate and binding, the rebels then extorted a "voluntary" public confession and penance from Louis with secret threats of violence to Judith and Charles and subsequently drew up documents attesting to the probity and solemn irrevocability of the feigned ritual. Francis Palgrave long ago provided the classic formulation of this "odious," ahistorical crime of passion:

> The charges [against Louis] . . . were futile, the arguments irrelevant,
> and the ceremonies and doctrines of the Church prostituted and
> perverted for the purpose of forwarding the parricidal projects
> entertained by Lothair and his brethren.—The pretended judgment
> was the worst of all social crimes, an act of force cloaked in the garb
> of justice, and therefore bringing justice into disrepute, and casting
> obloquy upon the very principles by which justice is sustained.[105]

Construed in this way, the events of 833 acquired their meaning through a calculated decision on the part of the bishops who understood the desertion of Louis by his troops specifically in terms of a judgment of God, and who pleaded, admonished, and ultimately coerced Louis to undergo penance in order to quell God's anger, saving both the realm and his own soul thereby—

not because they believed any of this but because of its immediate political expediency.

While such an interpretation imparts agency, it does so only at the expense of belief, for it implies that people either can ignore their inherited inventory of constituted patterns of meaning—that perpetual, unbidden bequest of the past to the present—or can selectively value those elements that are the most self-regarding.[106] In other words, this cynical interpretation of 833, first proffered by Louis' staunch defenders, presupposes that the rebels did not take religious belief seriously, that Louis performed penance only because he was coerced, and that the rebels manipulated the ritual to satisfy their immediate desire of removing Louis from the throne in order to claim it for themselves. This is why contemporary *fideles* of Louis deemed the actions especially sacrilegious and "unheard-of"; to the deeply Christian society of Louis' day, the rebels' "cunning argument," in the words of one author, appeared to have prostituted and perverted religious practice and belief, sacrificing them at the satanic altar of power politics.[107] This is also why Enlightenment authors condemned the rebels' actions as ruinous, for their beliefs were affronted as well. But unlike those of the Carolingian critics, their beliefs were not religious; one need only recall Voltaire's secret pleasure upon reading of the bitter rewards reaped by Wala and the pope for their participation in the rebellion. In Voltaire's view, their comeuppance was a welcome, but all too rare, exception to the rule since, as his study of history made manifest, most clerics customarily used religion to get away with murder.[108] Rather, *philosophes* such as Voltaire found the rebels' cunning argument offensive and pernicious because it had led to the decline of the Carolingian empire; that is, it acted in opposition to their cherished, secular belief in progress. From this perspective, religion had not been defiled in 833; on the contrary, it was considered a large part of the problem.

Despite these differences, both Carolingian and Enlightenment critics assumed a large degree of unbelief on the part of the rebellion; consequently, both groups understood Louis' abandonment and penance as the unfolding of a sacrilegious or pernicious plot. And as we have seen, both also frequently chose to represent this alleged dissimulation in theatrical terms. Over the last two centuries, still a third position has been staked out, one that views the rebels' almost unheard-of "estrangement" from the opposite end of the interpretive spectrum. From this perspective, their unbelief appears not as sacrilegious or pernicious—and, thus, damning—but as precociously modern and liberating, offering evidence that people in the past had managed to forsake their constitutive inheritance of meaning and transcend it.[109] Consequently, the rebels have been seen by some teleologically inclined historians—secure in their postabsolutist world of separated church and democratic state—not as traitors but as "revolutionaries" who made a "great ideological advance" by deliberately linking, for the purpose of legally removing a monarch, Louis' desertion with a judgment of God.[110] Hardly embedded in the grain of their particular historical milieu, with its own traditions and value systems governing right and wrong behavior, the rebels seemed to have transcended the norms of their time and "acted otherwise" because the norms themselves were in a state of flux, reminiscent of Émile Durkheim's anarchic, crisis period of "anomie."[111] As James Westfall Thompson once put it, although "the deposition of Louis the Pious . . . at Compiègne was irregular—as all political revolutions are," this irregularity is understandable in light of the larger historical context because, he reasoned, "the ninth century was a century of revolution. The old order of things was passing away and a new form of government, a new social structure, a new political philosophy was slowly coming into being."[112] While the body politic still vacillated between periods of homeostasis and crisis, each period of crisis now afforded the possibility of development along a teleological axis. The more things changed, the more they anticipated the present.

In short, by beginning with the premise of unbelief, all interpreters, past and present, no matter if they damn the rebels or praise them, refuse to take their claims seriously. Louis' performance of penance in 833 has always been understood as somehow false: at worst, that it was nothing more than the feigned display of willing contrition extorted from a captive under duress[113]; at best, that it was a sad and shameful instance of an early medieval case of the "Stockholm syndrome," a condition in which brainwashed hostages become sympathetic to and willingly comply with their captors. Moreover, the relatively common supernatural explanation offered repeatedly by Agobard, Paschasius, and others—that the sudden desertion of Louis on the Rotfeld had been a *iustum divinum iudicium*, a just divine judgment that testified to the emperor's iniquity and their own propriety[114]—has inspired few supporters, either then or now.[115] The Astronomer was sure that Louis' men had broken their oaths of fealty and "surged like a torrent" over to the sons' camp because they had been "partly distracted by bribes, partly seduced by promises, [and] partly frightened by threats,"[116] sordid motives that led the emperor's adherents to dub the site of the affair the Field of Lies.[117] Certainly this practice of subornation was conduct that Nithard later believed to be entirely "typical" (*mos solitus*) of Lothar.[118] Many modern scholars have agreed with and lionized Nithard (whose brusque reasoning has resonated with their own) for his apparently keen discernment of *Realpolitik*.[119] Because the rebels' explanation of divine intervention was (as far as we know) first introduced during Louis' public penance in October—three months after his desertion—supporters of the emperor, both medieval and modern, have disregarded it as a ploy by the cunning ecclesiastics who retroactively exploited the rhetoric of "God's just judgment" for their own interests.[120] Yet, what then should we make of Paschasius Radbertus's consistent explanation for the many other travails he described in his text—that such things had also happened surely "not by chance, but by the dispensation of divine judgment"?[121] The same reasoning can be observed of the rebels Agobard and Ebbo as well.[122] Even Louis the Pious himself, shortly after his ad hoc restoration ceremony in March 834, admitted to Abbot Hilduin of Saint-Denis that what had happened to him in 833 was "an event of mortal inconstancy (*humanae varietatis eventus*), which must always be acknowledged as a just judgment of God."[123] One begins to suspect that it is rather the modern historian who, in the recovery and dramatic retelling of the past, has either faithfully followed the loyalist tradition of its emplotted, cynical representation or transcended its cognitive world, retroactively projecting teleological, revolutionary insights into certain "precocious" minds of the past through the "benefit" of hindsight.[124] That few of the relatively numerous texts penned by the rebels to justify their actions have been examined in detail, let alone translated, only supports this suspicion.[125] Viewed in retrospect, the rebels' actions have always spoken louder than their words.

Rather than seek to determine whether the rebel bishops were self-interested hypocrites or reform-minded revolutionaries standing "outside" of history, a more fruitful endeavor is to examine their words and deeds within the discursive context of their time. Upon immersing ourselves in the depths of the ninth century and its many currents, it quickly becomes apparent that deep faith and power politics were not mutually exclusive but often conjoined,[126] and that characterizations of the bishops as either hypocritical or revolutionary are binaries stemming from a modern, Western, market-driven system of reasoning about motives and expediency. As Marshall Sahlins has pointed out, these poles rely on the logic of the "economic man," of people as "business-like social beings, bent on maximizing life's benefits and minimizing its costs."[127] Already by the late nineteenth century, Friedrich Nietzsche had rejected this utilitarian analytic whereby bourgeois life "turns culture into the hidden a priori of a calculus of pragmatic action"; with characteristic economy, he remarked sardonically, "Man does not strive after happiness. Only the Englishman does that."[128]

As Jean-Claude Schmitt, Patrick Geary, Darren Oldridge, and Carlo Ginzburg remind us, there are many other, seemingly strange kinds of social logic and systems of meaning in the past, which all require careful and attentive reconstruction.[129] Many are formal, explicit, and articulated by contemporaries with a great deal of precision, while still others are fragmentary and allusive, allowing us little recourse other than to circumstantial inference. Consequently, if we wish to understand rather than judge those involved in the events of 833, it is imperative that we first take seriously (though not credulously) their own interpretations, together with the social logic or "codes" by which these same interpretations were themselves informed.[130] We must make things strange.[131] As J. R. R. Tolkien implored an unsympathetic audience over seventy years ago, "In considering a period when literature was narrower in range and men possessed a less diversified stock of ideas and themes, one must seek to recapture and esteem the deep pondering and profound feeling that they gave to such as they possessed."[132] Certainly the worriers of the time left us a remarkably rich record with which to make such an attempt. Rather than look upon this material with disdain or self-congratulation, let us instead try to view it in the round, with a regard for the multipolar, the interactional, and the mediatory relationships always already at work within it.[133] To conclude—or rather, to begin again—let us now turn to these Carolingian worriers and their works with an eye not for judging but for understanding.[134]

PART II

Justifying

. . . You seem to start at the beginning . . .
—Jean-Paul Sartre, *Nausea*

CHAPTER 4

Documenting Duty's Demands

The shame of the Franks.
　　—Sole entry for the year 833 in numerous Carolingian annals

The shameful "Report of the bishops concerning the deposition of
Louis" . . .
　　—Henri Leclercq, Histoire des conciles

AS WE HAVE seen in Part I, thanks to the interpretive preeminence held by
the loyalist narratives about 833, the formal, explicit statements by the rebels
to justify and consign their deeds to posterity have long been neglected or
given short shrift by historians of Carolingian Europe.[1] In the many rue-
ful, tragic narratives of the realm's decline, for instance, only rarely has the
"shameful" account by the rebel bishops been awarded the pages—or the
respect—reserved for sources sympathetic to Louis,[2] such as Thegan's biography containing Louis' noble farewell speech to his men on the Rotfeld[3] or
the pious lament of the imprisoned emperor as supplied by Odilo.[4] Reluctant
to see the texts produced by the rebellion as containing anything other than
the moralistic rhetoric with which they cloaked their *Realpolitik* (for to take
this rhetoric at face value would risk embarrassment by, or complicity with,
the actions waged in its name), historians of Carolingian achievement and
failure have always condemned the episcopal accounts as little more than
sanctimonious propaganda.

For historians interested in a narrative of process, however, the accounts of the rebel bishops are a valuable resource. Indeed, they are as crucial for analyses of process and transformation as the accounts surveyed in Chapter 1 have been for analyses of Carolingian rise and decline, growth and decay. Deliberately written for posterity (a posterity of Christians the bishops believed forever their contemporaries in thought), the texts contain not only the justifications for the bishops' deeds but also the contemporary system of meaning upon which these same justifications relied, a system the bishops assumed would endure for all posterity.[5] Thus, what the episcopal accounts provide is nothing less than the crystallization of an idealized set of norms against which Louis was—and ultimately the bishops themselves would be— measured and found wanting.

In the following pages, we shall see that this normative system was itself, regardless of the bishops' belief in its perpetuity, by 833 only the latest expression of a dialectical process of social change and ideological transformation. So rapid was this process that the bishops themselves discerned its occurrence, although from their "privileged" perspective as the realm's moral watchmen they would perceive it at first with respect to the emperor's person and only then with respect to themselves. Indeed, the pernicious change that they believed had befallen both the emperor and the empire *in processu temporis*, over the course of time, was, ironically, an impression itself effected by—and thus serves as a key witness to—a subtle transformation in the bishops' *own* system of values. As J. M. Wallace-Hadrill once put it, "The actions of the bishops [in 833] matter less than their reasons, and their reasons are bound up with their feelings. Louis the Pious had shocked them in proportion as their feelings about the *vita apostolica* had become intensified."[6] Thus, to understand Louis' penance, one needs to know how and why this intensification of the bishops' feelings occurred.

However, before we examine this crucial correlation between the bishops' opinion of Louis and their esteem for the apostolic life (a correlation that will be taken up in Part III), we need to establish the normative grounds upon which the bishops legitimized their actions. Consequently, the structure of the value system as it stands within the episcopal accounts of 833 demands closer inquiry. What reasons did the rebels give for their actions, and on what basis and to what degree did they feel that these reasons were legitimate and compelling? That new manuscripts of the bishops' justificatory *Relatio* have recently come to light, manuscripts that predate the only other extant witness by nearly a century, makes an analysis of these long neglected texts all the more timely.[7]

This chapter investigates the official summary account of Louis' penance prepared by the rebel bishops, paying attention both to its intratextual dynamics and its appeals to extratextual sources of authority (see the appendix for an English translation of the *Relatio*). Several contemporary supporting texts penned by Bishop Agobard of Lyon, as well as a letter of rebuke to Louis' bishops from Pope Gregory IV will also be examined (Table 2).[8] As subsequent chapters shall demonstrate, this textual scrutiny is not so much an exercise as a necessity, for the most recent studies of Louis' penance formulate their understanding of what the events meant to Carolingian contemporaries primarily on the basis of these texts but without engaging them seriously.[9] Such cursory treatment has led these studies to overlook a fundamental component of the arguments proffered by the bishops—the duties and demands exacted by iniquity—which has in turn led to a narrow understanding of why Louis' "strange" penance ever occurred.

Fortuitous Survivors or Necessary Evils?

If the rebels drew up their texts to confirm Louis' egregious wrongs, to solemnize his willing abdication, and to commemorate his irrevocable conversion from warrior to penitent, then why—given that Louis was quickly restored and the rebellion soon crushed—were these now-opprobrious testaments preserved? Surely one would expect the loyalists to have destroyed extant copies of such "erroneous" records, whether by the traditional procedure for rendering legal documents inert—namely, by having them pierced through while gripped in the outstretched hands of their owner[10]—or by the equally formal ceremony of putting the documents to the torch.[11] Just as Agobard of Lyon believed that sycophants had led Louis astray by themselves erring and sending others into error (2 Tim. 3:13), his contemporaries held this same scriptural belief about the corruptive influence of false documents.[12]

What the preservation and duplication of the rebels' texts likely demonstrate is that they were considered by their successive owners to possess a constructive utility that outweighed their potential harm. As we have seen in Chapter 2, such consideration was given to the bishops' *Relatio*, which was preserved by Thegan or Walafrid Strabo and then copied by Reginbert of Reichenau as a didactic device. Framed first by Thegan's biography and again within Reginbert's series of historical texts, the "perverse" narrative demonstrated the terrible consequences of elevating slaves to noble offices (with an

TABLE 2. TEXTS JUSTIFYING THE REBELLIONS IN 830 AND 833 (**BOLDFACE**)

Texts	Key Events
	June 829, Reform council of Paris
	August 829, Louis the Pious redivides the empire
Agobard of Lyon, **_De divisione imperii_**	
	April 830, First rebellion of Lothar, Pippin, and Louis the German
	February 831, Louis the Pious redivides the empire
	September 832, Louis the Pious redivides the empire
Agobard of Lyon, **_De privilegio apostolicae sedis_** **Pope Gregory IV,** **_Epistola_** **Agobard of Lyon,** **_Liber apologeticus_** I	
	June 833, Louis the Pious is abandoned on the Rotfeld
Agobard of Lyon, **_Liber apologeticus_** II	
	October 833, Louis the Pious undertakes penance
Agobard of Lyon, **_Cartula_** **_Relatio episcoporum_**	
	March 834, Louis the Pious is restored at Saint-Denis
	February 835, Louis the Pious is re-crowned at Metz
Annales Bertiniani Thegan, _Gesta Hludowici imperatoris_	
	June 840, Louis the Pious dies
Astronomer, _Vita Hludowici imperatoris_ Nithard, _Historiae_	June 841, Battle of Fontenoy
	August 843, Treaty of Verdun
Paschasius Radbertus, _Epitaphium Arsenii_	
	Beginning of the tenth century
Odilo of Soissons, _Translatio Sancti Sebastiani_	

emphasis on Ebbo), testified to the general guilt of the rebels for their decep-
tion (again, emphasizing Ebbo), revealed the written guise that such a decep-
tion could assume (with an emphasis on forestalling any future attempts,
perhaps by Ebbo), and documented the history of Louis' trials and triumphs
in the unfolding of providence (with an emphasis, perhaps, on Louis the German's filial devotion). However, it is possible that the rebels' texts were also
preserved by grudging members of the rebellion themselves, some of whom
were granted clemency by Louis after his restoration.[13] This may explain the
survival of Agobard's texts written on behalf of the rebellion. Louis allowed
Agobard to return, after four years of exile in Italy, to his diocese of Lyon in
838, where he was later venerated uncanonically as a saint.[14] And, indeed, it
was in Lyon that the only known witness of Agobard's polemical texts regarding 833 would be discovered.[15] This favorable memory of Agobard, together
with a good deal of luck, may have kept his texts in a kind of revered isolation: the ninth-century Lyon manuscript survived, without any indication
of its having ever been copied. If the Tertullian-inspired thunder of "Saint"
Agobard's prose was long held in esteem, it may, ironically, have been this
very esteem that held his thunder in check.[16]

The survival of Pope Gregory IV's acrimonious epistle to Louis' loyal
bishops makes the circumstances in Lyon following the events of 833 even
more intriguing, for the missive is extant uniquely in the Lyon Agobard manuscript.[17] As Agobard's modern editor, Lieven van Acker, has pointed out,
the letter appears among a cluster of texts by Agobard regarding 833. This
grouping, suggests Van Acker, may reflect the existence of a dossier of texts
about the events that the Carolingian copyist of the manuscript used as his
exemplar—a dossier that at the very least consisted of five works by Agobard
(*De divisione imperii*; *De privilegio apostolicae sedis*; *Liber apologeticus* I and II;
and *Cartula de Ludovici imperatoris poenitentia*) and the epistle of Gregory.[18]
If by the mid-ninth century such a dossier existed in Lyon, its presence there
was likely thanks to Agobard himself. He may have assembled the dossier
after the controversial events to codify their righteousness and to document
his participation in them. If this hypothesis is correct, this would be yet another ninth-century compilation of texts about 833 to add to the list of those
already tentatively associated with Thegan, Walafrid, Reginbert, Ebbo, and
Hincmar in Chapter 2.

Prolegomena

Before turning to the bishops' narrative of Louis' penance, it should be useful to provide a brief summary of several other texts by the rebels that will be called upon occasionally for corroboration and clarification. These documents are found solely within the Lyon Agobard manuscript and collectively comprise the small dossier postulated by Van Acker. Their titles are modern editorial additions.[19] The first text, "On the Division of the Empire" (*De divisione imperii*), was written by Agobard likely shortly prior to the first uprising against Louis in 830.[20] In it, Agobard begs the emperor, in a cautious and humble tone, to reexamine his recent actions, specifically his repudiation of the lawful ordination made in 817 that, by the will of God and with the sanction of the pope and the people, had established Lothar as his heir to the imperial title. Agobard fears that Louis' imprudence will call down God's wrath; indeed, the emperor should be aware, he explains, that there is already sadness and even slanderous talk among his men because of the contradictory oaths they had been compelled to swear. As a loyal servant, Agobard feels it is his duty to forewarn Louis of the imminent dangers both to the realm and to the salvation of his very soul.

The next text is again by Agobard, entitled "On the Privilege of the Apostolic Seat" (*De privilegio apostolicae sedis*).[21] Written in April of 833, it is a response to a request from Louis the Pious that, as part of mustering the realm's forces, Agobard attend a general assembly called to defy and refute accusations being made against the emperor by his sons and the pope. Humbly declining this summons, Agobard suggests that Louis should rather read the passages from the church fathers appended to his reply and reconsider how much reverence an emperor traditionally owes to the pope. If the pope were traveling to the realm with the objective of fomenting dissension, concedes Agobard, certainly he deserves to be resisted with the force of arms. But since the pope was coming to restore peace and achieve reconciliation—to return the realm to the state Louis had established in 817 in accordance with God's will, the people's consent, and the pope's confirmation—he should be obeyed. It was for Louis' own good that he comply with this request, Agobard continues, for he has already endangered his soul through his ill-advised alteration of his sacred ordination. Agobard was willing to suffer the accusation of effrontery, he admitted, if he could help the emperor recover his esteemed reputation and save his soul.

Shortly after this letter by Agobard (probably in early June 833), Pope Gregory IV sent an indignant missive to those bishops who had heeded Louis' call.[22] From its contents, one can infer that it is the third (and only extant) letter in a series of epistolary exchanges between Louis' loyal bishops and Gregory. In the initial letter, Gregory seems to have called all those bishops standing with Louis to come before him upon his arrival in Francia and show him the obedience and respect that was his due as their spiritual father.[23] The bishops replied that they normally would have been overjoyed at the pope's presence, but in this instance were only saddened. They claimed (reports Gregory in his extant reply) that the pope had excommunication in mind, and they warned him not to dishonor his office by attempting such an act. They then reminded him of the oath of fealty he had sworn to the emperor and explained that the dispensation of the empire that Louis made in 817 needed revision to suit "present circumstances" (*rerum oportunitas*). They assured the pope that he would be received reverently if he were to come to Louis, who would tell him the truth about the recent events. Finally, they leveled a threat at Gregory, stating that, if he did not conform to their demands, they would place him under a ban, denying him any power or respect within their dioceses. They warned, explains Gregory in astonishment, that any ecclesiastics who allied themselves with him should know that they faced irrevocable (but unspecified) consequences.[24]

To these pronouncements, Gregory replied with his extant, belligerent letter. Outraged by the bishops' insolence, Gregory points out that papal authority is superior to and always preempts imperial commands. He asks them why they had neglected their duty as watchmen to remind Louis, using the authority of church fathers such as Gregory of Nanzianzus or Augustine, that, as a member of Christ's flock, he should show due humility to his shepherd, the pope.[25] Gregory also accuses them of many fallacies and contradictions. For instance, he admits that, as they say, he had sworn allegiance to the emperor; but, contrary to their claims, this was the very reason for his journey—to abide by this solemn oath. He had come to warn Louis in all good faith that his actions against the unity and peace of the church were placing his soul in peril. Thus, it was bitterly ironic that the bishops should accuse Gregory of infidelity and perjury since they, by ignoring their oaths and not warning Louis of his misdeeds, were themselves perjurers. Doubtless they were acting in accordance with their warped consciences, he reasons, consciences perverted by cupidity. As for their claim that the new division of the empire was necessitated by changed circumstances, Gregory shows nothing but contempt, remarking that it is doubly false: on the one hand, because the new division had clearly afflicted many evils on the realm; on the other hand, because no one had received indication that God's will had changed with respect to the first division and its ordination in 817.[26] To their threat of banning him, Gregory invokes an elaborate corporeal metaphor of Christ, the church, and the faithful to prove that members of the church cannot willingly separate themselves from its body and that there is a natural hierarchy descending from Christ's head to his beard (the apostles) to the hood of his garment to the garment itself (the various orders within the church). He then pronounces the bishops' threats empty and absurd, for the entire history of the church has never known anything of their like. As clever as they believed themselves to be, they did not realize that their threats only served to incriminate them. They had forgotten, concludes Gregory with a crass metaphor, that the more a cesspool is stirred, the greater the stench that is released.[27]

At about the same time that Gregory wrote to Louis' loyal bishops, Agobard shed his tone of humility to write what might be called an indignant manifesto to the world (*Liber apologeticus* I).[28] He begins his text with a striking proclamation:

> Hear this all peoples! Let the earth and her fullness hear, from the rising of the sun to its setting, from the north and from the sea; let all men learn and reflect at the same time on the fact that the sons of the lord and emperor Louis have been and are justly outraged, and that they properly mean and plan to cleanse their father's palace of its foul crimes and wicked factions, and to cleanse the kingdom of its most bitter and turbulent disturbances! Their great desire is that brotherly faith and fraternal sincerity, worthy of God and welcomed by all loyal people, may persist among them and endure unbroken![29]

Echoing Psalm 48:2–3, Agobard makes clear that the sons of Louis the Pious, righteous in their anger, are preparing to provide a remedy for the kingdom. To justify their indignation, he then offers a brief history of the realm under Louis, detailing how the emperor was made a cuckold by his shameless wife, Judith. This scandal had brought such disgrace upon the empire that the sons rose as one, chased the offenders from the palace, seized Judith, confined her to a cloister, and restored to their father both his throne and a fraction of his former dignity. Unfortunately, these good deeds were annulled, explains

Agobard, due to the excessive clemency of the sons.[30] For soon thereafter, Louis had been allowed to recall Judith to the palace, where she began again to work her evil, blinding Louis to the truth and setting him against his devoted sons. Under her sway, Louis compelled his people to swear multiple and contradictory oaths, which compounded to bring the realm to the brink of civil war. And all this was occuring, grieves Agobard, when the armies of the realm should rather be fighting the barbarian nations at its borders and extending the Christian faith.

But there was still more. Agobard reveals that he has learned of men at the emperor's side who are plotting his murder in order to divide the realm among themselves. He is sure that, unless God intervenes, the empire will be handed over to the barbarians, carved up among tyrants, or delivered to the Antichrist. "This is happening," he explains, "since the emperor, who ought to be undertaking just wars against barbarian kings, prepares to wage unjust wars against his sons, who love him."[31] Adding insult to injury, Judith remains at the palace and behaves childishly, he observes, bringing disrepute upon herself, staining the honor of both the palace and its priests, and diminishing the dignity of the realm as a whole. Agobard closes with an extended plea that everyone who loves God, the king, the kingdom, and peace should bend his every effort toward healing the realm of its wound without bloodshed. The only alternative is perdition.

Within a few months, sometime between the events on the Rotfeld (the end of June) and the assembly at Compiègne (the beginning of October), with Louis now sequestered in a cell, Agobard issued a follow-up to his bold manifesto. In this text (*Liber apologeticus* II) he alludes to his comments from 830, recalling the fact that falsehood is often expressed not only in words but also in deeds.[32] The emperor is an example of this truism, he continues, as Louis did not desist from sowing the seeds of scandal by his actions and, thus, overturned the peace and unity of the realm. This scandalous behavior would only have continued had God not intervened (on the Rotfeld) and miraculously stilled the chaos without conflict or the spilling of blood. This fact, explains Agobard, should set all to earnest prayer in praise of the Lord— that he had chosen to take mercy on his people. At this point, Agobard interrupts his narrative to explain the origin of the recent disorder, a cause "that should not be kept secret." He then relates the ignominious events of Louis' reign up to the revolt of 830 in much the same manner as he had in the first part of his manifesto. There are, however, some interesting additions and qualifications within this later version. Louis' first queen, Ermengard, had been a good wife, he recalls, one agreeable to the emperor in her faith and manners. When she died in 818, it was necessary that Louis marry again, remarks Agobard, in order that the emperor have a consort for the direction and smooth governance of both the palace and the realm. Yet "by a secret judgment of God" (*occultum Dei iudicium*), a phrase Agobard uses whenever something happens for no discernable reason, Louis chose Judith for his new wife, a woman who at first was quiescent but quickly became the cause of all the realm's troubles.[33] Responding to this plague set upon their father's house, the honorable sons eventually united and drove Judith and her minions into exile. Here, Agobard notes that a period of quasi rule began in the realm, for the sons rejoiced "as if" (*quasi*) their father were now free from the pit of his ruination (a qualification that suggests that in truth he was not free from it at all). Agobard then adds that after the sons had completed this deed—one "blameless and most deserving of everyone's praise"—they returned to their respective kingdoms. Yet, thanks to the devil, Judith was soon restored to the throne "as if" she were the emperor's legitimate wife (implying that she was not). This time no mention is made of the sons' excessive clemency being the cause of her return. The sons soon had no choice, explains Agobard, but to strike at the source of the crimes that were again multiplying throughout the realm. What should a good son have done in this situation, Agobard asks rhetorically? Feign ignorance? Remain silent? Do nothing?[34] No, rather they acted to "extirpate" Judith, that "restored root of all the evils," before their father became another Ahab or Samson, a righteous man made abominable by a wicked wife. Accounting for his own seemingly treasonous behavior, Agobard explains that those watchmen who boldly attempted to warn Louis of his own wickedness should be likened to the prophet Elijah or the priest Jehoiada, who rebuked offenders and compelled them to do penance, purging Jerusalem of its vice. As he puts it plainly, "we say these things so that we may show that good and bad men among the ancients correspond appositely with good and bad men among the present populace." Louis, the former emperor, should consider what had happened to him and the reasons for the events, continues Agobard, for he presently risks losing his right to the eternal kingdom, just as he has lost his right to the terrestrial one. He should heed God's judgment, he explains, "since nothing on this earth happens without a reason." He should follow the example of Job, who did not consent to his wicked wife but confuted her. He should emulate the piety of King Nebuchadnezzar and his deference to God. In other words, continues Agobard, these scriptural examples should be understood as a demonstration that Louis, too, had succumbed to an evil woman. Fortunately all is not lost; like those ancient kings, Louis still has a chance to secure his salvation, but only if he undertakes a sincere penance. Indeed, he ought to render the greatest thanks and praise to God, since the Lord determined that Louis would be succeeded not by an enemy or a stranger but by his own loving son, just as he had always desired. Everyone should now heed the words of the prophet Habakkuk, concludes Agobard, and keep silent in their dread and awe of God's sublime work in the realm.

The final text in the collection is an affidavit by Agobard, testifying to his presence at the council at Compiègne and Louis the Pious's subsequent penance at Saint-Médard in October 833.[35] Agobard notes that Lothar, as emperor and a lover of Christ, presided over the assembly of ecclesiastics and nobles at Compiègne. Dire necessity, he says, had compelled them all to meet and discuss the present troubles and determine what might be done to correct them. Addressing the first topic, Agobard reports that Louis' negligence was found to be the cause of the realm's problems. The second topic was addressed in two respects, in order of their importance: those things to be done for the good of the realm and those things to be done for the redemption of Louis' soul. It was clear that the solution to both problems lay in Louis' performing penance. But first, explains Agobard, the former emperor needed to be made aware of his spiritual illness. To this end, messengers were sent to Louis' cell to exhort him, bringing him a little book that detailed his crimes so that he might recognize his iniquity and seek penance. A short time later, Louis acceded to their recommendations. Prostrating himself before the bishops upon their return to his cell, he begged their assistance and indulgence. Soon thereafter, recalls Agobard, Louis performed a ritual penance, appearing before a large assembly in the abbey church of Saint-Médard and confessing numerous times to his sins. Remorseful in his mind and refreshed by his tears, he removed his sword-belt and royal garb and exchanged them for the rough habit of a penitent. "Rejoicing and feeling assured," recalls Agobard, Louis then asked the bishops to lead him, a stray sheep, back to the flock of the faithful. Agobard concludes the affidavit with his signature, confirming that he both took part in the proceedings it documented and agreed with them.

These are the five texts by the rebellion that have survived solely within the Lyon Agobard manuscript.[36] The final text by the rebels that sought to establish the definitive narrative about Louis' reign and its many wrongs is the summary account of the penance drawn up by the bishops, a *Relatio* that, as we have seen, was preserved and later reframed by Thegan or Walafrid

Strabo to support their loyalist counternarrative. As it aims to give the final word about the events of 833 and their meaning and appears to have attracted the attention of Louis' defenders (Agobard's apologies are unattested by his contemporaries), it is to this text that we should now turn.

The Bishops' *Relatio*: Form and Content

The text of the *Relatio* begins with a declaration by the bishops on the duties and responsibilities—collectively understood as their *ministerium*—that are constitutive of the episcopal office itself.[37] Foremost among these duties is the preservation of the fundamental precepts that lend the church its lasting strength, a responsibility that the bishops immediately note "is proper to know." This declaration implies rather forcefully that there are some who either do not or might not "properly know" or understand the charge of the episcopal office, a misunderstanding the *Relatio* now aims to correct.[38] Indeed, continue the bishops, this solemn charge was decreed by no less an authority than Christ himself, who bestowed upon them the power necessary to expedite their spiritual wardship. By quoting from Matthew's gospel (18:18–19), they then simultaneously define the nature of this power and demonstrate its incontrovertibility by locating it within scripture: as the vicars of Christ and the key bearers of the kingdom of heaven, the transcendental ability of binding and loosing remains theirs and theirs alone.[39]

Having established the general nature of their duty, the sublime authority from which it derives, and the heavenly charisma with which they are invested, the bishops then further clarify their ministry through an explanation, laden with pastoral metaphors, of what might act to threaten it— episcopal neglect. On the one hand, through the negligence of the bishops, the "sheep of Christ" might be denied the "food of life"; on the other hand, sheep straying in error might not be zealously pursued by the bishops and led back to the fold. The bishops quote the injunction of Saint Paul in his second epistle to Timothy to explain how the latter form of episcopal negligence is countered: errant sheep should be shepherded back through "reproving and entreating" (*arguendo* [et] *obsecrando*) (2 Tim. 4:2).[40]

The Pauline charge that the bishops here assign themselves serves two functions. First, it points to the specific bases on which the bishops ground their responsibility and authority. Second, it acts as a proleptic framing device, lending a familiar shape and set of expectations to their narrative about the "errant" Emperor Louis. In fact, these specific means by which to retrieve errant members of the flock, if Pauline in form, are actually Benedictine in content. Saint Benedict, in his Rule, insisted upon the observance of Paul's dictum by the head of the monastic community and provided details on the traits of those persons who were deserving of each Pauline imperative: the undisciplined and unruly are those in need of severe reproof (*durius arguere*), explained Benedict, while the obedient, mild, and patient are those specifically in need of entreaty (*obsecrare*), he continued, "so that they may become even better."[41] Doubtless, the bishops involved in the proceedings of 833 were well aware of Benedict's interpretation of Paul's command.[42] In 817, a large number of abbots and monks had assembled with the emperor at Aachen and decreed as inviolate a number of resolutions on monastic behavior; it was sometime between the date of this assembly and 847 that a summary of Benedict's thoughts on discipline—including his quotation of and commentary upon Paul's injunction to Timothy—was singularly added to numerous contemporary copies of the Aachen decree.[43] Moreover, in the years following 817, several contemporary Carolingian ecclesiastics, such as Smaragdus of Saint-Mihiel, Benedict of Aniane, Hildemar of Corbie/Civate, and a certain priest known only as Grimlaicus, would all write concordances of or commentaries on Benedict's Rule.[44] When taken together with the observation that—as we shall see momentarily—even the particular pastoral language used in the episcopal account of 833 is derivative of the language found in the very passage from Benedict's Rule that contains Paul's charge, such Carolingian interest in the Rule strongly suggests that the understanding of Paul's injunction in the episcopal account is specifically Benedictine.

This Benedictine qualification is significant because the quotation of Paul by the bishops is actually a truncation: in fact, Paul's ministerial command to Timothy (2 Tim. 4:2) is not bipartite but tripartite in nature: "reprove, entreat, rebuke" (*argue, obsecra, increpa*). That the bishops omitted the last of these three well-known imperatives from their declaration is no oversight[45] but rather an intentional and conspicuous lacuna, a kind of momentary suspension that establishes not so much the Pauline as the Benedictine grounds upon which the narrative of Louis' errors will be developed and brought to their necessary conclusion. For as Benedict had dictated in his Rule, those persons specifically deserving of rebuke are the *negligentes*, the negligent.[46] And as we shall see, it is the development of Louis' erroneous negligence that the bishops painstakingly document in their account and, consequently—and in precise terms—emend with rebuke.

The bishops follow their allusive quotation of Paul/Benedict with another quotation, one that not only refines the nature of their episcopal responsibilities but also stands as the most suggestive statement of how their account of Louis' penance should be understood. "If you shall not announce to the iniquitous man his iniquity," the bishops proclaim, paraphrasing the words of God that were uttered by the prophet Ezekiel, "and that same man will have died in his impiety, I shall require his blood from your hand" (Ezek. 3:18).[47] Here the threat posed by episcopal neglect, with the concomitant Pauline/Benedictine responsibility of reproving and entreating that such a situation demands, is given an absolute urgency; now even the righteousness and salvation of the bishops themselves are imperiled along with the sacred precepts. Negligence on their part, insist the bishops, makes them worse than the iniquitous person who perishes as a result of their carelessness. This, then, is the terrible cost of their "power of the keys"; they must never falter in their ministry and be ready to act at the slightest sign of error, or it is they on whom God will exact his terrible vengeance.

Yet, unlike the earlier quotation's casting of errants as unruly, negligent members of the flock—that is, strictly in the Benedictine terms of how they behave—the quotation from Ezekiel defines such truants in terms of how they are, characterizing them with the moral condition of "iniquity." As we shall see in Part III, this (from our perspective, subtle) nuance is the key to unlocking the ecclesiastical meaning of the events of 833. For this quotation—indeed, the entire opening declaration of the bishops' account—casts the immediate problem of Louis the Pious's governance in general scriptural terms, yet terms chosen and arranged to suit the particular justificatory narrative that the rebel bishops understood as the truth. As the bishops were well aware, it was a scriptural, justificatory truth that had been told before.

Role Models, Allusively

At the end of the fourth century, the church father Ambrose (339–397), bishop of Milan, employed in a similar fashion the same scriptural passages from Paul and Ezekiel in defense of his intervention in secular affairs. In two carefully crafted letters to the emperor Theodosius (347–395), Ambrose invoked these quotations to frame and support his unprecedented, daring, yet deferential demands that the emperor recognize his scandalous wrongs and do penance.[48] The Carolingian bishops' parallel usage in 833 of these same biblical quotations was no coincidence. In fact, apart from the letters of Ambrose and the Carolingian bishops' *Relatio*, there are few texts from the early Middle Ages in which these passages from Ezekiel and Paul are found clustered together.[49] Moreover, Ambrose's bold letters remained virtually unknown until the eighteenth century—but for the notable exception of Hincmar of Reims's quotations from them in the ninth.[50] Hincmar had read them (at Reims), and the rebel bishops may have, too (such as Ebbo, perhaps also at Reims). Certainly the bishops' appeals to Paul and Ezekiel serve a rhetorical, approbatory purpose analogous to that of Ambrose in his candid letters of conscience. By opting to define the nature of their ministry through the general foil of episcopal neglect, choosing the specific foil of neglected "strays," and then selecting scriptural quotations related to this constitutive foil that dictate precise traits, roles, and obligations, the bishops at once foreshadow and warrant the event of the "errant" Louis' penance in broad but definitive strokes. Like Theodosius, Louis was unaware of his iniquity; like the model bishop Ambrose, the rebel bishops were obligated to help the obdurate emperor know himself, for the sake of his salvation as well as their own; and like their function in Ambrose's letters, the lines from Paul and Ezekiel in the bishops' *Relatio* anchor and uphold what might otherwise be taken as insolence. Put another way, the bishops' opening declaration renders their ministry in strictly moral terms, implicates them in the terrestrial realm's immorality, and justifies their efforts toward its correction.[51] Iniquity arises from negligence but can be countered by zeal. Consequently, the narrative that follows in the episcopal account should be understood as, at the very least, an extreme case that attests to the truth of this fundamental, suprahistorical axiom.[52] Agobard's earlier equation of the rebel bishops' role with that of outspoken biblical figures, such as the prophet Elijah (3 Kings 21) or the priest Jehoiada (4 Kings 11), underscored the timelessness of this point.[53] In his letter to Theodosius, Ambrose himself had done much the same, equating his bold actions with the biblical figure of Nathan admonishing a repentant King David (2 Kings 12).[54]

The declarative opening of the episcopal *Relatio* then resumes. In order to combat negligence with zeal, reason the bishops, the shepherds of Christ must strive to maintain a state of "most prudent temperance" (*moderatio discretissima*). As their following statements make clear, by laboring continuously to maintain this temperance, the shepherds are rewarded with its associated graces, which they define by quoting Pope Gregory the Great: they can stand as partners with those of virtuous conduct and also stand firm against sinners and their vices.[55] Moreover, this temperance imparts them a sure and steady sense of direction for the circumspect performance of their ministry: on the one hand, it stirs them from any languor in their service, and, on the other hand, it keeps them immune from the profane influences of fawning and intimidation. The bishops then explain that the foregoing qualification and elaboration of their ministry have not been taken up simply for their own sake but rather to make manifest the particular purpose of this wardship within the unfolding of God's plan. Their goal of maintaining a most prudent temperance, they note, allows them to care for all those living in the present and sets an example to be followed and likewise perpetuated by vigilant shepherds of future generations.

Like the quotations of Paul/Benedict, Ezekiel, and perhaps Ambrose, the words of Gregory that appear in this opening declaration demand consideration. Just as those quotations function to establish the bedrock upon which the edifice of the bishop's ministry stands, Gregory's recommendations of humility and zeal are invoked to strengthen its framework. By appealing to the words of Gregory in the context of defining their office's duties, the bishops not only demonstrate the moral rectitude and patristic authority of their episcopal charge and recall its recent imperial sponsorship (Gregory's *Pastoral Care* had been promoted by Charlemagne and extolled by Louis the Pious),[56] but also reveal their awareness that Pope Gregory himself had utilized these same quotations from Ezekiel and Paul. In both his *Homilies on Ezekiel* and his book *Pastoral Care*, Gregory had refined his explanation of how to preach to certain types of "errants" by quoting and then glossing on Paul's command to Timothy to "reprove, entreat, rebuke." In *Homilies on Ezekiel*—like the letters of Ambrose, one of the few early medieval texts to cluster the passages from Ezekiel and Paul—the Pauline quotation and its gloss occur specifically in Gregory's commentary on Ezekiel 3:18–19, those passages that demand the iniquitous man be confronted with his iniquity.[57] Thus, the nature of the bishops' *ministerium*, while explicitly based on Paul and Ezekiel, was in its design and fabrication reliant on Benedict, Ambrose, and Gregory—as the bishops presumed their audience would recognize, mighty pillars indeed.[58]

The *Relatio* then returns to and extends its use of pastoral metaphors. The bishops begin by locating themselves as shepherds upon the field of God, namely, the church of Christ. Because the "Ancient Enemy," that is, Satan, is continually causing "ills" (*noxia*) of all kinds to sprout up in the field under their care, they maintain that it is their obligation to uproot such weeds with the "shepherd's hoe" (*sarculum pastorale*).[59] Once again, these lines are derivative not only of the Benedictine interpretation of Paul's mandate but also of the formal resolution from an imperial reform assembly held in 818/19:

> And since, through [Christ's] apostle [Paul], he deigned to name us his helpers, and the holy church his bride (in holy scripture she is called a garden [Song of Sol. 4:12]), [it] ought to be cultivated by daily exercises applied to the hoe of good work (*sarculo bonae operationis*), so that, just as injurious things always grow up in it [the church] just as in a good [fertile] field, thus may by work and good diligence [or study] ills (*noxia*) be uprooted and the useful planted.[60]

Having grounded the execution of their ministry both in Benedict's Rule and in this precedent set at an imperial assembly, the bishops then abandon metaphors and come straight to the point: there are wicked people, they submit, who either refuse to recognize good deeds when they are done or choose to interpret a benign act malignantly rather than delight in its truthfulness. Consequently, because the wicked would not hesitate to criticize the doers of good deeds, precautionary steps must be taken—namely, whenever the bishops have effected a good deed for the common weal through the performance of their collective ministry, they should commit it to writing, in accordance with ecclesiastical custom. As they explain, they can thereby preserve for posterity the fruit of their labors and eliminate any chance of criticism on the part of wicked gainsayers, who, whether now or in the future, might otherwise undermine the bishops' good works. In other words, with a carefully written instrument, they can obviate any potential counterclaims against their actions.

The opening declaration of the episcopal narrative ends here. Thus far, the *Relatio* has assumed a hallowed tone that defines episcopal duties, their nature, and their praxis in eternal, immutable, and constitutive terms, rather than in terms of expediency or contingency.[61] The bishops have established the unconditional justification for both the existence of their documentary account and the performance of the "good deed" it validates and preserves for posterity. This good deed, despite being the product of a contingency of a specific time and place, is certain to suffer the calumny reserved for such deeds in any age, imply the bishops, if not properly ratified. Thus, not only is the present legal document entirely necessary, but it is also entirely typical. Forestalling criticism of their good deed as having been an act unusual or unheard-of—that is, as a novel expedient—the bishops cast and interpret criticism itself as a perennial problem faced by shepherds of every age—a diabolical "weed" that confirms the wisdom behind the equally enduring ecclesiastical custom of deterrence through ratification. "Therefore," they explain in light of their prefatory remarks, "we determined that it was necessary for all the sons of the holy church of God, namely [those] in the present and in future times to know how we bishops. . . ."[62] What follows is the customary, requisite *Relatio* of their good deed—written in careful, incontrovertible language.

Remembering Louis' Sins

In contrast to their prefatory declaration with its timeless statements, the bishops begin the narrative of their salutary act by formally locating it in time and space. Indeed, this temporal and spatial contrast between the preface and the narrative of the deed is especially pronounced by the formulaic, notarial style of the *Relatio*'s preamble: "We bishops," it begins, "appointed under the authority of the Lord and most glorious Emperor Lothar, in the year since the incarnation of our Lord Jesus Christ, 833, twelfth indiction, in other words, in the first year of [the reign of] that same sovereign, generally assembled in the month of October at the palace of Compiègne."[63] After this mannered opening, the bishops recall that they had justified publicly the overriding demand of their duty. Approaching Lothar humbly, they took care to elucidate to the new emperor, his dignitaries, and everyone assembled at the council the exact nature of their episcopal responsibilities, the degree of power they wield, and the fate that awaits any who defy their admonitions—the fearsome yoke of damnation.

Having established their paramount authority over those things falling within the broad purview of their ministry, the bishops then come to the related matter at hand. The assembly had been called so that the bishops could fulfill their duty as watchmen and warn Lothar and the people about the untold offenses recently committed against God. These wrongs could be redressed and the Lord placated, they counseled, if an act of satisfaction were offered without delay. Here the bishops clearly foreshadow Louis' public penance, which they will describe later. For the moment, however, they note only that the nature of the offenses against God had become the main topic of consideration at the assembly. Thus, the narrative suggests that the specific act necessary to achieve satisfaction from God did not become evident until the precise nature of the offenses themselves had first been ascertained. Many things were scrutinized, explain the bishops, that had to do with the scandalization (*scandalum*) of the church, the calamity (*ruina*) of the populace, and the destruction (*interitus*) of the kingdom—a tripartite distinction that arises in the following paragraphs as a common refrain. What became readily apparent, they concluded, was that all these ills had been the terrible result of "negligence" (*negligentia*), something that the assembly resolved should be quickly remedied and then entirely shunned in the future.

The sole surviving affidavit of the penance, penned by Agobard, confirms the resolutions summarized in the bishops' account. True necessity, explains Agobard, had impressed upon everyone at the assembly that they should discuss with diligence "the peril of the realm, both in the present and its condition in the future."[64] The urgency, he continues, stemmed from the fact that the realm—which had been tottering for a long while—was recently being compelled to its ruin through negligence (*neglegentia*) and, what Agobard believed was a more accurate diagnosis, through listlessness (*ignavia*).

In both accounts, the consensus over negligence thus far pertained only to its salutary elimination both in the present and for the future. The source of such ruinous negligence, however, still needed reckoning before the corrective steps could be taken, satisfaction achieved, and order restored. To this end, the bishops declare that they then led everyone assembled in a collective act of remembrance. They began by recalling how the realm had been united and nobly enlarged by God both through the administration of Charlemagne and the peacemaking efforts of his predecessors. This achievement, they continued, had subsequently been—and here they are meticulous with their language—solemnly "entrusted" (*committere*) to the Lord Emperor Louis for the purpose of sustaining the general peace.[65]

Thus far, the bishops have provided the reader with a textbook narrative about the auspicious (if conspicuously pacific) rise of the Carolingian dynasty. Yet, as the more ominous remainder of their remembrance makes clear, the divine sponsorship and terrestrial success of the Carolingians had always been conditional. God had favored the realm and kept it in a state of peace for Louis and his subjects, they remembered, only so long as that sovereign had kept up his end of the demanding contract—that he would strive to please God, follow the examples of his ancestors, and yield to the counsel of his best men.[66] Of course, in spelling out these conditions by way of recollection, the bishops simultaneously adumbrate what Louis had failed to do—hence, the revocation of his rule—and what Lothar should keep well in mind as grave obligations now, in his new capacity as emperor, equally demanded of him.

If the general cause of the realm's recent ills was negligence, as the bishops now recalled, then its specific source was Louis' gradual failure to fulfill the obligations of his imperial contract. Agobard wasted little ink in making this fact clear: it was Lord Louis—one "formerly venerated as emperor"— who had been destructively negligent and idle, allowing himself to become ensnared and misled by the wiles of seducers.[67] In the bishops' *Relatio*, Louis' failure was treated in much detail. Over the course of time (*in processu temporis*), explained the bishops, Louis had become an embarrassment as a ruler and, thus, unworthy of that noble achievement of his ancestors. As a result of both his rashness (*inprovidentia*) and negligence (*negligentia*), everyone was only too aware of the disgrace Louis had brought upon himself, his people, and the realm. A sordid list of Louis' general wrongs then follows: Louis had "exercised negligently the duty entrusted to him under the Highest"[68]; he had rashly done or compelled to be done and negligently allowed to be done deeds displeasing to both God and men; he had tempted God through numerous execrable resolutions; he had scandalized the church; and, aside from countless other wrongs, he had most recently assembled the entire populace subject to him for no other purpose than their mutual destruction. Due to these wrongs, assure the bishops in closing, God had revoked the imperial power from Louis by a divine and just judgment.

Raging Silences

The foregoing act of remembrance, which identified Louis as the source of the ruinous negligence and, thus, as the ultimate cause of the realm's afflictions, ends here with the supernatural explanation of the emperor's sudden abandonment upon the Rotfeld. In other words, the bishops' public recollection of Louis' dysfunctional reign was generally chronological, moving somewhat vaguely from the decorous past to the unseemly present; indeed, this linearity is underscored by the bishops' emphasis of the fact that Louis had become ignominious "over the course of time." Louis had been entrusted with the peaceful governance of the realm, a charge that the bishops' statements imply he had initially expedited with due competence and care. It was only after a number of years that Louis had proved himself to be unworthy.[69]

As the extant documents by Agobard attest, this observation of Louis' iniquitous transformation was central to the rebels' justification for their actions. Agobard had earlier employed much the same language that would be used in the episcopal *Relatio* to describe this transformation. In his admonitory letter to the emperor in 830, for instance, he recalled how Louis had previously chosen to make his eldest son, Lothar, his consort and partner in the imperial title. Over the course of time (*in processu temporis*), whenever and wherever imperial letters were sent, they contained the names of both emperors. But later, according to Agobard, these sacred statutes were overturned because Louis' will had changed.[70] Although he provides no reason for Louis' apparent capriciousness, Agobard would again take up the emperor's change in greater detail in another highly partisan text, the *Liber apologeticus* he addressed to the four corners of the world shortly before the encounter on the Rotfeld. Louis, he there observed, had flourished while he remained in his palace and had been at peace because he fulfilled his marital duty. But over the course of days (*in processu vero dierum*), this honorable relationship had changed, at first becoming tepid and then frigid, notes Agobard with marked sexual innuendos. As a result, Queen Judith had turned to lasciviousness; since what was licit ceased, she sought that which was illicit, at first secretly and then shamelessly, until her indiscretions were known to the ends of the earth. As Agobard lamented, young men laughed about this matter, old men grieved, and the more discerning deemed it unbearable. Seeing their father's bed stained, the palace disgraced, the kingdom confused, and the name of the Franks benighted, Louis' discerning sons could tolerate no more and were reasonably moved (*zelus rationabilis*) to take action.[71]

Again, in a slightly later supplement to the same document, the *Liber apologeticus* II, Agobard pointed out that the problem with Louis had been one that developed gradually: after Louis' first wife, Ermengard, had died (in 818), he found another (in 819) who, in the initial years of their marriage, had been restrained (*premere*; *subdere*) by his vigor and power (diction suggesting that, although Judith appeared obedient during that period, it was only because she had been forced to behave this way). But over the course of time (*in processu temporis*), recalled Agobard, Queen Judith became an instigator of great disturbances, one who not only confounded and saddened but indeed had nearly killed such persons up to and including the sons of the emperor. No one could now mistake the fact, he continued, that gradually the palace had been dishonored, the splendor of the kingdom darkened, and the name of those ruling brought into disrepute.[72]

Unlike these valuable manifestos by Agobard, the episcopal accounts of the penance give no ostensible reason for Louis' embarrassing transformation over the course of time; explicit mention of Queen Judith, for instance, is nowhere to be found in either the affidavit by Agobard or the episcopal *Relatio*.[73] This silence is not surprising, however, for the bishops were certain that the ultimate culpability rested with Louis alone. Even Agobard's scathing attack of Judith in his other texts suggested as much, albeit indirectly. Although, in its early years, their marriage had displayed a promising future, the union soon became bankrupt and Judith licentious only because, Agobard insinuated, Louis no longer had been able to honor his marital debt and keep his wife subdued by his dominion (*virtus et potestas*) as her rightful husband and lord.[74] Doubtless, Agobard expected his audience to understand without difficulty what Pope Gregory the Great had already considered common knowledge in the sixth century: "Obviously . . . the temptation of the flesh burns hot in youth. But from the fiftieth year, the heat of the body begins to cool."[75] That carnal relations between Judith and Louis, the latter already forty-one when they married in 819, began to wane after the birth of their children (Gisela in 820; Charles in 823) thus had come as no surprise. That this natural development had led to Louis' gradual emasculation and the loss of control over his own household, however, was, in Agobard's estimation, particularly troubling. Why should something so obvious and banal have had such dire consequences? In his letter to the emperor in 830 on the division of the empire, Agobard had explained (using Ps. 7:10) that matters of the heart and loins are transparent to God, thereby underscoring his own sincerity but also intimating that others might have more to fear from such divine scrutiny below the belt (or beneath the gown).[76] Why had Louis not recognized the conspicuous wrongs his wife had been committing against him? How had he been so easily cuckolded, a condition to which Agobard may have alluded with his description of the proud and stubborn Louis' "hard horns" (*dura cornua*)?[77] "O Lord God of heaven and earth," he implored, "why have you allowed your most faithful Christian servant, our emperor, to come to such negligence that he does not wish to see the evils that threaten him from all sides? For he loves those hating him and hates those loving him."[78] To Agobard, all this could only have been the product of a "secret judgment of God" (*occultum Dei iudicium*).[79] (In his relentless search for truth—for, as he asserted, "there is nothing on this earth that happens without a reason"[80]—the explanation of a secret judgment of God was Agobard's customary way of admitting defeat.) Phenomena that occurred contrary to the terrestrial and divine laws governing the order of things—in cases when those laws otherwise had been faithfully followed—were simply the inscrutable manifestations of God's mysterious will.[81] Consequently, Louis' unwitting transformation into a cuckold remained as impenetrable as the depths of an abyss. Unable to be fathomed, its cause remained a secret.[82]

By attributing the source of the realm's problems to Louis' transformation, which was understood to lie behind Judith's wanton behavior, and characterizing this change as mysterious or secret, Agobard here remains conspicuously silent about rumors circulating at the time that ascribed Louis' hard-hearted blindness to enchantment.[83] Previously, at the great reform assembly of Paris in 829, the realm's bishops had insisted that sorcery and practitioners of pagan rites were chief among the many evils currently weakening the church and endangering the empire. In particular, they noted that diabolical illusions were used to poison people's minds to such an extent that they became oblivious to the injuries they were inflicting and, thus, were deemed by many to have become mad.[84] According to the Astronomer, writing in retrospect in 841, many nobles had alleged that Louis himself was the victim of such sorcery, which caused his blindness, led to his iniquitous change, and allowed Judith and the court chamberlain Bernard of Septimania to commit adultery with impunity.[85] The loyal biographer quickly discounted this supernatural explanation by noting that the nobles who had made such allegations of devilry in the palace were greedy, suggesting that they had fabricated their "inside information" because they hoped to be rewarded for providing Louis' sons with this "crucial" (but, in fact, false) intelligence.[86] Despite this cynical interpretation of the nobles as selfish maligners, the Astronomer's testimony attests to the fact that charges of sorcery surrounded the palace in the late 820s–early 830s. In the Annals of Saint-Bertin, the anonymous first annalist also claimed that treacherous nobles were to blame for instigating the rebellion but made no mention of sorcery. Rather, he noted that Bernard of Septimania's counsel to Louis to undertake a military campaign into Brittany during the days of Lent in 830 had already turned the general populace against the emperor, and thus had made the nobles' uprising all the more appealing.[87] Writing years later, well after Bernard's death in 844,[88] Paschasius Radbertus would be far more direct and say what the loyal annalist had dared not in the mid-830s—that in addition to confounding the people with his ill counsel, Bernard himself had been the great sorcerer responsible for Louis' blindness and delusions and, thus, had been the ultimate source of the rebels' indignation and wrath.[89] Thanks to spies Wala had planted within the palace,[90] it was learned that Bernard's enchantment of Louis was just one part of a larger plot: with his incantations, the chamberlain had divined a plan to slay the spellbound emperor so that it would appear he had died of his own infirmity and then follow this secret homicide with the murder of Louis' children, beginning with King Pippin.[91] Agobard, it seems, had already gotten wind of this plot in the early 830s and made public its general objectives: certain men known for their discernment, he explained in his Book of Apology, had verified that there were some at Louis' side who avidly desired the death of his sons and who were conspiring to harm the emperor and divide the kingdom among themselves.[92] Paschasius would later be more specific: it had been Bernard who wished "to destroy the emperor and annihilate all his progeny and take his wife [Judith] whom he had shamelessly polluted. If it had worked, with her he would have extended his reach throughout the empire, and either slain all the seigneurs of the land or subjugated them with wicked oppression. Otherwise he would have transported himself to Spain with her."[93] Had this incredible plan come to fruition, one can only guess what Bernard had in mind for Dhuoda, his learned wife dutifully overseeing their estates back home in Uzès.[94]

While we have no records that charge Dhuoda herself with witchcraft, Bernard's reputation as a sorcerer was imputed to other members of his family. At Chalon-sur-Saône in the summer of 834, while maneuvering against the combined might of his father and brothers' forces, Lothar ordered Bernard's sister Gerberga dragged from her convent, sealed in a barrel, and drowned as a witch in the Saône River.[95] Typically, this incident is invoked by modern historians to demonstrate the ruthlessness and spite of the rebels.[96] Yet the specific manner of Gerberga's execution carries deeper implications. If the Astronomer's explanation is true that the allegations of sorcery put forward by the "conscientious" nobles of the realm were nothing but a pretext for their rebellion, then why did the rebels attempt to stamp out such Bernardian sorcery even as they were on the defensive and their rebellion failing? The Astronomer makes no attempt to reconcile this apparent paradox when he adds the detail that Gerberga "was strangled by water *as a witch (venefica)*."[97] Thegan attributed the idea for the deed to the "impious wives" of Lothar's counselors[98] and concluded that it was but another instance of divine fulfillment: "With the holy you will be holy, and with the perverse, perverse" (Ps. 17:26). Although these loyalist authors provided their accounts of Gerberga's ghastly end as further compelling evidence against the rebels, the ritual manner of her execution suggests that it was more than a perverse parting shot. Perhaps the rebels' belief in Bernard's sorcery was not a pretext after all; perhaps when they drowned Gerberga as a witch, they believed it. Several other members of Bernard's family, whom Wala knew well, were apprehended by the rebellion, with some executed, one blinded, and others exiled.[99] Whether the charge against them was witchcraft as well the sources do not say.

In contrast to these many rumors and allegations swarming around the palace and its courtiers, the episcopal *Relatio* conspicuously devotes little attention to the reasons for Louis' scandalous transformation. (Later in the account, there is an oblique reference to "plots" his enemies had prepared against him.) [100] For the bishops' immediate purposes, it was enough to recognize that over time Louis had become an "iniquitous" man, which led to his negligent and imprudent behavior (both with respect to his household and the empire), which itself had offended God, elicited his wrath, and led to the wretched state of affairs. This was no great "mystery of iniquity" (2 Thess. 2:7) that demanded the genius of an Augustine to uncover its meaning.[101] Nor was it a case, as preached by Isidore of Seville two centuries earlier, of God's altering the king because of the wickedness of the people, giving them their just deserts for their sins.[102] Taking a more direct approach than Agobard, the bishops were above all interested in how to address Louis' manifestly iniquitous negligence, rather than in divining the reasons for it. And something had to be done, they insisted, for Louis' negligence was not only offending God but was spreading scandal throughout the realm as well, making the once noble church, empire, and people a laughingstock, even to their enemies.[103] Such scorn was usually unthinkable; as Louis' own exiled court poet had reminded him only a few years before, the Franks were intolerant of their enemies' jeers, silencing them in "Frankish style"—with a swift arrow through the throat.[104] Einhard provided a similar image of the Franks' fearsome reputation in his biography of Charlemagne; the great emperor, he recalled, had embodied the sardonic Greek proverb known to many others from bitter experience: "Have a Frank as a friend, never as a neighbor."[105] Equally passionate about the renown of the Franks, Agobard grieved over Louis' embarrassing misconduct; indeed, it was for this very reason, he warranted, that the emperor's sons had risen up out of understandable concern to restore the dignity of the imperial household and its illustrious name, an appellation that was, of course, tantamount to their own.[106] According to Agobard, they had undertaken this "irreproachable deed most deserving of praise" in order to return their father to peace and restore what little honor they might still salvage for him.[107]

Although neither Agobard nor the bishops display awareness of it in their texts, the need for Louis' palace to have been "cleansed" was deeply ironic. For a "cleansing of the palace" was one of Louis' first tasks upon assuming the reins of the empire. When he inherited sole possession of the throne after Charlemagne's death in 814, Louis arrived at Aachen with his Aquitainian court in tow and immediately swept his father's house clean of its "moral filth," driving some courtiers into exile while forcing others, many of his kin among them, to assume the tonsure or veil.[108] The rebels' claim that they had been compelled to cleanse Louis' court doubtless draws on these well-known deeds as a subtext.[109] Things had gone so wrong in the realm that the very ruler once renowned for his reforms had himself become the one in need of reform.

In short, the memory of Louis' reign in the episcopal account testifies as much to Louis' gradual change into an iniquitous, negligent emperor as it does to the shame correspondingly suffered by the realm. That Louis' iniquitous negligence had become, as the bishops stressed, increasingly obvious to everyone not only lent the strength of consensus to the claims made in the bishops' act of incriminating remembrance but also served as a foil, equally demonstrating just how blind the emperor had become.[110] Whatever had altered Louis—whether a secret judgment of God or the black magic of Bernard—he required nothing less than the most blatant display of God's judgment upon the Rotfeld to open his eyes once more to the truth. The bishops' urgent duty as the vicars of Christ was to expedite this divine judgment by making Louis cognizant of his iniquity, helping him appease God, and ensuring that he retained his discernment, both for the good of his salvation and for that of the realm formerly in his keep.[111] Similarly, in Agobard's affidavit, the protocol of these episcopal duties was made explicitly manifest. Casting his vote in agreement with those necessary resolutions that had been "determined usefully and laudably through discussion and consultation," Agobard supported taking action toward the benefit and integrity of the realm and the emperor.[112] Only then, he continued, did the bishops discuss the matter of Louis' soul.

A Salutary Legation

Closing their remembrance of Louis' wrongs, the bishops note in their *Relatio* that they had also kept in mind constructive thoughts, such as the precepts of God, their own duty to uphold these precepts, and the pious grants that

Louis himself had once commendably bestowed. The bishops' recollection of their episcopal charge at this particular moment in the summary account has an important function. By evoking the suprahistorical truth claims laid out in the *Relatio*'s preamble, these "afterthoughts" about both the precepts of God and the demands they exact together serve to justify the conscientious bishops' next step.

As the session of recollection, discussion, and interpretation at Compiègne concluded, it was at last decided that, through the dispensation of Lothar, a legation bearing the authority of the sacred assembly should be sent to Louis to remind him of his sins. This decision had been rendered, explained the bishops, so that Louis might gain a better awareness of the perilous condition of his soul. In other words, by helping him discern his iniquity, the bishops were acting in accordance with their charge as assigned in Ezekiel 3:18—that is, they were making sure that the iniquitous man was aware of his iniquity, thereby averting the visitation of God's wrath upon themselves for negligence. Moreover, these actions were taken not just in accordance with Ezekiel but again through its interpretation in Benedict's Rule. In his chapter "How Solicitous the Abbot Should Be for the Excommunicated," Benedict explains that, since it is not the healthy but the sick who need a physician (Matt. 9:12), the abbot should send to a delinquent brother *senpectae*, that is,

> brethren of mature years and wisdom, who may, as it were, secretly console the wavering brother and induce him to make humble satisfaction; comforting him that he may not "be overwhelmed by excessive grief" (2 Cor. 2:7), but that, as the Apostle says, charity may be strengthened in him (2 Cor. 2:8). And let everyone pray for him.[113]

Let there be no doubt, explain the bishops in their role as *senpectae*, or spiritual doctors, that Louis had been deprived of his terrestrial power by a judgment of God and through the authority of his bishops. Only by gaining an accurate appraisal of his spiritual health, they reasoned, could Louis fully appreciate that losing his throne was now the least of his worries. For the former emperor, eternal damnation was imminent.

A similar, more detailed description of this salutary legation is given in Agobard's affidavit. At Compiègne, it was resolved that a legation should go to Louis to exhort him for his errors, which, "by hastening through the ways of depravity and injustice," he had committed against the will of God. By means of this exhortation, it was hoped that Louis would apprehend his perilous condition, recognize the foulness of his deeds, and, as the prophet Isaiah had said, be led back to his heart (Isa. 46:8). Agobard was certain that, if Louis would commit himself in earnest to repeated acts of devotion and confession, then "he who had lost the earthly realm through many instances of negligence" could obtain indulgence from "the Lord and Omnipotent Judge, who is the most clement pardoner of crimes," and gain reassurance of his rightful place in heaven. For this reason, continues Agobard, the assembly of bishops at Compiègne drew up a little book (*libellus*) containing evidence of Louis' crimes and presented it to him. By confronting him with this indictment, they hoped that Louis would perceive in its contents, as though it were a kind of mirror, the wretchedness of his deeds and experience the type of self-awareness that scripture states is gained by a perfect penitent: "I know my iniquity, and my sin is always before me" (Ps. 50:5).[114]

The episcopal legation evidently met with success. After listening to the assembly's counsel and salutary admonitions, explains the *Relatio*, Louis willingly (*libenter*) agreed with their warnings and asked that he be given time to deliberate. Granting him a reprieve, the legation departed, but not before setting a date when they would expect an answer from Louis.

When the day for Louis' decision arrived (the *Relatio* does not indicate the duration of this interlude), the episcopal legation returned to hear his answer. Conspicuously describing him as congenial and cooperative (*venerabilis vir*),[115] they claim that they took care to admonish Louis diligently and reminded him of his tripartite transgressions: that Louis had offended God, scandalized the church, and tormented the people conditionally entrusted to him. Agobard gives a similar account: in order to expedite the process of Louis' recovery, the legation of bishops returned to Louis to impress upon him that they were beseeching God on his behalf. Commiserating with Louis' infirmities and afflictions, explained Agobard, they continuously supplicated the Lord to raise Louis up from his wretched state.

According to the episcopal *Relatio*, Louis willingly embraced (*libenter*) both the bishops' salutary admonition and their severe reproach (*exaggeratio*).[116] Indeed, he promised them that he would undergo a therapeutic judgment. But there was still more. Louis was so overcome with joy (*hilaris*) by their admonitions, recall the bishops, that he asked to speak immediately with his son Lothar. Although Lothar was already intending to meet with him soon, Louis implored his eldest son to make haste with his best men so that they might promptly undertake a mutual reconciliation in accordance with Christian doctrine. This meeting should occur first, Louis insisted, for it would allow them to purge any resentment from their hearts through a sincere request for forgiveness. Following this plea, Louis accepted the judgment of an ecclesiastical penance—one which, the author of the *Relatio* adds by way of transition, was done not long after this.

Agobard gives an analogous, if less detailed report of Louis' conversion: the old emperor neither refused the bishops' requests, claims Agobard, nor sought any delay. Rather, having regained the contrition of a humble heart, he prostrated himself effusively before his episcopal wards, doing so, Agobard notes, no fewer than three times. Displaying sincere recognition of his crimes, Louis beseeched the bishops' indulgence and the aid of their prayers. He then received their counsel and made a request to undertake penance, promising the bishops that he would fulfill assiduously whatever act of humility was demanded of him. Agobard explains that Louis was then made aware of the "law and order" of a public penance. Still Louis made no complaint, agreeing entirely with their sound judgment.[117]

Louis the Pious, Benito Cereno, and Ahab

It should come as no surprise that this sequence of events as presented by Agobard and the episcopal *Relatio* has given many readers pause. For the colloquy that took place between the bishops and Louis soon after his reprieve, and more specifically the claim that the former emperor's consent to undertake penance was gladly offered, has long been stigmatized as the most transparent sign of the rebels' "odious intrigue." Understood in light of the numerous later narratives about Louis' abandonment and penance by his supporters, the bishops' *Relatio* has always been thought to present a fictitious version of the events, one concealing the ugly truth that Louis' "happy" request for a penance was, in fact, the unhappy result of coercion. Indeed, this "sinister ruse" was—as we saw in Chapter 1—repeatedly the focus of Louis' defenders, who saw it as an element central to the "tragedy" of 833.[118] With his close study in 1904 of the many documents reporting the events of 833, Louis Halphen was only restating and refining within a modern scholarly context a conviction that had been firmly held for many centuries: that Louis' apparently willing compliance was actually the result of secret extortion and duress.[119]

Yet, what should one make of the fact that, not long after regaining his throne, Louis himself interpreted the deeds of 833 as having been undoubtedly a just judgment of God, an incident (*eventus*) by which he had been disciplined by the rod and shown "utterly glorious mercy" through the supportive staff of his family's great patron saint, Denis of Paris?[120] Or that upon his recovery he rapidly changed his public intitulature from the former "Louis Emperor Augustus, having been ordained by divine providence . . ." to read instead "Louis Emperor Augustus, having come into favor once more by divine clemency . . . ," thereby suggesting that he had indeed fallen out of divine favor and was now fashioning himself as another humbled and pure-hearted King Solomon of old?[121] Was it only empty flattery and poetic fancy when, in 826, Louis' exiled court poet Ermoldus Nigellus boasted with a striking vignette that, for habitually embracing the altar as a supplicant, laying himself prostrate before it in tears, and imploring Christ to grant him aid, the emperor was believed to have been awarded the reins of the empire?[122] In the same poem, Ermoldus would later even have Louis sententiously remind Pope Stephen IV that "the avenging Father corrected [the sinful people of Israel] with plagues and various tribulations; thus their lesson learned, they returned to the ancient laws. You see—when weakened—wretched people suddenly remember the Lord, and the Pious Caretaker readily welcomes them back."[123] Louis knew of what he spoke, for, as his admirers and critics alike agreed, he spent much time studying scripture—a fact about Louis that the poet expected his audience to know in order for his artful representation of the reverent emperor to have its fullest effect.[124]

When heard amid this constant refrain in praise of his piety and zealous devotion, perhaps Louis' conspicuous silence about being coerced by the rebels should prompt the consideration of what has long been thought unthinkable: that at the strident entreaties of the bishops about his many sins, the dire need for their expiation, and the damning consequences of their neglect, Louis may very well have freely, even joyously, submitted to his penance. The intervention of the supernatural in human affairs was, we should remember, a universally shared belief of the utmost importance in the early Middle Ages, one common to Louis, his opponents, and society at large.[125] Given the Catholic, confessional culture to which he belonged—indeed, that he himself had done so much to foster—Louis may have been convinced of his iniquity by the bishops' repeated admonitions and considered penance a means to render satisfaction to an angry God.[126] After all, the humility of penance was considered to be the ideal way to purge oneself and grow stronger in the process, as the example of King David and even the words of Christ himself attested, "He that humbleth himself shall be exalted" (Luke 14:11, 18:14; Matt. 23:12).[127] In fact, it is likely that Louis did believe in the annealing quality of penance, for, more than a decade earlier in 822, he had undertaken a self-inflicted public humiliation and penance in order to appease God for certain "public" offenses.[128] Although this was probably not the momentous, decisive act that, as Jules Michelet once thought, signaled a "new era of morality and the advent of conscience,"[129] the penance of 822 still betrays Louis' acute and solemn sensitivity to the direct relationship among the purity and degree of his own devotion, the realm's overall well-being, and the esteem of God. Sometime shortly after February 834, Louis recalled his recent penance at Soissons in similar terms of salutary, corrective chastisement: the same penance of 833 that the bishops represented in their account as a "shepherd's hoe" for the uprooting of iniquities in the field of God (which were kept from returning through careful, preemptive codification) was now understood by Louis in accordance with the Psalms (Ps. 22:4–6) as rather having been the "rod and staff" of God's instruction (via his special intercessor, Saint Denis). Hardly some early medieval version of Herman Melville's tormented, pathetic Captain Benito Cereno, compelled by the murderous gaze of his secretly mutinous crew to feign the appearance of possessing free will, Louis may actually have come to believe in his wrongs and knew of the power of penance to right them.[130] The same sincerity regarding the penance and its necessity can be applied to the rebels as well. As Agobard explained in his apology, Louis' sons only acted against him as swiftly as they had because they feared that their father might become another Ahab; having committed evil with his wife in view of the Lord, Ahab had also offered and undertaken a penance, but it came too late, only postponing God's vengeance temporarily until the reign of his hapless son.[131] Thus, as the experience of Ahab proved, and as Louis himself apparently acknowledged, only a sincere and immediate penance would be beneficial to all (and to his anxious sons in particular). Exactly what this urgent act of penance should have been interpreted to mean at the time of its performance, however, had itself not necessarily been agreed upon. For as we shall see, it appears that Louis, in accordance with the experience of his earlier salutary penance of 822, believed that undergoing the ritual humiliation of a public penance meant one thing, but to the rebel bishops it meant quite another.

The Implications of a Mutual Reconciliation

Just as free will, or at least its appearance, was a requisite part of the ritual of penance,[132] so, too, it seems, was the prefatory step of a mutual reconciliation. In order to expedite the rendering of a salutary judgment, explain the bishops, Louis requested a preliminary meeting with Lothar and his son's dignitaries so that he could make a pure and humble request for their forgiveness and ensure that no ill feelings remained between them. As the episcopal *Relatio* is then careful to note, this reconciliation was done "in accordance with Christian doctrine." Such assurance on the part of the bishops here is significant, for it underscores the fact that, with episcopal counsel, Louis was following the proper protocol for the assumption of a legitimate—and thus, effective—penance: everything was being done correctly. Moreover, his willing request to go through with the preparatory, doctrinal rite of reconciliation also suggests, in retrospect, that Louis had been fully aware of the gravity of what he was about to do—that to undergo penance was, like death, to leave the world behind. Only two years later, in 835, Louis, now in his late fifties, would be persuaded by his anxious advisors that he was nearing the hour of his death. Consequently, reports the Astronomer, Louis asked for another mutual reconciliation with Lothar and his magnates (including Wala of Corbie) so that he might remit whatever transgressions he had committed against them.[133] In 822, shortly before undertaking his first public penance, Louis had similarly made certain to reconcile himself with his brothers, whom he had ordered tonsured against their will.[134] Given sufficient forewarning of the moment of one's "departure"—whether this leave was taken by penance or by death—it was deemed necessary first to rid oneself of any unresolved differences with estranged family, friends, and colleagues.[135] Thus, the somber connotation of undertaking this final reconciliation was clear: a preliminary ritual cleansing was now underway for an extreme rite of passage whose performance was imminent. By including in their account the fact that Louis had abided by Christian doctrine with his request for such a mutual reconciliation in 833, the bishops were ensuring that there should be no misinterpretation among their readers over the meaning of what Louis had done; Louis himself had been aware of the irrevocable consequences of his formal actions, and had still performed them willingly. Like the rationale of "ecclesiastical custom" offered in the account's preamble to justify the codification and ratification of the penance, Louis' "doctrinal" request for reconciliation also seems to have been included to forestall gainsayers, who might otherwise question the legitimacy and meaning of Louis' (and the bishops') actions. Such discretion was well founded, for ambiguity and disagreement over the consequences of penance were known to be a problem.[136] Indeed, as we have seen in Chapter 1 and already in Louis' own letter about his adversities, a great deal of debate regarding the precise meaning of these same events at Saint-Médard was not long in coming.

The Narrative of Louis' Public Penance

At last, following their lengthy preliminary justifications, the two accounts come to Louis' performance of his penance, providing a vivid description of the ritual and its participants. In a long opening sentence, "Lord" Louis (*dominus*) is described in the episcopal *Relatio* entering the church of Holy Mary in Soissons, a place especially noteworthy, insist the bishops, for being the resting place of Saints Médard and Sebastian (the relics of Saint Sebastian had only recently come into the monastery's possession through a celebrated translation from Rome in 826, engineered by Abbot Hilduin[137]). Among the capacity crowd looking on were bishops, priests, deacons, clerics, as well as "Lord" Lothar (*dominus*), his nobles, and—assures the account—as many of the general populace as the church was able to accommodate. Under the intense scrutiny of this great and greatly diversified assembly, Louis fell upon a hair shirt in front of the altar and began to speak. Or rather, he began to give a confession. Agobard provides a condensed version of these same proceedings: Louis came into the church before the altar and sepulcher of the saints and, in the presence of the faithful, prostrated himself on a hair shirt and "confessed two and three and four times to everything in a clear voice with a copious effusion of tears."[138] The bishops' *Relatio* continues the narrative of this confession in more detail: due to his negligence, admitted Louis, he had unworthily discharged the duty entrusted to him. Such negligence, he explained, had offended God, scandalized the church, and led the people into disorder. Here, Louis was confessing—"in the presence of everyone," we are reminded—to the same tripartite transgressions about which the bishops had so diligently admonished him during their earlier, private visit to his cell.[139] Because of these transgressions, continued Louis and, more specifically, because these transgressions had been so severe that they required both a public and an ecclesiastical expiation, he said that he desired to undertake penance.[140] By this means, together with the aid and assistance of the Lord and his terrestrial keepers of the keys, he could perhaps merit the absolution of his great crimes.

Regardless of whether it had been scripted by the bishops or was the heartfelt expression of a deeply devout man wracked by his conscience and his concern for salvation, Louis' confession as it is represented here was meant to reveal much more than his open acknowledgment of guilt. As the bishops took care to make clear, Louis not only declared his own recognition and avowal of his wrongs but, in so doing, also confirmed a number of other certainties alleged within the *Relatio*: first, that he had chosen penance because it was the type of satisfaction best suited to the enormity of his offenses (which, we should recall, fell within the bishops' equally vast pastoral jurisdiction); second, that Louis himself also acknowledged the bishops' unrivaled powers of binding and loosing, which were mentioned in the preamble of the account as a constitutive, charismatic aspect of the episcopal office; and finally, that although he had neglected his own charge (*ministerium*), he trusted that the bishops would not neglect theirs.

Taking their cue, the bishops entered the ritual at this point to fulfill their salutary mandate. As his self-styled, Benedictine "spiritual doctors," they admonished Louis to acknowledge his errors openly.[141] Only by means of a pure and simple confession, they declared, could he gain a true remission of his sins. Thanks to his previous requests for forgiveness both in his cell and during his mutual reconciliation with Lothar, Louis was well prepared for this expiatory prescription from his "doctors" and again readily confessed that he had greatly offended God. The bishops then responded in turn with a remarkable harangue, holding forth on the disastrous consequences that come of dissimulation during penance.

Louis' Deceit and Its Consequences

Simultaneously addressing Louis, the crowd watching his penance, and the readers and listeners of the written record of the event, the bishops explain that a confession from Louis was necessary because his seemingly pious candor and comportment were not altogether trustworthy. Only three years earlier—but what already seemed to them "now long ago"—at another assembly at Compiègne, Louis had been anything but sincere in his response to

similar charges leveled against him. At that time, he had undoubtedly concealed things within himself, they proclaimed, and acted deceitfully in the
view of God.[142] Paschasius Radbertus would later express the same misgivings
about Louis' honesty at that assembly; when Louis acceded to the rebels'
demands in 830 and thanked them publicly for their salutary assistance, recalled Paschasius, he "may have hidden something in his heart."[143] Similarly,
even at his first public penance in 822, there were those who believed that
Louis had performed the ritual insincerely, having feigned his humility and
contrition. As Paschasius remembered soon after, in 826, many who had been
present at Attigny in 822 "contemplated Louis' willingness and perceived his
unwillingness."[144] Consequently, by demanding a preliminary, public confession from Louis now—in the conspicuous presence of the church's two
knowing saints—the bishops were taking careful steps to avoid suffering the
same disastrous consequences of those earlier, subverted assemblies. This was
the reason for their ready participation in a penance that Louis' supporters,
such as the Astronomer, would later insist was nothing but an unequivocal
case of double jeopardy, of "holding God to judge twice on the very same issue
(Nah. 1:9)."[145] The rebel bishops claimed that Louis' earlier attempts to merit
divine satisfaction through penance had been undermined and invalidated
by his duplicity.[146] As they announced (thereby also alerting any who might
still be unaware), it was presently known to everyone that, at the assembly
in 830, Louis had drawn near to God "with a false heart through pretense
and cunning," having achieved for his efforts nothing but the provocation
of God's wrath. Given these charges by the rebels of Louis' repeated penitential insincerity, the traditional, loyalist claim about the involuntary nature
of Louis' penance in 833 is thus highly ironic: for the rebels claimed to hold
the same suspicions about Louis' willingness during his previous penances
in 822 and 830 that his defenders would later hold about his free will during
the penance of 833. Indeed, the rebels' doubts about his sincerity in those two
previous rituals are the very reason they felt the penance in 833 needed to be
so necessary, urgent, and precise. Rather than having gained pardon for his
sins through those earlier attempts at penance, explained the bishops, Louis
had only provided further evidence of the scriptural truth that "dissemblers
and crafty men prove the wrath of God" (Job 36:13). Similar to what Louis'
biographer Thegan would insist a few years later, the bishops here discerned
in Louis the likeness of Job. Yet, in their view, this resemblance was due less
to his renowned patience, equanimity, and faith than to his arrogance—of
repeatedly trying to uphold his false humility before an all-knowing God.

As they were well aware, by invoking this passage from the book of Job, the bishops were also assuming for themselves the righteous role of Eliu, rebuking Job/Louis against any further such attempts to provoke the Almighty.

The Efficacy of Doctrinal Performance

Yet, even if Louis had previously performed penance for his sins disingenuously, as the bishops claimed, why had his contrived exterior expression of humility not worked to actuate the ritual and reshape his inner iniquitous state? What had gone wrong with those earlier attempts, whose failure consequently made necessary the exceedingly formal, manifestly "doctrinal" performance of a public penance in 833? One explanation for Louis' initial failures at penance is implied by the bishops' repeated emphasis in 833 upon their meticulous attention to doctrine: recall that Louis had requested a mutual reconciliation with his sons, as they pointed out, "in accordance with Christian doctrine," and that the bishops had drawn up their written record of the events "in accordance with ecclesiastical custom." Such scrupulousness on the part of the bishops is usually viewed by modern interpreters with suspicion, being understood as nothing more than an exaggerated, transparent attempt to justify and underscore the legitimacy of what the bishops knew to be an odious act.[147] But there is another way to interpret their outspoken insistence about the careful observance of doctrine and protocol at the ritual: as a method of ensuring that, unlike the previous, abortive attempts that had been marred or compromised, the present penance had rather been in all ways properly, and thus effectively, carried out.[148] From this perspective, the problem with Louis' earlier efforts at penance appears to have stemmed from the fact that they were not undertaken with due rigor and care. As the bishops stressed, Louis' unwillingness at those occasions was perceptible even to the common observer; "everyone" had been aware of Louis' duplicity both in 822 and in 830. Consequently, if it had been obvious from Louis' demeanor that he was insincere, then one could hardly expect his inner state to have been remedied by such an inept enactment of penitential humility.[149] The sacred rite had not been properly performed; thus Louis had not been suitably conditioned to approach God for forgiveness. At the penance in Soissons, however, the bishops believed that the rigorous adherence to doctrine would solve this problem and allow the former emperor to redeem both his soul and the realm he had placed in jeopardy. That such adherence would also eliminate potential ambiguities or loopholes by which the ritual might later be called into question only further reflected the propriety and efficacy of the solemn act.

Negligence and Fitting Rebuke

After listening to the bishops' Jobian admonition about the terrible, ineluctable consequences of dissimulation, Louis confessed to his particular sins. This confession, however, prompted yet another admonition from the bishops. Having carefully tailored it to suit his personal failings, the bishops scolded Louis both in speech and writing with what they called "fitting rebuke." Here at last is the completion of the bishops' partial quotation of Paul's command to "reprove" and "entreat" that appeared in the preamble of the account. When one recalls that Louis' confession was described by the bishops as characterized above all by the former emperor's admission of negligence and that the bishops conceived of the event they were describing in the Benedictine terms of obedience and correction, then the specific identification of their rebuke (*increpatio*) as "fitting," "deserving," or "worthy" is telling indeed. After all, negligence—as Benedict's Rule stipulates—was to be countered with Pauline rebuke.[150] The nature and degree of correction had to suit and be commensurate with the nature and degree of the infraction. As a contemporary Carolingian exegete remarked, "I believe that no clearer explanation of that saying by the Apostle [namely, 'Rebuke!' (2 Tim. 4:2)] can be found than that given by the Blessed Benedict [when he said], 'We admonish [the abbot] to rebuke and punish the negligent and stubborn.' "[151] Ironically, even Louis himself had once enjoined his servants to abide by the same Benedictine mandate by which he was now being disciplined: the first thing the *missi* should enquire when inspecting the condition of a realm, he had decreed at an assembly in 829, was "how those ruling the populace have attended to their charge (*ministerium*), so that we may know who, by virtue of their proper activity, are worthy of being excused. But those who, on account of their negligence (*negligentiae*), are deserving of correction and rebuke (*increpatio*) should in all ways be made evident to us."[152]

Unfortunately, all that remain of this exigent, corrective rebuke in the extant sources are general and vague references to its application, such as that by Louis quoted above, allowing little insight into either the manner in which the Pauline/Benedictine charge was executed or even the form that it took. For example, Charlemagne's cousin Wala, the abbot of Corbie and leading member of the rebellion, is known to have written a little book in 828 or 829 outlining the evils he believed were then arising within the realm. Reading it aloud "before the emperor, the senators, and all the prelates of the realm," Wala, we are told, not only informed them of "how evils were shooting up" and that all things were now "corrupted and disfigured," but he also enumerated for Louis and his courtiers "the duties of the various orders, one after another."[153] That Wala conspicuously associated the onset of the realm's current evils with the nature of each order's responsibilities suggests that he was attributing the widespread calamity to the prevalence of negligence. But because Wala's booklet of rebuke is lost to us, it is impossible to be sure.[154]

In the episcopal *Relatio*, on the other hand, the bishops provide a long and detailed qualification for their rebuke of Louis' negligence. Immediately following their formal tongue-lashing of the prospective penitent, they handed Louis a document (*cartula*) that contained a record of his sins for which he was being held responsible. The appearance of this list in the bishops' narrative at this precise moment was not fortuitous; here was the carefully written instrument of their corrective Pauline/Benedictine rebuke, coming hard on the heels of Louis' admission of negligence (recall that the bishops claimed to have rebuked him "both in speech and in writing"). Taking the charter in his hands—a document the nineteenth-century German playwright Karl Robe once called, as we saw in Chapter 3, "a poison for kings, that should still remain potent after a thousand years"—Louis read, or heard the bishops read, its contents aloud. The *Relatio* does not identify the reader.

The Episcopal Indictment

Summarized in the episcopal account as eight discrete chapters or entries— the *Relatio* itself supplies the (possibly interpolated) word *capitula* together with Roman numerals, and avows that the actual charter grasped by Louis contains all of what will follow in greater detail—the bishops' description of Louis' wrongs takes the form of a nightmarish annal of sin, as Roland Faulhaber observed more than half a century ago. Or rather, Faulhaber pointed out that the events it recounts are organized chronologically, moving from the early period of Louis' reign to his recent abandonment upon the Rotfeld.[155] However, given Paul Dutton's work on Carolingian dream narratives and the rise and influence of oneiric criticism in the ninth century, it is tempting to see the contents of the charter as something of a waking nightmare for Louis—a candid annal of sin after brazen sin, itself betraying the influence of earlier, indirect critiques of Louis' governance that had already been circulating for some time in the more circumspect form of dream and miracle narratives. Between the years 824 and 829, in addition to Wala's booklet of rebuke, there appeared no fewer than three "revelatory" accounts of Louis' poor kingship: a fantastic dream by an anonymous poor woman of Laon about various events between the years 814 and 824, including the first great crisis of Louis' reign; a dream by a blind monk about the Archangel Gabriel's special message for the emperor, dictated to the decrepit dreamer sequentially, in the form of a dozen or so mysterious "chapters"; and the harangue delivered at an exorcism by a learned, prolix demon in possession of a young peasant girl, disclosing the "true," historical reasons for the vast carnage and devastation he had been wreaking throughout the realm "for several years," he explained, "with eleven of my mates."[156] At least two of these accounts—those of the poor woman and the blind man—were said to have been brought to Louis' attention, though what effect they had on the emperor was difficult even for contemporaries to ascertain.[157] Similarly, in the mid-830s, Louis' wife, Judith, would learn of an oneiric history book, one dreamed by a loyal courtier that provided a far more comforting interpretation of current events—indeed, it may even have been an oneiric response to the damning history contained in the rebel bishops' indictment.[158] This is not the last we will hear of this ineffable history book or its inventive dreamer, Walafrid Strabo.

Confronted repeatedly with such lurid, fantastic narratives in the 820s, perhaps Louis thought the contents of the capitular charter of rebuke he held in his hands at Saint-Médard in 833 to be, if not strikingly similar to those earlier dream reports, then at least hauntingly familiar. What must be remembered, however, is that the bishops had ostensibly delivered their rebuke to Louis at Saint-Médard for a very specific reason—to correct his negligence, show him his iniquity, and save his soul thereby. This is the reason Agobard, in his affidavit of Louis' penance, referred to the bishops' indictment as a mirror; it was hoped that, by fixing his gaze upon its terrible contents, Louis would—as Agobard put it—recover his humility and contrition, recognize the sinfulness of his many misdeeds described in the charter, and thus become conscious of his own perilous, iniquitous condition.[159] Only then could he begin the long journey back to the faith and regain the prospect of salvation.[160] Thus, the bishops' indictment was no warped "prince's mirror" or *Fürstenspiegel*, those sanctioned texts intended to edify and shape the moral character of royal youth.[161] Neither was it the strident inner core of some dream text, stripped of its oneiric, delusory trappings and brought to the attention of the king in order to spark the reaction of desired reform. Nor was it another bill of wrongs, drawn up by Wala and his associates once again to urge discipline and correction. For the objective of the bishops' indictment was entirely different from the aims of those three genres of advisory literature that Louis had studied before but from which he had evidently learned so little.[162] To adopt an ancient metaphor of which the Carolingians were especially fond: if the *Fürstenspiegel* was designed to help plot the future course of the king (and, thus, the kingdom); dream criticism to correct his current, errant course by guidance supplied from the heavens; and Wala's "state-of-the-union" address to do much the same but by the terrestrial compass of tradition, experience, and dead reckoning, then the charter presented to Louis could be thought of as providing the penetrating, redemptive light of a beacon. In the spring of 833, shortly prior to the events upon the Rotfeld, Agobard, writing in defense of Pope Gregory IV, had employed similar language to warn Louis about the condition of his "ship" and the dangerous waters into which the emperor was sailing it. "Let your sublime prudence," begged Agobard,

> condescend to weigh these words of the Apostle: "In the last days perilous times will come" (2 Tim. 3:1). These perils the blessed Pope Gregory [the Great] had already deplored at a time when the situation was incomparably better than now, when he said: "I am so much tossed about by the waves of this world that I am unable to guide to port the old half-rotten ship whose governance the hidden plans of God have charged me with. Sometimes the waves beat on the bow; sometimes the foaming billows of the sea swell along the sides; sometimes the tempest blows against the stern; and amidst all this turmoil I see myself compelled sometimes to charge right down upon an obstacle, sometimes to tack and present the side of the ship to the menace of the waves. I sigh when I realize that as soon as my vigilance slackens, the bilge-water of vices will increase, and that, in the face of the storm that is raging, the rotten planks will sound the impending shipwreck." Alas! Alas! If the ship of the church and the planks from which it is made were already rotten then, in what state is it now?[163]

The charter of rebuke Louis now held in his hands was meant to supply him with diagnostic information about his present condition and heading.

Cast adrift in a sea of iniquity, alone amid a tempest, Louis might regain his bearings by means of the illuminating charter and begin to steer himself safely back on the course to salvation—but not by the same route, for he would no longer be taking the royal way. His was now the humble passage of a penitent.[164]

Chapter one of the bishops' indictment begins by referring back to the early years of Louis' reign and asserts that, even then, Louis had incurred the sin of sacrilege and murder. Commencing each of its subsequent three charges with the causal conjunction "*quod*," the entry first accuses Louis of having broken the solemn oath he had made to observe the grave admonition of his father, delivered by Charlemagne at Louis' coronation ceremony in 813. Because Louis, while standing before the altar, under divine invocation, and in front of priests and a great many others, had sworn at that time that he would always show peace both to his kindred and to the church, any transgression of this vow was consequently tantamount to sacrilege.[165] And transgress it he evidently had, for the entry then continues with the charge that Louis had thereafter rendered violence to his kinsmen (here perhaps referring to the forced enclaustration of his siblings during the palace "cleansing" in 814[166]) and, more specifically, that he had allowed his nephew King Bernard of Italy to be killed in 818, even though—as the indictment carefully points out—he could have freed him.[167] Finally, Louis' sacrilege was further compounded by his use thereafter of the heuristic practice of the "ordeal of the cross," namely, of holding one's arms outstretched to form the shape of a cross for a longer period than one's opponent. Louis allegedly employed this practice of divining truth in flagrant opposition to its prohibition sometime shortly after 817.[168] As the bishops' indictment notes, Louis had resorted to this banned method of adjudication—perhaps in a modified, though no less offensive form[169]—in order to avenge his indignation (*propter vindictam suae indignationis*).

To be sure, these were all extremely complex events, about which we know far too little. For instance, the veracity of the bishops' charge that Louis had contravened his own ban and employed the ordeal of the cross is difficult to determine due to the ambiguity of the contemporary sources.[170] The circumstances surrounding the revolt and subsequent death of Louis' nephew King Bernard of Italy are also largely uncertain. To take but one point of ambiguity: what influence should be ascribed to Louis' first wife, Ermengard, in the capture and murder of King Bernard? As two authors in the ninth century would later remark rather cryptically, Queen Ermengard had harbored animosity toward Bernard and, "unbeknownst to Louis," as one reported, had called him to the palace, only to have him blinded (from which wounds he would die shortly thereafter).[171] While modern scholars for the most part draw a causal link between Louis' formal dispensation of the empire in 817 in favor of his and Ermengard's three sons (the so-called *Ordinatio imperii*) and the dissatisfaction and revolt of Bernard (who allegedly felt stripped of his rightful inheritance by this dispensation), the bishops here make no such connection.[172] To them, the terrible events were sins that had resulted solely from Louis' negligence, which, it seems, predated the diabolical influence of either Judith or Bernard of Septimania. Louis had failed to observe his solemn promise to his father, allowed King Bernard to be killed, and was unmindful of his ban against the ordeal of the cross. Why the emperor was so angered that he chose to use the prohibited ritual is left unstated.

Chapter two of the charter continues the chronological record of Louis' sins, now charging him with having committed perjury. As an "author of scandal, disturber of the peace, and violator of oaths," Louis overturned the sworn treaty he had made with his sons (in 817), explain the bishops, a treaty that had been created by the resolution of the community and the consent of all his faithful men in order to ensure the peace and unity of the empire and the tranquility of the church. The former emperor had broken this salutary agreement on the basis of "unlawful authority" (*illicita potestas*), they then remark, a qualification that suggests not so much that Louis had actually tried to justify his breach of the solemn pact (a justification that is otherwise unattested) as it does the bishops' understanding and description of the treaty's violation in terms of notarial rhetoric. In fact, the phrase *illicita potestas* had often been used by Louis the Pious's own chancellery within legal instruments to characterize, in a formulaic manner, the temerity of those who would take authority into their own hands, without regard for law or consensus.[173]

After violating his earlier pact, continue the bishops, Louis then compelled his faithful men to swear another that was in opposition to the first treaty and oath. That the bishops describe Louis' *fideles* as having sworn only under duress was another way of saying that Louis' men had known the deed put before them was wrong. The implications of this cognizance, however, only become apparent with the bishops' following statement: that without doubt the true perjurer had been Louis. In the immediate, harsh light of Louis' certain guilt, the perjury extorted from his discerning *fideles* appears to pale in comparison. Unlike Louis, they had not been blind to the sacrilege of the act demanded of them. Nevertheless, their culpability for the transgression was soon made evident by its consequences: clearly the oath breaking had been displeasing to God, observe the bishops, because, after the collective violation, both Louis and his subjects no longer merited the blessing of peace, instead finding confusion and tumult their only rewards. Closing with another allusion to Gregory the Great's *Homilies on Ezekiel* (drawn once again specifically from the homily about showing the iniquitous man his iniquity), they explain that the ensuing "punishment of sin" (*poena peccati*)—that is, the resulting period of sin's giving birth to other pregnant sins that came of Louis' initial covetousness—had been nothing less than a judgment of God.[174]

Iniquity and the Fecundity of Sin

The characterization of the realm's condition in terms of Gregory the Great's concept of the self-perpetuating nature of sin is significant, for it provides a valuable clue about the otherwise implicit organizational principle guiding the capitular form of the bishops' record of rebuke. Apart from Roland Faulhaber's general observation that the contents of the indictment are organized chronologically, no other explanation for their arrangement has been offered. Why are Louis' various sins grouped into the eight distinct chapters as preserved by the account? Is there a unifying scheme unique to each chapter and/or one that is common to all of them? Gregory's notion of the fecundity of sin, which the bishops invoke at the end of Louis' second offense, satisfies these questions by suggesting the logic that influenced the author of the indictment, leading him to cluster events into separate chapters or "proofs" that each follow the narrative scheme of sin that engenders sin. In other words, the indictment appears to have been designed with several chronologically organized, distinct "genealogies" of sin in mind—accounts of Louis' major transgressions that display the sinful "offspring" they each yielded over the course of time.[175]

Thus, if we return to the first entry of the indictment, a kind of "familial" order can be observed within it, relating the events together into a short, discrete narrative or "lineage" of "kindred" offenses. By committing violence against his kinsmen, Louis broke his solemn promise to his father about their fair treatment. Thereafter (*postea*), explains the indictment, "on account of the avenging of his indignation," Louis demanded that some should undergo the ordeal of the cross—here was yet another sin, this one evidently begotten from a misguided attempt to vindicate himself of the previous homicide and perjury. Ordered to subdue his relatives, Louis' courtiers had carried out their charge only too well (at the urging of Queen Ermengard?), wounding King Bernard with a blow to his eyes that would soon prove fatal; thanks to an odd detail provided by Nithard a few years later, we even know the name of Bernard's murderer, a certain "Bertmund, governor of the province of Lyon."[176] Yet, as the indictment carefully states, men such as Bertmund were not to blame, for it was Louis who had negligently "allowed" Bernard to be slain, even though he could have freed him.[177] Despite the insistence by most of Louis' defenders that Bernard, as a "tyrant," only got what he deserved,[178] even Louis' loyal biographer Thegan would admit that the emperor "did not prohibit" (*non prohibuit*) his counselors from maiming Bernard. It was for this reason, continued Thegan, that, in accordance with the judgment of his bishops Louis had undertaken his unheralded penance in 822.[179] Perhaps it was also for this reason that Louis, indignant after learning of Bernard's unauthorized execution, had imposed the outlawed ordeal of the cross upon overzealous henchmen such as Bertmund in order to exercise his vengeance and anger, thereby committing his third sin (which was the progeny of his perjury, itself born of the initial violence against his kindred).[180] Jörg Jarnut's argument that the bishops were careful not to blame Louis directly for Bernard's murder because it was known that Lothar's mother, Queen Ermengard, had been partially responsible (and thus any such accusation would risk offending the new Emperor Lothar and his royal brothers) neglects to consider the mortal sin in its concatenate, narrative context, falling as it does in the first chapter of the indictment together with Louis' perjury and the violation of his own probative ban.[181] To the bishops, Louis' sin of reemploying the judgment of the cross was clearly related "by birth" to the sacrilege and negligence that had led to Bernard's murder.[182]

The remaining six chronological chapters of Louis' concatenate sins are organized in the same fashion, although they detail events that had occurred between the years 830 and 833. That the bulk of the charges against Louis fall in this brief period of Louis' "quasi-rule" only supports the claims made by the bishops that Louis had become a bad sovereign over the course of time, especially, it seems, after his feigned—and badly botched—attempt at penance in 830.

Chapter three of the indictment recalls Louis' military expedition of 830 into Brittany during the days of Lent. This expedition, explain the bishops—which was made in opposition to the Christian religion, contrary to Louis' own vow, and done without any public utility or specific necessity—was undertaken only because Louis had been deluded by the counsel of "wicked men," this being an oblique allusion to his new palace chamberlain Bernard of Septimania.[183] To make matters worse, Louis had ordered a general assembly to be held while the expedition was in such remote parts of the empire, even though it was Maundy Thursday (the Thursday before Easter), the time when the paschal sacraments "ought to be celebrated by all Christians."[184] All these wrongs—which Louis compelled his unwilling subjects to commit "inasmuch as he could"—had the pernicious effects, charged the bishops, of inciting the people to great murmuring, keeping the priests from their divinely ordained duties, and inflicting the heaviest burden upon the poor.

In chapter four, the bishops catalog Louis' numerous sins against his followers, which he committed in the wake of the ill-advised expedition to Brittany. Several of Louis' *fideles*, out of their concern for Louis' and his sons' salvation, and for the restoration of the tottering realm,[185] had come to the emperor in all humility and provided him with information they had discovered about the plots being prepared by his enemies. Their reward, explain the bishops, had been nothing but injury, dispossession, and exile—all this being another indirect allusion to Bernard of Septimania, his murderous plot, and the effects of the enchantment that blinded Louis to the evil surrounding him. Those who had been absent from this ad hoc tribunal, one that operated contrary to every law, both human and divine, Louis simply sentenced to death. Moreover, the judges in his service had certainly been led into rendering false judgment: as the bishops point out, priests and monks at the trial had been handed a predetermined verdict, while those ecclesiastics who were absent, like their lay counterparts, were condemned to death. For all these summary judgments made against divine and canonical authority, reasoned the bishops, Louis had incurred the sin of murder, and thus stood forth as a violator of divine and human laws.[186]

Chapter five focuses on the sin of perjury, alluding to the oaths sworn again to Louis by his repentant sons and followers at the tribunal described in the charter's previous chapter. Various oaths, which were contradictory and pernicious, assured the bishops, had been sworn unreasonably (*irrationabiliter*) by Louis' sons and the people in the wake of the unsuccessful rebellion of 830, all at Louis' order and command. As a result, the people entrusted to him suffered the stain of sin themselves. Yet it was clear that Louis had been the one who in fact suffered the sin of perjury, since the fraudulent oaths were justly turned back upon their author, who compelled them to have been sworn in the first place. What was more, the "purgation of the woman"—here an allusion to Judith and her ritual reinstatement in February 831[187]—unjust judgments, false testimonies, and outright perjuries had all been perpetrated with Louis' permission and in his presence. In an aside, the bishops note that, with respect to these crimes, Louis himself "knows how much he has offended God."[188]

Chapter six details the suffering born from the many expeditions by Louis within the realm entrusted to him, which he made "not only needlessly, but also injuriously, without counsel and utility," presumably during the campaigns mustered in late 832/33.[189] As the bishops recalled, a whole host of "almost unheard-of" disgraces had been perpetrated against the Christian populace during these expeditions, including murder, perjury, sacrilege, adultery, rape, and arson, committed within churches and across the empire. All these wrongs were also turned back upon their author, explained the bishops, just like the fraudulent oaths they had mentioned before.

Chapter seven recalls the reckless deeds undertaken by Louis during the troubles with his sons between 831 and 833. First, the emperor had divided his empire rashly and in accordance with nothing but his own liking—a division, note the bishops, that was thus made "in opposition to the common peace and the well-being of the entire empire."[190] Following this sin, Louis then compelled the entire populace to swear yet another oath, which bound them to act against his sons as though they were his enemies.[191] What was worse, explain the bishops, this compurgation had been altogether unnecessary, for Louis, in their view, could have appeased his sons if he had wished through both his paternal authority and the counsel of his faithful men.

Finally, conclude the bishops in their eighth chapter, all these evils and shameful deeds—committed by Louis as a result of his "negligence and heedlessness" (*negligentia et improvidentia*)—had led to both the perdition of the realm and the disgrace of the king. Yet, in addition to all this wretchedness, Louis had attempted to achieve the "pinnacle of woes" (*cumulus miseriarum*) by most recently assembling the populace under his dominion for the sole purpose of its mutual destruction (an expression used verbatim by the bishops earlier in the *Relatio*).[192] This deed was all the more execrable, noted the bishops in their interpretation of the recent events upon the Rotfeld, since Louis ought to have been a leader working for the welfare and peace of his people. Miraculously, the imminent massacre upon the Rotfeld had not come to pass, for divine grace decided to take pity on the suffering populace, bringing about their collective salvation in a way, marvel the bishops, "unheard-of, imperceptible, and which ought to be preached about in our time."[193]

Anxiety, Authority, and Overstatement

Following their capitular summary of Louis' indictment, the bishops observed that Louis made a confession, before God and his priests, that he had been the one responsible for all the wrongs that had just been enumerated. Declaring in tears that he had failed in all his duties, he then requested a public penance in order to render satisfaction to the church, which he had scandalized through his sins. Louis explained that, just as there had been scandal through his excessive negligence, likewise he now desired to set an example by undertaking a worthy penance. Handing over the record of his sins and confession to the priests "for future remembrance," Louis watched as they placed the document on the altar. Taking his cue, Louis then detached his sword-belt (*cingulum militiae*) and, following the bishops' lead, placed it upon the altar as well. In Agobard's affidavit, little is added to this account of the events, other than a description of Louis' restored state of mind. Louis had removed his weapons with his own hand, explained Agobard, and cast them to the foot of the altar. Possessing a remorseful mind, he accepted the sentence of a public penance, which was rendered through the imposition of the bishops' hands, together with the utterance of prayers and the singing of psalms.[194]

Like other aspects of Agobard's and the bishops' accounts, such as their interpretation of the Pauline imperatives and the related focus on negligence or the description of certain brethren as Louis' persistent coaxers and consolers, the representation of the ritual divestiture here closely resembles the language and guidelines provided by the Benedictine Rule—in this instance, with respect to the manner of receiving brethren into the monastic community.[195] Such affinities and fundamental similarities between the performance of penance and the adoption of the monastic life were recognized by many in the early Middle Ages, often leading the respective rites to be taken as "two of a kind."[196] In the rebels' accounts, the frequent allusions to the Benedictine Rule—indeed, the intertextual, a priori influence the Rule appears to have had on the accounts' overall form and content—suggest that the bishops at Saint-Médard also understood penance and monastic conversion in this way, a conflation that says something important about their hopes as well as their fears.[197]

At this point in their respective narratives, the affidavit of Agobard and the subsequent episcopal *Relatio* summarizing the events diverge (at least explicitly) on a crucial issue. Agobard's text merely states what had happened next at the ritual, a description once again conspicuously informed by the Benedictine terms of how an abbot should care for the excommunicated. Benedict, alluding to Luke 15:5, had commanded that an abbot should "imitate the loving example of the Good Shepherd who left the ninety-nine sheep in the mountains and went to look for the one sheep that had gone astray, on whose weakness he had such compassion that he deigned to place it on his own sacred shoulders and thus carry it back to the flock."[198] Agobard described the former emperor in like terms: "having removed his former clothes, and donning the clothes of a penitent, rejoicing and feeling assured, Louis asked that he be led back on the shoulders of the Most Pious Shepherd to the unity of the sheep that has been found and redeemed."[199]

The *Relatio*, on the other hand, not only notes the laying on of hands by the bishops, as well as Louis' exchange of his worldly clothes for a penitent's habit, but also explains, by quoting from a decretal of Pope Leo the Great (440–461), what all these symbolic acts should be understood to mean:

- Decretal of Pope Leo the Great (ca. 458/59)
  That no one may return to the secular military service after
  penance: It is altogether contrary to ecclesiastical rules to return
  to the secular military service after an act of penance, since the
  Apostle says: "No man, being a soldier to God, entangeleth himself
  with secular businesses" (2 Tim. 2:4). For he is not free from
  the snares of the Devil, who wishes to involve himself in secular
  military affairs.

  [Quod ad militiam saecularem post poenitentiam redire non debeat.
  Contrarium est omnino ecclesiasticis regulis post poenitentiae actionem
  redire ad militiam saecularem, cum Apostolus dicat: "Nemo militans
  Deo implicat se negotiis saecularibus." Unde non est liber a laqueis
  diaboli, qui se militia mundana voluerit implicare.][200]

- Leo's Decretal, as Quoted in the *Relatio* of Louis' Public Penance in 833
  . . . so that, after such and so great a penance, no one may ever
  return to the secular military service.

[. . . ut post tantam talemque poenitentiam, nemo ultra ad militiam secularem redeat.][201]

Typically, this statement in the bishops' account is taken by scholars to be, as Karl Leyser once put it, the one "which matters."[202] Long ago, Léon Levillain argued that it should be understood in accordance with the old title given to the bishops' account (by Pierre Pithou) of *exauctoratio*, or deposition. As he pointed out, the bishops' key statement parallels an article in Roman law that names as "deposed" one who has had his insignia of military rank ritually removed, thereby leaving him to be counted among the disgraced.[203] Recent studies, however, have looked to the bishops' frank, decisive statement for evidence to support broader claims: for some, it reveals the full extent to which public penance was considered "an acceptable and adroit method" for barring Louis' return to the *militia saecularis*,[204] while for others, it is a conspicuous benchmark by which to gauge and understand the changing relationship between lay and religious status in the early Middle Ages.[205]

Given this constant attention paid to the bishops' definitive statement, which is probably the part of the *Relatio* cited most frequently by scholars, it is surprising that so few have commented on it with respect to its capacity as a quotation—that is, as a self-conscious allusion to canon law, made to lend meaning, legitimacy, and authority to Louis' penance.[206] For it is this self-consciousness on the part of the bishops, this feeling of the need to explain and make explicit the consequences of a relatively common ritual—much like their feeling the need to note Louis' cooperative congeniality or to explain the basis, purview, power, and demands of their episcopal authority at the beginning of the account—that has made the statement (and the opening definition of their ministry) long seem "odd."[207] Here, "odd" is usually used as a euphemism for "fraudulent"; as Louis Halphen argued forcefully over a century ago, such self-conscious overstatement seems to suggest a cover-up by the bishops, who, knowing that their actions were wrong and would be met with suspicion, attempted to forestall resistance to their bold coup by exaggerating the legitimacy of the penance and their power to make it binding. Their quotation of the papal decretal, with all its weight of ecclesiastical authority, antiquity, tradition, and law, would seem to support this view.

As I have suggested in the previous pages, however, such overcompensation by the bishops need not be taken as evidence of a cover-up feebly masking ulterior motives. Because of the exceptionally high status of the person undergoing penance, the bishops' frequent overstatement may rather suggest genuine anxiety about the extent of their authority and their competence to protect the common good. So unusual were the circumstances and so atypical the penitent that, while the bishops felt secure in the moral rectitude of their actions, they may have been deeply apprehensive about their actual ability to carry them out.[208] After all, there were few precedents for expediting the judgment of God against men of Louis' rank, apart from biblical examples and the memory of Ambrose. And even those precedents were from the distant past and involved the likes of prophets and saints. Hardly an arrogant, overweening episcopacy boldly testing the limits of its power,[209] the bishops supporting the rebellion in 833 may rather have been sincerely fearful of failing in their duty (given all its dire consequences in this world and the next), trepidation that led them to overcompensate and exaggerate in the expression not only of their penitential authority but also with respect to the consequences of the penance itself. With the disastrous effects of the subverted rituals of 822 and 830 more apparent than ever, failure this time around was not an option.

Ironically, it was not the rebels but Louis' own loyal cohort of bishops who were considered high-handed and arrogant at the time; recall the belligerent letter from Pope Gregory IV to Louis' bishops shortly before their meeting on the Rotfeld, in which he expressed astonishment at the unheard-of threats and demands they dared make to him, their spiritual father.[210] Paschasius would later remember that Gregory had at first been "greatly surprised and frightened" by the bishops' unprecedented contumacy, for they had claimed to have "ancient canons" that supported their defiant stance.[211] Armed with these canons, the bishops made it known, added the Astronomer, that "if the pope was coming to excommunicate, he would go away excommunicated."[212] Only when Wala and Paschasius supplied Gregory with canons of his own, decretals "established by the authority of the holy fathers and assembled in writing by his [papal] predecessors," did the pope recover his confidence.[213] His belligerent letter to Louis' recalcitrant bishops followed soon thereafter.[214]

Like the anxious pope's ready reliance on ancient canons, the bishops' general tendency toward overstatement and their quotation of the Leonine decretal in particular may suggest an insecurity and uneasiness about their ability to secure the meaning of Louis' penance. Put another way, the quotation "that, after such and so great a penance, no one may ever return to the secular military service" was the hoped-for outcome of the ritual.[215] As many scholars have observed, the consequences of undertaking penance in the early Middle Ages, like the consequences of monastic conversion, were by no means irrevocable and often quite arbitrary; upon his reinstatement in 830, for instance, Louis gave those of his supporters who had been tonsured by the rebellion the option "to remain thus or to return to their former condition as they wished."[216] For the bishops in 833, then, the question was whether they had the authority to make their "good deed" (as they called it earlier in the *Relatio*) a lasting one. To this end, it appears they adopted the rhetorical strategy of making the hoped-for, irrevocable consequences of the penance appear typical and, thus, unequivocal. As they repeatedly assured themselves and everyone else in the present and future, while Louis' great responsibilities (and, thus, his great punishments) were commensurate with his great rank, he was still beholden to the same basic rules and standards as any other Christian.[217] In his capacity as a penitent, the difference, they stressed, lay in terms of degree rather than kind—a difference even apparent in the quotation itself. Pope Leo's original decretal simply stated that, after penance, no one may return to the secular military service; the bishops in 833, however, added intensifying adjectives and adverbs to the quotation to underscore the fact that Louis' great rank, coupled with his great sins, called for an equally great penance, the consequences of which were strengthened and secured in proportion with its unusual scale: "after *such and so great* a penance, no one may *ever* return." There were differences in degree, but the governing principle—that penance meant forfeiture of the secular life—remained the same. In this way, the consequences of the exceptional penance were made to seem unexceptional.

Even the very use of the quotation suggested such typicality. Hardly the calculated result of some tireless, careful search by the rebels for an obscure legal pretext by which they might legitimately depose Louis,[218] this papal decretal by Leo, the one "that matters," is, in fact, featured prominently within many contemporary penitential handbooks, such as that by Halitgar, bishop of Cambrai, compiled sometime between 816 and 831 at the request of Archbishop Ebbo.[219] "What troubles me greatly," Ebbo had explained to Halitgar, is that "the judgments for penitents are so confused in the books of our priests and are so diverse and at odds with one another without the support of any authority that they cannot be distinguished because of the lack of agreement."[220] In response to such widespread confusion, Ebbo, the leader of the ritual in 833, determined to make certain that the meaning of the penance at Saint-Médard, like its later codification in the bishops' *Relatio*, was in accordance with ancient "ecclesiastical custom"—custom that collections like Halitgar's were meant to make manifest.[221] Unlike the attempts in 822 and 830, this time Louis' penance had been canonically—thus, successfully—carried out. Recognizing the likelihood of confusion and error, the bishops invoked the papal decretal as the last of their proper, necessary measures to establish and affix a uniform, doctrinal meaning to the penance. Ebbo himself would later complain bitterly about just who was contributing to the confusion about such matters: "Clearly the modern authority of the palace has compelled the laity, both men and women, to assume the monastic habit of a penitent, only to allow them to return to their former secular status once peace has returned."[222] In stark contrast to this novel (and, thus, evil) practice, there had been nothing modern about the penance at Saint-Médard in 833. So far as Ebbo and the other rebel bishops were concerned, it was old, it was typical, it was binding, and thus it was right.[223]

Conclusions

Over the winding course of the textual analysis followed above, I have attempted to show why the traditional condemnation and neglect of the episcopal summary account of Louis' penance in 833 is unwarranted. While the *Relatio* purports to represent the events in suprahistorical terms, it actually provides a revealing snapshot of a specific "revivalist" strain of Carolingian episcopal ideology particular to its time and place. As we have seen, the rebel bishops carefully justified their involvement by using the materials of Ezekiel, Paul, Benedict, Ambrose, and Gregory the Great (himself the great promoter and popularizer of Benedict) to construct the edifice of a ministry both age-less and all-extensive.[224] The urgent demands of iniquity called for the use of their supreme powers of binding and loosing but only in accordance with their "most prudent temperance"; role models such as Gregory and Ambrose were invoked to point the way. Yet, the historical context in which such suprahistorical claims of authority and ministry were being pronounced reveals perhaps the greatest of the many great ironies characterizing Louis the Pious's reign: the particular "golden age" formulation of the rebel bishops' ministry was largely derived from a program of reform that Louis himself had fostered—and then allegedly forsaken "over the course of time." In Shakespeare's terms, one could say that, in 833, Louis was largely hoisted with his own petard. And as I have suggested, there is even the possibility that Louis himself might have agreed with this assessment.

That is, I have also argued that Louis' willingness to undergo penance, as reported by the episcopal *Relatio*, should not necessarily be taken as a sham and the result of coercion. Rather, Louis may have understood the bishops' harangues to perform penance in the same terms of the penances he had previously undertaken—as a ritual chastisement by which his errant rule might be corrected and made stronger. To the rebel bishops, however, Louis' penance in 833 was qualitatively different from those he had performed in the past; unlike his other, defective attempts, this time the rite was formally correct, effective, and, thus, salutary for the ailing realm. Such concern for ritual precision may even have carried over to the capitular indictment brought against him. Due to his iniquity, Louis had committed a number of sins, which begat more sins, and these begat still others. Perhaps the chapters of the indictment form an octad because of the equally eightfold nature of the cardinal sins: Louis' concatenate iniquity was numerologically consummate.[225] In the end, his "traditionally" performed penance amounted to nothing less than conversion and, thus, abdication. Certainly the bishops themselves underscored this transformation in status by their precise description of Louis' exchange of clothing—that Louis had given up his temporal clothes for the timeless hair shirt of a penitent. His dress symbolized the nature of his being; no longer a participant in a particular age, Louis had become a member of the order of penitents, one who was effectively dead to this world and could play no further part in it.[226]

If there is one sure fact amid all the inferences and hypotheses in the preceding pages, it is that the bishops' narrative survived the centuries and was re-copied; for all its traditional censure, the *Relatio* nevertheless appears to have remained of interest. But of what kind? Why? And for whom? We have seen that Walafrid Strabo and then Reginbert of Reichenau each had a hand in preserving the text, likely to incriminate the rebel bishops and to forestall any such deceptions in the future. That the *Relatio* was copied and transmitted without the names of the bishops who oversaw the penance at Saint-Médard, a list of signatories that the narrative itself says formed an integral part of the original document,[227] serves to support the inference of its having been preserved for generic, didactic purposes. What seems to have mattered was the general language, style, and form that such a "destructive fiction" could take, and not the historical specifics of its content, such as the identities of the attesters.

In the next chapter, we shall explore still other ninth-century accounts of 833, namely, those that would have little impact upon the memories of that year's events by later generations. Yet, although they are less vivid and dramatic than the influential narratives surveyed in Chapter 1, these accounts are no less valuable. Not only do they provide a useful foil by which to understand why narratives such as those by Thegan and the Astronomer would long be remembered, but they also shed light on the circumstances that gave contemporaries cause to remember the events of 833 and cause to forget. Perhaps there was more to the episcopal text's preservation and the omission of its signatories' names than first appears. For Ebbo would not be silenced. Which is precisely what had worried Thegan—and, with Ebbo's return in 840, what worried Walafrid Strabo all the more.

CHAPTER 5

Forgotten Memories

There seldom is any simple truth in treason.
　　　—*Carl Van Doren,* Secret History of the American Revolution

Just as an oar appears bent and broken to the ignorant when seen in
water, and a man's fingers seem much shorter when under water, or
rather, they seem to have been cut shorter so that they appear nearly
all the same length, as though having been mutilated—a phenomenon
the inexperienced can test in the bath—so verisimilitude has very often
deceived and deceives those who are careless. . . .
　　　—*Gottschalk of Orbais,* De "in" praepositione explanatio

APART FROM THE contemporary narrative accounts of the six writers surveyed in Chapter 1 and the justificatory manifestos penned by the rebel bishops examined in Chapter 4, there remain only a handful of ninth-century
authors who deemed the events of 833 worthy of note. Of these remaining
narratives—polemics written chiefly by the participants in the great controversy dogging the scapegoat of the rebellion, Ebbo of Reims—none would
have a significant impact upon later chroniclers and historians, and consequently upon the shape of the predominant and, as we have seen, largely
loyalist narrative.[1] Yet, despite their lackluster appeal, these same authors'
accounts reveal an understanding of Louis' troubles with his sons in terms
that, if not explicitly tragic or comic, were still highly fraught. The primary difference lay in the new concerns influencing—and in some cases,

TABLE 3. TEXTS DETAILING AND DISPUTING ARCHBISHOP EBBO'S LOSS OF THE SEE OF
REIMS IN 835 AND 841 (**BOLDFACE**)

Texts	Key Events
	June 829, Reform council of Paris
	August 829, Louis the Pious redivides the empire
Agobard of Lyon, *De divisione imperii*	
	April 830, First rebellion of Lothar, Pippin, and Louis the German
	February 831, Louis the Pious redivides the empire
	September 832, Louis the Pious redivides the empire
Agobard of Lyon, *De privilegio apostolicae sedis* Pope Gregory IV, *Epistola* Agobard of Lyon, *Liber apologeticus* I	
	June 833, Louis the Pious is abandoned on the Rotfeld
Agobard of Lyon, *Liber apologeticus* II	
	October 833, Louis the Pious undertakes penance
Agobard of Lyon, *Cartula Relatio episcoporum*	
	March 834, Louis the Pious is restored at Saint-Denis
	February 835, Louis the Pious is re-crowned at Metz
Ebbo of Reims, *Resignatio*	February 835, Ebbo resigns as archbishop
Annales Bertiniani Thegan, *Gesta Hludowici imperatoris*	
	June 840, Louis the Pious dies
	August 840, Ebbo is reinstated as archbishop of Reims
Walafrid Strabo, *Prologus* to Thegan, *GH* Astronomer, *Vita Hludowici imperatoris*	June 841, Battle of Fontenoy

	July 841, Ebbo flees Reims
Ebbo of Reims, *Apologetici*	
Nithard, *Historiae*	
	August 843, Treaty of Verdun
	844, Ebbo is heard and condemned by Pope Sergius II
	April 845, Hincmar is appointed bishop of Reims
	845, Ebbo is appointed bishop of Hildesheim
Lothar, *Epistola*	
Ebbo of Reims (?), *Epistola spuria*	
	March 851, Ebbo dies
Synod of Soissons, *Acta*	April 853, Synod of Soissons
Paschasius Radbertus, *Epitaphium Arsenii*	
Clerics of Reims, *Narratio*	
Hincmar of Reims, *Epistolae*	
Synod of Troyes, *Acta*	October–November 867, Synod of Troyes
Charles the Bald, *Epistola*	
Pope Hadrian II, *Epistolae*	
Hincmar of Reims, *Visio Bernoldi*	
	Beginning of the tenth century
Odilo of Soissons, *Translatio Sancti Sebastiani*	

influenced by—their accounts. Within a generation or two of the events, Louis' abandonment and penance had become conflated and established as an infamous—though by no means unequivocal—point of reference in popular memory, an *exemplum* to be mustered in support of an argument rather than a divine judgment itself the issue of dispute. The battleground of meaning may have shifted away from the Rotfeld and Saint-Médard, but these *lieux de mémoire* remained crucial support stations for later hermeneutic struggles.

What prompted by far the most frequent recall of 833 was the bitter controversy, spanning the 840s to the 860s, over the legitimacy of the episcopal ministry of Ebbo of Reims (Table 3). Encloistered in 835 by Louis after duly resigning his office, Ebbo all but disappears from the historical record until

840.[2] What little the sources from this intervening period do tell us about him, however, is worth reviewing, for it provides the context for the explosive dispute sparked by Ebbo's brief reinstatement as archbishop of Reims in 840/41, an ephemeral return that would instigate the repeated polemical remembrance of 833 over the course of the ninth century.[3]

The Case of Ebbo of Reims

According to the narrative set down in the first part of the Annals of Saint-Bertin (by an anonymous author loyal to Louis), Archbishop Ebbo stood out among all the rebels as a "kindler of false charges" against the emperor.[4] Cast as the archvillain of the events, he was—unlike Louis' ultimately contrite children—afforded little sympathy at the tale's end, falling as he does outside the scriptural, honorable father/spiteful son plot followed by the annalist. Whether Ebbo was assigned his principal role because he was the only prominent member of the rebellion to have been captured[5] or because Louis' penance at Saint-Médard had taken place within Ebbo's diocese, making him the de facto minister of the ritual[6] or because Ebbo really was the chief architect of the uprising is impossible to tell.[7] What is clear is his part in the annalist's colorful story. Ebbo served as an emblem of iniquity—a "standard bearer," wrote the annalist—whose narrative function was a foil, setting in bold relief by his ruin not only the triumphant equity synonymous with Louis' rule but also the equity of those ecclesiastics now acting on Louis' behalf against Ebbo—ecclesiastics whose loyalty to the old emperor might otherwise still be in doubt.[8]

Thus the annalist's focus lands on Ebbo only to resolve the drama on a celebratory note, with the didactic apologue of the bishop's fall. After Louis was freed from his captors—thanks to his remorseful sons Louis the German and Pippin—he effected a reconciliation with Lothar late in 834.[9] Louis is next found in the annal at a remarkable ceremony, alternately taking place at Metz and his nearby palace at Thionville, in February 835. There were two items on the agenda: first, a formal reinvestment of Louis with his crown before the altar, effectively counteracting and negating Louis' divestiture at Saint-Médard through a careful inversion of that earlier ritual; second, the resignation of Ebbo from his ecclesiastical office. As we shall return to the first item in detail in the next chapter, it is sufficient to note here that the various counteractions at Louis' restoration included not only his formal reinvestiture but also the production of documentation that mirrored, superseded, and thereby invalidated the legal instruments produced for the ritual in 833. There was even a singular indictment drawn up—like the *cartula* held by Louis in 833—that testified to the crimes of the leading malefactor, Archbishop Ebbo of Reims.[10]

In the annalist's account, Ebbo's resignation in 835 had required two steps. First, after Louis' reinvestment with his regalia at Metz, the "correct" narrative summary of the recent events was read aloud "publicly, to all who were present." Ebbo then "ascended a high place in that same church," explained the annalist, "and voluntarily confessed before everyone that the emperor had been unjustly deposed; that everything done against him had been iniquitously accomplished and plotted contrary to the course of complete equity; and that afterwards the emperor had been deservedly, justly, and worthily established again on his own throne of empire."[11] Following the proceedings, the assembly moved to the emperor's palace at Thionville. After confessing to a capital crime at a plenary session of the synod, Ebbo then "proclaimed his unworthiness of so great an office as that of bishop, and confirmed this in his own writing."[12] The annalist concluded his account by noting that Ebbo resigned in accordance with the consent of all. The other bishops were only too eager to voice their approval.

The narratives of Louis' biographers Thegan and the Astronomer add only a few details to this loyalist account of Ebbo's resignation. As we have seen, to Thegan, Ebbo epitomized the execrable practice of raising men of humble birth to positions of noble status within the church, an error he hoped his work would make clear to the emperor. After recounting Louis' release by Lothar at Saint-Denis in 834, Thegan remarks that the craven Ebbo immediately took flight.[13] Soon captured and imprisoned, "the most vile peasant" Ebbo was made to appear at Louis' palace in 835 where, in quick succession, he, at the urging of other bishops, admitted that he was no longer fit for his office and was thereupon "completely dismissed." In Thegan's estimation, this lenient punishment resulted from the other bishops' fear that, if they moved more firmly against him, Ebbo would become their betrayer (*proditor*) and testify to their complicity in the rebellion.[14] Concluding his remarks about Ebbo by suddenly switching to the present tense, Thegan laments that "there is still a need to correct this matter completely" because Ebbo's contrite abdication was clearly nothing more "than a show of false piety under the pretext of religion."[15] In other words, Ebbo's seemingly pious confession and magnanimous resignation were shrewd—and deplorably successful—contrivances; what was required, Thegan insisted, was the rendering of a just sentence upon Ebbo in accordance with the will of the holy fathers. For how could other such abominations be eliminated, Thegan implies, when their very quintessence in the form of Ebbo was still able to find such favorable treatment?[16]

The Astronomer notes less fervently that in 835 Louis had "made a complaint" at Thionville "against certain bishops involved in his deposition."[17] But of those he named, only Ebbo was present. When asked by Louis to give a reason for his actions, Ebbo himself complained that he alone was being intimidated, while others who had been in attendance were being ignored. At this point, some bishops at the assembly stepped forward to plead that those events had demanded their presence and that they had therefore taken part unwillingly and in all innocence. Hearing these words, explains the Astronomer, Ebbo became "sorely vexed" and sought counsel from other bishops. Shortly after this mysterious, unrecorded colloquy, Ebbo announced his unworthiness of the priesthood and abjured the privileges of his office. Having confirmed and subscribed the statement himself, he handed his confession to the bishops who duly remitted it to the emperor.[18]

Ebbo's Confession

Although none of the loyalists' texts formally endorsing Louis' reinvestiture in 835 have survived, the text of Ebbo's confession and resignation, mentioned in the reports of the annalist and two biographers, is extant in no fewer than nine manuscript witnesses, several even dating from the ninth century.[19] Characterizing himself as an "unworthy bishop," Ebbo begins his statement by acknowledging his awareness of both his mortal fragility and the gravity of his sins and expresses his desire to make a confession so that he might become worthy of penance and thereby merit a remedy for his ailing soul. Identifying his witnesses and confessors, namely, Archbishop Aiulf of Bourges and Bishops Badurad of Paderborn and Modoin of Autun, Ebbo underscores the fact that he had secretly confessed his sins to them and presently wishes to resign from his episcopal office. He recommends that another should be consecrated to serve in his stead, one "who can worthily preside over and be useful to the church, which I, an unworthy man, presided over until now." Closing with the preclusion that he was renouncing future claims to his office or appeals "by means of canonical authority," he signed the document in his new capacity as "I, Ebbo, formerly a bishop" (*quondam episcopus*).[20]

While Ebbo's resignation was reproduced by a number of contemporary authors within the body of their own texts (including some by Ebbo himself), several manuscript witnesses suggest that it had circulated initially as part of a booklet (*libellus*), one that authenticated Ebbo's signed confession by appending to its text (and thereby framing it) the official interpretation and endorsement of the many bishops who presided over the assembly at which it was delivered. According to this interpretive episcopal text, dictated by Bishop Jonas of Orléans to the notary Helias (the future bishop of Chartres), Ebbo's witnesses and confessors attested vociferously to the assembly that Ebbo had confessed his "particular crimes" to them and that he was henceforth banned from his pontifical office and the episcopal ministry. After rehearsing Ebbo's resignation again, the eight archbishops and thirty-five bishops each confirmed with their signature his irrevocable forfeiture of office, his vow to abstain from preaching, and his professed intention to regain God's favor through penance.[21]

The Enemy Within

If we pause to review the various reports of Ebbo's resignation, several impressions about the events of 833 can be gleaned. The accounts of the loyalists together with the public statement read aloud by the repentant Ebbo at Metz characterize the deeds of Louis' abandonment and divestiture as having been shameful, even capital, "crimes." A brief declaration, made at a general assembly of the realm's bishops at Aachen in February 836, would be more specific: it was now clear, they there decreed, that the transgressions of ecclesiastics, the perversion and infidelity of noblemen, and the improbity of Louis' sons had all been to blame for that "unheard-of crime"—one that had shaken the very foundations of sincerity and integrity.[22]

Moreover, both of Louis' biographers intimate that, although Ebbo had resigned, there was concern among Louis' supporters regarding the degree of complicity of those still in their ranks. Thegan, for instance, was certain that the conspicuous silence of the assembled bishops at Ebbo's resignation, a reticence that contributed to Ebbo's light punishment, had been due to the bishops' anxiety that Ebbo might otherwise divulge their part in the rebellion. To Thegan, it was the bishops' very silence that had in fact betrayed them.

The Astronomer's account is at once more circumspect and more damning, for it hints that Ebbo's "show of false piety" had actually been devised at the assembly itself—at the discreet urging of some of the recreant bishops. After his complaint about being singled out was rebutted by certain bishops who claimed that their duties had demanded their participation in Louis' penance, Ebbo sought counsel from other bishops in attendance. Soon thereafter he was ready with his confession and resignation. What the Astronomer is suggesting by this particular narrative sequence is that a deal had been struck: Ebbo would confess, take the fall himself, and not expose his co-conspirators, provided they would not press for punishment more severe than his resignation and performance of penance.[23] With this turn of events, perhaps the Astronomer was reminded of the proverb used sardonically to describe the solidarity of bishops: "a crow does not peck out the eye of another crow."[24]

Despite Ebbo's admission of guilt and signed forfeiture of office in 835, feelings of resentment still ran high about those who had disgracefully swayed with the political winds in 833/34. Ebbo had hardly been part of some "lunatic fringe." Indeed, at the council of Aachen in 836, the bishops themselves made a general confession that, "due to fear, cupidity, and various other kinds of inducement," they had "for the most part and in many ways greatly erred and eschewed [their] ministry" in 833. They acknowledged that closure could not be gained on the events—"they in no way seem to us complete and capable of being brought to a necessary conclusion," they explained—unless the honor of the church were restored and the (recently disgraced) authority of the bishops was both renewed and strengthened.[25] Here, in fact, was the objective of the council of Aachen: to make manifest a new, ecumenical plan for such "proper"—which was tantamount to fiercely loyal—episcopal conduct. Perhaps this is the reason the names of the bishops who had signed the episcopal *Relatio* of Louis' penance in 833 are conspicuously absent from the manuscripts that preserve it. A loyalist editor wished to save the text but not to incriminate its signatories, many of whom had since returned to their office and desired to bury an embarrassing past. As the bishops stressed at the council of Aachen, the emperor should rest assured that henceforth there were no enemies residing in their midst.[26]

Ebbo's Restoration and Expulsion

Even if attention had shifted from the scapegoat to his accomplices still lurking within the realm, Ebbo was not entirely forgotten. Shortly after his capture
in 834, rumors began to circulate among the loyalists that Lothar was seeking
to locate Ebbo and have him delivered to Italy "for the purpose of [causing]
new disturbances"; consequently, Louis ordered Ebbo to be shut away in the
monastery of Fulda, northeast of Mainz.[27] After being released to stand trial
in Thionville and Metz (where he confessed and resigned from office), the
former archbishop was returned to Fulda to fulfill his vow to perform penance.[28] But he was not to remain there for long. Soon transferred—for reasons unknown—to the care of Bishop Frechulf of Lisieux, Ebbo eventually
came into the custody of Boso, abbot of Fleury, who delivered him to Lothar
sometime before August 840.[29] For at that time, Lothar restored Ebbo to the
see he believed he had only temporarily forsaken.

About a month after the death of Louis the Pious in June 840, Lothar
ignored his exile in Italy and, at his brothers' expense, marched north to
seize control of the territories in Francia he considered part of his rightful
inheritance. Holding court at the palace of Ingelheim, he convened an assembly in August for the purpose of restoring Ebbo to his former office as
archbishop of Reims.[30] Proudly dating the assembly "in the first year of his
return, having been made the successor of his father in Francia,"[31] terms
that proclaimed his right to the imperial succession, Lothar announced that,
by his munificence, he was returning the episcopal pallium to Ebbo at the
behest of the archbishop's many followers from the church of Reims. Ebbo,
who had lost his episcopal power on Lothar's behalf (*pro causa nostra*), had
fulfilled his promise of penitential humility, the new emperor proclaimed,
and was ready to resume the duties of his divine office. As Lothar explained,
in allusion to Ebbo's recent experience, the Gospel confirms that he who
humiliates himself will not be condemned but exalted (Luke 18:14).[32] No
fewer than five archbishops and fifteen bishops, including seven who had
witnessed Ebbo's resignation in 835, then attested to Lothar's right reasoning
and his generosity of restoring Ebbo to office.[33] By the sixth of December,
nine bishops of the ecclesiastical province met at Reims and unanimously
declared the validity of Ebbo's restoration[34]; nearly half had been attesters at
Ebbo's resignation in 835.[35]

Over the next several months, Ebbo would act in his full capacity as archbishop of Reims, an office whose responsibilities included the ordination of new clerics. Although the exact number is unknown, somewhere between ten to fifteen ordinations were made by the seemingly restored archbishop in the first half of 841.[36] Of all the many deeds of Ebbo's long, embattled career, these ordinations would prove to be the most controversial. Soon after the infamous battle of Fontenoy on June 25, 841, when the allied armies of Charles the Bald and Louis the German finally clashed with the forces of their brother Lothar and nephew Pippin, decimating the pride of the Frankish nobility in a single day of fratricidal slaughter, Lothar began his retreat from the territory he had briefly arrogated from Charles.[37] Bereft of Lothar's protection, the hapless archbishop now suddenly found himself behind enemy lines. Not counting on receiving clemency from Charles, Ebbo took flight from Reims once more, eventually finding his way back to Lothar's court.[38] Ebbo's instincts were indeed correct, for by December 841 Charles called an assembly at Bourges to declare both the lasting validity of Ebbo's resignation in 835 and the current vacancy of the episcopal see at Reims.[39] By implication, the ordinations made by Ebbo during his uncanonical restitution were thus deemed invalid, at least for the moment. A year earlier, Walafrid Strabo, Charles's longtime supporter, had heralded the dangers of Ebbo's restitution by editing the compilation of Thegan's biography of Louis and the episcopal *Relatio* of Louis' penance in 833, which together offered a vivid reminder of the lowborn archbishop's cunning and lasting guilt. Walafrid's remarks in the preface he appended to each text leave no doubt that, as far as Walafrid was concerned, Ebbo's return in 840 meant nothing but still further fraudulence and vice.[40]

Ebbo's Defense and Its Failure

For the next four years, Ebbo would vehemently seek redress for the loss of his see, issuing strident manifestos defending the integrity of his maligned ministry. These "apologies" are actually two recensions of the same basic text, which Ebbo first wrote in 842 (in a rather opaque, infelicitous style) and then seems to have revised and reissued sometime shortly thereafter.[41] While they are too lengthy and detailed to be given full treatment here, a few major points—especially with respect to Ebbo's conception of the events of 833—can be drawn from them.[42] In both apologies, Ebbo begins with a description of the realm's condition in the 830s. Although the "first period" (*prima tempora*) of Louis' reign, he explains in the earlier draft, had been a time of prosperity and resplendence, it was ultimately shattered by "calamity beyond measure." Ebbo then characterizes this havoc in terms of divine indignation, pointing out the similarities between the nature of the recent crises and Christ's words to the apostles that brother will deliver brother unto death, a father his children, and that children will rise up against their parents (Matt. 10:21). Certainly the effects of this divine wrath were felt everywhere, he observes: numerous bishops and ecclesiastics of various orders were exiled, while many noblemen were likewise driven from their homelands. Still others of the lay nobility were compelled to assume the monastic habit. Nevertheless, these tribulations had to a certain extent proved rewarding, he reasoned, for the penitent were tempered and strengthened, while the stubborn were made aware of the terrible judgment that ineluctably awaits them. In his final estimation, the vast desolation had been necessary since what prosperity had allowed to become corrupt, adversity had salutarily purged.[43]

In the revised version of the apology, Ebbo begins with the declaration that everyone in the empire knows beyond all doubt that innumerable evils had risen up in the present age because of the ubiquity of sin. Calamity had affected rich and poor alike, explained Ebbo; orphans and widows found no mercy, while murder and arson were committed with impunity; justice was rare, and even rarer were those who had any interest in the Christian peace or reverence for the houses of God. Returning to the narrative sequence of his first draft, Ebbo then notes that many noblemen and ecclesiastics had suffered exile or imprisonment and that this reign of misery was clearly foretold in scripture as the righteous consequence of loving the trifles of this world.[44]

Following this introduction in both apologies, Ebbo then places himself and his past actions squarely within the historical context he has established: of a realm rampant with well-deserved suffering and vainglorious sin. In this narrative, all traces of culpability for the troubles of the 830s have been blurred by Ebbo and attributed to the realm as a whole: he had been just one among a multitude of sinners, he maintains, generally responsible for incurring God's wrath. Nowhere is the revolt against Louis ever mentioned.

By framing his sin in such broad terms, Ebbo lays the perfect grounds for his argument against his persecutors. Anyone who claims that he had been deposed in 835 is surely incorrect, Ebbo insists, for he had freely offered his resignation for the good of the realm, but only until the troubles had passed; unlike most, Ebbo had taken the high road and spared the realm additional anguish by withdrawing from office to do penance.[45] Thus, after seven years of humble satisfaction, he was canonically entitled to be reinstated in his ministry, which is indeed what had happened at the councils of Ingelheim and Reims in 840, he explains.[46] The real crime, argues Ebbo, is that he had been driven away from his see shortly thereafter and falsely condemned, despite having sacrificed so much for the realm.

In other words, Ebbo's apologies countered the loyalist framing of two earlier texts associated with him—the episcopal *Relatio* and his own *Resignatio*—and sought to uphold three interrelated claims. First, Ebbo should still be considered the acting bishop of Reims, as per his legitimate reinstatement in August 840. This claim of legitimacy was valid because of the equal veracity of his second claim: his resignation in 835 had been a temporary renunciation made under difficult circumstances, not a deposition.[47] This was true, he argues, because nowhere in his signed statement, which he (selectively) reproduces in both apologies, does he confess to having committed a crime.[48] Here was Ebbo's third claim: his signed confession was being misinterpreted in order to slander him, for it was not a testament condemning him of a crime but a token both of his renunciation and his avowal to undertake penance. Yet, this third and fundamental claim itself rested upon the contention that Ebbo had merely been, like everyone else, a "sinner" in those once prosperous, now perilous times. The difference was that Ebbo possessed the discernment to know the proper course. In other words, Ebbo sublimates the events of 833 into a general period of iniquitous disorder—the nature of which was understood by "everyone"—while simultaneously casting himself as a righteous imitator of Christ and the apostles, one who sacrificed himself so that equity might be restored. Thus, not only was Ebbo still the legitimate holder of his see, but he had made an exemplary renunciation as well. He was deserving not of condemnation, implies his apologies, but of emulation and applause.

Unfortunately for Ebbo, his arguments never did him much good. Although it is unknown whether Ebbo presented or intended to present the apologies at any particular occasion, his fate after his flight from Reims in 841 upon the advance of Charles the Bald's forces demonstrates that few were convinced by his claims. In early 844, Ebbo, together with his co-conspirator and partner in exile Archbishop Bartholomew of Narbonne, joined a legation consisting of Lothar's eldest son Louis and Archbishop Drogo of Metz on its way to Rome for a meeting with newly elected Pope Sergius II.[49] Duly gaining an audience before the pope, Ebbo and Bartholomew pleaded their case and begged for reconciliation and restoration to their sees. Despite their efforts, however, the two exiled bishops were rewarded nothing but further condemnation and a papal demotion to lay status.[50] If this was the occasion for which Ebbo had prepared his apology, his elaborate arguments had been devised in vain.[51]

Making matters worse for Ebbo, in April 845 at an assembly in Beauvais, a monk named Hincmar (806–882) was promoted by Charles the Bald and established as the new archbishop of Reims, an action that, from Charles's perspective, at last filled the vacancy caused by Ebbo's deposition ten years earlier.[52] Here was the event that would stoke the debate for the next two decades, for now Ebbo had a serious rival for his see, a competitor who would stop at nothing to uphold the canonical validity of his own promotion. Even after Ebbo's death in 851, Hincmar would not rest his case, for the iniquity of Ebbo had, in his opinion, only begotten further iniquity; all ordinations made by Ebbo during his brief reinstatement in 840/41 at Reims were invalid, Hincmar would clamor again and again, since Ebbo himself had been reinstated fraudulently. To believe otherwise meant calling Hincmar's own ordination into question, implying that he had usurped the office of the absent incumbent Ebbo. Many years of Hincmar's long career would be spent embroiled in disputes over the canonical status of those clerics ostensibly ordained by Ebbo in 840/41, some of whom would come to acquire powerful, even royal, patrons. Yet, if their canonical validity meant the legitimacy of Ebbo's ministry, and thus the illegitimacy of Hincmar's own episcopal tenure, it also implied that Ebbo's resignation in 835 had been offered freely rather than levied as a punishment. Thus, one is returned to the basic position presupposed by Ebbo in his apologies: he had never taken part in any crime (such as conspiracy against the emperor) but had merely been one more sinner caught up in a divine flood of iniquity. In short, accepting the validity of Ebbo's ordinations ultimately came at the expense of forgetting the particular significance of 833.

The Year 833 and the Legacy of Ebbo's Career

To be sure, the vicious (and verbose) quarrels from 845 to 867, first between Archbishops Ebbo and Hincmar and then between the indefatigable Hincmar and Ebbo's numerous ordained disciples, are a vast topic, deserving a separate study all their own.[53] To take but one example, the most audacious and complex set of forgeries from the ninth century, dubbed by modern scholars the "Pseudo-Isidorian decretals," may have been composed by clergy in Reims who remained loyal to Ebbo and attempted to correct the wrong done to him by "collecting" and "organizing" (i.e., fabricating, interpolating, and manipulating) canonical decretals to suit their case.[54] For our purposes, however, it is the remembrance of 833 in the context of the debate between Ebbo and Hincmar that is of interest.

Following his dismissal by Pope Sergius II in 844, Ebbo undertook several other legations for Lothar until somehow incurring his disfavor.[55] Shortly thereafter, one finds Ebbo under the protection of Lothar's brother, Louis the German, as the newly installed archbishop of Hildesheim, an office he would hold until his death in 851.[56] Yet, even in this post, Ebbo never lost sight of his cherished see of Reims. Despite the failure of his apologies and his appeal to the pope, Ebbo (or perhaps his disciples at Reims) argued his case at least one last, desperate time. For he (or they) now dared to forge a letter in the name of Pope Gregory IV, stating—in language, often verbatim, from Ebbo's apologies—that Ebbo had been deposed unjustly and now had papal permission to remain as bishop of Hildesheim until such time as was safe for him to return to his rightful see at Reims.[57] The calamities suffered by everyone, stated "Gregory," were divine punishments provoked by sin; those who had humbled themselves, such as Ebbo, "ought therefore to be applauded, not condemned."[58] Here, the author elided yet again the events of 833.[59] Unfortunately, this letter seems to have done its author little good; an anonymous hand of the ninth century noted in the margin of the single manuscript preserving the text that the papal letter was manifestly false (*mendax*).[60]

Sometime between 847 and 849, Lothar also wrote a letter that focused on Ebbo, his legitimacy, and his role in the events of 833. Addressing it to Pope Leo IV, Lothar now endorsed the right of Hincmar rather than Ebbo to the Reims archbishopric.[61] Certainly this change in perspective suited Lothar's present aims at reconciliation with his brother Charles the Bald.[62] Ebbo, he explained, had earlier incurred the wrath of Louis the Pious on account of his involvement with "certain factions and their disputes." Such quarreling had taken place, he recalled, during that "time of most wretched discord, which had lasted for a long while between us and our father," a period of strife caused by the devil working "through his attendants."[63] Yet, there should be no doubt, assured Lothar, that Ebbo had eventually been brought before Louis and had thereupon utterly banished himself from office. Lothar even sent copies of this signal act from the Reims archive for the pope's inspection to eliminate any suspicion of its validity. While Lothar's "diabolic" explana-

tion absolved Louis of liability for the decline of the realm and equally ex-
culpated Lothar of responsibility for his past ignominy, the devil's advocacy,
which Agobard and the Astronomer had both discerned in the events of the
830s, did not extend to Ebbo.[64] In Lothar's opinion, the bishop's fall had been
his own doing. Once again, Ebbo was at a loss for defenders. Even the devil
refused to claim him.

As we have seen, Ebbo argued time and again that he was innocent
of any crime, for he had been just one participant in a massive display of
malfeasance brought about by the realm's decadence[65]; in this narrative,
Louis' abandonment and penance were forgotten. In 853, however, the recently deceased Ebbo (d. 851) would be officially condemned at a synod
in Soissons by Hincmar, who made certain that his own position as the
archbishop of Reims was made even more secure by also deposing the group
of clerics "illegitimately" ordained by Ebbo in 840/41.[66] In this context,
Ebbo's part in the events of 833 was recalled to demonstrate exactly why
his subsequent condemnation had been irrevocable and, thus, why his later
ordinations were invalid: the emperor, who had been "falsely incriminated"
and "unjustly deposed" from his imperial seat, explained the synod, had
also been subjected to a public penance by Ebbo. This was the reason Ebbo
had been brought, in accordance with the canons, to make his confession
and resignation in 835. If there should be any doubt about this,[67] offers
Bishop Theoderich of Cambrai (a signatory witness at Ebbo's deposition)
in a summary account of the events he presented to the synod, then one
should simply look in the church archive of Metz to find the very booklet
that Ebbo signed and presented to the emperor.[68]

In the 860s, the clerics writing in defense of both Ebbo and their own
dubious ordinations would be more specific than Theoderich, admitting that
Ebbo had indeed taken part in the events of 833 but only because the monastery of Saint-Médard lay within his diocese, requiring him to supervise all
proceedings there.[69] What was more, he had imposed a public penance upon
Louis, explained the clerics, at the urgings of the bishops and nobles of the
realm. Thus, Ebbo had been charged with an excessive, enduring offense for
no other reason than that he had piously fulfilled the demands of his office—
demands so impiously impressed upon him by his peers. In the clerics' opinion, they held no reason to suspect that their own ordinations by Ebbo were
invalid since, as far as they knew, the bishop had been restored canonically
by Lothar in 840. Rather, they felt that Hincmar had been unwarranted—
indeed, rather spiteful—in banning them from their ministry.[70]

The Truths of the Matter

In 867, the long debate over Ebbo and the validity of his ordinations finally ended in compromise, with the devil once again being held responsible for the contemptible behavior of Louis' sons in 833. At a general synod in Troyes, convened on October 25, Hincmar—having recently alienated himself from both Pope Nicholas I and his own sovereign, Charles the Bald—was now forced to swallow his pride and concede that Wulfad, a prominent cleric who numbered among Ebbo's contested ordinations (and who was presently a favorite courtier of Charles), was worthy of office.[71]

Although there was no doubt among the assembly that Ebbo had been an impostor in 840/41, it was decreed that his ordinations of the unwitting clerics should stand firm. To demonstrate the reasoning behind this decision, which the synod was sending off to the pope for his consideration, a detailed account of the controversial events (presumably dictated by Hincmar) was drawn up, beginning with Louis' misfortunes in 833. By a just judgment of God and the odious work of the devil, explains the synod, the sons of Louis, together with a party of wicked men and Pope Gregory IV, whom Lothar had brought with him under the pretext of peacemaking, had all met upon the Rotfeld and there driven Louis from power. They then led him under heavy guard to the city of Soissons. What happened next was unequivocal to the synod: to make it believable to the populace that Louis had been driven from the kingdom deservedly, certain criminal charges were trumped up (*conficere*) against him. On this basis, the pretext (*praetextus*) of a public penance was invoked so that some bishops, including Ebbo, could judge Louis and succeed in barring him from the church. At the first sign of resistance, however, Lothar had abandoned his father at Saint-Denis and fled in terror. Shortly thereafter, continued the synod, Ebbo learned of Lothar's reversal and quickly took cover, thinking that he might lay low until a more auspicious time for flight presented itself. Soon discovered by the emperor's men, however, Ebbo was taken in custody to the monastery of Fulda to await trial.

At the assembly in 835, after Louis had been restored by common consent, continued the account, Ebbo signed in his capacity as archbishop an individual booklet, in which he acknowledged that the emperor had been disgraced and insolently deprived of the kingdom without regard for justice or the canons.[72] After this booklet had been compiled with those signed by the other bishops in attendance, the assembly moved within the church of

Metz, where Ebbo publicly condemned himself. The assembly then relocated to the palace of Thionville, where Ebbo confessed that he had wrongly incriminated the emperor. By assailing Louis with false crimes, he explained, he had deposed him from the kingdom, taken away his arms, and—against all the rules of the church—excluded the emperor from Christian society, even though Louis had "neither confessed to nor been convicted of anything." Perceiving that Louis was growing angry at his confession, Ebbo begged the assembly to conduct the remainder of his trial away from the emperor's presence. After Louis' withdrawal, a colloquy among the bishops soon determined that, in order to avoid the performance of violent, vindictive punishment and maintain the dignity of the episcopal office, the best course lay in Ebbo's offering his abdication of his own accord (*sponte*). Reading aloud what had been confessed to them in secret, the bishops proclaimed that they were in agreement with Ebbo's decision to give up his episcopal ministry.

The account by the Troyes synod continues with a narrative about the remainder of Ebbo's difficult career, revealing that in 845—the tenth year since Ebbo had "departed" from the see of Reims—Hincmar had been installed in his place in accordance with the sacred canons and the consent of the people. Yet, ten years later, recalled the synod, Lothar had sent a letter to Pope Leo IV requesting his assistance in "resolving" the "dispute" over Ebbo's ejection, thereby making it seem as though (*quasi*) there were still disagreement in Reims over Hincmar's ordination in place of Ebbo.

Although it was now clear, explains the synod, that Lothar had sent this letter only to fan the conflict he had been waging at that time with his brother Charles, there has unfortunately remained an uncertainty about the status of ordinations involving the see of Reims. In the synod's opinion, with which it hoped the pope would be in agreement, Ebbo had been cast out and excommunicated from his see; Hincmar had been legitimately installed in his stead; and the ordinations performed by Ebbo in 841 should be considered valid since the prospective clerics were unaware that Ebbo's restitution had been illegitimate.[73] As Hincmar admitted a year earlier (866) in an annal he was keeping (as continuator of the Annals of Saint-Bertin), the ordination of Wulfad and his colleagues from Reims had been valid because their case closely followed the precedents set by Meletius and the Donatists, as adjudicated and canonized in the early days of the church.[74] The same conciliar doctrine had likewise provided the synod of Troyes with a sure guide for their present judgment.

In a fascinating twist of events in the debate over Ebbo and his ordinations, the narrative composed by the synod of Troyes in 867 only reached Pope Nicholas I by way of Charles the Bald, who sent with it his own lengthy narrative of the debate for the pope's consideration.[75] Hincmar would later insist that Charles had broken the seals of the synod's report, found its contents not to his liking, and consequently forwarded his own letter—one written "in opposition to Hincmar" because "Hincmar had not ended up by being silenced at that synod, as Charles had wished."[76] Charles, however, claimed that the pope had, in fact, asked him for a report concerning the case of Ebbo. He was merely complying with the pontiff's wish, setting down, as he put it, "the truth of the matter" (*veritas rei*). In a narrative nearly as long as the synod's report, Charles provided a selective, rehabilitative history of Ebbo's career to make clear to the pope that Wulfad, a favorite courtier of Charles, who numbered among Ebbo's contested ordinations, was worthy of his office. This was true not just because of canonical precedents but also because Ebbo had—contrary to the account given by the synod—been unlawfully deposed in 835.

Beginning with an account of the lowborn Ebbo's remarkable rise to high office through the merits of his intelligence and education, Charles noted that when, at the "instigation of the devil," the people had risen up unsuccessfully in revolt in 830, Ebbo had remained faithful to his great patron, Louis the Pious. In 833, however, Ebbo had been part of the large group of bishops who—both willingly and unwillingly—followed the fickle populace that was seduced by Lothar's exhortations and enticements into abandoning Louis. After Judith had been sent to Italy and the young Charles, "not yet ten years old, as though guilty of numerous crimes," had been confined to the monastery of Prüm, Louis was marched into the monastery of Saint-Médard and, despite having "neither confessed to nor been convicted of anything," was barred from taking communion with the faithful.[77] Soon rescued by his remorseful followers, recalled Charles, Louis captured Ebbo before he could take flight and had him led to the church of Metz where the terrified bishop professed that an inequitable judgment had been rendered against the emperor. Before allowing the proceedings to continue, however, the bishops in attendance spoke up and convinced Louis that, if he wished to try Ebbo correctly, then he should do so only in the absence of the laity. Meanwhile, explained Charles, Ebbo had enjoined a messenger (whom Charles remembered had been a certain hermit named Framegaud) to carry to the Empress Judith a special ring she had given him upon Charles' birth. Although it was primarily meant as keepsake, so that the holy man would always remember her child in his prayers, the ring was also a promise of her future assistance: if Ebbo were ever to meet with misfortune, he should send the ring to Judith. Consequently, upon receiving the ring, Judith earnestly begged both the assembly of bishops and her husband to show mercy to the pitiful Ebbo.[78] Here, it seems, was the reason for the surprising leniency shown toward Ebbo in 835 that would so upset Louis' biographer Thegan. For after hearing the appeals of his wife, Louis, together with the episcopal assembly, then decreed that Ebbo should not suffer any punishment greater than that prescribed for him within his own confession.

In Charles's remembrance of the events, the immediate issue of gaining papal approval of his valued courtier Wulfad's episcopal status—approval that would overrule any protests by Hincmar—certainly contributed to the form and content of his narrative. Charles himself made this concern explicit, telling the pope that he had provided the lengthy sketch of Ebbo's career so that—despite what the pope may have already heard about Ebbo (from the synod's, i.e., Hincmar's, report)—he might decide for himself whether such things had any bearing on the case of Bishop Wulfad's canonical validity. Consequently, in order to make Wulfad's ordination by Ebbo in 840/41 appear as legitimate as possible (and simultaneously make Hincmar seem intransigent in proportion), Charles characterized Ebbo as an archbishop who had been unjustly vilified. This point bears repeating: little more than three decades after his father's humiliation at the hands of the same bishop and without a hint of irony, Charles portrays Ebbo with great sympathy in his letter[79]—the devil had been to blame for the shameful actions of persons whom Charles otherwise recalled as having been respectful and kind (Lothar) or brilliant, reverent, and keen (Ebbo).[80] Ebbo had at first remained loyal to Louis in 830, until at last succumbing—along with most other bishops in the realm—to the diabolically sweetened blandishments of Lothar in 833. After his capture, the astute Ebbo relied on the succor of Charles's mother, the "glorious Empress" Judith, who did not hesitate to act on his behalf. As a result, Louis had levied the light sentence that Ebbo must abide by the terms of his confession; subsequently, recalled Charles, the emperor had records of these proceedings sent to Pope Gregory IV for his inspection and approval. Here, Charles pauses to explain that, although he knows the pope received these records and had sent his answer in return, it was presently unknown to him what the papal decision had been. But surely, admits Charles (echoing a point made by Ebbo years earlier in his apology), if the pope had agreed with Louis' judgment regarding Ebbo, then Louis would have chosen another person to fill the vacancy in the Reims bishopric. The fact that the see had remained vacant for years after Ebbo's resignation, therefore, must mean that the pope had, in fact, not been in agreement with Louis' decision and that Louis consequently left the see vacant for Ebbo's eventual return.[81] Charles then abruptly concludes his account of Ebbo's career with the archbishop's restitution by Lothar in 840.

While Charles's nearly apologetic tale of Ebbo and his role in the rebellion is certainly remarkable, even more so are the king's timely silences: nowhere in his narrative does he make mention of Hincmar's ordination in 845 as the new archbishop of Reims (which Charles himself had endorsed); nor does he speak of Ebbo's flight from Reims in 841 due to his recovery of that city from the forces of his brother Lothar; nor does he claim to know what the pope's response had been to Louis' judgment against Ebbo. Indeed, some modern scholars believe this alleged epistolary exchange between Louis and Gregory IV in 835 was nothing but an invention on the part of Charles, devised in order to suggest the early papal endorsement of Ebbo's legitimacy as archbishop of Reims, thereby making Wulfad's later ordination by that same archbishop appear all the more valid.[82] Unless witnesses of this correspondence between Louis and the pope come to light, however, such charges will always remain putative.

As we have seen, both the synod of Troyes and Charles agreed that what had happened in 833 was associated with the devil (although the synod had understood it first as a judgment of God; what it was a judgment *for*, however, was never specified). Where they part in their narratives is, first, in the degree of their interpretation of that year's events and, second, in the fate of Ebbo during his trial in 835. Whereas the synod of Troyes provided a deeply suspicious view of the rebellion, characterizing its deeds as duplicitous and part of a larger iniquitous stratagem, Charles remained silent, noting simply that the rebels had barred Louis from the church. Upon coming to Ebbo's trial, the synod reported that Ebbo had confessed both to his insolence and to the fraudulence of his charges against the emperor. Here was where the two accounts in 867 diverged widely, for in Charles's letter Ebbo had not been condemned but rescued by the Empress Judith and allowed to resign.

The narratives from the synod and Charles, with their differing emphases and silences, ultimately mattered little to the pope. In November 867, Nicholas I died, and his successor Pope Hadrian II received the pair of accounts forwarded by Charles. Determined to settle the festering debate once and for all, Hadrian responded to both parties with letters of his own, explaining that he happily sanctioned their joint decision to allow Wulfad's ordination to stand.[83] But the case of Ebbo, he commanded, must henceforth be laid to rest. As Charles had noted in his letter, all but one of the bishops directly knowledgeable about the matter had already died. Consequently, insisted Hadrian, the dispute had now fallen within God's jurisdiction; as he put it, "Ebbo now either stands or has fallen by his Lord."[84] To continue the debate was to give precedence to human judgment over divine. And who would dare display such temerity, Hadrian wondered?

By 867, the immediate matter of Wulfad's legitimacy may have been decided, but, as the two accounts clearly attest, feelings about Ebbo's status still remained wildly at odds. Regardless of Pope Hadrian's decree, Hincmar would not let the matter of Ebbo rest, for he would later claim to have gained access to the outcome of Ebbo's divine trial in the next world.[85] According to an alleged vision in 877 by one of Hincmar's monks named Bernold, Ebbo and his colleagues were languishing feverishly in a nightmarish realm, filthy from head to toe and clothed in rags blackened and singed by purgatorial fire.[86] Begging Bernold's help, they explained that only by having the many people in the palace who were still speaking about them instead offer prayers on their behalf might they gain a less severe place of confinement. Bernold was able to fulfill this request, explained Hincmar, with the result that Ebbo and his colleagues were now clean, clothed in white robes, and residing under the gentle keep of Saint Ambrose—although, remarked Hincmar as a parting shot, all of them still lacked chasubles.[87] In other words, Ebbo remained demoted to lay status—as per the canonical and papal judgments of 835 and 844—even in the next world.[88] That the text of Bernold's vision immediately follows Ebbo's apology in one of the manuscripts that preserves it (as noted above in Chapter 2) underscores its function as a definitive "answer" to Ebbo's "fraudulent" claims. In his account of Bernold's vision, Hincmar even had a bitter parting shot for the recently deceased Charles the Bald (d. 877). For Bernold had also encountered Charles in the other world, not as a resplendent king but as a bloody, festering heap, with worms gnawing greedily at his body.[89] Calling out to Bernold, the grotesque king confessed what the self-righteous Hincmar had known all along: "Make your way to Bishop Hincmar and tell him this: Because I did not listen to the good advice that he and other faithful men gave me, for my faults I now suffer the punishment you see."[90] Charles had the last word in the debate, just as he had wished, but it was set down for the ages by the poison pen of Hincmar.[91] That, ultimately, was the truth of the matter.

Hincmar of Reims, Saint Ambrose, and the Value of Experience

During the 860s, Hincmar invoked Louis' troubles of the 830s not only in the context of the dispute over Ebbo but also as an unambiguous, memorable series of events that proved the supraimperial authority of the episcopacy. Dragged into the dispute over the validity of the divorce and remarriage of Lothar's son and namesake King Lothar II (and, thus, over the legitimacy of that desperate king's heirs by his new wife), Hincmar drafted a long treatise in answer to his petitioners' queries, arguing for the right of bishops to adjudicate over such delicate matters as the divorce of a king.[92] Here he cited, as just one among several historical examples of ecclesiastics' intervening propitiously in secular affairs, the public penance of Louis the Pious in 833: "[Nearly five centuries ago, Saint] Ambrose excluded the emperor Theodosius from the church on account of his sins and called him back by penance," explained Hincmar (an admirer of Ambrose's bold letters to that emperor). "In our era," he continued, "after the august, pious Louis, who had been ousted from the kingdom, [rendered] a satisfaction, the united episcopacy, with sounder counsel, and the consent of the people, restored him to the kingdom and the church."[93] In making this remarkable comparison, Hincmar was not speaking entirely from hearsay, for nearly three decades earlier he had been a young monk at Saint-Denis, where Louis the Pious was initially reinvested with his regalia in 834, and had even been present a year later at the synod of Thionville for Louis' solemn restoration ceremony.[94] As he remembered approvingly (and not a little vaguely), the bishops had had everything to do with Louis' eventual return. The rebel bishops who had "ousted" Louis in the first place, however, are here conspicuously passed over in silence by Hincmar (apart from their presence implied by Hincmar's comparative description of the bishops who restored Louis—that the loyal bishops had acted in accordance with *sounder* counsel). Certainly this momentary lapse in his account was no accident, for, as we have seen, much of Hincmar's career was spent combating the injurious claims by the "leader" of those bishops of the rebellion, Archbishop Ebbo of Reims. As Mayke de Jong has argued, for Hincmar "the events of 833 remained very much in the present"[95] but only insofar as

they symbolized both the improper employment of the episcopal prerogative (which, as we saw in the rebel bishops' *Relatio*, also took its cue from
Ambrose) and the dire consequences resulting from such abuse. It was rather
the honorable deeds of the loyal bishops in 834—who, in reinvesting Louis,
had acted with sounder counsel as the prudent ministers of the realm and its
people—that Hincmar believed should be seen as exemplary and in line with
the intentions of the church fathers, such as Ambrose.[96]

Hincmar would also demonstrate his absolute approval of the Ambrosian
episcopal conduct he had witnessed in 834/35 by imitating it literally.[97] When
Hincmar reports that Charles had hurried to Metz in 869 for his coronation
only after hearing the "wiser counsel" of men from that part of the realm, who
longed for his presence after the death of their own sovereign, doubtless the
bishop had sensed—if indeed had not stressed—the symbolic importance of
that particular destination[98]; for in his role as the impresario of Charles's coronation ceremony, Hincmar explicitly compared the proceedings in 869 with
Louis' recoronation at Metz in 835—emphasizing, as he had in response to the
earlier query regarding the divorce of Lothar II, the powerful role of episcopal
"unanimity" in his account.[99] As he now recalled, Louis had been deprived of
earthly authority by a faction of men only to return by the unanimity of the
bishops and the (renewed) fidelity of the populace. It had been before this very
altar of the protomartyr Stephen in Metz, exclaimed Hincmar, that Louis was
"restored to rulership with the crown of the realm by the priests of the Lord,
[and] with the acclamation of the faithful populace, just as we, who were present there, saw it [happen]."[100] To his recollection, the great concord among the
bishops demonstrated that no wolves had remained in their midst.

While it is difficult to know what Hincmar intended by inserting in
the account his brief aside about his own presence at Louis' recoronation, he
may have meant it to lend authority to the format and efficacy of the current
ceremony in 869. He himself had seen Louis restored to power before this
very altar at Metz, Hincmar seems to say, and thus knew first hand of the
benefits it had bestowed upon that emperor: following his restoration, Louis
had retained his sovereignty until the day of his death. Likewise, by following
his father's example and being crowned by bishops before the altar of the holy
Stephen, Charles could also expect an auspicious reign. That he would instead
die an ignominious death only eight years later (perhaps by poison), his stink-
ing corpse stuffed into a barrel, sealed with tar, wrapped in leather ("such was
the corpse's stench"), and finally buried in Nantua, far from the royal tombs
of Saint-Denis, Aachen, or Metz, in Hincmar's estimation only testified to

Charles's subsequent disregard of the solemn vows he had taken before the bishops, populace, and saint in 869.[101] Thanks to the vision of Bernold, Hincmar also knew that Charles's abject death was only the slightest hint of what had truly befallen him. Unlike Ebbo, he would not find company with the likes of Saint Ambrose; his only companions now were worms.

Remembering Then Again

Taking stock of the various accounts of 833 we have reviewed, the first impression is certainly of their selective, obliging nature. Ebbo's vague remembrance of the events suited his claims of his right to the episcopal office of Reims, while Hincmar's precise, damning recollection supported his own rights to that same see. In 836, the realm's anxious bishops recalled their part in the sordid events to appease and reassure the emperor that they had learned from their common mistake and would never make such an error again. The clerics of Reims ordained by Ebbo after his restitution, on the other hand, maintained that they had duly followed his directives only because they had been ignorant of what had occurred with their archbishop during the 830s; thus, they had never been at fault and should not be condemned. Over a decade later, King Lothar remembered the troubles of the 830s as the result of diabolical influence, an alibi that did not extend to the cunning, baseborn Ebbo. Consequently, Lothar felt justified in supporting his brother's choice of Hincmar as Ebbo's replacement for the Reims episcopate. That Lothar wished to effect a reconciliation with Charles at the time doubtless served to conduce a memory in favor of Charles's bishop. Likewise, King Charles himself would remember the trying events he had experienced as a child rather differently by the 860s when the matter of his prized courtier Wulfad's canonical legitimacy—as ordained by Ebbo—was suddenly at stake.

Despite their obliging appearance, however, these selective, rather timely memories should not lead one to conclude that they were always devised at the behest of immediate desires. For this would be to privilege intention over memory.[102] Rather, the same set of events often meant different things at different times to different—or even the same—people, and such malleable memories themselves served to shape desires and inform courses of action. Doubtless, the truth of the matter lies somewhere within the dialectical relationship between these two poles.[103] Hincmar of Reims, for instance, had a complex memory of the events of the early 830s, for he not only remembered them as the prime example of his archnemesis Ebbo's duplicity but also as a sequence of experiences that contributed to his own righteous episcopal identity; he had been present at Louis' restoration in 835, he declared during Charles's coronation ceremony in 869, and thus knew all the more about a bishop's constitutive powers and duties—and a king's.

No less variegated and demanding were the memories of a number of other contemporary ecclesiastics, who all remembered Louis' abandonment and penance in light of their immediate circumstances and needs and in accordance with their idiosyncratic sensibilities and experiences. Whether as a dramatic sequence of events that had clearly proved the supreme, Ambrosian authority of the episcopal office or as a memorable instance of Judith's depravity or Louis' pusillanimity, 833 continued to matter and be remembered. Yet, the enduring memory of the events would increasingly take a back seat to more pressing concerns in other, more immediate social dramas.

In short, most of the examples surveyed in Parts I and II demonstrate that by the late ninth century the memory of Louis' abandonment and penance had not yet hardened into a symbolic cliché. Only Regino of Prüm's laconic account suggests that the memory of Louis' troubles had been abraded away to a few basic facets—and only then in the heart of Francia, i.e., the region of Prüm, Trier, and Metz (places all falling, perhaps not coincidentally, within Archbishop Drogo's ambit). Despite the proliferation and predominance of the major loyalist narratives by Thegan and the Astronomer, sites like Soissons and Corbie to the west; Lyon, Vienne, and Bergamo to the south; and Hildesheim to the north all afforded the possibility of presenting independent versions of the events; Regino's presumption of what constituted "common knowledge" had not yet crystallized and become established across the realm. But it soon would be. As we saw in Chapter 2, by the eleventh century and the spread of the *chansons* about Charlemagne's hapless son, the memory of the events of 833 would be abraded still further to the point that annalists could simply supply the lapidary phrase "the shame of the Franks" for that year and assume that their readers would know what they meant. The contours of a collective memory about the events had largely been set.

Conclusions

In the numerous minor narratives surveyed above, we have witnessed at once both a variety of representations of the rebellions against Louis the Pious and a gradual, gathering consensus regarding them. Between the 850s and the 860s, the events of 833 were remembered by Hincmar of Reims as an example of the Ambrosian superiority of episcopal competence when bishops are drawn into secular affairs. Asked to advise on the divorce case of Lothar II, Hincmar cited as instances of episcopal authority the analogous cases of Ambrose's excommunication and readmission of Theodosius and the unanimous will of the bishops in 835 to effect the restoration of Louis the Pious. That Louis had been deposed in the the first place, however, was to Hincmar clearly an abuse of this authority; thanks to Bernold's vision of Ebbo's fate in the next world, he knew not only that Ebbo had suffered for this misdeed but also that the truculent bishop eventually found solace in the keep of Saint Ambrose. Only in death had Ebbo learned to follow the saint's example (a calumnious suggestion, given that the rebels had alluded to Ambrose in their justificatory texts, as we have seen in the bishops' *Relatio* of 833 and the *Epitaphium Arsenii*).

Another trend we have observed are the attempts by a number of authors to forget an inconvenient past, attempts that demonstrate its continuing recurrence in the Carolingian present. Many bishops were at pains to repress their complicity in the "shameful" events of 833—their conspicuous silence at Ebbo's trial and sentencing (in exchange for Ebbo's own silence about their guilt) and the absence of their names in the edited copy of the episcopal *Relatio* are mute testimony of this fact. In 836, with Ebbo safely sequestered in his penitential cell, the bishops attempted to purge themselves and their ranks through a collective confession at the Aachen ecumenical assembly; since everyone had been guilty—if only through intimidation or the demands of his office—and was now publicly repentant, no one (unless everyone) could now be held accountable for the misdeeds of 833 (Ebbo, who knew too much, was effectively muffled; Thegan, whistleblower though he was, was not brave enough to supply names).[104] The united Frankish episcopate could thus move forward in allegiance with the emperor to emend (and thereby efface) an embarassing past. Unfortunately for the bishops, Louis' death, civil war, and Ebbo's release and reinstatement soon dashed these plans. Yet, Ebbo's chance to speak freely did not lead to another round of incriminations, as the bishops had feared. Rather, Ebbo accounted for his actions in much the same way that they had in 836: everyone in the decadent realm had been guilty of the sin begat by its decadence, including Ebbo himself. He, however, had possessed sufficient discernment to humble himself before God and do penance in order to abate their communal punishment. In other words, Ebbo had preempted the bishops' collective confession with his own. Struggling to extricate himself from their damning narrative (as framed by both Jonas of Orléans and the first annalist of the Annals of Saint-Bertin in 835, Thegan in 836/37, and Walafrid Strabo in 840/41), Ebbo shrewdly attempted to situate his actions within the bishops' *own* reframing or counternarrative of the recent past, thereby ennobling his "prescient" self-sacrifice and beating them at their own game. Like the rest of the bishops, he wanted to remember and in the process to forget—something that, as we have seen, Hincmar was not about to let happen. The devil and his demons may have been behind the realm's woes during the 830s, but, as both Lothar and Hincmar (following the Astronomer) were careful to note, this "fact" did not exculpate Ebbo as it did them. Present concerns required Ebbo's guilt, a detail to which the devil could not lay claim.

Within his eleventh-century *passio* of Bishop Frideric's martyrdom, Odbert of Utrecht appears to have known either directly or indirectly the episcopal *Relatio* of 833, for he placed within Frideric's divinely inspired mouth a quotation from the book of Ezekiel, one that nearly parallels the quotation invoked by the rebel bishops in 833. In each case, God's moral imperative to Ezekiel was used as the primary justification for what otherwise might seem an act of great insolence ventured against Louis the Pious.[105] In the next chapter, we shall look closely at the discourse and system of logic employed by the rebels in their accounts, one implicit in the quotation from Ezekiel. What we will find is that this discourse was shared: not only his critics but Louis' supporters would also understand the events of 833 in terms of the binary conditions of equity and iniquity. Louis may have become the embodiment of iniquity to his critics, but to his supporters he was nothing less than equity incarnate.

PART III

Discoursing

. . . And in reality you have started at the end.
—Jean-Paul Sartre, *Nausea*

CHAPTER 6

Eloquence in Equity, Fluency in Iniquity

Tragedy disappears to the degree that an equitable settlement is possible.
  —*Goethe, as quoted by Chancellor Friedrich von Müller*

Beware and flee iniquity, love equity, practice justice.
  —*Dhuoda,* Liber manualis

IN A PATH-BREAKING article, Mayke de Jong remarked that the concepts and language used by the rebel bishops, both to define the problem with the realm and to justify their efforts in the early 830s to correct it, were also used by the emperor and his supporters.[1] Taking De Jong's observation of a common conceptual framework as a point of departure, this chapter will explore the formal, ecclesiastic interpretations of the events at the Field of Lies and Saint-Médard, and trace the development of a particular value system—shared among ecclesiastics, both pro- and anti-Louis—that informed these same interpretations. Beset by troubles both human and divine, Carolingian intellectuals struggled to understand and curtail the growing *iniquitas* of a king and a kingdom. As I intimated in the opening pages of Chapter 4, this seemingly traditional formulation of right and wrong order was itself, regardless of the belief in its perpetuity, by 833 only the latest result of a relatively rapid, dialectical process of social change and ideological transformation. Determining the nature of this shift, and when and why it took place, will be the focus of this concluding chapter.

In our examination, two great ironies of the many that characterize Louis the Pious's career will be explored. On the one hand, we will see that early in his reign Louis fostered an ideological program within which he would later find himself enframed. While this point has long been recognized by scholars, the conceptual apparatus of the program, and more specifically its relationship with the binary system of *aequitas/iniquitas*, has never been examined in detail. On the other hand, the pernicious change that the rebel bishops believed had come over both the emperor and the empire *in processu temporis*, over the course of time, was an impression, I shall argue, itself ironically brought about by a subtle transformation in the bishops' own system of values. Rather than view Louis as an emperor who gradually failed, we should shift our gaze to the criteria by which he was judged, with an eye for the way they changed over time, holding him up to ever-higher standards he was not prepared to meet.

By focusing on the transformation of a particular system of values, at least two other normative systems are necessarily implied from this diachronic perspective—that which came before and that which came after. In the years preceding Louis' ecclesiastical reforms, criticism or praise of great men was often expressed in terms of utility, a scale of values suggesting a relationship between historical action or inaction and a larger polity that such activity affected in time.[2] This was the pragmatic discourse—perhaps a product of the Carolingian Roman revival—that Louis' widespread program of religious renewal would come to overshadow. By the tenth century, however, after years of political instability and an increasing plurality both of kingdoms and of lords, current concerns would shift yet again, moving from the ostensibly eternal moral system of equity and iniquity promoted by Louis and his ecclesiastical advisors to a far more immediate quest for *auctoritas* or legitimate authority.[3]

It should be kept in mind that these discursive shifts occurred at different speeds among different people in different places. While the discussion that follows will for the most part speak in broad terms about such shifts, the reality was far less tidy, for the changes often took place not in isolation but with the new appearing close beside the old—indeed, the discourses were often vying in fierce competition. Patrick Geary has used the expression "historical slippage" to describe this asymmetrical process of discursive change and the gaps it will always leave in any totalizing view of a cultural system.[4] Perhaps more illuminating is the vivid example Paul Dutton has employed to call attention to this phenomenon of difference, to the way in which "individuals exist within a time, but may not always be of it or keep pace with its cultural changes and influences. Old scribes, we may usefully recall, were still writing late Caroline minuscule long after the new Gothic script had taken hold."[5] Consequently, when considering the appearance and influence of such "new scripts" and their "scribes," we should not forget the abiding persistence of "old hands" in their midst.

The Shadow King, the Negligent King, and the Tyrant

In 1957, François Ganshof needed no more than twelve pages to sketch the formative outline for all future studies of Louis the Pious and the contours of his reign.[6] Writing against the grain of centuries of learned opinion, Ganshof argued that Louis was not the enfeebled king that so many later historians required him to be for their arcing narratives. Rather, Louis inherited from his father a realm in desperate need of repair; that he had been unable to keep Charlemagne's already foundering empire from sinking under its own weight, declared Ganshof, should not be seen as a failure on his part.[7] On the contrary, the new emperor made a creative, even Herculean effort to preserve the great achievement of his forefathers—one that for all its zeal would still fall short. One momentous change instituted by Louis in support of this endeavor was the replacement of "the traditional, almost patrimonial idea of royal power" with "the 'non-historic' notion of the Empire which had developed in Church circles since the time of Gregory the Great." According to this latter notion, continued Ganshof, "the emperor—and this meant, of course, the Roman emperor—was endowed with a universal authority destined to protect the universal Church against the dangers which might threaten her, to spread the Christian faith, and to preserve its purity." In other words, Louis had altered the traditional conception of Frankish rulership. Due to his frequent communion with learned clerics, Louis opted to abandon the pragmatic, patrimonial notion of monarchy that was dependent on the historical person of the king and adopted in its place an otherwise "incompatible" ecclesiastical interpretation of sovereignty, "an abstract idea of royal power, which one might compare to the idea of the state."[8] Yet, this precocious ecclesiological experiment was short-lived: as Ganshof concluded, "we know that the concept of the *res publica*, as well as the notion of the unity of Empire, territorial integrity, and succession to the throne by way of primogeniture without partition, all crumbled during the troubled period between

829 and 843." That which came to supplant this unified system was described by Ganshof with two ominous words—"factional interests."⁹

In 1970, Edward Peters adopted the tripartite scheme of Carolingian political history sketched by Ganshof and refined it through a study of the terminology employed by continental writers of the ninth century to describe the monarchy.[10] Peters observed that the replacement of the Merovingian dynasty with that of the Carolingian line of kings—namely, the deposition of Childeric III in 751 by Louis' grandfather Pippin the Short—had been justified by Carolingian promoters in terms of Childeric's "uselessness" (*inutilitas*) and Pippin's ability and power (*potestas*).[11] As he put it, "Childeric III became the first conspicuous *rex inutilis*, not because his own inadequacy was especially greater than that of some of his predecessors, but because the distinction between *utilitas* and *inutilitas* in the person of the king had become a part of the historical background of the Carolingian world order."[12] This distinction would soon come to be replaced, argued Peters, by a set of Christian political ideas gradually introduced by the Carolingians themselves, a moral-legal system that focused on the idea of a Davidic "just king" (*rex iustus*). What followed was a period of striking changes for the Frankish monarchy, "none of which were more important than the ecclesiastically influenced structure of government and the ecclesiastical concept of the character of royal governance."[13] Here was another Carolingian "world order."

In order to gain a clearer picture of the momentous change that occurred under Louis the Pious, Peters suggested that a revealing comparison can be made by juxtaposing the deposition of Childeric III in 751 with that of Louis in 833. What becomes apparent is that Childeric had been disqualified from office because he was said to have lacked the *potestas* required of a proper king, and thus was effectively "useless." He was but a shadow of a king. With Louis the Pious, however, the royal *potestas* was clearly present, but he was judged to have perverted it. Such an abuse of sovereign power, when measured against the newly heightened moral standards of Christian kingship, was conceived by contemporaries typically in one of two ways: either the king acted flagrantly and willfully and, thus, was a savage tyrant, or else he failed to act righteously due to ineptitude or carelessness and, thus, became a *rex negligens*, a negligent king, who rarely used his *potestas* properly and on occasion allowed wicked men to use it improperly.[14] For Peters, there was no doubt that Louis had been a prime example of the latter type of morally deficient ruler, a negligent king. As the rebel bishops at Saint-Médard testified, he had incurred "so much disgrace and contempt through his rashness and negligence, that he not only came into grief with his friends, but even came into ridicule with his enemies." Louis "both did and compelled his people to do, or allowed to be done many things displeasing to God and men," they continued.[15] Both rash and negligent, Louis had been a fickle—and thus an unpredictable—sovereign, one who not only coerced his subjects to commit evil but was himself swayed by the wicked among them as well.[16]

Referring to the events of 833, Peters explained that "the purely ecclesiastical form of the proceedings against Louis the Pious was probably a result, *ironically*, of the [moral] reforms which the Carolingians had made in the structure of the Frankish church."[17] In other words, Louis' deposition on the basis of his negligence had been the ironic result of letting the moral terms and postulates he himself had fostered slip away from his control. Or as Stuart Airlie has characterized this process, Louis had "set in motion machinery with its own logic."[18]

A Brief History of Equity and Iniquity

While Peters showed with precision the terminology employed by Carolingian contemporaries to express different types of bad kingship, he was not as careful in illustrating—at least for Louis' reign—the ways in which good kingship had likewise been conceived and described. For the earlier period, Peters noted that a king such as Childeric was considered either "useful" (*utilis*) or "useless" (*inutilis*), while for the period following Louis' reign, rulers either possessed "courage" (*virtus*), "power" (*potestas*), and "worth" (*dignitas*), or else were deemed "unworthy" (*indignus*), displaying signs of "idleness" (*desidia*) and "inactivity" (*inertia*).[19] Between these two periods, bad kings were understood largely in moral terms of *negligens* and *iniquus*.[20] The antithesis of such depraved kingship, however, Peters left rather vague, describing it with the title *rex iustus*, a just king.[21]

In fact, Carolingian moralists were highly aware that to characterize a king as "iniquitous" had a very specific connotation, implying that he was the antithesis of a perfectly "equitable" ruler—one devoid of equity. Indeed, the binary system of *aequitas/iniquitas* was part of a larger moral discourse well known and current among the Carolingians by the mid-ninth century.[22] Yet, this particular binary opposition has gone mostly unrecognized by historians, being examined—when observed at all—in piecemeal fashion or as something of a curiosity.[23] Some have commented in general on the binary relationship between *aequitas* and *iniquitas* but have not explored the degree to which it was employed in Carolingian culture.[24] Others have observed the emphasis on *iniquitas* during Louis' reign and demonstrated many of the ways in which Carolingian writers expressed this moral condition, but without noting the commensurate frequency of its positive contrary.[25] Still others have perceived the prevalence of *aequitas* in what Jean Gaudemet called its "theologico-moral vein"—that is, as a moral condition rather than in its strict Roman legal sense—but have not recognized its relationship with iniquity.[26]

To be sure, both terms had their roots deep in the value systems of antiquity. Above all, the term *aequitas* was long employed within the semantic domain of Roman jurisprudence to express a very specific concept: the correcting or overruling of law in exceptional cases, where strict adherence to the letter of the law would, by reason of its inflexible universality, otherwise render an unintentional miscarriage of justice.[27] Put another way, to do *aequitas* meant to preserve the spirit of the law by bending its letter.[28] This juridical connotation of *aequitas* has received most of the scholarly attention, although there was another meaning of the term that is often overlooked. *Aequitas* was frequently associated with the legitimacy of mints, appearing regularly as a legend on Roman currency to guarantee its authenticity and value.[29]

At its core, and as its use on coinage was meant to suggest, the word *aequitas* carried the benign, eternal notions of fairness, steadiness, and right. Consequently, the term was employed often by classical authors in this abstract, qualitative sense as a virtue and coupled with *iniquitas*, its corresponding vice.[30] In 63 B.C.E. for instance, Cicero could matter-of-factly proclaim the antithetical relationship of the two qualities: *aequitas* among the virtues contends with *iniquitas* among the vices. And in arguing for the existence of the soul, Cicero would again invoke this pair of contraries, describing the types of men each quality characterized and the degree of discernment relative to each: "And what of the fact that the wisest men die with the greatest equanimity (*aequissimus*), the most foolish with the greatest iniquity (*iniquissimus*)," he asked rhetorically. "Is it not apparent to you that it is because the soul of the one, having a keener and wider vision, sees that it is setting out for a better place, while that of the other, being of duller sight, sees not its path?"[31]

As most studies of *aequitas* are quick to observe, the strict legal sense of the term would disappear in the West during the "decline" of the Roman Empire and not make a reappearance until its revival by canon lawyers in the twelfth century. In describing this narrative arc, these same studies themselves typically make the equivalent chronological leap without pause; because the legal connotations of *aequitas* lay dormant, most scholars have felt justified to pass over the long period of its "slumber" between Augustine and the twelfth century.[32] On the rare occasion that an examination of *aequitas* in this intervening period has been undertaken, it has nevertheless proceeded with the Roman juridical concept and its institutionalization firmly in hand as the criterion by which to evaluate transformation or degeneration in the term's meaning and use.[33]

While it is true that the presence of *aequitas* in its Roman juridical application gradually declined, the concomitant rise of Christianity ensured that the term would continue to appear with frequency during the early Middle Ages but in its broader sense, as demonstrated by Cicero. Solemnized and transmitted in the Latinity of scripture, *aequitas* maintained a robust existence as a moral concept of righteousness, being regularly paired with its binary of iniquity.[34] "The law of truth was in his mouth and iniquity was not found in his lips," proclaimed the Lord about the recipient of his covenant, for "he walked with me in peace, and in equity, and turned many away from iniquity" (Mal. 2:6). The moral binary resounded even more tersely in the Psalms: "Thou hast loved malice more than goodness, and iniquity rather than to speak equity" (Ps. 51:5). It comes as no surprise that the church fathers were conversant in this binary opposition: in his commentary on Psalm 63:7, Augustine warned that "feigned equity is not equity but double iniquity, both because it is iniquity and because it is feigning." Elsewhere, he explained that baptism is always sacred within both the just and the unjust man, being neither augmented by his *aequitas* nor diminished by his *iniquitas*.[35]

The appearance of the binary in scripture stems from the early conflation and translation of a number of Hebrew words standing for concepts such as right and wrong, good and evil, and the like, into two Greek terms. When scripture was translated yet again, this time from Greek into Latin, the binary terms of *aequitas* and *iniquitas* were chosen as the two words that came closest semantically to conveying the sense of the Greek binary *nomia* and *anomia*, legality and illegality. Theologians such as Augustine understood the meaning of these terms not in any narrow sense but in a way that was at once both broad and specific. *Iniquitas* did not strictly mean against the law but suggested a state of being completely outside of law; it was considered a violation of general moral principles, not of any particular moral code. *Anomia* and its Latin counterpart *iniquitas*, observes Marco Orrù, "lacked specific legalistic boundaries, [having] no connection with the written law, but referred to broader unwritten guiding principles of human conduct."[36] *Iniquitas*, and by association *aequitas*, described a moral condition rather than connoting any specific type of act.

The church fathers devoted considerable attention to what Saint Paul called the "mystery of iniquity" (2 Thess. 2:7) and the nature of its relationship with sin and came to two important conclusions. First, it was determined that law is the defining boundary separating *iniquitas* and *peccatum*, iniquity and sin. As Jerome stated, "Between *anomia*, that is iniquity, and sin, this matters—that iniquity is before the law, and sin is after the law [of Moses]."[37] While sin represented a transgression of Mosaic law, it still implied acting upon a correlative legal plane. Iniquity, on the other hand, was a "pre-legal," wicked state of being. The second distinction made by the fathers was hierarchical rather than qualitative, for they considered *iniquitas* to be the root cause of specific transgressions. Iniquity was understood to be the moral condition of the individual that gives birth to and directs the performance of sin. Ambrose made this distinction quite clear: "sin is the work of iniquity," he remarked, "and iniquity is the producer of the fault and crime."[38]

Ambrose knew also that *aequitas* was the corresponding condition contrary to *iniquitas* and explained its existence by means of an extraordinary anecdote. Relying on the redaction provided by Cicero in his treatise *De officiis*, Ambrose invoked the ancient fable told by Plato about the "Ring of Gyges" in order to demonstrate the superiority of Christian to pagan arguments over righteousness.[39] As Plato had "imagined," began Ambrose, the shepherd Gyges was out with his flock one day when he discovered a chasm in the earth. Descending into the deep, Gyges soon encountered a large iron horse with numerous small doors in its flanks. Opening one of the hatches and peering inside, the shepherd discovered to his amazement that within the statue lay a corpse, naked but for a gold ring on its finger.[40] "Desiring the gold," explains Ambrose, Gyges took the ring and returned to the surface. Sometime later, Gyges began to fiddle with the strange ring he was now wearing on his own finger and by chance turned it so that its bezel faced inward toward the palm of his hand. To his great surprise, the shepherd learned that he had become invisible; what was more, by returning the ring to its original position, he found that he could once again be seen. Recognizing the ring's great power and its even greater potential, Gyges immediately made off to the royal palace and, by means of the ring, committed adultery with the queen, slew the king, and took possession of the kingdom after murdering all those who posed a threat to his rule.[41]

Plato's lesson from this fable, explained Ambrose, was that if a wise man were given Gyges's ring, he would not use it as Gyges had to commit crimes with impunity. For the wise man knows that, were he to do so, he would be no more free from the stain of sin than if his acts were committed in plain view. That wise men consider the stain of sin far worse than the pain of punishment is undoubtedly true, continued Ambrose, because they recognize, along with the apostle Paul, that "the law is laid down not for the just but for the unjust" (1 Tim. 1:9). The just man has no concern for law and the consequences of its transgression since "he has within himself the law of his mind, and a rule of equity and justice (*aequitatis ac iustitiae suae norma*). Thus, he is not recalled from sin by fear of punishment, but by the rule of a virtuous life."[42] Now, all this, admits Ambrose, is certainly true.[43] But while the pagan Plato needed to invoke "the pretense of the ring" to demonstrate the truth that a perfectly just man is unerringly guided not by the punitive precepts of law but by the inner tribunal of his conscience, Ambrose proudly states that he can evince the same truth using "the true examples of good [biblical] men," such as David and John the Baptist.[44] "Where was the use of Gyges's ring in John's case," asks Ambrose defiantly,

> who would not have been put to death by Herod if he had kept silence? He could have kept silence before [Herod] so as to be both seen and yet not killed. But because he not only could not endure to sin himself to protect his own safety, but also could not bear and endure even another's sin, he brought about the cause of his own death [by boldly speaking out].[45]

Here, Ambrose was making the same argument about the grave demands of iniquity that he would invoke in his quietly defiant letter to the emperor Theodosius in 390 and that would later be raised by the rebel bishops against Louis in 833 with their quotation of Ezekiel 3:18.[46] By daring to speak their conscience, both Ambrose and the Carolingian bishops had acted wisely like John the Baptist, in accordance with the equity and justice of their own "inner tribunal." They would not be stained by the sin of inaction, whatever the cost.[47]

The two distinctions surveyed above, regarding the ontological relationship between equity and iniquity, and the hierarchical relationship between iniquity and sin, are of profound importance for understanding the ecclesiastical logic of Louis' penance in 833. Reformers at Louis' court recognized the moral, constitutive condition of equity that characterized Louis' right rule, as well as the inverse condition of iniquity that was ascribed to his misrule. As we have seen, the eight chapters of the indictment read aloud during Louis' penance testified to the sins increasingly "born" of this iniquity. Indeed, Louis' iniquitous behavior was especially troubling to the realm's discerning moral guardians, for, as Augustine had warned centuries earlier, by definition it posed twice the threat: "Feigned equity is not equity but double iniquity," the great church father pronounced, "both because it is iniquity and because it is feigning." To the rebel bishops, such twinned iniquity was precisely what Louis' previous attempts at penance in 822 and 830 had produced; feigning equity at the rituals, the duplicitous emperor had only exacerbated the strife, calling down God's wrath upon a realm already suffering from the punishment of sin. Conversely, to Louis' loyal bishops, such feigned equity was precisely what the rebels themselves had performed at the emperor's penance in 833 by assuming the fraudulent *personae* of "spiritual doctors." While the roles were different, the consequences of such dissimulation were deemed equally disastrous.[48]

The Movement Gains Momentum

In a wide-ranging study of early medieval moral discourse, Paul Fouracre demonstrated that the Carolingians adopted a moral-theological framework already well in place by the late seventh century. As he notes, the Merovingian kings of the sixth and seventh centuries were also described by their ecclesiastical counselors as monarchs who furthered *iustitia* and *aequitas*.[49] Moreover, a moral tract on rulership, the *De duodecim abusivis saeculi*, was written in Ireland sometime in the seventh century and circulated widely on the continent shortly thereafter; thanks to the tract's emphasis on the *rex iniquus* as one of the twelve execrable "abuses of the age," immense weight was placed on *aequitas* as a corresponding virtue of proper rulership.[50] By the late eighth century, this preexisting moral framework, argues Fouracre, was appropriated by the Carolingians, who used it with increasing frequency to fashion themselves as avatars of justice. This self-fashioning was expressed largely in terms of a rhetoric of reform, one "directed at religious life, in which the Frankish clergy were seen to be of low moral standard, the organisation of the church to be in need of renewal, and the Christian community to be in need of defenders. Improvement in these fields was the self-proclaimed duty

of the rulers, and this moral purpose not only justified but positively necessitated an expansion of their power."[51] It is precisely within this moral—if not
necessarily instrumental—program described by Fouracre that the numerous
changes instituted by Louis the Pious should be understood.

Early in his reign, Louis initiated a series of sweeping reforms that would
set its future direction. Dismayed over the poor moral condition of the empire he had inherited, the new, stern emperor purged the imperial palace
of "undesirables" (among whom included even—or perhaps especially—a
number of his own kindred) and, under the guidance of his advisor, the ascetic Aquitainian Abbot Benedict of Aniane, rapidly steered the realm onto a
course of renewal. Upon assuming control of his father's great empire, Louis
surrounded himself with a coterie of other Aquitainian Visigothic counselors, including Helisachar, Claudius of Turin, Theodulf and Jonas of Orléans,
Agobard of Lyon, Ebbo of Reims, and Benedict of Aniane.[52] In fact, many
of these ecclesiastic reformers had simply followed Louis north to the imperial palace, for they had already been serving as his courtiers in Aquitaine, a
frontier realm where he had lived most of his life as king: born in 778, Louis
had been sent by his father only three years later to the Aquitainian march,
where he remained until Charlemagne's death in 814.[53] Because of the relatively conservative form of Christianity he subsequently endorsed, Louis is
often understood as having fallen from an early age under the sway of these
doctrinaire "Aquitanian 'backwoodsmen,'" as Roger Collins has facetiously
called them, provincial puritans who, upon Louis' succession to the imperial
throne, introduced "a regime of almost Calvinistic morality in place of the
hedonistic house party that was Charles's Aachen."[54]

Although Collins exaggerates to underscore the point that Louis' policies
were, in his opinion, based not on the "utopian" dictates of such extremists,
but upon a more "pragmatic" consideration of politics, there is still much to
be said for the notion of a particularly austere Aquitainian influence upon
Louis. For from the time Louis was king of Aquitaine, it was the zealous
Visigothic warrior-turned-monk Benedict of Aniane who, until his death in
February 821, would have the emperor's ear. Between 816 and 819, at Benedict's recommendation, several assemblies were held at Aachen for the purpose
of standardizing the norms of religious observance. Largely concerned with
the Rule of Saint Benedict and its increasing neglect by a wayward people,
these councils, presided over by Louis and Benedict, stressed the rigorous application of and strict adherence to a uniform interpretation of the monastic
code.[55] According to his contemporary biographer, the charismatic Benedict

was at Louis' side so often during this time that "he began to wear away the palace floors" by his presence.[56] Indeed, the monks of Benedict's monastery of Inden (Kornelimünster), a cloister built for him at the emperor's command (in July 817) near the imperial palace of Aachen, would boast after his death that Benedict had

> had the greatest concern for the entire ecclesiastical order, whether monks, canons, or layfolk, but especially for monks. The Emperor [Louis] listened to all of his counsel willingly and accomplished it. Louis was called by some "the Monkish" (*Monachius*), [both] because he always called the monks "his own" out of love for the holy man [Benedict], and because he went so far as to declare himself openly "abbot" of this monastery [of Inden] after Benedict's death.[57]

While this anecdote, as remembered by Benedict's brethren, was certainly meant to suggest the intimacy and respect shared between Louis and Benedict, the particular imagery deployed within it is suggestive in still other ways. For the epithet *Monachius*, the Monkish, is one of only two such bynames given to Louis during his lifetime (we will examine the other appellation, *Equitatius*, in detail below).[58] Unfortunately, the two epithets have never been juxtaposed and analyzed in order to gain insight into the ways in which Louis fashioned himself or was fashioned by others in the hope of gaining his approval (and perhaps his coveted ear as well). In fact, the nicknames hang together in a rather specific sense—indeed, are two sides of the same coin—and say much about the nature of the reform movement promoted by Louis under Benedict's inspired and decidedly monastic guidance.

Equity and the Rule of Saint Benedict

With respect to Louis' penance in 833, scholars have long postulated that the bishops of the rebellion were aware of and took as a precedent for their own bold act the seemingly analogous event of the Visigothic King Wamba's penitential deposition in the late seventh century. In 680, a rival for Wamba's throne allegedly slipped him a drug that rendered him unconscious. While in this moribund state, the king was administered the last rite of penance, which was reserved for those on the threshold of death. Upon awakening, Wamba learned that he had been tonsured, clothed in a hair shirt, and was henceforth a member of the order of penitents. As such, he was dead to this world and was thus ineligible to rule as king. Convinced by those around him to sign documents ratifying the new, de facto state of affairs, he agreed to confirm the status of his rival (and alleged druggist) as the sovereign ruling in his stead. Wamba then retired to a monastery, never to be heard from again.[59]

Because the incident with Wamba took place within the realm of Visigothic Spain, some scholars have suggested that the Visigothic members of the rebellion in 833, such as Agobard of Lyon, may have known about the event and been familiar with the records documenting it.[60] While an awareness of Wamba's deposition may very well have played some unattested role in the actions of the Carolingian rebels (as did their awareness of Theodosius's penance in 390), it was not an exemplar necessary for engendering their bold deeds. For even without Wamba's "precedent," there was still a southern influence evident in the events of the 830s, one more pervasive and subtle than any such instrumental model borrowed from the Visigothic past.

The terms *aequitas* and *aequus* appear several times in the Benedictine Rule.[61] Used to describe the prudent temperance and discretion by which the abbot should govern the brethren of his house, *aequitas* for Benedict signified a sense of God's right order as manifest in the abbot's just behavior, equanimity, and aplomb. As the learned Hrabanus Maurus once remarked, *aequitas* was nothing other than a "form of discretion."[62] Ludo Milis has identified this condition of righteousness as a primary link in the constitutive hierarchical structure of cenobitical life, a series of bonds simultaneously descending from God through his equitable abbot to the monks, and ascending from the monks' humility and obedience to the abbot and thence to God[63]:

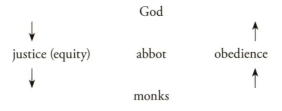

Complementary to Milis's formulation is Terrence Kardong's broader observation that the notion of equity in the Rule is analogous to its meaning in the Hebrew Psalms: that "'equity' like 'justice' starts as an attribute of Yahweh and works outward to the created order so that men can also be called 'equitable,' as in Ps. 16:2 [= 'Let my judgment come forth from thy countenance: let thy eyes behold the things that are equitable'].["64] Given its ancient, well-known binary relationship with *aequitas*, the concomitant appearance of iniquity as the general term for wrong in Benedict's Rule is unsurprising: "Let the prudent monk—so that he may avoid evil thoughts," commands Benedict, "always say in his heart: 'Then I shall be spotless before him, if I shall keep myself from my iniquity' (Ps. 17:24)."[65] The Carolingian monk Hildemar of Corbie/Civate in his commentary on the Rule similarly declared that "he who does not love [all his equally good monks] equally is not an equitable abbot, since he behaves more with iniquity than equity" (*magis iniquitatem . . . quam aequitatem*).[66]

When these observations on the salience of equity in the Benedictine Rule are taken together with the remarks of Thomas Noble on the monastic character of Louis the Pious's rulership, one source of the common conceptual ground in which so many of the struggles late in Louis' reign were rooted becomes clear. By embracing the monastic ethos of Benedict, Louis thereby endorsed a moral concept of order and rulership that was based on the moral-legal-theological binary of *aequitas* and *iniquitas*.

Noble long ago put out a call for others to refine his initial observations on the monastic tenor of Louis' rule. His most striking suggestion was that the monkish Louis—an emperor the contemporary court poet Ermoldus Nigellus once called *caesar et abba simul*—fashioned himself as the monarchial "abbot" of his realm and, as such, placed himself in the onerous intermediary "abbatial" position between God and his subjects.[67] Answering the call, Peter McKeon developed Noble's observations to what he considered their logical conclusion. In a bold, synthetic study on the general character of Louis' reign, McKeon claimed that if there is an argument to be made for the "tragedy" of Louis the Pious, it is specifically with respect to the allegedly paradoxical situation in which the emperor placed himself by conceiving of his rule in monastic terms.[68] According to McKeon, Louis' program "was doomed from the start, precisely because the theology it expressed was rooted in that which guided Louis himself." As ruler of his realm, Louis was required to guide those under his care. Yet, as a devout Christian, he was deeply conscious of his own unworthiness before God and placed himself on the same mortal plane as his brethren. Thus, Louis felt unqualified to lead them, while simultaneously having no one to turn to for his own guidance but those same, equally unworthy men whom he felt unqualified to lead: "To rule and guide others, he knew, one must rule himself." The problem lay in that the insecure Louis did not know how to rule himself and yet knew of no one better from whom he might take counsel—especially after the death in 821 of his longtime advisor Benedict of Aniane. This was Louis' "inescapable paradox," his impossible—and, thus, tragic—burden: "both to be an example to his people, and to make them an example for himself."[69]

Alluring as it may be, McKeon's argument is premised upon the same a priori notion of Louis' reign held by so many other critics: that it was a tragedy. What was new was his attempt to explicate in precise terms the paradox that had seemingly led to the long acknowledged "tragic" situation—that Louis' monastic self-fashioning was his own undoing and, thus, the undoing of the realm. Yet, if we are to take seriously Louis' monastic program of governance observed by Noble, McKeon, and several others,[70] then to claim that Louis fell victim to an "inescapable paradox" through his self-deprecating religiosity is unfair. For as "abbot" of his realm, Louis was deeply conscious not only of Benedict's custodial mandate but also of his recommendations on how an abbot might conduct his ministry properly and with assurance. Indeed, such guidelines for self-knowledge and right rule were likely what made Benedict's program so attractive to Louis in the first place. The Rule repeatedly reminds the abbot that he must govern with the utmost diligence and discretion, since he will eventually have to render an account to God for the condition of the souls of all those under his care.[71] By fearing the Lord's future questioning, the abbot will remain as concerned for those entrusted to him as he is for himself and, through the constant admonition and correction of others' vice, shall likewise be cleansed of his own.[72]

As "abbot" of his realm, Louis was intimately aware of Benedict's grave charge and attended to his ministerial responsibility for his subjects—his "brethren"—in earnest. In 818/19, for instance, he had the following statement affixed as the introduction to a set of comprehensive reforms for the empire:

> Since each person will render account for his deeds, and we especially—
> who stand equal to others in our mortal condition and greatly surpass
> them in the dignity of rule—who are going to render account on the
> day of strict examination not only for our graver commission but also
> for our sinful words and deeds, and even more for our thoughts, just as

holy scripture says, "Since he will examine your works and search out your thoughts." (Wis. 6:4)[73]

The similarity of Louis' admonition with that of Benedict to the would-be abbot of a monastery is striking. "The Abbot," warns Benedict,

> must always remember what he is, be mindful of his calling, and know that to whom more is committed, from him more is expected. . . . He should know that he must prepare himself to account for the souls in his care: however many monks that he knows are under his care, he should understand for certain that on Judgment Day he will without doubt have to render an account to the Lord for all of their souls, as well as his own.[74]

Such self-conscious concern is precisely what Bruno Candidus, a monk from the monastery of Fulda, would remember about Louis in the 840s shortly after his death: the emperor had been a knowledgeable overseer of monastic discipline, recalled Bruno, one who had readily intervened in the cloister's affairs to harangue its malcontents and rebuke the unruly.[75] Comparable in this respect was the Benedictine mandate that "negligence" was specifically to be countered with Pauline "rebuke," a mandate that Louis also delivered to his administrative assistants at an assembly in 829: the first thing the *missi* should inquire when inspecting the condition of a realm, he decreed, is "how those who ought to be ruling the populace have attended to their charge, so that we may know who, by virtue of their proper activity, are worthy of being excused. But those who, on account of their negligence, are deserving of correction and rebuke should in all ways be made evident to us."[76] Louis' promotion of the lowborn to high ecclesiastical office, as well as his tendency to show clemency, were acts likewise in keeping with Benedict's recommendations to an abbot: he should make no distinction of persons "unless it be one whom he finds better in good works or obedience" (chap. 2), and he should "exalt mercy above judgment, that he himself may obtain mercy" (chap. 64).[77]

As Louis became a lover of monks, espousing the particular Benedictine rule of order so dear to his Aquitainian advisors, he also became a promoter and defender of Benedictine equity, attributing the monastic rule's concept of equitable right order to all his dominion. In other words, to be *Monachius* was tantamount to being the perfectly just "abbot" of a monastically conceived and organized community.

A Carolingian Binary

Such equitable, Benedictine discretion would gain a heightened currency and valence in the years following Louis' reforms and would characterize not only the nature of Louis' rule but also the ethos and ideals of his ecclesiastical courtiers and advisors. Take, for example, the eventual spokesman for the rebellion in 833, Agobard of Lyon. Sometime shortly after the great reform councils of 817, Agobard penned a complaint to Louis on the multiplicity of laws in effect throughout the far-flung empire and the many problems that were constantly arising from this legal diversity.[78] Concluding his plea to the emperor, Agobard begged,

> would that it might please God the Almighty that everyone were ruled under one most pious king by one law, the same [law] according to which one lives and his neighbors also answer. It would indeed accomplish much on behalf of the concord of the city of God, and the equity of the people.[79]

While much can be said about this passage and about Agobard's treatise as a whole, what is of interest here is the general point that Agobard longed for a normative right order of things in terms of "concord" and (Benedictine) "equity."[80] Agobard would again call upon these same terms of order to describe Louis' first public penance in 822. "Behold, almighty God readied the thoughts of the Lord Emperor," explained Agobard to his seniors at the assembly of Attigny, "so that he might understand carefully the forces of his time [that are] concordant or discordant with equity (*vires consonas vel dissonas equitati*)."[81] Over the next few years, Louis would demonstrate that his devotion to equity was genuine; by 825, the entire realm was enjoined by the emperor to act in accordance with equity and concord, and his counts and bishops commanded to monitor it scrupulously, so that Louis might learn of any who shirked the proper dispensation of their duties.[82]

In a treatise on the nature of kingship written to Louis' son Pippin in 829, Bishop Jonas of Orléans, another southerner, would echo Agobard's and Louis' sentiments about equity and right order. "The royal ministry," Jonas advised the young king, "is specifically to govern the people of God, to rule with equity and justice, and to strive so that they may have peace and concord."[83] A few chapters later, Jonas states frankly, "It is established that the royal power should legislate for all his subjects according to the order of equity (*secundum aequitatis ordinem*)."[84]

Equity, we should recall, was only one half of the binary discourse. Carolingian intellectuals needed no such reminder. In his gloss on Ecclesiasticus 21:31, for example, Hrabanus Maurus observed that "gifts and money divert the judgments of judges away from the course of equity to the path of iniquity."[85] And as we have seen, Hildemar, in his commentary on Benedict's Rule, declared that some abbots behave "more with iniquity than equity."[86] Yet, it was more often Psalm 10:6—"he that loveth iniquity hateth his own soul"—that elicited commentary from exegetes on *iniquitas* and *aequitas*, for it raised the profound question of how one should understand the relationship between the will and the nature of the soul. Commenting on this psalm, Paschasius Radbertus noted that "iniquity is the hatred of oneself or one's neighbor and comes from the hatred of justice and equity."[87] In his apology, Ebbo gave a similar explanation of this psalm in defense of his own conscientious Christian loyalty and added that, in contrast to iniquity, equity is to love justice, to preserve with all one's heart the due statute and pact of love, so that one sets God on high and loves one's neighbor as much as oneself.[88] Ratramnus, like Paschasius a monk of Corbie, explored the soteriological implications of the psalm in more detail. Writing in the midst of a bitter controversy over the doctrine of predestination (ca. 850), he chose to follow the exegesis of the early medieval author Fulgentius on the self-fulfilling fate of those consumed with iniquitous hatred and loathing. Sinful souls, assured Ratramnus, are lost to hell by their own doing—such was the just price of human iniquity, a fact that by its self-evidence only served to underscore the divine *aequitas* of the Lord.[89] Gottschalk of Orbais, a Carolingian theologian who would be imprisoned for his unrepentant, Augustinian stance on predestination, also articulated this view but with characteristic economy: the Lord, as a just judge, considers the soul of each, asserted Gottschalk, adjudicating without any *iniquitas* and only the utmost *aequitas*.[90]

Ecclesiastics were not the only ones to use this particular binary discourse of right and wrong. In the early 840s an anonymous layman wrote a letter on the relationship among iniquity, equity, and demons. Having learned that his name had been slandered—more specifically, that he had been called an "imitator of demons"—at the court of Lothar and his wife, Ermengard, the nobleman defended himself with an impassioned explanation of the nature of the demonological. This clarification, he hoped, would expose the mendacity of any claims concerning his alleged demonic behavior:

> You [Queen Ermengard] said that an unexpected report had reached you, namely that I was trying to disturb the peace of the church and to overthrow fraternal concord; and you ascribed this work to demons. Demons, indeed, as is most obvious, take pleasure in dissension and the disturbing of good men, and are delighted by discord. And it is also true that whoever, stimulated by the zeal of malice, disturbs the peace-abiding church by impious efforts and desires the separation of true fraternity is made a partner of demons, the collaboration of which may the mercy of the Lord deign me worthy of immunity from forever. For he who seeks only his own justice does not desire universal discord. And therefore I do the work of demons not at all, since I seek not iniquity but rather equity and justice. For if reason is considered, a man who values iniquity, [who] renders injustice, [who] always puts forth discord to equity, and [who] never desists from this intention, more certainly ought to be said and believed to be a partner of demons, just as he [the slanderer] is who incites your lord [Lothar] so that [Lothar] may take action in such a manner against me.[91]

As much as he disliked having to state the obvious, the nobleman—whom Janet Nelson has argued should be identified as the influential court seneschal Adalhard[92]—felt that the charge leveled against him was serious enough to risk insulting the queen. By having to explain something that was well known, he was implying that Ermengard had been beguiled, was thereby acting irrationally, and had misunderstood what it meant to behave like a demon. He insisted that the queen would surely see through the calumny raised against him, if only she would consider the matter according to reason. Indeed, his letter was itself meant to guide her toward such rational discernment. Demons and those who are influenced by them, reasoned the nobleman, love iniquity and injustice and are relentless in their desire to foment discord over equity—characteristics Ermengard would recognize if she would but look again at those who were contributing to the slander and discord.

As the letter from the anonymous nobleman attests, people of the ninth century understood that where there reeked the brimstone of the devil and

his demons, the fires of iniquity also burned. During the 830s, even the demons themselves were attesting to the rampant iniquity of the realm. In his
account of the miracles that had transpired during the celebrated translation
of the relics of Saints Marcellinus and Peter (written ca. 830/31), the nobleman Einhard at times claimed to be relying on a number of small booklets
he had received from his servants, who had allegedly recorded the occurrence
of various wonders demonstrating the greater glory of his saints.[93] One report
in these booklets was particularly extraordinary, for it described the words of
an evil creature in possession of a young girl—an exceptionally loquacious
demon who called itself "Wiggo"[94]:

> The demon speaking through the girl said, "I am an assistant (*satelles*)
> and disciple of Satan, and I was for a long time a gate-keeper in
> the infernal regions, but for the last few years I and eleven of my
> companions have wreaked havoc upon the kingdom of the Franks. We
> have destroyed and utterly ruined grain, wine, and all the other crops
> that come from the earth for human use, just as we had been ordered
> to; we killed off herds [of cattle] with disease; [and] we let plague
> and pestilence loose among those people of yours. Indeed, all the
> misfortunes and evils, that people have been suffering from for a long
> time now, as they so deserved, fell upon them because of our actions
> and our assault."[95]

With Wiggo, we hear firsthand from one of those diabolic attendants later
blamed by Lothar for the perdition of the realm.[96] Unable to wreak havoc on
their own accord, explained Wiggo, he and his fellow unholy apostles had
appeared in this world only because they had been ordered to go. Wiggo
even corrected himself to make this point, claiming that they had not been
"allowed" to leave their stygian posts but had been "commanded" to do so.
When a priest, who had been called to exorcize the demon from the girl,
asked Wiggo why he and his infernal companions had been charged to torment the realm, Wiggo replied using moral language his audience knew only
too well: "because of the wickedness of this people and because of the various
iniquities of those appointed [to rule] over them."[97] But these were only introductory remarks. Relishing the opportunity to castigate his audience, Wiggo
then proceeded to describe those various iniquities with an eloquent tirade,
one that painted a truly hellish picture of Frankish society and its rulers.

Despite all its ghastly imagery, Wiggo's lurid description of the iniquities of the realm hardly took Einhard by surprise. For, as he "redacted" the episode involving Wiggo, what Einhard read must have confirmed what he already knew: the Frankish kingdom had become hell on earth.[98] How could he be surprised that demons such as Wiggo freely inhabited a world that had become so like their own? Rather, it was Wiggo's role as a teacher that to Einhard seemed truly astonishing and perverse. Closing his account of the episode, he lamented on the implications of the infernal orator's appearance and appointed task: "Alas! What a miserable state of affairs," interjects Einhard, "that our times have fallen so low that it is not good people, but evil demons who now instruct us. And those who [normally] incite us to vice and encourage us to commit crimes are now advising us to reform ourselves."[99] If there was a moral to be taken from the account, this is it. The nature of the messenger itself spoke as eloquently as its damning message. In a realm where iniquity had become the lingua franca, the people got the preacher they deserved, one who harangued them in terms they could understand. Only saints such as Marcellinus and Peter, concluded Einhard, could save them now.

The Demands of Iniquity: Conscience, Will, and Faith

To members of the rebellion in 833, the problem was equally clear: the realm was bowing beneath the heavy yoke of *iniquitas*.[100] As we saw in Chapter 4, Ebbo and the other rebel bishops justified their extraordinary action of expediting God's judgment against Louis in terms of his iniquity and the responsibility it placed upon them before God.[101] By loosely quoting the prophet Ezekiel (3:18), they professed their awareness of God's stringent imperative that "if you shall not relate to the iniquitous man his iniquity . . . I shall require his blood from your hand."[102] Consequently, the bishops, who shared with Louis the grave task of the realm's spiritual and moral governance, carefully enumerated what were—given the context of the penitential proceedings—not so much accusations as the incontrovertible facts of his iniquitous behavior.

But it was not the passage from Ezekiel alone that reminded the bishops of the moral demands of their episcopal *ministerium*. If Thomas Noble is correct that Louis conceived of himself as the realm's monarchial "abbot" and, through his continuous programs of Benedictine reform, made certain his subjects understood that he was serving in this "abbatial" role, then in

833 the directives of Benedict's Rule for the removal of a bad abbot assume a profound importance. "If the whole community should by mutual consent elect a person consenting to their—God forbid—vices," commands Benedict,

> and those vices in whatever way come to the attention of the bishop
> to whose diocese that place pertains, or to neighboring abbots or
> Christians, these [persons outside the monastery] should not permit the
> consent of the wicked to prevail, but should appoint an overseer worthy
> of God's House, knowing that they shall receive a good reward for this,
> if they do it chastely and with godly zeal; just as, on the contrary, they
> shall commit a sin if they neglect [to do] it.[103]

In this striking passage, Benedict not only calls for the replacement of an abbot who allows the vices of his community to thrive but even warrants episcopal intervention in the process.[104] Much like the passage by Ezekiel, Benedict insists that any bishop who perceives such wrongs in the monastic community but does nothing to stop them is himself made a sinner by his negligence. On the other hand, if the same watchman takes action in accordance with prudence and discretion, he will be rewarded. In 833, the Benedictine-inflected moral code that Louis had promoted over the course of his reign was here turned back upon him.

Bishop Agobard of Lyon also set the problems of the reign within the moral framework of the emperor's *iniquitas*. In his affidavit of the proceedings at Soissons, which he presented to Lothar as evidence of their propriety and necessity, Agobard certified that Louis was one who had required a "remission of iniquities."[105] He had already argued elsewhere that Louis was unwittingly inflicting a "wound" upon the realm through his iniquity.[106] Now, if Louis would just look into the salutary statement prepared by the bishops, counseled Agobard, he would see, as if in a mirror, the error of his ways and consequently undertake penance, just as it said in Psalm 50:5, "I know my iniquity and my sin is always before me."[107]

Similarly, Archbishop Ebbo, even after nine years of persecution, would continue to justify his apparent treason within the same ideological framework, which he and the rebellion had established earlier with the quotation from Ezekiel. Compelled like any truly righteous man to combat iniquity, Ebbo maintained that, in 833, he had attempted to meet the difficult demands of this moral imperative. He had not been ashamed (unlike Louis, who had to be coaxed) to admit his vice and say with the psalmist, "For I will declare my iniquity and I will think for my sin" (Ps. 37:19).[108] Having lost his episcopal see twice over the decade since Louis' penance, Ebbo had become all the more convinced of both the iniquity of the realm and the need for its correction. In his impassioned apology composed in 841 shortly after his second flight from Reims, Ebbo upheld his beliefs and accounted for the allegedly treasonous turn in his career. He was hardly surprised that, in a kingdom sinking under the weight of its own sin, the calumniation of his selfless sacrifice of penance as a criminal sentence had prevailed. For Ebbo knew that iniquity was itself tantamount to injustice. Scripture may say that "he who loves iniquity hates his own soul" (Ps. 10:6), but, as Ebbo noted in his revised apology, what this psalm actually means is clear: "He who does not love justice hates his own soul."[109] The terrible irony, of course, was that, for Ebbo, it was exactly this injustice, this iniquity still prevalent in the 840s, that not only led to his two depositions, but was also the very thing he and others, such as Abbot Wala of Corbie, had tried to correct at Soissons in 833. That was what galled.

At about the time that Ebbo was composing his bitter apology, Paschasius Radbertus was observing how the same widespread love of iniquity was causing the reputation of his hero, Abbot Wala, to be unjustly slandered. In Wala's defense, Paschasius turned such charges on their head to show that the very concepts of loyalty and faith were themselves being perverted.[110] Using a Pauline allusion, he explained that a truly righteous man such as Wala could only be considered iniquitous by those who themselves unwittingly cherish iniquity and who have replaced the selfless love of Christ and of one another (Gal. 5:6) with the uncharitable desire to pursue their own selfish—what Paschasius calls "earthly," "bestial," and "diabolical"—will. There are times, reasons Paschasius, "when faith is not faith, because it is not of love toward God and one's neighbor, but is of earthly, brutish remonstrance and diabolical obligation."[111] It is, therefore, quite clear, he continues,

> that anyone who cherishes injustice or agrees to it wickedly hates both his own soul and him with whom he indulgently agrees on behalf of iniquity (cf. Ps. 10:6). It follows plainly that fealty should not extend to what one might wish for, namely, to rise up against God's commandments at the behest of an earthly lord. Otherwise, by evil consent the faithless one will lose that faith which is brought to fruition through love for one's neighbor.[112]

In other words, true faith is the unconditional love of Christ and one's neighbors, while love for that which is unjust, covetous, and willful—such as supporting an earthly ruler against God's laws for one's own interest—is faith both base and diabolical (here Paschasius, like Ebbo, gives a juridical interpretation to Psalm 10:6). The divine obligation for action imposed by iniquity always takes precedence over the diabolical obligation for action imposed by terrestrial oaths. Perhaps Ebbo put it best in his apology when he quoted Christ's unequivocal statement that "he who is not with me is against me" (Luke 11:23).[113] In the dark days of the 830s, both Ebbo and Wala had been confronted with such a moment of decision, with all its conflicting loyalties, and both claimed to have taken the high road. For they had known that to be with Christ was to act on behalf of charity, not cupidity, on behalf of equity, not iniquity.[114]

Annealing Equity's Sword

When Louis' critics described the ruination of the realm in terms of iniquity, his defenders understood the particular imperial virtue being impugned. Indeed, in countering the charges of Louis' iniquity, his supporters worked specifically within the binary system that the condition of *iniquitas* suggested, taking care to stress the consummate imperial *aequitas* in the face of oppression and its immutability before any disrepute.[115]

The loyal abbot Hrabanus Maurus of Fulda, writing to Louis in his defense sometime shortly after the division of the rebel faction in 834, sought to counter the recent accusations of imperial *iniquitas* but did so by evaluating the effect of such iniquity upon the emperor's mind.[116] In a lengthy letter, Hrabanus provided numerous scriptural and historical examples testifying to the respect sons owe to their fathers and subjects to their kings. The sons of the emperors Constantine and Theodosius, he explained, had all known and honored the principle that one's patrimony is not obtained rightfully during the father's lifetime, "for there is no law, whether human or divine," assured Hrabanus, "that praises sons for banishing their parents from their homes and possessions through plundering and cheating; rather, [the law] teaches and advises the deserving to expect a future inheritance from their parents with reverence, humility, and honorable obedience."[117] Through such reminders, Hrabanus emphasized to the emperor that, in their recent revolt, Louis' sons had acted unlawfully and in shameful disrespect of their father.

Yet, like the members of the rebellion, Hrabanus could not deny that iniquity truly had been visited upon Louis. Indeed, he even invoked the same psalm that Agobard had referenced earlier to induce the emperor to recognize his wrongs—"I know my iniquity and my sin is always before me" (Ps. 50:5). Hrabanus, like Agobard, urged this same introspection, quoting this psalm in his letter to Louis to proclaim the great merits of one who has recognized his iniquity, confessed, and grown wiser thereby.[118] To underscore this point, he not only marched out a series of scriptural examples demonstrative of wisdom forged through iniquity but also opened and closed his treatise with an affirmation of Louis' "humble" and "devout" mind.[119] Hrabanus may have acknowledged the recent ascendance of iniquity, but, as scripture made clear, it was this same iniquity that, by annealing the emperor's mind, had ultimately been for the benefit of the realm. Louis himself appears to have agreed with this interpretation, for, shortly after his reinstatement at Saint-Denis in 834, the emperor explained that he had recently experienced an "event of mortal inconstancy" in which he had been disciplined and subsequently shown "utterly glorious mercy" by the divine rod and staff—here speaking allusively in the scriptural terms (Ps. 22:4) he was known to esteem.[120] However, there was still one more lesson Hrabanus urged the chastened emperor to take: he should show paternal clemency. Not to forgive his prodigal sons would demonstrate that he had ultimately learned little from his ordeal. And that Hrabanus could scarcely believe.[121]

Seven years later, following Louis' death and the subsequent slaughter committed by his sons on the battlefield of Fontenoy, Hrabanus felt it necessary, in light of the recent display of sordid rulership, to remind a friend about the proper nature of sovereignty. "There is a great difference," he explained to Bishop Otgar of Mainz, "between a seditious tyrant and a legitimate ruler, between one who strives to destroy the tranquility of Christian peace, and one who desires to defend with weapons equity against iniquity."[122] In his earlier letter of 834—which was described by a contemporary reader as an epistle of consolation to the emperor[123]—Hrabanus may also have thought about the events of 833 in these same binary terms, for after acknowledging Louis' tempered mind, he invoked as a foil the tyrannical behavior of Louis' rebellious sons. By marshaling a host of examples of iniquitous tyrants from the past (culled both from scripture and the *Historiae* of Augustine's pupil Orosius), Hrabanus cast in bold relief the strikingly similar iniquity displayed by Lothar, Pippin, and Louis the German in the present. The ignominious association implicitly stressed, by way of contrast, the emperor's righteous stance during the recent struggles—as an embattled, and ultimately triumphant, defender of equity.[124]

"Contrary to the Course of Complete Equity"

In his retrospective, typological account of the events leading up to Louis' restoration in 835, the anonymous first annalist of the Annals of Saint-Bertin told a gripping tale of loss and redemption—a story that not only spoke of the just deserts reaped by kings neglectful of their duties and by sons disobedient to their father, but also extolled the triumph of Louis' perfect *aequitas* over the assembled forces of iniquity.

Before examining the annalist's use of *aequitas*, a brief review of his narrative is helpful. Following Louis' penance at Soissons, explained the annalist, Lothar escorted his father first to Compiègne and then to Aachen, planning to remain there for the winter. But by February 834, Lothar's brothers Pippin and Louis the German had turned on him and with their armies marched on Aachen to free their captive father. According to the annalist, their tergiversation had been prompted by the feelings of compassion that Lothar's confinement and inhumane treatment of Louis had stirred. Forewarned, Lothar hastened to Paris with his father in thrall. Even during these desperate maneuvers, observed the annalist reprovingly, Lothar had kept Louis under the same form of cruel custody. When Lothar and his men arrived at Paris, to their dismay they found Pippin's army encamped on the opposite bank of the Seine. Strong winds and heavy rain had rendered the channels of the river impassable. Such fortune afforded Lothar little comfort, however, for word soon came that Louis the German was heading for Paris with an even larger army. Stricken with terror, the craven Lothar fled, explained the annalist, leaving his father behind in the hope of delaying any further pursuit.

On the following day, in the church of Saint-Denis, several bishops arrayed Louis with royal robes and weapons, effectively restoring his imperial dignity. After this impromptu ceremony, Louis spent the next several months pursuing Lothar, making manifest to all the top priority of his rule—the reestablishment of peace and concord throughout the realm.[125] Finally, by mid-August of 834, Lothar accepted his father's terms for reconciliation; after swearing oaths that neither he nor his followers would ever engage in such shameful behavior again, Lothar was granted the kingdom of Italy and his men shown the clemency for which the emperor was renowned.

Six months later, Louis called a general ecclesiastical council at his palace in Thionville. After the recent series of events had been discussed in full, the presiding bishops and abbots reached a consensus: all those in attendance should acknowledge Louis' status as their sovereign and lord. Once this decision had been codified, the bishops then moved the assembly to the church of Metz and there restored the crown to Louis' head "to the utmost joy of everyone," observed the annalist. To conclude the ceremony, the captive Ebbo was brought forward. The former archbishop of Reims,

> who had once been a kind of standard-bearer of that whole conspiracy, ascended a high place in that same church and voluntarily confessed before everyone that the emperor had been unjustly deposed; that everything done against him had been wickedly accomplished, and plotted contrary to the course of complete equity.[126]

There can be no doubt that this formal assembly on February 28, exactly one year after Lothar's flight from Paris, was meant to correct the earlier divestiture that had taken place at Soissons in October of 833. Indeed, the ceremony at Metz not only reveals that Louis and his supporters believed the "fraudulent" ritual at Soissons had been efficacious, and, thus, needed to be formally counteracted, but the similarity of the procedures at both ceremonies also suggests a belief in the efficacy of a literal ritual reversal[127]: voluntary confessions were read aloud from statements by the transgressors at each assembly, and episcopal affidavits were employed in both 833 (recall Agobard's short testament of Louis' iniquity) and 835 to certify the consensus and legitimacy of the proceedings. The argumentative frame made explicit by the annalist—if not by the assembly of loyal bishops themselves—to justify the reversal was no different in this respect, for it too was a mirror image of that moral-legal frame that had lent meaning to the events of 833: everything that had been done against Louis, Ebbo now admitted in 835, "had been wickedly (*inique*) accomplished, and plotted contrary to the course of complete equity (*contra totius tramitem aequitatis*)."[128] Just as Louis had voluntarily confessed his criminal iniquity before the assembly at Soissons, Ebbo now made a voluntary confession, before all who were present, of his own iniquitous "capital crime."

Yet, unlike Louis' earlier pronouncement, Ebbo's confession in 835 did more than testify to his and his co-conspirators' iniquity. Rather, he expressed their iniquitous deeds obliquely, as transgressions against and contrary to the course of complete equity—a righteous path presupposed and by contrast made implicitly synonymous with the direction of the realm under Louis' reign.

"There Was Written *Equitatius*"

While the loyal annalist countered accusations of Louis' *iniquitas* by indirectly asserting the emperor's unshakeable course of *aequitas*, another supporter rebuffed these same charges through the divination of Louis' equitable character and conscience. After the emperor's makeshift restoration at Saint-Denis and Judith's return from captivity in Italy, the loyal court poet Walafrid Strabo presented the empress with a short poem.[129] Within the opening lines of his verse, Walafrid reminded Judith of the horrors perpetrated throughout the realm during the recent "dominion of suffering." Worries for the side of right unceasingly filled the poet's breast. Indeed, he could not even find solace in what were—and here Walafrid foreshadows artfully—his "regularly prophetic dreams." But one night, he recalled, God drove away the dismal clouds of fear to reveal an auspicious sight. Before the wide eyes of the dreaming poet there appeared a sublime book. Walafrid discovered that its text, in alternating sections of verse and prose, spoke in plain language of matters pertaining to both the emperor and the empire. What especially caught his eye in the wondrous volume, however, were a striking illustration and its subtitle:

Caesaris hic nomen quadam sub imagine versum,	Here, under a certain image, the name of Caesar was changed, and
Proque sacro semper Ludowici Equitatius illic	there, for that ever sacred name of Louis, was written "*Equitatius.*"[130]

If the name beneath the emperor's image at first appeared strange to the wakeful reader, it hardly confounded the perceptive dreamer, for the qualitative cognomen *Equitatius* clearly characterized the emperor's person; after all, admitted Walafrid, things are known best by their ordinary operations and familiar deeds.[131] This correspondence soon became manifest as the poet quickened his reading: twinned treacherous desertion, a general state of sin, and double violation leaped from the pages, only to be followed by an equally evocative narrative of victorious perseverance and the ever retrievable honor of a ruler and his reign.[132] Simultaneously entranced and overwhelmed by the sublimity of the text, he stood at the brink of madness, when suddenly the tome was torn from his grasp. Reeling, Walafrid turned to discover that his savior was a mysterious monk, who now held the ineffable, omniscient book well away from his sight. The dreaming poet then began to wake, but not before his savior bid him farewell with an enigmatic speech:

Tristor ex oculis humor, quam tota decebat,	Tears sadder than it was right for any breast to bear fall from the eyes
Pectora, non longae passuri damna ruinae.	of one who will not suffer the misfortunes of a long overthrow.[133]

Although Walafrid struggled to retain the transcendental knowledge he had gleaned from the numinous manuscript, upon awakening he could remember little more than the emperor's epithet and the monk's parting words. It was the former fragment that the poet now analyzed for the empress, closing the poetic account of his dream with an attempt at interpretation. The appearance of *Equitatius* for Louis, explained Walafrid, was surely an omen of peace—recall that Walafrid had described his dreams to be prophetic—for the name foretold of a rapid abundance of virtue (*veloces virtutis opes*). Indeed, this auspicious interpretation of the emperor's true name was confirmed by the strange monk's farewell speech: oppressive burdens ought not aggrieve the man who endures overmuch, declared Walafrid, since he will make a swift return to rule. But all these fragments really only fell into place, the learned poet concluded, because he had ultimately witnessed the propitious dream portents "fulfilled in deeds." Whatever else his dream might reveal, suggested Walafrid in closing, it was now up to the empress to discern.

Perhaps Judith did find other meanings hidden in the cryptic dream poem, but its central message was perfectly clear. For the one thing that Walafrid conveniently remembered was surely the only thing one needed to remember: the revelation of Louis' true name, *Equitatius.*

While Walafrid expected Judith to infer from this epithet the meaning he intended, such fluency has been lost among later readers of his poem.

Walafrid was a man of his time, writing for royal readers of his time. The linguistic and cultural systems of reference shared among this interpretive community to impart meaning were no different in this respect, for they too were a unique product of their milieu, shaped through an ongoing dialectic between normative traditions and particular contingencies.[134] Consequently, modern scholars, far removed from this community, its concerns, and its shifting systems of referents, have only been able to postulate what Walafrid expected Judith to understand by the name *Equitatius*. Helena Siemes, for instance, argued that Walafrid meant to draw a connection between the image of Louis presented in his dream poem and the likeness of the sixth-century Ostrogothic king Theodoric described in one of Walafrid's earlier poems, *De imagine Tetrici* (composed in 829).[135] Both representations, contends Siemes, conjured up notions of a "Rider": on the one hand, the word *Equitatius* evoked and drew meaning from its near homonym *equitatus* (horseman); on the other hand, Walafrid's verse portrait of Theodoric focused on an equestrian statue of that Gothic king that stood in the poet's day before the royal palace at Aachen. According to Siemes, a deliberate association between the two images was made by the poet in order to contrast the wicked King Theodoric, whom Walafrid had previously vilified, with the salvific grace of Louis, a "Rider of men." This latter equestrian image Siemes borrowed from the contemporary exegesis of Hrabanus Maurus on a related passage in the Old Testament (Exodus 15:1); men, in their behavior and actions, Hrabanus explained, are like horses, upon which ride either the Lord or the devil and his demons.[136] Thus, as the leader of his people, Louis could also be thought of as their "Rider," concluded Siemes, their *Equitatius*, judiciously guiding them in imitation of an "equestrian" Christ.

Another modern interpreter of the poem, Hans Kamphausen, argued that, with the name *Equitatius*, Walafrid had expressed a complex idea through an etymological association: Louis was the embodiment of judiciousness and calm (*aequitas*), and he personified the best quality of a horse (*equus*)—controlled haste. The poet had dreamed of a man in whom these two attributes, *aequitas* and *equus*, were united and whose very name seemed to convey imminent consolation and hope.[137]

Paul Dutton also characterized Walafrid's poem to Judith as a work of consolation but suggested that the poet was being deliberately Boethian in his vision. Taking its transmission history into consideration, he noted that the dream poem usually follows Walafrid's complex poem *De imagine Tetrici* in the manuscripts within which it survives. In that earlier poem on the statue of Theodoric, Walafrid alluded to Boethius's great work *Consolation of Philosophy* and emphasized the comfort brought to those who are self-aware. Dutton suggested that Walafrid's dream poem to Judith was also cast in this Boethian mold, offering the empress philosophical reassurance and prophetic revelation.[138]

While the Boethian theme may have carried over into Walafrid's dream poem, the equestrian motif probably did not accompany it. In the poem vilifying Theodoric, Walafrid employed the metaphor commonly known to connote pride—that of a fallen horseman.[139] Likewise, in the poem to Judith, Walafrid utilized a vivid metaphor, one that would convey consolation and hope. The solution the poet found was not in the representation of Louis as a Christ-like "Rider of men" nor in his portrayal as the embodiment of alloyed equipoise and equine haste, for the subtle structure of Walafrid's poem rendered the reliance upon an equestrian motif unnecessary.

When Walafrid "previewed" the plans for the realm in the Lord's book of history past, present, and future, the sacred meaning of the events he saw there was essentially tantamount to their temporal interpretation, as rendered by the emperor's supporters shortly after the same events' occurrence. As we have seen, the anonymous annalist of the Annals of Saint-Bertin reported that Louis, an emperor who guided the realm along its righteous course, had first been wronged and then, by virtue of his customary patience and clemency, honorably restored. In the annalist's final estimation of those deeds, Ebbo and his co-conspirators had acted iniquitously, having taken insolent steps contrary to the course of complete equity. In the prophetic dream book of truth beheld by Walafrid, the story was the same. No matter that the poet was able to recall only a few details of God's future designs, for, as Walafrid knew, the suggestive fragments that he could remember for the empress were meaningful enough. He had read of a ruler he recognized to be Louis, though aptly identified as *Equitatius*. Twofold treachery, abandonment, sin, and seizure were the events that the text then disclosed, only to be followed by remarks on perseverance and a ruler's ever retrievable honor. On one level, these vague impressions confirmed that God himself had long ago set down in his book the same moral interpretation currently being promulgated by the emperor's supporters in their books (recall the adjudication of the events and the codification and wide proclamation of their meaning by Drogo and other bishops overseeing Louis' restoration at Metz). But on a deeper level, the fragments of Walafrid's dream revealed how myopic and vulgar such an interpretation really was; for even those fleeting impressions gained from the

Lord's book granted a more penetrating view of the truth than could ever be achieved by the feeble powers of mortal discernment. That Ebbo and his allies in 833 had acted iniquitously and in opposition to complete equity Walafrid's revelatory reading confirmed beyond doubt. That the emperor himself was the very apotheosis of the realm's equity, however, was an immediately recognizable truth only divulged to Walafrid during his brief encounter with the Lord's sublime book. What his dream seems to suggest is that, while the emperor's supporters at the recoronation assembly of 835 were correct in their interpretation of the recent events, they had not gleaned the more profound truth: when the rebel faction acted iniquitously, they had not just upset the righteous course of the realm but had striven to wrest control from its steady pilot—*Equitatius*, equity incarnate, Louis.[140] Among the emperor's contemporaries, it was his anonymous biographer who would come closest to gaining this quintessential insight: Louis had always been a lover of equity, the Astronomer would insist again and again, a pious ruler who always weighed matters carefully and with equitable balance.[141]

Buried within Eugen Wohlhaupter's study of equity and canon law published in 1931 is a subsection of four concise pages, titled "*Aequitas* postulated as a virtue of rulership in the Carolingian empire."[142] Noting that the dream poem by Walafrid on *Equitatius* should be understood in terms of equity, Wohlhaupter suggested that *aequitas* as an ideal virtue of Christian rulership had been introduced specifically during the reign of Louis the Pious.[143] What was more, he contended that this concept of order and right rule first made its appearance in the acts of the council of Paris drawn up by Jonas of Orléans in 829 (one of four great reform assemblies called by Louis the Pious and Lothar in that year).[144]

As we have seen, the concept of *aequitas* did indeed experience a particular appreciation and endorsement during Louis' reign, although not necessarily at the specific occasion of the Paris council, as Wohlhaupter claimed. Rather, what the record from the assembly in 829 documents is a lament to the emperor from his bishops often expressed in terms of equity and iniquity, whose moral theology—far from being devised as an ad hoc program—was already well developed and understood. Through their careful consideration of the Psalms in particular, Carolingian intellectuals often defined the moral binary in terms and degrees of one's love for Christ and neighbor and took its measure by its manifest effect on one's loyalty and will. The soul was caught in a struggle within the conscience, an interior zone of engagement as much dictated and defined by the rule of law and its absence as the exterior realm. Paschasius Radbertus was the one writer who consistently sounded the depths of conscience in search of an answer for the events of the 830s and their aftermath. Yet, as Wohlhaupter observed, by 829 the realm's bishops had already expressed their concerns in terms of iniquity, transgression, and conscience: since the realm was suffering deservedly, they harangued (and repeatedly quoted Ezekiel 3:18 and Gregory the Great to justify their bold speech[145]), on account of its iniquity, the only way forward was for everyone, regardless of rank, to fast for three days and engage in a collective examination of conscience. In this way, each might recognize how he had offended God and move swiftly to make amends through the satisfaction of penance.[146]

Thus, when the rebel bishops in 833 claimed that, in the performance of their grave deed, they were acting in accordance with their "most prudent discretion" (*moderatio discretissima*)—what Benedict in his Rule called the "mother of all virtues"[147]—it appears that they were following a Benedictine–Gregorian conception of conscience and its concomitant demands of corrective intervention. Quoting from Gregory the Great, they explained that they were kept on their course both by being checked through the practice of humility toward their peers and being goaded by the zeal of curbing the vices of sinners.[148] Yet, this characterization of their discretion is not entirely accurate, for, when the bishops made such a claim, they were referring specifically to their most prudent employment of that constitutive gift of the episcopal office—the power to bind and loose souls. It is only through the Benedictine–Gregorian notion of discretion, they explained, that they may wield their awesome power responsibly, conscientiously.

The bishops would eventually come to acknowledge that the basis for their prudent discretion derived not from a Benedictine or Gregorian notion of conscience but from what they called "Peter's Equity" (*aequitas Petri*).[149] It was Saint Peter on whom Christ had bestowed the power to bind and loose souls, and, through Peter, this power had become an apostolic, and then episcopal, privilege. In the middle of the fifth century, Pope Leo the Great (d. 461) first stated how this Petrine privilege should be wielded:

> This privilege of Peter resides wherever judgment has been passed in accordance with his equity (*ex ipsius aequitate*). And neither severity nor leniency is excessive where nothing is bound or loosed unless that which blessed Peter would bind or loose.[150]

The guiding episcopal precept of "Peter's Equity" required that the bishop, before daring to make any decision about when to use Peter's great privilege, must first ask himself how Peter, with his highest of standards, would act in the same situation. What is remarkable is that this mimetic model formalized by Pope Leo in the fifth century was not invoked again until the middle of the ninth. Archbishop Hincmar of Reims would quote from Pope Leo's definition no less than five times, while King Charles the Bald (through the pen of Hincmar) insulted Pope Hadrian by calling into question that pope's own adherence to Peter's Equity.[151] Although the bishops in 833 never use the term *aequitas* in their *Relatio* of Louis' penance, their description of the basis for their prudent ministry of Peter's privilege comes immediately after their quotation of Ezekiel, which justifies the need to show the iniquitous man his iniquity. Given the binary nature of iniquity and equity, when the bishops in 833 defined the conscientious ministry of their Petrine power in the Benedictine and Gregorian terms of zeal and humility, such a "counterbalanced" ministry is another way of saying that they were acting equitably (and thus in opposition to the iniquity of the man they sought to warn and correct). Recall Hrabanus Maurus' observation that *aequitas* was nothing other than a "form of discretion."[152] That the bishops grounded their conscience in the words of Gregory and Benedict rather than the judgment of Saint Peter, as Hincmar would only three decades later, demonstrates the abiding influence held by the reforms of Charlemagne, Louis the Pious, and Benedict of Aniane. The Carolingian bishops, even at their most daring in 833, had not yet tapped the "intrinsic" source for their own guidance—that they might act in accordance with an exclusively episcopal, Petrine exemplar.

Epilogue: Convictions Past and Present

> *Bad things befall one, good things come to pass, both happen.*
> [Accidunt mala, contingunt bona, eveniunt utraque.]
> —*Bede,* De orthographia

IN THE SECOND half of the ninth century, Sedulius Scottus, an Irish monk of Lothar's middle kingdom and sometime poet, penned sixteen verses on the binary relationship between equity and iniquity.[1] Cast in the form of a riddle (what Sedulius or perhaps a later interpolator called a "*problema*," whose solution, as Ludwig Traube noted long ago, is *iniquitas*), the poem questions the relationship between *aequum* and *verum*, the equitable and the true, raising doubts about the former and recalling the odious nature of its origins:

Nascitur ex aequo, quod iam mox abdicat aequum.	It is born from equity, but immediately rejects equity;
Sic ex non aequo nos aequum cernimus esse.	Thus, we see that equity is from [what is] not equity.
Si verum fuerit, quod et aequum, scire memento:	If the true were to be the same as the equitable, remember this:

Non erit inventum seu verum sive quod aequum.   neither what is true nor
                                               what is equitable will
                                               be found.[2]

In the years following the death of Louis the Pious, the combined experience of civil war, political instability, and general strife apparently led Sedulius to reconsider a familiar concept, one that was still being taken for truth but was now felt by some to be increasingly devoid of it. In Sedulius's estimation, equity was being perverted to the point where it now hardly differed from its intrinsic counterpart of iniquity.

At the beginning of the tenth century, the monk Flodoard of Reims retold the sequence of events that had led to Louis' restoration to the throne in 835 by inserting within his own work the relatively brief narrative for that year found in the Annals of Saint-Bertin. As Bernhard Simson recognized over a century ago, Flodoard or an early copyist reproduced the account of the annalist verbatim but for one small alteration, substituting *auctoritas* for the word *aequitas*.[3] Like Sedulius's poem, this subtle exchange of terms perhaps offers a rare glimpse of the dissatisfaction with and eventual transformation of Louis' normative system of equity. Flodoard had read and copied the account of Ebbo's deposition and Louis' return as given by the ninth-century annals, but understood—even if unconsciously, with just a slip of the pen— the events they reported in tenth-century terms; when the anonymous annalist explained that Ebbo confessed to having acted in 833 "contrary to the course of complete equity" (*aequitas*), Flodoard wrote that Ebbo had acted "contrary to the course of complete authority" (*auctoritas*).[4]

Taken together, the two examples sketched above may provide faint traces of the general transformation of Louis' ideological program of equity in its relationship with the changing political realities of the Carolingian realm. Fragmentation of Louis' empire among his sons and their successors led contemporaries such as Paschasius Radbertus to see and lament in this process the disappearance of the ideal of universal equity and the increase in arbitrary and conflicting modes of justice.[5] Sedulius Scottus appeared to be more cynical than despondent, noting that appeals to equity were still rather common during his day, but that equity itself had become something of a sham, being tailored to suit any perverse circumstance or expedient.[6] As he observed in his poem, "Lords prefer it when equity is false," for to deal in terms of equity meant that "the same thing now remains true, then appears false."[7] Truth had fallen away from equity, leaving equity itself now not far removed from its evil twin. By the early tenth century, Flodoard understood the deeds done to Louis as having been performed not against the course of equity—a condition that, as we have seen, Hrabanus Maurus, the first annalist of the Annals of Saint-Bertin, and Walafrid Strabo had all presumed as right, and in the wake of 833 still sought to recover for the realm—but against that of authority. With a multiplicity of lords and kingdoms, the focus in Flodoard's day, one that he projected anachronistically into the past, was on legitimate authority and how it might be recognized, rather than on a now impossible norm of universal equity. Here, one would do well to recall the plea of Bishop Agobard to Louis the Pious in 822 to institute that very norm:

> Would that everyone were ruled under one most pious king by one law, the same [law] according to which one lives and his neighbors also answer. It would indeed accomplish much on behalf of the concord of the city of God, and the equity of the people. But because it is an undertaking of such magnitude, and perhaps humanly impossible.[8]

Agobard dared the emperor to do the impossible, in terms he knew the emperor would understand. What Paschasius would see lacking in the 850s from the perspective of Corbie, Agobard had already desired by 820 from his point of view in Lyon and the emperor and his advisors had attempted to realize in the years between. The fleeting ideal of concord, unity, and equity had been harnessed momentarily, and then just as quickly been lost.

Put more broadly, Louis' promotion of equity went hand in hand not only with the Benedictine Rule but also with the notion of a transpersonal polity, a *res publica* that carried with it the correlatives of the *utilitas publica* or *utilitas populi*.[9] Both Louis' critics and his defenders were first and foremost moved by a concern for the realm, not just in terms of its law but in its disposition as *ecclesia*, as a state that was also coterminous with a religious society and, therefore, had to be ministered to and made healthy.[10] Note the repeated, solicitous references to the general or public *utilitas* in the rebel bishops' *Relatio* of 833.[11] In the quest for the health of the realm and the welfare of the people, purgative penance, accompanied by occasional strong-armed attempts at enlightening the blind sinner, was understood to be a key instrument. In the bishops' pastoral terms, penance often served as the conscientious shepherd's "hoe of good work."[12]

Such reminders regarding the extensive attention paid to the realm's health, both corporeal and spiritual, bring us back to a consideration of individuals, their beliefs, and—as has so often been the case in the preceding pages—their books. Frechulf, a loyal bishop of Lisieux, explained to Queen Judith in 829 that the history book he was sending for her son Charles's education was like a mirror in which the prince would be able to see what should be done and what should be avoided: "Enlightened by the deeds of the emperors, the triumphs of the saints, and the teachings of magnificent doctors, he will discover what to do cautiously and what to avoid shrewdly."[13] The past could provide guidance for the present in order to attain a more secure—and, hence, salutary—future, a relationship among the three aspects of time that was often conflated, crystallized, and polished to form the reflective surface of a mimetic mirror. Yet, while it is through this same formalizing process that both the selective relationship of past, present, and future preserved in the text and the historical context of their configuration were meant to be glazed over and effaced, these dynamic variables must not be overlooked; in each instance, it was the specific future desired by the historian that informed his equally specific, suggestive, and typically nostalgic presentation of the past. As we have seen, this was the case not only in the composition of historical narratives but also in their subsequent compilation into multiwork historical anthologies. God may have already written the future of his chosen people, the Franks, but the text of this teleological story was always subject to his emendation, something that wary Carolingian actors and advisors, writers and compilers kept well in mind.[14] When Walafrid Strabo informed Judith that, in a dream, he had been granted an opportunity to read God's great book and preview the fate of the king and kingdom within it, perhaps the queen wondered if he had seen any such divine emendations made to its text, changes like those another Carolingian dreamer had previously witnessed upon God's wall inscribed with the names of the elect.[15]

In a way, medical prognostication charts, which we encountered in the Introduction, were a clumsy, alternate means by which to gain momentary access to God's book and learn what he had inscribed there about the health of his people. That the chart in Fig. 1 is from a ninth-century book associated with Hincmar of Reims, one otherwise replete with numerous texts on the debate over the status of Ebbo and the Reims episcopate, is especially intriguing.[16] Was it merely by chance that the divinatory chart was included amid these texts? Or did their compiler understand there to be a connection among them? Hincmar had apparently practiced the art of intertextual juxtaposition and assemblage once before; by placing the damning vision of Bernold immediately after Ebbo's apology in another compilation, he thereby created sequential "chapters" that together told the true story of Ebbo's character, career, and its otherworldly conclusion.[17] Whether Hincmar also practiced the art of divination remains unknown.

One book whose texts were certainly meant to be read together for their cumulative salutary effect is the miscellany requested by Louis the Pious shortly after his ad hoc restoration ceremony at Saint-Denis in 834. We have already encountered Louis' letter of request for this volume several times in the preceding pages, for within it the emperor recalled his recent trials in 833 and interpreted them as experiences by which he had been chastened by God and restored to power through the Lord's love and mercy. But as Louis explains to his addressee, Abbot Hilduin of Saint-Denis, God had not intervened in these matters directly but had done so through his servant Saint Denis. Thanks to the great devotion shown to Denis by Louis' royal predecessors and Carolingian ancestors, devotion practiced with even greater fervor by Louis himself, the saint had long been a special protector of the Frankish kings and their subjects. This fact was made especially manifest after Louis' desertion by his troops on the Rotfeld, "an event of human inconstancy," proclaimed Louis, "which must always be acknowledged as a just judgment of God." For it had surely been no coincidence, he reasoned, that "we were restored and raised up once more by divine virtue" specifically "before the altar of our lord and most reverend father Denis." Having taken up his sword-belt again through the merits and consolation of the saint and "by the judgment and authority of the episcopacy," Louis rejoiced in knowing that he continued to be worthy of the support of Denis "up to the present day." To make this fact all the more certain, Louis now commanded Abbot Hilduin to compile a volume of various texts having to do with his abbey's great saint and to send it to him immediately. This was to be done in all haste, concluded Louis, "since we believe that we have the great and very sweetest, desirable pledge of the presence of that lord and consoler Denis, wherever we may be, if we speak in prayer, conversation, or reading, the words uttered with him or about him or by him."[18] The perils of this world could be surmounted with the help of Saint Denis, whose divine assistance was secured by means of Louis' special vademecum—eloquent testimony of a culture for which deep faith and power politics were inextricably conjoined.

Throughout the preceding pages we have looked at the events of 833 as a way to understand the relationships among historical consciousness, memory, and a variety of narrative modes. In Part I the many different narratives supplied by (chiefly ecclesiastical) contemporaries were examined in order to gain insight into the manifold ways in which Louis' troubles in 833 were interpreted and shaped by immediate concerns and idiosyncratic sensibilities. Biblical typology was largely the lens through which the events were understood, although the Benedictine interpretation of scripture, with its emphasis on obedience and humility, stability and correction, was also a guiding interpretive mode, often underlying other modes and lending them their narrative structure. In every instance, the events were depicted vividly—indeed, at times even dramatically—in order to draw attention to the fact that a great wrong had been committed. Yet, exactly who had committed the wrong or even what the wrong was understood to have been was a hotly contested matter.[19]

At the beginning of the tenth century, for instance, Odilo of Saint-Médard claimed that Louis the Pious, in his "prison diary," recalled having had a remarkable dream regarding such historical culpability. His illustrious benefactor Saint Sebastian, he said, had forewarned him in his sleep that he was soon to die and that the empire would consequently fall; but the saint had also been the bearer of happy news—God would not hold Louis responsible for its ruin. Of the many remarkable things found within Odilo's narrative, this royal dream is perhaps the most arresting, for it not only suggests that, by Odilo's time, the Carolingian empire was thought to have fallen, but by its divine reassurance of Louis' innocence it also implies that there were some, if not most, who held Louis to blame. Decades earlier, in 874, Louis' son Louis the German was himself said to have had a "terrifying" dream in which he saw his father in torment, pleading for his son's assistance in order that he might find release and attain salvation. According to the annalist who reported this royal dream, Louis the Pious had "deservedly been condemned to suffer penalties, since he would not correct the errors of those who had been entrusted to him while he could, even after he had been warned."[20] As we have seen, such incriminations would only mount over the centuries. Yet, already as early as the 850s, feelings about Louis' responsibility for the empire's wrongs ran high. Audradus, a strange suffragan bishop of Sens, in one of his numerous oracular dreams claimed at that time to have witnessed God at first interrogate Louis about his role in the realm's many troubles and, after hearing his testimony, consequently absolve the dead emperor of any guilt for its plight. Like the dream penned by Odilo, Audradus's dream about Louis' innocence with respect to the wrack and ruin of the empire seems not so much a declaration as a response; in Audradus's account, God ultimately held Louis' sons to blame for the realm's turmoil but only after first ridding himself, thanks to Louis' posthumous testimony, of the presumption that Louis was the one responsible for the conflict among them. God's initial belief in Louis' guilt doubtless reflected the terrestrial misgivings of his people. One need only recall Nithard's disgust, in the early 840s, with the anxious and indecisive Louis, whose constant need for counsel had done nothing but stoke the avarice and cupidity of his grasping sons.[21]

In the Introduction, I indicated that one theme of this study would be the discernment and nature of truth amid competing narratives. To previous generations of scholarship, this task of unraveling and discerning the truth was a relatively straightforward affair: one weighed the reliability of the authors and the corresponding value of their works and, consequently, made an informed critical judgment.[22] By comparing all the contemporary accounts of Louis' penance in 833—that is, those provided by the rebels as well as by the loyalists—Louis Halphen believed he could see truth in those points where the majority of the accounts are in harmony and pretense in those points where the accounts of the rebels seem especially pronounced in their disagreement with those of the loyalists. In other words, to Halphen's keen eye, the rebels gave themselves away at precisely those moments where they seem to be either exaggerating or protesting too much relative to the loyalist accounts, which he privileged as reliable and, thus, valuable for establishing his "discerning" point of view.[23] But what if, as I have suggested, we have no way of knowing which sources are more or less reliable? If what remains are fragments from the past that rarely engaged with one another,[24] that seem to present little hope of ever being fitted together into a recognizable whole? Rather than resign in despair from what must always be an impossible task, I maintain that some measure of truth can still be gleaned from these fragments—their irreconcilable narratives notwithstanding—if we look instead for the discourses of truth and falsehood, of right and wrong order, running through them. Like the book script that must have been common to the disparate scribes responsible for the reproduction and preservation of the various narratives about the events of 833, a particular discourse of right and wrong is the common truth that clusters many of the narratives themselves. Yet, this unifying discourse was never all-encompassing, for competing, discontinuous discourses, like book hands, were in play at different speeds at any given moment, with one slowing as another gained pace.[25] Nithard, we should recall, expressed his nostalgia for a terrifying useful king at about the same time that the Astronomer was extolling the merits of a clement equitable one.

By tracing the reception of a number of Carolingian narratives, which through writing and compiling the wrong of 833 sought to right it, we have also gained insight into the varieties of historical consciousness of a number of authors and eras, and observed the process by which the modern narratives of Carolingian rise and decline, growth and decay, have both shaped and been shaped by the events of that year. It was primarily due to an ironic congruence between dramatic Carolingian narratives and Enlightenment interest in drama that modern scholars have consistently represented Louis' abandonment and penance in terms of a duplicitous intrigue. Stigmatized as a "shameful tragedy" or an "odious comedy," the events have been treated traditionally by most historians, librettists, playwrights, and novelists—and, no doubt, eventually by filmmakers—with almost palpable distaste.

Yet by gaining an awareness first of the uncritical acceptance of the loyalist accounts of 833 by modern scholars, then of the reasons underlying this trusting reception, and finally of the Carolingian origins for the conventional version of the events, we have seen that the long-standing neglect of the contemporary accounts penned by the rebel bishops is unwarranted. By scrutinizing the bishops' *Relatio* of their grave deed, their justifications become clear: their hand was forced by Louis' iniquity and the scriptural demands this pernicious condition exacted from them. The indictment of Louis' sins summarized in the *Relatio* likewise seems to adhere to a logic associated with iniquity: the fecundity of Louis' sins was exhibited and retraced in eight chronological genealogies of crimes in order to evince his iniquitous condition. Finally, I have suggested that, even in the acts of its preparation and performance, Louis' penance was interpreted to mean different things by its different participants. Based on his previous experiences with penance, Louis perhaps believed that his penance in 833 was yet another opportunity to purge himself of his iniquity and grow wiser and stronger in the process. The rebel bishops, on the other hand, understood the penance primarily in Benedictine terms, viewing it in accordance with the intervention demanded of them for the removal of a negligent "abbot" from his office.

Moving beyond the episcopal *Relatio*, we explored the milieu of monastic reform that characterized Louis' reign and observed that the concept of iniquity understood by the bishops in 833 was merely one half of a moral binary. Equity/iniquity was the dichotomous discourse shared by supporters and critics alike to characterize Louis or his enemies. Although this moral binary system had an ancient pedigree, its particular salience during Louis' reign was the indirect product of his widespread program of monastic reform, for the concepts were inherent in the Benedictine Rule itself. Taking as our point of departure the observation that Louis conceived of his dominion in Benedictine terms, we witnessed that the bishops likewise understood their own ministry in terms of Benedictine discretion and "prudently" took action against Louis on account of his negligence. *Hludowicus* was judged in terms befitting an emperor also known as *Monachius* and *Equitatius*, two sides of the same coin. In 833, Caesar was rendered what was Caesar's and God what was God's.

Two decades ago, Randolph Starn and Natalie Zemon Davis sounded the following warning on the problematic relationship between history and memory: "If memory is an index of loss, and notoriously malleable besides, how can we remember truly? The obstacles are formidable—sheer forgetfulness, suggestibility, censorship, hindsight, conflicting recollections, the force of interests that frame whatever we remember. If we call on memory to inform or confirm present convictions, it may become an all too obliging mirror; if we do not, it becomes, or at least pretends to be, merely antiquarian."[26] In the preceding pages, there should be no doubt that I, like the many authors I have examined, have also called on a memory of 833 to inform present convictions. The choice of that year's momentous events was by no means the result of chance. That the various memories of 833, in the very process of their investigation, have often acted to disrupt, problematize, and produce tension in these convictions, however, gives me hope that the present study has been more honest than, as Starn and Zemon Davis have warned, all too obliging.[27]

(Latin text in C. M. Booker, "The Public Penance of Louis the Pious: A New
Edition of the *Episcoporum de poenitentia, quam Hludowicus imperator professus est, relatio Compendiensis* [833]," *Viator* 39, no. 2 [2008]: 1–19.)

WHAT FOLLOWS ARE the things that were done against the most Christian emperor Louis at the palace of Compiègne when he was deprived of the
kingdom for a time. These things were done from a partisan zeal for his overthrow, which should not be imitated, by Ebbo, the author of this evil, and by
the other bishops who were either working in error or acquiescing out of fear.
These things, however, should not be embraced as the decrees of a healthy
council but rejected as the work of a deadly contrivance.

Given all the precepts established in the Christian religion, it is proper to
know what the nature of the bishops' duties should be and what kind of
watchfulness and care for the well-being of all should be put upon them,
who are certainly the vicars of Christ and the key bearers of the kingdom of
heaven. Such great power was bestowed to them by Christ, so that *whatsoever* 5
*they shall bind upon earth, shall be bound also in heaven, and whatsoever they
shall loose upon earth, shall be loosed also in heaven* (Matt. 18:18–19). And in
how much danger are they placed, if they neglect to supply the food of life to
the sheep of Christ, and do not strive with all their might to lead those straying in error back to the way of truth, through *reproving and entreating* (cf. 2 10
Tim. 4:2), just as the prophet said: *If you shall not announce to the iniquitous*

man his iniquity, and that same man will have died in his impiety, I shall require
his blood from your hand (Ezek. 3:18), and many things akin to these [words]
relating to the pastoral wardenship, which are contained here and there in
15   the holy scriptures.

Therefore, with respect to the errors of sinners, these same shepherds of
Christ should avidly seek to maintain the most prudent temperance, so that
[on the one hand], in accordance with the example of blessed [Pope] Gregory
[the Great]'s teaching, *they may be through humility partners with those doing*
20   *well, but through the zeal of justice resolute against the vices of sinners* (*Pastoral*
Care, 2.1, 2.6); [and on the other hand] they may exercise their duty without
indolence or languor, and by disregarding temporal benevolence or terrestrial
fear, in order that they may wholesomely care for those of the present, and
may be an example of wholesomeness for those of the future.

25   But since, in the field of God, which is the church of Christ, all kinds of ills
do not cease to arise by the incitement of the Ancient Enemy, it is necessary that
they be utterly uprooted through the use of the shepherd's hoe. On account of
all those wicked persons, who, when good deeds are done, either do not wish
to understand [them as such] or rather understand [them] with wicked intent
30   instead of being delighted to embrace the truth itself, it seems fitting that these
same [episcopal] shepherds, whenever they might decide something in their assemblies concerning the common utility or public correction, should commit
it to documents, in accordance with ecclesiastical custom—namely, so that for
posterity they might completely cut off every ambiguity and opportunity of
35   fairly slandering or criticizing [them or their decision].

Therefore, we determined that it was necessary for all the sons of the
holy church of God, namely, [those] in the present and in future times, to
know how we bishops, appointed under the authority of the Lord and most
glorious Emperor Lothar, in the year since the incarnation of our Lord Jesus
40   Christ, 833, twelfth indiction, in other words, in the first year of [the reign
of] that same sovereign, generally assembled in the month of October at the
palace of Compiègne and came humbly to the above-mentioned sovereign. In
accordance with the demand of our duty, we took great care to make clear to
[Lothar] and his dignitaries and all the general populace who had gathered
45   together there of what nature the strength and power of the priestly duty is,
and what sort of damning punishment one deserves, who refuses to obey
priestly admonitions.

We then strove to warn as much the above-mentioned sovereign [Lothar]
as all his people that they might seek most faithfully to please the Lord, and,

for whatever things they had done to offend him, they might not delay to as- 50
suage [him] by means of [rendering] a satisfaction. Indeed, many things were
enumerated, which happened in this empire through negligence and which
pertained in markedly obvious ways to the scandalization of the church,
the calamity of the populace, and the destruction of the kingdom. [And] it
was [determined to be] necessary that these things [under consideration] be 55
emended quickly and in the future avoided in all ways.

Among other things, we remembered, and it was [thereby] recalled by
everyone, how the realm was both united and wondrously enlarged by God
through the administration of the most distinguished emperor of good
memory, Charles [the Great], and through the peacemaking effort of his 60
predecessors, and entrusted to the Lord Emperor Louis by God for the purpose of ruling under a great peace. And, since the Lord was protecting [the
realm] under this same peace, as long as the same sovereign [Louis] strove
to please God and was mindful to make use of the examples of his ancestors and yield to the counsel of good men, [the realm] would have remained 65
safe. [But it was also recalled] how, over the course of time, as was made
obvious to everyone, [Louis] came into so much disgrace and contempt
through [his] rashness and negligence that he not only came into grief with
[his] friends but even came into ridicule with [his] enemies. Since the same
sovereign [Louis] exercised negligently the duty entrusted to him under 70
the Highest, and [since] he both did and compelled [his people] to do, or
allowed to be done, many things, which were displeasing to God and men,
and [since] he provoked God on account of many execrable resolutions, and
scandalized the holy church and, though we omit other things, which are
countless, most recently assembled the entire populace under his dominion 75
for the purpose of [its] mutual destruction, and [since] the imperial power
was suddenly taken away from him by a divine and just judgment—[for all
these reasons] we, mindful of the precepts of God, and of our duty, and of
[Louis'] endowments, thought it fitting that, through the dispensation of
the above-mentioned sovereign Lothar, we should send a legation to [Louis] 80
on the authority of the sacred council. This legation would remind him of
his sins, so that he might acquire a definite appraisal of his health; [by recognizing that] he had been deprived of earthly power in accordance with
divine judgment and ecclesiastical authority [and was now] placed in dire
straights, he might strive to labor with all his might, lest he lose his own 85
soul. [As a result of] the legates' counsel and more wholesome admonitions,
[Louis] willingly offered [his] assent, requested a respite, and established a

day on which he would give them a definite answer concerning their wholesome reprimands.

90 When the above-written day was at hand, the same sacred council went in complete agreement to the same amenable man [Louis] and took care to admonish him diligently and to remind him of all the ways in which he had offended God, scandalized the holy church, and thrown the people entrusted to him into disorder. But he, freely welcoming their salutary ad-

95 monition and proper and fitting reproach, promised that he would be content with [their] sound advice with respect to all those things and would undergo a healing judgment. Moreover, joyful from so lofty and wholesome an admonition, he immediately beseeched his own sweet son, the august Lothar—who was quickly going to come to him—to put an end to any

100 delays and come with his best men, so that there might first be a mutual reconciliation between them in accordance with Christian doctrine. [Louis wished to make this immediate reconciliation] so that, if there was any envy or discord present in their hearts, a pure and humble request for forgiveness [on Louis' part] would purge [it]. Thereupon, in the presence of all

105 the people, he accepted the judgment of a penance in the priestly manner, which was done not long after this.

Then the same Lord Louis came into the basilica of Holy Mary mother of God, where the bodies of the saints lay—namely, Médard, a confessor of [both] Christ and priests, and also the most eminent martyr Sebastian.

110 Bishops, priests, deacons, and not a small crowd of clerics [all] stood [within the basilica]; also present were his son, the above-mentioned Lord Lothar, his noblemen, and all the general populace—that is, as many as that same basilica was able to hold within the sanctuary of its walls. Having prostrated [himself] upon a hair shirt before the holy altar, Louis confessed in the pres-

115 ence of everyone that he had exercised unworthily the duty duly entrusted to him, had offended God in many ways by this, had scandalized the church of Christ, and through his negligence had led the populace in many ways into disorder. Therefore, for the sake of a public and ecclesiastical expiation of such great sins, [Louis] said that he wished to attempt a penance, by which,

120 with the help of the Lord, he might deserve to obtain absolution of such great crimes through the ministry and assistance of those [bishops] to whom God has bestowed the power of binding and loosing. These same priests, as though spiritual doctors, admonished him wholesomely, so that he might openly confess his errors, declaring to [Louis] that a true remission of sins

125 would follow a pure and simple confession. Louis [then] acknowledged to

them that he had greatly offended God. [This confession was given] lest by chance he might conceal anything within [himself], or do something deceitful in the view of God, just as, for instance, it was known by everyone that he had done already long ago, [when he was] accused in the presence of the entire church at another sacred public assembly in the palace of Compiègne. [Moreover, the present confession was given] lest as then, and so now, by drawing near to God with a false heart through pretense and cunning, he call forth anger rather than a pardon for his sins, since scripture testifies that *dissemblers and crafty men prove the wrath of God* (Job 36:13). But after an admonition of this sort, he confessed that he had especially sinned in all these things, whereupon he was personally admonished by the above-mentioned priests—either in speech or in writing—and was reproached with fitting rebuke. [With respect to all his offenses] they [then] gave him a document, which he held in [his] hands, containing a summation of his sins, from which they might specifically confute him.

Chapter 1. Namely, just as it is preserved in more detail in the same document, [that he was responsible] for incurring the sin of sacrilege and murder because he did not strictly observe the fatherly exhortation and dreadful admonition, in accordance with his own promise—[a promise he] made to himself under divine invocation before the holy altar, in the presence of priests and among a great crowd of people; because he rendered violence to his brothers and kinsmen and allowed his nephew [Bernard], whom he was able to free, to be killed; and because, unmindful of his vow, he thereafter ordered that the symbol of holy religion be undertaken on account of the avenging of his indignation.

2. That he, being an author of scandal, disturber of the peace, and violator of oaths, broke on unlawful authority the treaty, which, for the purpose of the peace and unity of the empire and the tranquility of the church [and] by the resolution of the community and the consent of all his faithful men, had been made among his sons and confirmed through an oath. Because he compelled his faithful men to swear another oath, in opposition to that same first treaty and oath, without doubt he incurred the sin of perjury on account of the violation of such great oaths. Indeed, how much this deed was displeasing to God is perfectly clear, since afterward neither he nor the people subject to him deserved to have peace, but all were led into confusion, suffering by a just judgment of God the punishment of sin.

3. Since he, deluded by the counsel of wicked men, ordered that a general
165 expedition be undertaken, without any public utility or specific necessity,
during the days of Lent, in opposition to the Christian religion, and in opposition to his own vow; and he determined that a general assembly should
be held in the remote parts of his empire on Maundy Thursday, when the
Paschal sacraments ought to be celebrated by all Christians; [and during]
170 which expedition—inasmuch as he could—he compelled the people to great
murmuring, removed the priests of the Lord from their duties, [which is]
contrary to divine law, and inflicted the heaviest burden on the poor.

4. That he inflicted violence on several of his faithful men, who, out of their
175 loyalty [to Louis and his sons] and for the sake of Louis' and his sons' salvation
and for the recuperation of the tottering realm, had come to [Louis] humbly
and had given him information about plots [which his] enemies had prepared
against him. Against every law, divine and human, he deprived them of their
possessions, ordered them to be carried off into exile, sentenced those [who
180 were] absent to death, [and] led the judges without any doubt into false judgment. Contrary to divine and canonical authority, he imposed a predetermined judgment upon the priests of the Lord and monks and condemned
those [who were] absent, and by incurring this sin of murder, he stood forth
as a violator of divine and human laws.
185

5. Because of the various oaths, contrary to each other and pernicious, which,
at his order and command, had often been made irrationally by [his] sons and
by the people, he brought not a little stain of sin to the people entrusted to
him. Nevertheless, he [himself] had incurred the sin of perjury, since these
190 [oaths] were without doubt turned back rightly to [their] author, who compelled them to have been made. And on account of the purgation of the
woman [Judith], unjust judgments, false testimonies and perjuries, which by
his permission were perpetrated in his presence, he himself knows how much
he has offended God.
195

6. Concerning the various expeditions, which he made in the realm entrusted
to him not only needlessly, but also injuriously without counsel and utility,
during which without doubt great and innumerable disgraces were inflicted
upon the Christian people, namely, [acts of] murder and perjury, sacrilege,
200 adultery, rape, arson, done both in the churches of God and in various diverse
places, plunder and oppression of the poor. These deeds, which were done in

a manner that was wretched and almost unheard-of among Christians, are all turned back to [their] author, just as was said before.

7. On account of the divisions of the empire made by him rashly for his own liking in opposition to the common peace and the well-being of the entire empire, and also on account of the oath, which he compelled the entire populace to swear, that they should act against his sons just as against his enemies, even though he had been able to appease [his sons] by [his] paternal authority and the counsel of his faithful men.

8. That so many evils and disgraces, which are not able to be enumerated, were not enough for him, [evils] having been committed in the kingdom entrusted to him through his negligence and heedlessness, and that had obviously caused both the perdition of the realm and the disgrace of the king. But in addition, for the pinnacle of miseries, he most recently assembled together all the people of his dominion for [their] mutual destruction, although he ought to have been the leader of well-being and peace for the same people. [This mutual slaughter would have occurred] had not divine grace, in an unheard-of and imperceptible way and which ought to be preached about in our times, decided to take pity on [Louis'] people.

Therefore, for these things and with respect to all these things, which were mentioned above, [Louis] confessed with tears in the presence of God, the priests, and to all the people that he was the one responsible, and he declared that he had failed in all these things and sought a public penance, so that, to the church, which he had scandalized by committing sin, he might render satisfaction by doing penance; and just as there was a scandal by [his] being very negligent, likewise he declared that he wished to be an example by undertaking a fitting penance. After this confession, he gave to the priests the document of his sins and confession for future remembrance, which [document] they placed upon the altar. Thereupon, he detached [his] sword-belt, and placed it upon the altar, and stripping himself of the clothes of the age, he received the habit of a penitent through the laying on of the hands of the bishops, so that, *after such and so great a penance, no one may ever return to the secular military service* (Pope Leo the Great, *Ep.* 167).

And when these things had been done in this way, it was pleasing that each of the bishops [who was present] should include within documents of his own just how [all] these things were done and confirm it with his own signature and offer this confirmation to the above-mentioned sovereign Lothar for

240   the remembrance of this deed. At last, it seemed to all of us who were present that we should gather briefly and concisely into one [account] the sum of all the [episcopal] documents of such a great affair, and that we should confirm this gathering with the personal signatures of our own hands, just as the following [signatures] show has been done.

ABBREVIATIONS

Primary Sources

AA SS	Acta Sanctorum. Ed. Société des Bollandistes. 68 vols. Antwerp and Brussels, 1643–1940.
AB	*Annales de Saint-Bertin*. Ed. Félix Grat, Jeanne Vielliard, and Suzanne Clémencet. Paris, 1964.
AF	*Annales Fuldenses*. Ed. Georg H. Pertz and Friedrich Kurze. MGH, *SRG* 7. Hannover, 1891.
Agobard	Agobard of Lyon. *Opera omnia*. Ed. Lieven van Acker. *CCCM* 52. Turnhout, 1981.
ARF	*Annales regni Francorum*. Ed. Georg H. Pertz and Friedrich Kurze. MGH, *SRG* 6. Hannover, 1895.
Astronomer, *VH*	Astronomus, *Vita Hludowici imperatoris*. Ed. and trans. Ernst Tremp, *Thegan: Die Taten Kaiser Ludwigs; Astronomus: Das Leben Kaiser Ludwigs*. MGH, *SRG* 64. Hannover, 1995.
Benedict, *Regula*	Benedict. *Regula*. Ed. Rudolf Hanslik. *CSEL* 75. Vienna, 1977.
CCCM	Corpus Christianorum, Continuatio Medievalis. Turnhout, 1966–.

CCSL	Corpus Christianorum, Series Latina. Turnhout, 1953–.
CSEL	Corpus Scriptorum Ecclesiasticorum Latinorum. Vienna, 1866–.
Ebbo, *Apologeticus* 1	Ebbo of Reims. *Apologetici Ebonis forma prior*. Ed. Albert Werminghoff. MGH, *Conc.* 2(2):794–99. Hannover, 1908.
Ebbo, *Apologeticus* 2	Ebbo of Reims. *Apologetici Ebonis forma posterior*. Ed. Albert Werminghoff. MGH, *Conc.* 2(2):799–806. Hannover, 1908.
Einhard, *Translatio*	Einhard. *Translatio et miracula sanctorum Marcellini et Petri*. Ed. Georg Waitz. MGH, *SS* 15(1):238–64. Hannover, 1887.
Einhard, *VKM*	Einhard. *Vita Karoli Magni*. Ed. Oswald Holder-Egger. MGH, *SRG* 25. Hannover, 1911.
LCL	Loeb Classical Library
MGH	Monumenta Germaniae Historica
Capit.	Capitularia, Legum Sectio II, Capitularia Regum Francorum. 2 vols. Hannover, 1883, 1897.
Conc.	Concilia, Legum Sectio III. 6 vols. Hannover, 1893–2007.
Epist.	Epistolae. 8 vols. Hannover, 1887–1939.
PLAC	Poetae Latini Aevi Carolini. 4 vols. Hannover, 1881–99.
SRG	Scriptores Rerum Germanicarum in usum scholarum separatim editi. 78 vols. Hannover, 1871–2007.
SRL	Scriptores Rerum Langobardicarum et Italicarum, saec. 6–9. Hannover, 1878.

SRM	Scriptores Rerum Merovingicarum. 7 vols. Hannover, 1885–1951.
SS	Scriptores. 38 vols. Hannover, 1826–2007.
Nithard	Nithard, *Historiarum libri IV.* Ed. Philippe Lauer, *Nithard: Histoire des fils de Louis le Pieux.* Paris, 1926.
Odbert, *Passio*	Odbert. *Passio Friderici episcopi Traiectensis.* Ed. Oswald Holder-Egger. MGH, *SS* 15(1):342–56. Hannover, 1887.
Odilo, *Translatio*	Odilo of Saint-Médard. *Translatio sancti Sebastiani.* Ed. Oswald Holder-Egger. MGH, *SS* 15(1):377–91. Hannover, 1887.
Paschasius Radbertus, *Epitaphium*	Paschasius Radbertus. *Epitaphium Arsenii.* Ed. Ernst Dümmler. In *Abhandlungen der königlichen Akademie der Wissenschaften zu Berlin, Philologische und historische Klasse* 2:1–98. Berlin, 1900.
Paschasius Radbertus, *Exp. in Matheo*	Paschasius Radbertus. *Expositio in Matheo libri XII.* Ed. Beda Paulus. *CCCM* 56, 56A, 56B. Turnhout, 1984.
PL	Patrologiae Cursus Completus, Series Latina. Ed. J.-P. Migne. 221 vols. Paris, 1841–66.
Regino, *Chronicon*	Regino of Prüm, *Chronicon.* Ed. Friedrich Kurze. MGH, *SRG* 50. Hannover, 1890.
Relatio Comp.	*Episcoporum de poenitentia, quam Hludowicus imperator professus est, relatio Compendiensis.* Ed. C. M. Booker, "The Public Penance of Louis the Pious: A New Edition

of the *Episcoporum de poenitentia,
quam Hludowicus imperator
professus est, relatio Compendiensis*
(833)." *Viator* 39, no. 2 (2008):
1–19.

SC   Sources Chrétiennes. Paris, 1941–.

Thegan, *GH*   Thegan, *Gesta Hludowici
                            imperatoris*. Ed. and trans. Ernst
                            Tremp, *Thegan: Die Taten Kaiser
                            Ludwigs; Astronomus: Das Leben
                            Kaiser Ludwigs*. MGH, *SRG* 64.
                            Hannover, 1995.

Secondary Works

ABL   *Analecta Bollandiana*
ABR   *American Benedictine Review*
AG   *Archiv der Gesellschaft für ältere
                            deutsche Geschichtskunde*
AHR   *American Historical Review*
AHSS   *Annales: Histoire, Sciences Sociales*
AKG   *Archiv für Kulturgeschichte*
BEC   Bibliothèque de l'École des chartes
BHL   *Bibliotheca Hagiographica Latina*
BM   Böhmer, Johann F., and Engelbert
                            Mühlbacher. *Regesta Imperii*. Vol.
                            1: *Die Regesten des Kaiserreichs
                            unter den Karolingern, 751–918*.
                            2nd ed. Innsbruck, 1908.
BS   *Bibliotheca sanctorum*. 12 vols.
                            Rome, 1961–69.
BSAHSS   *Bulletin de la Société archéologique,
                            historique et scientifique de Soissons*
CCM   *Cahiers de civilisation médiévale,
                            X^e–XIIe siècles*
CH, ed. Godman and Collins   *Charlemagne's Heir: New Perspectives
                            on the Reign of Louis the Pious*

	(814–840). Ed. Peter Goodman and Roger Collins. Oxford, 1990.
Clavis AG	Jullien, Marie-Hélène, and Françoise Perelman. *Clavis scriptorum Latinorum medii aevi: Auctores Galliae, 735–987. CCCM.* Turnhout, 1994.
DA	*Deutsches Archiv für Erforschung des Mittelalters*
Depreux, *Prosopographie*	Depreux, Philippe. *Prosopographie de l'entourage de Louis le Pieux (781–840).* Sigmaringen, 1997.
DLB	*Dictionary of Literary Biography*
DRCH	*Dutch Review of Church History*
Dutton, *Carolingian Civ.*	Dutton, Paul E., ed. and trans. *Carolingian Civilization: A Reader.* 2nd ed. Peterborough, 2004.
Dutton, *Courtier*	Dutton, Paul E., ed. and trans. *Charlemagne's Courtier: The Complete Einhard.* Peterborough, 1998.
Dutton, *Mustache*	Dutton, Paul E. *Charlemagne's Mustache and Other Cultural Clusters of a Dark Age.* New York, 2004.
EHR	*English Historical Review*
EME	*Early Medieval Europe*
FMSt	*Frühmittelalterliche Studien*
Ganshof, *Carolingians*	Ganshof, François L. *The Carolingians and the Frankish Monarchy.* Trans. Janet Sondheimer. London, 1971.
HFM, ed. Scharer and Scheibelreiter	*Historiographie im frühen Mittelalter.* Ed. Anton Scharer and Georg Scheibelreiter. Vienna, 1994.
HJb	*Historisches Jahrbuch*
HT	*History and Theory*

HWJ	*History Workshop Journal*
IJCT	*International Journal of the Classical Tradition*
JEH	*Journal of Ecclesiastical History*
JMH	*Journal of Medieval History*
JML	*Journal of Medieval Latin*
JTS	*Journal of Theological Studies*
MA	*Le Moyen Âge*
MJb	*Mittellateinisches Jahrbuch*
MS	*Mediaeval Studies*
NA	*Neues Archiv der Gesellschaft für ältere deutsche Geschichtskunde*
NCMH 2	*New Cambridge Medieval History*, vol. 2, *c. 700–c. 900*. Ed. Rosamond McKitterick. Cambridge, 1995.
Nelson, *ASB*	Nelson, Janet L., ed. and trans. *The Annals of St.-Bertin*. Manchester, 1991.
Nelson, *Politics*	Nelson, Janet L. *Politics and Ritual in Early Medieval Europe*. London, 1986.
NYRB	*New York Review of Books*
PP	*Past and Present*
RB	*Revue Bénédictine*
RBPH	*Revue belge de philologie et d'histoire*
SAP	*Société des antiquaires de Picardie*
SCH	*Studies in Church History*
SE	*Sacris Erudiri*
Simson, *Jahrbücher*	Simson, B. von. *Jahrbücher des fränkischen Reiches unter Ludwig dem Frommen*. 2 vols. Leipzig, 1876.
SM	*Studi Medievali*
SP	*Studia Patristica*
SS Spoleto	Settimane di studio del Centro Italiano di Studi sull'Alto Medioevo. Spoleto, 1954–.

TRHS	*Transactions of the Royal Historical Society*
UP, ed. Hen and Innes	*The Uses of the Past in the Early Middle Ages.* Ed. Yitzhak Hen and Matthew Innes. Cambridge, 2000.
Wattenbach and Levison, *DGM*	Wattenbach, Wilhelm, and Wilhelm Levison. *Deutschlands Geschichtsquellen im Mittelalter: Vorzeit und Karolinger.* Weimar, 1952–73.

NOTES

Part epigraph phrases are taken from Jean-Paul Sartre, *Nausea*, trans. L. Alexander (1938; New York, 1964), 57.

INTRODUCTION

1. J.-B.-F. Descuret, *La médecine des passions, ou Les passions considérées dans leurs rapports avec les maladies, les lois et la religion* (Paris, 1841), 717–18; trans. M. S. Roth, "Dying of the Past: Medical Studies of Nostalgia in Nineteenth-Century France," *History and Memory* 3 (1991): 6–7.

2. Roth, "Dying of the Past," 7.

3. For additional studies on nostalgia, see M. S. Roth, "The Time of Nostalgia: Medicine, History and Normality in Nineteenth-Century France," *Time and Society* 1 (1992): 271–86; J. Starobinski, "The Idea of Nostalgia," *Diogenes* 54 (1966): 81–103; S. Boym, *The Future of Nostalgia* (New York, 2001); K. Brunnert, *Nostalgie in der Geschichte der Medizin* (Düsseldorf, 1984).

4. A. Momigliano, "History Between Medicine and Rhetoric," in idem, *Ottavo contributo alla storia degli studi classici e del mondo antico*, trans. R. Di Donato (Rome, 1987), 13–25.

5. P. E. Dutton, "Beyond the Topos of Senescence: The Political Problems of Aged Carolingian Rulers," in *Aging and the Aged in Medieval Europe*, ed. M. M. Sheehan (Toronto, 1990), 75; revised as "A World Grown Old with Poets and Kings," in Dutton, *Mustache*, 153. See also V. W. Turner, *Dramas, Fields, and Metaphors: Symbolic Action in Human Society* (Ithaca, N.Y., 1974), 24–29; J. E. Schlanger, *Les métaphores de l'organisme* (Paris, 1971), 175–89; R. Nisbet, *Social Change and History: Aspects of the Western Theory of Development* (Oxford, 1969), 3–11.

6. R. Starn, "Historians and 'Crisis,'" *PP* 52 (1971): 3–22; J. B. Shank, "Crisis: A Useful Category of Post-Social Scientific Historical Analysis?" *AHR* 113 (2008): 1090–99; and for the early twentieth-century origin of the term "homeostasis," D. Fleming, "Walter B. Cannon and Homeostasis," *Social Research* 51 (1984): 609–40.

7. Starn, "Historians and 'Crisis,'" 4; R. Koselleck, *Critique and Crisis: Enlighten-*

ment and the Pathogenesis of Modern Society (1959; Cambridge, Mass., 1988), 167 n. 31; and Hippocrates, *On Affections*, 8, ed. and trans. P. Potter, *LCL* (Cambridge, Mass., 1988), 5:16–17.

8. P. E. Dutton, "Awareness of Historical Decline in the Carolingian Empire, 800–887" (Ph.D. diss., University of Toronto, 1981), 19–64; S. F. Wemple, "Claudius of Turin's Organic Metaphor or the Carolingian Doctrine of Incorporations," *Speculum* 49 (1974): 222–37; J. L. Nelson, "On the Limits of the Carolingian Renaissance," in eadem, *Politics*, 49–67.

9. Agobard, *Liber apologeticus* I, 3, ed. Van Acker, 310.

10. Ermentarius, *Miracula sancti Philiberti*, 2, ed. O. Holder-Egger, MGH, *SS* 15(1):302.

11. Regino, *Chronicon*, s.a. 888, ed. Kurze, 129; trans. Dutton, *Carolingian Civ.*, 541. Cf. Dutton, "Beyond the Topos," 76 n. 8.

12. J. W. Thompson, *The Dissolution of the Carolingian Fisc in the Ninth Century* (Berkeley, Calif., 1935), 57–58; M. Bloch, *Feudal Society*, trans. L. A. Manyon (1939–40; Chicago, 1961), 109; L. Halphen, *Charlemagne and the Carolingian Empire*, trans. G. de Nie (1947; Amsterdam, 1977), 213; J. Dhondt, *Le haut moyen âge (VIIIe–XIe siècles)*, rev. ed. M. Rouche (Paris, 1968), 73.

13. H. Fichtenau, *Das karolingische Imperium: Soziale und geistige Problematik eines Grossreiches* (Zürich, 1949), 287; see also 184, 296. See Dutton, "Awareness of Historical Decline," 56–62; K. Brunner, *Oppositionelle Gruppen im Karolingerreich* (Vienna, 1979), 117.

14. G. Simons, *Barbarian Europe* (New York, 1968), 112.

15. F. L. Ganshof, "Charlemagne's Failure," in idem, *Carolingians*, 257–58. An early critic of the biological metaphor applied to the Carolingians was P. E. Schramm, *Kaiser, Könige, und Päpste: Gesammelte Aufsätze zur Geschichte des Mittelalters* (Stuttgart, 1968), 1:336–39.

16. The classic case of this resilience is the "decline and fall" or "decay" of the Roman Empire. See W. Goffart, "Zosimus, The First Historian of Rome's Fall," *AHR* 76 (1971): 414; P. Burke, "European Ideas of Decline and Revival, c. 1350–1500," *Parergon* 23 (1979): 3–8; idem, "Tradition and Experience: The Idea of Decline from Bruni to Gibbon," in *Edward Gibbon and the Decline and Fall of the Roman Empire*, ed. G. W. Bowersock, J. L. Clyde, and S. R. Graubard (Cambridge, Mass., 1977), 87–102; W. Rehm, *Der Untergang Roms in abendländischen Denken: Ein Beitrag zur Geschichtsschreibung und zum Dekadenzproblem* (Leipzig, 1930).

17. Dutton, "Awareness of Historical Decline," 6–7; D. A. Schön, "Generative Metaphor: A Perspective on Problem-Setting in Social Policy," in *Metaphor and Thought*, ed. A. Ortony (Cambridge, 1993), 137–63; G. Constable, "Medieval Latin Metaphors," *Viator* 38, no. 2 (2007): 1–20. For a brilliant analysis of the ways in which metaphors served to shape the thought of the Carolingians themselves, see K. F. Morrison, "*Unum ex multis*: Hincmar of Rheims' Medical and Aesthetic Rationales for Unification," *SS Spoleto* 27(2): 583–718.

18. Cf. W. B. Cannon, "Relations of Biological and Social Homeostasis," in idem, *The Wisdom of the Body* (London, 1932), 287–306; Fleming, "Walter B. Cannon and Homeostasis," 636–39.

19. Cf. R. A. Nye, "Metaphors of Pathology in the *Belle Epoque*: The Rise of a Medical Model of Cultural Crisis," in idem, *Crime, Madness, and Politics in Modern France: The Medical Concept of National Decline* (Princeton, N.J., 1984), 132–70; M. S. Roth, "Remembering Forgetting: *Maladies de la Mémoire* in Nineteenth-Century France," *Representations* 26 (1989): 49–68; F. W. Coker, *Organismic Theories of the State: Nineteenth Century Interpretations of the State as Organism or as Person* (New York, 1910). But see also J. Soll, "Healing the Body Politic: French Royal Doctors, History, and the Birth of a Nation 1560–1634," *Renaissance Quarterly* 55 (2002): 1259–86.

20. J.-C.-L. Simonde de Sismondi, *Histoire des français* (Paris, 1821), 1:xx; trans. W. Bellingham in Sismondi, *The French Under the Merovingians and the Carlovingians* (London, 1850), xxxvii.

21. Sismondi, *Histoire des français*, 3:4. P. C. F. Daunou, in his review of Sismondi's book, was struck by this passage; see *Journal des savants* (September 1821): 555.

22. On the "infection" of Sismondi's mother with nostalgia (ca. 1793), see P. Waeber, *Sismondi: Une biographie* (Geneva, 1991), 1:119–22; F. Palgrave, "Life and Works of Sismondi," *Quarterly Review* 72 (1843): 303–4. It was long observed by doctors that the Swiss were particularly susceptible to nostalgia: Starobinski, "The Idea of Nostalgia," 87–93.

23. Cf. P. de Lilienfeld, *La pathologie sociale* (Paris, 1896), 19; see also 53–68.

24. Paschasius Radbertus, *Expositio in Lamentationes Jeremiae*, 4.13, ed. B. Paulus, *CCCM*, 85:282; partial trans. E. S. Duckett, *Carolingian Portraits* (Ann Arbor, Mich., 1962), 189. Cf. the similar complaints by Paschasius, *Exp. in Matheo*, 11.24, 7, ed. Paulus, 56B:1159; idem, *Epitaphium*, 2.7, ed. Dümmler, 67.

25. Nithard, 4.7, ed. Lauer, 144; trans. Dutton, *Carolingian Civ.*, 331.

26. J. L. Nelson, "Public *Histories* and Private History in the Work of Nithard," *Speculum* 60 (1985): 281.

27. For just such a diagnosis, see B. W. Scholz, *Carolingian Chronicles* (Ann Arbor, Mich., 1972), 30; P. Depreux, "Nithard et la *Res Publica*: Un regard critique sur le règne de Louis le Pieux," *Médiévales* 22–23 (1992): 161. The literature on the rhetorical skills of the Carolingians is growing quickly. See *Strategies of Writing: Studies on Text and Trust in the Middle Ages*, ed. P. Schulte et al. (Turnhout, 2008); *Narrative and History in the Early Medieval West*, ed. E. M. Tyler and R. Balzaretti (Turnhout, 2006); *Texts and Identities in the Early Middle Ages*, ed. R. Corradini et al. (Vienna, 2006); *UP*, ed. Hen and Innes; M. S. Kempshall, "Some Ciceronian Models for Einhard's Life of Charlemagne," *Viator* 26 (1995): 11–37; P. E. Dutton, *The Politics of Dreaming in the Carolingian Empire* (Lincoln, Neb., 1994); J. M. Pizarro, *A Rhetoric of the Scene: Dramatic Narrative in the Early Middle Ages* (Toronto, 1989).

28. J. L. Nelson, "History-Writing at the Courts of Louis the Pious and Charles the Bald," in *HFM*, ed. Scharer and Scheibelreiter, 440. Cf. M. de Jong, "The Empire as *Ecclesia*: Hrabanus Maurus and Biblical *Historia* for Rulers," in *UP*, ed. Hen and Innes, 199–200.

29. As Boym, *The Future of Nostalgia*, xvi, has observed, "Nostalgia is not always about the past; it can be retrospective but also prospective. Fantasies of the past determined by needs of the present have a direct impact on realities of the future." See also Schön, "Generative Metaphor," 146; Dutton, *The Politics of Dreaming*, 210.

30. J. L. Nelson, "Translating Images of Authority: The Christian Roman Emperors in the Carolingian World," in eadem, *The Frankish World, 750–900* (1989; London, 1996), 97 n. 50. Such admirable willingness to question and revise her own convictions is characteristic of Nelson's scholarly career; see *Frankland: The Franks and the World of the Early Middle Ages: Essays in Honour of Dame Jinty Nelson*, ed. P. Fouracre and D. Ganz (Manchester, 2008).

31. Note the recent attention given specifically to Carolingian historiography and to Carolingian literacy in general: *Lay Intellectuals in the Carolingian World*, ed. P. Wormald and J. L. Nelson (Cambridge, 2007); R. McKitterick, *History and Memory in the Carolingian World* (Cambridge, 2004); *UP*, ed. Hen and Innes; *HFM*, ed. Scharer and Scheibelreiter; *Schriftlichkeit im frühen Mittelalter*, ed. U. Schaefer (Tübingen, 1993); *The Uses of Literacy in Early Mediaeval Europe*, ed. R. McKitterick (Cambridge, 1990); R. McKitterick, *The Carolingians and the Written Word* (Cambridge, 1989). Cf. C. F. Briggs, "Literacy, Reading, and Writing in the Medieval West," *JMH* 26 (2000): 397–420; P. J. Geary, "Oblivion Between Orality and Textuality in the Tenth Century," in *Medieval Concepts of the Past: Ritual, Memory, Historiography*, ed. G. Althoff et al. (Cambridge, 2002), 112.

32. See Dutton, *The Politics of Dreaming*, 208–24, 312 nn. 42–43, on the negative connotation of the phrase "*modernum tempus*." See also B. Stock, "Attitudes Towards Change," in idem, *The Implications of Literacy: Written Language and Models of Interpretation in the Eleventh and Twelfth Centuries* (Princeton, N.J., 1983), 472–76; H. Fichtenau, *Living in the Tenth Century: Studies in Mentalities and Social Orders*, trans. P. J. Geary (1984; Chicago, 1990), 383; A. J. Gurevich, *Categories of Medieval Culture*, trans. G. L. Campbell (1972; London, 1985), 124–25.

33. In a medical manuscript of the tenth century (Rome, Vat. Reg. lat. 1260, fol. 177r), the Greek term "*crisin*" is glossed as "*declinatio valitudinis*." *Corpus glossariorum Latinorum*, ed. G. Loewe and G. Goetz (Berlin, 1892), 3:599 l. 22.

34. On this point—namely, the binaries of the tyranny of custom and the freedom of agency—see N. B. Dirks, "The Policing of Tradition: Colonialism and Anthropology in Southern India," *Comparative Studies in Society and History* 39 (1997): 182–212.

35. S. Coupland, "'A Tale of Misfortune': The Hardships of Life in Ninth-Century Europe," *Medieval History* 3 (1993): 178–83.

36. On the interdependence of belief and agency, see G. Koziol, "A Father, His Son, Memory, and Hope: The Joint Diploma of Lothar and Louis V (Pentecost Monday, 979) and the Limits of Performativity," in *Geschichtswissenschaft und "Performative Turn": Ritual, Inszenierung und Performanz vom Mittelalter bis zur Neuzeit*, ed. J. Martschukat and S. Patzold (Cologne, 2003), 83–86; P. E. Dutton, "Thunder and Hail over the Carolingian Countryside," in Dutton, *Mustache*, 169–88.

37. F. S. Paxton, "*Signa Mortifera*: Death and Prognostication in Early Medieval

Monastic Medicine," *Bulletin of the History of Medicine* 67 (1993): 631–50; P. Riché, "La magie a l'époque carolingienne," *Comptes Rendus des Séances de l'Académie des Inscriptions et Belles-lettres* 1 (1973): 127–38; E. Wickersheimer, "Figures medico-astrologiques des IXe, X^e et XIe siècles," *Janus* 19 (1914): 157–77.

38. Of course, the ideal of just what was to be returned to through efforts of reform was itself the locus of change—and debate. Cf. the numerous reform movements during the Middle Ages seeking a return to an idealized primitive church: G. Olsen, "The Idea of the *Ecclesia Primitiva* in the Writings of the Twelfth-Century Canonists," *Traditio* 25 (1969): 61–86; M. E. Hönicke Moore, "Carolingian Bishops and Christian Antiquity: Distance from the Past, Canon-Formation, and Imperial Power," in *Learned Antiquity: Scholarship and Society in the Near-East, the Greco-Roman World, and the Early Medieval West*, ed. A. A. MacDonald et al. (Leuven, 2003), 175–84; G. B. Ladner, *The Idea of Reform: Its Impact on Christian Thought and Action in the Age of the Fathers* (1959; New York, 1967). For a lucid statement of this notion of change cast in terms of reform, see L. J. R. Milis, *Angelic Monks and Earthly Men: Monasticism and Its Meaning to Medieval Society* (Woodbridge, 1992), 14; and, in general, K. F. Morrison, *The Mimetic Tradition of Reform in the West* (Princeton, N.J., 1982); J. S. Preus, "Theological Legitimation for Innovation in the Middle Ages," *Viator* 3 (1972): 1–26.

39. S. MacLean, *Kingship and Politics in the Late Ninth Century: Charles the Fat and the End of the Carolingian Empire* (Cambridge, 2003), 1–11; E. J. Goldberg, *Struggle for Empire: Kingship and Conflict Under Louis the German, 817–876* (Ithaca, N.Y., 2006), 4–7.

40. On such medieval "paralysis," see J. Barish, *The Antitheatrical Prejudice* (Berkeley, Calif., 1981), 47–48; K. F. Morrison, *Tradition and Authority in the Western Church, 300–1140* (Princeton, N.J., 1969), 6–8.

41. E.g., J. L. Nelson, "A Tale of Two Princes: Politics, Text and Ideology in a Carolingian Annal," *Studies in Medieval and Renaissance History* n.s. 10 (1988): 115; P. Fouracre, "Carolingian Justice: The Rhetoric of Improvement and Contexts of Abuse," *SS Spoleto* 42(2): 774, 778, 784, 786–87; and the debate over Carolingian military "grand strategy": B. S. Bachrach, *Early Carolingian Warfare: Prelude to Empire* (Philadelphia, 2001), with reviews by C. R. Bowlus, *AHR* 107 (2002): 592–93; S. MacLean, *EME* 11 (2002): 175–76; W. Brown, *Speculum* 78 (2003): 454–56. For a masterful critique of the tendency to interpret past behavior in modern, Western terms of pragmatism and utility, see M. Sahlins, "Individual Experience and Cultural Order," in idem, *Culture in Practice: Selected Essays* (1982; New York, 2000), 277–91.

42. Athanasius, *Vita Antonii*, 3 (Latin trans. of Evagrius), *PL* 73, col. 128A; *Scripta Leonis, Rufini et Angeli Sociorum S. Francisci: The Writings of Leo, Rufino and Angelo, Companions of St. Francis*, 4, ed. and trans. R. B. Brooke (Oxford, 1970), 94–95.

43. But for a historiographical survey and critique of such narratives of transformation, see now the essays in *Journal of Late Antiquity* 1 (2008).

44. J. J. Contreni, "Carolingian Biblical Culture," in *Iohannes Scottus Eriugena: The Bible and Hermeneutics*, ed. G. Van Riel et al. (Leuven, 1996), 12. Cf. Goldberg, *Struggle for Empire*, 7–8, 13.

45. R. McKitterick, *The Frankish Kingdoms Under the Carolingians, 751–987* (London, 1983), 124. Cf. MacLean, *Kingship and Politics*, 3, on the traditional arc of Carolingian politics, and their trajectory as plotted within modern historiography.

46. E.g., P. R. McKeon, "The Empire of Louis the Pious: Faith, Politics, and Personality," *RB* 90 (1980): 50–62; L. K. Born, "The *Specula principis* of the Carolingian Renaissance," *RBPH* 12 (1933): 586.

47. Cf. McKitterick, *The Frankish Kingdoms*, 135–36.

48. The standard narrative of Louis' "error-ridden reign" can be found in almost any general survey of Carolingian history, the two consulted most frequently in English being Halphen, *Charlemagne*; P. Riché, *The Carolingians: A Family Who Forged Europe*, trans. M. I. Allen (1983; Philadelphia, 1993). On Louis and the fisc, the classic studies are J. Dhondt, *Études sur la naissance des principautés territoriales en France (IXᵉ–Xᵉ siècle)* (Bruges, 1948); Thompson, *The Dissolution*.

49. J. L. Nelson, "The Last Years of Louis the Pious," in *CH*, ed. Godman and Collins, 148.

50. As observed by P. Chevallard, *Saint Agobard, Archevêque de Lyon: Sa vie et ses écrits* (Lyon, 1869), 301. See also Sismondi, *Histoire des français*, 3:23–24.

51. On this approach, see G. Duby, *The Legend of Bouvines: War, Religion, and Culture in the Middle Ages*, trans. C. Tihanyi (1973; Berkeley, Calif., 1990); A. Boureau, *The Myth of Pope Joan*, trans. L. G. Cochrane (1988; Chicago, 2001); R. Darnton, "It Happened One Night," *NYRB* 51, no. 11 (24 June 2004): 60–64; and the film *Rashomon*, directed by Akira Kurosawa, 1950, together with D. Boyd, "Positions and Perspectives: Rashomon," in idem, *Film and the Interpretive Process* (New York, 1989), 51–73; W. D. Roth and J. D. Mehta, "The *Rashomon* Effect: Combining Positivist and Interpretivist Approaches in the Analysis of Contested Events," *Sociological Methods & Research* 31, no. 2 (2002): 131–73.

52. See C. L. Becker, "Everyman His Own Historian," *AHR* 37 (1932): 227: "the more of the past we drag into the specious present, the more an hypothetical, patterned future is likely to crowd into it also. Which comes first, which is cause and which effect, whether our memories construct a pattern of past events at the behest of our desires and hopes, or whether our desires and hopes spring from a pattern of past events imposed upon us by experience and knowledge, I shall not attempt to say." Cf. P. Buc, *The Dangers of Ritual: Between Early Medieval Texts and Social Scientific Theory* (Princeton, N.J., 2001), 256.

53. P. J. Geary, *Phantoms of Remembrance: Memory and Oblivion at the End of the First Millennium* (Princeton, N.J., 1994), 86–87, 98, 177; Dutton, "Thunder and Hail," in idem, *Mustache,* 169–88; P. Fouracre, "Cultural Conformity and Social Conservatism in Early Medieval Europe," *HWJ* 33 (1992): 152–61; Nelson, "On the Limits," in eadem, *Politics,* 49–67; E. Perroy, "Carolingian Administration," in *Early Medieval Society*, ed. S. L. Thrupp (New York, 1967), 129–46; E. Auerbach, *Mimesis: The Representation of Reality in Western Literature*, trans. W. R. Trask (1946; Princeton, N.J., 2003), 38–39, 559–61. But cf. M. Innes, "Introduction: Using the Past, Interpreting the Present, Influencing the

Future," in *UP*, ed. Hen and Innes, 8; S. Bagge, *Kings, Politics, and the Right Order of the World in German Historiography c. 950–1150* (Leiden, 2002), 4.

54. See Agobard, *De spe et timore*, ed. Van Acker, 430–31; Hrabanus Maurus, *Expositio in Matthaeum*, ed. B. Löfstedt, *CCCM*, 174:200–201; *Anonymi in Matthaeum*, ed. B. Löfstedt, *CCCM*, 159:72. More optimistic about medieval attitudes toward transforming the future are J. Le Goff, "Merchant's Time and Church's Time in the Middle Ages," in idem, *Time, Work and Culture in the Middle Ages*, trans. A. Goldhammer (1960; Chicago, 1980), 31; J.-C. Schmitt, "Appropriating the Future," trans. P. Rand, in *Medieval Futures: Attitudes to the Future in the Middle Ages*, ed. J. A. Burrow and I. P. Wei (Woodbridge, 2000), 11–12.

55. See P. R. McKeon, "817: Une année désastreuse et presque fatale pour les Carolingiens," *MA* 84 (1978): 5–12; F. L. Ganshof, "Some Observations on the *Ordinatio Imperii* of 817," in idem, *Carolingians*, 273–88, esp. 280 n. 73.

56. "*Quis custodiet ipsos custodes?*" Juvenal, 6.347–48.

57. See K. F. Morrison, "'Know thyself': Music in the Carolingian Renaissance," *SS Spoleto* 39(1): 369–483.

58. E. L. Fortin, "The Political Implications of St. Augustine's Theory of Conscience," in idem, *Classical Christianity and the Political Order: Reflections on the Theologico-Political Problem* (Lanham, Md., 1996), 65–84; A. Firey, "Blushing Before the Judge and the Physician: Moral Arbitration in the Carolingian Empire," in *A New History of Penance*, ed. A. Firey (Leiden, 2008), 173–200; I. van Renswoude, "The Sincerity of Fiction: Rather and the Quest for Self-Knowledge," in *Ego Trouble: Authors and Their Identities in the Early Middle Ages*, ed. R. McKitterick et al. (Vienna, forthcoming).

59. Einhard, *VKM*, 24, trans. Dutton, *Courtier*, 31; Thegan, *GH*, 19–20, trans. Dutton, *Carolingian Civ.*, 164–65. See also T. F. X. Noble, "The Monastic Ideal as a Model for Empire: The Case of Louis the Pious," *RB* 86 (1976): 235–50; E. K. Rand, "On the History of the *De Vita Caesarum* of Suetonius in the Early Middle Ages," *Harvard Studies in Classical Philology* 37 (1926): 40–48.

60. This privilege, of course, is increasingly being challenged and contested—for better and for worse—by many groups outside the academy; see C. Kent, "History: The Discipline of Memory—and of Forgetting," *The Structurist* 37–38 (1997–98): 38–39.

61. E.g., the concluding sentence of Geary, *Phantoms of Remembrance*, 181. But cf. idem, *The Myth of Nations: The Medieval Origins of Europe* (Princeton, N.J., 2002), 16.

62. Augustine, *Ep.* 28 (ca. 394/95), ed. A. Goldbacher, *CSEL*, 34:113; trans. C. White, *The Correspondence Between Jerome and Augustine of Hippo* (Lewiston, N.Y., 1991), 70.

CHAPTER 1. TELLING THE TRUTH ABOUT THE FIELD OF LIES

Epigraphs: Paschasius Radbertus, *Epitaphium*, 1, intro., ed. Dümmler, 21; trans. A. Cabaniss, *Charlemagne's Cousins: Contemporary Lives of Adalard and Wala* (Syracuse, N.Y.,

1967), 87; Herman Melville, *Benito Cereno,* in *The Writings of Herman Melville, The Northwestern-Newberry Edition*, vol. 9, *The Piazza Tales and Other Prose Pieces, 1839–1860* (Evanston, Ill., 1987), 46.

1. Described most explicitly in Agobard, *Liber apologeticus* I, II, ed. Van Acker, 309–19; Pope Gregory IV, *Ep.* 17, ed. E. Dümmler, MGH, *Epist.*, 5:228–32; *Relatio Comp.*, ed. Booker, 11–19. See E. Boshof, *Ludwig der Fromme* (Darmstadt, 1996), 182–91.

2. Many contemporary sources provide an account of this event. See *BM,* 366–68; Simson, *Jahrbücher,* 2:45–54. The best modern discussion remains T. F. X. Noble, "Louis the Pious and the Papacy: Law, Politics and the Theory of Empire in the Early Ninth Century" (Ph.D. diss., Michigan State University, 1974), 321–52.

3. *AB,* s.a. 833, ed. Grat et al., 10; trans. Nelson, *ASB,* 2.

4. On Ebbo, see Chapter 5.

5. On this episcopal *Relatio,* see C. M. Booker, "A New Prologue of Walafrid Strabo," *Viator* 36 (2005): 83–105; idem, "The Public Penance of Louis the Pious: A New Edition of the *Episcoporum de poenitentia, quam Hludowicus imperator professus est, relatio Compendiensis* (833)," *Viator* 39, no. 2 (2008): 1–19. I shall discuss the *Relatio* in detail in Chapter 4. For a translation of the text, see the Appendix.

6. *Relatio Comp.,* ed. Booker, 17; Appendix, l. 184.

7. *Relatio Comp.,* ed. Booker, 11–19; Agobard, *Cartula de Ludovici imperatoris poenitentia,* ed. Van Acker, 323–24. For a full catalog of contemporary sources documenting the penance, see *BM,* 369–71; Simson, *Jahrbücher,* 2:63–78. For modern analyses, P. Chevallard, *Saint Agobard, Archevêque de Lyon: Sa vie et ses écrits* (Lyon, 1869), 257–327; C. Barthélemy, "La déposition de Louis le Débonnaire," in idem, *Erreurs et mensonges historiques,* 4th ser. (Paris, 1873), 110–48; L. Halphen, "La pénitence de Louis le Pieux à Saint Médard de Soissons," in *Bibliothèque de la Faculté des Lettres de Paris XVIII, troisièmes mélanges d'histoire du Moyen Âge* (Paris, 1904), 177–85; repr. in idem, *A travers l'histoire du Moyen Age* (Paris, 1950), 58–66; F. Kern, *Gottesgnadentum und Widerstandsrecht im früheren Mittelalter* (1914; Darmstadt, 1967), 341–43; L. Halphen, *Charlemagne and the Carolingian Empire,* trans. G. de Nie (1947; Amsterdam, 1977), 194–210; M. David, *La souveraineté et les limites juridiques du pouvoir monarchique du IXᵉ au XVᵉ siècle* (Paris, 1954), 112–19; H.-X. Arquillière, *L'Augustinisme politique: Essai sur la formation des théories politiques du Moyen-Age,* 2nd ed. (Paris, 1955), 170–89; W. Ullmann, *The Carolingian Renaissance and the Idea of Kingship* (London, 1969), 43–70, esp. 64–70; E. Peters, *The Shadow King: Rex Inutilis in Medieval Law and Literature, 751–1327* (New Haven, Conn., 1970), 57–65; K. Bund, *Thronsturz und Herrscherabsetzung im Frühmittelalter* (Bonn, 1979), 405–23; T. Oberndorff, "Lodewijk de Vrome's afzetting in 833 en de religieuze motivatie der opstandige bisschoppen," *Aanzet* 8 (1990): 221–31; idem, "Lodewijk de Vrome's openbare boetedoening in 833: een kwestie van *ministeria*," *DRCH* 71 (1991): 1–36; L. Van Beckum, "Een keizer onttroond: Lodewijk de Vrome en zijn openbare boetedoening," *Utrechtse historische cahiers* 16 (1995): 61–78; Boshof, *Ludwig der Fromme,* 192–212; G. Althoff, "Das Privileg der *deditio,*" in idem, *Spielregeln der Politik im Mittelalter* (Darm-

stadt, 1997), 116–25; and, above all, M. de Jong, "Power and Humility in Carolingian Society: The Public Penance of Louis the Pious," *EME* 1 (1992): 29–52; eadem, "*Sacrum palatium et ecclesia*: L'autorité religieuse royale sous les Carolingiens (790–840)," *AHSS* 58 (2003): 1243–69.

8. A.-M.-P. Ingold, "L'Ochsenfeld: Ses antiquités, ses traditions," *Bulletin de la société pour la conservation des monuments historiques d'Alsace* 2nd ser. 1 (1863): 142. On Ingold, see *Dictionnaire de biographie française*, ed. M. Prévost et al. (Paris, 1994), 18:171–72, s.v. "Ingold, Auguste-Marie-Pierre."

9. Ingold, "L'Ochsenfeld," 141–43. See also J. D. Schöpflin, *L'Alsace illustrée*, French trans. L. Waldemar Ravenèz (Paris, 1849–52; repr. 1974), 3:320–23; X. Boyer, "Le Champ du Mensonge: An 833," *Revue d'Alsace* 2nd ser. 13 (1862): 49–108; C. Oberreiner, "Le Champ du Mensonge," *Revue d'Alsace* 2nd ser. 56 (1905): 345–49; G. Gravier, *Légendes d'Alsace* (Belfort, 1986), 1:69–72.

10. Ingold, "L'Ochsenfeld," 142. It is not surprising that the local popular memory of Louis' desertion was anti-Charles (if one accepts Ingold's interpretation), for the territory remained in the hands of Charles's half brothers and their sons throughout the ninth century. For a useful map, see J. L. Nelson, *Charles the Bald* (London, 1992), 320–21. Another early report of the legend has Louis himself, after discovering the desertion by his men, calling down a curse upon both the traitors and the field that "witnessed" their betrayal; F. J. Kiefer, *Die Sagen des Rheinlandes* (Cologne, 1845), 289–91.

11. For what follows, I have largely paraphrased the account reported in the memoirs of Charles Maurice de Talleyrand (1754–1838), bishop of Autun before the French Revolution and later a senior diplomat. See *Memoirs of the Prince of Talleyrand*, ed. D. de Broglie, trans. R. L. de Beaufort (New York, 1891), 2:75–77. Cf. R. Morrissey, *Charlemagne and France: A Thousand Years of Mythology*, trans. C. Tihanyi (1997; Notre Dame, Ind., 2003), 261.

12. Cf. the similar parallel drawn by the sixteenth-century Gallican author François de Clary, who saw in the collusion of Pope Gregory IV with the sons of Louis the Pious an antecedent for the "despicable" collusion between the Roman Church and the French Catholic League in his own day. F. de Clary, *Philippiques contre les bulles et autres pratiques de la faction d'Espagne* (1592; Tours, 1611), fol. 132v.

13. See Morrissey, *Charlemagne and France*, 250–65.

14. On Louis' occasional French epithet "le Débonnaire," and its connotations of excessive clemency, see P. Hyams, "What Did Henry III of England Think in Bed and in French About Kingship and Anger?" in *Anger's Past: The Social Uses of an Emotion in the Middle Ages*, ed. B. H. Rosenwein (Ithaca, N.Y., 1998), 112–20.

15. L. Rid, "Die Wiedereinsetzung Kaiser Ludwigs des Frommen zu St. Denis (1. März 834) und ihre Wiederholung zu Metz (28. Februar 835)," in *Festgabe Alois Knöpfler zur Vollendung des 70. Lebensjahres*, ed. H. M. Gietl and G. Pfeilschifter (Freiburg im Breisgau, 1917), 265–75.

16. G. B. de Mably, *Observations sur l'histoire de France*, 2.4, rev. ed. F. Guizot (1765; Paris, 1823), 1:145; J.-C.-L. Simonde de Sismondi, *Histoire des français* (Paris, 1821), 3:36;

trans. W. Bellingham, in Sismondi, *The French Under the Merovingians and the Carlovingians* (London, 1850), 309; J. C. Prichard, *The Life and Times of Hincmar, Archbishop of Rheims* (Oxford, 1849), 67; T. Greenwood, *Cathedra Petri: A Political History of the Great Latin Patriarchate* (London, 1859), 3:143, 146–47.

17. A. Kleinclausz, *L'Empire carolingien: Ses origines et ses transformations* (Paris, 1902), 318; F. Lot, *Naissance de la France* (Paris, 1948), 408. Cf. M. Bloch, *Feudal Society*, trans. L. A. Manyon (1939–40; Chicago, 1961), 192.

18. T. Schieffer, "Die Krise des karolingischen Imperiums," in *Aus Mittelalter und Neuzeit: Festschrift für Gerhard Kallen*, ed. J. Engel and H. M. Klinkenberg (Bonn, 1957), 13–14; J. Boussard, *The Civilization of Charlemagne*, trans. F. Partridge (New York, 1968), 203; R. Folz, *The Coronation of Charlemagne, 25 December 800*, trans. J. E. Anderson (1964; London, 1974), 189.

19. For the quotation, see *CH*, ed. Godman and Collins, viii. To cite just a few examples of such bleak portraits: J. T. Rosenthal, "The Public Assembly in the Time of Louis the Pious," *Traditio* 20 (1964): 31; R. Collins, *Early Medieval Europe, 300–1000* (New York, 1991), 299–300; A. Koch, *Kaiserin Judith: Eine politische Biographie* (Husum, 2005), 143.

20. J. L. Nelson, "The Last Years of Louis the Pious," in *CH*, ed. Godman and Collins, 148. Cf. P. E. Dutton, "Awareness of Historical Decline in the Carolingian Empire, 800–887" (Ph.D. diss., University of Toronto, 1981), 43–50, for the notable exceptions of modern scholars who—while still having thought in terms of an overarching Carolingian decline—argued for causes and moments of crisis other than the "ineptitude" of Louis and 833.

21. Nelson, "The Last Years," 159.

22. Nelson, "The Last Years," 148–49; S. Ashley, "The Power of Symbols: Interpreting Portents in the Carolingian Empire," *Medieval History* 4 (1994): 34–50. For Halley's comet and Louis' optimism regarding it, see the account by one of Louis' biographers, known to modern historians only as the "Astronomer" (so-called because of his self-professed astronomical learning), *VH*, 58, ed. Tremp, 518–25. A prudent courtier, the Astronomer was hesitant to offer his opinion on the comet. Cf. the reactions of the nobleman Einhard (Dutton, *Courtier*, 160–61); and Abbot Lupus of Ferrières (Dutton, *Carolingian Civ.*, 460).

23. E.g., Boshof, *Ludwig der Fromme*, 203; Koch, *Kaiserin Judith*, 143; J. Fried, *Donation of Constantine and Constitutum Constantini* (Berlin, 2007), 89. Cf. D. Ganz, "The Debate on Predestination," in *Charles the Bald: Court and Kingdom*, ed. M. Gibson and J. L. Nelson, 2nd ed. (London, 1990), 285.

24. Nelson, "The Last Years," 148. See also J. Canning, *A History of Medieval Political Thought, 300–1450* (London, 1996), 42–43, on the "long shadow" cast by the misinterpreted Augustinian theory of rulership, dubbed by H.-X. Arquillière "l'Augustinisme politique." Arquillière saw this theory realized most fully in the events of 833, an observation that has cast a long shadow of its own: L. Levillain, review of H.-X. Arquillière, *L'Augustinisme politique* (Paris, 1934), in *BEC* 96 (1935–36): 383–90; H.-X. Arquillière, "Réflexions sur

l'essence de l'augustinisme politique," in *Augustinus Magister: Congrès international augustinien, Paris, 21–24 Septembre 1954* (Paris, 1954), 2:994; idem, *L'Augustinisme politique*, 2nd ed. (Paris, 1955), 146, 200. Cf. A. Boureau, "Des politiques tirées de l'Écriture: Byzance et l'Occident," *AHSS* 55 (2000): 881–83.

25. On emplotment, see H. White, "Introduction: The Poetics of History," in idem, *Metahistory: The Historical Imagination in Nineteenth-Century Europe* (Baltimore, 1973), 1–38; idem, *The Content of the Form: Narrative Discourse and Historical Representation* (Baltimore, 1987), 1–57; idem, "Historical Emplotment and the Problem of Truth," in *Probing the Limits of Representation: Nazism and the "Final Solution"*, ed. S. Friedlander (Cambridge, Mass., 1992), 37–53; together with A. M. Dershowitz, "Life Is Not a Dramatic Narrative," in *Law's Stories: Narrative and Rhetoric in the Law*, ed. P. Brooks and P. Gewirtz (New Haven, Conn., 1996), 99–105.

26. On this approach, see R. Darnton, "It Happened One Night," *NYRB* 51, no. 11 (24 June 2004): 60–64; G. Piterberg, *An Ottoman Tragedy: History and Historiography at Play* (Berkeley, Calif., 2003); A. Boureau, *The Myth of Pope Joan*, trans. L. G. Cochrane (1988; Chicago, 2001); G. Duby, *The Legend of Bouvines: War, Religion, and Culture in the Middle Ages*, trans. C. Tihanyi (1973; Berkeley, Calif., 1990).

27. Ellen O'Gorman has also used the term "congruence" in this way in her important discussion on the implications of aligning primary (historical) narratives with only those secondary (fictive) narratives about the past that are permissible by the structures of power operative in the historian's present. See "Detective Fiction and Historical Narrative," *Greece and Rome* 46 (1999): 19–26.

28. Cf. R. Starn, "Meaning-Levels in the Theme of Historical Decline," *HT* 14 (1975): 1–31.

29. Cf. G. W. Bowersock, "Gibbon on Civil War and Rebellion in the Decline of the Roman Empire," in *Edward Gibbon and the Decline and Fall of the Roman Empire*, ed. G. W. Bowersock et al. (Cambridge, Mass., 1977), 31, on the similar way a particular metaphor employed by Gibbon both constrained and compelled him to charge Septimius Severus as the principal author of the decline of the Roman Empire. For the reference to Charlemagne's shoulders, see H.-X. Arquillière, *Saint Grégoire VII: Essai sur sa conception du pouvoir pontifical* (Paris, 1934), 121, embellishing a remark by Charlemagne's court scholar Alcuin.

30. L. Sergeant, *The Franks* (London, 1898), 298–99. For more recent examples, see J. Calmette, *L'effondrement d'un empire et la naissance d'une Europe IXᵉ–Xᵉ siècles* (Paris, 1941), 25, 52; Rosenthal, "The Public Assembly," 39 n. 60; F. L. Ganshof, "L'Empire Carolingien: Essence et Structure," in *Gesellschaft, Kultur, Literatur: Rezeption und Originalität im Wachsen einer europäischen Literatur und Geistigkeit*, ed. K. Bosl (Stuttgart, 1975), 202; P. R. McKeon, "The Empire of Louis the Pious: Faith, Politics, and Personality," *RB* 90 (1980): 50–62; I. Gobry, *Histoire des Rois de France: Louis Iᵉʳ, Premier successeur de Charlemagne* (Paris, 2002).

31. But cf. N. Staubach, "Das Herrscherbild Karls des Kahlen: Formen und Funktionen monarchischer Repräsentation im früheren Mittelalter," pt. I (Ph.D. diss., West-

fälischen Wilhelms-Universität, Münster, 1981), 30, who argues that the "spectacular" configuration of Louis' reign as a "tragedy" is only a relatively recent phenomenon, one that has the advantage of eliminating the assignment of culpability for the events. I shall return to Staubach's claims in Chapter 3.

32. Cf. R. M. Stein, "Literary Criticism and the Evidence for History," in *Writing Medieval History*, ed. N. F. Partner (London, 2005), 69–72, 75–76; N. F. Partner, "Notes on the Margins: Editors, Editions, and Sliding Definitions," in *The Politics of Editing Medieval Texts*, ed. R. Frank (New York, 1993), 15.

33. Cf. S. D. Troyan, *Textual Decorum: A Rhetoric of Attitudes in Medieval Literature* (New York, 1994); White, "Historical Emplotment," 42–43. Similar in their determinative qualities, and often complementary to emplotment in their use, are the various theatrical metaphors; see E. R. Curtius, *European Literature and the Latin Middle Ages*, trans. W. R. Trask (1948; New York, 1953), 138–44.

34. Cf. K. G. Heider, "The Rashomon Effect: When Ethnographers Disagree," *American Anthropologist* 90 (1988): 73–81, whose observations are equally relevant to historians past and present; P. Burke, "History of Events and Revival of Narrative," in idem, *New Perspectives on Historical Writing*, 2nd ed. (Cambridge, 2001), 283–300; Innes, "Introduction," in *UP*, ed. Hen and Innes, 1–8; T. Reuter, "Pre-Gregorian Mentalities," *JEH* 45 (1994): 465–74.

35. Although my use of the term emplotment suggests a clear reliance on the narrative theory of Hayden White, in practice I follow the specific formulation of White's theory by Piterberg, *An Ottoman Tragedy*, 58–68, who recognizes and compensates for White's modernist bias—that modern historians are ostensibly the only ones to give form, structure, and meaning to the historical record. On the ways in which the complexities of the information to be transmitted, together with an author's emotions and aspirations, all influence and occasionally act to defy the author's own ideology, see P. J. Geary, "Germanic Tradition and Royal Ideology in the Ninth Century: The 'Visio Karoli Magni,'" in idem, *Living with the Dead in the Middle Ages* (1987; Ithaca, N.Y., 1994), 49–76; idem, review of M. H. Heinzelmann, *Gregory of Tours: History and Society in the Sixth Century*, trans. C. Carroll (Cambridge, 2001), in *Speculum* 79 (2004): 198.

36. C. Pelling, "Epilogue," in *The Limits of Historiography: Genre and Narrative in Ancient Historical Texts*, ed. C. Shuttleworth Kraus (Leiden, 1999), 325–60; Stein, "Literary Criticism," 73. R. McKitterick and J. M. Pizarro have noted the ways in which early medieval authors often combined or synthesized interpretive modes; R. McKitterick, "Introduction: Sources and Interpretation," in *NCMH* 2:10–11; J. M. Pizarro, "Mixed Modes in Historical Narrative," in *Narrative and History in the Early Medieval West*, ed. E. M. Tyler and R. Balzaretti (Turnhout, 2006), 91–104.

37. On the rhetorical and literary skills of Carolingian authors and the ways these skills helped shape their representations of events, see *Narrative and History in the Early Medieval West*, ed. E. M. Tyler and R. Balzaretti (Turnhout, 2006); *UP*, ed. Hen and Innes; P. E. Dutton, *The Politics of Dreaming in the Carolingian Empire* (Lincoln, Neb., 1994); J. M. Pizarro, *A Rhetoric of the Scene: Dramatic Narrative in the Early Middle Ages*

(Toronto, 1989). See also J. Rider, *God's Scribe: The Historiographical Art of Galbert of Bruges* (Washington, D.C., 2001); S. Bagge, *Kings, Politics, and the Right Order of the World in German Historiography, c. 950–1150* (Leiden, 2002).

38. Rid, "Die Wiedereinsetzung," 265–75.

39. Nelson, "The Last Years," 147–59.

40. For a systematic (if cursory) analysis of the literary representations of the events of 833 within contemporary sources, see W. Kern, "Der Streit Ludwigs des Frommen mit seinen Söhnen im Lichte der augustinischen Geschichtsauffassung" (Ph.D. diss., Universität Greifswald, 1922); Chevallard, *Saint Agobard*, 208–13. On the importance of recognizing and explicating the rhetorical elements at work within any narrative representation of ritual performance, see P. Buc, "Ritual and Interpretation: The Early Medieval Case," *EME* 9 (2000): 183–210; idem, *The Dangers of Ritual: Between Early Medieval Texts and Social Scientific Theory* (Princeton, N.J., 2001).

41. The only exceptions are Mably, who also used the relatively obscure account of Andreas of Bergamo, and Kleinclausz, who also employed the account by Regino of Prüm. While it is true that, in addition to these loyalist narratives, Sismondi and Kleinclausz both made use of some of the extant texts produced by the rebellion, they did so only to condemn them, a trend that will be discussed in Chapter 3.

42. Notable exceptions to this rule are Kern, "Der Streit Ludwigs," 44–78; Chevallard, *Saint Agobard*, 208–13. See R. D. Ray, "Medieval Historiography Through the Twelfth Century: Problems and Progress of Research," *Viator* 5 (1974): 33–59.

43. Stein, "Literary Criticism," 72, emphases in original. See also Innes, "Introduction," 5.

44. On the authorship of the annals in the early 830s, see Nelson, *ASB*, 6–7. According to Nelson, "The Annals of St. Bertin," in eadem, *Politics*, 176; Nelson, *ASB*, 7, 25, one manuscript, Berlin, Deutsche Staatsbibliothek, Meerman lat. 141, which contains the annals from 830 to partway through 837, may have been copied for Drogo, archbishop of Metz and Louis' half brother, on whom see n. 255 below.

45. Nelson, "The Annals of St. Bertin," 175. For the manuscripts and transmission of the text, see the introduction by L. Levillain in *AB*, ed. F. Grat et al., xvi–lxxiv; F. L. Ganshof, "Notes critiques sur les *Annales Bertiniani*," in *Mélanges dédiés a la mémoire de Félix Grat* (Paris, 1949), 2:159–74; Nelson, *ASB*, 15–16. The Annals of Saint-Bertin (the name stems from the provenance of the earliest extant manuscript that contains them) are the continuation by some author of the royal palace in 830 of what are known as the "Royal Frankish Annals," an "official" log of Carolingian activities, whose author seems to have ceased his recording of events in 829 (as attested by the number of extant manuscripts of these annals that continue with other works after this year). On the Royal Frankish Annals, see R. McKitterick, *History and Memory in the Carolingian World* (Cambridge, 2004).

46. Nelson, "The Annals of St. Bertin," 175. On retrospective composition and compilation in annals, see S. Foot, "Finding the Meaning of Form: Narrative in Annals and Chronicles," in *Writing Medieval History*, ed. N. F. Partner (London, 2005), 88–108, esp.

97; R. McKitterick, "Constructing the Past in the Early Middle Ages: The Case of the Royal Frankish Annals," *TRHS* 6th ser. 7 (1997): 117.

47. *Annales Xantenses*, s.a. 833, ed. R. Rau, *Quellen zur karolingischen Reichsgeschichte* (Darmstadt, 1966), 2:340. On these annals, see H. Löwe, "Studien zu den Annales Xantenses," *DA* 8 (1951): 59–99.

48. I do not mean to deny the Annals of Xanten their own measure of narrativity; rather, the difference between them and the Annals of Saint-Bertin in this regard is one of degree rather than kind. Cf. the fact that the entry for 833 in the Annals of Xanten consists of 88 words, while the Annals of Saint-Bertin's entry contains 424.

49. Kern, "Der Streit Ludwigs," 66–68.

50. For the events described in this paragraph, see *AB*, s.a. 830–834, ed. Grat et al., 1–15; trans. Nelson, *ASB*, 21–31.

51. *AB*, s.a. 830, ed. Grat et al., 2. Murmuring (*murmuratio*) is a hypocritical act that is characteristic, in the Old Testament, of an ungrateful people and, in the New Testament, of the scribes and pharisees. See C. Casagrande and S. Vecchio, *Les péchés de la langue: Discipline et éthique de la parole dans la culture médiévale*, French trans. P. Baillet (1987; Paris, 1991), 181–86.

52. *AB*, s.a. 832, 833, ed. Grat et al., 6–7, 10; trans. Nelson, *ASB*, 25, 27. The annalist's use of the term *incentor*, like his use of *murmuratio*, is again indicative of his biblical mode of interpretation and representation of the events. Cf. 2 Macc. 4:1, together with contemporary Carolingian exegesis (e.g., Jonas of Orléans, *De institutione laicali*, *PL* 106, col. 155B), which follows Jerome (*PL* 26, col. 109B) in noting the specifically sinister, diabolic quality that serves to distinguish an *incentor* from an *auctor*. Another of the annalist's contemporaries, Thegan, a biographer of Louis the Pious and suffragan bishop of Trier, would quote 2 Macc. 4:1 in his description of Matfrid as the "*incentor malorum*" of the 830s. See n. 78 below.

53. *AB*, s.a. 834, ed. Grat et al., 13; trans. Nelson, *ASB*, 29.

54. Dutton, *The Politics of Dreaming*, 110.

55. Cf. E. Auerbach, *Mimesis: The Representation of Reality in Western Literature*, trans. W. Trask (1946; Princeton, N.J., 1953), 101; idem, *Figura*, in idem, *Scenes from the Drama of European Literature,* trans. R. Manheim (1959; Minneapolis, 1984), 11–76.

56. Ardo, *Vita Benedicti abbatis Anianensis*, prologus, ed. O. Holder-Egger, MGH, *SS*, 15(1):201.

57. *Regni divisio* (831), ed. A. Boretius and V. Krause, MGH, *Capit.*, 2:20–24, no. 194.

58. See Nithard, 1.4, ed. Lauer, 14; *AF*, s.a. 832, ed. Pertz and Kurze, 26; Astronomer, *VH*, 47, ed. Tremp, 470.

59. Ganz, "The Debate on Predestination," 285, has suggested that the typological model used by the first annalist was Job. However, the themes and particular vocabulary of the annals bear far more resemblance to the biblical tale about the aged patriarch Jacob, his covetous elder sons, and his younger, favorite sons Joseph and Benjamin by his second wife, Rachel (Gen. 29–50); cf. the use of the following words in both the annal

for the years 830–835 and the book of Genesis: *commota, compellere, custodia, machinatus, perterritus, pertinatio.* Moreover, Louis' second wife, Judith, and their son Charles had only recently been referred to as "Rachel" and "Benjamin" by the court poet Walafrid Strabo in 829; see *De imagine Tetrici,* vv. 147–48, ed. and trans. M. W. Herren, "The *De imagine Tetrici* of Walahfrid Strabo: Edition and Translation," *JML* 1 (1991): 127, 136. Louis himself had a special interest in Genesis; see M. Gorman, "Augustine Manuscripts from the Library of Louis the Pious: Berlin Phillipps 1651 & Munich CLM 3824," *Scriptorium* 50 (1996): 104. The annalist does not quote any specific passages from scripture. On the typological structure of medieval thought, see G. Spiegel, *The Past as Text: The Theory and Practice of Medieval Historiography* (Baltimore, 1997), 91–95; J. D. Dawson, *Christian Figural Reading and the Fashioning of Identity* (Berkeley, Calif., 2002), 83–137; and n. 55 above.

60. See Bagge, *Kings, Politics,* 7; H. Vollrath, "Konfliktwahrnehmung und Konfliktdarstellung in erzählenden Quellen des 11. Jahrhunderts," in *Die Salier und das Reich,* ed. S. Weinfurter (Sigmaringen, 1991), 3:279–96; eadem, "Oral Modes of Perception in Eleventh-Century Chronicles," in *Vox intexta: Orality and Textuality in the Middle Ages,* ed. A. N. Doane and C. B. Pasternack (Madison, Wis., 1991), 102–11.

61. *AB,* s.a. 832, ed. Grat et al., 8; trans. Nelson, *ASB,* 26.

62. On Thegan's intertextuality, see M. Innes, " 'He never even allowed his white teeth to be bared in laughter': The Politics of Humour in the Carolingian Renaissance," in *Humour, History and Politics in Late Antiquity and the Early Middle Ages,* ed. G. Halsall (Cambridge, 2002), 137–38; M. Innes and R. McKitterick, "The Writing of History," in *Carolingian Culture: Emulation and Innovation,* ed. R. McKitterick (Cambridge, 1994), 207, 209; E. Tremp, *Studien zu den* Gesta Hludowici imperatoris *des Trierer Chorbischofs Thegan* (Hannover, 1988), 21–63, 88–89; and n. 70 below. For the manuscripts and transmission of his text, see Tremp, *Studien zu den* Gesta.

63. Tremp, *Studien zu den* Gesta, 19–20.

64. Walafrid Strabo, prologus to Thegan, *GH,* ed. Tremp, 168. See Tremp, *Studien zu den* Gesta, 82–83; W. Berschin, *Biographie und Epochenstil im lateinischen Mittelalter* (Stuttgart, 1991), 3:225; Wattenbach and Levison, *DGM,* 335. On Walafrid as editor of Thegan's text, see Booker, "A New Prologue," 83–105; and Chapter 2.

65. Thegan, *GH,* 28, ed. Tremp, 216. Cf. the way Thegan, in his report of Louis' seemingly harsh tonsuring of Drogo and Hugh in 819 (*GH,* 24, ed. Tremp, 214–15), immediately attempts to counter any ill feelings that it might generate toward the emperor by means of a "flash forward," providing a brief snapshot of Drogo's and Hugh's future prosperity and honor thanks to Louis' munificence.

66. Thegan, *GH,* 20, ed. Tremp, 204–10. Thegan's comments continue to strike a nerve with some modern scholars; cf. Berschin, *Biographie und Epochenstil,* 3:226.

67. Tremp, *Studien zu den* Gesta, 82–83.

68. Thegan, *GH,* 44, 49, 58, ed. Tremp, 232, 242, 254; trans. Dutton, *Carolingian Civ.,* 170, 173, 175. See J. M. Wallace-Hadrill, *The Frankish Church* (Oxford, 1983), 237.

69. Thegan, *GH,* 42, ed. Tremp, 228–30; trans. Dutton, *Carolingian Civ.,* 170.

70. On the rhetorical function of direct speech in early medieval narrative, see Pizarro, *A Rhetoric of the Scene*, 62–108. Direct speech appears only three times in Thegan's biography (*GH*, 7, 16, 42), including Louis' speech upon the Rotfeld. However, of the three instances, Louis' Rotfeld speech is the only one that is not a quotation from scripture. As I note in Booker, "A New Prologue," 94; idem, "The Public Penance," 6; and Chapter 2, Thegan may be using this anecdote to refute the charge made by the rebellion in 833 that Louis' greatest sin had been in bringing his people together on the Rotfeld for the purpose of their mutual destruction. On the anecdote's enduring reception, see Chapter 4, n. 3.

71. Thegan, *GH*, 20, ed. Tremp, 206–8.

72. Tremp, *Studien zu den* Gesta, 87–88; P. Lehmann, "Der Einfluss der Bibel auf frühmittelalterliche Geschichtsschreiber," *SS Spoleto*, 10:135.

73. Thegan, *GH*, 20, ed. Tremp, 206–8; trans. Dutton, *Carolingian Civ.*, 165. Cf. Wallace-Hadrill, *The Frankish Church*, 237.

74. Thegan, *GH*, 42, ed. Tremp, 231 n. 218.

75. Thegan, *GH*, 44, ed. Tremp, 236; trans. Dutton, *Carolingian Civ.*, 172. Cf. Ganz, "The Debate on Predestination," 285. Innes, "He never even allowed," 148–54, argues that Thegan sought to depict Louis as acting in imitation of Christ. On the understanding of Job in the Middle Ages, see L. L. Besserman, *The Legend of Job in the Middle Ages* (Cambridge, Mass., 1979), esp. 166–67 n. 1.

76. Tremp, *Studien zu den* Gesta, 88. For a broad survey on medieval historiography as the careful and studied interpretation of God's will, see K. F. Werner, "Gott, Herrscher und Historiograph: Der Geschichtsschreiber als Interpret des Wirkens Gottes in der Welt und Ratgeber der König (4. bis 12. Jahrhundert)," in Deus qui mutat tempora: *Menschen und Institutionen im Wandel des Mittelalters*, ed. E. D. Hehl et al. (Sigmaringen, 1987), 1–31.

77. Cf. Thegan, *GH*, 9, 44, ed. Tremp, 190, 232. For other instances of fulfillment, see *GH*, 49, 52, 54, ed. Tremp, 242, 244, 248. See also the concluding sentence of Einhard, *VKM*, 33, ed. Holder-Egger, 41.

78. On ruthless ambition and insolence as innate qualities of the lowborn, see Thegan, *GH*, 20, 50, ed. Tremp, 204–8, 242–44. On Matfrid, see *GH*, 55, ed. Tremp, 250. Cf. the description of Ebbo as the *incentor* by the first annalist of the Annals of Saint-Bertin in n. 52 above. On the bishops, see *GH*, 44, ed. Tremp, 232. For the rebels as instruments of God, see J. L. Nelson, "Kingship, Law, and Liturgy in the Political Thought of Hincmar of Rheims," in eadem, *Politics*, 135.

79. Thegan, *GH*, 44, ed. Tremp, 238; trans. Dutton, *Carolingian Civ.*, 172. See S. Airlie, "Bonds of Power and Bonds of Association in the Court Circle of Louis the Pious," in *CH*, ed. Godman and Collins, 200–204.

80. Thegan, *GH*, 44, ed. Tremp, 232–36; trans. Dutton, *Carolingian Civ.*, 171–72; following Virgil, *Aeneid*, 6.625–27. Cf. Tremp, *Studien zu den* Gesta, 89; Wallace-Hadrill, *The Frankish Church*, 237. On the intertextual allusion here to the rebel bishops' *Relatio* of Louis' penance in 833, see Booker, "The Public Penance," 6.

81. Thegan, *GH*, 56, ed. Tremp, 252.

82. Thegan, *GH*, 20, ed. Tremp, 208; trans. Dutton, *Carolingian Civ.*, 166.

83. Thegan, *GH*, 50, ed. Tremp, 242–44. For the "happy ending," see Innes and McKitterick, "The Writing of History," 209.

84. Tremp, *Studien zu den* Gesta, 76, describes the prospect of Ebbo's regaining his episcopal office as the primary "nerve" of Thegan's endeavor and intent. In fact, this would be the primary concern of Thegan's first editor, Walafrid Strabo, in making his edition of the text; see Booker, "A New Prologue," 95–96, and Chapter 2.

85. Thegan, *GH*, 20, ed. Tremp, 204. Cf. the criticism of Louis' overzealous absorption in scripture by Paschasius Radbertus, *Epitaphium*, 2.2, 2.17, ed. Dümmler, 63, 88.

86. Thegan, *GH*, 50, ed. Tremp, 242. See also *GH*, 20, ed. Tremp, 206.

87. J. L. Nelson, "History-Writing at the Courts of Louis the Pious and Charles the Bald," in *HFM*, ed. Scharer and Scheibelreiter, 438–39; Innes and McKitterick, "The Writing of History," 209; Innes, "He never even allowed," 135.

88. Thegan, *GH*, 58, ed. Tremp, 254.

89. Paschasius Radbertus, *Exp. in Matheo*, 3, praefatio, ed. Paulus, 56:233. See J. D. A. Ogilvy, "*Mimi, Scurrae, Histriones*: Entertainers of the Early Middle Ages," *Speculum* 38 (1963): 611–12; H. A. Kelly, *Ideas and Forms of Tragedy from Aristotle to the Middle Ages* (Cambridge, 1993), 57–58.

90. Astronomer, *VH*, 49, ed. Tremp, 480. Kelly, *Ideas and Forms*, 50–61, has surveyed the sparing and generally confused usage of the term *tragoedia* in the early Middle Ages but is unaware of its employment here by the Astronomer.

91. For the manuscripts and transmission of the text, see E. Tremp, *Die Überlieferung der* Vita Hludowici imperatoris *des Astronomus* (Hannover, 1991). On the identity of the Astronomer, see n. 129 below.

92. E. Tremp, "Thegan und Astronomus, die beiden Geschichtsschreiber Ludwigs des Frommen," in *CH*, ed. Godman and Collins, 695; Berschin, *Biographie und Epochenstil*, 3:230–31. Like Thegan, the Astronomer occasionally uses direct speech to enliven certain scenes (*VH*, 15, 19, 58, 63, 64), though I am unable to discern why he chose these scenes in particular, apart from someone's making an observation in each instance (cf. n. 99 below).

93. Significantly, the Astronomer did not make use of the biography by Thegan; cf. W. Nickel, "Untersuchungen über die Quellen, den Wert und den Verfasser der Vita Hludowici des Astronomus" (Ph.D. diss., Universität Berlin, 1919), 13–14. On the Astronomer's sources, see Astronomer, *VH*, ed. Tremp, 69–98.

94. Astronomer, *VH*, ed. Tremp, 91–93. Tremp (following Nickel) claims that any similarities between the Astronomer's text and the account of 830–834 in the Annals of Saint-Bertin are merely coincidental, since they both describe the same basic set of events. Yet, cf. the following statement in the Annals (*AB*, s.a. 831, ed. Grat et al., 4): "*Hlotharium in Italiam, Pipinum in Aquitaniam, Hludowicum in Baioariam ire permisit*," with that by the Astronomer regarding the same event (*VH*, 46, ed. Tremp, 464): "*Hlotharium in Italiam, Pippinum in Aquitaniam, Hludowicum in Baioariam ire permisit*." For the suggestion of notes available in the palace archive, see Innes and McKitterick, "The Writing of History," 210.

95. By slipping in knowing asides, the Astronomer foreshadows the failure and eventual exposure of the rebels' scheme during the very act of narrating it: *VH*, 48, 49, ed. Tremp, 472, 480. Note that the Astronomer's explicit evaluation of the events as a tragedy occurs at a moment in his narrative when he is describing the news a visiting embassy from Constantinople will carry back to their emperor about the realm of the Franks.

96. Cf. Dershowitz, "Life Is Not a Dramatic Narrative," 99–105; A. Lane, "This Is Not a Movie: Same Scenes, Different Story," *New Yorker* (24 September 2001): 79–80.

97. Kelly, *Ideas and Forms*, 50–61. See also D. Dox, *The Idea of the Theater in Latin Christian Thought: Augustine to the Fourteenth Century* (Ann Arbor, Mich., 2004).

98. On tragedy as an interpretive mode in the Middle Ages, see H. A. Kelly, "Interpretation of Genres and by Genres," in *Interpretation: Medieval and Modern*, ed. P. Boitani and A. Torti (Woodbridge, 1993), 107–22; T. M. S. Lehtonen, "History, Tragedy, and Fortune in Twelfth-Century Historiography, with Special Reference to Otto of Freising's *Chronica*," in *Historia: The Concept and Genres in the Middle Ages*, ed. T. M. S. Lehtonen and P. Mehtonen (Helsinki, 2000), 29–49; R. Kaiser, "Guibert de Nogent und der Bischofsmord in Laon (1112): Augenzeuge, Akteur, Dramaturg," in *Bischofsmord im Mittelalter/Murder of Bishops*, ed. N. Fryde and D. Reitz (Göttingen, 2003), 121–57.

99. On Louis as another Christ, cf. the Astronomer's report of Louis' near-death experience in 817 (from which he was saved "by God to whom he was a beloved son") with that provided by the Royal Frankish Annals, his source for this passage: Astronomer, *VH*, 28, ed. Tremp, 372–74; *ARF*, s.a. 817, ed. Pertz and Kurze, 146. See also Astronomer, *VH*, 62, ed. Tremp, 542, likening Louis to the monastic Good Shepherd (cf. Benedict, *Regula*, 27); H. Siemes, "Beiträge zum literarischen Bild Kaiser Ludwigs des Frommen in der Karolingerzeit" (Ph.D. diss., Universität Freiburg, 1966), 57–62; and Astronomer, *VH*, 64, ed. Tremp, 552, like the evangelists Mark and Matthew on Christ's death (Mk. 15:34; Mt. 27:46), reporting Louis' last words in the vernacular. Ganz, "The Debate on Predestination," 285, has alleged that the typological model used by the Astronomer was Job (cf. Astronomer, *VH*, 46, ed. Tremp, 466), while Dutton, *The Politics of Dreaming*, 110, has suggested David and his sons (cf. Astronomer, *VH*, 55, ed. Tremp, 508). The strong allusions made by the Astronomer to the likeness of Louis and Christ—in terms of their corporeal demeanor and terrestrial fate—is perhaps a reflection of the intense sponsorship that the cult of Christ the Savior enjoyed during Louis' reign; see P. Le Maitre, "Image du Christ, Image de L'Empereur: L'Exemple du culte du Saint Sauveur sous Louis le Pieux," *Revue d'histoire de l'église de France* 68 (1982): 201–12.

100. Astronomer, *VH*, prologus, ed. Tremp, 280–84. As Tremp observes (284 n. 15), the Astronomer quotes Virgil, *Aeneid*, 4.19, for his suggestion of Louis' *culpa* in the specific sense of "weakness." Cf. n. 111 below.

101. Berschin, *Biographie und Epochenstil*, 3:230.

102. Astronomer, *VH*, prologus, ed. Tremp, 284; trans. A. Cabaniss, *Son of Charlemagne* (Syracuse, N.Y., 1961), 31.

103. Astronomer, *VH*, 42, ed. Tremp, 444. Cf. *VH*, 33, 39, 45.

104. Astronomer, *VH*, prologus, ed. Tremp, 284. On the irony of this passage, see

Siemes, "Beiträge," 96–97. The Astronomer's understanding of this "fault" not as a weakness but as a strength is supported by the scriptural context from which he draws his quotation of Paul: see 2 Cor. 12:9–10.

105. Astronomer, *VH*, prologus, ed. Tremp, 284. The Astronomer's use here of the term *aemulus* only serves to underscore the Pauline context and associations of this passage, as it is a word especially prevalent in Paul's epistles.

106. Cf. Astronomer, *VH*, 44, ed. Tremp, 458.

107. For a striking contemporary account using irony to stress the depravity of the times, see Chapter 6, nn. 94–95, on Einhard's concluding thoughts about the tongue-lashing delivered to the populace by the demon Wiggo.

108. On the Astronomer's cautious employment of the terms *fortuna* (*VH*, 2, ed. Tremp, 288), *infortunatus* (*VH*, 20, ed. Tremp, 342), and *infortunium* (*VH*, 2, 49, ed. Tremp, 288, 482), see Siemes, "Beiträge," 92–93. Perhaps the Astronomer is here betraying the influence of Boethius, *De consolatione Philosophiae*, 2.2: "What else does the clamor of tragedies bewail but Fortune overthrowing happy kingdoms with an unexpected blow?"

109. Wallace-Hadrill, *The Frankish Church*, 235. See also E. Tremp, "Zwischen 'stabilitas' und 'Mutatio Regni': Herrschafts- und Staatsauffassungen im Umkreis Ludwigs des Frommen," in *La royauté et les élites dans l'Europe carolingienne*, ed. R. Le Jan (Lille, 1998), 119.

110. Astronomer, *VH*, 44, ed. Tremp, 456; trans. Cabaniss, *Son of Charlemagne*, 89. This proverb is not listed by H. Walther, *Proverbia sententiaeque latinitatis Medii Aevi: Lateinische Sprichwörter und Sentenzen des Mittelalters in alphabetischer Anordnung*, ed. P. G. Schmidt (Göttingen, 1963–86), though it is clearly based on the classical proverb of "dog's eloquence" (*canina facundia*); cf. Isidore of Seville, *Sententiae*, 3.56, PL 83, col. 728A; trans. O. O'Donovan and J. L. O'Donovan, *From Irenaeus to Grotius: A Sourcebook on Christian Political Thought, 100–1625* (Grand Rapids, Mich., 1999), 209.

111. Astronomer, *VH*, 44, ed. Tremp, 456, quoting Virgil, *Aeneid*, 4.172, to express their *culpa* in the specific sense of "guilt." Cf. n. 100 above.

112. Astronomer, *VH*, 45, 48, ed. Tremp, 462, 472. Cf. Kern, "Der Streit Ludwigs," 51–65.

113. Astronomer, *VH*, 44, 45, 47–48, 52, ed. Tremp, 456, 458, 460, 462, 468, 476, 496.

114. Astronomer, *VH*, 48, ed. Tremp, 472; trans. Cabaniss, *Son of Charlemagne*, 96.

115. Astronomer, *VH*, 45, 47, 48, 52, ed. Tremp, 460, 468, 476–78, 496.

116. Astronomer, *VH*, 45, ed. Tremp, 462.

117. Astronomer, *VH*, 51, ed. Tremp, 486, trans. Cabaniss, *Son of Charlemagne*, 101. Although it is generally ignored by Cabaniss and Tremp in their translations, the use of the term *sane* by the Astronomer is often revealing of the biographer's feelings about many of the events he describes.

118. Tremp, *Die Überlieferung der* Vita, 128–56; Astronomer, *VH*, ed. Tremp, 67–68, accounts for the inclusion of Lothar's "reasonable" rebuttal by arguing that the Astronomer originally composed the biography for Lothar in the winter of 840/41—hence, his

sympathetic portrait here of Lothar—but decided to present it instead to Charles the Bald after the battle of Fontenoy, 25 June 841. E. Screen, "The Importance of the Emperor: Lothar I and the Frankish Civil War, 840–843," *EME* 12 (2003): 27, has also observed that the Astronomer's text "is not unsympathetic to Lothar's claims, and may have been written or commissioned by someone within Lothar's circle." On p. 27 n. 11, she mentions Archbishop Drogo of Metz as possibly having commissioned the work. Cf. J. L. Nelson, "Carolingian Royal Funerals," in *Rituals of Power: From Late Antiquity to the Early Middle Ages*, ed. F. Theuws and J. L. Nelson (Leiden, 2000), 159 n. 117, and n. 44 above.

119. Astronomer, *VH*, 48, 49, ed. Tremp, 478, 482. Cf. Engelbert, *Versus de bella quae fuit acta Fontaneto*, stanza 5, ed. E. Dümmler, MGH, *PLAC*, 2:138.

120. Berschin, *Biographie und Epochenstil*, 3:230.

121. S. Airlie, "Private Bodies and the Body Politic in the Divorce Case of Lothar II," *PP* 161 (1998): 29–31; M. Richter, *The Formation of the Medieval West: Studies in the Oral Culture of the Barbarians* (Dublin, 1994), 125–45; K. F. Morrison, " 'Know Thyself': Music in the Carolingian Renaissance," *SS Spoleto* 39(1): 369–483; J. O. Fichte, *Expository Voices in Medieval Drama* (Nürnberg, 1975), 6.

122. Dox, *The Idea of the Theater*; and A. J. Frantzen, "Drama and Dialogue in Old English Poetry: The Scene of Cynewulf's *Juliana*," *Theatre Survey* 48 (2007): 99–119, provide a good historiographical survey of this tradition. See also R. W. Vince, *Ancient and Medieval Theatre: A Historiographical Handbook* (Westport, Conn., 1984).

123. See Dox, *The Idea of the Theater*; Kelly, *Ideas and Forms*; H. Jürgens, *Pompa diaboli: Die lateinischen Kirchenväter und das antike Theater* (Stuttgart, 1972).

124. Morrison, " 'Know Thyself': Music."

125. On medieval attitudes toward Terence, see C. Symes, "The Performance and Preservation of Medieval Latin Comedy," *European Medieval Drama* 7 (2003): 29–50; J. B. Holloway, "Slaves and Princes: Terence Through Time," in *The Influence of the Classical World on Medieval Literature, Architecture, Music, and Culture*, ed. F. Fajardo-Acosta (Lewiston, N.Y., 1992), 34–53; P. Theiner, "The Medieval Terence," in *The Learned and the Lewed: Studies in Chaucer and Medieval Literature*, ed. L. D. Benson (Cambridge, Mass., 1974), 231–47; E. K. Rand, "Early Mediaeval Commentaries on Terence," *Classical Philology* 4 (1909): 359–89. For Carolingian illuminated manuscripts of Terence, see C. R. Dodwell, *Anglo-Saxon Gestures and the Roman Stage* (Cambridge, 2000); L. W. Jones and C. R. Morey, *The Miniatures of the Manuscripts of Terence Prior to the Thirteenth Century*, 2 vols. (Princeton, N.J., 1930–31).

126. Einhard, *Translatio*, 3.16, ed. Waitz, 254; trans. Dutton, *Courtier*, 106. On the theatrical connotations of the term *persona*, see M. H. Marshall, "Boethius' Definition of *persona* and Mediaeval Understanding of the Roman Theater," *Speculum* 25 (1950): 471–82. Note also Einhard's unusual reference to and quotation of Vitruvius's comments on *scenographia* and stagecraft; Dutton, *Courtier*, 143.

127. J. L. Borges, "Averroës' Search," in idem, *Labyrinths: Selected Stories and Other Writings* (1949; New York, 1964), 148–55.

128. See Dox, *The Idea of the Theater*; Kelly, *Ideas and Forms*.

129. Scholars have made many conjectures regarding the identity of the Astrono-mer, ranging from the long-held medieval conviction that he was Einhard (Astronomus, *VH*, ed. Tremp, 53), to the palace notary Hirminmaris (J. G. von Eckhart, *Commentarii de rebus Franciae orientalis et episcopatus Wirceburgensis . . .* [Würzburg, 1729], 323), to the archchaplain Hilduin (M. Buchner, "Entstehungszeit und Verfasser der 'Vita Hludowici des Astronomen'," *HJ* 60 [1940]: 14–45), to the Irish monk Dicuil (Depreux, *Prosopographie*, 114), to archbishop Jonas of Orléans (M. M. Tischler, *Einharts Vita Karoli: Studien zur Entstehung, Überlieferung und Rezeption* [Hannover, 2001], 2:1109). I find it surprising, however, that no one, to my knowledge, has suggested Walafrid Strabo (808–849) as a possible candidate, for Walafrid is known to have been at court for nearly a decade (829–838) as a tutor to Charles the Bald; remained firmly loyal to Louis and Judith; read and carefully edited the biographies of Charlemagne by Einhard and Louis the Pious by Thegan at about the time the Astronomer's text was written; been sympathetic to Lothar in the winter of 840/41 (while exiled in Speyer, Walafrid wrote to Lothar for assistance; MGH, *PLAC*, 2:413–15, no. 76); and kept a vademecum filled with extracts and notes concerning medical and astronomical matters (subjects about which the Astronomer proudly displays his learning in his text). See Booker, "A New Prologue"; W. M. Stevens, "Walahfrid Strabo—A Student at Fulda," *Canadian Historical Association, Historical Papers* (1971): 13–20; B. Bischoff, "Eine Sammelhandschrift Walahfrid Strabos (Cod. Sangall. 878)," in idem, *Mittelalterliche Studien: Ausgewählte Aufsätze zur Schriftkunde und Literaturgeschichte* (1950; Stuttgart, 1967), 2:38–41.

130. On the narrative demands made by such interpretive modes, see White, "Historical Emplotment," 42–43; Dershowitz, "Life Is Not a Dramatic Narrative."

131. K. Young, *The Drama of the Medieval Church* (Oxford, 1933), 1:6.

132. In other words, the use of the term *traguedia* in the biography did not elicit commentary by contemporaries as being in any way noteworthy or unusual, as did Einhard's use of the rare word *dicaculus* in his biography of Charlemagne; see D. Ganz, "Einhard's Charlemagne: The Characterisation of Greatness," in *Charlemagne: Empire and Society*, ed. J. Story (Manchester, 2005), 51 n. 67.

133. While J. Matthews, "Peter Valvomeres, Re-Arrested," in *Homo Viator: Classical Essays for John Bramble*, ed. M. Whitby et al. (Bristol, 1987), 277–84; T. D. Barnes, *Ammianus Marcellinus and the Representation of Historical Reality* (Ithaca, N.Y., 1998), 11–19; and T. P. Wiseman, *Roman Drama and Roman History* (Exeter, 1998), have asked similar questions about drama and its influence upon the interpretive modes of the ancient and late antique Romans, and Piterberg, *An Ottoman Tragedy*, of the early modern Ottomans, no one has yet examined the Carolingians in this light, despite their clear fascination with drama. Modern Carolingian studies are also largely devoid of performativity as a category of analysis, which is particularly regrettable, given that members of the royal court regularly communicated using classical and biblical nicknames; see M. Garrison, "The Social World of Alcuin: Nicknames at York and at the Carolingian Court," in *Alcuin of*

York: Scholar at the Carolingian Court, ed. L. A. J. R. Houwen and A. A. MacDonald (Groningen, 1998), 59–79; eadem, "*Praesagum nomen tibi*: The Significance of Name-Wordplay in Alcuin's Letters to Arn," in *Erzbischof Arn von Salzburg*, ed. M. Niederkorn-Bruck and A. Scharer (Vienna, 2004), 107–27.

134. On Nithard and his work, see S. Airlie, "The World, the Text, and the Carolingian: Royal, Aristocratic, and Masculine Identities in Nithard's *Histories*," in *Lay Intellectuals in the Carolingian World*, ed. P. Wormald and J. L. Nelson (Cambridge, 2007), 51–76; Screen, "The Importance of the Emperor," 25–51; K. Leyser, "Three Historians," in idem, *Communications and Power in Medieval Europe* (London, 1994), 1:19–26; J. L. Nelson, "Ninth-Century Knighthood: The Evidence of Nithard," in eadem, *The Frankish World, 750–900* (1989; London, 1996), 75–87; eadem, "Public *Histories* and Private History in the Work of Nithard," *Speculum* 60 (1985): 251–93; K. Sprigade, "Zur Beurteilung Nithards als Historiker," *Heidelberger Jahrbücher* 16 (1972): 94–105. For older studies, see Wattenbach and Levison, *DGM*, 353–56.

135. Leyser, "Three Historians," 25.

136. On Nithard's text as the exception that proves the rule with respect to the relative interest in secular and sacred historiography during the early Middle Ages, see M. de Jong, "The Empire as *Ecclesia*: Hrabanus Maurus and Biblical *Historia* for Rulers," in *UP*, ed. Hen and Innes, 199–200. Modern scholars have consistently viewed Nithard's text as a unique window through which to discern the *Realpolitik* that lay behind the events of the 830s–840s. I shall discuss the implications of this usage in Chapter 3. Cf. Reuter, "Pre-Gregorian Mentalities," 472. It has long been thought that Nithard's work survives in only one manuscript of the late ninth century (Paris, B.N.F. lat. 9768) and in an incomplete copy of this manuscript made in the fifteenth (Paris, B.N.F. lat. 14663). Yet, much remains to be said about the transmission and reception of Nithard's text; see C. M. Booker, "An Early Humanist Edition of Nithard, *De dissensionibus filiorum Ludovici Pii*: Troyes, Médiathèque de l'Agglomération Troyenne, 3203," *Revue d'histoire des textes*, forthcoming.

137. Nithard, 2, prologus, ed. Lauer, 36.

138. Nithard, 1, prologus, ed. Lauer, 2.

139. Nithard, 1.5, ed. Lauer, 22. Cf. Screen, "The Importance of the Emperor," 29, 47.

140. Nithard, 4.5, ed. Lauer, 136.

141. Nithard, 1.3, 1.4, ed. Lauer, 12, 18.

142. Nithard, 1.4, ed. Lauer, 16.

143. A distinction observed by P. Depreux, "Nithard et la *Res Publica*: Un regard critique sur le règne de Louis le Pieux," *Médiévales* 22–23 (1992): 149–61. For additional studies on Nithard's political vocabulary, see Y. Sassier, "L'utilisation d'un concept romain aux temps carolingiens: La *res publica* aux IXe et Xe siècles," *Médiévales* 15 (1988): 17–29; W. Wehlen, *Geschichtsschreibung und Staatsauffassung im Zeitalter Ludwigs des Frommen* (Lübeck, 1970), 61–78, 96–105.

144. Nelson, "Public *Histories*," 289.

145. Nithard, 4.7, ed. Lauer, 144; trans. Dutton, "Awareness of Historical Decline," 253.

146. On the date of Nithard's death, see Nelson, "Public *Histories*," 291–93; C. Treffort, "Nithard, petit-fils de Charlemagne: Note sur une biographie controversée," *SAP* 632 (1994): 427–34. On Nithard's remains, H. Bernard, "A Saint-Riquier sur les traves de Nithard," *SAP* 632 (1994): 405–8; H. Guy, "Anthropologie médico-légale des restes présumés de Nithard, petit-fils de Charlemagne," *SAP* 632 (1994): 409–14.

147. Nelson, "History-Writing at the Courts," 440.

148. Nithard, 4.7, ed. Lauer, 142–44; trans. Dutton, *Carolingian Civ.*, 331.

149. On the careers of these courtiers, see Depreux, *Prosopographie*; J.-P. Brunterc'h, "Moines bénédictins et chanoines réformés au secours de Louis le Pieux (830–834)," *Bulletin de la société nationale des antiquaires de France*, seance du 12 mars (1986): 70–85.

150. Nithard, 1.3, ed. Lauer, 8.

151. Cf. Nithard's closing critique of Charles's selfish marriage to Ermentrude, which had been arranged only "because [Charles] believed that with [Ermentrude's father] Adalhard's help he could win over a large part of the people to himself"; Nithard, 4.6, trans. Dutton, *Carolingian Civ.*, 330–31. On Nithard's feelings toward Adalhard, see n. 153 below.

152. See n. 150 above. Cf. also Nithard, 1.2.

153. Near the end of Book 2 (9), Nithard criticizes Charles for making a tactical mistake: by unwisely heeding the counsel of the minority of his men and choosing to rendezvous with his mother rather than march immediately against Lothar, Charles allowed Lothar to spread damaging rumors. Later in his work (4.6), Nithard accuses Louis the Pious's chief counselor, the seneschal Adalhard, of having ruined the empire by his manipulative prodigality; see Nelson, "Public *Histories*"; C. M. Booker, "*Imitator daemonum dicor*: Adalhard the Seneschal, Mistranslations, and Misrepresentations," *Jahrbuch für internationale Germanistik* 33 (2001): 114–26.

154. Nithard, 1, prologus, 1.1, ed. Lauer, 2, 4.

155. For *terror* and medieval rulership, see G. Althoff, "*Ira Regis*: Prolegomena to a History of Royal Anger," trans. W. Brown, in *Anger's Past: The Social Uses of an Emotion in the Middle Ages*, ed. B. Rosenwein (Ithaca, N.Y., 1998), 61; L. Wallach, "The Political Theories of Alcuin," in idem, *Alcuin and Charlemagne: Studies in Carolingian History and Literature* (Ithaca, N.Y., 1959), 8, 16–18. In 829 and again in the early 830s, Bishop Jonas of Orléans, *Concilium Parisiense* (829), 56, ed. A. Werminghoff, MGH, *Conc.*, 2(2):651; idem, *De institutione regia*, 4, ed. A. Dubreucq, *SC*, 407:198, counseled that a king must "prevent injustices by the terror which he inspires." Cf. Isidore of Seville, *Sententiae*, 3.47, *PL* 83, col. 717B.

156. Nithard, 1.1, ed. Lauer, 4.

157. Nithard, 4.7, ed. Lauer, 144; trans. Dutton, *Carolingian Civ.*, 331.

158. Cf. Leyser, "Three Historians," 20, 26. H. Patze, "Iustitia bei Nithard," in *Festschrift für Hermann Heimpel zum 70. Geburtstag am 19, September 1971* (Göttingen, 1973), 3:163, was the first to note the implications of Nithard's placing the remembrance of

Charlemagne at the beginning and end of the work. Nithard's use of direct speech is another marker of his rhetorical sophistication; appearing only three times in the work (1.7, 3.5, 4.1), in each instance it is used to underscore the gravity of oath swearing in public assemblies.

159. Nithard, 4.7, ed. Lauer, 144, posited a direct relationship between the actions of men and the forces of nature. Thus, if the foul weather described at the end of his work was a reflection of the perverse iniquity of the realm, the implication was that it could just as well be remedied through a renewal of sober propriety. Cf. the Astronomer's account of Louis' restoration at Saint-Denis in March 834 and its effect on the weather, *VH*, 51; trans. Dutton, *Carolingian Civ.*, 264. Like the Astronomer, Nithard also makes use of the term *fortuna*; see Nelson, "Public *Histories*," 268; and n. 108 above.

160. Cf. M. de Jong, "The Emperor Lothar and his *Biblioteca Historiarum*," in *Media Latinitas*, ed. R. I. A. Nip et at. (Turnhout, 1996), 233.

161. The text, entitled *Epitaphium Arsenii* (*BHL* 8761), is incomplete, surviving in only one manuscript, Paris, B.N.F. lat. 13909, fols. 1–112, saec. IX med., Corbie provenance. For analysis and the dates of its composition, see C. Verri, "Il libro primo dell'*Epitaphium Arsenii* di Pascasio Radberto," *Bullettino dell'istituto storico italiano per il Medio Evo e archivio muratoriano* 103 (2000–01): 33–131; D. Ganz, "The *Epitaphium Arsenii* and Opposition to Louis the Pious," in *CH*, ed. Godman and Collins, 537–50; idem, *Corbie in the Carolingian Renaissance* (Sigmaringen, 1990), 112–20, 145; H. Mayr-Harting, "Two Abbots in Politics: Wala of Corbie and Bernard of Clairvaux," *TRHS* 5th ser. 40 (1990): 217–37; K. F. Morrison, "'Christ in Us, Moving Toward the Father': Paschasius Radbertus's View of History," in idem, *The Mimetic Tradition of Reform in the West* (Princeton, N.J., 1982), 121–35; P. von Moos, *Consolatio: Studien zur mittellateinischen Trostliteratur über den Tod und zum Problem der christlichen Trauer* (Munich, 1971), 3(1):140–46, 3(2):100–106. For a survey of Paschasius's career and works, see H. Peltier, *Pascase Radbert, Abbé de Corbie: Contribution à l'étude de la vie monastique et de la pensée chrétienne aux temps carolingiens* (Amiens, 1938).

162. Paschasius Radbertus, *Epitaphium*, 1, intro., ed. Dümmler, 19; trans. A. Cabaniss, *Charlemagne's Cousins: Contemporary Lives of Adalard and Wala* (Syracuse, N.Y., 1967), 84.

163. On the dialogic form of the text, see Verri, "Il libro primo," 34 n. 4. That Paschasius's text is written in two parts is likely a reflection of his primary model, the two-part funeral oration by Saint Ambrose on the death of his brother Satyrus (*De excessu fratris Satyri*); see Ganz, "The *Epitaphium Arsenii*," 543. Verri, "Il libro primo," also notes that the text borrows from the ancient genres of the funeral elegy (35 n. 5), the letter of consolation (35 n. 6), and the *epitaphium* (35 n. 7). The dialogic form may also derive from a theatrical model; Corbie is known to have possessed a manuscript containing the plays of Terence in which the abbreviated names of the interlocutors are written in red rustic capitals (Paris, B.N.F. lat. 7900), the same format in which they are written in the lone manuscript of the *Epitaphium Arsenii*.

164. See, for example, Paschasius Radbertus, *Epitaphium*, 2.8, ed. Dümmler, 70.

On the importance of reputation in the Middle Ages, see *Fama: The Politics of Talk and Reputation in Medieval Europe*, ed. T. Fenster and D. L. Smail (Ithaca, N.Y., 2003); E. Peters, "Wounded Names: The Medieval Doctrine of Infamy," in *Law in Mediaeval Life and Thought*, ed. E. B. King and S. J. Ridyard (Sewanee, Tenn., 1990), 43–89.

165. After Louis' reinstatement in March 834, Wala fled to Italy, becoming abbot of the monastery of Saint-Columban at Bobbio. In May 836, he was recalled to an assembly at Thionville by Louis the Pious and formally pardoned. He then returned to Bobbio, where he died from an epidemic in August 836. See Paschasius Radbertus, *Epitaphium*, 2.23, ed. Dümmler, 94; Astronomer, *VH*, 55, ed. Tremp, 506; Ganz, *Corbie*, 115; L. Weinrich, *Wala: Graf, Mönch und Rebell: Die Biographie eines Karolingers* (Lübeck, 1963), 88.

166. For the comparison of Wala with Jeremiah, see Paschasius Radbertus, *Epitaphium*, I, intro., 1.1, 1.2, 1.23, 2.2, 2.5, 2.8, 2.15, ed. Dümmler, 19–20, 22, 23–24, 53, 62, 66, 71, 82; and Verri, "Il libro primo," 55–57. However, as Mayr-Harting, "Two Abbots in Politics," 220–22, has observed, Wala's character is also modeled in important ways after the Rule of Saint Benedict.

167. Paschasius Radbertus, *Epitaphium*, 2.8, ed. Dümmler, 70; trans. Cabaniss, *Charlemagne's Cousins*, 163–64. Paschasius's formulation of Wala as another Jeremiah reflects his general belief that his age mirrored the age of that prophet; at the time he was writing the *Epitaphium*, Paschasius also wrote a work of exegesis on the book of Lamentations, in which he demonstrated how many of its prophecies were being fulfilled in the present. See E. A. Matter, "The Lamentations Commentaries of Hrabanus Maurus and Paschasius Radbertus," *Traditio* 38 (1982): 150 n. 54.

168. Paschasius Radbertus, *Epitaphium*, 2.14, 2.15, ed. Dümmler, 81, 83.

169. Paschasius Radbertus, *Epitaphium*, 2.18, ed. Dümmler, 89.

170. Paschasius Radbertus, *Epitaphium*, 2.15, ed. Dümmler, 82; trans. Cabaniss, *Charlemagne's Cousins*, 181–82.

171. Paschasius Radbertus, *Epitaphium*, 2.8, ed. Dümmler, 70; trans. Cabaniss, *Charlemagne's Cousins*, 163.

172. Paschasius Radbertus, *Epitaphium*, 2.17, ed. Dümmler, 85–88. On these alleged letters, see Ganz, "The *Epitaphium Arsenii*," 545–47.

173. Paschasius Radbertus, *Epitaphium*, 2.19, ed. Dümmler, 90.

174. Paschasius Radbertus, *Epitaphium*, 2.17, ed. Dümmler, 88.

175. See Paschasius Radbertus, *Epitaphium*, 2.20, ed. Dümmler, 91, quoting from Job 12:6, 12:13–14, 12:16–21, 12:24–25, 23:13.

176. Paschasius Radbertus, *Epitaphium*, 2.18, ed. Dümmler, 88. To my knowledge, no connections have been demonstrated between Corbie and the manuscript transmission of these texts. Ganz, "The *Epitaphium Arsenii*," 541, 547–48, has argued that Paschasius knew Nithard's work and that "the *Epitaphium* implicitly criticizes Nithard's attempt to understand the preconditions for 843 [i.e., the Treaty of Verdun]."

177. Paschasius Radbertus, *Epitaphium*, 1.3, ed. Dümmler, 25; trans. Cabaniss, *Charlemagne's Cousins*, 93. The quotation is from Terence, *Phormio*, 5.8.57.

178. Paschasius quotes from all six books of Terence (none of which contain the word *vertigo*) throughout Book One: *Epitaphium*, 1, intro., 1.2, 1.3, 1.8, 1.11, 1.21, 1.22, 1.28, ed. Dümmler, 19, 24–25, 32, 38, 50–52, 58. Although Ganz, "The *Epitaphium Arsenii*," 537–50, has raised doubts about their traditionally assigned dates of composition, the two books of the *Epitaphium Arsenii* are generally believed to have been written by Paschasius at different moments in his career. The fact that Paschasius quotes from Terence only in his first book suggests that he had access to a manuscript of Terence's plays only during the composition of Book One, an implication that supports the notion of the text's production during two periods (though it is odd that Paschasius does not repeat some quotations from the first book within the second; he had already repeated several quotations in the first book itself). As it is generally held that Paschasius wrote Book One sometime soon after the death of Wala (August 836)—i.e., while Paschasius was still at Corbie, and thus prior to his temporary move to Saint-Riquier (in 849) and eventual return to Corbie—perhaps a manuscript of Terence's plays was present in the Corbie library only during the first half of the ninth century and was unavailable upon Paschasius's return to that monastery in the 850s. Corbie is known to have had two copies of Terence by the eleventh century; see B. Bischoff, "Hadoardus and the Manuscripts of Classical Authors from Corbie," in *Didascaliae*, ed. S. Prete (New York, 1961), 54–55 n. 33.

179. Cf. Paschasius Radbertus, *Epitaphium*, 2.6, 2.7, ed. Dümmler, 66, 68.

180. Paschasius Radbertus, *Epitaphium*, 2.6, ed. Dümmler, 66; trans. Cabaniss, *Charlemagne's Cousins*, 157. Cf. also *Epitaphium*, 2.20, ed. Dümmler, 91, quoting Job 12:25.

181. Cabaniss, *Charlemagne's Cousins*, 20–21; Ganz, "The *Epitaphium Arsenii*," 543.

182. On the presence of the works of Terence at Corbie, see n. 178 above. In his lament for Wala, Paschasius quotes not only Terence, but also the *Apocolocyntosis* of Seneca, a first-century satire on the Emperor Claudius (indeed, his quotations are the earliest witness of this text: *Epitaphium*, 1, intro., ed. Dümmler, 20–22). See R. Roncali, "Seneca satirico nel nono-dodicesimo secolo," *Belfagor* 25 (1970): 694–95; Ganz, *Corbie*, 116–17; idem, "The *Epitaphium Arsenii*," 543. For Paschasius's ambivalent interest in drama, see n. 89 above, and Paschasius Radbertus, *Exp. in Matheo*, 4.6, 2, ed. Paulus, 56:366–67; 7.14, 3, ed. Paulus, 56A:734. Such ambivalence is not unusual, for Augustine himself would at times argue, on the one hand, that theater was without any value for the Christian and, on the other hand, that it could be used to explain Christian truths; cf. Dox, *The Idea of the Theater*, 11–29; J. A. Barish, *The Antitheatrical Prejudice* (Berkeley, Calif., 1981), 58–59.

183. Paschasius Radbertus, *Epitaphium*, ed. Dümmler, 7; Mayr-Harting, "Two Abbots in Politics," 224; Ganz, "The *Epitaphium Arsenii*," 541–42. On the use of nicknames "as a *Geheimsprache* to relate sensitive information," see Garrison, "*Praesagum nomen tibi*," 111 n. 16. That Paschasius used the pseudonyms to cloak identity is problematic, for he also provided the actual names of Pope Eugenius II and Lothar's wife, Queen Ermengard, within the text (*Epitaphium*, 1.28, 2.24, ed. Dümmler, 58, 97).

184. Paschasius Radbertus, *Epitaphium*, 2.1, ed. Dümmler, 61; trans. Cabaniss,

Charlemagne's Cousins, 149. Cf. idem, *Epitaphium*, 1, prologus. Paschasius's cloaking of the characters need not imply that his text was meant to circulate outside the monastery (cf. Ganz, "The *Epitaphium Arsenii*," 538). On one level, the pseudonyms were simply a precautionary measure, for one never knew where a text might end up. Monks such as Paschasius, eager to find, borrow, and copy manuscripts for their own library, were all too familiar with the truism that books have their own fates.

185. On Paschasius's knowledge of Ambrose, see Ganz, "The *Epitaphium Arsenii*," 542–43, and n. 163 above.

186. Honorius (384–423) and Gratian (b. 388–died in infancy) were sons of Theodosius I; the Gratian better known to history (359–383) was the son of Valentinian I; Justina (b. ca. 350–d. 388), the second wife of Valentinian I, had Ambrose tutor her son Valentinian II, only to persecute him later; Arsenius (354–450) was the tutor of Arcadius and Honorius, sons of Theodosius I. In ca. 394, Arsenius fled to the Egyptian desert to become a hermit.

187. Ganz, "The *Epitaphium Arsenii*," 541–42.

188. On the memory of Theodosius's penance, see R. Schieffer, "Von Mailand nach Canossa: Ein Beitrag zur Geschichte der christlichen Herrscherbusse von Theodosius der Grosse bis zu Heinrich IV," *DA* 28 (1972): 333–70; H. Koch, "Die Kirchenbusse des Kaisers Theodosius der Grosse in Geschichte und Legende," *HJ* 28 (1907): 257–77; and on the memory of Theodosius in general, J. L. Nelson, "Translating Images of Authority: The Christian Roman Emperors in the Carolingian World," in eadem, *The Frankish World, 750–900* (1989; London, 1996), 89–98. The Astronomer, *VH*, 35, ed. Tremp, 406, compared Louis the Pious with Theodosius when describing the emperor's first public penance in 822.

189. According to C. Foss, "The Empress Theodora," *Byzantion* 72 (2002): 175, Justinian's wife Theodora was remembered in the medieval West "as a malevolent and heretical force who interfered with the church."

190. For the memory of Justinian II in the West, see *Liber Pontificalis*, 84 (Iohannes V)–90 (Constantinus), ed. L. Duchesne (Paris, 1955), 1:366–95, esp. 86.9 (p. 374) and 90.6 (pp. 390–91); Paul the Deacon, *Historia Langobardorum*, 6.11, 6.31, ed. L. Bethmann and G. Waitz, MGH, *SRL*, 168, 175.

191. Paschasius Radbertus, *Epitaphium*, 1, intro., ed. Dümmler, 18–20; trans. Cabaniss, *Charlemagne's Cousins*, 83, 85–86; alluding to Cicero, *De inventione rhetorica*, 2.1. See Morrison, "Christ in Us," 126–27.

192. On the early medieval meaning of *persona*, see Marshall, "Boethius' Definition of *Persona*," 471–82; Morrison, "'Know Thyself': Music." For Paschasius's development of "character"—a complex topic that relates directly to his writings on the Eucharist—see C. Chazelle, "Figure, Character, and the Glorified Body in the Carolingian Eucharistic Controversy," *Traditio* 47 (1992): 1–36; B. Stock, *The Implications of Literacy: Written Language and Models of Interpretation in the Eleventh and Twelfth Centuries* (Princeton, N.J., 1983), 259–72; and n. 196 below. For its rhetorical foundations and use by Augustine, see A. Cizek, "Der 'Charakterismos' in der *Vita Adalhardi* des Radbert von Corbie,"

Rhetorica 7 (1989): 185–204; N. M. Haring, "St. Augustine's Use of the Word *Character*," *MS* 14 (1952): 79–97.

193. As Verri, "Il libro primo," 43 n. 26, 47 n. 37, 50 n. 51, points out, the name of one interlocutor, Chremes, is the name of a character in several of Terence's comedies (*Andria, Heautontimorumenos, Eunuchus, Phormio*), while the name of another, Adeodatus, is that of an interlocutor—Saint Augustine's son—in Augustine's early, dialogic works *De vita beata* and *De magistro*. The interlocutor Theophrastus bears the name of Aristotle's disciple, who wrote an extensive work on the various character-types from which a dramatic work might draw. Paschasius likely knew of Theophrastus through Cicero; cf. Ganz, *Corbie*, 113; C. B. Schmitt, "Theophrastus in the Middle Ages," *Viator* 2 (1971): 252–70; and n. 191 above on Cicero. On the other interlocutors in the text (Paschasius, Severus, and Allabigus), see Verri, "Il libro primo," 43–52.

194. See Augustine, *De civitate Dei*, 5.9; F. J. Crosson, "Esoteric versus Latent Teaching," *Review of Metaphysics* 59 (2005): 80. Cf. I. van Renswoude, "The Sincerity of Fiction: Rather and the Quest for Self-Knowledge," in *Ego Trouble: Authors and Their Identities in the Early Middle Ages*, ed. R. McKitterick et al. (Vienna, forthcoming). In fact, "Paschasius" was a cognomen adopted by Radbertus; whether he wished thereby to associate himself with an early sixth-century saintly deacon of Rome bearing the same name, mentioned by Gregory the Great (*Dialogues*, 4.40), or a late sixth-century monk Paschasius of Dumio, who translated lives of the Desert Fathers from Greek to Latin is uncertain; see C. W. Barlow, *Iberian Fathers*, vol. 1, *Martin of Braga, Paschasius of Dumium and Leander of Seville*, Fathers of the Church 62 (Washington, D.C., 1969).

195. Ganz, "The *Epitaphium Arsenii*," 549.

196. On Paschasius as exegete, see C. Chazelle, "Exegesis in the Ninth-Century Eucharist Debate," in *The Study of the Bible in the Carolingian Era*, ed. C. Chazelle and B. Van Name Edwards (Turnhout, 2003), 167–87; W. Otten, "Between Augustinian Signs and Carolingian Reality: The Presence of Ambrose and Augustine in the Eucharistic Debate Between Paschasius Radbertus and Ratramnus of Corbie," *DRCH* 80 (2000): 137–56; Chazelle, "Figure, Character," 1–36; Matter, "The Lamentations Commentaries," 137–63.

197. On this ability to "speak freely" or "speak boldly" (*parrhesia*), see P. Brown, *Power and Persuasion in Late Antiquity: Towards a Christian Empire* (Madison, Wis., 1992), 61–70, and 111 for Ambrose; C. Rapp, *Holy Bishops in Late Antiquity: The Nature of Christian Leadership in an Age of Transition* (Berkeley, Calif., 2005), 67, 83–84, 220–21, 266–73. Cf. I. van Renswoude, " 'The Word Once Sent Forth Can Never Come Back': Trust in Writing and the Dangers of Publication," in *Strategies of Writing: Studies on Text and Trust in the Middle Ages*, ed. P. Schulte et al. (Turnhout, 2008), 399; A. Murray, *Reason and Society in the Middle Ages* (Oxford, 1978), 393–99; and in general, M. Foucault, *Fearless Speech* (1983; Los Angeles, 2001). On the relationship between *parrhesia* and drama, see Buc, *The Dangers of Ritual*, 133.

198. Paschasius Radbertus, *Epitaphium*, 2.1, ed. Dümmler, 61. Cf. Fried, *Donation of Constantine*, 97.

199. Paschasius Radbertus, *Epitaphium*, 2.15, ed. Dümmler, 82; trans. Cabaniss, *Charlemagne's Cousins*, 182. See Ganz, "The *Epitaphium Arsenii*," 544; and Introduction, n. 58.

200. Paschasius Radbertus, *Epitaphium*, 1, intro., ed. Dümmler, 21; trans. Cabaniss, *Charlemagne's Cousins*, 88.

201. Paschasius Radbertus, *Epitaphium*, 1, intro., ed. Dümmler, 21; trans. Cabaniss, *Charlemagne's Cousins*, 87. Cf. idem, *Epitaphium*, 1.26.

202. As J. Habermas, *The Structural Transformation of the Public Sphere*, trans. T. Burger (1962; Cambridge, Mass., 1989), 90 n. 6, observed, conscience was equated with truth until the seventeenth century, when Hobbes equated it with opinion. But cf. Pope Gregory IV, *Ep.* 17, ed. E. Dümmler, MGH, *Epist.*, 5:230, ll. 20–23.

203. Paschasius Radbertus, *Epitaphium*, 2.12, ed. Dümmler, 79; trans. Cabaniss, *Charlemagne's Cousins*, 176. Cf. Gregory the Great, *Dialogues*, 2.3, trans. M. L. Uhlfelder (Indianapolis, 1967), 8–11.

204. Paschasius Radbertus, *Epitaphium*, 2.11, ed. Dümmler, 78; trans. Cabaniss, *Charlemagne's Cousins*, 175. See S. A. Stofferahn, "A New Majesty: Paschasius Radbertus, Exile, and the Masters' Honor," in *Medieval Monks and Their World: Ideas and Realities*, ed. D. Blanks et al. (Leiden, 2006), 49–69. On the ideal of self-knowledge in the ninth century, see Morrison, " 'Know Thyself': Music."

205. Paschasius Radbertus, *Epitaphium*, 1.3, ed. Dümmler, 25; trans. Cabaniss, *Charlemagne's Cousins*, 92–93.

206. Paschasius Radbertus, *Epitaphium*, 2.8, ed. Dümmler, 68.

207. Paschasius Radbertus, *Epitaphium*, 2.11, ed. Dümmler, 78. See also idem, *Epitaphium*, 2.12. Cf. the advice of Sedulius Scottus to King Lothar II (ca. 855–859) on "The Art and Diligence by Which a Transitory Kingdom Can Remain Stable," which employs the same binary, *vertigo* and *stabilitas*: *De rectoribus Christianis*, 3, ed. S. Hellmann, *Sedulius Scottus* (Munich, 1906), 27–28. On the monastic ideal of *stabilitas*, see A. de Vogüé, " 'To Persevere in the Monastery unto Death' (Stability in St. Benedict and Others)," *Word and Spirit* 16 (1994): 125–58; Tremp, "Zwischen 'stabilitas' und 'Mutatio Regni'," 111–27.

208. Mayr-Harting, "Two Abbots in Politics," 225.

209. Paschasius Radbertus, *Epitaphium*, 2.2, 2.17, ed. Dümmler, 63, 88. For Thegan's view, cf. n. 85 above. I shall return to Louis' monastic character in Chapter 6.

210. Paschasius Radbertus, *Epitaphium*, 2.2, 2.3, ed. Dümmler, 63–65. See Ganz, "The *Epitaphium Arsenii*," 544 n. 42.

211. Paschasius Radbertus, *Epitaphium*, 2.15, ed. Dümmler, 82; trans. Cabaniss, *Charlemagne's Cousins*, 181. On Wala's engagement with secular politics, see Mayr-Harting, "Two Abbots in Politics," 223–26; Fried, *Donation of Constantine*, 97.

212. Odilo, *Translatio*, 44, ed. Holder-Egger, 388–91; *BHL* 7545; abridged French trans. B. Zeller, *La succession de Charlemagne: Louis le Pieux, 814–840* (Paris, 1883), 91–94. The section of the account containing Louis' narrative has long been known as the *Conquestio domni Hludowici imperatoris*, a title taken from the first of two rubrics appearing

in a manuscript of the eleventh century (Vat. Ottobon. 3064, fols. 227–28): *Conquestio domni Chludovici imperatoris et augusti piissimi de crudelitate et defectione et fidei ruptione militum suorum et de horrendo scelere filiorum suorum in sui deiectione et depositione patrato.* The second rubric states, *De auxilio sancti martiris Sebastiani expetito et sibi experto et de revelatione obitus sui.* For the full text of the work, see *PL* 132, cols. 575–628. For the date ca. 900, see F. Lifshitz, "The 'Exodus of Holy Bodies' Reconsidered: The Translation of the Relics of St. Gildard of Rouen to Soissons," *ABL* 110 (1992): 335–37. On Odilo, see *Saint-Médard: Trésors d'un abbaye royale,* ed. D. Defente (Paris, 1996), 29, 92–94.

213. F. Palgrave, *The History of Normandy and of England* (London, 1878), 1:730. Cf. Wattenbach and Levison, *DGM,* 296 n. 2.

214. Thegan, *GH,* 19, ed. Tremp, 204. See P. C. Jacobsen, "Formen und Strukturen der lateinischen Literatur der ottonischen Zeit," *SS Spoleto,* 38(2): 944; Innes, "He never even allowed," 131–56.

215. See E. Müller, "Die Nithard-Interpolation und die Urkunden- und Legendenfälschungen im St. Medardus-Kloster bei Soissons," *NA* 34 (1909): 703–4. On the translation of Sebastian's remains to Saint-Médard, see P. J. Geary, *Furta Sacra: Thefts of Relics in the Central Middle Ages,* rev. ed. (Princeton, N.J., 1991), 40–41; J. M. H. Smith, "Old Saints, New Cults: Roman Relics in Carolingian Francia," in *Early Medieval Rome and the Christian West,* ed. J. M. H. Smith (Leiden, 2000), 323–27.

216. See the remark by Holder-Egger in his introduction to the text, MGH, *SS,* 15(1):378.

217. On monastic memory at Saint-Médard, see Müller, "Die Nithard-Interpolation," and, in general, P. J. Geary, "Monastic Memory and the Mutation of the Year Thousand," in *Monks and Nuns, Saints and Outcasts: Essays in Honor of Lester K. Little,* ed. B. Rosenwein and S. Farmer (Ithaca, N.Y., 2000), 19–36.

218. Müller, "Die Nithard-Interpolation," 707–8; *Saint-Médard,* 70–71. The abbey of Saint-Étienne in Choisy-au-Bac is 30 kilometers west of Soissons.

219. Odilo, *Translatio,* 43, ed. Holder-Egger, 387. Cf. Müller, "Die Nithard-Interpolation," 703.

220. M. Gaillard, "L'éphémère promotion d'un mausolée dynastique: La sépulture de Louis le Pieux à Saint-Arnoul de Metz," *Médiévales* 33 (1997): 141–51; Nelson, "Carolingian Royal Funerals," 155–60; R. Melzak, "Antiquarianism in the Time of Louis the Pious and Its Influence on the Art of Metz," in *CH,* ed. Godman and Collins, 629–40.

221. Odilo, *Translatio,* 43, ed. Holder-Egger, 387–88. Little is known of this alleged visit by Louis and Judith to Saint-Médard in 827. A charter attesting to Louis' gift of the abbey of Saint-Étienne in Choisy-au-Bac to Saint-Médard during this year is thought to be a forgery by Odilo, one "corroborated" by his equally fictitious account of its creation in his *Translatio,* 43, ed. Holder-Egger, 388. See *BM,* 330–31 (no. 842); Müller, "Die Nithard-Interpolation," 704–8. It is believed that the Gospel book presented by Louis to Saint-Médard during his visit is the extant deluxe manuscript Paris, B.N.F. lat. 8850, the "Soissons Gospels." See *Saint-Médard,* 63 n. 65.

222. Odilo, *Translatio,* 44, ed. Holder-Egger, 388.

223. To my knowledge, the only other attempt at an explanation is *Saint-Médard*, 57.

224. Odilo, *Translatio*, 44, ed. Holder-Egger, 389.

225. Odilo, *Translatio*, 44, ed. Holder-Egger, 389.

226. On the identity of Teuther, see E. Boshof, *Erzbischof Agobard von Lyon: Leben und Werke* (Cologne, 1969), 210, which supports the conjecture by Holder-Egger (MGH, SS, 15(1):390 n. 1) that "Louis" is here describing events that took place in September/October 838. See also B. Bischoff, *Katalog der festländischen Handschriften des neunten Jahrhunderts* (Wiesbaden, 2004), 2:383, no. 3870.

227. Odilo, *Translatio*, 45, ed. Holder-Egger, 391.

228. Jacobsen, "Formen und Strukturen," 943. Note also the important autobiographical work of the tenth-century bishop Rather of Verona; see Van Renswoude, "The Sincerity of Fiction." On the genre of autobiography in the Middle Ages, see J. Rubenstein, "Biography and Autobiography in the Middle Ages," in *Writing Medieval History*, ed. N. F. Partner (London, 2005), 22–41.

229. E.g., *AB*, s.a. 833–34, ed. Grat et al., 10–11; Thegan, *GH*, 43–45, ed. Tremp, 230–39.

230. Odilo, *Translatio*, 44, ed. Holder-Egger, 389. A few lines later, Louis explains that the means for his escape was contrived only "between the deep sighs of my heart" (*inter alta cordis suspiria*).

231. According to a letter by L. G. Cahier written in 1821, *BSAHSS* 9 (1855): 142, the inscription stated: "Hélas! je suis bien prins de doleur que je dure mourir me . . ." The remainder was illegible. Cahier's argument against Louis as its author was based on his observation that the letters of the inscription, which could still be read "easily" in his day, were in a script of a period much later than the time of Louis' captivity. Cf. Palgrave, *The History of Normandy*, 1:730.

232. The owner of Saint-Médard in 1803 was Nicolas Geslin (1758–1832), a tanner, who had moved his business onto the grounds of the monastery. See Cahier, *BSAHSS* 9 (1855): 132; Letter from Henri Congnet, dean of Soissons, 15 August 1866, in P. Guérin, *Les petits Bollandistes: Vies des saints* (Paris, 1876), 16:528; and *Saint-Médard*, 304, 354. The monastery was purchased from Geslin's heirs in 1840 and converted to a sanatorium for several decades, during which time its storied past was promoted just as vigorously through the sale of souvenirs; see *Saint-Médard*, 307.

233. White, *The Content of the Form*, 7. Cf. Foot, "Finding the Meaning," 91–92.

234. Augustine, *De doctrina Christiana*, 2.36, ed. and trans. R. P. H. Green, *Augustine: De doctrina Christiana* (Oxford, 1995), 118–19.

235. See *BS*, 12:1381, s.v. "Wala." Wala was listed among the names of the saints at Corbie but does not appear to have had his own cult; B. Coquelin, *Historiae regalis abbatiae Corbeiensis compendium* (Amiens, 1846), 16, 70. Cf. Weinrich, *Wala*, 89.

236. On the question of audience, see W. J. Ong, "The Writer's Audience Is Always a Fiction," *PMLA* 90 (1975): 9–21; Buc, *The Dangers of Ritual*, 249–50; R. McKitterick, *History and Its Audiences* (Cambridge, 2000); eadem, *History and Memory*; W. S. van

Egmond, "The Audience of Early Medieval Hagiographical Texts," in *New Approaches to Medieval Communication*, ed. M. Mostert (Turnhout, 1999), 41–67.

237. P. J. Geary, "Frühmittelalterliche Historiographie: Zussamenfassung," in *HFM*, ed. Scharer and Scheibelreiter, 541. In response to Geary, see *UP*, ed. Hen and Innes; McKitterick, *History and Memory*; D. S. Bachrach, "Memory, Epistemology, and the Writing of Early Medieval Military History: The Example of Bishop Thietmar of Merseburg (1009–1018)," *Viator* 38, no. 1 (2007): 63–90.

238. Nithard, 3, prologus, ed. Lauer, 80; trans. Dutton, *Carolingian Civ.*, 349.

239. On Nithard's concerns with rumor, see n. 153 above, and Nelson, "Public Histories." For the "contest waged with words rather than weapons," see J. L. Nelson, "The Search for Peace in a Time of War: The Carolingian Brüderkrieg, 840–843," in *Träger und Instrumentarien des Friedens im hohen und späten Mittelalter*, ed. J. Fried (Sigmaringen, 1996), 108.

240. On the many implications of open textual transmission in the Middle Ages, see E. P. Goldschmidt, *Medieval Texts and Their First Appearance in Print* (London, 1943), 86–121. Cf. the rare, proactive attempts to control the interpretation of their work by Augustine, *Retractationes*, prologus, ed. A. Mutzenbecher, *CCSL*, 57:5–7; Gregory of Tours, *Libri Historiarum X*, 10.31, ed. B. Krusch and W. Levison, MGH, *SRM*, 1(1):536. See Van Renswoude, "The Word Once Sent Forth," 411–12; M. H. Heinzelmann, *Gregory of Tours: History and Society in the Sixth Century*, trans. C. Carroll (1994; Cambridge, 2001), 94–101.

241. M. Trenchard-Smith, "*Furibunda silentia*: The 'Raging Silences' of the Testimony of Dhuoda, Countess of Septimania" (unpublished paper, UCLA, 1997), 6. Cf. Paschasius Radbertus, *Epitaphium*, 1.3, ed. Dümmler, 25. On authorial strategies of indirection, see P. J. Geary, "Medieval Archivists as Authors: Social Memory and Archival Memory," in *Archives, Documentation, and Institutions of Social Memory: Essays from the Sawyer Seminar*, ed. F. X. Blouin, Jr., and W. G. Rosenberg (Ann Arbor, Mich., 2006), 106–13; P. E. Dutton, "Whispering Secrets to a Dark Age," in Dutton, *Mustache*, 129–50, esp. 147–50; idem, *The Politics of Dreaming*; J. Fenster, *Fictions of Advice: The Literature and Politics of Counsel in Late Medieval England* (Philadelphia, 1996), 1–14; Auerbach, *Mimesis*, 89; H. Speier, "The Communication of Hidden Meaning," in idem, *The Truth in Hell and Other Essays on Politics and Culture, 1935–1987* (1977; New York, 1989), 189–212.

242. See n. 129 above.

243. Cf. Dutton, *Courtier*, xx–xxii.

244. Terentianus Maurus, *De syllabis*, v. 1286, ed. J.-W. Beck (Göttingen, 1993), 122, 518–20; L. Quicherat, "Un autre proverbe mal compris," in idem, *Mélanges de philologie* (Paris, 1879), 325–28.

245. On the interdependence of the written and the spoken, see P. J. Geary, "Oblivion Between Orality and Textuality in the Tenth Century," in *Medieval Concepts of the Past: Ritual, Memory, Historiography*, ed. G. Althoff et al. (Cambridge, 2002), 111–22. On rumor, see, in general, *Fama: The Politics of Talk*; M. Bloch, "Réflexions d'un historien sur les fausses nouvelles de la guerre," *Revue de synthèse historique* 33 (1921): 41–57; and, for

the ninth century, Dutton, "Whispering Secrets," and "Thunder and Hail," both in Dutton, *Mustache*, 129–50, 169–88; Nelson, "Public *Histories*"; F. Lot, "Le monastère inconnu pillé par les Normands en 845 (comment les rumeurs se propageaient au IXᵉ siècle)," *BEC* 70 (1909): 433–45.

246. Paschasius Radbertus, *Epitaphium*, 2.18, ed. Dümmler, 88. Cf. n. 176 above.

247. See Tremp, "Thegan und Astronomus," 691–700; and the maps of textual transmission in idem, *Studien zu den Gesta*, 209; idem, *Die Überlieferung der* Vita, 157.

248. On this point, see Nelson, "Public *Histories*." While it is true that local meanings and invented memories can cumulatively have a supralocal effect, as demonstrated by A. G. Remensnyder, *Remembering Kings Past: Monastic Foundation Legends in Medieval Southern France* (Ithaca, N.Y., 1995), this does not appear to have been the case with the idiosyncratic accounts of Nithard, Paschasius, and Odilo.

249. On Wala at Herford, where the abbess Swanahild translated his remains in the late eleventh century, see *BS*, 12:1381, s.v. "Wala"; *Kalendarium Benedictinum: Die Heiligen und Seligen des Benediktinerorderns und seiner Zweige*, ed. A. M. Zimmermann (Metten, 1938), 3:4–8. For the reception history of Nithard's text, see Booker, "An Early Humanist Edition." Contrary to Odilo's claims, Louis explained in a letter shortly after the events of 833 that he was certain he had Saint Denis to thank for his rapid return to the throne; see the Epilogue, n. 18.

250. Geary, "Frühmittelalterliche Historiographie," 541–42; De Jong, "The Empire as *Ecclesia*"; Heinzelmann, *Gregory of Tours*; J. Rubenstein, *Guibert of Nogent: Portrait of a Medieval Mind* (New York, 2002); Buc, *The Dangers of Ritual*.

251. See n. 191 above. See also Dutton, *Mustache*, xvi.

252. Cf. M. Vessey, "History, Fiction, and Figuralism in Book 8 of Augustine's *Confessions*," in *The Cultural Turn in Late Ancient Studies: Gender, Asceticism, and Historiography*, ed. D. B. Martin and P. Cox Miller (Durham, N.C., 2005), 237–57. Mary Garrison has noted the "bold and original" fusion of hermeneutic modes in the thought of Alcuin; see "The Bible and Alcuin's Interpretation of Current Events," *Peritia* 16 (2002): 82. See also n. 36 above.

253. See n. 220 above.

254. R. Schieffer, "Ludwig 'der Fromme': Zur Entstehung eines karolingischen Herrscherbeinamens," *FMSt* 16 (1982): 61.

255. On Drogo, see S. Glansdorff, "L'évêque de Metz et archichapelain Drogon (801/802–855)," *RBPH* 81 (2003): 945–1014; C. Pfister, "L'archevêque de Metz Drogon (823–856)," in *Mélanges Paul Fabre: Études d'histoire du Moyen Age* (Paris, 1902), 101–45; Depreux, *Prosopographie*, 163–67; *Clavis AG*, 1:307–9. On his presence at the Rotfeld, see *AB*, s.a. 833, ed. Grat et al., 9 n. "g" in apparatus.

256. See J. A. Schmoll gen. Eisenwerth, "Das Grabmal Kaiser Ludwigs des Frommen in Metz," *Aachener Kunstblätter* 45 (1974): 75–96; with the studies in n. 220 above. Louis himself had chosen a stone sarcophagus for his close friend and adviser Benedict of Aniane upon his death in 821: Ardo, *Vita Benedicti*, 42, ed. Holder-Egger, 219.

257. Dutton, *The Politics of Dreaming*, 111. Nelson, "Carolingian Royal Funerals,"

156–57, argues that Louis and Judith, rather than Drogo, were responsible for the selection of the sarcophagus no later than 829. Whatever its meaning to the imperial couple at that time (if one accepts Nelson's argument), to Drogo, the iconography of the sarcophagus surely took on new shades after the turmoil of the 830s.

CHAPTER 2. THE SHAME OF THE FRANKS

Epigraphs: C. H. Cooley, *Human Nature and the Social Order* (New York, 1902), 309; H. Quentin, *Les martyrologes historiques du Moyen Age: Etude sur la formation du martyrologe Romain* (Paris, 1908), 232.

1. See S. A. Airlie, "'Sad Stories of the Death of Kings': Narrative Patterns and Structures of Authority in Regino of Prüm's *Chronicle*," in *Narrative and History in the Early Medieval West*, ed. E. M. Tyler and R. Balzaretti (Turnhout, 2006), 105–31; H.-H. Kortüm, "Weltgeschichte am Ausgang der Karolingerzeit: Regino von Prüm," in *HFM*, ed. Scharer and Scheibelreiter, 499–513; K. F. Werner, "Zur Arbeitsweise des Regino von Prüm," *Die Welt als Geschichte* 19 (1959): 96–116; H. Löwe, "Regino von Prüm und das historische Weltbild der Karolingerzeit," in idem, *Von Cassiodor zu Dante* (1952; Berlin, 1973), 149–79.

2. On Adalbero of Augsburg, see K. F. Werner, "3. A[dalbero]," in *Lexikon des Mittelalters*, ed. R. Auty et al. (Munich, 1980), 1:93. For Regino's sources, see Regino, *Chronicon*, ed. Kurze, vii–ix. For Ado's martyrology, see *Le martyrologe d'Adon*, ed. J. Dubois and G. Renaud (Paris, 1984).

3. Note the decrease in the use of source material after 814 by Ado in his *Chronicon* (composed after 869), ed. G. H. Pertz, MGH, *SS*, 2:317–26 (which are only extracts; for the entire work, see *PL* 123, col. 23–138). On Ado, see *Le martyrologe d'Adon*, xii–xix; *Clavis AG*, 1:30–36; W. Kremer, "Ado von Vienne: Sein Leben und seine Schriften" (Ph.D. diss., Friedrich-Wilhelms Universität, Bonn, 1911).

4. Regino, *Chronicon*, ed. Kurze, 73, quoting Jerome, *Contra Rufinam*, 2.25.

5. For the title of his second book, the "*Liber de gestis regum Francorum*," see Regino, *Chronicon*, ed. Kurze, 40. See also Werner, "Zur Arbeitsweise des Regino," 98.

6. On these concerns by Regino, see Werner, "Zur Arbeitsweise des Regino," 98–99.

7. Regino, *Chronicon*, s.a. 880, ed. Kurze, 117. See P. E. Dutton, *The Politics of Dreaming in the Carolingian Empire* (Lincoln, Neb., 1994), 240; idem, "Awareness of Historical Decline in the Carolingian Empire, 800–887" (Ph.D. diss., University of Toronto, 1981), 22.

8. It has been argued that Regino's primary source for the years following 814 were the Annals of Prüm (which for these years are no longer extant). As Friedrich Kurze contended, the long-lost contents of this annal for the ninth century can seemingly be surmised by a comparison of Regino's text with the information given for these same

years in other extant annals, which themselves apparently depend upon either the Annals of Prüm or a lost exemplar as their common source (cf. the *Annales Stabulenses*, MGH, *SS*, 13:39–43, and the later recension of the *Annales Prumienses*, MGH, *SS*, 15[2]:1289–92). See Regino, *Chronicon*, ed. Kurze, viii–ix. However, as Werner, "Zur Arbeitsweise des Regino," 96–116, noted, all these annals may rather themselves rely upon Regino's account, which itself relies upon a lost source.

9. Regino, *Chronicon*, s.a. 888, ed. Kurze, 129; trans. Dutton, *Carolingian Civ.*, 541.

10. This erroneous chronology (Regino assigns the years 836 and 837 to events that occurred in 818; 838 and 839 to events from 833 to 835) is thought to be the result of Regino's deliberate attempt to create an uninterrupted sequence of entries out of the supposedly erratic and arbitrary information provided by his source. Cf. Regino, *Chronicon*, ed. Kurze, ix, following P. Schulz, "Die Chronik des Regino vom Jahre 813 an" (Ph.D. diss., Friedrichs-Universität, Halle-Wittenberg, 1888). Werner, "Zur Arbeitsweise des Regino," 97 n. 5, on the other hand, views the error as the eventual, cumulative result of slips in memory and their oral transmission.

11. Regino, *Chronicon*, s.a. 838–839, ed. Kurze, 74; partial trans. *François Hotman Francogallia*, ed. and trans. R. E. Giesey and J. H. M. Salmon (Cambridge, 1972), 491.

12. Kortüm, "Weltgeschichte am Ausgang," 499–513. See also N. Staubach, "Geschichte als Lebenstrost: Bemerkungen zur historiographischen Konzeption Ottos von Freising," *MJb* 23 (1988): 66–67.

13. Kortüm, "Weltgeschichte am Ausgang," 505 n. 40. Cf. Werner, "Zur Arbeitsweise des Regino," 98–99, on the quantitative disparity of Regino's chronicle. In Kurze's edition, the years 813–37 (Werner's "first part" of this section of the work) take up one and a half pages (!), while the remaining years to 906 take up another 78 pages.

14. W.-R. Schleidgen, *Die Überlieferungsgeschichte der Chronik des Regino von Prüm* (Mainz, 1977), 4–6, and n. 20.

15. Schleidgen, *Die Überlieferungsgeschichte*, 5–6 n. 20. Cf. Löwe, "Regino von Prüm," 165.

16. Ado of Vienne, *Chronicon*, ed. Pertz, 2:321. Ado's depiction of Judith as a wicked consort is perhaps the earliest explicit criticism of the empress by an author not directly associated with the uprisings of the 830s. Although Agobard of Lyon and Paschasius Radbertus of Corbie both composed scathing critiques of Judith, they were closely affiliated with the rebel party. See E. Ward, "Agobard of Lyons and Paschasius Radbertus as Critics of the Empress Judith," *SCH* 27 (1990): 15–25; G. Bührer-Thierry, "La reine adultère," *CCM* 35 (1992): 299–312.

17. While Regino's sympathies appear to lie with the hapless emperor—he describes the members of the rebellion as "conspirators" and also notes that Louis was given an "honorable" burial—such feelings may also have become part of a "common knowledge" about Louis. For the conspirators, see Regino, *Chronicon*, s.a. 839, ed. Kurze, 74; for Louis' honorable burial, s.a. 840, ed. Kurze, 74.

18. Odbert, *Passio*, ed. Holder-Egger, 342–56; *BHL* no. 3157. On Odbert's text, see

P. Corbet, "Interdits de parenté, hagiographie et politique: La *passio Friderici episcopi Traiectensis* (ca. 1024)," *Ius Commune: Zeitschrift für europäische Rechtsgeschichte* 23 (1996): 1–98.

19. Frideric was a participant at the council of Mainz in 829 and the recipient of a commentary on the book of Joshua, which Hrabanus Maurus respectfully dedicated to him between 826 and 829. See W. J. Alberts and S. Weinfurter, "Trajectum (Utrecht)," in *Series episcoporum ecclesiae catholicae occidentalis, V. Germania*, vol. 1, *Archiepiscopatus Coloniensis*, ed. O. Engels and S. Weinfurter (Stuttgart, 1982), 176–77; *Oorkondenboek van het sticht Utrecht*, ed. S. Muller and A. C. Bouman (Utrecht, 1920), 1:63–69, nos. 58–62.

20. O. Holder-Egger, in MGH, *SS*, 15(1):352 nn. 2, 4, remarks that the elements of Odbert's account for 833 are taken from Thegan, *GH*, 42, and Regino, *Chronicon*, s.a. 838. See also pp. 348 n. 2 and 352 n. 6, where Odbert appears to refer the reader directly to Ebbo's apology (on which, see below and Chapter 5). For Odbert's use of Thegan's text, see E. Tremp, *Studien zu den* Gesta Hludowici imperatoris *des Trierer Chorbischofs Thegan* (Hannover, 1988), 137–38. Odbert's erroneous dating of the event to 838 follows the chronological error by Regino in his chronicle. On Odbert's knowledge of the episcopal *Relatio*, cf. Odbert, *Passio*, 9, ed. Holder-Egger, 348, quoting Ezek. 33:8; with the *Relatio Comp.*, ed. Booker, 11, quoting Ezek. 3:18. Following the quotation, both texts resume their narrative with the causal conjunction *quapropter*.

21. Odbert, *Passio*, 17, ed. Holder-Egger, 352. Cf. C. Vogel, "La discipline pénitentielle en Gaule des origines au IXe siècle: Le dossier hagiographique," *Revue des sciences religieuses, universitaire Strasbourg* 30 (1956): 5–6.

22. Corbet, "Interdits de parenté," 30–98.

23. For Frideric's birth, training, and rise to the episcopate, see Odbert, *Passio*, 1–6, ed. Holder-Egger, 344–46. For his appointment as bishop, *Passio*, 7–8, ed. Holder-Egger, 346–47. For his meeting with Louis at the palace, *Passio*, 9, ed. Holder-Egger, 347–48.

24. Odbert, *Passio*, 9, ed. Holder-Egger, 347.

25. Corbet, "Interdits de parenté," 22–24, has discussed Odbert's exchange between Frideric and Louis and demonstrated its affinities with contemporary Ottonian and Salian formulas of "imperial theocracy." However, Corbet does not offer an explanation for the fish-eating analogy. Odbert has Frideric himself note that, by first removing all the bad parts in the head, one can move more rapidly from the head to the tail. Cf. Paschasius Radbertus, *Epitaphium*, 1.11, ed. Dümmler, 39; C. Wickham, "Ninth-Century Byzantium Through Western Eyes," in *Byzantium in the Ninth Century: Dead or Alive?* ed. L. Brubaker (Aldershot, 1998), 255; J. Schneider, "Die Geschichte vom gewendeten Fisch," in *Festschrift Bernhard Bischoff*, ed. J. Autenrieth and F. Brunhölzl (Stuttgart, 1971), 218–25.

26. On Odbert's use of the term *neptis* to mean cousin rather than niece, see Corbet, "Interdits de parenté," 32–33.

27. Odbert, *Passio*, 9, ed. Holder-Egger, 347–48.

28. Odbert, *Passio*, 10–11, ed. Holder-Egger, 348–49.

29. Odbert, *Passio*, 12, ed. Holder-Egger, 349–50.

30. Odbert, *Passio*, 15, ed. Holder-Egger, 351.

31. Odbert, *Passio*, 16, ed. Holder-Egger, 351–52.

32. Odbert, *Passio*, 17, ed. Holder-Egger, 352.

33. Odbert, *Passio*, 18, ed. Holder-Egger, 353–54. Cf. M. M. Gauthier, "Le meurtre dans la cathédrale: Thème iconographique médiéval," in *Thomas Beckett, Actes du colloque de Sédières*, ed. R. Foreville (Paris, 1975), 247–53.

34. This is a subject that demands further study. For some brief remarks, see Corbet, "Interdits de parenté," 84.

35. Corbet, "Interdits de parenté," 61–68, 87–90. See also S. Weinfurter, *The Salian Century*, trans. B. M. Bowlus (1991; Philadelphia, 1999), 22–24; T. Reuter, *Germany in the Early Middle Ages, c. 800–1056* (London, 1991), 226.

36. Such strict observance, however, was not necessarily true of all ecclesiastics at the time; Archbishop Pilgrim of Cologne, for instance, confirmed and crowned Gisela as Conrad's legitimate wife and queen upon Aribo's refusal to do so. For a survey of the vast topic of consanguinity, incest, marriage, and the coalescence of related prohibitions during the eleventh-century reform movement, see C. B. Bouchard, "Consanguinity and Noble Marriages in the Tenth and Eleventh Centuries," *Speculum* 56 (1981): 268–87, together with J. Goody, *The Development of the Family and Marriage in Europe* (Cambridge, 1983), 134–46; Corbet, "Interdits de parenté," 31–37, 87–92. On incest and consanguinity in the early Middle Ages, see M. de Jong, "To the Limits of Kinship: Anti-incest Legislation in the Early Medieval West (500–900)," in *From Sappho to De Sade: Moments in the History of Sexuality*, ed. J. Bremmer (London, 1989), 36–59; D. Herlihy, "Making Sense of Incest: Women and the Marriage Rules of the Early Middle Ages," in *Law, Custom, and the Social Fabric in Medieval Europe*, ed. B. S. Bachrach and D. Nicholas (Kalamazoo, Mich., 1990), 1–16. On the differing medieval methods of calculating degrees of blood kinship, see E. Champeaux, "*Jus sanguinis*: Trois façons de calculer le parenté au moyen âge," *Revue historique de droit français et étranger* 4th ser. 12 (1933): 241–90.

37. For the ecclesiastical opposition to Conrad II's election, see Corbet, "Interdits de parenté," 78–87. For Odbert's prefatory dedication (in verse), see Odbert, *Passio*, ed. Holder-Egger, 344; and for the circumstances of its composition, Corbet, "Interdits de parenté," 84–87. On the beginnings of the Salian dynasty and Conrad II's election, see Weinfurter, *The Salian Century*, 1–43.

38. Cf. E. Archibald, "Gold in the Dungheap: Incest Stories and Family Values in the Middle Ages," *Journal of Family History* 22 (1997): 133–49; eadem, "Incest in Medieval Literature and Society," *Forum for Modern Language Studies* 25 (1989): 1–15.

39. Both the period when and the means by which the *chansons de geste* were created have long been an issue of debate. For a useful introduction, see S. Amer, "Epic and Beast Epic," in *Literature of the French and Occitan Middle Ages: Eleventh to Fifteenth Centuries*, ed. D. Sinnreich-Levi and I. S. Laurie, *DLB*, 208:285–95; with N. Dass, *The Crowning of Louis: A New Metrical Translation of the Old French Verse Epic* (Jefferson, N.C., 2003), 1–14; J. M. Ferrante, *Guillaume d'Orange: Four Twelfth-Century Epics* (New York, 1974),

1–61; U. T. Holmes, Jr., "The Post-Bédier Theories on the Origins of the *Chansons de Geste*," *Speculum* 30 (1955): 72–81. For the historical figure who served as inspiration for the poetic character of William, see J. Frappier, *Les chansons de geste du cycle de Guillaume d'Orange* (Paris, 1955), 1:65–87; *Entre histoire et épopée: Les Guillaume d'Orange (IXe–XIIIe siècles)*, ed. L. Macé (Toulouse, 2006).

40. B. Guidot, *Recherches sur la chanson de geste au XIIIe siecle* (Aix-en-Provence, 1986), 1:155–69, esp. 159–60. This theme is not present in all the poems of the William cycle, but only begins with the poem *Couronnement de Louis*. See D. Boutet, "La pusillanimité de Louis dans *Aliscans*: Idéologie ou *topos* de cycle? Topique, structure et historicité," *MA* 103 (1997): 277.

41. A. Adler, "The Dubious Nature of Guillaume's Loyalty in *Le Couronnement de Louis*," *Symposium* 2 (1948): 179–91; J. Frappier, "Les thèmes politiques dans le *Couronnement de Louis*," in *Mélanges de linguistique romane et de philologie médiévale offerts à M. Maurice Delbouille* (Gembloux, 1964), 2:195–206; idem, *Les chansons de geste*, 2:145–47; Boutet, "La pusillanimité de Louis."

42. Cf. W. Van Emden, "Kingship in the Old French Epic of Revolt," in *Kings and Kingship in Medieval Europe*, ed. A. J. Duggan (Exeter, 1993), 305–50.

43. R. Van Waard, "*Le Couronnement de Louis* et le principe de l'hérédité de la couronne," *Neophilologus* 30 (1946): 52–58.

44. Van Waard, "*Le Couronnement de Louis*." Cf. Frappier, *Les chansons de geste*, 2:57–59, who suggests the perhaps more judicious date of ca. 1131–1150.

45. Van Waard, "*Le Couronnement de Louis*," 55. However, there was a recoronation of Louis by Pope Stephen IV in 816, two years after Charlemagne's death; see Thegan, *GH*, 16, ed. Tremp, 196.

46. Van Waard's argument was refined by K.-H. Bender, *König und Vasall: Untersuchungen zur Chanson de Geste des XII. Jahrhunderts* (Heidelberg, 1967), 43–67.

47. E. R. Curtius, "Über die altfranzösische Epik IV: Zum Couronnement Louis," *Romanische Forschungen* 62 (1950): 342–49, demonstrated the parallels between the *Couronnement* and Thegan, *GH*, 6, 7, 20, 44, 50; Einhard, *VKM*, 30; and Charlemagne's capitulary of 802, ed. A. Boretius, MGH, *Capit.*, 1:91–99, no. 33. Cf. D. Scheludko, "Neues über das Couronnement Louis," *Zeitschrift für französische Sprache und Literatur* 55 (1931): 425–71.

48. Cf. G. A. Beckmann, "Die erste Branche des Couronnement Louis und die drei Typen epischer 'Historizität'," *Germanisch-Romanische Monatsschrift*, NF 24 (1974): 385–408.

49. Cf. Frappier, *Les chansons de geste*, 2:77–78; Tremp, *Studien zu den Gesta*, 143–44.

50. Such contradictory information would act as an impediment to the poet's representation of the coronation only if his understanding of texts from the past (what we consider "historical sources") was similar to ours—a correlation that is problematic at best. See S. Fleischman, "On the Representation of History and Fiction in the Middle Ages," *HT* 22 (1983): 278–310.

51. See R. Louis, "L'Épopée française est carolingienne," in *Colloquios de Ronces-valles, Agosto 1955* (Saragossa, 1956), 425–27, citing Abbo of Fleury, Rodulfus Glaber, and Pope Urban II. This list can easily be expanded through an examination of the numerous medieval authors who used the biographies of Louis by Thegan and the Astronomer. See the reception surveys by E. Tremp, "Thegan und Astronomus, die beiden Geschichts-schreiber Ludwigs des Frommen," in *CH*, ed. Godman and Collins, 691–700; idem, *Studien zu den Gesta*, 128–49; idem, *Die Überlieferung der* Vita Hludowici imperatoris *des Astronomus* (Hannover 1991), 5–48. See also R. Schieffer, "Ludwig 'der Fromme': Zur Entstehung eines karolingischen Herrscherbeinamens," *FMSt* 16 (1982): 61 n. 24.

52. Schieffer, "Ludwig 'der Fromme,'" 58–73, and esp. 72. See also G. Leidinger, "Ludovicus Pius," in *Aus der Geisteswelt des Mittelalters*, ed. A. Lang et al. (Münster, 1935), 1:196–203; and H. Hummer, "The Identity of *Ludouicus Piissimus Augustus* in the *Praefatio in Librum Antiquum Lingua Saxonica Conscriptum*," *Francia* 31, no. 1 (2004): 11, who, with Schieffer, rightly observes that Louis was known as *piissimus augustus* during his lifetime; however, this epithet was used not as an individual nickname but as a part of his regnal titulature. Recall Schieffer's observation (p. 61) that Louis' epithet appears more frequently in those sources that have their origins geographically proximate to the city of Metz, Louis' burial place.

53. A. W. Lewis, *Royal Succession in Capetian France: Studies on Familial Order and the State* (Cambridge, Mass., 1981), 48.

54. Louis, "L'Épopée française," 411–43, esp. 426–27. For the historical Bernard of Septimania, see Depreux, *Prosopographie*, 137–39; L. Malbos, "La capture de Bernard de Septimanie," *MA* 76 (1970): 5–13; J. Calmette, *De Bernardo sancti Guillelmi filio (?–844)* (Toulouse, 1902); and n. 39 above. A tantalizing hint of the historical memory in the late eleventh century of Bernard and his wife Dhuoda is provided by T. N. Bisson, "Unheroed Pasts: History and Commemoration in South Frankland before the Albigensian Cru-sades," *Speculum* 65 (1990): 297–98.

55. For the manuscripts of Odbert's work, see M. Carasso-Kok, *Repertorium van verhalende historische bronnen uit de Miiddeleeuwen* (Gravenhage, 1981), 33–34; Corbet, "Interdits de parenté," 13 n. 40; MGH, *SS*, 15(1):343.

56. Corbet, "Interdits de parenté," 15–17; William of Malmesbury, *Gesta pontificum Anglorum*, 1.6, ed. N. E. S. A. Hamilton (London, 1870), 11–15. For William's understand-ing of the term *tragedia*, see H. A. Kelly, *Ideas and Forms of Tragedy from Aristotle to the Middle Ages* (Cambridge, 1993), 91–92.

57. Corbet, "Interdits de parenté," 16; William of Malmesbury, *Gesta pontificum Anglorum*, 1.6, ed. Hamilton, 13–14.

58. Odo Aribert, *Narratio de morte Bernardi*, ed. M. Bouquet, *Recueil des historiens des Gaules et de la France* (Paris, 1870), 7:286–87; Dutton, *The Politics of Dreaming*, 101. On Odo Aribert, see U. Chevalier, *Répertoire des sources historiques du Moyen Age: Bio-Bibliographie* (Paris, 1905), 1:311, s.v. "Aribert (Odon)"; Calmette, *De Bernardo*, 108–11.

59. Otto of Freising, *Chronica sive Historia de duabus civitatibus*, 5.34, ed. A. Hof-

meister, MGH, *SRG*, 45:259; trans. C. C. Mierow, *The Chronicle or History of the Two Cities* (New York, 1966), 356. Cf. Regino, *Chronicon*, s.a. 838, ed. Kurze, 74.

60. For Suger's close relationship with Louis VII, especially regarding Louis' coronation, see E. A. R. Brown, *"Franks, Burgundians, and Aquitanians" and the Royal Coronation Ceremony in France* (Philadelphia, 1992), 34–53.

61. *Vita Sugerii*, 1, ed. A. L. de la Marche, *Oeuvres complètes de Suger* (Paris, 1867), 382; G. Spiegel, "History as Enlightenment: Suger and the *Mos Anagogicus*," in *Abbot Suger and Saint-Denis*, ed. P. L. Gerson (New York, 1986), 151. Apart from a description of ecclesiastical privileges granted by Louis the Pious, to my knowledge Suger recalled Louis only once more in his extant works, attributing the dissension of the later ninth century to "the sons of [Charlemagne's] son, namely Louis the Pious" (*Oeuvres complètes de Suger*, ed. De la Marche, 160, 115).

62. As I shall demonstrate in Chapter 4, this is one of the charges leveled against Louis in 833. See Ward, "Agobard of Lyons and Paschasius," 15–25; Bührer-Thierry, "La reine adultère," 299–312.

63. Ferrante, *Guillaume d'Orange*, 70, v. 259; 131–32, vv. 2408–9, 2427–28.

64. Ferrante, *Guillaume d'Orange* (Louis' weeping) 127, v. 2247; 131, v. 2413, 2417; (Louis' cowardly deeds) 111, vv. 1708–9; 128–29, vv. 2311–15.

65. Ferrante, *Guillaume d'Orange*, 66, vv. 89–98. As T. F. X. Noble has demonstrated, the impression of Louis as "monkish" has endured for many centuries; see "Louis the Pious and His Piety Re-Reconsidered," *RBPH* 58 (1980): 297–316. For Charlemagne in the *chansons de geste*, see R. Morrissey, *Charlemagne and France: A Thousand Years of Mythology*, trans. C. Tihanyi (1997; Notre Dame, 2003), 43–78, and 65–66 for the *Couronnement*.

66. Ferrante, *Guillaume d'Orange*, 139, v. 2671.

67. Ferrante, *Guillaume d'Orange*, 66–67, vv. 99–149.

68. Ferrante, *Guillaume d'Orange*, 111, vv. 1692–93. See also 70, v. 246; 104, vv. 1467–68.

69. The traitors in the poem have often been seen as vague reflections of Abbot Wala, Counts Matfrid of Orléans and Hugh of Tours, and other figures who participated in the rebellions against Louis the Pious. See E. Langlois, *Le Couronnement de Louis* (Paris, 1888), iv–lxxv; L. Willems, *L'Élément historique dans le Couronnement Looïs* (Gand, 1896); Scheludko, "Neues über das Couronnement"; Louis, "L'Épopée française"; Beckmann, "Die erste Branche."

70. Cf. P. Haidu, *The Subject Medieval/Modern: Text and Governance in the Middle Ages* (Stanford, 2004), 66–68, on the *Couronnement*'s textualization of the period's political unconscious.

71. Van Waard, "*Le Couronnement de Louis*," 54.

72. *Annales Alamannici*, ed. W. Lendi, *Untersuchungen zur frühalemannischen Annalistik* (Freiburg, 1971), 176. The entries in this work for the years 802–56, which are very sparse, were likely recorded all at once by a single annalist working at Reichenau in the third quarter of the ninth century; for the manuscript, Stiftsarchiv St. Gallen,

Zürcher Abt. X, Nr. 1, fols. 90v–91r, see Lendi, *Untersuchungen*, 83–84, and for a tenth-century copy, 134–35. The *Annales Alamannici* are the source for the 833 entry in the *Annales Weingartenses*, ed. G. H. Pertz, MGH, *SS*, 1:65; *Annales Einsidlenses*, ed. G. H. Pertz, MGH, *SS*, 3:139; and *Annales Formoselenses*, ed. G. H. Pertz, MGH, *SS*, 5:35. See P. Grierson, *Les annales de Saint-Pierre de Gand et de Saint-Amand* (Brussels, 1937), XLIV–LII.

73. Ferrante, *Guillaume d'Orange*, 113, vv. 1775–76.

74. Ferrante, *Guillaume d'Orange*, 112, vv. 1747–55.

75. Frappier, "Les thèmes politiques," 2:206.

76. See L. K. Little, "Pride Goes Before Avarice: Social Change and the Vices in Latin Christendom," *AHR* 76 (1971): 16–49. Cf. Ferrante, *Guillaume d'Orange*, 111, vv. 1692–96.

77. Cf. J. Dunbabin, "Discovering a Past for the French Aristocracy," in *The Perception of the Past in Twelfth-Century Europe*, ed. P. Magdalino (London, 1992), 1.

78. D. Foote, "How the Past Becomes a Rumor: The Notarialization of Historical Consciousness in Medieval Ovieto," *Speculum* 75 (2000): 815.

79. Cf. J. J. Duggan, "Medieval Epic as Popular Historiography: Appropriation of Historical Knowledge in the Vernacular Epic," in *Grundriss der romanischen Literaturen des Mittelalters*, ed. H. U. Gumbrecht et al. (Heidelberg, 1986), 11:285–311.

80. On the *Grandes Chroniques*, see G. Spiegel, *The Chronicle Tradition of Saint-Denis: A Survey* (Brookline, Mass., 1978); eadem, *Romancing the Past: The Rise of Vernacular Prose Historiography in Thirteenth-Century France* (Berkeley, Calif., 1993); eadem, *The Past as Text: The Theory and Practice of Medieval Historiography* (Baltimore, 1997); A. D. Hedeman, *The Royal Image: Illustrations of the* Grandes Chroniques de France, *1274–1422* (Berkeley, Calif., 1991); Morrissey, *Charlemagne and France*, 90–95.

81. On the myth of the Franks' Trojan origins, see E. A. R. Brown, "The Trojan Origins of the French and the Brothers Jean du Tillet," in *After Rome's Fall: Narrators and Sources of Early Medieval History*, ed. A. C. Murray (Toronto, 1998), 348–84; and I. Wood, "Defining the Franks: Frankish Origins in Early Medieval Historiography," in *Concepts of National Identity in the Middle Ages*, ed. S. Forde et al. (Leeds, 1995), 47–57.

82. Hedeman, *The Royal Image*, 1–3; Spiegel, *The Chronicle Tradition*, 88–89.

83. On the relationship between the royal ideology of Saint Louis and the composition of the *Grandes Chroniques*, see J. Le Goff, *Saint Louis* (Paris, 1996), 566–68; B. Guenée, "Les Grandes Chroniques de France: Le Roman aux roys (1274–1518)," in *Les Lieux de mémoire*, ed. P. Nora (Paris, 1986), 2(1):189–214; Hedeman, *The Royal Image*, 1–6.

84. *Grandes Chroniques de France*, ed. J. Viard (Paris, 1927), 4:ii–v.

85. As Viard observed (*Grandes Chroniques de France*, 4:112 n. 2), Louis' confession is not included within Paris, B.N.F. lat. 5925, the manuscript containing the Latin text upon which Primat based much of the *Grandes Chroniques* and from which he drew the Astronomer's account. On this manuscript and its relationship with the *Grandes Chro-*

niques, see Spiegel, *The Chronicle Tradition*, 68–71; Tremp, *Die Überlieferung der* Vita, 42–43.

86. *Grandes Chroniques de France*, ed. Viard, 4:ii–v.

87. *Grandes Chroniques de France*, ed. Viard, 4:112; Tremp, *Die Überlieferung der* Vita, 43. Primat's redaction covers only one half of the confession "recorded" by Odilo, namely, the "complaint" (*conquestio*) of Louis over the cruelty of his sons and treachery of his *fideles*, which was rubricated as a discrete section in one of the extant manuscripts; see Chapter 1, n. 212.

88. *Grandes Chroniques de France*, ed. Viard, 4:112–13, which follows the rubric for this section as found in a manuscript of Odilo's text. See the previous note.

89. *Grandes Chroniques de France*, ed. Viard, 4:112–17. The author repeatedly describes the events with terms such as *grief* and *tribulation*, 113; *doleur*, 114–15; *dolenz et tristres*, 119; *dolenz* and *grief*, 122; *tristre et dolent*, 127. The text's modern editor, Viard, believed Odilo's report of Louis' confessional narrative to be authentic and reliable (p. 112 n. 2).

90. For the interest of Charles V in the *Grandes Chroniques*, see Hedeman, *The Royal Image*, 95–133; Spiegel, *The Chronicle Tradition*, 122, esp. nn. 274–75. For the manuscript and miniature in Fig. 8 (Paris, B.N.F. fr. 2813, saec. XIV), see Hedeman, *The Royal Image*, 95–133, 244–48, and 245, no. 45.

91. See R. McKitterick, "The Study of Frankish History in France and Germany in the Sixteenth and Seventeenth Centuries," *Francia* 8 (1980): 557–58; with B. Gordon, "The Changing Face of Protestant History and Identity in the Sixteenth Century," in *Protestant History and Identity in Sixteenth-Century Europe*, ed. B. Gordon (Aldershot, 1996), 1–22. As Dutton, "Awareness of Historical Decline," 28, has noted, the ninth-century eucharistic controversy was also a matter of great interest to sixteenth-century religious reformers.

92. This spurious decretal is known as the *Decretum Hadriani*, ed. L. Weiland, MGH, *Constitutiones et acta publica imperatorum et regum* (Hannover, 1893), 1:657–60, no. 446. See G. W. Marx, "Louis I (The Pious, or 'Le Débonnaire'): A Personal Reassessment of the Man Through the Events in His Reign" (Ph.D. diss., New York University, 1971), 355–56, esp. n. 85; R. L. Benson, *The Bishop-Elect* (Princeton, N.J., 1968), 233 n. 18; W. Ullmann, *The Growth of Papal Government in the Middle Ages* (London, 1965), 353 n. 4. In addition to listing the three extant manuscript witnesses of the *Decretum Hadriani* (beginning in the twelfth century), Weiland notes (p. 658) the various medieval sources that reproduced or referred to it (starting from the eleventh century), including, among others, Landulf, *Historia Mediolanensis*, 2.11; Ivo of Chartres, *Panormia*, 8.135; Gratian, *Decretum*, 1.lxiii.22; Sigebert of Gembloux, *Chronicon*, s.a. 773; William of Malmesbury, *Gesta regum Anglorum*, 2.202.

93. Marx, "Louis I," 355–56, esp. n. 87.

94. Marx, "Louis I," 358–59, and n. 92.

95. On Hotman, see Morrissey, *Charlemagne and France*, 132–36; McKitterick, "The

Study of Frankish History," 558–59; D. R. Kelley, *Foundations of Modern Historical Scholarship* (New York, 1970), 106–12; *François Hotman Francogallia*, 3–134.

96. *François Hotman Francogallia*, 241, quoting Regino, *Chronicon*, s.a. 838.

97. *François Hotman Francogallia*, 341.

98. For additional accounts of 833, see the remarks by Archbishop Adam of Bremen in the eleventh century (*Gesta Hammaburgensis ecclesiae pontificum*, 1.22, ed. B. Schmeidler, MGH, *SRG*, 2:28), and Hugh of Fleury in the twelfth (*Historia regum Francorum*, 20, ed. G. H. Pertz, MGH, *SS*, 9:401). To fortify their arguments, the polemicists involved in the Investiture Controversy of the eleventh and twelfth centuries occasionally recalled the "deposition" of both Emperor Louis the Pious and Archbishop Ebbo of Reims; see MGH, *Libelli de lite imperatorum et pontificum*, ed. E. Dümmler et al. (Hannover, 1891–97), 1:289, 362, 386–88; 2:44–45; 3:738.

99. *François Hotman Francogallia*, 489. To support this statement, Hotman goes on to cite the testimony of Ekkehard, Michael Ritius, Otto of Freising, and Regino of Prüm.

100. Cf. the early remark by Nithard, 1.4, ed. Lauer, 18, that Judith was not allowed back to the "royal bed" (*thorus regius*) until she publicly swore an oath regarding her "innocence of the offenses with which she had been charged." Nithard presumed his audience knew the nature of these offenses and thus left them unspecified; the allusion to the royal bed was likely enough of a hint. See J. L. Nelson, "Early Medieval Rites of Queen-Making and the Shaping of Medieval Queenship," in *Queens and Queenship in Medieval Europe*, ed. A. J. Duggan (Woodbridge, 1997), 304 n. 17; eadem, *Charles the Bald* (London, 1992), 130; Chapter 1, n. 153; and n. 16 above. Odbert's story about Louis and Judith's consanguinity and the cost of Frideric's vigilance would become an anecdote well known among late medieval and early modern historians. See Marx, "Louis I," 338–39, esp. n. 47.

101. Cf. the remarks of Giesey and Salmon in *François Hotman Francogallia*, 53.

102. Of course, the long-accepted "tragic" story of 833 is itself a counternarrative about the events of that year, for it was composed by the emperor's supporters largely as a rebuttal to, and with the intent to undermine and condemn, those texts initially composed by the rebels to justify both their extreme deeds and their seemingly seditious cause. Cf. J. Fried, *Donation of Constantine and Constitutum Constantini* (Berlin, 2007), 91. On history and counternarrative, see A. Funkenstein, "History, Counterhistory, and Narrative," in *Probing the Limits of Representation: Nazism and the "Final Solution"*, ed. S. Friedlander (Cambridge, Mass., 1992), 66–81.

103. *AB*, s.a. 835, ed. F. Grat et al., 15–16; trans. Nelson, *ASB*, 32. See R. McKitterick, "Introduction: Sources and Interpretation," in *NCMH* 2:6; L. Rid, "Die Wiedereinsetzung Kaiser Ludwigs des Frommen zu St. Denis (1. März 834) und ihre Wiederholung zu Metz (28. Februar 835)," in *Festgabe Alois Knöpfler zur Vollendung des 70. Lebensjahres*, ed. H. M. Gietl and G. Pfeilschifter (Freiburg im Breisgau, 1917), 265–75.

104. For the textual transmission and influence of the biographies of Louis the Pious

by Thegan and the Astronomer, see Chapter 1, n. 247; and n. 51 above. Cf. P. J. Geary, *Before France and Germany: The Creation and Transformation of the Merovingian World* (New York, 1988), 221–26, on the similar type of narrative "victory" achieved by Carolingian authors on the "uselessness" of the Merovingian kings.

105. For much of what follows on Walafrid and his editorial work, see C. M. Booker, "A New Prologue of Walafrid Strabo," *Viator* 36 (2005): 83–105.

106. Walafrid's prologue to Thegan's text survives in two witnesses: Copenhagen, Universitätsbibliothek, AM 830 4°, fol. 97r (dating from 1496); and Pierre Pithou's printed source collection, *Annalium et historiae Francorum ab anno Christi DCCVIII ad annum DCCCCXC scriptores coaetanei XII* . . . (Paris, 1588), pt. 2, 93–94. See Tremp, *Studien zu den Gesta*, 114, 164, 172. For the Latin text, see Thegan, *GH*, ed. Tremp, 168–75. For a partial English trans., see E. S. Duckett, *Carolingian Portraits: A Study in the Ninth Century* (Ann Arbor, Mich., 1962), 149.

107. Booker, "A New Prologue," 95 n. 62.

108. See Booker, "A New Prologue," 91; and the Appendix.

109. For the catalog and its date, see Booker, "A New Prologue," 89. For Thegan as compiler, see Booker, "The Public Penance," 5–6.

110. Booker, "A New Prologue," 94; idem, "The Public Penance," 6; and Chapter 1, n. 69.

111. Booker, "A New Prologue," 95.

112. See n. 72 above.

113. Booker, "A New Prologue," 96.

114. These manuscripts being the ninth-century "Reginbert codex 36" and the late medieval "Petershausen Thegan codex," which have been lost but not before a copy was made of the latter by the humanist Konrad Peutinger in 1508 and printed in 1588 by Pierre Pithou. See Booker, "A New Prologue," 89–90, and 87 nn. 25–26; M. M. Tischler, *Einharts Vita Karoli: Studien zur Entstehung, Überlieferung und Rezeption* (Hannover, 2001), 1:873–83. Recall, however, Odbert of Utrecht's use of Thegan's text and possible use of the bishops' *Relatio* (see n. 20 above). Did Odbert have access to these texts in a compilation, one that—given the clear sympathies he shows for the rebels—lacked Walafrid's censorious editorial remarks?

115. On this compilation, which consisted of the following texts—*Chronicon de sex aetatibus mundi; Annales Laureshamenses, 703–770; Annales regni Francorum, 771–818;* Thegan, *Gesta Hludowici imperatoris*; and the episcopal *Relatio* of Louis' penance—see Booker, "A New Prologue," 88–90, 96–97; Tischler, *Einharts Vita Karoli*, 1:428–29, 875–77. On Reginbert and the library of Reichenau, see K. Preisendanz, "Reginbert von der Reichenau: Aus Bibliothek und Skriptorium des Inselklosters," *Neue Heidelberger Jahrbücher* NF (1952–1953): 1–49; idem, "Aus Bücherei und Schreibstube der Reichenau," in *Die Kultur der Abtei Reichenau* (Munich, 1925), 2:657–83. On Walafrid's exile from Reichenau, see Booker, "A New Prologue," 84 nn. 9–10.

116. Note, for instance, the favorable treatment Thegan gives to Louis the German, observing again and again that the young Louis was his father's "beloved namesake"

and faithful supporter: Thegan, *GH*, 36–37, 39, 45–48, 54–55, 57. See Tremp, *Studien zu den Gesta*, 79–81; M. Innes and R. McKitterick, "The Writing of History," in *Carolingian Culture: Emulation and Innovation*, ed. R. McKitterick (Cambridge, 1994), 209. On Louis the German's activities in 840–841 and his seizure of Reichenau, see E. J. Goldberg, *Struggle for Empire: Kingship and Conflict Under Louis the German, 817–876* (Ithaca, N.Y., 2006), 96.

117. The historical interests of Louis the German have not been studied to the same degree as those of his father or brothers. But see B. Bischoff, "Bücher am Hofe Ludwigs des Deutschen und die Privatbibliothek des Kanzlers Grimalt," in idem, *Mittelalterliche Studien* (Stuttgart, 1981), 3:187–212.

118. Booker, "A New Prologue," 88–90.

119. Pithou, *Annalium et historiae Francorum . . . scriptores*, table of contents (no. XIII, "*Acta impiae et nefandae exauctorationis eiusdem Ludovici Imperatoris apud Compendium Anno DCCCXXII* [sic]"), and for the account itself, printed in chronological order vis-à-vis the other texts Pithou included in the book, 2:136–48. On Pithou, the best study remains P.-J. Grosley, *Vie de Pierre Pithou avec quelques mémoires sur son père et ses frères* (Paris, 1756). For modern biographies, see Booker, "A New Prologue," 93 n. 50. On Gallican historiography, see J. H. M. Salmon, "Clovis and Constantine: The Uses of History in Sixteenth-Century Gallicanism," *JEH* 41 (1990): 584–605.

120. There were no fewer than nine printings of the *Relatio* made in the seventeenth century; see Booker, "The Public Penance," 9–10.

121. S. Binius, *Concilia generalia et provincialia* (Cologne, 1606), 3(1):575. Cf. the justification of Claude Fauchet for including the text in his volume of French "antiquities," *Fleur de la maison de Charlemaigne, qui est la continuation des Antiquitez françoises, contenant les faits de Pépin et ses successeurs depuis l'an 751 jusques à l'an 840, . . .* (Paris, 1601), 232 (bk. 3, chp. 11); 237 (bk. 3, chp. 12).

122. J. Sirmond, *Concilia antiqua Galliae* (Paris, 1629), 2:687, who characterized the sentiment of "Einhard" with these words. However, Sirmond here followed medieval tradition in erroneously ascribing to the biographer of Charlemagne the later, anonymous biography of Louis by the Astronomer. On this tradition, see Astronomer, *VH*, ed. Tremp, 53. For the rhetorical use of Einhard as a "wise man" to lend authority to historical truth claims, see C. M. Booker, review of P. E. Dutton, *Charlemagne's Courtier: The Complete Einhard* (Peterborough, Ont., 1998), in *Comitatus* 30 (1999): 186 n. 16.

123. London, British Library, 1058.b.12: Pierre Pithou, *Annalium et historiae Francorum ab anno Christi DCCVIII ad annum DCCCCXC scriptores coaetanei XII . . .* , 2nd ed. (Frankfurt, 1594), 328, 322. See Kelley, *Foundations of Modern Scholarship*, 264. On p. 330 of his Pithou volume Casaubon also wrote "*O lugubre spectaculum!*" a terse, poignant characterization of Louis' penance that would become predominant in the following centuries.

124. L. d'Achéry, *Spicilegium* (Paris, 1666), 7:175. On d'Achéry, see the *Dictionnaire de biographie française* (Paris, 1933), 1:324–25, s.v. "2. Achery."

125. As reported in M. Bouquet, *Recueil des historiens des Gaules et de la France* (1749;

Paris, 1870), 6:254 (a). The manuscript is Vat. Pal. lat. 576 (saec. IX ex.), on which see n. 127 below.

126. See Ebbo, *Apologeticus* 1, ed. Werminghoff, 794–99. I shall return to Ebbo's apology and the context of its composition in Chapter 5.

127. On this manuscript, Vat. Pal. lat. 576, and its contents, see L. Bethmann, "Nachrichten über die . . . Sammlungen von Handschriften und Urkunden Italiens," *AG* 12 (1858–74): 337–38; E. Stevenson and G.-B. De Rossi, *Codices Palatini Bibliothecae Vaticanae* (Rome, 1886), 190–91; H. Fuhrmann, *Einfluss und Verbreitung der pseudoisidorischen Fälschungen* (Stuttgart, 1973), 2:268–69 n. 79. On Hincmar, see J. Devisse, *Hincmar, archevêque de Reims, 845–882*, 3 vols. (Geneva, 1975–76); H. Schrörs, *Hinkmar Erzbischof von Reims* (Freiburg, 1884). For a sketch of his career, see Duckett, *Carolingian Portraits*, 202–64.

128. On this manuscript, Wolfenbüttel, Helmst. 32, and its contents, see *Die Handschriften der herzoglichen Bibliothek zu Wolfenbüttel*, ed. O. von Heinemann (Wolfenbüttel, 1884), 22–24, no. 35. It was first utilized for an edition of Ebbo's apology by J. J. Maderus, *M. Adami, scriptores vetusti, Historia ecclesiastica: religionis propagatae gesta, ex Hammaburgensi potissimum atque Bremensi ecclesiis . . .* (Helmstadt, 1670), 235–45.

129. For the mandate (ca. 822) (fols. 194r–195v), see MGH, *Epist.*, 5:68–70. On Ebbo's mission, see J. T. Palmer, "Rimbert's *Vita Anskarii* and Scandinavian Mission in the Ninth Century," *JEH* 55 (2004): 235–56.

130. For the maxims, beginning *"Hoc est bonum quod non potest invitus amittere"* and ending *"Qui victoriam cupit, milites imbuat diligenter,"* see fol. 131v. Cf. the summary of Vegetius' text by Hrabanus Maurus, *De procinctu Romanae miliciae*, ed. E. Dümmler, *Zeitschrift für deutsches Alterthum* 15 (1872): 443–51. For the extract from the *Dialogues* of Sulpicius Severus (2.11–12), see fols. 130r–131r.

131. On Sirmond's transcription, Paris, B.N.F. nouv. acq. lat. 469, and its contents, see M. van der Lugt, "Tradition and Revision: The Textual Tradition of Hincmar of Reims' *Visio Bernoldi* with a New Critical Edition," *Bulletin du Cange* 52 (1994): 133–34. The manuscript used by Sirmond is thought to have perished in the fire that consumed the monastery of Hérivaux (30 km north of Paris in Luzarches) on 18 October 1632. See Van der Lugt, "Tradition and Revision," 135.

132. A. Werminghoff, "Ein neuer Text des Apologeticum Ebonis," *NA* 25 (1900): 363–78; Ebbo, *Apologeticus* 2, ed. Werminghoff, 799–806.

133. Van der Lugt, "Tradition and Revision," 135. On Sirmond's fidelity to his exemplar, see Werminghoff, "Ein neuer Text," 363.

134. Van der Lugt, "Tradition and Revision," 137, claims that the principle governing the arrangement of the texts in the manuscript "seems to have been geographical." On Hincmar's moral theology as evinced in the *Visio Bernoldi*, see Van der Lugt, "Tradition and Revision," 112–13 n. 10.

135. On the *Visio Bernoldi*, see Dutton, *The Politics of Dreaming*, 183–94; Van der Lugt, "Tradition and Revision."

136. Vat. Pal. lat. 576 was created "perhaps in the vicinity of Reims" according to

Fuhrmann, *Einfluss und Verbreitung*, 2:268–69 n. 79; W. Hartmann, ed., MGH, *Conc.*, 3:256. Wolfenbüttel, Helmst. 32 was likely created in Hildesheim, according to Von Heinemann, *Die Handschriften*, 24; A. Werminghoff, ed., MGH, *Conc.*, 2(2):794. Ebbo was appointed bishop of Hildesheim by Louis the German in 845, an office he held until his death in 851; see H. Goetting, *Das Bistum Hildesheim: Die Hildesheimer Bischöfe von 815–1221* (Berlin, 1984), 72–79. Might the exemplar used by the eleventh-century compiler in Hildesheim, one containing Ebbo's apology, the maxims from Vegetius, the extract from Sulpicius Severus' *Dialogues*, and Ebbo's papal mandate, have been assembled by Ebbo himself while at Hildesheim?

137. Von Heinemann, *Die Handschriften*, 24. The note is on fol. 192v.

138. For a list of editions, see Werminghoff, ed., MGH, *Conc.*, 2(2):794.

139. See C. Le Cointe, *Annales ecclesiastici Francorum* (Paris, 1683), 8:633–36.

140. E. Dumont, "Les fausses décretales," *Revue des questions historiques* 1 (1866): 421 n. 1; and, quoting Dumont in full, C. Barthélemy, "La déposition de Louis le Débonnaire," in idem, *Erreurs et mensonges historiques* 4th ser. (Paris, 1873), 114.

141. For a biographical sketch of Mabillon, see R. Avis, "Jean Mabillon (1632–1707)," in *Medieval Scholarship: Biographical Studies on the Formation of a Discipline*, ed. H. Damico and J. B. Zavadil (New York, 1995), 1:15–32.

142. Paschasius Radbertus, *Epitaphium*, ed. Dümmler, 16; H. Peltier, *Pascase Radbert, Abbé de Corbie: Contribution à l'étude de la vie monastique et de la pensée chrétienne aux temps carolingiens* (Amiens, 1938), 98–99; J. Staub, *Studien zu Iotsalds Vita des Abtes Odilo von Cluny* (Hannover, 1999), 41–42. For a description of the manuscript (Paris, B.N.F. lat. 13909), see Chapter 1, n. 161.

143. J. Mabillon, *Acta sanctorum ordinis Sancti Benedicti saec. iv* (Paris, 1677), 1:453; repr. in *PL* 120, col. 1557A. As Staub, *Studien zu Iotsalds Vita*, 37–42, has shown, Abbot Iotsald of Saint-Claude—a monastery that had close associations with Saint-Arnoul de Crépy—may have utilized the *Epitaphium Arsenii* in the eleventh century as a literary model for his *vita* of Abbot Odilo of Cluny. Palmer, "Rimbert's *Vita Anskarii*," 244, has suggested that Archbishop Rimbert of Hamburg-Bremen had access to the *Epitaphium Arsenii* while writing his *Vita Anskarii* between 869 and 876.

144. Mabillon, *Acta sanctorum Sancti Benedicti*, 1:453; repr. in *PL* 120, col. 1559B–C.

145. See Paschasius Radbertus, *Epitaphium*, ed. Dümmler, 17, listing its use by G. W. Leibniz, *Annales imperii occidentis Brunsvicenses*, ed. G. H. Pertz, *Gottfried Wilhelm Leibniz: Gesammelte Werke*, I, 1 (Hannover, 1843); F. Funck, *Ludwig der Fromme* (Frankfurt am Main, 1832); A. Himly, *Wala et Louis le Débonnaire* (Paris, 1849). But see also J.-M.-F. Frantin, *Louis-le-Pieux et son siècle* (Paris, 1839); and Barthélemy, "La déposition de Louis," 110–48. Before Dümmler's edition, the text of the *Epitaphium Arsenii* was printed only a handful of times, first in full by Mabillon in 1677 (repr. in *PL* 120, col. 1557–650) and then in abridged selections by Le Cointe, *Annales ecclesiastici Francorum*, 8:126–32; Bouquet, *Recueil des historiens*, 6:279–92; Pertz, MGH, *SS*, 2:533–69. See *BHL* 8761.

146. Leibniz, *Annales imperii*, s.a. 830, 831, 833, ed. Pertz, 402, 413, 426. Leibniz's treatment of the text was more ambivalent than dismissive, for, if he did not quite trust Paschasius's interpretation of events, he still gave great weight to the words of Wala as reported by Paschasius; cf. *Annales imperii*, s.a. 830, ed. Pertz, 399.

147. For his characterization of 833 as a "tragedy," see Leibniz, *Annales imperii*, s.a. 833, ed. Pertz, 428, 432. For Louis' penance as a "scene" from an "opprobrious drama," s.a 833, ed. Pertz, 431. For his use of Louis' "confession" from Odilo, s.a. 833, ed. Pertz, 427–28. For his quotation of Louis' speech to his men on the Rotfeld, s.a. 833, ed. Pertz, 425. On Leibniz's tragic emplotment of the events, see N. Staubach, "'Des grossen Kaisers kleiner Sohn': Zum Bild Ludwigs des Frommen," in *CH*, ed. Godman and Collins, 701–21, esp. 709–12. For a comprehensive history of Leibniz's composition of the *Annales* based on rich archival material, see L. Davillé, *Leibniz Historien* (Paris, 1909), 274–333, esp. 567 n. 1, 642 n. 3.

148. For a study of Masson's career, see P. Ronzy, *Un humaniste italianisant, Papire Masson (1544–1611)* (Paris, 1924). Masson was a close friend of Pithou; see Ronzy, *Un humaniste italianisant*, 539–41.

149. The manuscript found by Masson now bears the shelfmark Paris, B.N.F. lat. 2853 (saec. IX); see P. Lauer, *Catalogue général des manuscrits latins* (Paris, 1952), 3:164–65. For Masson's brief account of his discovery, see the preface to his edition of the manuscript, *Sancti Agobardi episcopi ecclesiae Lugdunensis opera . . .* (Paris, 1605), repr. in *PL* 104, col. 18B. See also P. Chevallard, *Saint Agobard, Archevêque de Lyon: Sa vie et ses écrits* (Lyon, 1869), 11–12, and Agobard, ed. Van Acker, LI–LII, esp. n. 270, which provides literature in support of Van Acker's statement that "the manuscript unequivocally came from Lyon." However, as Van Acker notes (LII, LV–LVI), the manuscript also resided for a time in the library of Cluny, according to a twelfth-century library catalog from that monastery.

150. For these texts and the numerous manuscripts within which they survive, see Agobard, ed. Van Acker, 335–67. For a brief summary of the debate between Amalarius and Agobard, see Duckett, *Carolingian Portraits*, 109–20; A. Cabaniss, "Agobard and Amalar," in idem, *Judith Augusta: A Daughter-in-Law of Charlemagne and Other Essays* (New York, 1974), 97–105.

151. These *testimonia* are conveniently assembled in *PL* 104, col. 13–16; A. Bressolles, *Saint Agobard: Evêque de Lyon (769–840)* (Paris, 1949), 43–46.

152. Of the twenty-five texts that comprise Agobard's *opera omnia* edited by Van Acker, nineteen derive solely from Masson's manuscript; only Van Acker's numbers 4 (*De privilegio et iure sacerdotii*), 8 (*De spe et timore*), 15 (*De quorundam inlusione signorum*), 17 (*De fidei veritate et totius boni institutione*), 24 (*De antiphonario*), and 25 (*Contra libros quatuor Amalarii*) are extant in other witnesses.

153. This view was even taken by Masson himself; Agobard's participation in the revolt, he admitted, had left "la tache qui obscurcit la glorieuse vieillesse de l'évêque." See Ronzy, *Un humaniste italianisant*, 559–60. Cf. the similar remarks of Martin Bouquet nearly 150 years later, *Recueil des historiens*, 6:xiv–xv. For a review of the historiographical

tradition of Agobard's "rationalism," see E. Boshof, *Erzbischof Agobard von Lyon* (Cologne, 1969), 8–10, 173 n. 14.

154. Masson, *Sancti Agobardi*, 378–80. The modern edition of the text is Agobard, *Cartula de Ludovici imperatoris poenitentia*, ed. Van Acker, 323–24.

155. *Relatio Comp.*, ed. Booker, 19; Appendix, ll. 236–44.

156. Agobard's *cartula* was published eight times during the seventeenth century alone. See the list of source collections within which it was reprinted (and its author condemned) by A. Werminghoff, "Verzeichnis der Akten fränkischer Synoden von 742–843," *NA* 24 (1899): 489; with the complementary list in Agobard, ed. Van Acker, LXII n. 282.

157. On the intense interest in recovering and printing the records of the medieval past during the seventeenth century, see McKitterick, "The Study of Frankish History," 556–72; O. Ranum, *Artisans of Glory: Writers and Historical Thought in Seventeenth-Century France* (Chapel Hill, N.C., 1980); N. Edelman, *Attitudes of Seventeenth-Century France Toward the Middle Ages* (New York, 1946).

158. Étienne Baluze meticulously reedited the works of Agobard found in the manuscript discovered by Masson, publishing an edition that would not only withstand the test of time for 230 years but would also stimulate interest among his contemporaries in Agobard's texts; see E. Baluze, *Sancti Agobardi archiepiscopi Lugdunensis opera* . . . (Paris, 1666). For Dupleix, see S. Dupleix, *Histoire générale de France* (1621; Paris, 1648), 1:430–35, as cited by Bressolles, *Saint Agobard*, 13–14. For a survey of seventeenth-century accounts that detail 833 and Agobard's damning complicity, see Bressolles, *Saint Agobard*, 11–18; Chevallard, *Saint Agobard*, 212–22. The reception of Agobard's works is far more complex than what can only be touched on here and is a topic that would reward further study; for a useful point of departure, including remarks about the seventeenth-century view of Agobard as an early medieval precursor to Calvin, see Ronzy, *Un humaniste italianisant*, 559–64.

159. J.-B. de Bossuet, *Defensio declarationis cleri Gallicani*, 2.6.21 (1682; Luxembourg, 1730), 211; as cited by Bressolles, *Saint Agobard*, 14 nn. 2, 3. See also Chevallard, *Saint Agobard*, 215, 413–14 n. 59.

160. T. Raynaud, *Hagiologium Lugdunense complectens ea quae de sanctis Lugduni praesidibus* (Lyon, 1662), 25–28. See also Bressolles, *Saint Agobard*, 15–16. For the uncanonical veneration of Agobard (the origins of which are unknown) on June 6 within the locale of Lyon and the polemics it would generate in the eighteenth century, see Boshof, *Erzbischof Agobard*, 1–4, 306–9; Bressolles, *Saint Agobard*, 15–18; Chevallard, *Saint Agobard*, 16–19, 213–22, 376–82 n. 24; *BS* 1:420–21; *AA SS*, Iunius (Paris, 1695), 1:748–49.

161. Raynaud, *Hagiologium Lugdunense*, 27. The controversial text, entitled *De picturis et imaginibus*, is found in Masson, *Sancti Agobardi*, 212–55; Agobard, ed. Van Acker, 149–81. See Bressolles, *Saint Agobard*, 73–77; H. C. Lea, *Studies in Church History* (Philadelphia, 1869), 27 n. 2.

162. Raynaud, *Hagiologium Lugdunense*, 28; Bressolles, *Saint Agobard*, 16. Raynaud admitted that this alleged penance by Agobard is unattested.

163. As documented by Bressolles, *Saint Agobard*, 16–25. Cf. Bouquet, *Recueil des historiens*, 6:xxv, who claims that Raynaud's attempts to defend Agobard were made in vain.

164. Alcuin, *Ep.* 249, ed. E. Dümmler, MGH, *Epist.*, 4:403; see H. Fichtenau, *The Carolingian Empire*, trans. P. Munz (1949; Oxford, 1957), 171.

165. See K. Hampe, "Zum Streite Hincmars von Reims mit seinem Vorgänger Ebo und dessen Anhängern," *NA* 24 (1898): 180–95; and Chapter 5. By the eleventh century one author noted that Ebbo had a "*fama ambigua*"; see Adam of Bremen, *Gesta hammaburgensis ecclesiae pontificum*, 1.22(24), ed. Schmeidler, 28; Palmer, "Rimbert's *Vita Anskarii*," 250. Recall that Odbert of Utrecht used Ebbo's apology in the eleventh century and referred to him defensively and with reverence as "a truly God fearing man"; see Odbert, *Passio*, 17, ed. Holder-Egger, 352.

166. See W. Berschin, *Biographie und Epochenstil im lateinischen Mittelalter* (Stuttgart, 1991), 3:226; Chevallard, *Saint Agobard*, 438–39 n. 96. Note the positive way Ebbo is characterized in modern discussions of the major Carolingian artworks linked to Reims, such as the Utrecht Psalter or the "Ebbo Gospels": C. Chazelle, "Archbishops Ebo and Hincmar of Reims and the Utrecht Psalter," *Speculum* 72 (1997): 1055–77; C. R. Dodwell, *Pictorial Arts of the West, 800–1200* (New Haven, Conn., 1993), 64–67; with the literature cited therein.

167. J. Rubenstein "Putting History to Use: Three Crusade Chronicles in Context," *Viator* 35 (2004): 133; Dutton, *Courtier*, xxxi–xxxii; and the studies cited in Booker, "A New Prologue," 97 n. 72.

168. On the possession of the manuscript at some point by Cluny, see n. 149 above.

169. Masson, *Sancti Agobardi*, praefatio, repr. in *PL* 104, col. 18B. Masson printed the texts in the same sequence found in the manuscript; Van Acker printed the texts in chronological order.

170. Masson, *Sancti Agobardi*, 354–77. See Ronzy, *Un humaniste italianisant*, 560–61.

171. See Masson, *Sancti Agobardi*, "Synopsis: *De comparatione utriusque regiminis*"; French trans. in Ronzy, *Un humaniste italianisant*, 560–61.

172. Baluze, *Sancti Agobardi*, 2:111; repr. in *PL* 104, col. 291–92. See Bressolles, *Saint Agobard*, 40 n. 3.

173. Baluze, *Sancti Agobardi*, 1, praefatio ad lectorem; repr. in *PL* 104, col. 11D. For additional comments by Baluze on Masson's cluster of texts, "*De comparatione utriusque regiminis ecclesiastici et politici*," see Baluze, *Sancti Agobardi*, 2:111; repr. in *PL* 104, col. 291–92; Bressolles, *Saint Agobard*, 40 n. 3.

CHAPTER 3. HISTRIONIC HISTORY, DEMANDING DRAMA

Epigraphs: G. Duby, *The Legend of Bouvines: War, Religion, and Culture in the Middle Ages*, trans. C. Tihanyi (1973; Berkeley, Calif., 1990), 1–2; Hincmar of Reims, *De ordine palatii*, 3, ed. T. Gross and R. Schieffer, *MGH, Fontes iuris Germanici antiqui in usum scholarum, separatim editi* 3 (Hannover, 1980), 52; trans. Dutton, *Carolingian Civ.*, 521 (chp. 10); quoting chp. 6 of Pseudo-Cyprian, *De XII abusivis saeculi.*

1. P. E. Dutton, "Awareness of Historical Decline in the Carolingian Empire, 800–887" (Ph.D. diss., University of Toronto, 1981), 28; P. Burke, "Tradition and Experience: The Idea of Decline from Bruni to Gibbon," in *Edward Gibbon and the Decline and Fall of the Roman Empire*, ed. G. W. Bowersock et al. (Cambridge, Mass., 1977), 87–102; R. Starn, "Meaning-Levels in the Theme of Historical Decline," *HT* 14 (1975): 7.

2. R. Starn, "Historians and 'Crisis,'" *PP* 52 (1971): 3–22; L. Gossman, "Anecdote and History," *HT* 42 (2003): 148.

3. Cf. the definition of "spectacle" in the *Dictionnaire de l'académie française* (Paris, 1835), 2:775. See also P. Hernadi, "Re-Presenting the Past: A Note on Narrative Historiography and Historical Drama," *HT* 15 (1976): 45–51, at 45.

4. Burke, "Tradition and Experience," 97. On the early medieval understanding of the relationship between terrestrial disorder and divine disfavor, see R. Meens, "Politics, Mirrors of Princes and the Bible: Sins, Kings and the Well-Being of the Realm," *EME* 7 (1998): 345–57; D. Ganz, "Theology and the Organization of Thought," in *NCMH* 2:767–73; P. E. Dutton, *The Politics of Dreaming in the Carolingian Empire* (Lincoln, Neb., 1994).

5. Charles de Secondat, baron de Montesquieu, *De l'Esprit des loix*, 31.20–34 (1748; ed. G. Truc [Paris, 1956], 2:379–403). See J. B. Bury, *The Idea of Progress* (New York, 1932), 144–48; Dutton, "Awareness of Historical Decline," 28; R. Morrissey, *Charlemagne and France: A Thousand Years of Mythology*, trans. C. Tihanyi (1997; Notre Dame, Ind., 2003), 206–10.

6. Voltaire, *Essai sur les moeurs et ésprit des nations et sur les principaux faits de l'histoire depuis Charlemagne jusqu'à Louis XIII*, 23 (1756; ed. R. Pomeau [Paris, 1963], 371–75). See Bury, *The Idea of Progress*, 148–53; Dutton, "Awareness of Historical Decline," 29; Morrissey, *Charlemagne and France*, 203–6.

7. G. B. de Mably, *Observations sur l'histoire de France*, 2.4 (1765; ed. F. Guizot [Paris, 1823], 1:144–53). See J. K. Wright, *A Classical Republican in Eighteenth-Century France: The Political Thought of Mably* (Stanford, Calif., 1997), 142–61; Dutton, "Awareness of Historical Decline," 28–29; Morrissey, *Charlemagne and France*, 210–16.

8. F. W. J. Hemmings, *Theatre and State in France, 1760–1905* (Cambridge, 1994); R. M. Isherwood, *Farce and Fantasy: Popular Entertainment in Eighteenth-Century Paris* (New York, 1986); J. Lough, *Paris Theatre Audiences in the Seventeenth and Eighteenth Centuries* (Oxford, 1957).

9. Hemmings, *Theatre and State in France*, 7.

10. Hemmings, *Theatre and State in France*, 4. For the audience totals, see Lough, *Paris Theatre Audiences*, 163–268, esp. 174. For other popular spectacles in Paris, see Isherwood, *Farce and Fantasy*.

11. Hemmings, *Theatre and State in France*, 4; Lough, *Paris Theatre Audiences*, 174;

and above all S. Maza, *Private Lives and Public Affairs: The Causes Célèbres of Prerevolutionary France* (Berkeley, Calif., 1993), 60–67. Note the observation by C. Ginzburg, *History, Rhetoric, and Proof* (Hanover, N.H., 1999), 101–2, that "the very availability of a narrative device can generate—either directly or indirectly, by raising a silent veto—a specific approach to research."

12. M. H. Waddicor, "Montesquieu and the Theatre," in *Studies in Eighteenth-Century French Literature*, ed. J. H. Fox et al. (Exeter, 1975), 307–17; J. Tarraube, *Montesquieu auteur dramatique* (Paris, 1982); H. Lagrave et al., *Études sur Montesquieu: Montesquieu, personnage de théâtre et amateur de théâtre* (Paris, 1974).

13. M. Carlson, *Voltaire and the Theatre of the Eighteenth Century* (Westport, Conn., 1998), xv.

14. Mably, *Observations*, 2.4, ed. Guizot, 1:144–45.

15. *Lettres à Madame la Marquise de P . . . sur l'opéra* (Paris, 1741), 90–91, 110. On this work and its attribution to Mably (it was published anonymously), see Wright, *A Classical Republican*, 217 n. 3.

16. P.-A. C. Beaumarchais, "Préface du Mariage de Figaro" (Paris, 1785), in idem, *Théâtre complet*, ed. G. d'Heylli and F. de Marescot (Paris, 1870), 3:9. Coming full circle, J. Calmette, *L'effondrement d'un empire et la naissance d'une Europe IXe–Xe siècles* (Paris, 1941), 39, would see in Wala the character of Basile from Beaumarchais' *Mariage de Figaro*.

17. Cf. M. Innes, "Introduction: Using the Past, Interpreting the Present, Influencing the Future," in *UP*, ed. Hen and Innes, 5; M. de Jong, "Transformations of Penance," in *Rituals of Power: From Late Antiquity to the Early Middle Ages*, ed. F. Theuws and J. L. Nelson (Leiden, 2000), 190; and the observation by Dutton, "Awareness of Historical Decline," 64, that historians often "unwittingly repeat what they have discovered in Carolingian sources as though ninth-century history [really] was the dramatic story of calamity and dire circumstances which the Carolingians [themselves] tell." I would modify Dutton's observation slightly to state that such unwitting repetition of the Carolingians' dramatic story occurred largely thanks to the appeal of the story's vivid, dramatic formulation.

18. Montesquieu, *De l'Esprit*, 31.23, ed. Truc, 2:384. For Montesquieu's awareness of Aristotle's definition of tragedy, see Waddicor, "Montesquieu and the Theatre," 312. For contemporary notions on the relationship between pity and tragedy, see J. de Laporte, *Dictionnaire dramatique, contenant l'histoire des théâtres, les règles du genre dramatique, les observations des maîtres célèbres et des réflexions nouvelles . . .* (Paris, 1776), 2:429–31, s.v. "pitie." For the genre of tragedy in the eighteenth century, see De Laporte, *Dictionnaire dramatique*, 3:290–307, s.v. "tragédie."

19. Voltaire, *Essai sur les moeurs*, 23, ed. Pomeau, 372.

20. Mably, *Observations*, 2.4, ed. Guizot, 1:139, 141, 144–45. For contemporary notions of the *comédie d'intrigue*, see De Laporte, *Dictionnaire dramatique*, 2:425–26, s.v. "piéces d'intrigue."

21. See V. Burrus, "'In the Theater of This Life': The Performance of Orthodoxy in Late Antiquity," in *The Limits of Ancient Christianity: Essays on Late Antique Thought and Culture in Honor of R. A. Markus*, ed. W. E. Klingshirn and M. Vessey (Ann Arbor, Mich., 1999), 80–96; R. Kraemer, "'Sing Us a Palinode': The Controversy Between Augustine and Jerome over the Meaning of Galatians 2:11–14," in *And Every Tongue Confess: Essays in Honor of Norman Nagel*, ed. G. S. Krispin and J. D. Vieker (Dearborn, Mich., 1990), 38–60; F. Amory, "Whited Sepulchres: The Semantic History of Hypocrisy to the High Middle Ages," *Recherches de théologie ancienne et médiévale* 53 (1986): 19–25. For the dispute's reception during the Middle Ages, see P. Zagorin, *Ways of Lying: Dissimulation, Persecution, and Conformity in Early Modern Europe* (Cambridge, Mass., 1990), 15–37.

22. On the *theatrum mundi*, see E. R. Dodds, *Pagan and Christian in an Age of Anxiety* (Cambridge, 1965), 8–12; E. R. Curtius, *European Literature and the Latin Middle Ages*, trans. W. R. Trask (1948; New York, 1953), 138–44.

23. Burrus, "'In the Theater of This Life.'"

24. Burrus, "'In the Theater of This Life.'" 89. See R. Van Dam, "'Sheep in Wolves' Clothing': The Letters of Consentius to Augustine," *JEH* 37 (1986): 515–35.

25. See Chapter 1, n. 11. On the relationship between French theater and politics in the late eighteenth century, see Maza, *Private Lives*; P. Friedland, *Political Actors: Representative Bodies and Theatricality in the Age of the French Revolution* (Ithaca, N.Y., 2002).

26. G. W. F. Hegel, Letter to Immanuel Niethammer, 29 April 1814, ed. J. Hoffmeister, *Briefe von und an Hegel* (Hamburg, 1953), 2:28, no. 233; trans. C. Butler and C. Seiler, *Hegel: The Letters* (Bloomington, Ind., 1984), 307. For Hegel's views on tragedy and drama, see Butler and Seiler, *Hegel*, 650–61; *Hegel on Tragedy*, ed. A. Paolucci and H. Paolucci (Smyrna, N.Y., 2001); H. White, *Metahistory: The Historical Imagination in Nineteenth-Century Europe* (Baltimore, 1973), 81–131.

27. Hegel, Letter to Niethammer, ed. Hoffmeister, 2:28; trans. Butler and Seiler, *Hegel*, 307.

28. G. W. F. Hegel, *The Philosophy of History*, trans. J. Sibree (New York, 1956), 29–33. On Hegel and the "Cunning of Reason" (*List der Vernunft*), see K. Löwith, *Meaning in History* (Chicago, 1949), 52–59; A. Funkenstein, *Theology and the Scientific Imagination from the Middle Ages to the Seventeenth Century* (Princeton, N.J., 1986), 202–5.

29. Astronomer, *VH*, 49, ed. Tremp, 480, calls the events of 833 an "almost unheard-of tragedy" and an "unheard-of crime." Thegan, *GH*, 44, ed. Tremp, 232, says that the rebels "did unheard-of things" and "said unheard-of things" to Louis during his incarceration; this is the only passage in Thegan's biography where he uses the term "*inauditus.*" At a general assembly of the realm's bishops in 836, *Concilium Aquisgranense*, 66, ed. A. Werminghoff, MGH, *Conc.*, 2(2):723, the events of 833 were referred to as an "unheard-of crime." The rebels used the same language of horrified astonishment when referring to Louis' iniquities: *Relatio Comp.*, ed. Booker, 18,

"done in a manner that was wretched and almost unheard-of among Christians"; Paschasius Radbertus, *Epitaphium*, 2.8, ed. Dümmler, 69, "ills which were scarcely heard of before."

30. Cf. P. Buc, *The Dangers of Ritual: Between Early Medieval Texts and Social Scientific Theory* (Princeton, N.J., 2001), 242–43.

31. For such contemporary claims about the events of 833 having been a sham, see *AB*, s.a. 835, ed. Grat et al., 17; Thegan, *GH*, 44, 56, ed. Tremp, 234–36, 252; Astronomer, *VH*, 48, 49, ed. Tremp, 472, 480; Nithard, 1.4, ed. Lauer, 14; Synod of Troyes (867), ed. W. Hartmann, MGH, *Conc.*, 4:233. On medieval conceptions of dissimulation and hypocrisy, see Amory, "Whited Sepulchres," 5–39; Zagorin, *Ways of Lying*, 15–37. On theatrical *personae* in the ninth century, see M. H. Marshall, "Boethius' Definition of *persona* and Mediaeval Understanding of the Roman Theater," *Speculum* 25 (1950): 473; K. F. Morrison, "'Know Thyself': Music in the Carolingian Renaissance," *SS Spoleto*, 39(1): 378–79.

32. In his loyalist narrative, the Astronomer foreshadows the failure and eventual exposure of the rebels' "cunning scheme" by slipping in knowing asides during the act of its telling: *VH*, 48, 49, ed. Tremp, 472, 480. Cf. the similar use of foreshadowing by Thegan, Chapter 1, n. 65.

33. On hypocrisy, the manipulation of ritual, and their relationship with the devil, see Buc, *The Dangers of Ritual*, 106, 259, 240, "medieval thinkers were well aware of the possibility of power politics; unlike Machiavelli or Hobbes, they considered any instrumentalization of religion, even outward, a devilish perversion." Cf. the role of the devil in the accounts of 833 by the Annals of Saint-Bertin and the Astronomer, Chapter 1, nn. 52, 112.

34. Meens, "Politics, Mirrors of Princes"; Ganz, "Theology and the Organization"; Dutton, *The Politics of Dreaming*; M. de Jong, "*Imitatio Morum*: The Cloister and Clerical Purity in the Carolingian World," in *Medieval Purity and Piety: Essays on Medieval Clerical Celibacy and Religious Reform*, ed. M. Frassetto (New York, 1998), 49–80.

35. On Enlightenment anticlericalism, see P. Gay, *The Enlightenment: An Interpretation. The Rise of Modern Paganism* (New York, 1966); but cf. S. J. Barnett, *The Enlightenment and Religion: The Myths of Modernity* (Manchester, 2003).

36. G. C. Schürmann, *Ludovicus Pius oder Ludewig der Fromme*, ed. H. Sommer, Publikation älterer praktischer und theoretischer Musikwerke 17 (Leipzig, 1890). On Schürmann's career and works, see G. F. Schmidt, *Die frühdeutsche Oper und die musikdramatische Kunst Georg Caspar Schürmanns*, 2 vols. (Regensburg, 1933–34); H. Sommer, "Die Oper Ludwig der Fromme von Georg Caspar Schürmann," *Monatshefte für Musik-Geschichte* 14 (1882): 48–51; idem, "Zur Schürmann'schen Oper 'Ludovicus Pius'," *Monatshefte für Musik-Geschichte* 24 (1892): 137–39.

37. See the list of Schürmann's operas (most of which are no longer extant), including *Claudio ed Agrippina*, *Heinrich der Löwe*, *Heinrich der Vogler*, and *Orlando furioso*, in *The New Grove Dictionary of Opera*, ed. S. Sadie (London, 1992), 4:257. Cf. R. McKitterick, "Edward Gibbon and the Early Middle Ages in Eighteenth-Century Europe," in

Edward Gibbon and Empire, ed. R. McKitterick and R. Quinault (Cambridge, 1997), 180–82. On Brunswick as a leading center of opera under the direction of Schürmann, see G. Flaherty, *Opera in the Development of German Critical Thought* (Princeton, N.J., 1978), 132–35.

38. Schürmann, *Ludovicus Pius*, Act I, Scene 1.

39. Within the printed editions and studies of the opera, no indication is given of which sources—primary and/or secondary—Simonetti employed in the composition of his libretto. Its dialogue and plot offer no identifiable references, allusions, or parallels to particular sources.

40. Anonymous letter to the *Braunschweigische Anzeigen*, 9 June 1745, p. 752, as quoted by Flaherty, *Opera in the Development*, 134. On this sentiment, cf. McKitterick, "Edward Gibbon," 174–89.

41. G. W. Marx, "Louis I (The Pious, or 'Le Débonnaire'): A Personal Reassessment of the Man Through the Events in His Reign" (Ph.D. diss., New York University, 1971), 364–93; Dutton, "Awareness of Historical Decline," 31–42; Morrissey, *Charlemagne and France*, 250–65.

42. See J. Wiltenburg, "True Crime: The Origins of Modern Sensationalism," *AHR* 109 (2004): 1377–404. Calmette, *L'effondrement d'un empire*, was uncertain whether to characterize the events of Louis' reign in terms of the theater (39, 44, 51, 53, 55–56, 62, 79, 93), a novel (40), or a film (61).

43. L.-A.-F. de Marchangy, *La Gaul poétique, ou L'histoire de France considérée dans rapports avec la poésie, l'éloquence et les beaux-arts* (Paris, 1815), 4:1–50. See Morrissey, *Charlemagne and France*, 265–69; A. Taylor, "Was There a Song of Roland?" *Speculum* 76 (2001): 34.

44. Marchangy, *La Gaul poétique*, 4:2, 9–10.

45. Marchangy, *La Gaul poétique*, 4:24. Marchangy employed an array of primary and secondary sources as the building blocks for his dramatization of Louis' career. He was familiar with and cited nearly all the contemporary Carolingian works that discussed the events of 833, including the extant texts written by the rebellion, such as the bishops' *Relatio*, Agobard's *Cartula*, and Paschasius Radbertus's *Epitaphium Arsenii*. Moreover, Marchangy displayed a fine critical sense, noting (20 n. 3) that the text given by Odilo, purporting to be the complaint written by Louis himself, should not be attributed to the emperor. The secondary literature he employed was the standard nationalist French narratives of the day by Mézeray, Daniel, Cordemoy, Velly, Legendre, Moreau, Mably, Rivet, and Radier (9 n. 2; 10 n. 1).

46. Marchangy, *La Gaul poétique*, 4:25. In the latter reference Marchangy is citing the play *Der Tod Adams: Ein Trauerspiel*, published in 1757 by the German dramatist and poet Friedrich Gottlieb Klopstock.

47. Marchangy, *La Gaul poétique*, 4:25.

48. Marchangy, *La Gaul poétique*, 4:19, 30 n. 1.

49. Marchangy, *La Gaul poétique*, 4:415–16 n 1.

50. Marchangy, *La Gaul poétique*, 4:25–26. Cf. Chapter 1, n. 22.

51. Marchangy, *La Gaul poétique*, 4:26–50. In addition to the work of Sophocles and Klopstock, Marchangy was inspired by the seventeenth-century French dramatist Pierre Corneille; he imagined (46 n. 1) one part of his sketch of the tragedy of Louis the Pious to resemble Act IV, Scene 4 from Corneille's tragedy *Mort de Pompée* (1643).

52. Marchangy, *La Gaul poétique*, 4:37.

53. Marchangy, *La Gaul poétique*, 4:49–50. Cf. the dying words of Bishop Frideric in Odbert's *passio*, Chapter 2, n. 33.

54. Taylor, "Was There a Song of Roland?" 33–34.

55. M.-X.-V. Drap-Arnaud, *Louis I (Le Débonnaire), ou Le Fanatisme au IXᵉ siècle, Tragédie en cinq actes* (Paris, 1822), xxiii n. 1, praising the work of Marchangy as the source of his inspiration. For a survey of Drap-Arnaud's career, see *Biographie universelle ancienne et moderne*, ed. L. G. Michaud et al. (Paris, 1811–62), 11:304–5, s.v. "Drap-Arnaud, Victor-Marc-Xavier"; *Dictionnaire de biographie française*, ed. R. d'Amat and R. Limouzin-Lamothe (Paris, 1967), 11:732–33, s.v. "Drap-Arnaud, Prudent-Marc-Xavier-Victor."

56. For a study of French theater and the many attempts by the state to control it in the nineteenth century, see Hemmings, *Theatre and State in France*. For an inventory of censored plays (which does not include this play by Drap-Arnaud), see O. Krakovitch, *Les pièces de théâtre soumises a la censure (1800–1830)* (Paris, 1982). For Drap-Arnaud's remarks about the events as "appalling," see idem, *Louis I (Le Débonnaire)*, xxiii; for "fanaticism cloaked by the mantle of religion," vii.

57. Drap-Arnaud, *Louis I (Le Débonnaire)*, xiv–xv. For his work as a "national tragedy," vi.

58. Drap-Arnaud, *Louis I (Le Débonnaire)*, xi. For Louis' divestiture as a "heart-rending convulsion," xvii. Drap-Arnaud notes (ix nn. 1, 2; xi n. 1) that he read of Louis' divestiture in the account given by Thegan in the edition of Pierre Pithou.

59. Cf. the criticism of the play made in the *Journal des théâtres, de la littérature et des arts* (16 June 1822), under the rubric "Correspondance"; and Drap-Arnaud's response in the preface to his published script, *Louis I (Le Débonnaire)*, xii. Cf. the similar remarks on the dangerous influence of spectacles on the passions, in J.-B.-F. Descuret, *La médecine des passions, ou Les passions considérées dans leurs rapports avec les maladies, les lois et la religion* (Paris, 1841), 112–13. For additional remarks by Drap-Arnaud in defense of his play, see n. 61 below.

60. Drap-Arnaud supported himself as a playwright not through the success of his works (all were failures at the theater) but through a pension awarded to him by the royal family for his loyalty; he had served as an organizer in the resistance against Napoleon.

61. Drap-Arnaud, *Louis I (Le Débonnaire)*, xxiv (emphasis in original). Drap-Arnaud also published as pamphlets two rebuttals to the censorship of his play: M.-X.-V. Drap-Arnaud, *Aux gens de lettres de toutes les opinions; première réponse à l'article diffamatoire publié le 16 juin dans le Journal des Théâtres* (Paris, 1822); idem, *Notice à mes concitoyens de la Garde nationale* (Paris, 1831).

62. See Chapter 1, n. 232.

63. J. Michelet, *Le Moyen Âge: Histoire de France*, bk. 2, chap. 3, ed. C. Mettra (1833; Paris, 1981), 158.

64. Michelet, *Le Moyen Âge*, ed. Mettra, 157. Michelet was particularly fond of Shakespeare: see O. A. Haac, *Les principes inspirateurs de Michelet* (New Haven, Conn., 1951), 121, and the scattered references in Michelet's journal, *Jules Michelet, Journal, Tome I (1828–1848)*, ed. P. Viallaneix (Paris, 1959), 53, 115, 129. Cf. J. R. Williams, *Jules Michelet: Historian as Critic of French Literature* (Birmingham, Ala., 1987), 18; Dutton, "Awareness of Historical Decline," 35–36.

65. J.-M.-F. Frantin, *Louis-le-Pieux et son siècle* (Paris, 1839), 2:38, 45, 55.

66. A. Himly, *Wala et Louis le Débonnaire* (Paris, 1849), 165–66, 176–77.

67. X. Boyer, "Le Champ du Mensonge: An 833," *Revue d'Alsace* 2nd ser. 13 (1862): 49.

68. Boyer, "Le Champ du Mensonge," 81. For the antagonists and their masks, 77. For additional theatrical language, 58, 59, 73, 77, 80–81, 102.

69. Boyer, "Le Champ du Mensonge," 103.

70. See Chapter 1, nn. 8–10.

71. L. A. Warnkönig and P. A. F. Gerard, *Histoire des Carolingiens* (Brussels, 1862), 2:62. On p. 62, they also note the "drame de Compiègne." Eleven years later, C. Barthélemy, "La déposition de Louis le Débonnaire," in idem, *Erreurs et mensonges historiques*, 4th ser. (Paris, 1873), 117, 139 n. 1, would relate the direct relevance of the "well-known" affairs of 833 to current events in his own time—namely, the Franco-Prussian War and its aftermath.

72. K. Robe, *Ludwig der Fromme: Historisches Schauspiel* (Berlin, 1862). I have consulted the copy at Syracuse University in the Leopold von Ranke Special Collections of the Bird Library.

73. Robe, *Ludwig der Fromme*, 52 (Judith as a lioness); 62 (Louis' cry for Wala's head); 65 (Lothar's referring to Caesar and the Rubicon).

74. Robe, *Ludwig der Fromme*, 79 (for the number of troops); 108 (for Louis' brooding and self-reflection).

75. Robe, *Ludwig der Fromme*, 83, 112.

76. Robe, *Ludwig der Fromme*, 126, 137, 140.

77. Robe, *Ludwig der Fromme*, 121, 140–41.

78. E. von Wildenbruch, *Die Karolinger: Trauerspiel in vier Akten* (Berlin, 1881), 1. Cf. the motto on the title page of the play: "Motto: / Der Historiker liest im Buch der Geschichte die Zeilen, / Zwischen den Zeilen den Sinn liest / und erklärt der Poet." For a study of Von Wildenbruch's career, see B. Litzmann, *Ernst von Wildenbruch*, 2 vols. (Berlin, 1913–16).

79. For references to what is "natural" and "unnatural," see Wildenbruch, *Die Karolinger*, 22, 27, 56, 60–63, 81–82, 85, 97, 109, 115, 117–18, 122, 125, 129, 132, 135.

80. Wildenbruch, *Die Karolinger*, 117–18.

81. Wildenbruch, *Die Karolinger*, 135. This is an old theme: cf. M. Clanchy, "Law and Love in the Middle Ages," in *Disputes and Settlements: Law and Human Relations in the West*, ed. J. Bossy (Cambridge, 1983), 47–67.

82. Wildenbruch, *Die Karolinger*, 74.

83. Wildenbruch, *Die Karolinger*, 117. W. Kern, "Der Streit Ludwigs des Frommen mit seinen Söhnen im Lichte der augustinischen Geschichtsauffassung" (Ph.D. diss., Universität Greifswald, 1922), 5, also noted the significance of this passage.

84. E. Mühlbacher, *Deutsche Geschichte unter den Karolingern* (Darmstadt, 1896), 390–91, 396, 399, 404.

85. L. von Ranke, *Weltgeschichte* (Leipzig, 1896), 3:297. On this work, see L. Krieger, *Ranke: The Meaning of History* (Chicago, 1977), 320–43; S. Bann, *The Clothing of Clio: A Study of the Representation of History in Nineteenth-Century Britain and France* (Cambridge, 1984), 8–31; White, *Metahistory*, 163–90.

86. See nn. 75, 83 above. On Ranke's affinity for drama and its influence upon his narratives, see P. Gay, *Style in History* (New York, 1974), 59–94.

87. For Ranke's copy of Robe's play, see n. 72 above.

88. Perhaps no better example of a quintessentially modern representation of the events is the account in 1919 by Georgette Leblanc, the symbolist artist, actress, and companion of the French Nobel Prize-winning poet and playwright Maurice Maeterlinck. Leblanc recast Louis' troubled career in the form of a vignette about one of her own pets! See G. Leblanc-Maeterlinck, *Maeterlinck's Dogs*, trans. A. Teixeira de Mattos (London, 1919), 3–18, "Louis the Debonnair." For two historical novels that treat the events of 833, see G. Ellert, *Ich Judith bekenne* (Vienna, 1952); D. W. Cross, *Pope Joan: A Novel* (New York, 1996), 174–77.

89. Cf. this tendency with the remarks of Staubach in n. 99 below.

90. M. Gardner, *The Annotated Alice: Alice's Adventures in Wonderland & Through the Looking Glass by Lewis Carroll* (New York, 1960), 46–47. As Gardner notes (46 n. 1), the "dusty" passage recited by the mouse was taken from H. Chepmell, *Short Course of History* (London, 1862), 143–44. Carroll makes explicit that it is not the medieval events themselves that are dry but the way they are narrated by his contemporaries; during the mouse's speech, a member of its audience criticizes its narrative style.

91. Gay, *Style in History*, 59–94.

92. Cf. H. Fichtenau, *Das karolingische Imperium: Soziale und geistige Problematik eines Grossreiches* (Zürich, 1949), 264, 271, 279, 280, 285; W. Ullmann, *The Carolingian Renaissance and the Idea of Kingship* (London, 1969), 69; J. M. Wallace-Hadrill, *The Frankish Church* (Oxford, 1983), 233; R. Schieffer, *Die Karolinger* (Stuttgart, 1992), 131–33, 135; E. Boshof, *Ludwig der Fromme* (Darmstadt, 1996), 1, 191, 210, and 202, which is nearly a word-for-word reiteration of his comments on the event 27 years earlier in E. Boshof, *Erzbischof Agobard von Lyon: Leben und Werke* (Cologne, 1969), 251.

93. L. Halphen, *Charlemagne et l'empire carolingien* (Paris, 1947), 291, 297; E. S. Duckett, *Carolingian Portraits: A Study in the Ninth Century* (Ann Arbor, Mich., 1962), 45; R. Folz, *The Coronation of Charlemagne 25 December 800*, trans. J. E. Anderson

(1964; London, 1974), 189; Marx, "Louis I," 222–23; P. Zumthor, *Charles le Chauve* (Paris, 1981), 65–66; K. Deschner, *Kriminalgeschichte des Christentums* (Reinbek bei Hamburg, 1998), 5:80, 82, 84, 90–91; P. Depreux, "Louis le Pieux reconsidéré? À propos des travaux récents consacrés à 'l'héritier de Charlemagne' et à son règne," *Francia* 21, no. 1 (1994): 185.

94. For just a few, see J.-P. Charpentier, *Essai sur l'histoire littéraire du moyen age* (Paris, 1833), 365; F. Monnier, *Histoire des luttes politiques et religieuses dans les temps carolingiens* (Paris, 1852), 132; E. Dümmler, *Geschichte des ostfränkischen Reiches* (Leipzig, 1862), 1:78; P. Chevallard, *Saint Agobard, Archevêque de Lyon: Sa vie et ses écrits* (Lyon, 1869), 304; M. David, *La souveraineté et les limites juridiques du pouvoir monarchique du IXe au XVe siècle* (Paris, 1954), 119; J.-H. Bauchy, *Récits des temps carolingiens* (Paris, 1973), 216; *Saint-Médard: Trésors d'un abbaye royale*, ed. D. Defente (Paris, 1996), 57; I. Gobry, *Histoire des Rois de France: Louis Ier, Premier successeur de Charlemagne* (Paris, 2002), 210; A. Koch, *Kaiserin Judith: Eine politische Biographie* (Husum, 2005), 143 (following Boshof in n. 92 above); J. Fried, *Donation of Constantine and Constitutum Constantini* (Berlin, 2007), 91.

95. E. Magnou-Nortier, *Foi et Fidélité: Recherches sur l'évolution des liens personnels chez les Francs du VIIe au IXe siècle* (Toulouse, 1976), 74; eadem, "L'enjeu des biens ecclésiastiques dans la crise du IXe siècle," in *Aux sources de la gestion publique*, ed. E. Magnou-Nortier (Lille, 1995), 2:247.

96. E. Magnou-Nortier, "La tentative de subversion de l'État sous Louis le Pieux et l'oeuvre des falsificateurs (2e partie)," *MA* 105 (1999): 623, 629, 640 and n. 47. For a critique, see G. Schmitz, "Echte Quellen—falsche Quellen: Müssen zentrale Quellen aus der Zeit Ludwigs des Frommen neu bewertet werden?" in *Von Sacerdotium und Regnum: Geistliche und weltliche Gewalt im frühen und hohen Mittelalter: Festschrift für Egon Boshof zum 65. Geburtstag*, ed. F.-R. Erkens and H. Wolff (Cologne, 2002), 275–300.

97. As E. A. Wood, *Performing Justice: Agitation Trials in Early Soviet Russia* (Ithaca, N.Y., 2005), has demonstrated, Stalin's show-trials, with their terror, brutality, and Manichean outlook, must be understood within their particular historical context, as an outgrowth of an earlier practice of "agitation trials" staged to elicit dialogue on social ills and rouse support for the new regime. If there is a parallel to be drawn between the Soviet show-trials and Louis' public penance, it would rather be in their use of biblical similes—Nikolai Bukharin was known as the "Benjamin" of the Bolshevik party, while Leon Trotsky was referred to as "Judas-Trotsky"; see Wood, *Performing Justice*, 209, 218. Cf. C. M. Booker, "The Demanding Drama of Louis the Pious," *Comitatus* 34 (2003): 174.

98. Cf. Maza, *Private Lives*, 14; P. Brooks, *The Melodramatic Imagination: Balzac, Henry James, Melodrama and the Mode of Excess* (New Haven, Conn., 1995), vii–xx, 1–23.

99. N. Staubach, "Das Herrscherbild Karls des Kahlen: Formen und Funktionen monarchischer Repräsentation im früheren Mittelalter," part I (Ph.D. diss., Westfälis-

chen Wilhelms-Universität, Münster, 1981), 30, has argued, on the contrary, that the "tragic" configuration of the events is advantageous precisely because it does *not*, in his view, hold a single person or group responsible for the internal crises that appeared during Louis' reign. Rather, he contends that a dramatic emplotment simultaneously discloses the basic nature of the conflict and allows one to measure the relative value of the objective for which the characters in the "tragedy" strove, regardless of their ultimate success or failure in achieving it. He concludes that the problem of understanding the internal dynamics of the "tragedy of Louis the Pious" takes on a greater urgency the more its events are assigned a fundamental, broadly enveloping function, one that serves to extend the events' essential historical meaning across Louis' reign in order to make it comprehensible. As the survey in the preceding pages has shown, I would agree only with the last of Staubach's claims: the greater the size of the "problem" that the events of 833 have been used to "solve," the greater has been the urgency to understand the events themselves.

100. This tradition of a general demonization of the rebellion has occasionally provoked vehement retorts, e.g., Barthélemy, "La déposition de Louis," 134. According to a papal letter printed opposite its title page, Pope Pius IX officially endorsed Barthélemy's work.

101. See the arguments supplied by Agobard, *Liber apologeticus* I, II, ed. Van Acker, 309–19; idem, *Cartula*, ed. Van Acker, 323–24; Pope Gregory IV, *Ep.* 17, ed. E. Dümmler, MGH, *Epist.*, 5:228–32; *Relatio Comp.*, ed. Booker, 11–19; Ebbo of Reims, *Apologeticus* 1, 2, ed. Werminghoff, 794–806; Paschasius Radbertus, *Epitaphium*, ed. Dümmler, 1–98. See also Boshof, *Ludwig der Fromme*, 182–91.

102. E.g., factors usually related to the passions, such as (religious) fanaticism opposed to (secular) rationalism or natural law opposed to human (conventional) law (cf. the plays by Drap-Arnaud and Wildenbruch or the study by Calmette, in nn. 16, 55, 78 above). On the embodiment of such passions in drama, see J. Montagu, *The Expression of the Passions: The Origin and Influence of Charles Le Brun's* Conférence sur l'expression générale et particulière (New Haven, Conn., 1994), 52–53.

103. That the Carolingians represent *the* pivotal point in medieval, and perhaps all, Western history is certainly an overstatement. That they are used to represent *a* pivotal point, however, is evinced by their position as a transitional "bridge" between late antiquity and the Middle Ages in many grand historical narratives of Western Europe (as well as in many survey courses on the history of Western civilization). Where, then, does this leave the events of 833: as the pivotal moment of Carolingian history, which is itself seen as a pivotal era in the history of the West? Although it is rarely put so explicitly (though see K.-F. Werner, "Hludovicus Augustus: Gouverner l'empire chrétien—Idées et réalités," in *CH*, ed. Godman and Collins, 15), this is what weighs upon nearly all modern accounts of 833, lending them such gravity and contributing to their urgency and high drama. Cf. the remarks on the relative historical significance of Carolingian civilization by P. E. Dutton, "Res Carolinae," *IJCT* 4 (1997): 99–110; R. E. Sullivan, "The Carolingian Age: Reflections on Its Place in the History of the Middle Ages," *Speculum* 64 (1989): 267–306.

104. M. de Jong, "Power and Humility in Carolingian Society: The Public Penance of Louis the Pious," *EME* 1 (1992): 30. See also S. Airlie, "Private Bodies and the Body Politic in the Divorce Case of Lothar II," *PP* 161 (1998): 6–7.

105. F. Palgrave, *The History of Normandy and of England* (London, 1878), 1:295.

106. Cf. G. Koziol, "A Father, His Son, Memory, and Hope: The Joint Diploma of Lothar and Louis V (Pentecost Monday, 979) and the Limits of Performativity," in *Geschichtswissenschaft und "Performative Turn": Ritual, Inszenierung und Performanz vom Mittelalter bis zur Neuzeit*, ed. J. Martschukat and S. Patzold (Cologne, 2003), 83–86; J. E. Toews, "Intellectual History After the Linguistic Turn: The Autonomy of Meaning and the Irreducibility of Experience," *AHR* 92 (1987): 892.

107. E.g., *AB*, s.a. 835, ed. Grat et al., 16–17; Astronomer, *VH*, 49, ed. Tremp, 480. See Buc, *The Dangers of Ritual*, 237–47, 259.

108. See n. 6 above; and J. L. Nelson, "Inauguration Rituals," in eadem, *Politics*, 290, regarding the projection of Enlightenment cynicism back into the early Middle Ages. See also J. L. Nelson, "Public *Histories* and Private History in the Work of Nithard," *Speculum* 60 (1985): 285.

109. Cf. Calmette, *L'effondrement d'un empire*, 48: "Mais un tel paradoxe, en pleine ère carolingienne n'est-il pas frappé d'anachronisme? En vérité, Wala est un moderne. Il devance étonnamment les siècles." On the problem of transcendence, see L. Patterson, "On the Margin: Postmodernism, Ironic History, and Medieval Studies," *Speculum* 65 (1990): 88, esp. n. 5.

110. Ullmann, *The Carolingian Renaissance*, 68–69; J. M. Wallace-Hadrill, "The 'Via Regia' of the Carolingian Age," in idem, *Early Medieval History* (1965; Oxford, 1975), 192; J. Boussard, *The Civilization of Charlemagne*, trans. F. Partridge (New York, 1968), 202; T. Schieffer, "Die Krise des karolingischen Imperiums," in *Aus Mittelalter und Neuzeit: Festschrift für Gerhard Kallen zum 70. Geburtstag*, ed. J. Engel and H. M. Klinkenberg (Bonn, 1957), 12; H.-X. Arquillière, *L'Augustinisme politique: Essai sur la formation des théories politiques du Moyen-Âge*, 2nd ed. (Paris, 1955), 146, 200; idem, "Réflexions sur l'essence de l'augustinisme politique," in *Augustinus Magister: Congrès international augustinien, Paris, 21–24 Septembre 1954* (Paris, 1954), 2:994; E. Delaruelle, "En relisant le 'De institutione regia' de Jonas d'Orleans: L'entrée en scène de l'épiscopat carolingien," in *Mélanges d'histoire du moyen age dédiés à la mémoire de Louis Halphen* (Paris, 1951), 187; H. H. Milman, *History of Latin Christianity* (London, 1883), 3:141–42. On the way the "antagonistic dualism" of church and state anachronistically informs this view, see M. de Jong, "*Sacrum palatium et ecclesia*: L'autorité religieuse royale sous les Carolingiens (790–840)," *AHSS* 58 (2003): 1245–46.

111. Cf. N. Pleasants, "Free to Act Otherwise? A Wittgensteinian Deconstruction of the Concept of Agency in Contemporary Social and Political Theory," *History of the Human Sciences* 10, no. 4 (1997): 24–25. For the application of anomie theory to sources from the Middle Ages, and the methodological problems that undermine it, see B. Rosenwein, *Rhinoceros Bound: Cluny in the Tenth Century* (Philadelphia, 1982), with reviews by H. E. J. Cowdrey, *AHR* 88 (1983): 99; P. Horden, *EHR* 100 (1985): 156–57.

112. J. W. Thompson, *The Dissolution of the Carolingian Fisc in the Ninth Century* (Berkeley, Calif., 1935), 26–27.

113. Cf. the observations of N. B. Dirks, "The Policing of Tradition: Colonialism and Anthropology in Southern India," *Comparative Studies in Society and History* 39 (1997): 188.

114. See *Relatio Comp.*, ed. Booker, 14; Appendix, ll. 76–77, 83–84, 219–21; Agobard, *Liber apologeticus* II, 8, 12, 13, ed. Van Acker, 315, 318, 319; Paschasius Radbertus, *Epitaphium*, 2.18, 2.19, ed. Dümmler, 88, 90.

115. E.g., C. C. Fauriel, *Histoire de la gaule méridionale* (Paris, 1836), 4:140. However, in Louis' confessional "complaint," Odilo has Louis himself, while brooding in his cell, admit that his abandonment had been a judgment of God: "[Although] hurt and mocked in many ways by people whom I had never hurt, I was well aware of my own evil deeds, and thinking that I was suffering this rightfully, because of God's most equitable judgment, I tolerated this matter with equanimity." Odilo, *Translatio*, 44, ed. Holder-Egger, 388.

116. Astronomer, *VH*, 48, ed. Tremp, 476; trans. A. Cabaniss, *Son of Charlemagne* (Syracuse, N.Y., 1961), 97. The Astronomer refers to the event as a "*defectio*." Cf. *AB*, s.a. 833, ed. Grat et al., 9; Walafrid Strabo, prologus, to *Relatio Comp.*, ed. Booker, 11; Nithard, 1.4, ed. Lauer, 16; Charles the Bald, *Epistola Nicolao papae directa* (867), ed. W. Hartmann, MGH, *Conc.*, 4:240.

117. *AB*, s.a. 833, ed. Grat et al., 9 n. "c" in apparatus; Thegan, *GH*, 42, ed. Tremp, 228; Walafrid Strabo, table of contents (chap. 42), to Thegan, *GH*, ed. Tremp, 174; Astronomer, *VH*, 48, ed. Tremp, 474.

118. Nithard, 2.1, 2.3, 2.7; ed. Lauer, 36–38, 44–46, 58. On Lothar's habitual practice of subornation, see K. Leyser, "Three Historians," in idem, *Communications and Power in Medieval Europe* (London, 1994), 1:25–26; Nelson, "Public *Histories*," 267.

119. Nithard's lay view is usually taken by modern, secular scholars as that which bears closest resemblance to the truth about the events. Cf. Leyser, "Three Historians," 26; Wallace-Hadrill, *The Frankish Church*, 239; B. Scholz and B. Rogers, *Carolingian Chronicles* (Ann Arbor, Mich., 1970), 24, 26; H. Kuhn, "Das literarische Porträt Ludwigs des Frommen" (Ph.D. diss., Universität Basel, 1930), 29; and, already, Montesquieu, *De l'Esprit*, 31.22, ed. Truc, 2:382.

120. Cf. J. L. Nelson, "Violence in the Carolingian World and the Ritualization of Ninth-Century Warfare," in *Violence and Society in the Early Medieval West*, ed. G. Halsall (Woodbridge, 1998), 97–98; eadem, "The Search for Peace in a Time of War: The Carolingian Brüderkrieg, 840–843," in *Träger und Instrumentarien des Friedens im hohen und späten Mittelalter*, ed. J. Fried (Sigmaringen, 1996), 98, 107–8; R. McKitterick, *The Frankish Kingdoms Under the Carolingians, 751–987* (London, 1983), 170–72; Ullmann, *The Carolingian Renaissance*, 69–70; L. Halphen, *Charlemagne and the Carolingian Empire*, trans. G. de Nie (1947; Amsterdam, 1977), 194–206; idem, "La pénitence de Louis le Pieux à Saint Médard de Soissons," in idem, *A travers l'histoire du Moyen Age* (1904; Paris, 1950), 58–66.

121. Paschasius Radbertus, *Epitaphium*, 1.6, ed. Dümmler, 28–29; trans. Cabaniss, *Charlemagne's Cousins*, 99. Cf. also *Epitaphium*, 2, intro., 2.1, 2.8, 2.10, 2.20.

122. For Agobard, see Chapter 4, nn. 80–82; for Ebbo, Chapter 5.

123. Louis the Pious, *Ep.* 19, ed. E. Dümmler, MGH, *Epist.*, 5:326; *BHL* 2172. On this letter (and the response it elicited from Hilduin), see G. P. A. Brown, "Politics and Patronage at the Royal Abbey of Saint-Denis (814–98): The Rise of a Royal Patron Saint" (Ph.D. diss., New College, Oxford University, 1989), 207–17, 283–329.

124. On this point, see T. Reuter, "The 'Imperial Church System' of the Ottonian and Salian Rulers: A Reconsideration," *JEH* 33 (1982): 347–74; F. Oakley, "Celestial Hierarchies Revisited: Walter Ullmann's Vision of Medieval Politics," *PP* 60 (1973): 1–48; K. Davis, "National Writing in the Ninth Century: A Reminder for Postcolonial Thinking about the Nation," *Journal of Medieval and Early Modern Studies* 28 (1998): 618, 624, 634 n. 27, 635 n. 37; eadem, review of A. P. Smyth, *King Alfred the Great* (New York, 1995), *Medievalia et Humanistica* n.s. 24 (1997): 211–15.

125. See the texts cited in n. 114 above. Of these texts, only the *Epitaphium Arsenii* by Paschasius Radbertus has been translated; see Cabaniss, *Charlemagne's Cousins*.

126. Buc, *The Dangers of Ritual*, 240–45, 258–59. See also S. MacLean, "Ritual, Misunderstanding, and the Contest for Meaning: Representations of the Disrupted Royal Assembly at Frankfurt (873)," in *Representations of Power in Medieval Germany 800–1500*, ed. B. Weiler and S. MacLean (Turnhout, 2006), 97–119.

127. M. Sahlins, "Individual Experience and Cultural Order," in idem, *Culture in Practice: Selected Essays* (1982; New York, 2000), 278. Cf. Buc, *The Dangers of Ritual*, 238.

128. Sahlins, "Individual Experience," 279, citing F. Nietzsche, *The Twilight of the Idols*, trans. R. J. Hollingdale (1889; London, 1990), 33. See also J. Anomaly, "Nietzsche's Critique of Utilitarianism," *Journal of Nietzsche Studies* 29 (2005): 1–15.

129. J.-C. Schmitt, "Religion, Folklore, and Society in the Medieval West," in *Debating the Middle Ages*, ed. L. K. Little and B. Rosenwein (1988; Malden, Mass., 1998), 376–87; P. J. Geary, *Living with the Dead in the Middle Ages* (Ithaca, N.Y., 1994); idem, *Furta Sacra: Thefts of Relics in the Central Middle Ages*, rev. ed. (Princeton, N.J., 1991); D. Oldridge, *Strange Histories: The Trial of the Pig, the Walking Dead, and Other Matters of Fact from the Medieval and Renaissance Worlds* (London, 2005); C. Ginzburg, *The Cheese and the Worms: The Cosmos of a Sixteenth-Century Miller*, trans. J. Tedeschi and A. Tedeschi (Baltimore, 1980).

130. C. Ginzburg, "Checking the Evidence: The Judge and the Historian," in *Questions of Evidence: Proof, Practice, and Persuasion Across the Disciplines*, ed. J. Chandler et al. (Chicago, 1994), 290–303. See also G. Koziol, "Truth and Its Consequences: Why Carolingianists Don't Speak of Myth," in *Myth in Early Northwest Europe*, ed. S. O. Glosecki (Tempe, Ariz., 2007), 71–103; and Airlie, "Private Bodies," 31, on taking Carolingian political rhetoric seriously.

131. C. Ginzburg, "Making It Strange: The Prehistory of a Literary Device," in idem, *Wooden Eyes: Nine Reflections on Distance*, trans. M. Ryle and K. Soper (1996; New York,

2001), 1–23. Cf. Chevallard, *Saint Agobard*, 315–16; Milman, *History of Latin Christianity*, 3:139, 141, on the "strangeness" of 833.

132. J. R. R. Tolkien, "Beowulf: The Monsters and the Critics," in idem, *The Monsters and the Critics and Other Essays* (1936; London, 1983), 10. Cf. W. Goffart, *The Narrators of Barbarian History (A.D. 550–800)* (Princeton, N.J., 1988), 436.

133. Schmitt, "Religion, Folklore, and Society," 382.

134. Cf. C. W. Bynum, "In Praise of Fragments: History in the Comic Mode," in eadem, *Fragmentation and Redemption: Essays on Gender and the Human Body in Medieval Religion* (New York, 1991), 23.

CHAPTER 4. DOCUMENTING DUTY'S DEMANDS

Epigraphs: *Annales Alamannici*, ed. W. Lendi, *Untersuchungen zur frühalemannischen Annalistik* (Freiburg, 1971), 176; *Annales Weingartenses*, ed. G. H. Pertz, MGH, *SS*, 1:65; *Annales Einsidlenses*, ed. G. H. Pertz, MGH, *SS*, 3:139; *Annales Formoselenses*, ed. G. H. Pertz, MGH, *SS*, 5:35; C. J. Hefele, *Histoire des conciles d'après les documents originaux,* revised, with notes by H. Leclercq (Paris, 1911), 4(1):87 n. 1.

1. The *Relatio* drawn up by the rebel bishops has traditionally been known by the title appended by Pierre Pithou in 1588 (found in his descriptive table of contents): "Proceedings of Emperor Louis the Pious's shameful and impious deposition" (*Acta impiae et nefandae exauctorationis Ludovicii Pii imperatoris*). While the text survived into the modern era apparently through two manuscript copies (both have since been lost), it has undergone no fewer than twenty printings since its first publication by Pithou; see C. M. Booker, "The Public Penance of Louis the Pious: A New Edition of the *Episcoporum de poenitentia, quam Hludowicus imperator professus est, relatio Compendiensis* (833)," *Viator* 39, no. 2 (2008): 1–10. Despite this deluge of printings, and unlike other important Carolingian texts, the text has never been fully translated.

2. E.g., G. W. Leibniz, *Annales imperii occidentis Brunsvicenses*, s.a. 833, ed. G. H. Pertz, *Gottfried Wilhelm Leibniz: Gesammelte Werke*, I, 1 (Hannover, 1843), 428–30; J. Michelet, *Le Moyen Age: Histoire de France*, bk. 2, chp. 3, ed. C. Mettra (1833; Paris, 1981), 158; J.-C.-L. Simonde de Sismondi, *Histoire des français* (Paris, 1821), 3:26–27; A. Himly, *Wala et Louis le Débonnaire* (Paris, 1849), 176–77; F. Lot, *Naissance de la France* (Paris, 1948), 334; L. Halphen, *Charlemagne and the Carolingian Empire*, trans. G. de Nie (1947; Amsterdam, 1977), 206; and T. F. X. Noble, "Louis the Pious and the Papacy: Law, Politics and the Theory of Empire in the Early Ninth Century" (Ph.D. diss., Michigan State University, 1974), 347, 350, all summarize or quote from the bishops' *Relatio* but do so only to show its wickedness and shamefulness, mendacity and absurdity.

3. There is a clear correlation between the explicitly dramatic emplotment of the events of 833 and Thegan's report of Louis' address to his men on the Rotfeld. It is nearly axiomatic that, whenever a narrator includes Louis' speech in a recounting of the events,

an explicit reference to the events as some kind of drama is soon to follow (though the reverse is not as often the case). See Himly, *Wala et Louis*, 165; F. Monnier, *Histoire des luttes politiques et religieuses dans les temps carolingiens* (Paris, 1852), 124; J. Calmette, *L'effondrement d'un empire et la naissance d'une Europe IXe–Xe siècles* (Paris, 1941), 56; J.-H. Bauchy, *Récits des temps carolingiens* (Paris, 1973), 216.

4. The following scholars used Odilo's text sympathetically to convey the emperor's plight: Leibniz, *Annales imperii*, s.a. 833, ed. Pertz, 427–28; F. Funck, *Ludwig der Fromme* (Frankfurt am Main, 1832), 136; L. von Ranke, *Weltgeschichte* (Leipzig, 1896), 3:296; F. Palgrave, *The History of Normandy and of England* (London, 1878), 1:275, 293.

5. Cf. E. Peters, *The Shadow King: Rex Inutilis in Medieval Law and Literature, 751–1327* (New Haven, Conn., 1970), 58; M. de Jong, "Monastic Prisoners or Opting Out? Political Coercion and Honour in the Frankish Kingdoms," in *Topographies of Power in the Early Middle Ages*, ed. M. de Jong et al. (Leiden, 2001), 294.

6. J. M. Wallace-Hadrill, "The 'Via Regia' of the Carolingian Age," in idem, *Early Medieval History* (1965; Oxford, 1975), 192. Cf. J. L. Nelson, "Bad Kingship in the Earlier Middle Ages," *Haskins Society Journal* 8 (1996): 14; eadem, "Kingship, Law, and Liturgy in the Political Thought of Hincmar of Rheims," in Nelson, *Politics*, 144; W. Ullmann, *The Growth of Papal Government in the Middle Ages* (London, 1965), 169.

7. Booker, "The Public Penance," 1–10. I use the expression "come to light" rather than "discovered" because the "new" witnesses have long been known but—in keeping with the traditional distaste for the rebels' deeds—have either been quietly passed over or noted perfunctorily, without comment or analysis. See C. M. Booker, "A New Prologue of Walafrid Strabo," *Viator* 36 (2005): 88 n. 27; idem, "The Public Penance," 4–5 n. 14.

8. Agobard, *De divisione imperii*, ed. Van Acker, 247–50; idem, *De privilegio apostolicae sedis*, ed. Van Acker, 303–6; idem, *Liber apologeticus* I, II, ed. Van Acker, 309–19; idem, *Cartula*, ed. Van Acker, 323–24; Pope Gregory IV, *Ep.* 17, ed. E. Dümmler, MGH, *Epist.*, 5:228–32.

9. Since the foundational work by E. Boshof, *Erzbischof Agobard von Lyon: Leben und Werk* (Cologne, 1969), a close examination of these texts has remained a desideratum. Cf. M. Rubellin, "Vision de la société chrétienne à travers la confession et la pénitence au IXe siècle," in *Pratiques de la confession* (Paris, 1983), 64 n. 33; J.-M. Moeglin, "Rituels et 'Verfassungsgeschichte' au Moyen Âge: A propos du livre de Gerd Althoff, Spielregeln der Politik im Mittelalter," *Francia* 25, no. 1 (1998): 248–49.

10. On the ritual act of *transpunctio*, see H. Brunner and C. F. von Schwerin, *Deutsche Rechtsgeschichte* (1928; Berlin, 1958), 2:562 nn. 12–13; J. L. Nelson, "Dispute Settlement in Carolingian West Francia," in *The Settlement of Disputes in Early Medieval Europe*, ed. W. Davies and P. Fouracre (Cambridge, 1986), 57–58.

11. Cf. *Admonitio generalis* (March 789), 78, ed. A. Boretius, MGH, *Capit.*, 1:60, no. 22; *Concilium Parisiense* (829), 32, ed. A. Werminghoff, MGH, *Conc.*, 2(2):633.

12. Agobard, *Cartula*, ed. Van Acker, 323. Cf. the remarks of Charlemagne, in his *Admonitio generalis* (March 789), 78, ed. Boretius, 1:60, on the specifically Pauline justification for the burning of spurious, uncanonical documents.

13. Of the ecclesiastics known to have participated in the rebellion, several were later allowed to return to their offices: Agobard to Lyon and Bernard to Vienne in 838/39 (Depreux, *Prosopographie*, 406–8; Astronomer, *VH*, 57; Ado of Vienne, *Chronicon*, *PL* 123, col. 135D), Heribald to Auxerre in 838 (Depreux, *Prosopographie*, 241–42), and Hilduin to Saint-Denis perhaps as early as 834 (Depreux, *Prosopographie*, 250–56). Jesse of Amiens, Helias of Troyes, and Wala of Corbie (who was formally pardoned by Louis) all died from a plague in Italy late in 836 (Depreux, *Prosopographie*, 408–9; Astronomer, *VH*, 56). Bartholomew of Narbonne and Ebbo of Reims were both banned from office (Depreux, *Prosopographie*, 169–74; Simson, *Jahrbücher*, 2:138 n. 3), though after Louis' death Ebbo persisted to regain his see, acquiring it again briefly in 840 (see Chapter 5). In 835, Hildemann of Beauvais cleared himself of accusations alleging his disloyalty to the emperor during the days of the rebellion (Simson, *Jahrbücher*, 2:137 n. 3).

14. See Chapter 2, n. 160.

15. Paris, B.N.F. lat. 2853. On this manuscript, see Chapter 2, n. 149.

16. The relationship between the local cult of Agobard and the preservation of his texts in Lyon is a subject in need of close study. After the Treaty of Verdun in 843, the region of Lyon remained in the hands of Lothar and his sons until 870, when Charles the Bald obtained it and granted it to his brother-in-law Boso. For the influence of Tertullian's literary style on Agobard (who owned a rare copy of the works of this church father, which is extant: the "Codex Agobardinus," Paris, B.N.F. lat. 1622, saec. IX), see A. Cabaniss, "Agobard of Lyons," *Speculum* 26 (1951): 50 n. 12; Boshof, *Erzbischof Agobard*, 167; P. Buc, *The Dangers of Ritual: Between Early Medieval Texts and Social Scientific Theory* (Princeton, N.J., 2001), 244 n. 185. On the Codex Agobardinus, see P. Lauer, *Catalogue général des manuscrits latins* (Paris, 1940), 2:95–96.

17. Paris, B.N.F. lat. 2853, fols. 192v–197r.

18. Agobard, ed. Van Acker, XXI. The texts appear in Paris, B.N.F. lat. 2853 in the following order: *De divisione imperii* (fols. 187r–190r); *De privilegio apostolicae sedis* (fols. 190r–192v); Epistle of Pope Gregory IV (fols. 192v–197r); *Liber apologeticus* I (fols. 197r–200r), *Liber apologeticus* II (fols. 200r–206r); *Cartula de Ludovici poenitentia* (fols. 206r–208v).

19. As Van Acker notes (LII), there is a table of contents from the late ninth/early tenth century at the front of the manuscript (fol. 1v). Unfortunately, it is incomplete, giving titles only for the following texts in Van Acker's edition in the order that they appear in the manuscript: Van Acker nos. 5, 11, 12, 6, 14, 2, 4, 1, 18, 10, 15, 13, 23, 9, 7, 3, 17. Should any significance be ascribed to the fact that this table of contents concludes just before the collection of Agobard's "political" texts (listed above in n. 18) begins? On the different scribal hands discernible in the manuscript, see Van Acker, LI.

20. Agobard, *De divisione imperii*, ed. Van Acker, 247–50. See Van Acker, XLIII–XLIV; Boshof, *Erzbischof Agobard*, 200–205; F. L. Ganshof, "Some Observations on the *Ordinatio Imperii* of 817," in idem, *Carolingians*, 273–88.

21. Agobard, *De privilegio apostolicae sedis*, ed. Van Acker, 303–6. See Van Acker, XLV; Boshof, *Erzbischof Agobard*, 217–21.

22. Pope Gregory IV, *Ep.* 17, ed. Dümmler, 228–32. On this text, see Van Acker, XXI–XXII; Boshof, *Erzbischof Agobard*, 225–28; Noble, "Louis the Pious and the Papacy," 321–52; Ullmann, *The Growth of Papal Government*, 167–72; H.-X. Arquillière, *L'Augustinisme politique: Essai sur la formation des théories politiques du Moyen-Âge*, 2nd ed. (Paris, 1955), 179–89; idem, "Sur la formation de la 'theocratie' pontificale," in *Mélanges d'histoire du moyen âge, offerts à M. Ferdinand Lot par ses amis et ses élèves* (Paris, 1925), 18–21.

23. Among those bishops remaining loyal to Louis, Noble, "Louis the Pious and the Papacy," 329 n. 17, has identified Drogo of Metz, Modoin of Autun, Willeric of Bremen, Aldric of Le Mans, Otgar of Mainz, Hildi of Verdun, Bernold of Strasbourg, Verendarius of Chur, Heriric of Saint-Laumer de Blois, Christian of Saint-Germain d'Auxerre, Hrabanus Maurus, and Jonas of Orléans.

24. The language that Gregory provides as the bishops' reply bears a resemblance to the language and style of Bishop Jonas of Orléans (cf. *De institutione regia*, 8, ed. A. Dubreucq, *SC*, 407:220–24), a supporter of Louis known to have been the episcopal *dictator* at several ecclesiastical councils, including Louis' restoration ceremony at Thionville and Metz in 835. See Dubreucq, 40–42; and Depreux, *Prosopographie*, 276–77.

25. Pope Gregory IV, *Ep.* 17, ed. Dümmler, 229, quotes from Gregory of Nanzianzus, *Orationes*, 17.8–9, and asks, with (mock?) surprise, why the bishops had not shown to the emperor the portrait of the just ruler in Augustine, *De civitate Dei*, 5.24, which he then also quotes. This query supports the notion that Gregory was replying to a letter from Jonas, for Jonas had recently quoted (in 831) the same passage from Augustine in his *speculum principis* for King Pippin, *De institutione regia*, 17, ed. Dubreucq, 282–84.

26. Cf. Ganshof, "Some Observations," 281, 288 n. 75.

27. Cf. Augustine, *De civitate Dei*, 1.8.

28. Agobard, *Liber apologeticus* I, ed. Van Acker, 309–12. See Van Acker, XLIV–XLV; Boshof, *Erzbischof Agobard*, 228–39; P. E. Dutton, *The Politics of Dreaming in the Carolingian Empire* (Lincoln, Neb., 1994), 102–3; G. Bührer-Thierry, "La reine adultère," *CCM* 35 (1992): 299–312; E. Ward, "Agobard of Lyons and Paschasius Radbertus as Critics of the Empress Judith," *SCH* 27 (1990): 15–25; A. Cabaniss, *Agobard of Lyons: Churchman and Critic* (Syracuse, N.Y., 1953), 86–87, 89, 106; A. Bressolles, *Saint Agobard: Evêque de Lyon (769–840)* (Paris, 1949), 40–42.

29. Agobard, *Liber apologeticus* I, 1, ed. Van Acker, 309.

30. Agobard, *Liber apologeticus* I, 2, ed. Van Acker, 310.

31. Agobard, *Liber apologeticus* I, 4, ed. Van Acker, 311.

32. Agobard, *Liber apologeticus* II, ed. Van Acker, 315–19. See Van Acker, XLIV–XLV; Boshof, *Erzbischof Agobard*, 241–46; and the studies in n. 28 above.

33. On the Carolingian representation of Louis' selection of Judith as his new wife, see M. de Jong, "Bride Shows Revisited: Praise, Slander and Exegesis in the Reign of the Empress Judith," in *Gender in the Early Medieval World: East and West, 300–900*, ed. L. Brubaker and J. M. H. Smith (Cambridge, 2004), 257–77.

34. This sequence of rhetorical questions by Agobard (*Liber apologeticus* II, 9, ed. Van Acker, 316) is reminiscent of Ambrose's letter to Theodosius requesting the emperor to do penance for the massacre he sanctioned at Thessalonica in 390; cf. Ambrose, *Ep. extra collectionem* 11 [Maur. 51], 3, ed. M. Zelzer, *CSEL* (Vienna, 1982), 82(3):212–13; trans. J. H. W. G. Liebeschuetz, *Ambrose of Milan: Political Letters and Speeches* (Liverpool, 2005), 264: "What in the circumstances was I to do? Hear nothing? . . . Disclose what I heard? . . . Was I to hold my tongue?" Ambrose then supports his answers to these questions by paraphrasing Ezekiel 3:18. On this letter, see nn. 48–50, 54 below.

35. Agobard, *Cartula*, ed. Van Acker, 323–24. See Van Acker, XLVI; Boshof, *Erzbischof Agobard*, 247–51.

36. However, there is an additional, fragmentary text in Paris, B.N.F. lat. 2853 (fols. 208v–212r), that immediately follows the cluster of texts relating to 833 and may be linked to them—namely, Agobard's treatise addressed to Ebbo of Reims titled "On Hope and Fear" (*De spe et timore*), ed. Van Acker, 145–47. A much longer, but still fragmentary, witness of the text was discovered in 1985; see J.-P. Bouhot, "Le manuscrit Angers, B. M. 277 (268) et l'opuscule *De spe et timore* d'Agobard de Lyon," *Revue des études Augustiniennes* 31 (1985): 227–41; Agobard, ed. Van Acker, 428–54.

37. For the Latin text of the bishops' account, see the *Relatio Comp.*, ed. Booker, 10–19. For an English trans., see Appendix.

38. M. de Jong, "Power and Humility in Carolingian Society: The Public Penance of Louis the Pious," *EME* 1 (1992): 40 n. 46.

39. At the reform council of Paris in 829, the bishops claimed this power as their prerogative, using nearly the same diction (in this instance, however, they call themselves the *vicarii apostolorum*): *Concilium Parisiense* (829), prologus, ed. Werminghoff, 2(2):608, 673. On this council, which is cited below frequently, see M. de Jong, "*Ecclesia* and the Early Medieval Polity," in *Staat im frühen Mittelalter*, ed. S. Airlie et al. (Vienna, 2006), 129–31; M. E. Jegen, "Jonas of Orléans (c. 780–843): His Pastoral Writings and Their Social Significance" (Ph.D. diss., Saint Louis University, 1967), 242–98; M. E. Moore, "A Sacred Kingdom: Royal and Episcopal Power in the Frankish Realms (496–846)" (Ph.D. diss., University of Michigan, 1993), 290–310; W. Hartmann, *Die Synoden der Karolingerzeit im Frankenreich und in Italien* (Paderborn, 1989), 179–87. Bishop Jonas of Orléans linked penance and absolution to the episcopal privilege of binding and loosing: see his *De institutione laicali*, 1.15, *PL* 106, col. 151–52; discussed by D. F. Appleby, "Sight and Church Reform in the Thought of Jonas of Orleans," *Viator* 27 (1996): 29.

40. *Relatio Comp.*, ed. Booker, 11; Appendix, ll. 9–10. Cf. the similar use of this quotation by Theodulf of Orléans, *Capitulare* I (798–817/18), 28, ed. P. Brommer, MGH, *Capitula episcoporum* (Hannover, 1984), 1:125.

41. Benedict, *Regula*, 2.25, ed. Hanslik, 25.

42. On the ambiguous lines separating the canonical and monastic life in the ninth century, see T. L. Amos, "Monks and Pastoral Care in the Early Middle Ages," in *Religion, Culture, and Society in the Early Middle Ages*, ed. T. F. X. Noble and J. J. Contreni (Kalamazoo, Mich., 1987), 165–80; G. Constable, "Monks and Canons in Carolingian

Gaul: The Case of Rigrannus of Le Mans," in *After Rome's Fall: Narrators and Sources of Early Medieval History*, ed. A. C. Murray (Toronto, 1998), 320–36.

43. *Collectio capitularis Benedicti Levitae monastica*, 80, ed. J. Semmler, *Corpus consuetudinum monasticarum* (Sieburg, 1963), 1:553–54, no. 24a; J. Semmler, "Zur Überlieferung der monastischen Gesetzgebung Ludwigs des Frommen," *DA* 16 (1960): 377–78. For the assembly of 817 and the primary role played by Benedict of Aniane, see Semmler "Zur Überlieferung"; R. McKitterick, *The Frankish Kingdoms Under the Carolingians, 751–987* (London, 1983), 112–24.

44. For commentary on Benedict's inclusion of Paul's command, see Smaragdus of Saint-Mihiel, *Expositio in regulam S. Benedicti*, 2.20, ed. A. Spannagel and P. Engelbert, *Corpus consuetudinum monasticarum* (Sieburg, 1974), 8:71; Benedict of Aniane, *Concordia regularum*, 5.1, ed. P. Bonnerue, *CCCM*, 168A:65; Hildemar of Corbie/Civate, *Expositio regulae S. Benedicti*, ed. R. Mittermüller, *Vita et regula SS. P. Benedicti una cum expositione regulae* (Regensburg, 1880), 3:107–12; Grimlaicus, *Regula solitariorum*, 53, *PL* 103, col. 644B–D.

45. For instance, Dhuoda, a devout contemporary laywoman, was knowledgable of them as a triad; Dhuoda, *Liber manualis*, 4.8, ed. P. Riché, *SC*, 225*bis*:254. According to his biographer, Benedict of Aniane made Paul's three imperatives the cornerstone of his monastic teaching and widespread reforms; Ardo, *Vita Benedicti abbatis Anianensis*, 44, ed. O. Holder-Egger, MGH, *SS*, 15(1):220.

46. Benedict, *Regula*, 2.25, ed. Hanslik, 25.

47. *Relatio Comp.*, ed. Booker, 11; Appendix, ll. 11–13. This passage from Ezekiel was used frequently in the ninth century to define the obligations of the episcopal office. Cf. R. Reynolds, "A Ninth-Century Treatise on the Origins, Office, and Ordination of the Bishop," *RB* 85 (1975): 330, ll. 48–53; Hrabanus Maurus, *De institutione clericorum*, 1.5, ed. D. Zimpel, *Freiburger Beiträge zur mittelalterlichen Geschichte* (Frankfurt am Main, 1996), 7:299; *Concilium Parisiense* (829), 5, ed. Werminghoff, 2(2):612–14; H. Mordek, *Bibliotheca capitularium regum Francorum manuscripta* (Munich, 1995), 769, 777. On the bishop as watchman and the responsibilities of the office, see C. Leyser, "'Let Me Speak, Let Me Speak': Vulnerability and Authority in Gregory's Homilies on Ezekiel," in *Gregorio Magno e il suo tempo* (Rome, 1991), 2:169–82; idem, "Vulnerability and Power: The Early Christian Rhetoric of Masculine Authority," *Bulletin of the John Rylands University Library of Manchester* 80 (1998): 159–73; M. H. Hoeflich, "The Speculator in the Governmental Theory of the Early Church," *Vigiliae Christianae* 34 (1980): 120–29; C. Mohrmann, "Episkopos-Speculator," in eadem, *Études sur le latin des chrétiens* (Rome, 1977), 4:232–52.

48. Ambrose, *Ep. 74/Extra collectionem* 1A [Maur. 40], to Theodosius (winter, 388/89), ed. Zelzer, 82(3):54–73; trans. Liebeschuetz, *Ambrose of Milan*, 95–111; idem, *Ep. extra collectionem* 11 [Maur. 51], to Theodosius (390), ed. Zelzer, 82(3):212–18; trans. Liebeschuetz, *Ambrose of Milan*, 262–69. On these letters (regarding events at Callinicum and Thessalonica, respectively), see N. B. McLynn, *Ambrose of Milan: Church and Court in a Christian Capital* (Berkeley, Calif., 1994), 298–330.

49. I know of their joint appearance only in Gregory the Great, *Homiliae in Hieze-chihelem prophetam*, 1.11.15, ed. M. Adriaen, *CCSL*, 142:175–76; Caesarius of Arles, *Sermo* 4, ed. G. Morin, *CCSL*, 103:23; idem, *Sermo* 145, ed. Morin, *CCSL*, 104:596; idem, *Sermo* 230, ed. Morin, *CCSL*, 104:912; Eutropius, *Ep.* (*ad Petrum papam de districtione monacho-rum*), *PL* 80, col. 15C–D; Boniface, *Ep.* 78 (*ad Cuthbertem*) ed. M. Tangl, MGH, *Episto-lae selectae in usum scholarum, separatim editae* (Berlin, 1916), 1:166–67; and the work of Hincmar of Reims, cited below.

50. R. Schieffer, "Von Mailand nach Canossa: Ein Beitrag zur Geschichte der christ-lichen Herrscherbusse von Theodosius der Grosse bis zu Heinrich IV," *DA* 28 (1972): 346–47, 357–58; Liebeschuetz, *Ambrose of Milan*, 44–45. In 860, Hincmar would demonstrate his knowledge of Ambrose's two letters, quoting extensively from them to argue for the duties of a bishop. See Hincmar, *De divortio Lotharii regis et Theutbergae reginae*, respons. 7 (Anhang), ed. L. Böhringer, MGH, *Conc.*, 4(1):78, 253–54. Cf. K. Heidecker, "Why Should Bishops Be Involved in Marital Affairs? Hincmar of Rheims on the Divorce of King Lothar II (855–869)," in *The Community, the Family, and the Saint: Patterns of Power in Early Medieval Europe*, ed. J. Hill and M. Swan (Turnhout, 1998), 229–30; Y. Sassier, "Le roi et la loi chez les penseurs du royaume occidental du deuxième quart du IXe à la fin du XIe s.," *CCM* 43 (2000): 266.

51. M. de Jong, "What Was *Public* about Public Penance? *Paenitentia Publica* and Justice in the Carolingian World," *SS Spoleto*, 44(2): 866, 897.

52. Cf. the definition of a bishop's duties by Jonas of Orléans, *De institutione laicali*, 1.18, *PL* 106, col. 156–58, discussed by Jegen, "Jonas of Orléans," 231, 238; Hincmar of Reims, *De ordine palatii*, 2, ed. T. Gross and R. Schieffer, MGH, *Fontes iuris Germanici antiqui in usum scholarum, separatim editi* (Hannover, 1980), 3:42–43; and n. 47 above.

53. Agobard, *Liber apologeticus* II, 11, ed. Van Acker, 317.

54. Ambrose, *Ep. extra collectionem* 11 [Maur. 51], to Theodosius (390), 7–10, ed. Zelzer, 82(3):214–16; trans. Liebeschuetz, *Ambrose of Milan*, 265–67. It has been postu-lated that when Ambrose sent this letter to Theodosius, he attached to it his work *De apo-logia prophetae David*, a discussion on the penitential fiftieth psalm. See P. Brown, *Power and Persuasion in Late Antiquity: Towards a Christian Empire* (Madison, Wis., 1992), 111; P. Hadot, *Ambroise de Milan: Apologie de David*, SC, 239:37–43; S. Hamilton, "A New Model for Royal Penance? Helgaud of Fleury's *Life of Robert the Pious*," *EME* 6 (1997): 189–200. On Carolingian knowledge of the *De apologia prophetae David*, see Sassier, "Le roi et la loi," 266 n. 44; H. Yagello, "Histoire, exégèse et politique: L'apologie de David d'Ambroise de Milan et les Carolingiens," *Sources: Revue de l'Association Histoire au présent* 49–50 (1999): 103–22.

55. *Relatio Comp.*, ed. Booker, 11–12; Appendix, ll. 18–21, citing Gregory the Great, *Regula pastoralis*, 2.1, 2.6, ed. F. Rommel, *SC*, 382:174, 202; idem, *Registrum epistularum*, 1, *Ep.* 24, ed. D. Norberg, *CCSL*, 140:23, 29. Cf. Hildemar, *Expositio regulae S. Benedicti*, ed. Mittermüller, 3:119–20.

56. As F. S. Hoyt, "The Carolingian Episcopate: Concepts of Pastoral Care as Set Forth in the Capitularies of Charlemagne and His Bishops (789–822)" (Ph.D. diss., Yale

University, 1975), 267, has noted, Charlemagne, in a series of five councils in 813, enjoined all bishops to know Gregory the Great's *Pastoral Care*. This enjoinder was taken seriously—note the frequent reference to Gregory in the reform council of Paris in 829: *Concilium Parisiense* (829), 4, 11–12, 29, ed. Werminghoff, 2(2):611–12, 617–19, 632. See B. Judic, "La tradition de Grégoire le Grand dans l'idéologie politique carolingienne," in *La royauté et les élites dans l'Europe carolingienne*, ed. R. Le Jan (Lille, 1998), 17–57, esp. 40–47.

57. Gregory the Great, *Homiliae in Hiezechihelem prophetam*, 1.11.15, ed. Adriaen, 175–76; idem, *Regula pastoralis*, 3.16, ed. Rommel, 356. Cf. C. Leyser, *Authority and Asceticism from Augustine to Gregory the Great* (Oxford, 2000), 163. On Gregory's interpretation of the "exegetical contract" by which ecclesiastics are bound, see R. A. Markus, *Gregory the Great and His World* (Cambridge, 1997), 17–33; Leyser, "Let Me Speak, Let Me Speak," 2:169–82.

58. On the development of episcopal *ministerium* in the early ninth century, see Moore, "A Sacred Kingdom," 248–310; C. Margalhan-Ferrat, "Le concept de 'ministerium' entre littérature spéculaire et législation carolingienne," in *Specula principum*, ed. A. de Benedictis and A. Pisapia (Frankfurt am Main, 1999), 121–57; De Jong, "Power and Humility," 39–43; T. Oberndorff, "Lodewijk de Vrome's openbare boetedoening in 833: een kwestie van *ministeria*," *DRCH* 71 (1991): 1–36; O. Guillot, "L'exhortation au partage des responsabilités entre l'empereur, l'épiscopat et les autres sujets vers le milieu du règne de Louis le Pieux," in *Prédication et propagande au Moyen Age: Islam, Byzance, Occident* (Paris, 1983), 87–110.

59. Cf. the use of the term *sarculum* by Paschasius Radbertus, *Epitaphium*, 1.4, ed. Dümmler, 26.

60. *Proemium generale ad capitularia tam ecclesiastica quam mundana* (818–819), ed. A. Boretius, MGH, *Capit.*, 1:274, no. 137. On this assembly, see Hartmann, *Die Synoden der Karolingerzeit*, 161–64. Cf. the pastoral language in *Relatio Comp.*, ed. Booker, 12; Appendix, ll. 25–27; and the chapter on discipline from Benedict's Rule, as found in Carolingian capitularies, *Collectio capitularis Benedicti Levitae monastica*, 80, ed. J. Semmler, *Corpus consuetudinum monasticarum* (Sieburg, 1963), 1:553–54, no. 24a [= Benedict, *Regula*, 2.25–26, ed. Hanslik, 25–26].

61. Peters, *The Shadow King*, 61. Cf. P. Burke, "The Sense of Anachronism from Petrarch to Poussin," in *Time in the Medieval World*, ed. C. Humphrey and W. M. Ormrod (Rochester, N.Y., 2001), 160.

62. *Relatio Comp.*, ed. Booker, 12; Appendix, ll. 36–38.

63. *Relatio Comp.*, ed. Booker, 12; Appendix, ll. 38–42. A misprint here in Pithou's *editio princeps* of the *Relatio*—for centuries its sole witness—giving the ungrammatical *super imperio* instead of *sub imperio* has long been accepted without question, reprinted numerous times, and used as evidence of the bishops' "revolutionary" supra-imperial aspirations and ideology. See Booker, "A New Prologue," 92–93.

64. Agobard, *Cartula*, ed. Van Acker, 323.

65. On the ideal of peace in the Carolingian era, see R. Bonnaud-Delamare, *L'idée*

de la paix à l'époque Carolingienne (Paris, 1939); J. L. Nelson, "The Search for Peace in a Time of War: The Carolingian Brüderkrieg, 840–843," in *Träger und Instrumentarien des Friedens im hohen und späten Mittelalter*, ed. J. Fried (Sigmaringen, 1996), 87–114.

66. On this contract, see W. Parsons, "The Medieval Theory of the Tyrant," *Review of Politics* 4 (1942): 134–35; J. Van Engen, "Sacred Sanctions for Lordship," in *Cultures of Power: Lordship, Status, and Process in Twelfth-Century Europe*, ed. T. N. Bisson (Philadelphia, 1995), 213; and in particular, O. Guillot, "Une *ordinatio* méconnue: Le capitulaire de 823–825," in *CH*, ed. Godman and Collins, 455–86; idem, "L'exhortation au partage," 87–110. The contract was made explicit to Louis at the Council of Paris in 829: *Concilium Parisiense* (829), 59, ed. Werminghoff, 2(2):655.

67. Agobard, *Cartula*, ed. Van Acker, 323.

68. *Relatio Comp.*, ed. Booker, 13–14; Appendix ll. 70–71. Cf. Peters, *The Shadow King*, 60.

69. See Nelson, "Bad Kingship," 13, on kings that "go to the bad." Cf. Paschasius Radbertus, *Epitaphium*, 2.4, ed. Dümmler, 65.

70. Agobard, *De divisione imperii*, 4, ed. Van Acker, 248–49.

71. Agobard, *Liber apologeticus* I, 2, ed. Van Acker, 309.

72. Agobard, *Liber apologeticus* II, 8, ed. Van Acker, 316.

73. Though there is an oblique reference to Judith later in the bishops' collective account; *Relatio Comp.*, ed. Booker, 18; Appendix, ll. 191–92; and n. 187 below.

74. Cf. Nelson, "Bad Kingship," 15; Ward, "Agobard of Lyons and Paschasius," 19.

75. Gregory the Great, *Dialogues*, 2.2, ed. A. de Vogüé, *SC*, 260:138; trans. M. L. Uhlfelder, *The Dialogues of Gregory the Great Book Two: Saint Benedict* (Indianapolis, 1967), 7.

76. Agobard, *De divisione imperii*, 2, ed. Van Acker, 247. Cf. Paschasius Radbertus, *Epitaphium*, 1.26, ed. Dümmler, 56.

77. Agobard, *Liber apologeticus* I, 2, ed. Van Acker, 310. On horns as symbolic not only of stubborness and pride but also of a cuckold, the "*cornutus adulter*," see the satirical treatise by G. Rogers, *The Horn Exalted, or Roome for Cuckolds* (London, 1661).

78. Agobard, *Liber apologeticus* I, 4, ed. Van Acker, 311.

79. Agobard, *Liber apologeticus* II, 8, ed. Van Acker, 316.

80. Agobard, *Liber apologeticus* II, 12, ed. Van Acker, 318. Cf. G. Koziol, "Truth and Its Consequences: Why Carolingianists Don't Speak of Myth," in *Myth in Early Northwest Europe*, ed. S. O. Glosecki (Tempe, Ariz., 2007), 71–103.

81. Cf. H. Vollrath, "Oral Modes of Perception in Eleventh-Century Chronicles," in *Vox intexta: Orality and Textuality in the Middle Ages*, ed. A. N. Doane and C. B. Pasternack (Madison, Wis., 1991), 107–11; P. E. Dutton, "Thunder and Hail over the Carolingian Countryside," in Dutton, *Mustache*, 180, 187.

82. Cf. Agobard, *De divinis sententiis contra iudicium Dei*, 5–6, ed. Van Acker, 34, 43; idem, *De grandine et tonitruis*, 16, ed. Van Acker, 15, alluding to Ps. 35:7.

83. For much of what follows, see Bührer-Thierry, "La reine adultère," 299–312; Ward, "Agobard of Lyons and Paschasius," 15–25; P. Stafford, *Queens, Concubines, and*

Dowagers: The King's Wife in the Early Middle Ages (Athens, Ga., 1983), 18–20, 93–94; M. Blöcker, "Frauenzauber—Zauberfrauen," *Zeitschrift für schweizerische Kirchengeschichte* 76 (1982): 29–32. Note that impotence was regarded as the possible result of sorcery; thus, Agobard's insinuations of Louis' impotence may also have been an indirect allusion to sorcery worked upon the emperor. See J. A. Brundage, *Law, Sex, and Christian Society in Medieval Europe* (Chicago, 1987), 144–45.

84. *Concilium Parisiense* (829), 69(2), ed. Werminghoff, 2(2):669; P. Riché, *Daily Life in the World of Charlemagne*, trans. J. A. McNamara (1973; Philadelphia, 1978), 183–84. See also P. Riché, "La magie a l'époque carolingienne," *Comptes Rendus des Séance de l'Académie des Inscriptions et Belles-lettres* 1 (1973): 129; Blöcker, "Frauenzauber—Zauberfrauen," 29–30.

85. Astronomer, *VH*, 44, ed. Tremp, 456. On Bernard, count of Septimania, whom Louis appointed to the office of palace chamberlain in 829, see E. S. Duckett, *Medieval Portraits from East and West* (Ann Arbor, Mich., 1972), 197–218; J. Wollasch, "Eine adlige Familie des frühen Mittelalters: Ihr Selbstverständnis und ihre Wirklichkeit," *AKG* 39 (1957): 150–88; J. Calmette, "La famille de Saint Guilhem," *Annales du Midi* 18 (1906): 145–65; and Chapter 2, n. 54. On the close relations that were expected between a queen and the chamberlain for the proper execution of their duties, see Hincmar of Reims, *De ordine palatii*, 22, ed. Gross and Schieffer, 3:72–74.

86. Astronomer, *VH*, 44, ed. Tremp, 456.

87. *AB*, s.a. 830, ed. Grat et al., 1–2. On this expedition, see T. Scharff, *Die Kämpfe der Herrscher und der Heiligen: Krieg und historischer Erinnerung in der Karolingerzeit* (Darmstadt, 2002), 122; J. M. H. Smith, *Province and Empire: Brittany and the Carolingians* (Cambridge, 1992), 77–79; A. Chédeville and H. Guillotel, *La Bretagne des saints et des rois Vᵉ–Xᵉ siècle* (Ouest, 1984), 223–29; Simson, *Jahrbücher*, 1:341–43; and nn. 183–84 below.

88. On Bernard's death (he was executed by Charles the Bald), see L. Malbos, "La capture de Bernard de Septimanie," *MA* 76 (1970): 5–13.

89. Paschasius Radbertus, *Epitaphium*, 2.9, ed. Dümmler, 71–72. Cf. *Epitaphium*, 2.17, ed. Dümmler, 88.

90. Paschasius Radbertus, *Epitaphium*, 2.8, ed. Dümmler, 69. See P. E. Dutton, "Whispering Secrets to a Dark Age," in Dutton, *Mustache*, 133.

91. Paschasius Radbertus, *Epitaphium*, 2.8, 2.9, ed. Dümmler, 69, 72.

92. Agobard, *Liber apologeticus* I, 4, ed. Van Acker, 311.

93. Paschasius Radbertus, *Epitaphium*, 2.10, ed. Dümmler, 73; trans. A. Cabaniss, *Charlemagne's Cousins: Contemporary Lives of Adalard and Wala* (Syracuse, N.Y., 1967), 168. For Paschasius's strident and repeated charges of adultery between Judith and Bernard, see *Epitaphium*, 2.7–9, ed. Dümmler, 67–73. On the alleged plot, see Calmette, *L'effondrement d'un empire*, 39–40; L. Weinrich, *Wala: Graf, Mönch und Rebell: Die Biographie eines Karolingers* (Lübeck, 1963), 72.

94. On Dhuoda, see M. Thiébaux, *Dhuoda, Handbook for Her Warrior Son, Liber Manualis* (Cambridge, 1998); C. Neel, *Handbook for William: A Carolingian Woman's*

Counsel for Her Son (Lincoln, Neb., 1991); with S. A. Stofferahn, "The Many Faces in Dhuoda's Mirror: The *Liber Manualis* and a Century of Scholarship," *Magistra* 4 (1998): 89–134.

95. This event reverberates through the sources: *AB*, s.a. 834, ed. Grat et al., 14; Thegan, *GH*, 52, ed. Tremp, 244; Astronomer, *VH*, 52, ed. Tremp, 496; Nithard, 1.5, ed. Lauer, 20, 22; compiled in Simson, *Jahrbücher*, 2:107–8. See R. Collins, "Pippin I and the Kingdom of Aquitaine," in *CH*, ed. Godman and Collins, 375; S. Wemple, *Women in Frankish Society: Marriage and the Cloister, 500 to 900* (Philadelphia, 1981), 95; Riché, "La magie," 131; Calmette, "La famille de Saint Guilhem," 155–56.

96. Cf. Calmette, *L'effondrement d'un empire*, 59.

97. Astronomer, *VH*, 52, ed. Tremp, 496, my emphasis.

98. Thegan, *GH*, 52, ed. Tremp, 244. This statement by Thegan, if it is to be believed, raises the question of why the wives of Lothar's counselors were in Chalon-sur-Saône at all.

99. In 831, Bernard's brother Aribert (Heribert) was blinded and his cousin Odo sent into exile (Astronomer, *VH*, 45, ed. Tremp, 460). In 834 at Chalon-sur-Saône, in addition to Gerberga's execution, three men among the prisoners were singled out for beheading: Bernard's brother Gozhelm, another possible relative Senila, and Louis the Pious's vassal Madalelm (*AB*, s.a. 834, ed. Grat et al., 14; Astronomer, *VH*, 52, ed. Tremp, 496; Nithard, 1.5, ed. Lauer, 20, 22). On these relatives, see Wollasch, "Eine adlige Familie," 181–85; Calmette, "La famille de Saint Guilhem," 145–65; C. B. Bouchard, *"Those of My Blood": Constructing Noble Families in Medieval Francia* (Philadelphia, 2001), 181–91. Wala knew Bernard's family well (*pace* Bouchard, *"Those of My Blood"*, 186); according to Paschasius, Wala held great respect for Bernard's father, William of Gellone, and had even been married to Bernard's sister (likely Rothlindis)! See Paschasius Radbertus, *Epitaphium*, 2.8, ed. Dümmler, 69; Calmette, "La famille de Saint Guilhem," 156–57; Weinrich, *Wala*, 18.

100. *Relatio Comp.*, ed. Booker, 17; Appendix, ll. 174–78.

101. On the riddle posed by Saint Paul's remark about the "mystery of iniquity" and the medieval attempts to uncover its meaning, see G. B. Ladner, *The Idea of Reform: Its Impact on Christian Thought and Action in the Age of the Fathers* (1959; New York, 1967), 278–79.

102. Isidore of Seville, *Sententiae*, 3.48.11, *PL* 83, col. 720B. Cf. Jonas of Orléans, *Concilium Parisiense* (829), 55, ed. Werminghoff, 2(2):651; idem, *De institutione regia*, 3, ed. Dubreucq, 196.

103. For a discussion of *scandalum* in the *Relatio*, see De Jong, "Power and Humility," 36–52; eadem, "What Was *Public*," 897–901; eadem, *"Sacrum palatium et ecclesia*: L'autorité religieuse royale sous les Carolingiens (790–840)," *AHSS* 58 (2003): 1265–69; J.-M. Moeglin, "Pénitence publique et amende honorable au Moyen Age," *Revue historique* 298 (1997): 234–35.

104. Ermoldus Nigellus, *In honorem Hludowici*, 1.396–401, ed. E. Faral, *Ermold le Noir: Poème sur Louis le Pieux et épitres au roi Pépin* (Paris, 1964), 34. Cf. also Ermol-

dus's many proud references to the esteemed reputation of the Franks: 1.66–69, 1.372–81, 2.654, 2.846–47, 2.1152, 3.1256–57, 3.1836–37.

105. Einhard, *VKM*, 16, ed. Holder-Egger, 20; trans. Dutton, *Courtier*, 26.

106. At the reform council of Paris in 829, the bishops advised Louis that he should be especially mindful of the counselors he would choose—that they should be men considered honorable inside the realm and held in high esteem by those outside it. The result of selecting such men would be a palace whose renown would inspire as much those within the realm as those without; *Concilium Parisiense* (829), 91(24), ed. Werminghoff, 2(2):678.

107. Agobard, *Liber apologeticus* I, 2, ed. Van Acker, 309–10; idem, *Liber apologeticus* II, 8, ed. Van Acker, 316. Cf. Astronomer, *VH*, 44, ed. Tremp, 456.

108. See R. Collins, "Charlemagne and His Critics, 814–829," in *La royauté et les élites dans l'Europe carolingienne*, ed. R. Le Jan (Lille, 1998), 193–211; J. L. Nelson, "Women at the Court of Charlemagne: A Case of Monstrous Regiment?" in eadem, *The Frankish World, 750–900* (1993; London, 1996), 223–42; Dutton, *The Politics of Dreaming*, 54, 279 n. 11; E. Boshof, *Ludwig der Fromme* (Darmstadt, 1996), 93–94.

109. Cf. Dutton, *The Politics of Dreaming*, 101–2.

110. *Relatio Comp.*, ed. Booker, 13; Appendix, ll. 52–54, 66–69.

111. Appleby, "Sight and Church Reform," 11–33, is helpful for the contextualization of this aspect of the bishops' *ministerium*.

112. Agobard, *Cartula*, ed. Van Acker, 323.

113. Benedict, *Regula*, 27.2–4, ed. Hanslik, 89–90.

114. Agobard, *Cartula*, ed. Van Acker, 324.

115. On the connotation of the term *venerabilis* in the context of penance, see F. Bussini, "L'intervention de l'évêque dans la réconciliation des pénitents, d'après les trois 'postulationes' d'un archidiacre romain du Ve–VIe siècle," *Revue des sciences religieuses, Université de Strasbourg* 42 (1968): 334. Cf. C. F. Du Cange, *Glossarium mediae et infimae latinitatis* (Niort, 1885), s.v. *venerabilis* (= *consentaneus*).

116. The use of the word *exaggeratio* here in the unusual sense of "severe reproach," rather than to connote its typical meaning of "exaggeration," may perhaps provide a clue about the author of the *Relatio*.

117. Agobard, *Cartula*, ed. Van Acker, 324.

118. Cf. *AB*, s.a. 833–834, ed. Grat et al., 10–11; Thegan, *GH*, 43–44, ed. Tremp, 230–32; Astronomer, *VH*, 49, ed. Tremp, 482; Charles the Bald, *Epistola Nicolao papae directa* (867), ed. W. Hartmann, MGH, *Conc.*, 4:240.

119. L. Halphen, "La pénitence de Louis le Pieux à Saint Médard de Soissons," in idem, *A travers l'histoire du Moyen Age* (1904; Paris, 1950), 58–66.

120. Louis the Pious, *Ep.* 19, ed. E. Dümmler, MGH, *Epist.*, 5:325–27, here alluding to Ps. 22:4–6. On this letter (and the response it elicited from Hilduin), see D. Luscombe, "Denis the Pseudo-Areopagite in the Middle Ages from Hilduin to Lorenzo Valla," in *Fälschungen im Mittelalter* (Hannover, 1988), 1:133–43; G. P. A. Brown, "Politics and Patronage at the Royal Abbey of Saint-Denis (814–98): The Rise of a Royal Patron Saint"

(Ph.D. diss., New College, Oxford University, 1989), 207–17, 283–329. Cf. the similar remarks in 836 by Abbot Lupus of Ferrières, *Ep.* 4, ed. P. K. Marshall, *Servati Lupi epistulae* (Leipzig, 1984), 9, that the "judgment of God can be seen as an absolutely certain sign of [his] mercy rather than [his] anger." On *eruditio* in the context of penance (relying upon 2 Tim. 3:16), see Ladner, *The Idea of Reform*, 313 n. 38. As Ladner notes (at 402–3), the concept of "linking progress, understood in a Christian spiritual sense, to *eruditio*," has its basis in Augustine, *De civitate Dei*, 10.14.

121. On this change in title and its evocation of King Solomon and the purity of his heart known to God (3 Kings 8:39), see H. Wolfram, *Intitulatio II: Lateinische Herrscher- und Fürstentitel im neunten und zehnten Jahrhundert* (Vienna, 1973), 64–65, 172; R. Schmidt, "Zur Geschichte des fränkischen Königsthrons," *FMSt* 2 (1968): 57–62.

122. Ermoldus Nigellus, *In honorem Hludowici*, 1.618–21, ed. Faral, 48–50. Cf. P. Godman, "Louis 'the Pious' and His Poets," *FMSt* 19 (1985): 263.

123. Ermoldus Nigellus, *In honorem Hludowici*, 2.990–93, ed. Faral, 78; trans. C. D. Fleiner, "In Honor of Louis the Pious, A Verse Biography by Ermoldus Nigellus (826): An Annotated Translation" (Ph.D. diss., University of Virginia, 1996), 168–69.

124. Cf. Thegan, *GH*, 20, ed. Tremp, 204; Paschasius Radbertus, *Epitaphium*, 2.2, 2.17, ed. Dümmler, 63, 88.

125. R. Bartlett, *Trial by Fire and Water* (Oxford, 1986), 153–66; Dutton, *Courtier*, xxv, xxx; idem, "Res Carolinae," *IJCT* 4 (1997): 107; P. J. Geary, "Humiliation of the Saints," in idem, *Living with the Dead in the Middle Ages* (Ithaca, N.Y., 1994), 109–10.

126. Cf. S. MacLean, "Ritual, Misunderstanding, and the Contest for Meaning: Representations of the Disrupted Royal Assembly at Frankfurt (873)," in *Representations of Power in Medieval Germany 800–1500*, ed. B. Weiler and S. MacLean (Turnhout, 2006), 97–119; D. Bachrach, "Confession in the *Regnum Francorum* (742–900): The Sources Revisited," *JEH* 54 (2003): 3–22; De Jong, "Monastic Prisoners," 293, 315–16. But note the comments of De Jong, "*Sacrum palatium et ecclesia*," 1266.

127. See P. E. Dutton and H. L. Kessler, *The Poetry and Paintings of the First Bible of Charles the Bald* (Ann Arbor, Mich., 1997), 82–84; G. Koziol, *Begging Pardon and Favor: Ritual and Political Order in Early Medieval France* (Ithaca, N.Y., 1992), 169; R. Deshman, "The Exalted Servant: The Ruler Theology of the Prayerbook of Charles the Bald," *Viator* 11 (1980): 385–417. In the late 820s, an anonymous biographer of Alcuin recalled that that holy man had once quoted this same line from scripture to express his great esteem for Louis' manifest humilty; *Vita Alcuini*, 15, ed. W. Arndt, MGH, *SS*, 15(1):193. Saint Benedict began his chapter on humility by quoting this scriptural passage; Benedict, *Regula*, 7.1, ed. Hanslik, 43.

128. On this event, see O. Guillot, "Autour de la pénitence publique de Louis le Pieux (822)," *Cahiers de l'Institut d'Anthropologie Juridique* 3 (1999): 281–313; Boshof, *Ludwig der Fromme*, 148–50; Koziol, *Begging Pardon and Favor*, 100–103; T. F. X. Noble, "Louis the Pious and His Piety Re-Reconsidered," *RBPH* 58 (1980): 312–13; Schieffer, "Von Mailand nach Canossa," 354–55; G. W. Marx, "Louis I (The Pious, or 'Le Débonnaire'): A Personal Reassessment of the Man Through the Events in His Reign" (Ph.D.

diss., New York University, 1971), 238–61; Halphen, *Charlemagne*, 172–74; Simson, *Jahrbücher*, 1:177–82.

129. Michelet, *Le Moyen Âge: Histoire de France*, ed. Mettra, 157. Cf. Halphen, *Charlemagne*, 173.

130. To my knowledge, Arquillière, *L'Augustinisme politique*, 177 n. 2, was the first to suggest that Louis' penance was sincere (although perhaps not "*hilaris*"). Cf. P. R. McKeon, "Archbishop Ebbo of Reims (816–835): A Study in the Carolingian Empire and Church," *Church History* 43 (1974): 441–42. I reference Herman Melville's *Benito Cereno* because the bishops' *Relatio* has traditionally been read with suspicion similar to that ultimately validated in Melville's masterful tale. See *The Writings of Herman Melville, The Northwestern-Newberry Edition*, vol. 9, *The Piazza Tales and Other Prose Pieces 1839–1860* (Evanston, Ill., 1987), 46–117; M. Rohrberger, "Point of View in 'Benito Cereno': Machinations and Deceptions," *College English* 27 (1966): 541–46.

131. Agobard, *Liber apologeticus* II, 9–11, ed. Van Acker, 316–18, alluding to 3 Kings 21:25–29. See also Stafford, *Queens, Concubines, and Dowagers*, 19.

132. On the way the correct external expression made the penitential ritual binding, effected its power, and served to shape the interior state of the penitent, see M. de Jong, *In Samuel's Image: Child Oblation in the Early Medieval West* (Leiden, 1996), 259–64; eadem, "Transformations of Penance," 189–90, 220; eadem, "What Was *Public*," 886–93; eadem, "Power and Humility," 41–42, 49–50; MacLean, "Ritual, Misunderstanding," 105–6; Koziol, *Begging Pardon and Favor*, 316–21. Cf. Jonas of Orléans, *De institutione laicali*, 1.17–20, *PL* 106, col. 154–66.

133. Astronomer, *VH*, 54, ed. Tremp, 504–6.

134. *ARF*, s.a. 822, ed. Pertz and Kurze, 158.

135. Cf. F. S. Paxton, *Christianizing Death: The Creation of a Ritual Process in Early Medieval Europe* (Ithaca, N.Y., 1990), on the adoption of penance shortly before death for the purpose of reconciliation with God. See also De Jong, "Transformations of Penance," 197–99; eadem, "What Was *Public*," 870.

136. See De Jong, "Power and Humility," 33, 44–45, 49; eadem, "What Was *Public*," 870, 874, 884–85; eadem, "Transformations of Penance," 185, 206–7; eadem, "Monastic Prisoners," 293, 304, 318. Cf. the corrective prescription of Charlemagne, in his programmatic capitulary for his *missi* in 802 (*Capitulare missorum generale*, 32, ed. A. Boretius, MGH, *Capit.*, 1:97), that one who murders his kinsman must undertake penance in the way directed by his bishop "without any misunderstanding" (*absque ulla ambiguitate*).

137. Geary, *Furta Sacra*, 40–41; J. M. H. Smith, "Old Saints, New Cults: Roman Relics in Carolingian Francia," in *Early Medieval Rome and the Christian West*, ed. J. M. H. Smith (Leiden, 2000), 323–27.

138. Agobard, *Cartula*, ed. Van Acker, 324.

139. Cf. *Relatio Comp.*, ed. Booker, 13–15; Appendix, ll. 52–54, 92–94, 115–18.

140. On the formal language for requesting a penance, see B. Poschmann, *Penance and the Anointing of the Sick*, trans. F. Courtney (1951; New York, 1964), 87.

141. For the metaphor of "spiritual doctors," see Benedict, *Regula*, 27.1, 2, ed. Hans-

lik, 89; and its contemporary use by Jonas of Orléans, *De institutione laicali*, 1.10, *PL* 106, col. 140; together with Ullmann, *The Carolingian Renaissance*, 64–65, 191; Jegen, "Jonas of Orléans," 237. See also F. S. Paxton, "Curing Bodies—Curing Souls: Hrabanus Maurus, Medical Education, and the Clergy in Ninth-Century Francia," *Journal of the History of Medicine and Allied Sciences* 50 (1995): 230–52; and Chapter 3, n. 30.

142. Like Louis' first public penance in 822, there is relatively little scholarship on this important event due to its laconic treatment within the sources. See Boshof, *Ludwig der Fromme*, 184; K. Bund, *Thronsturz und Herrscherabsetzung im Frühmittelalter* (Bonn, 1979), 403; Halphen, *Charlemagne*, 189–90; E. S. Duckett, *Carolingian Portraits: A Study in the Ninth Century* (Ann Arbor, Mich., 1962), 39–41; Simson, *Jahrbücher*, 1:352–54.

143. Paschasius Radbertus, *Epitaphium*, 2.10, ed. Dümmler, 73.

144. Paschasius Radbertus, *Vita sancti Adalhardi*, 51, *PL* 120, col. 1535A. Cf. Noble, "Louis the Pious and His Piety," 312 n. 66. Several contemporary annals give parallel reports that Louis undertook penance not spontaneously but only after having received counsel from his priests. See *ARF*, s.a. 822, ed. Pertz and Kurze, 158; *AF*, s.a. 822, ed. Pertz and Kurze, 22; *Annales Sithienses*, s.a. 822, ed. G. Waitz, MGH, *SS*, 13:38.

145. Astronomer, *VH*, 49, ed. Tremp, 480–82; trans. Dutton, *Carolingian Civ.*, 262.

146. Cf. T. Zotz, "Zusammenfassung I," in *Formen und Funktionen öffentlicher Kommunikation im Mittelalter*, ed. G. Althoff (Stuttgart, 2001), 466.

147. Cf. De Jong, "What Was *Public*," 865–66; eadem, "Power and Humility," 42, who has also questioned this interpretive tradition.

148. Cf. MacLean, "Ritual, Misunderstanding," esp. 105–10.

149. On comportment and the visible signs of the body—"the worshiper's physical posture, the tone of her words, and the nature of her expression"—as the primary indicators for both true and false devotion, see R. Targoff, "The Performance of Prayer: Sincerity and Theatricality in Early Modern England," *Representations* 60 (1997): 49–69.

150. Benedict, *Regula*, 2.25, ed. Hanslik, 25.

151. Smaragdus, *Expositio in regulam S. Benedicti*, 2.25, ed. Spannagel and Engelbert, 8:72.

152. *Capitula de missis instruendis* (829), ed. A. Boretius and V. Krause, MGH, *Capit.*, 2:8. Louis' son Charles the Bald would also quote this Benedictine correlation with approval in a letter of 872 to Pope Hadrian II (*PL* 124, col. 884C). For the imprint that the Benedictine code of behavior left upon the Carolingian elite, see V. L. Garver, "The Influence of Monastic Ideals upon Carolingian Conceptions of Childhood," in *Childhood in the Middle Ages and the Renaissance: The Results of a Paradigm Shift in the History of Mentality*, ed. A. Classen (Berlin, 2005), 67–85; De Jong, *In Samuel's Image*, 245–52; and upon Louis the Pious in particular, T. F. X. Noble, "The Monastic Ideal as a Model for Empire: The Case of Louis the Pious," *RB* 86 (1976): 235–50; idem, "Louis the Pious and His Piety," 297–316; R. Deshman, "*Benedictus Monarcha et Monachus:* Early Medieval Ruler Theology and the Anglo-Saxon Reform," *FMSt* 22 (1988): 231, 239–40.

153. Paschasius Radbertus, *Epitaphium*, 2.1, ed. Dümmler, 61.

154. On Wala's "*scedula*," and the degree to which its contents were reproduced by

Paschasius in his *Epitaphium Arsenii*, see D. Ganz, "The *Epitaphium Arsenii* and Opposition to Louis the Pious" in *CH*, ed. Godman and Collins, 545–46; Weinrich, *Wala*, 62–63; F. L. Ganshof, "Am Vorabend der ersten Krise der Regierung Ludwigs des Frommen: Die Jahre 828 und 829," *FMSt* 6 (1972): 44.

155. R. Faulhaber, *Der Reichseinheitsgedanke in der Literatur der Karolingerzeit bis zum Vertrag von Verdun* (Berlin, 1931), 59 n. 26. Simson, *Jahrbücher*, 2:70, observed that the list included sins that fell within the general categories of "*sacrilegium, homicidium, et periurium.*" In the revised and augmented second edition of Arquillière, *L'Augustinisme politique*, 173, it was still claimed that Louis' crimes listed in the indictment, "se suivent sans aucun ordre logique et plusieurs font double emploi." Cf. C. de Clercq, "La législation religieuse franque depuis l'avènement de Louis le Pieux jusqu'aux fausses décrétales," *Revue de droit canonique* 5 (1955): 271, "huit articles assez confus."

156. See Dutton, *The Politics of Dreaming*, 67–80, 93–100; and for the possible contents of Gabriel's *capitula*, 97, 219–22.

157. Dutton, *The Politics of Dreaming*, 111, for the possibility of the report of the poor woman's dream having reached Louis; 94, on Einhard's belief that "of the things that [the blind man's account of Gabriel's *capitula*] commanded or advised [Louis] to do, he bothered to accomplish few." Louis the German was later said (in 874) to have had a dream in which he saw his father suffering torments in hell because he had failed to comply with Gabriel's instructions as delivered by Einhard; see Dutton, *The Politics of Dreaming*, 219–22; and the Epilogue.

158. Walahfrid Strabo, *Ad eandem de quodam somnio*, ed. Dümmler, MGH, *PLAC*, 2:379–80, no. 24; German trans. K. Langosch, *Lyrische Anthologie des lateinischen Mittelalters* (Darmstadt, 1968), 108–11. See Dutton, *The Politics of Dreaming*, 104–7; and Chapter 6.

159. Agobard, *Cartula*, ed. Van Acker, 324.

160. Cf. K. F. Morrison, "Interpreting the Fragment," in *Hermeneutics and Medieval Culture*, ed. P. J. Gallacher and H. Damico (New York, 1989), 27–37.

161. H. H. Anton, *Fürstenspiegel und Herrscherethos in der Karolingerzeit* (Bonn, 1968), 86 n. 50, believed that the bishops' indictment was like any other *Fürstenspiegel*, a mirror in which the noble onlooker could see "*quid agere—quid cavere debeat.*" Cf. De Jong, "Power and Humility," 41. For the genre of the *Fürstenspiegel* in general, see Anton, *Fürstenspiegel und Herrscherethos*; Wallace-Hadrill, "The 'Via Regia' of the Carolingian Age," 181–200; L. K. Born, "The *specula principis* of the Carolingian Renaissance," *RBPH* 12 (1933): 583–612.

162. Louis had been the recipient of a *Fürstenspiegel* between 812 and 815, when he was in his late thirties, one written by Smaragdus of Saint-Mihiel, *Via regia*, PL 102, col. 933–70; M. L. W. Laistner, "The Date and the Recipient of Smaragdus' *Via Regia*," *Speculum* 3 (1928): 392–97. As we have seen, Louis was well acquainted with critical dream texts and Wala's *scedula*, both of which were brought to his attention in the late 820s.

163. Agobard, *De privilegio apostolicae sedis*, 6, ed. Van Acker, 305–6; quoting Gregory the Great, *Ep.* 1.41; trans. Halphen, *Charlemagne*, 197.

164. Cf. Wallace-Hadrill, "The 'Via Regia' of the Carolingian Age," 181–200. As O. D. Watkins, *A History of Penance* (London, 1920), 1:366, 408, observed, Saint Jerome (*Ep.* 77) characterized the act of penance as that which rescues lost souls cast adrift by their "shipwreck" (*naufragium*).

165. On Louis' coronation, see Boshof, *Ludwig der Fromme*, 87–90; J. L. Nelson, "The Lord's Anointed and the People's Choice: Carolingian Royal Ritual," in eadem, *The Frankish World, 750–900* (1987; London, 1996), 113–14.

166. For this "Säuberungsaktion," see n. 108 above.

167. For Bernard's revolt, capture, and punishment, see G. Bührer-Thierry, "'Just Anger' or 'Vengeful Anger'? The Punishment of Blinding in the Early Medieval West," in *Anger's Past: The Social Uses of an Emotion in the Middle Ages*, ed. B. H. Rosenwein (Ithaca, N.Y., 1998), 81–91; P. Depreux, "Das Königtum Bernhards von Italien und sein Verhältnis zum Kaisertum," *Quellen und Forschungen aus Italienischen Archiven und Bibliotheken* 72 (1992): 1–25; K. F. Werner, "*Hludovicus Augustus:* Gouverner l'empire chrétien—Idées et réalités," in *CH*, ed. Godman and Collins, 37–50; J. Jarnut, "Kaiser Ludwig der Fromme und König Bernhard von Italien: Der Versuch einer Rehabilitierung," *SM* 3rd ser. 30 (1989): 637–48; T. F. X. Noble, "The Revolt of King Bernard of Italy in 817: Its Causes and Consequences," *SM* 3rd ser. 15 (1974): 315–26. Cf. the punishment of blinding for killing one's relatives, dictated by Charlemagne to his *missi*, in the *Capitulare missorum generale* (802), 37, ed. A. Boretius, MGH, *Capit.*, 1:98.

168. At an ecclesiastical council in 818–819, Louis commanded that bishops and other orders of the church should observe and teach that the ordeal of the cross was to be forbidden, "lest that [symbol], which is glorified by the Passion of Christ, be held in contempt by the temerity of anyone." *Capitulare ecclesiasticum* (818–819), 27, ed. A. Boretius, MGH, *Capit.*, 1:279. See F. L. Ganshof, *Frankish Institutions Under Charlemagne*, trans. B. Lyon and M. Lyon (Providence, R.I., 1968), 88–89; idem, "L'épreuve de la croix' dans le droit de la monarchie franque," in *Studi in onore di Alberto Pincherle* (Rome, 1967), 217–31; Boshof, *Erzbischof Agobard*, 46.

169. In the record of the repartition of territories among his sons in 831 (*Regni divisio*, 10, ed. A. Boretius and V. Krause, MGH, *Capit.*, 2:23), itself largely derivative of the *Divisio regnorum* of Charlemagne in 806 (14, ed. A. Boretius, MGH, *Capit.*, 1:129), Louis proclaimed that "in order to settle the doubtful question [in dispute], the will of God and the truth of the matter shall be sought by the *vexillum crucis*." This is a word for word repetition of chapter 14 from the record of Charlemagne's partition of the realm in 806, except that the new expression "*vexillum crucis*" was substituted in place of "*iudicium crucis.*" It is uncertain what this slight change means: Did Louis reinstitute the judgment of the cross in 831, or was this simply an accidental—and thus meaningless—"quasi-literal reprise" of a chapter from Charlemagne's edict of 806, as Ganshof, "L'épreuve de la croix'," 230 n. 55, believed? Should "*vexillum crucis*" simply be translated as "sign of the cross," or should it be rendered more literally as "banner of the cross?" And if it was the latter, does this new terminology consequently reflect a careful change introduced by Louis in the procedure's execution—of a banner bearing a cross (or fragment of the True

Cross) now used somehow in lieu of the extension of one's arms for the divining of truth? For the latter view, see E. J. Goldberg, "'More Devoted to the Equipment of Battle than the Splendor of Banquets': Frontier Kingship, Martial Ritual, and Early Knighthood at the Court of Louis the German," *Viator* 30 (1999): 62 n. 89; H. Fischer, "Die offene Kreuzhaltung im Rechtsritual," in *Festschrift Artur Steinwenter* (Graz, 1958), 3:52 n. 115. See also C. Erdmann, *The Origin of the Idea of Crusade*, trans. M. W. Baldwin and W. Goffart (1935; Princeton, N.J., 1977), 35–39.

170. In his exhaustive article on the judgment of the cross, Ganshof, "L''épreuve de la croix' dans le droit," 217–31, overlooked the reference in the bishops' account of 833 to Louis allegedly having used this form of the ordeal (an oversight which helps to account for his certainty [at 230 n. 55] that Louis' decree in 831 was nothing more than a copyist's error). On the peculiar reception of Louis' ban of the *iudicium crucis*, see T. Head, "Saints, Heretics, and Fire: Finding Meaning through the Ordeal," in *Monks and Nuns, Saints and Outcasts: Religion in Medieval Society*, ed. S. Farmer and B. H. Rosenwein (Ithaca, N.Y., 2000), 227.

171. See H. Houben, "*Visio cuiusdam pauperculae mulieris:* Überlieferung und Herkunft eines frühmittelalterlichen Visionstextes (mit Neuedition)," *Zeitschrift für die Geschichte des Oberrheins* 124 (1976): 31–42 (text composed ca. 820s); Andreas of Bergamo (after 877), *Historia*, 6, ed. G. Waitz, MGH, *SRL*, 225. Cf. Dutton, *The Politics of Dreaming*, 72–73; Werner, "*Hludovicus Augustus*: Gouverner l'empire chrétien," 43; Jarnut, "Kaiser Ludwig der Fromme," 638, 643–44, 648.

172. For the standard narrative of Bernard's revolt, see Noble, "The Revolt of King Bernard," 315–26; R. McKitterick, *History and Its Audiences* (Cambridge, 2000), 4–26, esp. 16 n. 17. On the *Ordinatio imperii*, see Ganshof, "Some Observations," 273–88; P. R. McKeon, "817: Une année désastreuse et presque fatale pour les Carolingiens," *MA* 84 (1978): 5–12.

173. Cf. the use of the formula "*illicita potestas*" in three charters recording endowments made by Louis: *pro monasterio Cormaricensi* (816), *PL* 104, col. 1041D; *pro monasterio Solemniacensi* (817), *PL* 104, col. 1065C; *pro Turonensi s. Martini ecclesia* (817), *PL* 104, col. 1068B. See T. Sickel, *Regesten der Urkunden der ersten Karolinger (751–840)* (Vienna, 1867), 2:117, no. 111; 2:113, no. 97.

174. The phrase "*poena peccati*" is often translated as punishment *for* sin, which is incorrect. As Gregory explained, and as the bishops in 833 were well aware, sin itself is to be understood as dual in nature, as at once both an act and a punishment. Cf. Gregory the Great, *Homiliae in Hiezechihelem prophetam*, 1.11.24, ed. Adriaen, 142:179–81, trans. T. Gray, *The Homilies of St. Gregory the Great on the Book of the Prophet Ezekiel* (Etna, Calif., 1990), 137–38, on the meaning of the "punishment of sin," using the sin of perjury as part of his example: "Therefore theft which proceed[s] from covetousness and [brings] forth perjury [is] both a sin and a punishment of sin for the preceding guilt, and a sin and a cause of sin for the subsequent guilt, because born of one it [gives] birth to the other." See also Paschasius Radbertus, *Epitaphium*, 2.6, ed. Dümmler, 67.

175. For the generative, concatenate nature of sin—which usually begins with

one of the seven or eight cardinal sins (this number changes during the Middle Ages)—see A. L. Kellogg, "An Augustinian Interpretation of Chaucer's Pardoner," *Speculum* 26 (1951): 465–68; S. Wenzel, "The Seven Deadly Sins: Some Problems of Research," *Speculum* 43 (1968): 4–5. Following Alcuin, *De virtutibus et vitiis, PL* 101, col. 613–38, many ninth-century authors acknowledged the eight cardinal sins as subjects essential to both confession and penance; cf. the bishops' remarks at the councils in 813 at Reims, cap. 13, and Châlon-sur-Saône, cap. 32, ed. A. Werminghoff, MGH, *Conc.*, 2(1):255, 279; Theodulf of Orléans, *Capitulare* I (798–817/18), 31, ed. Brommer, 1:128–29; Jonas of Orléans, *De institutione laicali*, 3.6, *PL* 106, col. 247A–B; Halitgar of Cambrai, *De vitiis et virtutibus et de ordine poenitentium*, 1, *PL* 105, col. 657–70; Hrabanus Maurus, *De virtutibus et vitiis*, ed. W. Lazius, *Fragmenta quaedam Caroli Magni imp. rom. aliorumque incerti nominis de veteris ecclesiae ritibus ac ceremoniis* (Antwerp, 1560).

176. Nithard, 1.2, ed. Lauer, 6–8. See Depreux, *Prosopographie*, 417, s.v. "Bermond."

177. In the late 820s, within a letter of complaint to Count Matfrid of Orléans on the many injustices at the imperial palace and Matfrid's unwitting complicity in them, Agobard would lionize Count Bertmund as a model courtier, as one who had appointed an excellent deputy reknowned for his love of God, equity, and justice. In boasting of such a virtuous Lyonnais deputy, is Agobard indirectly alluding to himself? See Agobard, *De iniusticiis (ad Matfredum)*, ed. Van Acker, 225–27; trans. W. L. North, www.fordham. edu/halsall/source/agobard2.html [accessed 8 August 2008].

178. *Chronicon Moissiacense*, s.a. 817 (noting Bernard's "tyranny"), ed. G. H. Pertz, MGH, *SS*, 1:312–13; *ARF*, s.a. 818 (in the entry for 817, Bernard's "tyranny" is mentioned), ed. Pertz and Kurze, 148; Astronomer, *VH*, 30, 35, ed. Tremp, 384, 406. But for a critical account, see Houben, "*Visio cuiusdam pauperculae mulieris*," 41–42.

179. Thegan, *GH*, 23, ed. Tremp, 212. Cf. *GH*, 22, ". . . his counselors blinded Bernard as well as [Bernard's] instigators . . ." See also Astronomer, *VH*, 35, ed. Tremp, 406. Tremp (213 n. 144) believes Thegan's remarks to be an indirect criticism of Louis, while Jarnut, "Kaiser Ludwig der Fromme," 647, thinks that Thegan was actually mitigating Louis' guilt by having his counselors bear the brunt of the blame.

180. At the Paris reform council in 829, the bishops had specifically warned against the illegitimate exercise of vengeance (*vindicta*): *Concilium Parisiense* (829), 84(17), ed. Werminghoff, 2(2): 675–76. On royal *indignatio*, cf. *Concilium Moguntinum* (847), 6, ed. A. Boretius and V. Krause, MGH, *Capit.*, 2:177.

181. See Jarnut, "Kaiser Ludwig der Fromme," 648.

182. Unaware of the genealogical logic governing the list of Louis' sins, Simson, *Jahrbücher*, 1:389 n. 8, 2:70 n. 6 was uncertain how to explain this part of the text.

183. On this expedition, and the resistance it met with the populace, cf. *AB*, s.a. 830, ed. Grat et al., 1–2. The annalist conspicuously notes that "it was Bernard the Chamberlain [Bernard of Septimania] who was the strongest advocate of this [expedition]." See n. 87 above.

184. The only other source which provides details about this event—noting that the

placitum was held in Rennes—are the *Annales Mettenses priores*, s.a. 830, ed. B. Simson, MGH, *SRG*, 10:95–97.

185. *Relatio Comp.*, ed. Booker, 17, "*pro . . . regnique nutantis recuperatione. . . .*" Cf. the use of this same metaphor by Agobard, *Cartula*, ed. Van Acker, 323, "*quod regnum, quia iam diu nutabat. . . .*"

186. *Relatio Comp.*, ed. Booker, 17; Appendix, ll. 174–84. On this tribunal, see *AB*, s.a. 830–831, ed. Grat et al., 1–4; *Annales Mettenses priores*, s.a. 830, ed. Simson, 95–97.

187. The reference to the "purgation of the woman" is usually understood to mean the purgation offered by Queen Judith to absolve herself of the charges of adultery leveled by the rebellion. Cf. *AB*, s.a. 831, ed. Grat et al., 4. On this episode, see Bührer-Thierry, "La reine adultère," 299–312. Due to a misprint in Pithou's *editio princeps* of the text, which gives the reading "*mulierum*" (*Relatio Comp.*, ed. Booker, 18), scholars have long attempted to explain what the bishops meant by speaking about Judith's purgation in the plural; cf. Simson, *Jahrbücher*, 2:72 n. 3.

188. *Relatio Comp.*, ed. Booker, 18; Appendix, ll. 193–94.

189. *Relatio Comp.*, ed. Booker, 18; Appendix, ll. 196–97. On the campaigns, see *AB*, s.a. 832–833, ed. Grat et al., 6–8.

190. *Relatio Comp.*, ed. Booker, 18; Appendix, ll. 205–7. For this new division, see the *Regni divisio* (831), ed. Boretius and Krause, 2:20–24.

191. According to Simson, *Jahrbücher*, 2:45, this oath swearing took place at Worms in June 833.

192. *Relatio Comp.*, ed. Booker, 18–19; Appendix, ll. 216–17. Cf. ll. 75–76.

193. *Relatio Comp.*, ed. Booker, 19; Appendix, ll. 219–21. Cf. the similar remarks about the miracle on the Rotfeld by Agobard, *Liber apologeticus* II, 8, ed. Van Acker, 315.

194. On the particularly Gregorian valence of such compunction during penance, see C. Straw, *Gregory the Great: Perfection in Imperfection* (Berkeley, Calif., 1988), 218–35.

195. Benedict, *Regula*, 58.17–29, ed. Hanslik, 149–51.

196. De Jong, "Power and Humility," 32, 43–45. See also De Jong, "Transformations of Penance," 203–8, 217–20; eadem, "What Was *Public*," 871, 892.

197. Note that the Benedictine Rule gives repeated warnings of the dire consequences an abbot must face if he is negligent in caring for the material and spiritual health of his brethren; see Benedict, *Regula*, 2, 3, 31, 36, 55, 63, 64, 65.

198. Benedict, *Regula*, 27.8–9, ed. Hanslik, 91.

199. Agobard, *Cartula*, ed. Van Acker, 324. Van Acker neglects to note that Louis' request reflects not only Luke 15:5, but more specifically its invocation in the *Regula* of Benedict.

200. Pope Leo I, *Ep.* 167 (*ad Rusticum Narbonensem episcopum*), *PL* 54, col. 1206C–7A (= *Collectio Dionysio-Hadriana*, 24, *PL* 67, col. 290A).

201. *Relatio Comp.*, ed. Booker, 19; Appendix, ll. 234–35.

202. K. Leyser, "Early Medieval Canon Law and the Beginnings of Knighthood,"

in idem, *Communications and Power in Medieval Europe: The Carolingian and Ottonian Centuries* (1984; London, 1994), 64.

203. L. Levillain, review of H.-X. Arquillière, *L'Augustinisme politique* (Paris, 1934), in *BEC* 96 (1935–36): 389, citing Justinian's *Digest*, 3.2.2.2, ed. T. Mommsen and P. Krueger, *Corpus Iuris Civilis* (Berlin, 1954), 1:66, "*Sed et si eum exauctoraverit, id est insignia militaria detraxerit, inter infames efficit.*"

204. De Jong, "Power and Humility," 50–51; eadem, *In Samuel's Image*, 261–62.

205. Ullmann, *The Carolingian Renaissance*, 66–67; Peters, *The Shadow King*, 59–60; R. Le Jan, "Frankish Giving of Arms and Rituals of Power: Continuity and Change in the Carolingian Period," in *Rituals of Power: From Late Antiquity to the Early Middle Ages*, ed. F. Theuws and J. L. Nelson (Leiden, 2000), 299–300.

206. That Boretius and Krause, in their edition of 1897 for the MGH, give no indication that the statement is a quotation may partially account for the lack of commentary. However, several scholars have alluded to the statement as a "canon" or "decretal," suggesting that they understood its source to be self-evident and thus unworthy of elaboration or further comment; cf. Sismondi, *Histoire des français* (Paris, 1821), 3:30; J. C. Prichard, *The Life and Times of Hincmar, Archbishop of Rheims* (Oxford, 1849), 54; E. Dümmler, *Geschichte des ostfränkischen Reiches* (Leipzig, 1862), 1:85 n. 1. Leyser, "Early Medieval Canon Law," 61, recognized it to be a decretal by Leo.

207. Leyser, "Early Medieval Canon Law," 64.

208. On such anxiety on the part of the bishops, see De Jong, "Power and Humility," 44, 51.

209. De Jong, "*Sacrum palatium et ecclesia*," 1245–46, gives a good overview of this tradition of a "théocratie épiscopale" in the historiography, to which I would add the long-standing editorial preference for the erroneous reading of "*super imperio*" in the bishops' account; see n. 63 above. See also De Jong, "Power and Humility," 41, 49–51; eadem, "Transformations of Penance," 189.

210. Pope Gregory IV, *Ep.* 17, ed. Dümmler, 5:228–32; and n. 22 above.

211. Paschasius Radbertus, *Epitaphium*, 2.16, ed. Dümmler, 84. For the claim of the bishops having "ancient canons," see Astronomer, *VH*, 48, ed. Tremp, 474.

212. Astronomer, *VH*, 48, ed. Tremp, 474.

213. Paschasius Radbertus, *Epitaphium*, 2.16, ed. Dümmler, 84. J. Fried, *Donation of Constantine and Constitutum Constantini* (Berlin, 2007), 98–102, sees this moment as the first appearance of a "first draft" of the Pseudo-Isidorian decretals.

214. On this episode, see W. Ohr, "Zwei Fragen zur älteren Papstgeschichte," *Zeitschrift für Kirchengeschichte* 24 (1903): 333–52 (Ohr believed Agobard wrote the papal letter in Gregory's name); J. Fried, "Ludwig der Fromme, das Papsttum und die fränkische Kirche," in *CH*, ed. Godman and Collins, 267–73; idem, *Donation of Constantine*, 98–102.

215. Leyser, "Early Medieval Canon Law," 64.

216. Astronomer, *VH*, 46, ed. Tremp, 466. On the consequences of penance, see

De Jong, "What Was *Public*," 874, 884–85; eadem, "Monastic Prisoners," 304. See also Bachrach, "Confession in the *Regnum Francorum*," 9–10.

217. Wallace-Hadrill, "The 'Via Regia' of the Carolingian Age," 192.

218. As would be the case with the canon lawyers seeking to defend Henry IV in 1085; see Vollrath, "Oral Modes of Perception," 109–10.

219. See Halitgar of Cambrai, *De vitiis et virtutibus et de ordine poenitentium*, 3.7, *PL* 105, col. 678C. Hrabanus Maurus knew this decretal; see his *Liber ad Otgarium*, 40, *PL* 112, col. 1424C. It is also found in the *Collectio Dionysio-Hadriana*, 24, *PL* 67, col. 290A; and in the capitulary collection of Benedictus Levita, 2.338, *PL* 97, col. 785A. On Halitgar and his compilation, see R. McKitterick, *The Frankish Church and the Carolingian Reforms, 789–895* (London, 1977), 170–72; S. Hamilton, *The Practice of Penance, 900–1050* (Woodbridge, 2001), 46–47; R. Meens, "The Frequency and Nature of Early Medieval Penance," in *Handling Sin: Confession in the Middle Ages*, ed. P. Biller and A. J. Minnis (York, 1998), 40–47, and for manuscripts containing his work, 55–61; C. van Rhijn and M. Saan, "Correcting Sinners, Correcting Texts: A Context for the *Paenitentiale pseudo-Theodori*," *EME* 14 (2006): 30, 33–34, 38–39. On the *Collectio Dionysio-Hadriana* and the collection of Benedictus Levita, see L. Kéry, *Canonical Collections of the Early Middle Ages (ca. 400–1140): A Bibliographical Guide to the Manuscripts and Literature* (Washington, D.C., 1999), 13–20, 117–22.

220. Ebbo, *Ep. ad Halitgarium*, ed. E. Dümmler, MGH, *Epist.*, 5:617; trans. P. J. Payer, *Sex and the Penitentials: The Development of a Sexual Code, 550–1150* (Toronto, 1984), 181 n. 61. On the expectation in the ninth century that most priests should know how to use a penitential, see A. Angenendt et al., "Counting Piety in the Early and High Middle Ages," in *Ordering Medieval Society: Perspectives on Intellectual and Practical Modes of Shaping Social Relations*, ed. B. Jussen, trans. P. Selwyn (Philadelphia, 2001), 31–32; Y. Hen, "Knowledge of Canon Law Among Rural Priests: The Evidence of Two Carolingian Manuscripts from Around 800," *JTS* 50 (1999): 117–34.

221. Whether Ebbo himself was the author of the bishops' *Relatio* is unknown, but it is certain that he was a leading participant in the affair and likely knew about the "irrevocable" consequences of penance from (among other sources) Halitgar's collection of ancient canons. For Ebbo's letter to Halitgar requesting the compilation, together with Halitgar's reply, see MGH, *Epist.*, 5:616–17. In an ironic twist, Halitgar's penitential would later play a significant role in the discussion regarding the legitimacy of the deposition and reinstallation of Ebbo himself; see R. Kottje, *Die Bußbücher Halitgars von Cambrai und des Hrabanus Maurus: Ihre Überlieferung und ihre Quellen* (Berlin, 1980), 86–90, 173–74, 228–30, 233–37; and Chapter 5.

222. Ebbo, *Apologeticus* 1, ed. Werminghoff, 799; trans. De Jong, "What Was *Public*," 885. Ironically, Ebbo himself had been charged with such "perjury"; cf. Thegan, *GH*, 44, ed. Tremp, 236 and 237 n. 245. On the negative connotation of the term "*modernum*," see the Introduction, n. 32.

223. On the idealized "golden age" of the Church Fathers projected and deployed

by Carolingian bishops, see De Jong, "Transformations of Penance," 185–224; M. E. Hönicke Moore, "Carolingian Bishops and Christian Antiquity: Distance from the Past, Canon-Formation, and Imperial Power," in *Learned Antiquity: Scholarship and Society in the Near-East, the Greco-Roman World, and the Early Medieval West*, ed. A. A. MacDonald et al. (Leuven, 2003), 175–84; Appleby, "Sight and Church Reform," 26–33; Halphen, *Charlemagne*, 188–92; and Chapter 6.

224. Cf. W. Otten, "The Texture of Tradition: The Role of the Church Fathers in Carolingian Theology," in *The Reception of the Church Fathers in the West: From the Carolingians to the Maurists*, ed. I. Backus (Leiden, 1997), 1:3–50. For Carolingian interest in Gregory, see Judic, "La tradition de Grégoire le Grand," 17–57.

225. On the symbolic value of the number eight in the early Middle Ages, see W. Haubrichs, *Ordo als Form: Strukturstudien zur Zahlenkomposition bei Otfrid von Weissenburg und in karolingischer Literatur* (Tübingen, 1969), 188–90; *Lexikon der mittelalterlichen Zahlenbedeutungen*, ed. H. Meyer and R. Suntrup (Munich, 1987), 565–80. Cf. the remarks by the ecclesiastics Cathulf and Sedulius Scottus on the "eight pillars" of good government: Cathulf, *Ep. ad Carolem* (c. 775), ed. E. Dümmler, MGH, *Epist.*, 4:503; Sedulius Scottus, *De rectoribus Christianis*, 10, ed. S. Hellmann, *Sedulius Scottus* (Munich, 1906), 49–50.

226. See M. Moore, "The King's New Clothes: Royal and Episcopal Regalia in the Frankish Empire," in *Robes of Honor: The Medieval World of Investiture*, ed. S. Gordon (New York, 2001), 109–10. On Louis' royal robe of state, see P. E. Dutton, "Evidence That Dubthach's Priscian Codex Once Belonged to Eriugena," in *From Athens to Chartres: Neoplatonism and Medieval Thought*, ed. H. J. Westra (Leiden, 1992), 18–20. On the symbolism of the sword-belt (*cingulum militiae*) and its removal, see Le Jan, "Frankish Giving of Arms," 299–300; Leyser, "Early Medieval Canon Law." Cf. S. Airlie, "Narratives of Triumph and Rituals of Submission: Charlemagne's Mastering of Bavaria," *TRHS* 6th ser. 9 (1999): 115, 118. See also the comments on clothing and documentation in Benedict, *Regula*, 58.26–29, ed. Hanslik, 151.

227. *Relatio Comp.*, ed. Booker, 19; Appendix, ll. 240–44.

CHAPTER 5. FORGOTTEN MEMORIES

Epigraphs: C. Van Doren, *The Secret History of the American Revolution* (New York, 1941), 143; Gottschalk of Orbais, *De "in" praepositione explanatio*, ed. C. Lambot, *Oeuvres théologiques et grammaticales de Godescalc d'Orbais* (Louvain, 1945), 375.

1. In addition to the polemics on Ebbo's legitimacy, the late ninth-century works by Ado of Vienne and Andreas of Bergamo touch on the events of 833 in ways that deserve greater scrutiny. See Ado of Vienne, *Chronicon*, ed. G. H. Pertz, MGH, *SS*, 2:321; and Andreas of Bergamo, *Historia*, 7, ed. G. Waitz, MGH, *SRL*, 225–26, who depicts a charged confrontation, using direct speech, between Louis the Pious and Bishop Angilbert of

Milan over the emperor's rough treatment of Lothar. On Andreas's account, see R. Balza-retti, "Spoken Narratives in Ninth-Century Milanese Court Records," in *Narrative and History in the Early Medieval West*, ed. E. M. Tyler and R. Balzaretti (Turnhout, 2006), 11–37. On Ado, see Chapter 2, n. 3.

2. The details of Ebbo's capture remain hazy. Several ninth-century sources claim that, after hearing of Louis' liberation at Saint-Denis in March 834, Ebbo fled the mon-astery of Saint-Bâle near Reims by river (because he was afflicted with gout) and sailed to Paris. It was there that two of Louis' men, Rothad of Soissons and Erchanrad of Paris, found him and delivered him to the emperor. See Ebbo, *Apologeticus* 1, ed. Werminghoff, 795; idem, *Apologeticus* 2, ed. Werminghoff, 801; the so-called *Narratio clericorum Remen-sium* (written ca. 860s), ed. A. Werminghoff, MGH, *Conc.*, 2(2):807; Charles the Bald, *Epistola Nicolao papae directa* (867), ed. W. Hartmann, MGH, *Conc.*, 4:240; Synod of Troyes (867), ed. W. Hartmann, MGH, *Conc.*, 4:233. In the middle of the tenth century, Flodoard of Reims would claim that Ebbo had taken flight via the rivers with a band of Northmen, carrying with him the treasures of his church; Flodoard, *Historia Remensis ecclesiae*, 2.20, ed. M. Stratmann, MGH, *SS*, 36:184. H. Schrörs, *Hinkmar Erzbischof von Reims* (Freiburg, 1884), 28–29 n. 11, notes that the two scenarios are not mutually exclu-sive. Recall that Ebbo had established relations with the Northmen through his earlier proselytizing mission in Scandinavia, sanctioned by Louis the Pious in 822; on this mis-sion, see Chapter 2, n. 129.

3. For a survey of Ebbo's career, see P. R. McKeon, "Archbishop Ebbo of Reims (816–835): A Study in the Carolingian Empire and Church," *Church History* 43 (1974): 437–47; H. Goetting, *Das Bistum Hildesheim: Die Hildesheimer Bischöfe von 815–1221* (Berlin, 1984), 56–84; Depreux, *Prosopographie*, 169–74, no. 78; G. F. S. Schweinsberg, "Reims in merowingischer Zeit: Stadt, Civitas, Bistum" (Ph.D. diss., Rheinischen Friedrich-Wilhelms-Universität, Bonn, 1971), 181–92. For Ebbo's extant texts, see *Clavis AG*, 1:27–33.

4. *AB*, s.a. 833, ed. Grat et al., 10.

5. In a failed expedition against Lothar's forces in 834, several of Louis' men, includ-ing Counts Odo of Orléans and William of Blois, Abbot Theoto of Saint-Martin, and an otherwise unknown figure named Fulbert, were slain. See *AB*, s.a. 834, ed. Grat et al., 13; Astronomer, *VH*, 52, ed. Tremp, 492–94; Nithard, 1.5, ed. Lauer, 20.

6. This is the explanation given by the *Narratio clericorum Remensium*, ed. Wer-minghoff, 2(2):807. Cf. D. Ganz, "The Debate on Predestination," in *Charles the Bald: Court and Kingdom*, ed. M. Gibson and J. L. Nelson, 2nd ed. (London, 1990), 285; Sim-son, *Jahrbücher*, 2:75 n. 3.

7. Cf. W. Hartmann, *Die Synoden der Karolingerzeit im Frankenreich und in Italien* (Paderborn, 1989), 188 n. 24. Recall that in his prologue to the episcopal *Relatio*, Walafrid Strabo named Ebbo as the "author of this evil." Flodoard of Reims would claim that Lothar rewarded Ebbo for his efforts with the monastery of Saint-Vaast in Arras; Flodo-ard, *Historia Remensis ecclesiae*, 2.20, ed. Stratmann, 184.

8. Cf. J. L. Nelson, "The Annals of St. Bertin," in eadem, *Politics*, 175.

9. K. Bund, *Thronsturz und Herrscherabsetzung im Frühmittelalter* (Bonn, 1979), 423–28; L. Rid, "Die Wiedereinsetzung Kaiser Ludwigs des Frommen zu St. Denis (1. März 834) und ihre Wiederholung zu Metz (28. Februar 835)," in *Festgabe Alois Knöpfler zur Vollendung des 70. Lebensjahres*, ed. H. M. Gietl and G. Pfeilschifter (Freiburg im Breisgau, 1917), 265–75.

10. *AB*, s.a. 835, ed. Grat et al., 16. On the production of documents at the assembly in 835, see Nelson, *ASB*, 32; R. McKitterick, "Introduction: Sources and Interpretation," in *NCMH* 2:6. On such staged counterassemblies, see S. MacLean, "Ritual, Misunderstanding, and the Contest for Meaning: Representations of the Disrupted Royal Assembly at Frankfurt (873)," in *Representations of Power in Medieval Germany 800–1500*, ed. B. Weiler and S. MacLean (Turnhout, 2006), 113 and n. 59.

11. *AB*, s.a. 835, ed. Grat et al., 16–17; trans. modified slightly from Nelson, *ASB*, 32–33.

12. *AB*, s.a. 835, ed. Grat et al., 17. As J. Devisse, *Hincmar, archevêque de Reims, 845–882* (Geneva, 1975), 1:81–83, notes, by confessing to a *"capitale crimen,"* renouncing his right to the episcopal office, and agreeing to undertake penance for seven years, Ebbo implied that the nature of his crime was in some way sexual.

13. Thegan, *GH*, 48, ed. Tremp, 242.

14. Thegan, *GH*, 56, ed. Tremp, 252, and the literature cited by Tremp, 253, nn. 308–9.

15. Thegan, *GH*, 56, ed. Tremp, 252.

16. As I shall demonstrate below, this grievance by Thegan is perhaps an indirect criticism of the influence wielded by Louis' second wife, Judith. As a letter from Charles the Bald in 867 would later make clear, Ebbo's punishment amounted to nothing more than his resignation and enclaustration in 835 primarily because of Judith's sympathy and timely intercession for him. If Thegan had knowledge of this intercession by Judith, his remarks would be the earliest criticism of the empress by an author not directly associated with the rebellion. Cf. Chapter 2, n. 100.

17. Astronomer, *VH*, 54, ed. Tremp, 500.

18. Astronomer, *VH*, 54, ed. Tremp, 502. See E. Boshof, *Ludwig der Fromme* (Darmstadt, 1996), 212. Cf. the Astronomer's use of the term *irrevocabiliter* here with his earlier, derisive use of the term (*VH*, 49, ed. Tremp, 482) when describing how the rebels characterized Louis' penance in 833.

19. For the text of Ebbo's *Resignatio*, see A. Werminghoff, ed., MGH, *Conc.*, 2(2):701–3; French trans., Devisse, *Hincmar, archevêque de Reims*, 1:77. While it is true that none of the texts concerned with Louis' reinvestiture in 835 has survived, Richard Jackson has argued persuasively that one of these formal texts—the *ordo* for Louis' recoronation at Metz—served as the model for and can be detected within Charles the Bald's own coronation *ordo* of 869. See *Ordines Coronationis Franciae*, ed. R. A. Jackson (Philadelphia, 1995), 1:87–109; R. A. Jackson, "Who Wrote Hincmar's Ordines?" *Viator* 25 (1994): 31–52. See also the brief acclamation in an undated letter to Louis written perhaps by Einhard (*Ep.* 66, ed. K. Hampe, MGH, *Epist.*, 5:142; trans. Dutton, *Courtier*, 162–63).

20. Ebbo, *Resignatio*, ed. Werminghoff, 2(2):702.

21. In three manuscripts, Laon, Bibliothèque municipale 407 (saec. IX ex.), fols. 159–60; Brussels 5417–5422 (saec. X), fols. 113–15; and Rome, Vat. Pal. lat. 576 (saec. IX), fols. 33–34, the word *libellus* is used in titles describing this mixed text of Ebbo's resignation followed by the episcopal commentary and signatures. In a booklet presented by Theoderich of Cambrai to the synod of Soissons in 853 (ed. W. Hartmann, MGH, *Conc.*, 3:290–93), Theoderich would note that Bishop Jonas of Orléans had dictated much of the proceedings of 835 to the notary Helias, who had thereafter titled the booklet.

22. *Concilium Aquisgranense* (836), 66, ed. A. Werminghoff, MGH, *Conc.*, 2(2):723. On this council, see Boshof, *Ludwig der Fromme*, 231–32; Hartmann, *Die Synoden der Karolingerzeit*, 190–94; H. H. Anton, *Fürstenspiegel und Herrscherethos in der Karolingerzeit* (Bonn, 1968), 218–31.

23. In this regard, the bishops named by both Ebbo and the episcopal assembly as Ebbo's witnesses and confessors—Archbishops Aiulf of Bourges and Notho of Arles; Bishops Theoderich of Cambrai, Achard of Noyon, Badurad of Paderborn, and Modoin of Autun—are perhaps worthy of special scrutiny. For Badurad and Modoin, see Depreux, *Prosopographie*, 116–18, 333–34. Flodoard of Reims, *Historia Remensis ecclesiae*, 2.20, ed. Stratmann, 185–87, would protest that the bishops had not "urged" Ebbo but merely counseled him to act in accordance with the ancient sacred canons "of Africa" so that the dignity of his office would not be polluted. Ebbo had then followed their counsel and "willingly" resigned. These same canons, explained Flodoard, had also dictated the various protocols of Ebbo's resignation, including the number of witnesses and confessors. Cf. the report by Theoderich of Cambrai in the booklet he presented to the synod of Soissons in 853 (ed. Hartmann, 3: 290–93), which Flodoard used as the basis for his account.

24. "*Corvus oculum corvi non eruet.*" Gregory of Tours, *Libri historiarum X*, 5.18, ed. B. Krusch and W. Levison, MGH, *SRM*, 1:219.

25. *Concilium Aquisgranense* (836), 24, 66, ed. Werminghoff, 2(2):710, 723.

26. Cf. Boshof, *Ludwig der Fromme*, 232; and Anton, *Fürstenspiegel und Herrschererethos*, 231, who sees in this remedial council of 836 the "triumph" of the theological moral-legal agenda of "political Augustinianism."

27. This information is derived from a seventeenth-century synopsis (by Georgius Colvenerius) of letters from the ninth-century abbot of Fulda, Hrabanus Maurus, which have since been lost: *Epistolarum Fuldensium fragmenta*, 13, ed. E. Dümmler, MGH, *Epist.*, 5:520.

28. In a letter to Pope Nicholas I in 867, ed. Hartmann, MGH, *Conc.*, 4:241, Charles the Bald would claim that, shortly after the proceedings of 835, his father had enjoined Abbot Gotafrid of Gregorienmünster to deliver documents detailing Ebbo's "deposition" to Pope Gregory IV in order to obtain that pope's confirmation and approval. Charles explains that, although he knows Gotafrid succeeded in delivering the documents, by 867 Gregory's response had been lost, and it was currently unknown to him what the papal decision about Ebbo had been. This "lost report" by Pope Gregory IV is believed by

modern scholars to have been a fabrication on the part of Charles; see Simson, *Jahrbücher*, 2:135; Depreux, *Prosopographie*, 220–21.

29. As reported by the *Narratio clericorum Remensium*, ed. Werminghoff, 2(2):808. One factor behind Ebbo's mysterious transfer from Fulda may have been the sympathy of Fulda's abbot, Hrabanus Maurus, for him. Hrabanus would later write letters of recommendation on Ebbo's behalf, as well as a letter to console Ebbo over his continuing misfortunes. See *Epistolarum Fuldensium fragmenta*, 13–14, ed. Dümmler, 5:520–21. On Boso, see *Narratio clericorum Remensium*, ed. Werminghoff, 2(2):808; Synod of Troyes (867), ed. Hartmann, 4:234.

30. L. Halphen, *Charlemagne and the Carolingian Empire*, trans. G. de Nie (1947; Amsterdam, 1977), 216; Hartmann, *Die Synoden der Karolingerzeit*, 197–98; H. Fuhrmann, "Die Synoden von Ingelheim," in *Ingelheim am Rhein: Forschungen und Studien zur Geschichte Ingelheims*, ed. J. Autenrieth (Stuttgart, 1964), 156–58. For the political context, see J. L. Nelson, *Charles the Bald* (London, 1992), 105–9.

31. *Concilium Ingelheimense* (840), ed. A. Werminghoff, MGH, *Conc.*, 2(2):793.

32. Cf. Chapter 4, n. 127.

33. *Concilium Ingelheimense*, ed. Werminghoff, 2(2):791–93. The seven bishops at both assemblies were archbishops Drogo of Metz, Otgar of Mainz, and Hetti of Trier, and Bishops Frothar of Toul, Badurad of Paderborn, Ado of Valenciennes, and Ratold of Strasbourg. In addition to his leading presence at Ebbo's resignation in 835, Drogo had remained with his half brother Louis the Pious on both the Rotfeld in 833 and at his deathbed in June 840. By August 840, as his participation in the council of Ingelheim attests, Drogo had chosen Lothar as his new lord. See Devisse, *Hincmar, archevêque de Reims*, 1:87 n. 275. For Drogo's career, see Chapter 1, n. 255.

34. The record of this assembly survives only as it was copied (or fabricated?) within an apology written by Ebbo in 842 (itself surviving in two recensions), defending his right to the see of Reims. See Ebbo, *Apologeticus* 1, ed. Werminghoff, 797–98; Ebbo, *Apologeticus* 2, ed. Werminghoff, 805–6. It was also reproduced (likely by way of Ebbo's apology) in the *Narratio clericorum Remensium*, ed. Werminghoff, 2(2):809–10. For the argument of its fabrication (by Ebbo), see A. Werminghoff, "Ein neuer Text des Apologeticum Ebonis," *NA* 25 (1900): 363–78.

35. Of the forty-three bishops who had participated in Ebbo's resignation in 835, Theoderich of Cambrai, Rothad of Soissons, Hildemann of Beauvais, and Raganar of Amiens are here attested as also having been signatories to his restoration. The other five attesters at Reims in 840 were Bishops Simeon of Laon, Erpwin of Senlis, Emmo of Noyon, Folcuin of Therouanne, and Lupus of Châlons. Cf. the two redactions of the assembly in the two recensions of Ebbo's apology, ed. Werminghoff, 2(2):798, 805–6. For a useful map of ecclesiastical provinces in Carolingian Francia, see R. McKitterick, *The Frankish Kingdoms Under the Carolingians, 751–987* (London, 1983), 372–73.

36. These ordinations are noted only in several later sources, which do not agree on the number of clerics ordained. Cf. *Narratio clericorum Remensium*, ed. Werminghoff, 2(2):810–13, which mentions at least fourteen; the record of the synod of Soissons from

853 (ed. Hartmann, 3:266), which mentions thirteen by name; and a letter of Hincmar of Reims in 866 (*Ep.* 185, ed. E. Perels, MGH, *Epist.*, 8[1]:189), which mentions only nine.

37. Like the events of 833, the battle of Fontenoy has long been an object of historical reflection. Cf. Nelson, *Charles the Bald*, 1–2, on the obelisk erected in 1860 to commemorate the site for nationalistic concerns; and R. Darnton, *The Great Cat Massacre: And Other Episodes in French Cultural History* (New York, 1984), 167, on the timely remembrance of the battle in the eighteenth century as a successful means by which to gain employment! Within many modern historical narratives, the events of 833 are seen as the unsettling prelude to the battle at Fontenoy, a conflict long believed to have been directly responsible for the decline of the Carolingian empire; cf. J. L. Nelson, "The Last Years of Louis the Pious," in *CH*, ed. Godman and Collins, 155–56.

38. These details are only reported later, in the *Narratio clericorum Remensium*, ed. Werminghoff, 2(2):812. Ebbo was soon granted the monasteries of Stavelot and Bobbio by Lothar; see Hincmar, *Ep.* 198 (867), ed. Perels, 8(1):211; Synod of Troyes (867), ed. Hartmann, 4:235.

39. On the uncertain date of this assembly (for which no contemporary records survive), see Schrörs, *Hinkmar Erzbischof von Reims*, 35 n. 35; 278 n. 41. Hincmar mentions the assembly in a letter from 866; see Hincmar, *Ep.* 186, ed. Perels, 8(1):192.

40. For Walafrid's prefaces, see Thegan, *GH*, ed. Tremp, 168–75; C. M. Booker, "A New Prologue of Walafrid Strabo," *Viator* 36 (2005): 83–105; and Chapter 2.

41. See Werminghoff, "Ein neuer Text," 363–78. Werminghoff demonstrated that Ebbo revised and reissued his apology so that he could bolster his argument by including additional forged and interpolated material in the later draft. For what occasion/s Ebbo revised his apology was/were never addressed in Werminghoff's study. On the discovery and publication of the two texts, see Chapter 2.

42. Apart from the remarks of Werminghoff, Schrörs, Devisse, and K. Hampe, "Zum Streite Hincmars von Reims mit seinem Vorgänger Ebo und dessen Anhängern," *NA* 24 (1898): 180–95, there has been little written on Ebbo's apologies. This neglect is unwarranted, for the texts would reward further study.

43. Ebbo, *Apologeticus* 1, ed. Werminghoff, 794–95.

44. Ebbo, *Apologeticus* 2, ed. Werminghoff, 800.

45. Cf. Ebbo, *Apologeticus* 1, ed. Werminghoff, 795–96; idem, *Apologeticus* 2, ed. Werminghoff, 800–804.

46. Cf. Ebbo, *Apologeticus* 1, ed. Werminghoff, 797, 799; idem, *Apologeticus* 2, ed. Werminghoff, 803–4.

47. Cf. Ebbo, *Apologeticus* 1, ed. Werminghoff, 796; idem, *Apologeticus* 2, ed. Werminghoff, 802–3.

48. Cf. Ebbo, *Apologeticus* 1, ed. Werminghoff, 797. After quoting his confession from 835, Ebbo argues that "if anyone decrees that I ought to be condemned on account of this charter [namely, Ebbo's signed confession], devised under various types of duress, then he will similarly be able to condemn me with respect to all my writings, in which I never do justice to myself, but in subscribing [my name] always declare myself

an 'unworthy bishop'." Ebbo is here referring to the fact that the only statement that can be construed as condemnatory in his confession is his remark that he was an "unworthy bishop" (*indignus episcopus*). But, he protests, if this is all there is with which to condemn him, then he should be condemned for everything he has ever written because he always refers to himself with humility as an "unworthy bishop." This is something of a sleight of hand by Ebbo, for, in his quotation of his 835 confession, he conveniently leaves out the subscription he had originally made in which he also declared himself to be "formerly a bishop" (*quondam episcopus*). In their quotation of Ebbo's resignation, Theoderich of Cambrai (ed. Hartmann, 3:290–93) and Flodoard of Reims (*Historia Remensis ecclesiae*, 2.20 [ed. Stratmann, 186]) both include Ebbo's subscription. The *Narratio clericorum Remensium*, ed. Werminghoff, 2(2):808, like Ebbo, omits the subscription.

49. On this legation, see *The Lives of the Ninth-Century Popes (Liber Pontificalis)*, trans. R. Davis (Liverpool, 1995), 81–82 n. 31; McKeon, "Archbishop Ebbo of Reims," 445–46. On Bartholomew, who would be permanently banned from office, see Simson, *Jahrbücher*, 2:138 n. 3; E. Boshof, *Erzbischof Agobard von Lyon: Leben und Werk* (Cologne, 1969), 261–62 n. 34. In the 840s, within his poetic lament on the division of the empire, Florus of Lyon would characterize Bartholomew as an esteemed man who was exiled, "still languishing sadly at his old wound." See P. Godman, *Poetry of the Carolingian Renaissance* (Norman, Okla., 1985), 266–67 (v. 37).

50. *Liber pontificalis*, 104 (Sergius II), ed. L. Duchesne (Paris, 1955), 2:90; trans. Davis, *The Lives of the Ninth-Century Popes*, 81–82. The monk Guntbald (mentioned by Nithard as a favorite of Louis the Pious) was later called upon by Pope Sergius II in 846 to intervene in the bitter dispute between Ebbo and Hincmar; see J.-P. Brunterc'h, "Moines bénédictins et chanoines réformés au secours de Louis le Pieux (830–834)," *Bulletin de la société nationale des antiquaires de France*, seance du 12 mars (1986): 73 n. 11.

51. The papal condemnation of Ebbo and Bartholomew as recorded in the *Liber pontificalis* was quoted later in the *libellus* of Theoderich of Cambrai (ed. Hartmann, 3:293) as irrefutable proof of Ebbo's prior condemnation in 835. The papal condemnation was also mentioned by Hincmar in a letter from 867 (*Ep.* 200, ed. Perels, 8[1]:224).

52. On Hincmar, see Devisse, *Hincmar, archevêque de Reims*; Schrörs, *Hinkmar Erzbischof von Reims*; E. S. Duckett, *Carolingian Portraits: A Study in the Ninth Century* (Ann Arbor, Mich., 1962), 202–64. Hincmar would later be criticized by the pope for having violated his monastic vows when he became archbishop. See K. F. Morrison, "*Unum ex multis*: Hincmar of Rheims' Medical and Aesthetic Rationales for Unification," *SS Spoleto*, 27(2): 607 n. 112.

53. For summaries of this contest, see *The Lives of the Ninth-Century Popes*, trans. Davis, 195–97; Duckett, *Carolingian Portraits*, 202–64. The standard examinations are Devisse, *Hincmar, archevêque de Reims*, 1:91–100; 2:603, 611–28; Schrörs, *Hinkmar Erzbischof von Reims*, 273–92.

54. J. M. Wallace-Hadrill, *The Frankish Church* (Oxford, 1983), 275–76; H. Fuhrmann, *Einfluss und Verbreitung der pseudoisidorischen Fälschung* (Stuttgart, 1972), 1:191–95. E. Magnou-Nortier, "La tentative de subversion de l'État sous Louis le Pieux

et l'oeuvre des falsificateurs," *MA* 105 (1999): 331–65, 615–41, sees the Pseudo-Isidorian decretals as part of a massive program of falsification undertaken by the "sore losers" of the rebellion in 833. J. Fried, *Donation of Constantine and Constitutum Constantini* (Berlin, 2007), 70, 92, 98–102, understands Wala and Paschasius Radbertus as the authors of the false decretals, which they offered to Pope Gregory IV to support his position on the Rotfeld in June 833; see Chapter 4, nn. 213–14.

55. Cf. Hincmar, *Ep.* 198 (867), ed. Perels, 8(1):211; Synod of Troyes (867), ed. Hartmann, 4:235; and Flodoard of Reims, *Historia Remensis ecclesiae*, 2.20, ed. Stratmann, 189, who all claim that Ebbo's dismissal was due to his refusal to travel to the Byzantine East as part of a legation for Lothar (recall that Ebbo was afflicted with gout). See Goetting, *Das Bistum Hildesheim*, 71–72.

56. As noted by the Synod of Troyes (867), ed. Hartmann, 4:235. Cf. the letter of consolation from Hrabanus Maurus to Ebbo at some point during the latter's time at Hildesheim, *Epistolarum Fuldensium fragmenta*, 14, ed. Dümmler, 5:521. On Ebbo at Hildesheim, see Goetting, *Das Bistum Hildesheim*, 72–79. See also the compilation of texts he may have assembled while in residence there, discussed in Chapter 2, nn. 128–30.

57. The spurious letter was edited by K. Hampe, MGH, *Epist.*, 5:81–84. See also Hampe, "Zum Streite Hincmars," 180–95; McKeon, "Archbishop Ebbo of Reims," 447 n. 91; Goetting, *Das Bistum Hildesheim*, 73–74; S. Scholz, *Transmigration und Translation: Studien zum Bistumswechsel der Bischöfe von der Spätantike bis zum hohen Mittelalter* (Cologne, 1992), 117–30. Hampe pointed out that much of the letter is also derivative of the letter from Pope Paschal to Ebbo in 822, authorizing his proselytization mission to the North; see Chapter 2, n. 129. Recall that this papal letter from Paschal is preserved within the Hildesheim compilation, mentioned in the previous note.

58. Pope Gregory IV, *Ep.* 15 (*Epistola spuria*), ed. Hampe, 5:82.

59. Recall that, according to the Astronomer, Gregory had departed from those same events "with heavy grief." See Chapter 1, n. 119.

60. Pope Gregory IV, *Ep.* 15 (*Epistola spuria*), ed. Hampe, 5:81 n. 8. The letter survives in Laon, Bibliothèque municipale 407 (saec. IX ex.), fol. 161. On the hand of the marginalia, see W. Hartmann, "Fälschungsverdacht und Fälschungsnachweis im früheren Mittelalter," in *Fälschungen im Mittelalter* (Hannover, 1988), 2:119 n. 22. Cf. the letter by Hincmar of Reims in 867 (*Ep.* 200, ed. Perels, 8(1):224), in which Hincmar states his recent awareness of the letter and his doubts about its authorship by the pope. Earlier in the year, at the Synod of Troyes (867), ed. Hartmann, 4:235, Hincmar spoke of the letter and stated that he was forwarding it to Pope Nicholas I for his inspection.

61. Lothar, *Epistola Leoni papae directa*, ed. A. Hirsch-Gereuth, MGH, *Epist.*, 5:609–11; W. Ullmann, *The Growth of Papal Government in the Middle Ages* (London, 1965), 172–73.

62. Lothar's letter itself was meant as a gesture toward this end, containing a request for the pope to allow Charles's man, Hincmar, the right of donning the pallium, a vestment symbolically certifying his authority over the episcopal office so hotly contested

between the two kings since Ebbo's deposition in 835. See Devisse, *Hincmar, archevêque de Reims*, 1:38–39.

63. Lothar, *Epistola Leoni papae directa*, ed. Hirsch-Gereuth, 5:610.

64. Cf. Agobard, *Liber apologeticus* II, 9, ed. Van Acker, 316; Astronomer, *VH*, 45, 48, ed. Tremp, 462, 472. As Tremp observed (473 n. 697), the language of Lothar's letter appears to reflect the influence of the Astronomer, *VH*, 48.

65. Cf. the similar reasoning of Ado of Vienne, *Chronicon*, ed. Pertz, 2:320–21: "the long period of peace occasioned treachery, treachery [occasioned] rebellion, rebellion [occasioned] the perdition of the empire."

66. C. Chazelle, "Archbishops Ebo and Hincmar of Reims and the Utrecht Psalter," *Speculum* 72 (1997): 1055–77, has argued that the creation of the ninth-century Utrecht Psalter should be seen in the context of Hincmar's ongoing struggle to establish his legitimate possession of his office as archbishop of Reims. Her discussion of the image in the manuscript depicting an early church council and its association with the ninth-century councils held by Hincmar to ensure his legitimacy accords well with the tenor of episcopal reform during the ninth century, which was fashioned in terms of a revival of the primitive church.

67. Responding to a query ca. 853–856 from his friend Bishop Heribald of Auxerre (who had formerly been a member of the rebellion in 833 until having been granted clemency by Louis in 838), Hrabanus Maurus would express his doubts about what had happened to Ebbo: "In regard to the deposition and restitution of Bishop Ebbo of Reims, it is not necessary for me to answer your question. Let those who did this thing [to Ebbo] decide whether it was done justly or unjustly. For when I, an unworthy man, was established in the bishopric of the Mainz church, I found him in possession of the episcopal see in Saxony [i.e., Hildesheim], and I did not prohibit him from acting as its chief minister, since I had heard that he had been restored to his office by the Holy See; and so up to the end of his life he remained in that office." Hrabanus goes on to say that, at the request of his brethren, he had recently sent a letter to Hincmar about Ebbo because he had heard that Hincmar had banned from office the clerics ordained by Ebbo in 841. He promises Heribald that as soon as he hears back about this letter, he will inform him of Hincmar's response. See Hrabanus Maurus, *Ep.* 56 (34), ed. E. Dümmler, MGH, *Epist.*, 5:514.

68. See the *libellus* presented by Theoderich of Cambrai to the synod of Soissons in 853 (ed. Hartmann, 3:290). Soon after Theoderich's damning booklet was read aloud to the synod in 853 (by Lupus of Ferrières), Fredebertus of Reims, one of the clerics present at the restoration of Ebbo to Reims in December 840, rose up and read aloud from his own booklet. Fredebertus claimed that several suffragan bishops from Reims had arrived in December bearing official letters from Lothar, and had subsequently restored Ebbo in 840; thus, Fredebertus and his companions had held no suspicion about the illegitimacy of the act. He then showed the synod those very letters, which—incredibly—appeared to be signed by Theoderich of Cambrai and several other bishops who were currently present at the Soissons synod for the purpose of condemning Ebbo. The synod immediately judged the letters to be patently and utterly spurious. See the Synod of Soissons, 853 (ed.

Hartmann, 3:273–74); together with Devisse, *Hincmar, archevêque de Reims*, 1:93; Hartmann, "Fälschungsverdacht," 111–20. Both Ebbo (in his apologies) and Ebbo's ordained clerics (in their narrative) claimed that Theoderich had participated in Ebbo's restoration. On Theoderich's shifting political alliances and the unusual political and ecclesiastical situation of Cambrai during the Carolingian civil wars, see P. W. Finsterwalder, "Eine parteipolitische Kundgebung eines Anhängers Lothars I.," *NA* 47 (1928): 413–15.

69. See the *Narratio clericorum Remensium*, ed. Werminghoff, 2(2):807. The author/s of this text and the occasion for which it was written are unknown. Its contents, however, place it within the disputes raging between 853 and 867 over Ebbo's restoration and subsequent ordinations. See Fuhrmann, *Einfluss und Verbreitung*, 1:208–9 n. 43.

70. *Narratio clericorum Remensium*, ed. Werminghoff, 2(2):806–14.

71. Synod of Troyes (867), ed. Hartmann, 4:232–38. On this synod, see Hartmann, *Die Synoden der Karolingerzeit*, 320–21. For the political context, see P. R. McKeon, *Hincmar of Laon and Carolingian Politics* (Urbana, Ill., 1978), 57–64. Apart from his role in the dispute between Hincmar and Charles and his service as tutor for Charles's son Carloman, Wulfad is a rather elusive figure. See J. Marenbon, "Wulfad, Charles the Bald and John Scottus Eriugena," in *Charles the Bald: Court and Kingdom*, ed. M. Gibson and J. L. Nelson (London, 1981), 375–80.

72. This booklet was one of the many affidavits written, signed, and compiled by the bishops in 835 at Thionville to counteract the legal instruments produced by the rebellion in 833, as reported by the Annals of Saint-Bertin, s.a. 835; see Nelson, *ASB*, 32.

73. Synod of Troyes (867), ed. Hartmann, 4:235–38.

74. *AB*, s.a. 866, ed. Grat et al., 128; trans. Nelson, *ASB*, 132 and n. 15. For Hincmar as an annalist, see Nelson, "The Annals of St. Bertin," 182–92; eadem, "A Tale of Two Princes: Politics, Text, and Ideology in a Carolingian Annal," *Studies in Medieval and Renaissance History*, n.s. 10 (1988): 105–41.

75. Charles the Bald, *Epistola Nicolao papae directa* (867), ed. Hartmann, 4:239–43.

76. *AB*, s.a. 867, ed. Grat et al., 138; trans. Nelson, *ASB*, 141.

77. Charles the Bald, *Epistola Nicolao papae directa* (867), ed. Hartmann, 4:240. As Simson, *Jahrbücher*, 2:68 n. 6; and L. Halphen, "La pénitence de Louis le Pieux à Saint Médard de Soissons," in idem, *A travers l'histoire du Moyen Age* (1904; Paris, 1950), 63 n. 3, observed, Charles seems to have borrowed the expression about Louis' "neither having confessed to nor been convicted of anything" (*nec confessum nec ab aliquo convictum*) from the report of the Troyes synod (*nec confessum nec convictum*), both of which reflect the influence of the account by the Astronomer, *VH*, 49, ed. Tremp, 482 (*nec confitentem neque convictum*).

78. See E. Ward, "Caesar's Wife: The Career of the Empress Judith, 819–829," in *CH*, ed. Godman and Collins, 211–12. Nothing more is known of Framegaud, the hermit allegedly chosen by Ebbo to deliver the promise ring to Judith.

79. Cf. Devisse, *Hincmar, archevêque de Reims*, 1:78 n. 238, 87 nn. 273–74, where he notes correctly Charles's positive characterization of Ebbo; with idem, *Hincmar,*

368 NOTES TO PAGES 201–203

archevêque de Reims, 2:627 n. 402, where he claims erroneously that Charles's portrayal of Ebbo is equally as severe as that given by Hincmar in the account of the synod of Troyes in 867.

80. Charles the Bald, *Epistola Nicolao papae directa* (867), ed. Hartmann, 4:239–41. Ebbo had similarly been praised for his fidelity and the extent of his learning by the exiled court poet Ermoldus Nigellus in the 820s; see his poem, *In honorem Hludowici* (written ca. 826), 4.1906–2237, ed. E. Faral, *Ermold le Noir: Poème sur Louis le Pieux et épitres au roi Pépin* (Paris, 1964), 146–70.

81. Charles the Bald, *Epistola Nicolao papae directa* (867), ed. Hartmann, 4:241. Cf. the observation of Ebbo, *Apologeticus* 1, ed. Werminghoff, 797; idem, *Apologeticus* 2, ed. Werminghoff, 803.

82. Simson, *Jahrbücher*, 2:135; Depreux, *Prosopographie*, 220–21. Schrörs, *Hinkmar Erzbischof von Reims*, 32 and n. 27, deemed the letters plausible but provided no satisfactory reason for his position. Devisse, *Hincmar, archevêque de Reims*, 1:85–86, refrains from making any decision. See n. 28 above.

83. Pope Hadrian II, *Ep.* 3, to the synod of Troyes (2 Feb. 868), and *Ep.* 7, to Charles the Bald (23 Feb. 868), ed. E. Perels, MGH, *Epist.*, 6:699–700, 704–7.

84. Pope Hadrian II, *Ep.* 7, to Charles the Bald (23 Feb. 868), ed. Perels, 6:705.

85. P. E. Dutton, *The Politics of Dreaming in the Carolingian Empire* (Lincoln, Neb., 1994), 183–94.

86. See the *Visio Bernoldi*, ed. M. van der Lugt, "Tradition and Revision: The Textual Tradition of Hincmar of Reims' *Visio Bernoldi* with a New Critical Edition," *Bulletin du Cange* 52 (1994): 109–49.

87. Dutton, *The Politics of Dreaming*, 184–85. As both Dutton and Van der Lugt point out, in his dream Bernold also encounters, among others, a suffering figure by the name of "Jesse." Dutton, *The Politics of Dreaming*, 188–89, states that this person remains unidentified, a position also taken by Van der Lugt, "Tradition and Revision," 113 and n. 11, only after discounting the claim by C. Carozzi, *Le voyage de l'âme dans l'Au-delà d'après la littérature latine (V^e–XIIIe siècles)* (Rome, 1994), 357, that Jesse should be identified as Ebbo's co-conspirator Bishop Jesse of Amiens, who died while in exile in Italy in 836. Despite Van der Lugt's misgivings, I believe Carozzi's identification to be plausible. The more interesting question is why Hincmar would neglect to include among these purgatorial figures the enduring source of so many of his troubles, Bishop Wulfad, who died in 876.

88. L. Nees, "The Illustrated Manuscript of the *Visio Baronti* [*Revelatio Baronti*] in St. Petersburg (Russian National Library, cod. Lat. Oct.v.I.)," in *Court Culture in the Early Middle Ages*, ed. C. Cubitt (Turnhout, 2003), 115–19, speculates that Hincmar made a "peace offering" to Ebbo after the latter's death through the production of an illuminated copy of a Merovingian dream text, the *Visio Baronti*, which speaks favorably about a certain monk Ebbo, "a man of noble birth."

89. Dutton, *The Politics of Dreaming*, 186–88.

90. *Visio Bernoldi*, rec. "C", 3, ed. Van der Lugt, "Tradition and Revision," 144; trans. Dutton, *The Politics of Dreaming*, 186.

91. As Dutton, *The Politics of Dreaming*, 230–33, observes, there was still another critical dream text about Ebbo composed between 877 and 888 at Reims, the *Visio Raduini*, ed. O. Holder-Egger, *NA* 11 (1886): 262–63. It was included by Flodoard in his *Historia Remensis ecclesiae*, 2.19, ed. Stratmann, 182–83.

92. Hincmar of Reims, *De divortio Lotharii regis et Theutbergae reginae*, which survives in a sole copy from the ninth century, Paris, B.N.F. lat. 2866. Additional work remains to be done on the poor reception of this text. Cf. the remarks of L. Böhringer, MGH, *Conc.*, 4(1):31; S. Airlie, "Private Bodies and the Body Politic in the Divorce Case of Lothar II," *PP* 161 (1998): 12.

93. Hincmar of Reims, *De divortio Lotharii*, respons. 6 (Anhang), ed. Böhringer, 4(1):247. Cf. K. Heidecker, "Why Should Bishops Be Involved in Marital Affairs? Hincmar of Rheims on the Divorce of King Lothar II (855–869)," in *The Community, the Family, and the Saint: Patterns of Power in Early Medieval Europe*, ed. J. Hill and M. Swan (Turnhout, 1998), 230; Y. Sassier, "Le roi et la loi chez les penseurs du royaume occidental du deuxième quart du IXe à la fin du XIe s.," *CCM* 43 (2000): 266. On Hincmar's interest in Ambrose's letters, see Chapter 4, n. 50.

94. Hincmar of Reims, *De divortio Lotharii regis*, respons. 2, ed. Böhringer, 4(1):125; Depreux, *Prosopographie*, 257–58. Flodoard of Reims, *Historia Remensis ecclesiae*, 3.1, ed. Stratmann, 191, claimed that Hincmar had been at the Rotfeld and, together with his mentor Hilduin of Saint-Denis, refrained from defecting. Cf. McKeon, *Hincmar of Laon*, 11.

95. M. de Jong, "Power and Humility in Carolingian Society: The Public Penance of Louis the Pious," *EME* 1 (1992): 51–52.

96. For Hincmar's general knowledge of Ambrose, see Dutton, *The Politics of Dreaming*, 308–9 n. 124. On his Ambrosian "insistence on the division between the juridical competence of royal courts and that of the episcopal," see Morrison, "*Unum ex multis*: Hincmar," 27(2):680–82.

97. For Hincmar's participation in Charles's coronation in 869, see J. L. Nelson, "Hincmar of Reims on King-Making: The Evidence of the *Annals of St. Bertin*, 861–882," in *Coronations: Medieval and Early Modern Monarchic Ritual*, ed. J. M. Bak (Berkeley, Calif., 1990), 22–26; Morrison, "*Unum ex multis*: Hincmar," 27(2):683–718.

98. *AB*, s.a. 869, ed. Grat et al., 157; trans. Nelson, *ASB*, 157 and n. 14.

99. See *Ordines Coronationis Franciae*, ed. Jackson, 1:87–109; Jackson, "Who Wrote Hincmar's Ordines?" 31–52. The coronation proceedings were inserted by Hincmar into his annal entry for the year 869; see *AB*, s.a. 869, ed. Grat et al., 163.

100. *Ordo* of Charles the Bald, ed. Jackson, *Ordines Coronationis Franciae*, 1:104–5.

101. On Charles's death and burial, see J. L. Nelson, "La mort de Charles le Chauve," *Médiévales* 31 (1996): 53–66; eadem, "Carolingian Royal Funerals," in *Rituals of Power*

from Late Antiquity to the Early Middle Ages, ed. F. Theuws and J. L. Nelson (Leiden, 2000), 161–66.

102. Cf. R. McKitterick, *History and Its Audiences* (Cambridge, 2000), 24.

103. C. L. Becker, "Everyman His Own Historian," *AHR* 37 (1932): 227.

104. Cf. the later remark of Hincmar of Reims, *De regis persona et regio ministerio*, 33, *PL* 125, col. 856C (quoting Pope Innocent I), regarding the fact that when a sin is universal among a people it must be disregarded since an entire realm cannot be punished.

105. See Chapter 2, nn. 20, 114.

CHAPTER 6. ELOQUENCE IN EQUITY, FLUENCY IN INIQUITY

Epigraphs: Letter of Friedrich von Müller, June 6, 1824, ed. R. Grumach, *Kanzler Friedrich von Müller, Unterhaltungen mit Goethe* (Munich, 1982), 127; as slightly abbreviated by K. Jaspers, *Philosophische Logik*, vol. 1, *Von der Wahrheit* (1947; Munich, 1958), 951; and translated in K. Jaspers, *Tragedy Is Not Enough*, trans. H. A. T. Reiche et al. (Boston, 1952), 86; Dhuoda, *Liber manualis*, 4.8, ed. P. Riché, *SC* (Paris, 1991), 225bis:244.

1. M. de Jong, "Power and Humility in Carolingian Society: The Public Penance of Louis the Pious," *EME* 1 (1992): 40. Cf. G. Alföldy, "The Crisis of the Third Century as Seen by Contemporaries," *Greek, Roman, and Byzantine Studies* 15 (1974): 110.

2. Cf. M. H. Hoeflich, "The Concept of *Utilitas Populi* in Early Ecclesiastical Law and Government," *Zeitschrift der Savigny-Stiftung für Rechtsgeschichte, Kanonistische Abteilung* 67 (1981): 36–74; E. Peters, *The Shadow King: Rex Inutilis in Medieval Law and Literature, 751–1327* (New Haven, Conn., 1970).

3. Cf. G. Koziol, "Lord's Law and Natural Law," in *The Medieval Tradition of Natural Law*, ed. H. J. Johnson (Kalamazoo, Mich., 1987), 103–17; idem, *Begging Pardon and Favor: Ritual and Political Order in Early Medieval France* (Ithaca, N.Y., 1992); O. Guillot, "Le concept d'autorité dans l'ordre politique français issu de l'an mil," in *La notion d'autorité au Moyen Âge: Islam, Byzance, Occident* (Paris, 1982), 127–40.

4. P. J. Geary, *Living with the Dead in the Middle Ages* (Ithaca, N.Y., 1994), 34. Cf. G. Duby, "Ideologies in Social History," in *Constructing the Past: Essays in Historical Methodology*, ed. J. Le Goff and P. Nora (1974; Cambridge, 1985), 158–59.

5. Dutton, *Mustache*, xiv; cf. 92. E. A. R. Brown has also observed such differences, noting that the historical sources themselves rarely correspond in their affinity for, and projection of, a particular structural model of social order. See "Georges Duby and the Three Orders," *Viator* 17 (1986): 51–64.

6. F. L. Ganshof, "Louis the Pious Reconsidered," in idem, *Carolingians*, 261–72.

7. Ganshof sketched the problematic inheritance left to Louis by Charlemagne in his essay, "Charlemagne's Failure," in Ganshof, *Carolingians*, 256–60.

8. Ganshof, "Louis the Pious Reconsidered," 263.

9. Ganshof, "Louis the Pious Reconsidered," 267. J. L. Nelson, "The Last Years of

Louis the Pious," in *CH*, ed. Godman and Collins, 147–59, was the first to respond to Ganshof's partial rehabilitation of Louis with a call for further rehabilitation, arguing that Louis' later years, which Ganshof condemned (829–840), are also in need of reconsideration.

10. Peters, *The Shadow King*.

11. Peters, *The Shadow King*, 47. See also R. McKitterick, "The Illusion of Royal Power in the Carolingian Annals," *EHR* 115 (2000): 1–20; *Der Dynastiewechsel von 751: Vorgeschichte, Legitimationsstrategien und Erinnerung*, ed. M. Becher and J. Jarnut (Münster, 2004).

12. Peters, *The Shadow King*, 48.

13. Peters, *The Shadow King*, 57.

14. Peters, *The Shadow King*, 60–61.

15. *Relatio Comp.*, ed. Booker, 13–14; Appendix, ll. 67–72.

16. J. L. Nelson, "Bad Kingship in the Earlier Middle Ages," *Haskins Society Journal* 8 (1996): 9–15, 21–22. See also L. Halphen, *Charlemagne and the Carolingian Empire*, trans. G. de Nie (1947; Amsterdam, 1977), 175.

17. Peters, *The Shadow King*, 65, my emphasis; see also 51. Cf. P. E. Dutton, *The Politics of Dreaming in the Carolingian Empire* (Lincoln, Neb., 1994), 78; P. Chevallard, *Saint Agobard, archevêque de Lyon: Sa vie et ses écrits* (Lyon, 1869), 319.

18. S. Airlie, "Private Bodies and the Body Politic in the Divorce Case of Lothar II," *PP* 161 (1998): 26. On this "machinery" and its relationship with "political Augustinianism," cf. J. M. Wallace-Hadrill, "The 'Via Regia' of the Carolingian Age," in idem, *Early Medieval History* (1965; Oxford, 1975), 192. See also Chapter 1, n. 24.

19. Peters, *The Shadow King*, 48, 66–71. For additional remarks on *virtus*, 22–23.

20. Peters, *The Shadow King*, 63–64.

21. Peters, *The Shadow King*, 60; see also 16–17.

22. E. Wohlhaupter, *Aequitas canonica: Eine Studie aus dem kanonischen Recht* (Paderborn, 1931), 32–35.

23. Cf. M. Orrù, *Anomie: History and Meanings* (Boston, 1987), 56.

24. M. Donnini, "Sul Lessico Giuridico nelle Fonti Altomedievali: Polisemia ed Esattezza di Significato in un Latino fra Letteratura e Diritto," *SS Spoleto* 44(1): 1226; Orrù, *Anomie*, 56; A. Wallace-Hadrill, "The Emperor and His Virtues," *Historia* 30 (1981): 302–3; R. Foreville, "Aux origines de la renaissance juridique: Concepts juridiques et influences romanisantes chez Guillaume de Poitiers, biographe du conquérant," *MA* 58 (1952): 59; C. Lefebvre, *Les pouvoirs du juge en droit canonique: Contribution historique et doctrinale à l'étude du canon 20 sur la méthode et les sources en droit positif* (Paris, 1938), 169.

25. Dutton, *The Politics of Dreaming*, 290 n. 54; G. Bührer-Thierry, "La reine adultère," *CCM* 35 (1992): 299–312.

26. J. Gaudemet, "Tradition romaine et reflexion chretienne: Le concept d'*aequitas* au IVe siecle," *Apollinaris* 63 (1990): 203; J. L. Nelson, "Kings with Justice, Kings Without Justice: An Early Medieval Paradox," *SS Spoleto*, 44(2): 799 n. 9; Koziol, *Begging*

Pardon and Favor, 218–21, 226–27; W. Ullmann, *The Carolingian Renaissance and the Idea of Kingship* (London, 1969), 58–59. F. Pringsheim, "Römische *Aequitas* der christlichen Kaiser," in *Acta congressus iuridici internationalis* (Rome, 1935), 1:121–52, is foundational.

27. The literature on this subject is massive. For an introduction, see *Aequitas and Equity: Equity in Civil Law and Mixed Jurisdictions*, ed. A. M. Rabello (Jerusalem, 1997); together with the rich bibliography by O. Bucci, "Per una storia dell'equita," *Apollinaris* 63 (1990): 257–317.

28. For a stimulating account of "doing equity," see W. I. Miller, "Clint Eastwood and Equity: Popular Culture's Theory of Revenge," in *Law in the Domains of Culture*, ed. A. Sarat and T. R. Kearns (Ann Arbor, Mich., 1998), 161–202.

29. A. Wallace-Hadrill, "Galba's *Aequitas*," *Numismatic Chronicle* 141 (1981): 20–39.

30. Cf. Orrù, *Anomie*, 55–56.

31. Cicero, *In Catilinam*, 2.25, ed. C. MacDonald, *LCL* (Cambridge, Mass., 1977), 94; idem, *De senectute*, 23.83, trans. modified slightly from W. A. Falconer, *LCL* (Cambridge, Mass., 1923), 94–95. See Wallace-Hadrill, "The Emperor and His Virtues," 302–3.

32. E.g., *Aequitas and Equity*, ed. Rabello; L. J. Riley, *The History, Nature, and Use of Epikeia in Moral Theology* (Washington, D.C., 1948); G. H. Haas, *The Concept of Equity in Calvin's Ethics* (Waterloo, 1997), 17–27; G. R. Evans, *Law and Theology in the Middle Ages* (London, 2002), 85–90. This list can easily be multiplied.

33. E.g., E. Kaufmann, *Aequitatis iudicium: Königsgericht und Billigkeit in der Rechtsordnung des frühen Mittelalters* (Frankfurt am Main, 1959).

34. Koziol, *Begging Pardon and Favor*, 218–21, 226–27; Gaudemet, "Tradition romaine," 191–204; P. Landau, "*Aequitas* in the *Corpus Iuris Canonici*," in *Aequitas and Equity: Equity in Civil Law and Mixed Jurisdictions*, ed. A. M. Rabello (Jerusalem, 1997), 128–30; Orrù, *Anomie*.

35. Augustine, *Ennarationes in psalmos*, 63.11, ed. E. Dekkers and J. Fraipont, *CCSL*, 39:814; idem, *De baptismo*, 6.5.7, ed. M. Petschenig, *CSEL*, 51(1):303; as noted by Lefebvre, *Les pouvoirs du juge*, 169. On Augustine's conception of *aequitas*, see Haas, *The Concept of Equity*, 24–27; A. E. McGrath, "Divine Justice and Divine Equity in the Controversy Between Augustine and Julian of Eclanum," *Downside Review* 101 (1983): 312–19; Wohlhaupter, *Aequitas canonica*, 30–31.

36. Orrù, *Anomie*, 43–44, 55–56, and for the quotation, 44–45.

37. Jerome, *Commentaria in Osee prophetam*, 2.8.14, ed. M. Adriaen, *CCSL*, 76:90; cited by Orrù, *Anomie*, 44.

38. Ambrose, *De Apologia prophetae David*, 1.13 (62), ed. P. Hadot, *SC*, 239:164; cited by Orrù, *Anomie*, 44. On Carolingian knowledge of this work, see Chapter 4, n. 54. Cf. also Isidore of Seville, *Differentiae*, 1.299, *PL* 83, col. 41A–B.

39. See Ambrose, *De officiis*, 3.5, ed. M. Testard, *Saint Ambroise: Les devoirs* (Paris, 1992), 2:93–98; following Cicero, *De officiis*, 3.9; who followed Plato, *The Republic*,

2.359–61. On the Gyges anecdote and its reception, see K. F. Smith, "The Tale of Gyges and the King of Lydia," *American Journal of Philology* 23 (1902): 261–82, 361–87; idem, "The Literary Tradition of Gyges and Candaules," *American Journal of Philology* 41 (1920): 1–37.

40. There has been much (fruitless) speculation about the symbolism of the equine statue and the corpse lying within it, e.g., R. Hollander, "The Golden Ring of Gyges: A Note on 'The Republic' (II 359)," *Eos* 71 (1983): 211–13.

41. Herodotus, *Histories*, 1.8–19, told another version of this tale, in which Gyges was able to commit his crime with impunity not by using a magic ring but by colluding with the queen and hiding behind the door in the royal bedchamber in order to slay the unsuspecting King Candaules. This version was dramatized in antiquity as a tragedy; see R. Travis, "The Spectation of Gyges in P. Oxy. 2382 and Herodotus Book 1," *Classical Antiquity* 19 (2000): 330–59. J. R. R. Tolkien, of course, also told his own version of the Gyges tale; cf. C. M. Booker, "Byte-Sized Middle Ages: Tolkien, Film, and the Digital Imagination," *Comitatus* 35 (2004): 148 n. 8.

42. Ambrose, *De officiis*, 3.5, ed. Testard, 2:95. Cf. Wallace-Hadrill, "The 'Via Regia' of the Carolingian Age," 194.

43. On the distinction Ambrose often makes between *lex mentis* and *lex carnis*, see B. Maes, *La loi naturelle selon Ambroise de Milan* (Rome, 1967), 178; Wohlhaupter, *Aequitas canonica*, 30.

44. On the potency of moral fables—the force Ambrose was attempting to overcome with his biblical, "true" account—see A. Laird, "Ringing the Changes on Gyges: Philosophy and the Formation of Fiction in Plato's *Republic*," *Journal of Hellenic Studies* 121 (2001): 12–29; U. Langer, "The Ring of Gyges in Plato, Cicero, and Lorenzo Valla: The Moral Force of Fictional Examples," in *Res et Verba in der Renaissance*, ed. E. Kessler and I. MacLean (Wiesbaden, 2002), 131–45.

45. Ambrose, *De officiis*, 3.5, ed. Testard, 2:95; trans. H. de Romestin, *A Select Library of Nicene and Post-Nicene Fathers*, 2nd ser. (New York, 1896), 10:73.

46. For Ambrose's letter to Theodosius, see Chapter 4, nn. 48, 50. Cf. Odilo's account of Judith's distress regarding her sinful silence, Chapter 1, n. 221.

47. The Gyges fable was known to the Carolingians likely through the *De officiis* of Cicero and Ambrose. See D. Ganz, "The Debate on Predestination," in *Charles the Bald: Court and Kingdom*, ed. M. Gibson and J. L. Nelson, 2nd ed. (London, 1990), 296–97; M. Winterbottom, "The Transmission of Cicero's *De officiis*," *Classical Quarterly* 43 (1993): 215–42; Ambrose, *De officiis*, ed. Testard, 1:52–60.

48. Cf. Ardo, *Vita Benedicti abbatis Anianensis*, 26, ed. O. Holder-Egger, MGH, SS, 15(1):210, on the "suitable" punishment incurred by several women who mocked an abbot by taking turns standing where he was accustomed to stand in a church and mimicking his posture for prayer.

49. P. Fouracre, "Carolingian Justice: The Rhetoric of Improvement and Contexts of Abuse," *SS Spoleto*, 42(2): 771–803. The groundwork for this study was done by E. Ewig, "Zum christlichen Königsgedanken im Frühmittelalter," in *Das Königtum: Seine geistigen*

und rechtlichen Grundlagen (Lindau, 1954), 7–73, esp. 19–23. See also J. M. Wallace-Hadrill, "The Seventh Century" in idem, *Early Germanic Kingship in England and on the Continent* (Oxford, 1971), 48.

50. H. H. Anton, *Fürstenspiegel und Herrscherethos in der Karolingerzeit* (Bonn, 1968), 68. See also idem, "Pseudo-Cyprian: *De duodecim abusivis saeculi* und sein Einfluss auf den Kontinent, inbesondere auf die karolingischen Fürstenspiegel," in *Die Iren und Europa im früheren Mittelalter*, ed. H. Löwe (Stuttgart, 1982), 568–617; M. E. Moore, "La monarchie carolingienne et les anciens modèles irlandais," *AHSS* 51 (1996): 313–16. For an English translation of chapter 9 from the work, detailing the qualities of the "unjust king," see M. L. W. Laistner, *Thought and Letters in Western Europe, A.D. 500–900* (Ithaca, N.Y., 1957), 144–45.

51. Fouracre, "Carolingian Justice," 774–75.

52. E. Boshof, *Ludwig der Fromme* (Darmstadt, 1996), 105–6; Koziol, *Begging Pardon and Favor*, xiii–xiv, 177–78; J. M. Wallace-Hadrill, *The Frankish Church* (Oxford, 1983), 229–30, 263–66; J. Semmler, "*Renovatio Regni Francorum*: Die Herrschaft Ludwigs des Frommen im Frankenreich 814–829/830," in *CH*, ed. Godman and Collins, 140–42. On the influence of Visigothic southerners in the Carolingian realm, see P. Riché, "Les réfugiés wisigoths dans le monde carolingien," in *L'Europe, héritière de l'Espagne wisigothique*, ed. J. Fontaine and C. Pellistrandi (Madrid, 1992), 177–83.

53. On Aquitaine under Louis' reign (781–814), see P. Wolff, "L'Aquitaine et ses marges," in *Karl der Grosse*, ed. W. Braunfels (Düsseldorf, 1965), 1:269–306; L. Auzias, *L'Aquitaine carolingienne (778–987)* (Toulouse, 1937), 3–76.

54. R. Collins, "Charlemagne and His Critics, 814–829," in *La royauté et les élites dans l'Europe carolingienne*, ed. R. Le Jan (Lille, 1998), 203.

55. For an overview of these councils, see Halphen, *Charlemagne*, 161–62; Wallace-Hadrill, *The Frankish Church*, 263–66; R. McKitterick, *The Frankish Kingdoms Under the Carolingians, 751–987* (London, 1983), 106–24; W. Hartmann, *Die Synoden der Karolingerzeit im Frankenreich und in Italien* (Paderborn, 1989), 153–64.

56. Ardo, *Vita Benedicti*, 35, ed. Holder-Egger, 15(1):215. On Benedict, see P. Engelbert, "Benedikt von Aniane und die karolingische Reichsidee: Zur politischen Theologie des Frühmittelalters," in *Cultura e spiritualità nella tradizione monastica*, ed. G. Penco (Rome, 1990), 67–103; R. Grégoire, "Benedetto di Aniane nella riforma monastica carolingia," *SM* 3rd ser. 26 (1985): 573–610; J. Semmler, "Benedictus II: Una Regula—Una Consuetudo," in *Benedictine Culture, 750–1050*, ed. W. Lourdaux and D. Verhelst (Louvain, 1983), 1–49; Boshof, *Ludwig der Fromme*, 39–49, 120–26.

57. Ardo, *Vita Benedicti*, 42, ed. Holder-Egger, 15(1):219; trans. A. Cabaniss, *The Emperor's Monk* (Elms Court, 1979), 96. On Louis' close relationship with Benedict, cf. Ermoldus Nigellus, *In honorem Hludowici*, 2.1184–1253, ed. E. Faral, *Ermold le Noir: Poème sur Louis le Pieux et épîtres au roi Pépin* (Paris, 1964), 92–96. On the abbey at Kornelimünster, see C. B. McClendon, *The Origins of Medieval Architecture: Building in Europe, A.D. 600–900* (New Haven, Conn., 2005), 162.

58. On the later nickname "Pius," see Chapter 2, n. 52.

59. *Concilium Toletanum* XII, 1, ed. J. Vives, *Concilios Visigóticos e Hispano-Romanos* (Barcelona, 1963), 385–87. See R. L. Stocking, *Bishops, Councils, and Consensus in the Visigothic Kingdom, 589–633* (Ann Arbor, Mich., 2000), 186–89; M. de Jong, "Adding Insult to Injury: Julian of Toledo and His *Historia Wambae*," in *The Visigoths from the Migration Period to the Seventh Century: An Ethnographic Perspective*, ed. P. Heather (San Marino, Calif., 1999), 373–402; F. S. Paxton, *Christianizing Death: The Creation of a Ritual Process in Early Medieval Europe* (Ithaca, N.Y., 1990), 73–74 n. 103.

60. De Jong, "Power and Humility," 42; Ullmann, *The Carolingian Renaissance*, 69–70 n. 1.

61. T. Kardong, "*Justitia* in the Rule of Benedict," *Studia monastica* 24 (1982): 68–71. Kardong notes *aequitas* and its cognate forms such as *aequalis* in the Rule at Prologus, 47; 2.20, 22; 3.11; 11.11; 18.20; 31.17; and the title of 34. Cf. U. K. Jacobs, *Die Regula Benedicti als Rechtsbuch: Eine rechtshistorische und rechtstheologische Untersuchung* (Cologne, 1987), 147–53.

62. Hrabanus Maurus, *Commentaria in Ezechielem*, 12.33, *PL* 110, col. 833B. Cf. idem, *De universo*, 6.1, *PL* 111, col. 160C. On *discretio* in the Rule, see Benedict, *Regula*, 64.19, ed. Hanslik, 166; Jacobs, *Die Regula Benedicti als Rechtsbuch*, 149–53; E. Scholl, "The Mother of Virtues: *Discretio*," *Cistercian Studies Quarterly* 36 (2001): 389–401; C. Straw, *Gregory the Great: Perfection in Imperfection* (Berkeley, Calif., 1988), 15 n. 60.

63. L. Milis, "Dispute and Settlement in Medieval Cenobitical Rules," *Bulletin de l'institut historique Belge de Rome* 60 (1990): 43–63; idem, "Topsy-Turvy Morality: Obedience as a Regulator of Social Behavior," in *Peasants and Townsmen: Studia in honorem Adriaan Verhulst*, ed. J.-M. Duvosquel and E. Thoen (Ghent, 1995), 651–61; idem, "Rejecting Power, Gaining Power," in *The Growth of Authority in the Medieval West*, ed. M. Gosman et al. (Groningen, 1999), 83–96. Cf. T. Kardong, "Self-Will in Benedict's Rule," *Studia monastica* 42 (2000): 319–46.

64. Kardong, "*Justitia* in the Rule," 68–69.

65. Benedict, *Regula*, 7.18, ed. Hanslik, 47.

66. Hildemar, *Expositio regulae S. Benedicti*, ed. R. Mittermüller, *Vita et regula SS. P. Benedicti una cum expositione regulae* (Regensburg, 1880), 3:106. On Hildemar, see M. de Jong, "Growing Up in a Carolingian Monastery: Magister Hildemar and His Oblates," *JMH* 9 (1983): 99–128.

67. Ermoldus Nigellus, *In honorem Hludowici*, 2.1248–49, ed. Faral, 96; T. F. X. Noble, "The Monastic Ideal as a Model for Empire: The Case of Louis the Pious," *RB* 86 (1976): 242–50. Cf. Milis, "Dispute and Settlement," 55.

68. P. R. McKeon, "The Empire of Louis the Pious: Faith, Politics, and Personality," *RB* 90 (1980): 50–62.

69. McKeon, "The Empire of Louis," 59–61. For McKeon's characterization of the reign as a "tragedy," 52.

70. J. M. Wallace-Hadrill, "Charles the Bald and Alfred," in idem, *Early Germanic Kingship in England and on the Continent* (Oxford, 1971), 136; McKitterick, *The Frankish*

Kingdoms, 124; R. Deshman, "The Exalted Servant: The Ruler Theology of the Prayerbook of Charles the Bald," *Viator* 11 (1980): 385–417; M. Innes, "'He never even allowed his white teeth to be bared in laughter': The Politics of Humour in the Carolingian Renaissance," in *Humour, History and Politics in Late Antiquity and the Early Middle Ages,* ed. G. Halsall (Cambridge, 2002), 144, 147, 155–56; and the studies in Chapter 4, n. 152.

71. Noble, "The Monastic Ideal," 242–43. For warnings to the abbot about his spiritual responsibility, see Benedict, *Regula,* 2.6–7, 30–31, 34, 37–40; 3.11; 63.3; 64.7; 65.22.

72. Benedict, *Regula,* 2.39–40, ed. Hanslik, 28–29.

73. *Proemium generale ad capitularia tam ecclesiastica quam mundana* (818/19), ed. A. Boretius, MGH, *Capit.,* 1:274, as noted by Noble, "The Monastic Ideal," 244.

74. Benedict, *Regula,* 2.30, 37–38, ed. Hanslik, 26, 28.

75. Bruno Candidus, *Vita Eigilis,* 9–10, ed. G. Waitz, MGH, *SS,* 15(1):225–28; M. de Jong, "*Sacrum palatium et ecclesia:* L'autorité religieuse royale sous les Carolingiens (790–840)," *AHSS* 58 (2003): 1249–50.

76. *Capitula de missis instruendis* (829), ed. A. Boretius and V. Krause, MGH, *Capit.,* 2:8. Cf. Benedict, *Regula,* 2.25, ed. Hanslik, 25. See Chapter 4, n. 152.

77. Cf. Noble, "The Monastic Ideal," 247–48; S. Airlie, "Bonds of Power and Bonds of Association in the Court Circle of Louis the Pious," in *CH,* ed. Godman and Collins, 200–201. The contemporary lay noblewoman Dhuoda also considered the Rule a useful mimetic model. In her handbook of salutary behavior she sent to her sixteen-year-old warrior son at court, Dhuoda advised a monastic program of study of the Psalms and frequently included scriptural passages characteristic of Benedict's Rule, such as 2 Tim. 4:2 ("Reprove, Entreat, Rebuke") and Ezekiel 3:18 (the obligation to combat iniquity), viewing them as appropriate to secular life. Thanks to Benedict of Aniane's constant teaching and close counsel, the "monkish" emperor Louis seems to have thought so, too. See C. Neel, ed. and trans., *Dhuoda: Handbook for William: A Carolingian Woman's Counsel for Her Son* (Lincoln, Neb., 1991), 136 n. 205. For Ezek. 3:18 and 2 Tim. 4:2, see Dhuoda, *Liber manualis,* 4.8, ed. P. Riché, *SC,* 225bis:246 n. 1; 254. On Dhuoda's monastic ethos, see M. A. Claussen, "Fathers of Power and Mothers of Authority: Dhuoda and the *Liber manualis,*" *French Historical Studies* 19 (1996): 794–802; M. A. Mayeski, "A Mother's Psalter: Psalms in the Moral Instruction of Dhuoda of Septimania," in *The Place of the Psalms in the Intellectual Culture of the Middle Ages,* ed. N. van Deusen (Albany, N.Y., 1999), 139–51.

78. Agobard, *Adversus legem Gundobadi,* ed. Van Acker, 19–28.

79. Agobard, *Adversus legem Gundobadi,* 14, ed. Van Acker, 28. Cf. P. Riché, *The Carolingians: A Family Who Forged Europe,* trans. M. I. Allen (1983; Philadelphia, 1993), 175.

80. Cf. Fouracre, "Carolingian Justice," 792–93. On order and disorder in terms of concord and discord, see M. de Jong, "The Empire as *Ecclesia:* Hrabanus Maurus and Biblical *Historia* for Rulers," in *UP,* ed. Hen and Innes, 225; K. F. Morrison, "'Know Thyself': Music in the Carolingian Renaissance," *SS Spoleto,* 39(1): 369–483.

81. Agobard, *De dispensatione ecclesiasticarum rerum*, 4, ed. Van Acker, 122. Cf. also his remark about the "adversaries of equity" in his treatise *De grandine et tonitruis*, 14, ed. Van Acker, 13.

82. *Admonitio ad omnes regni ordines* (823–825), 14, ed. A. Boretius, MGH, *Capit.*, 1:305. On this *ordinatio*, see O. Guillot, "Une *ordinatio* méconnue: Le Capitulaire de 823–825," in *CH*, ed. Godman and Collins, 455–86.

83. Jonas of Orléans, *De institutione regia*, 4, ed. A. Dubreucq, *SC*, 407:198.

84. Jonas of Orléans, *De institutione regia*, 8, ed. Dubreucq, 220. Cf. W. Parsons, "The Medieval Theory of the Tyrant," *Review of Politics* 4 (1942): 134.

85. Hrabanus Maurus, *Commentaria in Ecclesiasticum*, *PL* 109, col. 900D.

86. Hildemar, *Expositio regulae S. Benedicti*, ed. Mittermüller, 3:106.

87. Paschasius Radbertus, *Exp. in Matheo*, 8.18.28, ed. Paulus, 56A:914. Paschasius also applied this definition to the issue of conscience and hierarchies of loyalty; *Epitaphium*, 1.3, ed. Dümmler, 24. See n. 113 below.

88. Ebbo, *Apologeticus* 2, ed. Werminghoff, 801.

89. Ratramnus, *De praedestinatione Dei*, 2, *PL* 121, col. 50A, following Fulgentius, *Ad Monimum*, 1.6.3, ed. J. Fraipont, *CCSL*, 91:7.

90. Gottschalk, *De praedestinatione*, 9.1, ed. C. Lambot, *Oeuvres théologiques et grammaticales de Godescalc d'Orbais* (Louvain, 1945), 202. Cf. J. Wetzel, "Snares of Truth: Augustine on Free Will and Predestination," in *Augustine and His Critics: Essays in Honour of Gerald Bonner*, ed. R. Dodaro and G. Lawless (London, 2000), 129. On Gottschalk, see D. E. Nineham, "Gottschalk of Orbais: Reactionary or Precursor of the Reformation?" *JEH* 40 (1989): 1–18. For the predestination controversy of the ninth century, see Ganz, "The Debate on Predestination," 283–302.

91. Letter from an anonymous nobleman to Queen Ermengard (ca. 840–843), ed. E. Dümmler, MGH, *Epist.*, 5:343–44, no. 27.

92. J. L. Nelson, "The Search for Peace in a Time of War: The Carolingian Brüderkrieg, 840–843," in *Träger und Instrumentarien des Friedens im hohen und späten Mittelalter*, ed. J. Fried (Sigmaringen, 1996), 102–4. Cf. C. M. Booker, "*Imitator daemonum dicor*: Adalhard the Seneschal, Mistranslations, and Misrepresentations," *Jahrbuch für internationale Germanistik* 33 (2001): 114–26; and Chapter 1, n. 153.

93. Einhard, *Translatio*, ed. Waitz, 239–64; trans. Dutton, *Courtier*, 69–130; Dutton, *The Politics of Dreaming*, 91–98; M. Bondois, *La translation des Saints Marcellin et Pierre* (Paris, 1907). On the date of its composition, see Dutton, *Courtier*, xxiv–xxx.

94. On this episode, see Dutton, *The Politics of Dreaming*, 95–98; Bondois, *La translation des Saints*, 87, 93–99.

95. Einhard, *Translatio*, 3.14, ed. Waitz, 253; trans. Dutton, *Courtier*, 104.

96. Recall that, in the letter he wrote to Pope Leo IV sometime between 847 and 849 regarding Ebbo and Hincmar, Lothar admitted that the devil, working "through his attendants" (*per satellites suos*), had caused that "time of most wretched discord" in the 830s; Lothar, *Ep. Leoni papae directa*, ed. A. Hirsch-Gereuth, MGH, *Epist.*, 5:609–11. See Chapter 5, n. 61.

97. Einhard, *Translatio*, 3.14, ed. Waitz, 253.

98. Dutton, *The Politics of Dreaming*, 96.

99. Einhard, *Translatio*, 3.14, ed. Waitz, 254; trans. Dutton, *Courtier*, 105.

100. Dutton, *The Politics of Dreaming*, 290 n. 54, has also observed that "after the 820s this [sc., *iniquitas*] was to be a frequent theme." Cf. Bührer-Thierry, "La reine adultère," 299–312, on the moral discourse of iniquity in the 820–830s. For more general remarks, see Peters, *The Shadow King*, 57–71.

101. *Relatio Comp.*, ed. Booker, 12, 13; Appendix, ll. 25–27, 54–56 (on necessity); Ebbo, *Apologeticus* 2, ed. Werminghoff, 801; Agobard, *Cartula*, ed. Van Acker, 323. On the moral imperative of Carolingian justice, see R. McKitterick, "Perceptions of Justice in Western Europe in the Ninth and Tenth Centuries," *SS Spoleto*, 44(2): 1075–104; Fouracre, "Carolingian Justice," 771–803.

102. *Relatio Comp.*, ed. Booker, 11; Appendix, ll. 11–13.

103. Benedict, *Regula*, 64.3–6, ed. Hanslik, 163–64.

104. Recall that Ebbo's ordained clerics would later claim that Ebbo had only participated in the divestiture of Louis in 833 because, as archbishop, he had been responsible for the direction of any such proceedings taking place within his diocese. See Ganz, "The Debate on Predestination," 285; Simson, *Jahrbücher*, 2:75 n. 3; and Chapter 5, nn. 6, 69. On the intervention of bishops in the affairs of monasteries, see G. Constable, "The Authority of Superiors in Religious Communities," in *La notion d'autorité au Moyen Âge: Islam, Byzance, Occident* (Paris, 1982), 189–210, esp. 196.

105. Agobard, *Cartula*, ed. Van Acker, 324.

106. Agobard, *Liber apologeticus* I, 6, ed. Van Acker, 312. Cf. Paschasius Radbertus, *Exp. in Matheo*, 5.9.13, ed. Paulus, 56A:522–23, "*Ad hoc quippe vulneratus est propter iniquitates nostras.*"

107. Agobard, *Cartula*, ed. Van Acker, 324. Note the further attention Agobard gives to the problem of iniquity and sin in a long letter written to Ebbo, ca. 823–835, *De spe et timore*, ed. Van Acker, 429–54, esp. 432 and 454 where he begins to discuss Ezek. 3:17–18 (at which point the manuscript unfortunately breaks off *in medias res*). See Chapter 4, n. 36.

108. Ebbo, *Apologeticus* 2, ed. Werminghoff, 801; idem, *Apologeticus* 1, ed. Werminghoff, 795.

109. Ebbo, *Apologeticus* 2, ed. Werminghoff, 801. Around the same time, Dhuoda, in her handbook for her son William, would also quote this psalm, exhorting him to practice justice, love equity, and hate iniquity. See Dhuoda, *Liber manualis*, 4.8, ed. Riché, 225*bis*:244.

110. Paschasius Radbertus, *Epitaphium*, 1.3, ed. Dümmler, 24.

111. Paschasius Radbertus, *Epitaphium*, 1.3, ed. Dümmler, 25; trans. A. Cabaniss, *Charlemagne's Cousins: Contemporary Lives of Adalard and Wala* (Syracuse, N.Y., 1967), 92.

112. Paschasius Radbertus, *Epitaphium*, 1.3, ed. Dümmler, 24; trans. Cabaniss, *Charlemagne's Cousins*, 92.

113. Ebbo, *Apologeticus* 2, ed. Werminghoff, 801.

114. H. Mayr-Harting, "Two Abbots in Politics: Wala of Corbie and Bernard of Clairvaux," *TRHS* 5th ser. 40 (1990): 225, 236–37, D. Ganz, "The *Epitaphium Arsenii* and Opposition to Louis the Pious" in *CH*, ed. Godman and Collins, 544–45.

115. As Dhuoda would remind her son, "set opposites against opposites"; Dhuoda, *Liber manualis*, 4.2, ed. Riché, 225*bis*:206. The observation of D. A. Schön, "Generative Metaphor: A Perspective on Problem-Setting in Social Policy," in *Metaphor and Thought*, ed. A. Ortony (Cambridge, 1993), 150, that "the ways in which we set social problems determine both the kinds of purposes and values we seek to realize, and the directions in which we seek solutions" pertains no less to the ninth century than to the twenty-first.

116. On Hrabanus's political stance in the 830s, see M. Perrin, "La représentation figurée de César-Louis le Pieux chez Raban Maur en 835: Religion et idéologie," *Francia* 24, 1 (1997): 39–64; B.-S. Albert, "Raban Maur, l'unité de l'empire et ses relations avec les carolingiens," *Revue d'histoire ecclésiastique* 86 (1991): 7–16; E. Sears, "Louis the Pious as *Miles Christi*: The Dedicatory Image in Hrabanus Maurus's *De laudibus sanctae crucis*," in *CH*, ed. Godman and Collins, 622.

117. Hrabanus Maurus, *Ep.* 15.4, ed. E. Dümmler, MGH, *Epist.*, 5:409. Cf. Sears, "Louis the Pious as *Miles Christi*," 622.

118. Cf. Hrabanus Maurus, *Ep.* 15.9, ed. Dümmler, 5:412–13; Agobard, *Cartula*, ed. Van Acker, 324. Note Hrabanus's frequent quotation of scriptural passages containing the word *iniquitas*, esp. in 15.9 and 15.11.

119. Hrabanus Maurus, *Ep.* 15.9, ed. Dümmler, 5:412–13 (wisdom forged through iniquity); 15, proem., ed. Dümmler, 5:404; and 15.12, ed. Dümmler, 5:415 (humble and devout mind).

120. See Chapters 1, n. 85; 4, n. 124.

121. Hrabanus's letter soon found favor with Louis, for the emperor not only requested a detailed study from Hrabanus on the virtues and vices but also commended into his care the disgraced former bishop Ebbo. For Hrabanus's treatise, see the (sole complete) edition by W. Lazius, *Fragmenta quaedam Caroli Magni Imp. Rom. aliorumque incerti nominis de veteris Ecclesiae ritibus ac ceremoniis* (Antwerp, 1560), 190–306; and the commentary by Sears, "Louis the Pious as *Miles Christi*," 622–23.

122. Hrabanus Maurus, *Liber ad Otgarium*, ed. E. Dümmler, MGH, *Epist.*, 5:464. On this letter, see Albert, "Raban Maur, l'unité de l'empire," 20. Hrabanus would later repeat these remarks ca. 853–856 in a letter to Bishop Heribald of Auxerre, a former conspirator of 833, who had been granted clemency by Louis the Pious; see Hrabanus Maurus, *Poenitentiale ad Heribaldum*, 4, *PL* 110, col. 472D. Cf. F. H. Russell, *The Just War in the Middle Ages* (Cambridge, 1975), 31–32.

123. The reference to Hrabanus's letter was made sometime in the mid-840s by his biographer, Rudolf of Fulda, *Miracula sanctorum in Fuldensis ecclesias translatorum*, 15, ed. G. Waitz, MGH, *SS*, 15(1):341.

124. Hrabanus Maurus, *Ep.* 15.3, ed. Dümmler, 5:406–8. Perhaps Hrabanus's famous

illustration of the emperor, in his work *In honorem sanctae crucis*, should be understood in terms of Louis as a defender of equity and Christian peace, armed against the destructive forces of tyrannical iniquity. A recent study has argued persuasively that it was created as a royal gift soon after Louis' recoronation assembly in February 835; Perrin, "La représentation figurée," 39–64. See also C. Chazelle, *The Crucified God in the Carolingian Era: Theology and Art of Christ's Passion* (Cambridge, 2001), 129–31. Note that Paris, B.N.F. lat. 2423 is thought to be the actual presentation copy from Hrabanus to the emperor; see Perrin, "La représentation figurée," 58–59.

125. In the wake of Louis' recovery of the throne, the annalist often employs the verb "*disponere*" when speaking of the emperor's productive activities: *AB*, s.a. 834, 835, 837, 839, ed. Grat et al., 15, 17, 21, 27. Perhaps this is a useful stylistic criterion for determining the location of the long-postulated break in authorship of the annals during the 830s.

126. *AB*, s.a. 835, ed. Grat et al., 16–17; trans. modified slightly from Nelson, *ASB*, 32–33.

127. Cf. De Jong, "Power and Humility," 43; S. MacLean, "Ritual, Misunderstanding, and the Contest for Meaning: Representations of the Disrupted Royal Assembly at Frankfurt (873)," in *Representations of Power in Medieval Germany 800–1500*, ed. B. Weiler and S. MacLean (Turnhout, 2006), 113 and n. 59.

128. *AB*, s.a. 835, ed. Grat et al., 16–17. Charles the Bald, in a letter to Pope Nicholas I thirty-two years later (867), ed. W. Hartmann, MGH, *Conc.*, 4:240, would also remember Ebbo's confession at Metz in this way; the archbishop admitted to having rendered an inequitable judgment (*non equum . . . iudicium*) against Charles's father at Soissons in 833. Cf. Hincmar of Reims, in his treatise from 881, *De ordine palatii*, 5, ed. T. Gross and R. Schieffer, MGH, *Fontes iuris Germanici antiqui in usum scholarum, separatim editi* (Hannover, 1980), 3:70–71, and n. 160, that one duty of the count of the palace was to lead perverse judgments back to the course of equity (*ad aequitatis tramitem reduceret*).

129. Walafrid Strabo, *Ad eandem* [sc., Judith] *de quodam somnio*, ed. E. Dümmler, MGH, *PLAC*, 2:379–80; German trans. K. Langosch, *Lyrische Anthologie des lateinischen Mittelalters* (Darmstadt, 1968), 108–11. For linguistic commentary, see A. Önnerfors, "Philologisches zu Walahfrid Strabo," *MJb* 7 (1972): 85–87; idem, *Mediaevalia: Abhandlungen und Aufsätze* (Frankfurt am Main, 1977), 111–13.

130. Walafrid Strabo, *De quodam somnio*, vv. 24–25, ed. Dümmler, 2:379.

131. Walafrid Strabo, *De quodam somnio*, v. 28, ed. Dümmler, 2:379. For another instance of Walafrid's commenting on the power of images, see his work *De exordiis et incrementis quarundam in observationes ecclesiasticis rerum*, 8, ed. and trans. A. L. Harting-Correa (Leiden, 1996), 80–81. Cf. also Paschasius Radbertus, *Epitaphium*, 1.11, ed. Dümmler, 39, referring to his guarded literary portrait of Wala. For the early medieval belief that all things have a "true name" that reflects their intrinsic nature or essence, see P. Dronke, *Women Writers of the Middle Ages: A Critical Study of Texts from Perpetua († 203) to Marguerite Porete († 1310)* (Cambridge, 1984), 5.

132. Cf. Walafrid's reference to the ruler's (Louis') "ever-retrievable honor" (*decus*

reparabile semper) with the laconic characterization of the events of 833 in several contemporary annals (stemming from Reichenau) as "the shame of the Franks" (*francorum dedecus*). See Chapter 2, n. 72.

133. Walafrid Strabo, *De quodam somnio*, vv. 36–37, ed. Dümmler, 2:380; trans. Dutton, *The Politics of Dreaming*, 106.

134. On allusive messages within interpretive communities, see P. E. Dutton, "Whispering Secrets to a Dark Age," in idem, *Mustache*, 148–50.

135. H. Siemes, "Beiträge zum literarischen Bild Kaiser Ludwigs des Frommen in der Karolingerzeit" (Ph.D. diss., Universität Freiburg, 1966), 165–68. For the *De imagine Tetrici*, see M. W. Herren, "The '*De imagine Tetrici*' of Walahfrid Strabo: Edition and Translation," *JML* 1 (1991): 118–39; idem, "Walahfrid Strabo's *De imagine Tetrici*: An Interpretation," in *Latin Culture and Medieval Germanic Europe*, ed. R. North and T. Hofstra (Groningen, 1992), 25–41.

136. Hrabanus Maurus, *Commentaria in Exodum IV*, 2.4, *PL* 108, col. 68B. Cf. J. W. Smit, "The *Equitatio super undas*," in idem, *Studies on the Language and Style of Columba the Younger (Columbanus)* (Amsterdam, 1971), 190–97.

137. H. J. Kamphausen, *Traum und Vision in der lateinischen Poesie der Karolingerzeit* (Frankfurt am Main, 1975), 151–53.

138. Dutton, *The Politics of Dreaming*, 106.

139. Herren, "The '*De imagine Tetrici*' of Walahfrid Strabo," 123, 132, vv. 42–45. See L. K. Little, "Pride Goes Before Avarice: Social Change and the Vices in Latin Christendom," *AHR* 76 (1971): 31–39; A. Katzenellenbogen, *Allegories of the Virtues and Vices in Medieval Art* (London, 1939).

140. Due to the poem's apotheosization of an interpretation identical to that rendered by the bishops attending Louis' restoration at Metz in February 835, Walafrid may have composed the poem somewhat later than the date usually assigned to it. Rather than during the period immediately after Judith's return from captivity in Italy (834), perhaps it was composed shortly after the February 835 assembly at Metz. The Metz restoration assembly could thus be one of the propitious events Walafrid had glimpsed in his prophetic dream that had been "fulfilled in deeds."

141. Astronomer, *VH*, 38, 54, ed. Tremp, 424, 504 (lover of equity); *VH*, 23, 38, 59, 60, ed. Tremp, 354, 424, 526, 530 (equitable balance). Cf. the remarks above on the Astronomer's identity, Chapter 1, n. 129.

142. Wohlhaupter, *Aequitas canonica*, 32–35.

143. Cf. the critique of E. Kaufmann, *Aequitatis iudicium: Königsgericht und Billigkeit in der Rechtsordnung des frühen Mittelalters* (Frankfurt am Main, 1959), 33. Kaufmann argued that by the early Middle Ages *aequitas* already had a venerable tradition of being linked theocratically to the state, a political-theological commingling which had occurred long before the time of the Carolingians. Judging the Carolingian use of the term by the criterion of Roman legal standards, he declared that the expression of *aequitas* during Louis' reign was simply formulaic, carrying no specific institutional meaning.

144. Of the four councils, Paris, Lyon, Mainz, and Toulouse, only the acts of the Paris council survive: *Concilium Parisiense* (829), ed. A. Werminghoff, MGH, *Conc.*, 2(2):605–80. See Chapter 4, n. 39. It is unfortunate that Jonas's record of the Paris council has not been translated, for it provides perhaps the sharpest picture of the ecclesiological conception of Louis' rule and its problems.

145. *Concilium Parisiense* (829), 5, ed. Werminghoff, 2(2):612–14, quoting from Ezek. 3:18 four times. For the citations of Gregory, see B. Judic, "La tradition de Grégoire le Grand dans l'idéologie politique carolingienne," in *La royauté et les élites dans l'Europe carolingienne*, ed. R. Le Jan (Lille, 1998), 42–43.

146. *Concilium Parisiense* (829), ed. Werminghoff, 2(2):667. See M. E. Jegen, "Jonas of Orléans (c. 780–843): His Pastoral Writings and Their Social Significance" (Ph.D. diss., Saint Louis University, 1967), 288–89; D. Ganz, "Theology and the Organization of Thought," *NCMH* 2:768. In his report of Wiggo's unholy sermon, Einhard (or his source) also understood that the problem lay in the court of conscience; the language and themes of the demon's harangue were largely patterned after the text of Jonas of Orléans's report of the council in 829. See Dutton, *The Politics of Dreaming*, 99; Bondois, *La translation des Saints*, 94.

147. See n. 62 above.

148. *Relatio Comp.*, ed. Booker, 11–12; Appendix, ll. 16–24, citing Gregory the Great, *Regula pastoralis*, 2.1, 2.6, ed. F. Rommel, *SC*, 382(2):174, 202; idem, *Registrum epistularum*, 1, *Ep.* 24, ed. D. Norberg, *CCSL*, 140:23, 29. Cf. Hildemar, *Expositio regulae S. Benedicti*, ed. Mittermüller, 3:119–20, who also quoted these lines from Gregory on the counterbalances of humility and zeal in his commentary on the abbot's discretion and the nature of his duties.

149. Wohlhaupter, *Aequitas canonica*, 35 n. 1; G. H. Tavard, "Episcopacy and Apostolic Succession According to Hincmar of Reims," *Theological Studies* 34 (1973): 594–623; K. F. Morrison, *Tradition and Authority in the Western Church, 300–1140* (Princeton, N.J., 1969), 162, 246, 262; idem, *The Two Kingdoms: Ecclesiology in Carolingian Political Thought* (Princeton, N.J., 1964), 93–94, 104.

150. Pope Leo I, *Tractatus* 83(2), ed. A. Chavasse, *CCSL*, 138A:520–21; idem, *Tractatus* 4(3), ed. A. Chavasse, *CCSL*, 138:19–20.

151. Hincmar of Reims, *De presbyteris criminosis*, PL 125, col. 1107B; idem, *Ep.* 26 *(ad Adrianum papam)*, PL 126, col. 183B; idem, *Ep.* 32 *(ad Ioannem papam)*, PL 126, col. 243C–D; idem, *Opusculum LV capitulorum*, 20, ed. R. Schieffer, MGH, *Conc.*, 4(2):222; idem, *Liber expostulationis*, 26, ed. W. Hartmann, MGH, *Conc.*, 4:464. For the letter of Charles by Hincmar, see *Ep.* 8 *(ad Adrianum papam)*, PL 124, col. 894B–D. See also Tavard, "Episcopacy and Apostolic Succession," 616–17; J. L. Nelson, "'Not Bishops' Bailiffs but Lords of the Earth': Charles the Bald and the Problem of Sovereignty," in eadem, *The Frankish World, 750–900* (1991; London, 1996), 133–43.

152. See n. 62 above.

EPILOGUE

Epigraph: Bede, *De orthographia*, ed. H. Keil, *Grammatici Latini* (1880; Hildesheim, 1961), 7:264 l. 20; trans. C. D. Lanham, "Writing Instruction from Late Antiquity to the Twelfth Century," in *A Short History of Writing Instruction: From Ancient Greece to Modern America,* ed. J. J. Murphy (Mahwah, N.J., 2001), 87.

1. N. Staubach, "Das Rätsel des Sedulius Scottus: Bemerkungen zur Neuausgabe seiner Carmina," *Francia* 21, no. 1 (1994): 213–26; R. Düchting, *Sedulius Scottus: Seine Dichtungen* (Munich, 1968), 176–77.

2. Sedulius Scottus, *Carmina*, 64, vv. 5–8, ed. J. Meyers, *CCCM*, 117:105. For Traube's solution to the riddle, see MGH, *PLAC*, 3:219. For an English translation, which should be used with caution (cf. Dutton, *Mustache*, 244 n. 159), see E. G. Doyle, *Sedulius Scottus: On Christian Rulers and The Poems* (Binghamton, N.Y., 1983), 159.

3. Simson, *Jahrbücher*, 2:130 n. 6. There are no variants for this word in any manuscripts of either Flodoard's text or the Annals of Saint-Bertin.

4. Flodoard of Reims, *Historia Remensis ecclesiae*, 2.20, ed. M. Stratmann, MGH, *SS*, 36:185. Others have investigated the notion of *auctoritas* in the ninth century but not in its capacity as a substitute for *aequitas*. See M. David, *La souveraineté et les limites juridiques du pouvoir monarchique du IXe au XVe siècle* (Paris, 1954), 116 n. 35; O. Guillot, "Le concept d'autorité dans l'ordre politique français issu de l'an mil," in *La notion d'autorité au Moyen Age: Islam, Byzance, Occident* (Paris, 1982), 127–40; idem, "L'exhortation au partage des responsabilités entre l'empereur, l'épiscopat et les autres sujets vers le milieu du règne de Louis le Pieux," in *Prédication et propagande au Moyen Age: Islam, Byzance, Occident* (Paris, 1983), 87–110; Y. Sassier, "Le roi et la loi chez les penseurs du royaume occidental du deuxième quart du IXe à la fin du XIe s.," *CCM* 43 (2000): 257–73.

5. Paschasius Radbertus, *Epitaphium*, 2.17, ed. Dümmler, 85. In the first book of the *Epitaphium Arsenii*, which was written in the late 830s, Paschasius at that time appears to have still presupposed a unifying, viable state of equity in the realm. The persecutors of Wala were lacking in truth, he explained (*Epitaphium*, 1.26, ed. Dümmler, 57), being so corrupt that, as Isaiah had said (Is. 59:14), "equity cannot enter them." In other words, *aequitas* was not yet absent from the realm; just wanting in its offenders. Cf. D. Ganz, "The *Epitaphium Arsenii* and Opposition to Louis the Pious" in *CH*, ed. Godman and Collins, 546.

6. Cf. Paschasius's remarks on the role of the will in this process, in Chapter 1, nn. 199–201.

7. Sedulius Scottus, *Carmina*, 64, vv. 13, 15, ed. Meyers, 105.

8. Agobard, *Adversus legem Gundobadi*, 14, ed. Van Acker, 28.

9. H.-W. Goetz, "Die Wahrnehmung von 'Staat' und 'Herrschaft' im frühen Mittelalter," in *Staat im frühen Mittelalter*, ed. S. Airlie et al. (Vienna, 2006), 39–58; K. Leyser, "Three Historians," in idem, *Communications and Power in Medieval Europe: The*

Carolingian and Ottonian Centuries (London, 1994), 20–21; P. Depreux, "Nithard et la *Res Publica*: Un regard critique sur le règne de Louis le Pieux," *Médiévales* 22–23 (1992): 149–61; Y. Sassier, "L'utilisation d'un concept romain aux temps carolingiens: La *res publica* aux IXe et Xe siècles," *Médiévales* 15 (1988): 17–29; J. L. Nelson, "Legislation and Consensus in the Reign of Charles the Bald," in eadem, *Politics*, 108 n. 80; 202 n. 28; M. H. Hoeflich, "The Concept of *Utilitas Populi* in Early Ecclesiastical Law and Government," *Zeitschrift der Savigny-Stiftung für Rechtsgeschichte, Kanonistische Abteilung* 67 (1981): 36–74; W. Wehlen, *Geschichtsschreibung und Staatsauffassung im Zeitalter Ludwigs des Frommen* (Lübeck, 1970); J. Gaudemet, "Utilitas Publica," *Revue historique de droit français et étranger* 4 (1951): 465–99.

10. M. de Jong, "*Ecclesia* and the Early Medieval Polity," in *Staat im frühen Mittelalter*, ed. S. Airlie et al. (Vienna, 2006), 113–32.

11. *Relatio Comp.*, ed. Booker, 12, 17, 18; Appendix, ll. 32, 165, 197.

12. Cf. Chapter 4, nn. 59–60.

13. Frechulf of Lisieux, *Historiae*, 2, prologus ad Iudith, ed. M. I. Allen, *CCCM*, 169A:437; trans. Dutton, *Carolingian Civ.*, 256. On Frechulf, see *Frechulfi Lexouiensis episcopi Opera omnia*, ed. M. I. Allen, *CCCM*, 169.

14. M. Innes and R. McKitterick, "The Writing of History," in *Carolingian Culture: Emulation and Innovation*, ed. R. McKitterick (Cambridge, 1994), 215–17, understand this tension between teleology and political counsel/criticism differently, claiming that in order "to offer intelligent comment on contemporary politics and make realistic judgments [in the ninth century] one had to put this fact [of the Frankish monarchy as God's chosen instrument] firmly in the back of one's mind." Cf. M. Innes, "The Classical Tradition and Carolingian Historiography: Encounters with Suetonius," *IJCT* 3 (1997): 281–82; and M. de Jong, "The Empire as *Ecclesia*: Hrabanus Maurus and Biblical *Historia* for Rulers," in *UP*, ed. Hen and Innes, 198–99, who takes up this point with respect to Frechulf's *Chronicon*.

15. See the "Vision of the Poor Woman of Laon," trans. Dutton, *Carolingian Civ.*, 203–4, written sometime in the 820s (i.e., while Louis the Pious was still alive), which stated that, although Louis the Pious's name was inscribed in the otherworldly wall of those who would attain salvation, it was nearly effaced because "the killing of Bernard [Louis' nephew] led to the obliteration of that name." See P. E. Dutton, *The Politics of Dreaming in the Carolingian Empire* (Lincoln, Neb., 1994), 67–80.

16. On the contents of the manuscript, Laon, Bibliothèque municipale 407, see *Catalogue général des manuscrits des bibliothèques publiques des départements* (Paris, 1849), 1:209–11. The instructions and chart are on fols. 136v–137r. See the Introduction, n. 37. This manuscript also uniquely contains the letter from Pope Gregory IV regarding Ebbo's right to the see of Reims, together with the marginal note of its fraudulence. See Chapter 5, n. 57.

17. See Chapter 2, nn. 134–35.

18. Louis the Pious, *Ep.* 19, ed. E. Dümmler, MGH, *Epist.*, 5:325–27; *BHL* 2172. See Chapters 3, n. 123; 4, n. 120; 6, n. 121. The ninth-century manuscript used by Dümmler

for his edition of this letter (Phillipps 16339) now bears the shelfmark Berlin, Ms. Theol. Lat. Oct. 159. For Hilduin's reply to Louis' request, see Hilduin, *Ep.* 20, ed. E. Dümmler, MGH, *Epist.*, 5:327–35; *BHL* 2173; E. A. R. Brown, "*Gloriosae*, Hilduin, and the Early Liturgical Celebration of St. Denis," in *Medieval Paradigms: Essays in Honor of Jeremy Duquesnay Adams*, vol. 2, ed. S. Hayes-Healy (New York, 2005), 39–82; M. Lapidge, "The Lost '*Passio Metrica S. Dionysii*' by Hilduin of Saint-Denis," *MJb* 22 (1987): 56–79; G. P. A. Brown, "Politics and Patronage at the Royal Abbey of Saint-Denis (814–98): The Rise of a Royal Patron Saint" (Ph.D. diss., New College, Oxford University, 1989), 207–17, 283–329.

19. Sixty years ago, Heinrich Fichtenau, *The Carolingian Empire*, trans. P. Munz (1949; Oxford, 1957), 176, summed up this contest and its different perspectives with precision: "The conservatives looked upon the reformers as utopian doctrinaires; while the reformers saw in the conservatives no more than corrupt opportunists."

20. *AF*, s.a. 874, ed. Pertz and Kurze, 82; trans. T. Reuter, *The Annals of Fulda* (Manchester, 1992), 73–74. For details on this royal dream, its intertextuality, and the response it elicited, see Dutton, *The Politics of Dreaming*, 219–24.

21. On Audradus, see Dutton, *The Politics of Dreaming*, 128–56, esp. 143–45. Cf. Chapter 1, n. 150; and Lothar's claims, Chapter 5, n. 63.

22. See, for example, *Parallel Source Problems in Medieval History*, ed. F. Duncalf and A. C. Krey (New York, 1912), vii–xii, 7–8.

23. The episcopal *Relatio*'s description of the captive Louis' agreeing to undertake a humiliating public penance "willingly" and "with joy" was, for Halphen, a perfect example of this telling phenomenon; see L. Halphen, "La pénitence de Louis le Pieux à Saint Médard de Soissons," in idem, *A travers l'histoire du Moyen Age* (1904; Paris, 1950), 58–66.

24. On the early medieval understanding of texts as instruments or weapons—clubs used to bang the truth into the heads of one's enemies—cf. the complementary observations of H. Vollrath, "Oral Modes of Perception in Eleventh-Century Chronicles," in *Vox intexta: Orality and Textuality in the Middle Ages*, ed. A. N. Doane and C. B. Pasternack (Madison, Wis., 1991), 110; N. Hathaway, "Compilatio: From Plagiarism to Compiling," *Viator* 20 (1989): 27–28; D. E. Nineham, "Gottschalk of Orbais: Reactionary or Precursor of the Reformation?" *JEH* 40 (1989): 6 n. 23. As we have seen, the "textual swords" of the polemicists of 833 crossed only rarely.

25. Cf. Dutton, *Mustache*, xiv.

26. R. Starn and N. Z. Davis, "Introduction," *Representations* 26 (1989): 4.

27. "Hope is justified only by faith which justifies itself. Perhaps both grow only on the ruins of all-too-human beliefs and expectations, on the fruitful soil of despair of what is subject to illusions and deceptions." K. Löwith, *Meaning in History* (Chicago, 1949), 206.

SELECT BIBLIOGRAPHY

MANUSCRIPT SOURCES

Berlin, Deutsche Staatsbibliothek zu Berlin, Preussischer Kulturbesitz
    Meerman lat. 141
    MS theol. lat. oct. 159

Brussels, Bibliothèque royale
    MS 5417–5422

Copenhagen, Universitätsbibliothek
    AM 830 4°

Laon, Bibliothèque municipale
    MS 407

London, British Library
    1058.b.12: Pierre Pithou, *Annalium et historiae Francorum ab anno Christi DCCVIII ad annum DCCCCXC scriptores coaetanei XII. . . .* 2nd ed. Frankfurt, 1594.

Paris, Bibliothèque nationale de France
    fr. 2813
    lat. 1622
    lat. 2423
    lat. 2853
    lat. 2866
    lat. 5925
    lat. 7900
    lat. 8850
    lat. 9768
    lat. 13909
    lat. 14663
    nouv. acq. lat. 469

Rome, Biblioteca apostolica vaticana
  otto. lat. 3064
  pal. lat. 576
  reg. lat. 1260

St Gallen, Stiftsarchiv
  Zürcher Abt. X, Nr. 1

Wolfenbüttel, Herzog August Bibliothek
  Helmsted. 32

PRINTED PRIMARY SOURCES

Adam of Bremen. *Gesta hammaburgensis ecclesiae pontificum.* Ed. Bernhard Schmeidler. MGH, *SRG* 2. Hannover, 1917.

Admonitio ad omnes regni ordines (823–825). Ed. Alfred Boretius. MGH, *Capit.* 1:303–7, no. 150. Hannover, 1883.

Admonitio generalis (789). Ed. Alfred Boretius. MGH, *Capit.* 1:52–62, no. 22. Hannover, 1883.

Ado of Vienne. *Chronicon.* Ed. Georg H. Pertz. MGH, *SS* 2:317–26, Hannover, 1829. For the entire work, see *PL* 123, col. 23–138.

Agobard of Lyon. *Adversus legem Gundobadi.* Ed. Lieven van Acker. *CCCM* 52:19–28. Turnhout, 1981.

_____. *Cartula de Ludovici imperatoris poenitentia.* Ed. Lieven van Acker. *CCCM* 52:323–24. Turnhout, 1981.

_____. *De dispensatione ecclesiasticarum rerum.* Ed. Lieven van Acker. *CCCM* 52:121–42. Turnhout, 1981.

_____. *De divinis sententiis contra iudicium Dei.* Ed. Lieven van Acker. *CCCM* 52:31–49. Turnhout, 1981

_____. *De divisione imperii.* Ed. Lieven van Acker. *CCCM* 52:247–50. Turnhout, 1981.

_____. *De grandine et tonitruis.* Ed. Lieven van Acker. *CCCM* 52:3–15. Turnhout, 1981.

_____. *De iniusticiis.* Ed. Lieven van Acker. *CCCM* 52:225–27. Turnhout, 1981.

_____. *De privilegio apostolicae sedis.* Ed. Lieven van Acker. *CCCM* 52:303–6. Turnhout, 1981.

_____. *De spe et timore.* Ed. Lieven van Acker. *CCCM* 52:145–47, 429–54. Turnhout, 1981.

_____. *Liber apologeticus* I, II. Ed. Lieven van Acker. *CCCM* 52:309–12, 315–19. Turnhout, 1981.

_____. *Opera omnia.* Ed. Lieven van Acker. *CCCM* 52. Turnhout, 1981.

Alcuin. *Epistola ad Carolem imperatorem* (801–802). Ed. Ernst Dümmler. MGH, *Epist.* 4:401–4, no. 249. Berlin, 1895.

Ambrose. *De apologia prophetae David.* Ed. Pierre Hadot. *SC* 239. Paris, 1977.

_____. *De officiis.* Ed. Maurice Testard. *Saint Ambroise: Les devoirs.* 2 vols. Paris, 1984, 1992.

_____. *Epistolae.* Ed. Michaela Zelzer. *CSEL* 82(3). Vienna, 1982.

Andreas of Bergamo. *Historia.* Ed. Georg Waitz. MGH, *SRL* 1:220–30. Hannover, 1878.

Annales Alamannici. Ed. Walter Lendi. *Untersuchungen zur frühalemannischen Annalistik.* Freiburg, 1971.

Annales Bertiniani. Ed. Félix Grat, Jeanne Vielliard, and Suzanne Clémencet. *Annales de Saint-Bertin.* Paris, 1964. Ed. and trans. Janet L. Nelson. *The Annals of St.-Bertin.* Manchester, 1991.

Annales Einsidlenses. Ed. Georg H. Pertz. MGH, *SS* 3:137–49. Hannover, 1839.

Annales Formoselenses. Ed. Ludwig Bethmann. MGH, *SS* 5:34–36. Hannover, 1844.

Annales Fuldenses. Ed. Georg H. Pertz and Friedrich Kurze. MGH, *SRG* 7. Hannover, 1891.

Annales Mettenses priores. Ed. Bernhard von Simson. MGH, *SRG* 10. Hannover, 1905.

Annales Prumienses. Ed. Oswald Holder-Egger. MGH, *SS* 15(2):1289–92. Hannover, 1888.

Annales regni Francorum. Ed. Georg H. Pertz and Friedrich Kurze. MGH, *SRG* 6. Hannover, 1895.

Annales Sithienses. Ed. Georg Waitz. MGH, *SS* 13:34–38. Hannover, 1881.

Annales Stabulenses. Ed. Georg Waitz. MGH, *SS* 13:39–43. Hannover, 1881.

Annales Weingartenses. Ed. Georg H. Pertz. MGH, *SS* 1:64–67. Hannover, 1826.

Annales Xantenses. Ed. Reinhold Rau. *Quellen zur karolingischen Reichsgeschichte* 2:340–71. Darmstadt, 1966.

Anonymi. *In Matthaeum.* Ed. Bengt Löfstedt. *CCCM* 159. Turnhout, 2003.

Anonymus. *Epistola ad Ermengardem.* Ed. Ernst Dümmler. MGH, *Epist.* 5:343–44, no. 27. Berlin, 1899.

Ardo. *Vita Benedicti abbatis Anianensis.* Ed. Oswald Holder-Egger. MGH, *SS* 15(1):198–220. Hannover, 1887.

Astronomus. *Vita Hludowici imperatoris.* Ed. Ernst Tremp. *Thegan: Die Taten Kaiser Ludwigs; Astronomus: Das Leben Kaiser Ludwigs.* MGH, *SRG* 64. Hannover, 1995.

Athanasius. *Vita Antonii* (Latin trans. by Evagrius). *PL* 73, col. 125–69.

Augustine. *De baptismo.* Ed. Michael Petschenig. *CSEL* 51(1). Vienna, 1908.

_____. *De civitate Dei.* Ed. Bernard Dombart and Alphons Kalb. *CCSL* 47–48. Turnhout, 1955.

_____. *De doctrina Christiana.* Ed. and trans. Roger P. H. Green. *Augustine: De doctrina Christiana.* Oxford, 1995.

_____. *Enarrationes in psalmos.* Ed. Eligius Dekkers and Johannes Fraipont. *CCSL* 39. Turnhout, 1956.

_____. *Epistulae.* Ed. Alois Goldbacher. *CSEL* 34. Vienna, 1895.

_____. *Retractationes.* Ed. Almuth Mutzenbecher. *CCSL* 57. Turnhout, 1984.

_____. *Sermones. PL* 38–39.

Benedict. *Regula.* Ed. Rudolf Hanslik. *CSEL* 75. Vienna, 1977.

Benedict of Aniane. *Concordia regularum*. Ed. Pierre Bonnerue. *CCCM* 168–168A. Turnhout, 1999.

Boniface. *Epistolae*. Ed. Michael Tangl. MGH, *Epistolae selectae in usum scholarum, separatim editae* 1. Berlin, 1916.

Bruno Candidus. *Vita Eigilis*. Ed. Georg Waitz. MGH, *SS* 15(1):221–33. Stuttgart, 1887.

Caesarius of Arles. *Sermones*. Ed. Germain Morin. *CCSL* 103–4. Turnhout, 1953.

Capitula de missis instruendis (829). Ed. Alfred Boretius and Victor Krause. MGH, *Capit.* 2:7–9, no. 187. Hannover, 1897.

Capitulare ecclesiasticum (818–819). Ed. Alfred Boretius. MGH, *Capit.* 1:275–80, no. 138. Hannover, 1883.

Capitulare missorum generale (802). Ed. Alfred Boretius. MGH, *Capit.* 1:91–99, no. 33. Hannover, 1883.

Cathulf. *Epistola ad Carolem* (775). Ed. Ernst Dümmler. MGH, *Epist.* 4:501–5, no. 7. Berlin, 1895.

Charles the Bald. *Epistola Adriano papae directa* (872). *PL* 124, col. 881C–896B.

_____. *Epistola Nicolao papae directa* (867). Ed. Wilfried Hartmann. MGH, *Conc.* 4:239–43. Hannover, 1998.

Chronicon Moissiacense. Ed. Georg H. Pertz. MGH, *SS* 1:280–313. Hannover, 1826.

Cicero. *De senectute*. Ed. and trans. William A. Falconer. *De senectute. De amicitia. De divinatione*. *LCL*. Cambridge, Mass., 1923.

_____. *In Catilinam*. Ed. and trans. C. MacDonald. *In Catilinam 1–4. Pro Murena. Pro Sulla. Pro Flacco: B. Orations*. *LCL*. Cambridge, Mass., 1977.

Collectio capitularis Benedicti Levitae monastica. Ed. Josef Semmler. *Corpus consuetudinum monasticarum* 1. Sieburg, 1963.

Collectio Dionysio-Hadriana. *PL* 67, col. 139–346.

Concilium Aquisgranense (836). Ed. Albert Werminghoff. MGH, *Conc.* 2(2):704–24, no. 56. Hannover, 1908.

Concilium Cabillonense (813). Ed. Albert Werminghoff. MGH, *Conc.* 2(1):273–85, no. 37. Hannover, 1906.

Concilium Ingelheimense (840). Ed. Albert Werminghoff. MGH, *Conc.* 2(2):791–93, no. 61. Hannover, 1908.

Concilium Moguntinum (847). Ed. Alfred Boretius and Victor Krause. MGH, *Capit.* 2:173–84, no. 248. Hannover, 1890.

Concilium Parisiense (829). Ed. Albert Werminghoff. MGH, *Conc.* 2(2):605–80, no. 50. Hannover, 1908.

Concilium Remense (813). Ed. Albert Werminghoff. MGH, *Conc.* 2(1):253–58, no. 35. Hannover, 1906.

Concilium Toletanum XII. Ed. José Vives. *Concilios Visigóticos e Hispano-Romanos*. 380–410. Barcelona, 1963.

Couronnement de Louis. Trans. Joan M. Ferrante. *Guillaume d'Orange: Four Twelfth-Century Epics*. New York, 1974.

Decretum Hadriani. Ed. Ludwig Weiland. MGH, *Constitutiones et acta publica imperatorum et regum* 1:657–60, no. 446. Hannover, 1893.

Dhuoda. *Liber manualis.* Ed. Pierre Riché. *SC* 225bis. Paris, 1991.

Divisio regnorum (806). Ed. Alfred Boretius. MGH, *Capit.* 1:126–30, no. 45. Hannover, 1883.

Ebbo of Reims. *Apologetici Ebonis forma posterior.* Ed. Albert Werminghoff. MGH, *Conc.* 2(2):799–806. Hannover, 1908.

____. *Apologetici Ebonis forma prior.* Ed. Albert Werminghoff. MGH, *Conc.* 2(2):794–99. Hannover, 1908.

____. *Epistola ad Halitgarium* (830). Ed. Ernst Dümmler. MGH, *Epist.* 5:616–17, no. 2. Berlin, 1899.

____. *Resignatio.* Ed. Albert Werminghoff. MGH, *Conc.* 2(2):701–3. Hannover, 1908.

Einhard. *Epistolae.* Ed. Karl Hampe. MGH, *Epist.* 5:105–45. Berlin, 1899.

____. *Translatio et miracula sanctorum Marcellini et Petri.* Ed. Georg Waitz. MGH, *SS* 15(1):238–64. Hannover, 1888.

____. *Vita Karoli Magni.* Ed. Oswald Holder-Egger. MGH, *SRG* 25. Hannover, 1911.

Engelbert. *Versus de bella quae fuit acta Fontaneto.* Ed. Ernst Dümmler. MGH, *PLAC* 2:138–39. Berlin, 1884.

Episcoporum de poenitentia, quam Hludowicus imperator professus est, relatio Compendiensis. Ed. Alfred Boretius and Victor Krause. MGH, *Capit.* 2:51–55, no. 197. Hannover, 1897. Ed. Courtney M. Booker. "The Public Penance of Louis the Pious: A New Edition of the *Episcoporum de poenitentia, quam Hludowicus imperator professus est, relatio Compendiensis* (833)." *Viator* 39, no. 2 (2008): 1–19.

Ermentarius. *Miracula sancti Philiberti.* Ed. Oswald Holder-Egger. MGH, *SS* 15(1):297–303. Hannover, 1887.

Ermoldus Nigellus. *In honorem Hludowici.* Ed. Edmond Faral, *Ermold le Noir: Poème sur Louis le Pieux et épitres au roi Pépin.* Paris, 1964.

Eutropius. *Epistola ad Petrum papam de districtione monachorum. PL* 80, col. 15–20.

Flodoard. *Historia Remensis ecclesiae.* Ed. Martina Stratmann. MGH, *SS* 36. Hannover, 1998.

Frechulf of Lisieux. *Historiae.* Ed. Michael I. Allen. *CCCM* 169–169A. Turnhout, 2002.

Fulgentius. *Ad Monimum libri III.* Ed. Johannes Fraipont. *CCSL* 91. Turnhout, 1968.

Gottschalk. *De praedestinatione.* Ed. Cyrille Lambot. *Oeuvres théologiques et grammaticales de Godescalc d'Orbais.* 180–258. Louvain, 1945.

Grandes Chroniques de France. Vol. 4. Ed. Jules Viard. Paris, 1927.

Gregory of Tours. *Libri historiarum X.* Ed. Bruno Krusch and Wilhelm Levison. MGH, *SRM* 1(1). Hannover, 1937.

Gregory the Great. *Dialogi.* Ed. Adalbert de Vogüé. *SC* 260. Paris, 1978–80.

____. *Homiliae in Hiezechihelem prophetam.* Ed. Marcus Adriaen. *CCSL* 142. Turnhout, 1971.

____. *Registrum epistularum.* Ed. Dag Norberg. *CCSL* 140. Turnhout, 1982.

____. *Regula pastoralis.* Ed. Floribert Rommel. *SC* 382. Paris, 1992.

Gregory IV. *Epistola ad regni Francorum episcopos.* Ed. Ernst Dümmler. MGH, *Epist.* 5:228–32, no. 17. Berlin, 1899.

____. *Epistola spuria.* Ed. Karl Hampe. MGH, *Epist.* 5:81–84, no. 15. Berlin, 1899.

Grimlaicus. *Regula solitariorum.* PL 103, col. 573–664.

Hadrian II. *Epistolae.* Ed. Ernst Perels. MGH, *Epist.* 6:691–765. Berlin, 1925.

Halitgar of Cambrai. *De vitiis et virtutibus et de ordine poenitentium.* PL 105, col. 651–94.

Hildemar of Corbie/Civate. *Expositio regulae S. Benedicti.* Ed. Rupertus Mittermüller. *Vita et regula SS. P. Benedicti una cum expositione regulae.* 3 vols. Regensburg, 1880.

Hilduin, *Epistola ad Hludowicum Pium imperatorem.* Ed. Ernst Dümmler, MGH, *Epist.* 5:327–35, no. 20. Berlin 1899.

Hincmar of Reims. *De divortio Lotharii regis et Theutbergae reginae.* Ed. Letha Böhringer. MGH, *Conc.* 4(1). Hannover, 1992.

____. *De ordine palatii.* Ed. Thomas Gross and Rudolf Schieffer. MGH, *Fontes iuris Germanici antiqui in usum scholarum, separatim editi* 3. Hannover, 1980.

____. *De presbyteris criminosis.* PL 125, col. 1093–110.

____. *De regis persona et regio ministerio.* PL 125, col. 833–56.

____. *Epistolae.* Ed. Ernst Perels. MGH, *Epist.* 8(1). Berlin, 1939. See also *PL* 126, col. 9–280.

____. *Liber expostulationis.* Ed. Wilfried Hartmann. MGH, *Conc.* 4:420–87. Hannover, 1998.

____. *Opusculum LV capitulorum.* Ed. Rudolf Schieffer. MGH, *Conc.* 4(2):99–361. Hannover, 2003.

____. *Visio Bernoldi.* Ed. Maaike van der Lugt. "Tradition and Revision: The Textual Tradition of Hincmar of Reims' *Visio Bernoldi* with a New Critical Edition." *Bulletin du Cange* 52 (1994): 109–49.

Hippocrates. *On Affections.* Ed. and trans. Paul Potter. *Affections, Diseases. LCL.* Cambridge, Mass., 1988.

Hrabanus Maurus. *Commentaria in Ecclesiasticum.* PL 109, col. 763–1126.

____. *Commentaria in Exodum.* PL 108, col. 9–246.

____. *Commentaria in Ezechielem.* PL 110, col. 497–1084.

____. *De institutione clericorum.* Ed. Detlev Zimpel. *Freiburger Beiträge zur mittelalterlichen Geschichte* 7. Frankfurt am Main, 1996.

____. *De procinctu Romanae miliciae.* Ed. Ernst Dümmler. *Zeitschrift für deutsches Alterthum* 15 (1872): 443–51.

____. *De universo.* PL 111, col. 9–614.

____. *De virtutibus et vitiis.* Ed. Wolfgang Lazius. *Fragmenta quaedam Caroli Magni imp. rom. aliorumque incerti nominis de veteris ecclesiae ritibus ac ceremoniis.* Antwerp, 1560.

____. *Epistolae.* Ed. Ernst Dümmler. MGH, *Epist.* 5:379–516. Berlin, 1899.

____. *Epistolarum Fuldensium fragmenta.* Ed. Ernst Dümmler. MGH, *Epist.* 5:517–33. Berlin, 1899.

_____. *Expositio in Matthaeum*. Ed. Bengt Löfstedt. *CCCM* 174–174A. Turnhout, 2000.

_____. *Liber ad Otgarium*. Ed. Ernst Dümmler. MGH, *Epist.* 5:462–65, no. 32. Berlin, 1899.

_____. *Poenitentiale ad Heribaldum*. *PL* 110, col. 467–94.

Hugh of Fleury. *Historia regum Francorum monasterii sancti Dionysii*. Ed. Georg H. Pertz. MGH, *SS* 9:395–406. Hannover, 1851.

Isidore of Seville. *Differentiae*. *PL* 83, col. 9–98.

_____. *Sententiae*. *PL* 83, col. 537–738.

Jerome. *Commentaria in Osee prophetam*. Ed. Marcus Adriaen. *CCSL* 76. Turnhout, 1969.

Jonas of Orléans. *Concilium Parisiense* (829). See *Concilium Parisiense* (829).

_____. *De institutione laicali*. *PL* 106, col. 121–278.

_____. *De institutione regia*. Ed. Alain Dubreucq. *SC* 407. Paris, 1995.

Justinian. *Digesta*. Ed. Theodor Mommsen and Paul Krueger. *Corpus Iuris Civilis*. 3 vols. Berlin, 1954.

Leo the Great. *Epistolae*. *PL* 54, col. 551–1218.

_____. *Tractatus*. Ed. Antoine Chavasse. *CCSL* 138–138A. Turnhout, 1973.

Liber pontificalis. Ed. Louis Duchesne. *Le Liber pontificalis: Texte, introduction, commentaire*. 3 vols. Paris, 1955–57.

Lothar. *Epistola Leoni papae directa* (ca. 847–49). Ed. Adolf von Hirsch-Gereuth. MGH, *Epist.* 5:609–11, no. 46. Berlin, 1899.

Louis the Pious. *Epistola Hilduino abbati directa* (ca. 834–35). Ed. Ernst Dümmler. MGH, *Epist.* 5:325–27, no. 19. Berlin, 1899.

Lupus of Ferrières. *Epistulae*. Ed. Peter K. Marshall. Leipzig, 1984.

Narratio clericorum Remensium. Ed. Albert Werminghoff. MGH, *Conc.* 2(2):806–14. Hannover, 1908.

Nithard. *Historiarum libri IV*. Ed. Philippe Lauer. *Nithard: Histoire des fils de Louis le Pieux*. Paris, 1926.

Odbert. *Passio Friderici episcopi Traiectensis*. Ed. Oswald Holder-Egger. MGH, *SS* 15(1):342–56. Hannover, 1887.

Odilo of Saint-Médard. *Translatio sancti Sebastiani*. Ed. Oswald Holder-Egger. MGH, *SS* 15(1):377–91. Hannover, 1887. For the entire work, see *PL* 132, col. 575–628.

Odo Aribert. *Narratio de morte Bernardi*. Ed. Martin Bouquet. *Recueil des historiens des Gaules et de la France* 7:286–87. Paris, 1870.

Otto of Freising. *Chronica sive Historia de duabus civitatibus*. Ed. Adolf Hofmeister. MGH, *SRG* 45. Hannover, 1912.

Paschasius Radbertus. *Epitaphium Arsenii*. Ed. Ernst Dümmler. *Abhandlungen der königlichen Akademie der Wissenschaften zu Berlin, Philologische und historische Klasse* 2 (1900): 1–98.

_____. *Expositio in Lamentationes Jeremiae*. Ed. Beda Paulus. *CCCM* 85. Turnhout, 1988.

_____. *Expositio in Matheo libri XII*. Ed. Beda Paulus. *CCCM* 56, 56A, 56B. Turnhout, 1984.

_____. *Vita sancti Adalhardi*. *PL* 120, col. 1507–56.

Paul the Deacon. *Historia Langobardorum*. Ed. Ludwig Bethmann and Georg Waitz. MGH, *SRL* 1:12–187. Hannover, 1878.

Proemium generale ad capitularia tam ecclesiastica quam mundana (818–19). Ed. Alfred Boretius. MGH, *Capit.* 1:273–75, no. 137. Hannover, 1883.

Ratramnus of Corbie. *De praedestinatione Dei*. *PL* 121, col. 11–80.

Regino of Prüm. *Chronicon*. Ed. Friedrich Kurze. MGH, *SRG* 50. Hannover, 1890.

Regni divisio (831). Ed. Alfred Boretius and Victor Krause. MGH, *Capit.* 2:20–24, no. 194. Hannover, 1897.

Rudolf of Fulda. *Miracula sanctorum in Fuldensis ecclesias translatorum*. Ed. Georg Waitz. MGH, *SS* 15(1):328–41. Hannover, 1887.

Scripta Leonis, Rufini et Angeli Sociorum S. Francisci: The Writings of Leo, Rufino and Angelo Companions of St. Francis. Ed. and trans. Rosalind B. Brooke. Oxford, 1970.

Sedulius Scottus. *Carmina*. Ed. Jean Meyers. *CCCM* 117. Turnhout, 1991.

_____. *De rectoribus Christianis*. Ed. Siegmund Hellmann, *Sedulius Scottus* (Munich, 1906).

Smaragdus of Saint-Mihiel. *Expositio in regulam S. Benedicti*. Ed. Alfred Spannagel and Pius Engelbert. *Corpus consuetudinum monasticarum* 8. Sieburg, 1974.

_____. *Via regia*. *PL* 102, col. 933–70.

Synod of Soissons (853). Ed. Wilfried Hartmann. MGH, *Conc.* 3:253–93, no. 27. Hannover, 1984.

Synod of Troyes (867). Ed. Wilfried Hartmann. MGH, *Conc.* 4:229–45, no. 24. Hannover, 1998.

Terentianus Maurus. *De syllabis*. Ed. Jan-Wilhelm Beck. Göttingen, 1993.

Thegan. *Gesta Hludowici imperatoris*. Ed. Ernst Tremp. *Thegan: Die Taten Kaiser Ludwigs; Astronomus: Das Leben Kaiser Ludwigs*. MGH, *SRG* 64. Hannover, 1995.

Theoderich of Cambrai. *Libellus*. See Synod of Soissons (853).

Theodulf of Orléans. *Capitulare I* (798–817/818). Ed. Peter Brommer. MGH, *Capitula episcoporum* 1:73–142. Hannover, 1984.

Visio Raduini. Ed. Oswald Holder-Egger. *NA* 11 (1886): 262–63.

Vita Alcuini. Ed. Wilhelm Arndt. MGH, *SS* 15(1):182–97. Hannover, 1887.

Vita Sugerii. Ed. A. Lecoy de la Marche. *Oeuvres complètes de Suger*, 377–411. Paris, 1867.

Walafrid Strabo. *Ad eandem [Iudith] de quodam somnio*. Ed. Ernst Dümmler. MGH, *PLAC* 2:379–80, no. 24. Berlin, 1884.

_____. Chapter Headings to Thegan, *Gesta Hludowici imperatoris*. Ed. Ernst Tremp. *Thegan: Die Taten Kaiser Ludwigs; Astronomus: Das Leben Kaiser Ludwigs*. MGH, *SRG* 64:168–74. Hannover, 1995.

_____. *De imagine Tetrici*. Ed. and trans. Michael W. Herren. "The *De imagine Tetrici* of Walahfrid Strabo: Edition and Translation." *JML* 1 (1991): 118–39.

_____. *Prologus* to Thegan, *Gesta Hludowici imperatoris*. Ed. Ernst Tremp. *Thegan: Die Taten Kaiser Ludwigs; Astronomus: Das Leben Kaiser Ludwigs*. MGH, *SRG* 64:168. Hannover, 1995.

William of Malmesbury. *Gesta pontificum Anglorum.* Ed. N. E. S. A. Hamilton. London, 1870.

SELECT SECONDARY SOURCES

Airlie, Stuart. "Private Bodies and the Body Politic in the Divorce Case of Lothar II." *PP* 161 (1998): 3–38.

_____. "Bonds of Power and Bonds of Association in the Court Circle of Louis the Pious." In *Charlemagne's Heir: New Perspectives on the Reign of Louis the Pious (814–840)*, ed. Peter Godman and Roger Collins, 191–204. Oxford, 1990.

Anton, Hans Hubert. *Fürstenspiegel und Herrscherethos in der Karolingerzeit.* Bonn, 1968.

Appleby, David F. "Sight and Church Reform in the Thought of Jonas of Orleans." *Viator* 27 (1996): 11–33.

Arquillière, Henri-Xavier. *L'Augustinisme politique: Essai sur la formation des théories politiques du Moyen-Age.* 2nd ed. Paris, 1955.

Auerbach, Erich. *Mimesis: The Representation of Reality in Western Literature.* Trans. Willard R. Trask. Princeton, N.J., 2003.

Baluze, Étienne. *Sancti Agobardi archiepiscopi Lugdunensis opera. . . .* Paris, 1666.

Barthélemy, Charles. "La déposition de Louis le Débonnaire." In idem, *Erreurs et mensonges historiques* 4th ser. 110–48. Paris, 1873.

Becker, Carl L. "Everyman His Own Historian." *AHR* 37 (1932): 221–36.

Berschin, Walter. *Biographie und Epochenstil im lateinischen Mittelalter.* 5 vols. Stuttgart, 1986–2001.

Böhmer, Johann F., and Engelbert Mühlbacher. *Regesta Imperii.* Vol. 1, *Die Regesten des Kaiserreichs unter den Karolingern, 751–918.* 2nd ed. Innsbruck, 1908.

Booker, Courtney M. "An Early Humanist Edition of Nithard, Troyes, Médiathèque de l'Agglomération Troyenne, 3203, *De dissensionibus filiorum Ludovici Pii*": *Revue d'histoire des textes* (forthcoming).

_____. "The Public Penance of Louis the Pious: A New Edition of the *Episcoporum de poenitentia, quam Hludowicus imperator professus est, relatio Compendiensis* (833)." *Viator* 39, no. 2 (2008): 1–19.

_____. "A New Prologue of Walafrid Strabo." *Viator* 36 (2005): 83–105.

_____. Review of Gabriel Piterberg, *An Ottoman Tragedy: History and Historiography at Play* (Berkeley, Calif., 2003). *Comitatus* 35 (2004): 265–71.

_____. "The Demanding Drama of Louis the Pious." *Comitatus* 34 (2003): 170–75.

_____. "*Imitator daemonum dicor*: Adalhard the Seneschal, Mistranslations, and Misrepresentations." *Jahrbuch für internationale Germanistik* 33 (2001): 114–26.

Boshof, Egon. *Ludwig der Fromme.* Darmstadt, 1996.

_____. *Erzbischof Agobard von Lyon: Leben und Werke.* Cologne, 1969.

Boureau, Alain. *The Myth of Pope Joan.* Trans. Lydia G. Cochrane. Chicago, 2001.

Boyer, X. "Le Champ du Mensonge: An 833." *Revue d'Alsace* 2nd ser. 13 (1862): 49–108.

Bressolles, Adrien. *Saint Agobard: Evêque de Lyon (769–840)*. Paris, 1949.

Brown, Giles P. A. "Politics and Patronage at the Royal Abbey of Saint-Denis (814–98): The Rise of a Royal Patron Saint." Ph.D. diss., New College, University of Oxford, 1989.

Buc, Philippe. *The Dangers of Ritual: Between Early Medieval Texts and Social Scientific Theory*. Princeton, N.J., 2001.

Bührer-Thierry, Geneviève. "La reine adultère." *CCM* 35 (1992): 299–312.

Burke, Peter. "Tradition and Experience: The Idea of Decline from Bruni to Gibbon." In *Edward Gibbon and the Decline and Fall of the Roman Empire*, ed. Glen W. Bowersock, John Clive, and Stephen R. Graubard, 87–102. Cambridge, Mass., 1977.

Chevallard, P. *Saint Agobard, Archevêque de Lyon: Sa vie et ses écrits*. Lyon, 1869.

Corbet, Patrick. "Interdits de parenté, hagiographie et politique: La *passio Friderici episcopi Traiectensis* (ca. 1024)." *Ius Commune: Zeitschrift für europäische Rechtsgeschichte* 23 (1996): 1–98.

Corradini, Richard, Rob Meens, Christina Pössel, and Philip Shaw, eds. *Texts and Identities in the Early Middle Ages*. Vienna, 2006.

Darnton, Robert. "It Happened One Night." *NYRB* 51, no. 11 (24 June 2004): 60–64.

De Jong, Mayke. "*Ecclesia* and the Early Medieval Polity." In *Staat im frühen Mittelalter*, ed. Stuart Airlie, Walter Pohl, and Helmut Reimitz, 113–32. Vienna, 2006.

_____. "*Sacrum palatium et ecclesia*: L'autorité religieuse royale sous les Carolingiens (790–840)." *AHSS* 58 (2003): 1243–69.

_____. "Monastic Prisoners or Opting Out? Political Coercion and Honour in the Frankish Kingdoms." In *Topographies of Power in the Early Middle Ages*, ed. Mayke de Jong, Frans Theuws, and Carine van Rhijn, 291–328. Leiden, 2001.

_____. "The Empire as *Ecclesia*: Hrabanus Maurus and Biblical *Historia* for Rulers." In *The Uses of the Past in the Early Middle Ages*, ed. Yitzhak Hen and Matthew Innes, 191–226. Cambridge, 2000.

_____. "Transformations of Penance." In *Rituals of Power: From Late Antiquity to the Early Middle Ages*, ed. Frans Theuws and Janet L. Nelson, 185–224. Leiden, 2000.

_____. "What Was *Public* About Public Penance? *Paenitentia Publica* and Justice in the Carolingian World." In *La giustizia nell'alto Medioevo (secoli IX–XI)*, Settimane di studio 44(2): 863–904. Spoleto, 1997.

_____. *In Samuel's Image: Child Oblation in the Early Medieval West*. Leiden, 1996.

_____. "Power and Humility in Carolingian Society: The Public Penance of Louis the Pious." *EME* 1 (1992): 29–52.

Defente, Denis, ed. *Saint-Médard: Trésors d'un abbaye royale*. Paris, 1996.

Depreux, Philippe. *Prosopographie de l'entourage de Louis le Pieux (781–840)*. Sigmaringen, 1997.

Dershowitz, Alan M. "Life Is Not a Dramatic Narrative." In *Law's Stories: Narrative and Rhetoric in the Law*, ed. Peter Brooks and Paul Gewirtz, 99–105. New Haven, Conn., 1996.

Devisse, Jean. *Hincmar, archevêque de Reims, 845–882*. 3 vols. Geneva, 1975–76.

Dirks, Nicholas B. "The Policing of Tradition: Colonialism and Anthropology in Southern India." *Comparative Studies in Society and History* 39 (1997): 182–212.

Drap-Arnaud, Marc-Xavier-Victor. *Louis I (Le Débonnaire), ou Le Fanatisme au IXᵉ siècle, tragédie en cinq actes.* Paris, 1822.

Duby, Georges. *The Legend of Bouvines: War, Religion, and Culture in the Middle Ages.* Trans. Catherine Tihanyi. Berkeley, Calif., 1990.

Duckett, Eleanor S. *Carolingian Portraits: A Study in the Ninth Century.* Ann Arbor, Mich., 1962.

Dutton, Paul E. *Charlemagne's Mustache and Other Cultural Clusters of a Dark Age.* New York, 2004.

———. *Carolingian Civilization: A Reader.* 2nd ed. Peterborough, 2004.

———. *Charlemagne's Courtier: The Complete Einhard.* Peterborough, 1998.

———. *The Politics of Dreaming in the Carolingian Empire.* Lincoln, Neb., 1994.

———. "Awareness of Historical Decline in the Carolingian Empire, 800–887." Ph.D. diss., University of Toronto, 1981.

Ferrante, Joan M. *Guillaume d'Orange: Four Twelfth-Century Epics.* New York, 1974.

Fouracre, Paul. "Carolingian Justice: The Rhetoric of Improvement and Contexts of Abuse." In *La Giustizia nell'alto Medioevo (Secoli V–VIII)*, Settimane di studio, 42(2): 771–803. Spoleto, 1995.

Fried, Johannes. *Donation of Constantine and Constitutum Constantini.* Berlin, 2007.

Ganshof, François L. *The Carolingians and the Frankish Monarchy.* Trans. Janet Sondheimer. London, 1971.

———. "L''épreuve de la croix' dans le droit de la monarchie franque." In *Studi in onore di Alberto Pincherle*, 217–31. Rome, 1967.

Ganz, David. "The Debate on Predestination." In *Charles the Bald: Court and Kingdom*, ed. Margaret Gibson and Janet L. Nelson. 2nd ed. 283–302. London, 1990.

———. "The *Epitaphium Arsenii* and Opposition to Louis the Pious." In *Charlemagne's Heir: New Perspectives on the Reign of Louis the Pious (814–840)*, ed. Peter Godman and Roger Collins, 537–50. Oxford, 1990.

Geary, Patrick J. "Frühmittelalterliche Historiographie: Zussamenfassung." In *Historiographie im frühen Mittelalter*, ed. Anton Scharer and Georg Scheibelreiter, 539–42. Vienna, 1994.

———. *Phantoms of Remembrance: Memory and Oblivion at the End of the First Millennium.* Princeton, N.J., 1994.

Giesey, Ralph E., and John H. M. Salmon, trans. and eds. *François Hotman Francogallia.* Cambridge, 1972.

Godman, Peter, and Roger Collins, eds. *Charlemagne's Heir: New Perspectives on the Reign of Louis the Pious (814–840).* Oxford, 1990.

Goldberg, Eric J. *Struggle for Empire: Kingship and Conflict Under Louis the German, 817–876.* Ithaca, N.Y., 2006.

Guillot, Olivier. "Autour de la pénitence publique de Louis le Pieux (822)." *Cahiers de l'Institut d'Anthropologie Juridique* 3 (1999): 281–313.

_____. "L'exhortation au partage des responsabilités entre l'empereur, l'épiscopat et les autres sujets vers le milieu du règne de Louis le Pieux." In *Prédication et propagande au Moyen Age: Islam, Byzance, Occident*, 87–110. Paris, 1983.

Halphen, Louis. *Charlemagne and the Carolingian Empire*. Trans. Giselle de Nie. Amsterdam, 1977.

_____. "La pénitence de Louis le Pieux à Saint Médard de Soissons." In *Bibliothèque de la Faculté des Lettres de Paris XVIII, troisièmes mélanges d'histoire du Moyen Âge*, 177–85. Paris, 1904; reprinted in idem, *À travers l'histoire du Moyen Âge*, 58–66. Paris, 1950.

Hartmann, Wilfried. *Die Synoden der Karolingerzeit im Frankenreich und in Italien*. Paderborn, 1989.

Hedeman, Anne D. *The Royal Image: Illustrations of the* Grandes Chroniques de France, *1274–1422*. Berkeley, Calif., 1991.

Heider, Karl G. "The Rashomon Effect: When Ethnographers Disagree." *American Anthropologist* 90 (1988): 73–81.

Hen, Yitzhak, and Matthew Innes, eds. *The Uses of the Past in the Early Middle Ages*. Cambridge, 2000.

Hoeflich, Michael H. "The Concept of *Utilitas Populi* in Early Ecclesiastical Law and Government." *Zeitschrift der Savigny-Stiftung für Rechtsgeschichte, Kanonistische Abteilung* 67 (1981): 36–74.

_____. "The Speculator in the Governmental Theory of the Early Church." *Vigiliae Christianae* 34 (1980): 120–29.

Innes, Matthew. "'He never even allowed his white teeth to be bared in laughter': The Politics of Humour in the Carolingian Renaissance." In *Humour, History and Politics in Late Antiquity and the Early Middle Ages*, ed. Guy Halsall, 131–56. Cambridge, 2002.

_____. "Introduction: Using the Past, Interpreting the Present, Influencing the Future." In *The Uses of the Past in the Early Middle Ages*, ed. Yitzhak Hen and Matthew Innes, 1–8. Cambridge, 2000.

Innes, Matthew, and Rosamond McKitterick. "The Writing of History." In *Carolingian Culture: Emulation and Innovation*, ed. Rosamond McKitterick, 193–220. Cambridge, 1994.

Jacobs, Uwe K. *Die Regula Benedicti als Rechtsbuch: Eine rechtshistorische und rechtstheologische Untersuchung*. Cologne, 1987.

Jegen, Mary E. "Jonas of Orléans (c. 780–843): His Pastoral Writings and Their Social Significance." Ph.D. diss., Saint Louis University, 1967.

Judic, Bruno. "La tradition de Grégoire le Grand dans l'idéologie politique carolingienne." In *La royauté et les élites dans l'Europe carolingienne*, ed. Régine Le Jan, 17–57. Lille, 1998.

Jullien, Marie-Hélène, and Françoise Perelman. *Clavis scriptorum Latinorum medii aevi: Auctores Galliae, 735–987*. CCCM. Turnhout, 1994.

Kardong, Terrence. "Justitia in the Rule of Benedict." *Studia monastica* 24 (1982): 43–73.

Kaufmann, Ekkehard. *Aequitatis iudicium: Königsgericht und Billigkeit in der Rechtsordnung des frühen Mittelalters.* Frankfurt am Main, 1959.

Kelly, Henry Ansgar. *Ideas and Forms of Tragedy from Aristotle to the Middle Ages.* Cambridge, 1993.

Kern, Walter. "Der Streit Ludwigs des Frommen mit seinen Söhnen im Lichte der augustinischen Geschichtsauffassung." Ph.D. diss., Universität Greifswald, 1922.

Koch, Armin. *Kaiserin Judith: Eine politische Biographie.* Husum, 2005.

Koziol, Geoffrey. "A Father, His Son, Memory, and Hope: The Joint Diploma of Lothar and Louis V (Pentecost Monday, 979) and the Limits of Performativity." In *Geschichtswissenschaft und "Performative Turn": Ritual, Inszenierung und Performanz vom Mittelalter bis zur Neuzeit,* ed. Jürgen Martschukat and Steffen Patzold, 83–103. Cologne, 2003.

_____. *Begging Pardon and Favor: Ritual and Political Order in Early Medieval France.* Ithaca, N.Y., 1992.

Kuhn, Heinrich. "Das literarische Porträt Ludwigs des Frommen." Ph.D. diss., Universität Basel, 1930.

Ladner, Gerhart B. *The Idea of Reform: Its Impact on Christian Thought and Action in the Age of the Fathers.* New York, 1967.

Le Jan, Régine. "Frankish Giving of Arms and Rituals of Power: Continuity and Change in the Carolingian Period." In *Rituals of Power: From Late Antiquity to the Early Middle Ages,* ed. Frans Theuws and Janet L. Nelson, 281–309. Leiden, 2000.

Leibniz, Gottfried Wilhelm. *Gesammelte Werke.* Vol. I, pts. 1–4, *Annales imperii occidentis Brunsvicenses,* ed. Georg H. Pertz. Hannover, 1843–47.

Leyser, Conrad. "'Let Me Speak, Let Me Speak': Vulnerability and Authority in Gregory's Homilies on Ezekiel." In *Gregorio Magno e il suo tempo,* 2:169–82. Rome, 1991.

Leyser, Karl. "Early Medieval Canon Law and the Beginnings of Knighthood." In idem, *Communications and Power in Medieval Europe: The Carolingian and Ottonian Centuries,* 51–71. London, 1994.

Louis, René. "L'épopée française est carolingienne." In *Colloquios de Roncesvalles, Agosto 1955,* 327–460. Saragossa, 1956.

MacLean, Simon. "Ritual, Misunderstanding, and the Contest for Meaning: Representations of the Disrupted Royal Assembly at Frankfurt (873)." In *Representations of Power in Medieval Germany, 800–1500,* ed. Björn Weiler and Simon MacLean, 97–119. Turnhout, 2006.

McKeon, Peter R. "The Empire of Louis the Pious: Faith, Politics, and Personality." *RB* 90 (1980): 50–62.

_____. "Archbishop Ebbo of Reims (816–835): A Study in the Carolingian Empire and Church." *Church History* 43 (1974): 437–47.

McKitterick, Rosamond. *History and Memory in the Carolingian World.* Cambridge, 2004.

_____. *The Frankish Kingdoms Under the Carolingians, 751–987.* London, 1983.

_____, ed. *New Cambridge Medieval History.* Vol. 2, *c. 700–c. 900.* Cambridge, 1995.

_____. "The Study of Frankish History in France and Germany in the Sixteenth and Seventeenth Centuries." *Francia* 8 (1980): 556–72.

Mably, Gabriel Bonnet de. *Observations sur l'histoire de France.* 1765. 3 vols. Rev. ed. François Guizot. Paris, 1823.

Marchangy, Louis-Antoine-François de. *La Gaule poétique, ou L'histoire de France considérée dans rapports avec la poésie, l'éloquence et les beaux-arts.* 8 vols. Paris, 1813–17.

Marx, Gene W. "Louis I (The Pious, or 'Le Débonnaire'): A Personal Reassessment of the Man Through the Events in His Reign." Ph.D. diss., New York University, 1971.

Masson, Jean-Papire. *Sancti Agobardi episcopi ecclesiae Lugdunensis opera. . . .* Paris, 1605.

Mayr-Harting, Henry. "Two Abbots in Politics: Wala of Corbie and Bernard of Clairvaux." *TRHS* 5th ser. 40 (1990): 217–37.

Meens, Rob. "Politics, Mirrors of Princes and the Bible: Sins, Kings and the Well-Being of the Realm." *EME* 7 (1998): 345–57.

Montesquieu, Charles de Secondat, baron de. *De l'esprit des loix.* 1748. Ed. Gonzague Truc. Paris, 1956.

Moore, Michael E. "La monarchie carolingienne et les anciens modèles irlandais." *AHSS* 51 (1996): 307–24.

_____. "A Sacred Kingdom: Royal and Episcopal Power in the Frankish Realms (496–846)." Ph.D. diss., University of Michigan, 1993.

Morrison, Karl F. "'Know thyself': Music in the Carolingian Renaissance." In *Committenti e produzione artistico-letteraria nell'alto medioevo occidentale*, Settimane di studio 39(1): 369–483. Spoleto, 1992.

_____. "'Christ in Us, Moving Toward the Father': Paschasius Radbertus's View of History." In idem, *The Mimetic Tradition of Reform in the West*, 121–35. Princeton, N.J., 1982.

_____. "*Unum ex multis:* Hincmar of Rheims' Medical and Aesthetic Rationales for Unification." In *Nascita dell'Europa ed Europa Carolingia: Un'equazione da verificare*, Settimane di studio, 27(2): 583–718. Spoleto, 1981.

Morrissey, Robert. *Charlemagne and France: A Thousand Years of Mythology.* Trans. Catherine Tihanyi. Notre Dame, 2003.

Nelson, Janet L. "Bad Kingship in the Earlier Middle Ages." *Haskins Society Journal* 8 (1996): 1–26.

_____. "The Search for Peace in a Time of War: The Carolingian Brüderkrieg, 840–843." In *Träger und Instrumentarien des Friedens im hohen und späten Mittelalter*, ed. Johannes Fried, 87–114. Sigmaringen, 1996.

_____. "History-Writing at the Courts of Louis the Pious and Charles the Bald." In *Historiographie im frühen Mittelalter*, ed. Anton Scharer and Georg Scheibelreiter, 435–42. Vienna, 1994.

_____. "The Last Years of Louis the Pious." In *Charlemagne's Heir: New Perspectives on the Reign of Louis the Pious (814–840)*, ed. Peter Godman and Roger Collins, 147–59. Oxford, 1990.

_____. *Politics and Ritual in Early Medieval Europe.* London, 1986.

____. "Public *Histories* and Private History in the Work of Nithard." *Speculum* 60 (1985): 251–93.

Noble, Thomas F. X. "Louis the Pious and His Piety Re-Reconsidered." *RBPH* 58 (1980): 297–316.

____. "The Monastic Ideal as a Model for Empire: The Case of Louis the Pious." *RB* 86 (1976): 235–50.

____. "Louis the Pious and the Papacy: Law, Politics and the Theory of Empire in the Early Ninth Century." Ph.D. diss., Michigan State University, 1974.

____. "The Revolt of King Bernard of Italy in 817: Its Causes and Consequences." *SM* 3rd ser. 15 (1974): 315–26.

Orrù, Marco. *Anomie: History and Meanings.* Boston, 1987.

Peters, Edward. *The Shadow King: Rex Inutilis in Medieval Law and Literature, 751–1327.* New Haven, Conn., 1970.

Piterberg, Gabriel. *An Ottoman Tragedy: History and Historiography at Play.* Berkeley, Calif., 2003.

Pithou, Pierre. *Annalium et historiae Francorum ab anno Christi DCCVIII. ad ann. DCCCCXC. scriptores coaetanei XII.* Paris, 1588.

Pizarro, Joaquín M. *A Rhetoric of the Scene: Dramatic Narrative in the Early Middle Ages.* Toronto, 1989.

Raynaud, Théophile. *Hagiologium Lugdunense complectens ea quae de sanctis Lugduni praesidibus.* Lyon, 1662.

Reuter, Timothy. "Pre-Gregorian Mentalities." *JEH* 45 (1994): 465–74.

Riché, Pierre. *The Carolingians: A Family Who Forged Europe.* Trans. Michael I. Allen. Philadelphia, 1993.

____. "La magie a l'époque carolingienne." *Comptes Rendus des Séance de l'Académie des Inscriptions et Belles-lettres* 1 (1973): 127–38.

Rid, Ludger. "Die Wiedereinsetzung Kaiser Ludwigs des Frommen zu St. Denis (1. März 834) und ihre Wiederholung zu Metz (28. Februar 835)." In *Festgabe Alois Knöpfler zur Vollendung des 70. Lebensjahres,* ed. Heinrich M. Gietl and Georg Pfeilschifter, 265–75. Freiburg im Breisgau, 1917.

Robe, Karl. *Ludwig der Fromme: Historisches Schauspiel.* Berlin, 1862.

Sahlins, Marshall. "Individual Experience and Cultural Order." In idem, *Culture in Practice: Selected Essays,* 277–91. New York, 2000.

Scharer, Anton, and Georg Scheibelreiter, eds. *Historiographie im frühen Mittelalter.* Vienna, 1994.

Schieffer, Rudolf. "Ludwig 'der Fromme': Zur Entstehung eines karolingischen Herrscherbeinamens." *FMSt* 16 (1982): 58–73.

____. "Von Mailand nach Canossa: Ein Beitrag zur Geschichte der christlichen Herrscherbusse von Theodosius der Grosse bis zu Heinrich IV." *DA* 28 (1972): 333–70.

Schrörs, Heinrich. *Hinkmar Erzbischof von Reims.* Freiburg, 1884.

Schürmann, Georg Caspar. *Ludovicus Pius oder Ludewig der Fromme.* Ed. Hans Sommer. Publikation älterer praktischer und theoretischer Musikwerke 17. Leipzig, 1890.

Siemes, Helena. "Beiträge zum literarischen Bild Kaiser Ludwigs des Frommen in der Karolingerzeit." Ph.D. diss., Universität Freiburg, 1966.

Simson, Bernhard von. *Jahrbücher des fränkischen Reiches unter Ludwig dem Frommen*. 2 vols. Leipzig, 1876.

Sismondi, Jean-Charles-Léonard Simonde de. *Histoire des français*. 31 vols. Paris, 1821–44; vols. 1–2 trans. William Bellingham, in Sismondi, *The French Under the Merovingians and the Carlovingians*. London, 1850.

Starn, Randolph. "Meaning-Levels in the Theme of Historical Decline." *HT* 14 (1975): 1–31.

_____. "Historians and 'Crisis'." *PP* 52 (1971): 3–22.

Stein, Robert M. "Literary Criticism and the Evidence for History." In *Writing Medieval History*, ed. Nancy F. Partner, 67–87. London, 2005.

Tremp, Ernst. *Die Überlieferung der* Vita Hludowici imperatoris *des Astronomus*. Hannover, 1991.

_____. "Thegan und Astronomus, die beiden Geschichtsschreiber Ludwigs des Frommen." In *Charlemagne's Heir: New Perspectives on the Reign of Louis the Pious (814–840)*, ed. Peter Godman and Roger Collins, 691–700. Oxford, 1990.

_____. *Studien zu den* Gesta Hludowici imperatoris *des Trierer Chorbischofs Thegan*. Hannover, 1988.

Tyler, Elizabeth M., and Ross Balzaretti, eds. *Narrative and History in the Early Medieval West*. Turnhout, 2006.

Ullmann, Walter. *The Carolingian Renaissance and the Idea of Kingship*. London, 1969.

Van Waard, Roelof. "*Le Couronnement de Louis* et le principe de l'hérédité de la couronne." *Neophilologus* 30 (1946): 52–58.

Verri, Chiara. "Il libro primo dell'*Epitaphium Arsenii* di Pascasio Radberto." *Bullettino dell'istituto storico italiano per il Medio Evo e archivio muratoriano* 103 (2000–2001): 33–131.

Vollrath, Hanna. "Oral Modes of Perception in Eleventh-Century Chronicles." In *Vox intexta: Orality and Textuality in the Middle Ages*, ed. Alger N. Doane and Carol Braun Pasternack, 102–11. Madison, Wis., 1991.

Voltaire. *Essai sur les moeurs et ésprit des nations, et sur les principaux faits de l'histoire depuis Charlemagne jusqu'à Louis XIII*. 1756. Ed. René Pomeau. Paris, 1963.

Wallace-Hadrill, John Michael. *The Frankish Church*. Oxford, 1983.

_____. "The *Via regia* of the Carolingian Age." In idem, *Early Medieval History*, 181–200. Oxford, 1975.

Ward, Elizabeth. "Agobard of Lyons and Paschasius Radbertus as Critics of the Empress Judith." *SCH* 27 (1990): 15–25.

Wattenbach, Wilhelm, and Wilhelm Levison. *Deutschlands Geschichtsquellen im Mittelalter: Vorzeit und Karolinger*. Weimar, 1952–73.

Werner, Karl Ferdinand. "*Hludovicus Augustus:* Gouverner l'empire chrétien—Idées et réalités." In *Charlemagne's Heir: New Perspectives on the Reign of Louis the Pious (814–840)*, ed. Peter Godman and Roger Collins, 3–123. Oxford, 1990.

White, Hayden. "Historical Emplotment and the Problem of Truth." In *Probing the Limits of Representation: Nazism and the "Final Solution"*, ed. Saul Friedlander, 37–53. Cambridge, Mass., 1992.

____. *The Content of the Form: Narrative Discourse and Historical Representation*. Baltimore, 1987.

Wildenbruch, Ernst von. *Die Karolinger: Trauerspiel in vier Akten*. Berlin, 1881.

Wohlhaupter, Eugen. *Aequitas canonica: Eine Studie aus dem kanonischen Recht*. Paderborn, 1931.

Wormald, Patrick, and Janet L. Nelson, eds. *Lay Intellectuals in the Carolingian World*. Cambridge, 2007.

INDEX

Aachen, 9, 79, 141, 154, 223–24, 238, 242;
    council of (836), 189–90, 206, 208, 325 n.
    29, 361 n. 22, 361 n. 26
Abelard, Peter, 56
d'Achéry, Luc, 94, 96–98, 317 n. 124
actors, 37, 119
Adalbero, bishop of Augsburg, 69
Adalbold, bishop of Utrecht, 77
Adalhard the seneschal, 231, 295 nn. 151, 153
Adam of Bremen, 315 n. 98, 322 n. 165
Ademar, lost *vita* of Louis the Pious by, 34
Adeodatus, 47, 300 n. 193
Ado, bishop of Vienne, 69, 73, 306 n. 3, 358
    n. 1; criticism of Judith by, 307 n. 16
aemulus, 291 n. 105
aequitas (equity), 187, 194, 209, 214, 217–22,
    225–26, 228–31, 236–49, 254; *aequitas
    Petri* (Peter's Equity), 245–46
agency, 6, 8, 123, 276 nn. 31, 34, 276 36, 277
    n. 41, 333 n. 111
Agobard, bishop of Lyon, 121, 124–25, 131,
    143, 153, 168, 197, 223, 225, 229, 234, 237,
    249; *Cartula de Ludovici imperatoris
    poenitentia*, 139, 147–48, 150, 154–57, 161,
    167, 175–76, 234, 239, 321 n. 156; *De divi-
    sione imperii*, 134, 149–50; *De privilegio
    apostolicae sedis*, 134; *De spe et timore*, 340
    n. 36, 378 n. 107; as dramatic villain, 121;
    Liber apologeticus I, 136–37, 149, 152; *Liber
    apologeticus* II, 137–39, 149, 159; manu-
    script discovered in Lyon, 98, 101–4, 133,
    320 n. 149 organic metaphor by, 3, 137,
    234; pardon by Louis the Pious, 100, 133;
    as precursor to Calvin, 321 n. 158; "ratio-
    nality," 99, 320 n. 153; reputation, 98–101;
    uncanonical veneration of in Lyon, 100,

133, 321 n. 160, 338 n. 16; use of organic
    metaphor, 3, 137, 234
Ahab, 138, 159
Aiulf, bishop of Bourges, 188
Alcuin, 100, 348 n. 127
Alemannia, 9
Alsace, 26, 116
Amalarius, 98
Ambrose, Saint, 45–47, 142–44, 178, 180,
    203–8, 220–21, 296 n. 163, 340 n. 34;
    De apologia prophetae David, 342 n. 54;
    reception of letters of, 143
Andreas of Bergamo, 358 n. 1
Annales Alamannici, 312 n. 72
annals, writing of, 29, 83, 92–93, 285 n. 46
Annals of Prüm, 306 n. 8
Annals of Saint-Bertin, 24, 26–29, 34, 36,
    199, 248, 289 n. 94; on Ebbo's resigna-
    tion, 186–87, 239; first annalist of, 16,
    26–29, 63, 90–91, 151, 209, 238–39, 243,
    249, 285 n. 44; manuscript transmission,
    63, 66, 285 n. 45
Annals of Xanten, 26–27, 286 n. 48
anomia, anomie, 124, 219–20, 333 n. 111. *See
    also* metaphors
anonymity, 63
Anthony, Saint, 8
Aquitaine, 29, 154, 223
Aribo, bishop of Mainz, 77
Aristotle, 37, 108
Arneis d'Orléans, 82
Arnulf, Saint, 56, 70
Arsenius, 45–47
The "Astronomer," 24, 34–39, 42, 44–45, 47,
    53, 63, 65–66, 91, 108–9, 111, 124, 160, 163,
    178, 182, 197, 207, 209, 244, 253;

ACKNOWLEDGMENTS

IN A BOOK about remembering, it is only fitting that I leave a memento of the long process of its composition, an obsession that has consumed more than a decade of my life.

At the turn of the twenty-first century, the history of Carolingian Europe is still largely unknown in North America; telling someone that you study Carolingian history stands a good chance of eliciting the question, "Which Carolina—North or South?" Medieval European history, on the other hand, is a period and culture seemingly much more familiar, thanks to the imagined, fanciful version of the Middle Ages represented in novels, computer games, role-playing games, music, and films. This tenacious romanticization is impressed in the minds not only of North Americans (for whom the material remains of the Middle Ages are absent), but, increasingly, of people throughout the world by way of the global consumption of American entertainment. Why this is so is the topic for another book. I raise it here because my goal in this book—of reading Carolingian history against the grain; of searching for, and then trying to understand on their own terms, those moments that seem to resist modern attempts at interpretation—has no doubt been shaped, in ways both formative and antipathetic, by this prevalence of American medievalism. It is a latent influence, whose effects I have only recently begun to recognize.

Far clearer have been the lasting impressions made by my teachers. Bonnie Volkman taught me early *why* learning is important, doing so largely by example and through her love of the Middle Ages. What I learned from Bonnie was refined and given direction at UC Santa Barbara, where I had the great fortune of studying with Sharon Farmer, C. Warren Hollister, Jeffrey Burton Russell, Walter Capps, and Robert Babcock. The topic of this book was conceived at UCLA, another superb public school. Sustaining a tradition of medieval studies in Los Angeles, Patrick Geary, Richard Rouse, Bengt

Löfstedt, Teofilo Ruiz, and Claudia Rapp were exemplary teachers and role models. In particular, Patrick Geary set my standard for what it means to be a medievalist: learned in both the broad theory and technical minutiae of the discipline, consistently creative and original, Patrick practices and communicates his scholarship responsibly, humanely, and with discernment. Richard Rouse and Bengt Löfstedt, each in his own inimitable way, showed me from my first days at UCLA what it means to produce exacting scholarship, and to think about history not just through the evidence of texts, but also—but always—in terms of the material media and language through which it is expressed. I am also happy to include Paul Dutton of Simon Fraser University among this group of mentors. Weathering more than a decade of my questions with good cheer, Paul has been a paragon of selfless scholarship, always willing to provide encouragement, advice, and criticism. It is to Paul's book on the politics of dreaming that I owe much of my fascination with the Carolingians, and with Louis the Pious's "theater of illusions" in particular. It is also one of the few books on medieval history that brings me pleasure as a conspiring reader and anguish as an aspiring writer.

Several other scholars played a significant role in the writing of this book. Jason Glenn and Geoffrey Koziol each read an enormous early version of the text and provided much insightful commentary. Thanks to their efforts, Thomas F. X. Noble and an anonymous reader saw a leaner version of the manuscript, and generously offered still more astute advice. I am deeply grateful for the time they all took away from their own work to give attention to mine. In addition, Darren Bayne, Susanna Braund, Alejandra Bronfman, Keith Bunnell, Guy Geltner, Eric Goldberg, Meg Leja, Neil McLynn, Roxanne Panchasi, Paige Raibmon, Helmut Reimitz, Arlene Sindelar, Margaret Trenchard-Smith, Richard Unger, Irene van Renswoude, Mark Vessey, Max Withers, and Helene Yagello-Knupffer each assisted me in one fashion or another, more often than not by answering an obscure question, tracking down a more obscure reference, or procuring photocopies of a most obscure tome.

In this last respect, the interlibrary loan team at the University of British Columbia has frequently worked wonders in satisfying my many odd requests. But a number of other institutions have also been critical to the completion of this study. The spectacular Getty Research Institute in Los Angeles is where I wrote the initial draft; the impressive collections and congenial research environment of the Institute, combined with the resources of the Charles E. Young Research Library at UCLA, made possible at its inception the broad scope of my project. Gaps in research were later filled with the assistance of the Biblioteca Apostolica Vaticana; the Bibliothèque nationale de France; the Bird Library at Syracuse University; the British Library; the Burgerbibliothek Bern; the Department of Manuscripts of the Biblioteka Uniwersytecka, Uniwersytet Wrocławski, Poland; the Deutsche Staatsbibliothek, Berlin; the Herzog August Bibliothek, Wolfenbüttel; the Institut de recherche et d'histoire des textes, Paris; the Médiathèque de l'agglomération Troyenne; the Musée de Soissons; the Musées de Metz; the National Library of Russia, Saint Petersburg; and the St. Gallen Stiftsarchiv. The quarterly California Medieval History Seminar at the Huntington Library granted me the opportunity to see work in progress by some of the world's best medieval historians, and to test preliminary work of my own.

Earlier versions of parts of Chapters 1 and 3 appear in Courtney M. Booker, "Histrionic History, Demanding Drama: The Penance of Louis the Pious in 833, Memory, and Emplotment," in *Vergangenheit und Vergegenwärtigung: Frühes Mittelalter und europäische Erinnerungskultur,* ed. Helmut Reimitz and Bernhard Zeller, Forschungen zur Geschichte des Mittelalters (Vienna, in press). Earlier versions of parts of Chapter 2 appear in Courtney M. Booker, "The Public Penance of Louis the Pious: A New Edition of the *Episcoporum de poenitentia, quam Hludowicus imperator professus est, relatio Compendiensis* (833)," *Viator* 39, no. 2 (2008): 1–19; idem, "A New Prologue of Walafrid Strabo," *Viator* 36 (2005): 83–105. All are reprinted by permission.

Perhaps the greatest reward from writing this book has been the friends I have made in the process. Many have already been listed above, but there are several who warrant special mention. Eugene Sheppard and the Center for Exilic Studies have often provided stimulating conversation and hospitality during the peregrinations of this *Homo viator.* Blair Sullivan has frequently acted as the welcome goad for many papers and travels that I might otherwise not have composed and undertaken. Scott McDonough and Clementine Oliver have each offered sardonic critiques and dining adventures, a wholesome combination that has sustained me over the course of the journey. Finally, I am pleased to thank my colleagues and many excellent students in Vancouver at the University of British Columbia: the History department, the Medieval Studies program, the annual Medieval Workshop, and the medieval studies colloquium, *Vivarium,* have been a constant source of inspiration.

If the Middle Ages is an era of mystery to many, then the notion of writing about a single year in the medieval past has only deepened this feeling among my friends and family. Yet, while they may not have always understood, they have all been understanding to a fault. Kevin Attell and Rich Scramaglia know what it's like to descend into the depths of the earth and climb the barrier peaks, while Cathal Murray and Mauri Skinfill appreciate more than most the scrutiny of arcane records. Maria, Richard, and Natalie Birch; Randall and Amy Booker; June and Enzo Zeppa; and Kuem Sun, Harry, and Grace Cho have been unfailingly supportive between my all too infrequent visits. My warmest thanks go to every one of them.

Susan Cho is the heart and soul of this book, breathing life into its litany of the long dead. Her presence hovers between the lines of every page; where they ring true, it is thanks to her discrimination and refinement. My father, Phillip Gerald Booker, did not live to know this work, but his passion for the performance of the past has also infused it. While he was spared listening to me speak about tragedy for years, Susan was not. This book is dedicated to her not only in gratitude, but also as a testament of the promise that the coming years will be shared together in joy.